Praise for *The Essential G...*
Getting Your Book Published

"A must-have for every aspiring writer . . . Thorough, forthright, quite entertaining."
— KHALED HOSSEINI, bestselling author of *And the Mountains Echoed* and *The Kite Runner*

"Before you write your own book, read this one. Arielle Eckstut and David Henry Sterry understand the process of publishing—their advice will help you envision and frame your work so that publishers will be more likely to perceive its value."
— JONATHAN KARP, president and publisher, Simon & Schuster

"I had no idea that the code of publishing would be as hard to decipher as the secret language of adolescent girls. If only I had [*The Essential Guide to Getting Your Book Published*] when I started writing!"
— ROSALIND WISEMAN, author of *Queen Bees and Wannabees*, the book that inspired the movie *Mean Girls*

"I started with nothing but an idea, and then I bought this book. Soon I had an A-list agent, a near six-figure advance, and multiple TV deals in the works. Buy it and memorize it. This tome is the quiet secret of rock star authors."
— TIMOTHY FERRISS, bestselling author of *The 4-Hour Workweek*

"If there was ever a team who can put a writer on track to get published, it's David and Arielle. Their advice is clear, direct, simple to implement, and best of all, it comes with a good dose of wit and humor. There is not a duo on the planet I can recommend more highly than David and Arielle. If you're dying to get published you'll want to hang on every word they put in print!"
— JOANNEH NAGLER, author of *The Debt-Free Spending Plan: An Amazingly Simple Way to Take Control of Your Finances Once and for All*

"There is no way I would have landed a book deal without these two brilliant industry pros and their insider knowledge! This is not a mere guide. Eckstut and Sterry have—chapter and verse—written the bible for would-be authors of every stripe and genre."
— YLONDA GAULT, author of *Child, Please: How Mama's Old-School Lessons Helped Me Check Myself Before I Wrecked Myself*

"I cannot emphasize enough how well this book prepared me for the path to getting published. It warns writers about inevitable ups and downs, but it kept me from having to learn about the publishing world through frustrating trial and error. It also provided much-needed encouragement through some initial rejections. Now that my book is published, I've run into many people wanting to know how the whole thing works, and I always refer them to this book."
— ROXANNA ELDEN, author of *See Me After Class*

"I was lucky to get The Book Doctors' help in person when I won Pitchapalooza. But you don't have to win to get their help. It's all in this invaluable book. It's the first thing I recommend as a writer and librarian when people ask me, 'How do I get published?'"
—CATHY CAMPER, author of *Lowriders in Space*

"Smart, funny, readable, thorough, and, indeed, essential, the advice in *The Essential Guide to Getting Your Book Published* gave my proposal its voice, got me to the right publisher, walked me through contract negotiations, and even helped me pick an outfit when I finalized the deal. The book talked me down during angst-ridden moments. It gave me a good idea about the reality of publishing. I recommend it all the time. This book made my book happen."
—ANN RALPH, author of *Grow a Little Fruit Tree: Simple Pruning Techniques for Small-Space, Easy-Harvest Fruit Trees*

"This is the book that has helped me every step of way in writing, marketing, and publishing my first book. Any time I had a question—whether it was about working with my editor, agent, or publicist—I knew where I could find the answer. My copy has been earmarked, bookmarked, highlighted, annotated, and loved. Arielle and David are the best guides around if you are looking to get your book out in the world. And as a bookseller, I love putting *The Essential Guide* in the hands of writers and aspiring authors. I know that I'm giving them the best possible resource for understanding the ever-changing publishing landscape."
—MELISSA CISTARO, author of *Pieces of My Mother: A Memoir*

"We can tell you exactly where we'd be without The Book Doctors' *The Essential Guide to Getting Your Book Published*: without an agent, without a publisher, and without a book! Of all the advice we received throughout this long and winding road toward publishing, Arielle Eckstut and David Henry Sterry's expert guidance, skilled coaching, and practical wisdom were, without question, the most valuable. Ready to get that book of yours published? Step 1: Buy this very essential guide."
—MAGGIE CHOTAS and BETSY POLK JOSEPH, authors of *Power Through Partnership: How Women Lead Better Together*

"Once I ratcheted up the nerve to self-publish my first novel, I realized there were two ways to do it: Close my eyes, hold my breath, and hit the publish button, or learn everything I needed to know to do it professionally and successfully. I opted for the latter, bought *The Essential Guide to Getting Your Book Published*, and read it from cover to cover. Then I rolled up my sleeves and got to work. As a result, my book hit #1 on Amazon's commercial fiction list."
—EVA LESKO NATIELLO, author of *The Memory Box*

"You can't get published if you don't properly convey your ideas to agents and publishers. Before I read *The Essential Guide to Getting Your Book Published*, my proposal basically read, 'Dude, I've got this really cool football thing I'm doing.' David and Arielle taught me how to communicate on a professional level."
—JACKSON MICHAEL, author of *The Game Before the Money: Voices of the Men Who Built the NFL*

"*The Essential Guide to Getting Your Book Published* was my mentor, tutor, and inspiration in writing *The Custom-Fit Workplace*. The guidance for writing a proposal, crafting a pitch, building a platform, and developing a promotion plan was, quite simply, indispensable."

—NANETTE FONDAS, author of *The Custom-Fit Workplace: Choose When, Where, and How to Work and Boost Your Bottom Line*

"We had been working on our first project for several years, on our own, and struggling without any guidance. We were really discouraged by the entire process. Without *The Essential Guide to Getting Your Book Published*, we'd still be stuck in literary limbo. Now, with two books published, we're working on our third!"

—AYESHA MATTU and NURA MAZNAVI, authors of *Love, InshAllah: The Secret Love Lives of American Muslim Women* and *Salaam, Love: American Muslim Men on Love, Sex, and Intimacy*

"This book led me to publication and beyond: I wrote my nonfiction proposal exactly as the authors suggested, and the first publisher who read it sent me a contract. This truly 'essential guide' helped me navigate the terms of the contract, the launch, the publication, and book events from coast to coast. It is a treasure trove of ideas, a valuable reference, and a lot of fun to read."

—LEE WILSON, author of *Rebel on Pointe: A Memoir of Ballet and Broadway*

"If you've spent years on your manuscript, you'd be foolish not to spend a weekend with this book. The fact-based, no-nonsense approach will help you focus your energy in the right places."

—DEIRDRE VERNE, author of *Drawing Conclusions* (A Sketch in Crime Mystery)

"WARNING: Reading this book may cause increased productivity, completed manuscripts, and book deals! In *The Essential Guide*, Arielle and David share some of the most important insider information that will get you to the finish line quickly and efficiently without losing your own unique voice. We know because this is just what happened to us with our first book."

—HETH WEINSTEIN and JED WEINSTEIN, authors of *Buskers: The On-the-Streets, In-the-Trains, Off-the-Grid Memoir of Two New York City Street Musicians*

"Publishing your novel can be a full-time job, from crafting the best pitch, a synopsis, query letters, marketing strategies, and websites. Writing the book might be the easiest part. Having *The Essential Guide to Getting Your Book Published* is like having a job coach by your side whispering the right answers in your ear. It's invaluable."

—MICHAEL GURLEY, author of *The Long Season*

"I curled up in a big chair and read [*The Essential Guide to Getting Your Book Published*] like a novel. Written with insight and humor, it takes us through the writing process from idea to sequel. I wish I had a book this thorough and thoughtful and downright indispensable for every aspect of my life."

—KAREN CUSHMAN, author of Newbery Award winner *The Midwife's Apprentice* and Newbery Award runner-up *Catherine, Called Birdy*

"This is a terrific book. It's practical, it's fun to read, and it totally demystifies the publishing process. Whether you are just setting out to write a book, or already have several published books under your belt, you will find this an invaluable resource. There is no doubt in my mind that it will become a standard of the industry, sitting right alongside *Writer's Market* and *The Chicago Manual of Style*. (And let me tell you—it's a much better read than either of those books could ever dream of being!)"
    —RICK BEYER, author of *The Greatest Stories Never Told Series*

"You know all those books sitting on your shelf about how to get published? Well, you can finally unload them at your garage sale because this book is all you'll ever need. A to Z, soup to nuts, this is the most comprehensive guide available on how to become a published author."
    —NANCY LEVINE, author of *The Tao of Pug*

"[*The Essential Guide to Getting Your Book Published*] offers aspiring authors refreshingly honest, knowledgeable, and detailed advice on not only how to get published, but how to deal with every phase of the publishing process, constructively and realistically. It's an invaluable resource for anyone who dreams about having his/her book not only published, but published well."
    —JAMIE RAAB, publisher, Grand Central

"From coming up with an idea to promoting the finished book, these insiders tell you what you need to know and inspire you to do it—with wit, charm, and a thorough knowledge of what they write."
    —AMY CHERRY, editor, W.W. Norton

"[*The Essential Guide to Getting Your Book Published*] is a Rosetta Stone for authors, a guide that takes the mystery and uncertainty out of getting your book published. This book takes you inside the publishing industry and reveals what makes it tick. Prospective authors, listen up: If you want your book to see the light of day, read this one."
    —LARRY DOSSEY, M.D., author of *The Extraordinary Healing Power of Ordinary Things*, *Reinventing Medicine*, and *Healing Words*

"It's not very often that a person can say that a book or its authors changed their life, but I can definitely say that about Arielle and David. From forming the perfect pitch to figuring out the mysteries of marketing, for every writer, this book is essential!"
    —DEBRA DOCKTER, author of *Deadly Design*

The
Essential
Guide to
Getting
Your Book
Published

The Essential Guide to Getting Your Book Published

How to Write It, Sell It, and Market It...Successfully!

By Arielle Eckstut and
David Henry Sterry

WORKMAN PUBLISHING • NEW YORK

Library of Congress Cataloging-in-Publication Data is available.

ISBN: 978-0-7611-6085-4

Originally published as *Putting Your Passion into Print,* now revised and updated.

Cover design by David Matt
Interior design by Sara Edward-Corbett
Author photo © Ryan Brooks

Workman books are available at special discounts when purchased in bulk for premiums and sales promotions as well as for fund-raising or educational use. Special editions or book excerpts can also be created to specification. For details, contact the Special Sales Director at the address below or send an email to specialmarkets@workman.com.

Workman Publishing Co., Inc.
225 Varick Street
New York, NY 10014-4381

workman.com

WORKMAN is a registered trademark of Workman Publishing Co., Inc.

Printed in the United States of America
First printing June 2015

10 9 8 7 6 5

To Joann Eckstut and Stan Eckstut
and in memory of Maureen Moreland
for always encouraging us to follow our passions

To Olive, we thought this book was our baby until you came along!

And in memory of Peter Workman, who helped countless authors put their passion into print

While we had no problem divulging our own missteps, pratfalls and furious anger, it didn't seem fair to air other people's dirty laundry. So we've added the odd "unnamed author story" to our book. To fully protect these unnamed authors, we've changed some details and/or created composite stories. We'd hate to put an abrupt end to anyone's publishing career just to help other people start theirs!

We would like to gratefully acknowledge André Bernard for granting us permission to reprint a portion of his fabulous book Rotten Rejections: A Literary Companion (Chrysalis Books, 2002).

Contents

PART II

Taking Care of Business

"Nothing leads
so straight to
futility as literary
ambitions without
systematic
knowledge."

—*H.G. Wells*

Introduction

"The world of books is undergoing its most profound structural shift since Gutenberg."

—*John Makinson, chairman, Penguin Random House*

FIVE YEARS AGO, WE WROTE an updated edition of a book we wrote five years before that called *Putting Your Passion into Print*. Welcome to the even more updated edition. Why a *new* new edition after only five years? Because the world has been turned upside down since 2010. And the book business is dizzy from landing on its head.

For hundreds of years, a book has been a bunch of words, symbols and maybe some pictures printed on paper and bound between two covers held together by a sturdy spine. Suddenly, that's no longer true. In fact, at this very moment, you may be reading this very book on an e-reader that weighs in at less than a pound and contains everything from the *Iliad* to *Freakonomics* to *Captain Underpants*.

There's been a sea change in how we communicate. Social networking no longer means meeting for cocktails and hobnobbing at parties. It means logging hours in front of a computer screen. (Cocktails optional.) Research may mean a trip to the library, but it also means beaming into a search engine.

In fact, search engines were at the root of our title change. While we were oh so attached to the poetry of the first title for this book, *Putting Your Passion into Print,* we had to face the fact that it wasn't search-friendly. Our book wasn't finding its readers (or vice versa). Never a good thing for an author. Which gets us back to the fact that the world has radically changed. And these changes mean lots of great news to all current and future authors. In fact, after interviewing everyone from the CEO of Harlequin to the former editor in chief of Simon & Schuster, from a top search engine optimization expert to a number of social networking gurus, from literary giants like Margaret Atwood and Neil Gaiman to a whole host of self-publishing success stories, we've come to believe that this is the greatest time in history to write a book.

When we started working on this newest edition, we, like many authors, were feeling a little panicky and slightly depressed about the state of publishing and the future of books. But we have arrived at an undeniable conclusion: Today's writers have the chance to disseminate their ideas more easily and to larger groups of people than ever before. Back in the 15th century, printed books cost an arm, a leg, a couple of eyes and a few brains. Now rich and poor alike are able to buy and read books. In fact, many authors are offering up their books for free, which may sound crazy at first. But a free book, given to the right person at the right time, may be one of the best business decisions of your life.

Writers now have breathtaking new ways of connecting with and getting their work directly into the hands of readers. And they no longer have to rely on a small group of publishing experts in order to get published. Because there is now *no barrier* to publishing. "The opportunities for authors are boundless and growing exponentially every year," says Michael Cader, creator of Publishers Lunch and Publishers Marketplace, the leading online newsletter and resource for the industry. "The only downside is that the written world is an increasingly crowded place. Thus the contemporary paradox: It is both easier than ever and harder than ever to attract an audience for any particular piece of writing. And the corollary: It is also both easier than ever and harder than ever to make money from any particular piece of writing."

Yes, authors are now swimming in an ocean with a seemingly infinite number of fish, many of whom are much, much bigger than they are. Without a map and a paddle, it's all too easy to get lost at sea. That's where we come in. We have literally traveled from the Redwood Forests to the Gulf Stream Waters helping people to get their books published. Successfully. Grizzled veterans of the publishing jungle who were looking to avoid the author-eating beasts their next time around, and newbies dreaming of bestsellerdom. Doctors, lawyers and entrepreneurs. MFAs, Ph.D.s and high school dropouts. World War II veterans and goth teenagers. Professors and preschool teachers. Soccer moms and ex-cons. Nine-year-olds and 99-year-olds. Their writing spanned every bookstore category: fiction (literary, sci-fi, thrillers, romance, mysteries, graphic novels and more), narrative nonfiction, memoir, health, inspiration, parenting, religion, business, cookbooks, children's books of every kind—picture books, middle grade, young adult, new adult—the list goes on and on. . . . We know what you're up against. Our mission is to help you navigate the waters and land happily on the sunny shores of publishing.

What This Book Is and What It Is Not

Just so we're clear: This book is not about how to be or become a writer. It is a step-by-step, blow-by-blow explanation of how to take an idea you're passionate about, develop a book out of it, get it published and deliver it into the hands, heads and hearts of readers all over the world.

From figuring out the right idea to locating and landing an agent; to selling your book to the appropriate publisher or self-publishing; to understanding your contract; to getting P-A-I-D; to actually sitting down and writing your book; to becoming savvy about publicity, marketing, e-media and social networking; to setting up your website; to planning and executing a magnificent event where you sell beaucoup books; to getting online reviews; to making a promotional video that will make its way around the World Wide Web; to planting your flag on bestseller lists, *The Essential Guide to Getting Your Book Published* is your all-in-one guide to publishing.

Sprinkled among all these nuts and bolts are juicy nuggets of insider information from seasoned industry professionals: authors, agents, editors, publishers, publicists, social networking gurus, bookstore owners, website wizards, booksellers and many more.

What Does Passion Have to Do with It?

As we mentioned, the title to the first edition of this book was *Putting Your Passion into Print*. Passion isn't usually the first item on the list of requirements for writing a book. But here's a fact: Getting a book written, published, bought and read is hard work. And it's so much harder if you're writing about something you don't care that much about.

Passion will help you keep on keeping on. Passion is contagious. Whether it's on the page or flowing through your publicity and marketing efforts, passion excites and moves people. Passion will help you attract agents, publishers, booksellers and readers. It will help you sell books. And have fun. After all, what good is any of it if you're not having fun?

Probably the most important reason we decided to write this book is that we are utterly passionate about showing people how to get successfully published, whether they want to self-publish a limited number of books, go for a fat advance from a big publisher or anything in between. We've seen over and over the joy that publishing a book can bring and how it can change people's lives. But it helps to have the right guide dog to help you across the street. We are honored to be your dog.

Who Are We to Tell You What to Do?

B etween us, we've written 25 books in a wide range of categories: fiction, memoir, practical nonfiction, sports, science and humor. We've written for both adults and kids. We've led workshops on how to get published all across America, including at Stanford University's Continuing Studies program, where we taught for years before moving back to the East Coast.

Arielle was a literary agent who worked in New York City, the mecca of publishing, for a decade before opening up the West Coast office of the Levine Greenberg Rostan Literary Agency, where she is now an agent-at-large. She's midwifed dozens of first-time authors, as well as seventh-, eleventh- and twentieth-time authors. She's worked with every major publishing house and sold millions of dollars' worth of books.

Arielle is also a successful entrepreneur. She cofounded LittleMissMatched, a company that began by selling socks that don't match in packs of three and quickly became an iconic brand. LittleMissMatched started on a shoestring and is now a multimillion-dollar corporation with stores in Disney World, Disneyland, and on Fifth Avenue in New York City. Arielle has dealt with all the issues that crop up in the worlds of wholesale and retail. The worlds that publishers and booksellers live in. So she has an intimate knowledge of how the business of publishing works, from bottom to top and side to side. And by working outside of the industry, she got a shocking understanding of how backwards publishing can be—and an enlightening sense that authors don't always have to play by the rules of the publishing business.

David is a bestselling author whose books have appeared on the cover of *The New York Times Book Review* and been translated into a dozen languages. Film rights to his writing have been optioned by major Hollywood players.

David has also been a professional actor, screenwriter, live event producer and media coach for 20 years. In fact, he turned one of his books, *Chicken,* into a one-man show that had its international debut at the famed Edinburgh Theater Festival Fringe, where it was named the number one show in the U.K. by *The Independent,* one of Britain's top newspapers.

What do acting, screenwriting and helping people with their presentation skills have to do with writing a book? A lot. We live in a time when the way you present yourself and your book (to a literary agent, a publisher, the media, a book-store, the public, your e-friends) can be as important as what's *in* your book. After two decades of working with everyone from Michael Caine to Zippy the Chimp, years of pitching projects to film studios and producers large and small, and years of hawking everything from Big Macs to Publishers Clearing House, David has learned the art of selling himself. Borrowing from this knowledge will help you sell your book.

Together, we have appeared in and on hundreds of publications and media outlets, including *USA Today, The New York Times,* NPR's *Morning Edition, Business Week, Redbook, Entrepreneur, Details, New York Magazine, Fox Business News,* HBO, CNN and even QVC.

The previous paragraphs were the sum of our publishing history prior to writing the last edition of this book. But a lot has happened since. When we launched *The Essential Guide to Getting Your Book Published,* we were lucky enough to be sent on a major tour by our publisher. We knew we didn't want to do a traditional reading at bookstores. We knew we *did* want to create an event that would attract the attention of the media and the audience that would be passionate about our book. So we invented Pitchapalooza, the *American Idol* of books. Here's what happens: Writers get one minute to pitch their book to a panel of experts (us being two of those experts). At the end, we crown a winner, who receives an introduction to an agent or editor who is a match for that particular book.

Pitchapalooza was a hit, attracting the attention of *The New York Times, The Wall Street Journal, The Washington Post* and numerous other media outlets across the country. Today, dozens of Pitchapalooza winners and participants have signed with agents or been published by top-drawer publishers. We'll introduce you to some of these winners in the book.

We've traveled all over the country going to bookstores and falling in love with booksellers, presenting at book fairs, libraries and writers' conferences. We estimate that we've now heard more than 10,000 pitches for every kind of book you could ever possibly imagine. And many that you couldn't. We were shocked by how many great writers had great ideas but just didn't know anyone in publishing. Or didn't quite know how to explain what their book was. Or had a strong draft but needed a good, stiff edit. So we decided to start a business called The Book Doctors, taking the principles of this book and applying them to real writers. We've helped people figure out the right idea; how to pitch it effectively; how to identify comparable titles in their category of the bookstore; how to come up with a great title; how to write a slam dunk proposal; how to lure and land the right agent and publisher; how to self-publish; how to promote and market their work; how to decide what to write next; and how to build a career. We also have edited (and many times re-edited) hundreds and hundreds of manuscripts. We found we loved working with writers in this way. It was such a joy watching, over and over, how talented amateurs could turn into professionally published authors if they were given the right tools and worked their butts off. The bottom line? You'd be hard-pressed to come up with a publishing problem we haven't dealt with in one way or another.

Where It All Began

It's not like we set out to write a book about how to get published. It was the natural result of the process of publishing our first two books. In fact, we owe *The Essential Guide to Getting Your Book Published* to the famous Negro Leagues baseball player Satchel Paige and the great authoress Jane Austen.

A lovingly framed poster of Leroy "Satchel" Paige in mid-pitch was hanging on David's living room wall when Arielle, who was David's agent at the time and is now his wife, first walked into his house. She pointed to the poster and asked, "Who's that guy?"

"Oh, that's Satchel Paige," replied David. "He's been my hero since I was a little kid. He was the greatest pitcher in history. One of the funniest comedians of the 20th century. And one of the deepest philosophers America's ever produced. He was like Mark Twain, Yogi Berra and Richard Pryor rolled into one."

Arielle looked at David and said: "There's gotta be a book there."

And there was. It was called *Satchel Sez: The Wit, Wisdom, and World of Leroy "Satchel" Paige.* And we wrote it.

Soon thereafter, Arielle took a very important taxi ride. It must be understood that Arielle is a Jane Austen fanatic of the highest order and has been since she was just a tyke. She'd always wanted to write a book about her idol but assumed that since she didn't have a Ph.D. in English Literature, her dream would be forever unfulfilled. Until one day, in the aforementioned taxi, when a friend said, "Wouldn't it be funny if someone discovered sex scenes from Jane Austen's books that had been edited out?" At that moment, a galaxy of light-bulbs lit up over Arielle's head and a little inner voice said:

"There's a book there."

While she had ignored similar little voices many times over the years, Arielle was determined not to let this idea wriggle away. Eighteen months later *Pride and Promiscuity: The Lost Sex Scenes of Jane Austen* was born.

Writing our books was a blast. And brutally hard. A mental triathlon. There was always so much to do, and so few hours to do it in. But creating our books changed our lives. We were invigorated, full of purpose and energy, alive creatively, mentally, soulfully. It was an education. About ourselves. About each other. And about the publishing business. While Arielle had agented dozens of books, we were both author virgins. Publishing had its way with us, for better and for worse. Joy abounded. But there was also pain.

When it was time to birth our beautiful babies, we asked ourselves how we were going to get people to pay attention to them. Have events in bookstores, we thought, since that's what you're supposed to do. Bookstores informed us that if we could get Mr. Paige or Ms. Austen to come to our events, they would be glad to have us. This presented a seemingly insurmountable problem, since both of our subjects had been dead for many years. We were discouraged, but we didn't panic; after all, we had our publishers behind us, big corporations with sleek publicity machines primed to make bestsellers out of our books.

When we met with our publisher for *Satchel Sez,* we were extremely enthusiastic and optimistic. We arrived armed with delectable pastries. We had formulated what we thought was a brilliant marketing scheme. We'd have Satchel Paige Days at stadiums all over the country. Minor league, major league. We'd have Satchel Trivia Quizzes on the Jumbotron, complete with book giveaways; Negro Leagues Museum tie-ins for merchandising; charity events with Boys and Girls Clubs. We could see it all so clearly. We were raring to go, ready, willing and able to throw our books into our car and drive all over America to sell them one at a time.

Then reality hit us like a shovel, right between the eyes.

When we went in to talk to the publicity and marketing team, the publicity and marketing team wasn't there. It was only our editor and one guy from publicity. Don't get us wrong, the guy from publicity was a great person. Still is. But he didn't have time to do some elaborate Satchel Paige Day thing at baseball stadiums. He had 10 other books to publicize that week, and another 10 the next week, and another 10 the week after that. And no budget to send us out on tour. No point in touring, really, unless we could somehow resuscitate ol' Satch. Nobody, he told us, would want to come out to a Satchel event in a bookstore. "Baseball events don't work in bookstores," he proclaimed as confidently as he would have said, "The earth revolves around the sun."

Mind you, our publicist did what he was supposed to do, and he did it well. He sent our book out to radio, newspaper and TV people all over America, and he followed up with phone calls. We did probably 50 radio interviews, from National Public Radio to some obscure 100-watt station in Guam (we're big in Guam). Still, we knew where our core audience was. They were at baseball games. So we got a list of all the stadiums in the United States and started cold-calling them. But when we finally got the right person on the phone, he'd tell us it was already too late and ask if we wanted to buy advertising space at the stadium. We tried to convince major league baseball to get in on Satchel Paige Days, maybe on his birthday. Amazingly enough, we got close. But we struck out. We tried to get stadium vendors to sell the book. We succeeded in two places, but we were hoping for 200. We tried to partner with the Negro Leagues Museum. We whiffed once again.

Meanwhile, Arielle was experiencing what was now a familiar frustration with her book. Not having Jane Austen with her in the flesh was proving a formidable obstacle to getting people to come to a bookstore event. Then, on top of it all, her editor, the main champion of her book, moved to another publishing house and her sweet young book was suddenly a miserable orphan.

We felt dumb as a sack of hammers.

Soon thereafter we were at a party, and we accidentally let it slip that Arielle was a literary agent. The word buzzed madly through the room: *There's a book agent in the house!* Arielle was inundated for the umpteenth time. Like a dateless cheerleader at an all-boys high school mixer, she was hit upon all night. As we headed home, we reflected on the seemingly insatiable thirst we'd seen exhibited by the public for the answer to this question:

HOW DO I GET MY BOOK PUBLISHED?

"Aha," we said. We'll do a seminar about how to get a book published! In bookstores. We'll use our own books as examples of how to develop a book out of something you're passionate about. We'll throw back the curtain and show people the little man behind the scary Wizard in publishing.

Thus was born Putting Your Passion into Print: The Idea.

It took dozens and dozens of the coldest of calls, but we finally got our first bite. A booking. At a bookstore in a strip mall in a town you forget even as you're driving through it. But our ball was rolling. We used that booking to leverage others. Boom! We had a 16-bookstores-in-24-days tour.

Thus was born Putting Your Passion into Print: The Tour.

Luckily, we had no idea what we were getting ourselves into. We just tossed copies of our books and promotional materials into our car and off we went. And what an education we got. From people like Mary Gleysteen of the Eagle Harbour Bookstore on Bainbridge Island, Washington, who packed the room full of her smart and lovely customers. And from Maria Muscarella at the Barnes & Noble in Vancouver, who brought all 50 members of her writing group. And from Kate Cerino at Paulina Springs Book Company in Sisters, Oregon, who *did* want to do an event about Satchel Paige and filled her gem of a store with 35 people, almost all of whom had seen Satchel play. (For the full story, see pages 372–373.)

We also visited stores that didn't have our books, hadn't done one thing to let anyone know we were coming and seemed shocked to see us. The worst one was a rainy night in Oregon, when zero people showed up. Zero. And the store didn't even give us a complimentary beverage. But even this cloud had a silver lining. It was the night of the last game of the World Series, and David had been heartbroken about having to miss the early innings. In fact, he'd been secretly hoping we could cut out early—he just didn't think it would be *that* early.

In all, we drove about 3,000 miles. Saw spectacular country. Met amazing people of every ilk. Saw some elk. Sold many books. Witnessed brilliant flashes of wit and imagination. Listened to droning folks who didn't know when to say when. But mostly we were overwhelmed by how many people all over America:

- Want to write and publish a book,
- Are starved to have the smoke and mirrors removed from the publishing process, or
- Have previously written a book, watched it die on the vine and are determined to prevent history from repeating itself.

A few months after our tour, a high school friend of Arielle's mentioned our workshop to a colleague who was a producer at NPR's *Talk of the Nation*. Intrigued, and knowing so many aspiring writers herself, the producer asked us to come on the show. It was wild to watch the switchboard light up with calls from every nook and cranny of the country. The segment was such a success that Arielle was asked back for a follow-up interview later that week.

The Payoff

All during our tour, David kept repeating, like a man possessed, that he thought our workshop would make for a great book. But Arielle pooh-poohed the idea, coming up with all the lame excuses people use to stop themselves from achieving success and having fun. The only difference being that Arielle's self-doubt was probably even more severe than the average person's because she's a literary agent. And literary agents, like editors, are trained from an early age to say no, to figure out why a book won't work. So they found themselves playing the parts of Rock and Hard Place.

Well, just as Arielle was about to put the kibosh on David's idea once and for all, serendipity reared its pretty head. Arielle happened to be meeting with the editorial staff of Workman Publishing (yes, check the spine). Her boss, Jim Levine, the founder of the Levine Greenberg Rostan Literary Agency, was also in the meeting, and he told Peter Workman about our *Talk of the Nation* appearance. Peter said, "That's a proposal I'd be interested in seeing."

Thus was born *Putting Your Passion into Print:* The Book.

And now here we are, 10 years later. We are down to five major publishers, with the behemoth merger of Random House and Penguin. Amazon is now a publisher and controls the majority of the ebook marketplace. The fastest-selling book in history is *Fifty Shades of Grey,* a book that was published by the tiniest of tiny publishers—just a quarter step from self-publishing.

Nowadays many publishers seem more concerned with a writer's platform, how many Twitter followers and Facebook friends an author has, than how good his book is. Traditional publishing seems to be shrinking, even as there are more and more ways to get published. So, now we give you this third edition. See you again in another five years, when we'll all be downloading books directly into our brains.

How to Get Successfully Published Today

With so many ways to get published today, the process can be exceedingly confusing. But when you break down these many different ways, they sort themselves out into just three primary paths: 1) "The Big 5" publishing houses: HarperCollins, Penguin Random House, Simon & Schuster, Hachette, and Macmillan, 2) independent presses that range in size from the hefty W.W. Norton to the many university presses to the numerous one-person shops, and 3) self-publishing.

In our combined 35 years of experience in the publishing business as agents, writers and book doctors, we have walked down all three paths—and we have the corns, calluses and blisters to prove it. To help you avoid such injuries, we want to give you a quick primer that'll help you start to sort out which path is best for you. The rest of the book will go into far more detail on each of these paths, but we've found that laying out the basics is often enough to at least eliminate one that you know is *not* right for you.

1. The Big Five

B ecause publishing has gone from being a gentleman's business to being owned and operated by corporations, you have a much better chance of getting your book published if you are Snooki from *Jersey Shore* hawking your new diet manifesto than if you're an unknown (or even established but not famous) writer who's written a brilliant work of literary fiction. And because the corporatized publishing world continues to shrink at an alarming rate, there are fewer and fewer slots available, and the competition is every bit as fierce for those ever-dwindling spots. Add to this the fact that unless you are related to or sleeping with Mister Harper or Mister Collins, you will need to find an agent. The best agents tend to take on new clients who are at the very top of the cream of the crop. Even new agents who are trying to establish themselves take on only a tiny percentage of what they are pitched.

Writers who haven't been published by The Big 5 assume that once they get a deal with one of these big fish, they'll be able to sit in their living rooms and wait for their publishers to set up interviews with Ellen DeGeneres and Stephen Colbert. They assume they'll be sent on a multiple-city tour, where thousands of adoring readers will buy their books, ask for their autograph and shower them with the love and adoration they so richly deserve. We tell them from hard-won experience that this is almost never the case. But if your book needs both reviews by major media and placement in hundreds of bookstores to succeed, then put on your goggles, cap, and fins and see if you can swim with the big guys. Although your dream tour may be just that—a dream—it is true that if your book starts to take off, The Big 5 have the power and connections to turn your book into an instant hit.

2. Independent Presses

T hese publishers almost always specialize in a certain kind of book and appeal to a niche audience (as opposed to The Big 5, who are generalists and, in theory at least, publish books for everyone). That's not to say they can't be big companies. Workman, the publisher of this book, is one of the most successful publishers in the world. They've published everything from *What to Expect When You're Expecting* to *1,000 Places to See Before You Die* to the Sandra Boynton oeuvre. But many independent publishers tend to be small and run by individuals who are passionate about the subjects that they are publishing. A good number of these publishers are very well respected, and their books get reviewed in the largest and most prestigious publications in the world.

Because they have far fewer books on their lists, chances are, you're going to be the big spring book from your independent publisher. We speak from experience that it is so much better to be the big spring book from a well-respected independent press than it is to be book number 2,478 from publishers like Penguin Random House because they've got Stephen King, Bill Clinton and Snooki to promote. And the great news is, you don't have to have an agent when querying most independent publishers. Almost all indies expect writers to submit directly to them.

One major downside: Most independent publishers have limited resources. If, for some reason, you should happen to catch literary lightning in a bottle and your book blows up, an independent press may not be able to capitalize on your book's success. They may not have the bookers for Ellen and Colbert on speed-dial. And often they have to do very small print runs, so there's a good chance your book will sell out of its printing very quickly and there will be no print books immediately available.

3. Self-Publishing

This approach has recently been dubbed "independent" or "indie" publishing, not to be confused with independent presses. More than ever, writers are choosing to embrace the independent spirit of self-publishing. Many are not even going after agents or publishers. Why? Because they don't want to spend years being rejected; because they see opportunities in the market and want a bigger share of the pie than publishers offer; because they want full control of their book; for some, because they just want a relic of their work to share with friends and family. And many writers choose self-publishing because they don't want to wait for the *slooooooow* publishing machine. If you start looking for an agent or publisher right now, it can take years to find one (that is, if you *do* find one). Then after you get a book deal, it's typically going to take between 18 months and two years for your book to come out.

The good news about self-publishing is that you get to do everything you want with your book. The bad news is that you *have* to do everything. And as with any entrepreneurial project, you can spend between $0.00 to hundreds of thousands of dollars.

Whatever publishing approach you choose, you have to be the engine that drives your book's train. And the principles underlying successfully published books are remarkably similar.

The Four Principles of Successful Publishing

Roaming from coast to coast, talking with book people from the biggest publishers to the smallest, from bestselling authors to writers who have never been published, we've come to the conclusion that publishing success comes from following four basic principles. To our delight, even with all the dizzying changes these past 10 years have wrought, these exact same principles still apply. Enjoy!

1. Research

It's crucial to know what books are out there and to have an idea of who might publish and sell your book. Most important, who will read it and how are you going to get it onto their bookshelves or e-readers? Research will help you answer all those questions. It will be your guide through every stage of the publishing process, and with a little bit of luck it will help your book rise to the top of the publishing barrel.

If you systematically research every part of the book publishing process, you will be way ahead of your competitors. Most people simply do not do the research it takes to get a book published and sold. Let us be clear: Research takes a lot of hard work, but if you put the time in, your odds of getting published will go from nearly nil to extremely decent.

No Stone Unturned

Jackson Michael had a passion. Football. Specifically football as it was played professionally before the game became a multi-billion-dollar industry. And he wanted to write a book about it. He'd never published a book before. He wasn't even a professional writer, but he was a master at research.

First, Jackson went to his local independent bookstore, to his local library, and to online bookstores to find out what was already written on the subject. He found out that there were similar books but nothing exactly like what he was writing. Then he started researching players. Through his research, he was able to track down football Hall-of-Famer Carl Eller. He interviewed the legendary defender who played for the Minnesota Vikings in the 1960s and '70s, getting a completely new perspective on one of the most iconic plays in the history of the National Football League (NFL). Once he had this interview under his belt, he used it to contact other players he had researched. One interview led to another interview, which led to another, until a fascinating oral history was born.

Once Jackson had enough material for a proposal, he started researching statistics on the NFL. His proposal included everything from viewership ratings to population statistics to team revenues. It took many drafts, but once he was done, he had an airtight case on why this book should be published and that a large audience was waiting to read it.

Then it was time to submit the book to agents and independent publishers. "I researched every publisher and agent I contacted. One key bit of study is the submission guidelines. Simply following guidelines won't win a yes, but not following them could garner an immediate no."

Jackson also researched publishers' catalogs and clearly spelled out how his book would fit each one's list. "One publisher didn't publish sports books but did publish oral histories. In the query, I stated that I understood they didn't publish football books but that at its root this was an oral history that touched on racial issues and labor history—topics they *were* interested in."

Ultimately, Jackson got three offers for his book, *The Game Before the Money,* and ultimately signed with The University of Nebraska Press. "I think going the extra mile with research helped open those doors."

2. Network

The Carnegie Institute of Technology has long studied success and has concluded that, even in profoundly technical professions like engineering, only 15% of financial success stems from technical skills. A whopping 85% is due to "human engineering," or people skills. Publishing is no exception. Finding the right agent and publisher, creating buzz, reaching your readers and selling books are all, in very large part, dependent upon people skills. *Networking.*

If you are someone who naturally has the gift of gab, or has developed your in-person networking skills, fabulous. If you, like many writers, are challenged in the human engineering area, networking may yield slightly more enjoyment than a root canal with a migraine headache. But compared with days of yore, when you actually had to go out to parties, readings and conferences to meet the

Networking Mash-Up

Kristine Asselin was hoping to break into writing for children after she'd finished several manuscripts. She attended a one-day workshop sponsored by the New England chapter of the Society for Children's Book Writers and Illustrators (SCBWI). "It rocked my world. Before then, I had no idea that writers and illustrators came together to learn from each other." Soon after that fall workshop, she attended her first regional conference. At first it was difficult for her because she was an unknown, unpublished, uncertain writer who didn't know if she had what it took. "But everyone I met treated me like a 'real' writer." She found that hanging out with other writers, ranging from people who just dreamed of one day writing a book to successful authors with dozens of books under their belts, turned out to be a blast.

Kris also used cyber-networking to move her publishing career forward. It all started with National Novel Writing Month (NaNoWriMo). Every November, hundreds of thousands of writers write a 50,000-word novel in one month. Their motto: no plot, no problem. (We'll talk more about NaNoWriMo later.) Through networking with this worldwide writing group, Kris was able to turn off the critic in her head and write fast. "I loved fast-drafting without my inner editor!" By the end of November, she'd completed a young adult (YA) novel.

Kris edited and re-edited the book, got it off to critique partners, and finally felt ready to launch it into the world. In a perfect example of networking at the speed of light, she pitched a novel during #PitMad (a pitch party on Twitter), attracting the interest of Meredith Rich, an editor at Bloomsbury Spark. Meredith read the book and asked to speak with Kris. This conversation led to another about a different book Kris had completed. Meredith offered Kris a contract for *that* book, *Any Way You Slice It.* Though a bit circuitous, Kris did get her book deal through a Twitter pitch!

Networking over cyberspace. Networking in person. Nowadays, there are so many ways to reach and connect with people from all walks of the publishing world. "We all have different styles, and not everything works for everyone," Kris says. "Take workshops, take classes, read blogs, read books in your chosen genre, have your friends give you writing prompts. Put yourself out there. Be generous. That's how good things happen!"

people who might help you get your book published, today's networkers have it made. There are now approximately a squazillion places to connect with people online. At last, you can network uncombed, unkempt and in your jammies, after taking a 30-second commute to your computer. All the while doing what comes naturally to you: *writing*.

3. Write

One of our all-time favorite bookstores is Books & Books in Miami. Cross its threshold and you're sure to rub elbows with the literati, whether you know it or not. We asked Books & Books owner Mitchell Kaplan about the importance of good writing and, unsurprisingly, his author-centric brain instantly produced a perfect gem. The protagonist of this true story is a long-time writer. He's on a book tour and, having just finished reading from his new book, opens up the room for questions. A man in his sixties raises his hand and asks, "I'm about to retire from a long career as a cardiac surgeon and I'm thinking about becoming a novelist. What advice do you have for me?" The author pauses, then asks back, "I'm just about to retire from a long career as a

The Man Who Just Kept Writing

Tamim Ansary has been a writer for 35 years. When he first got out of college, he volunteered at a local collective weekly newspaper where he could write anything he wanted and get it published every week. He didn't get paid for this writing, but he amassed enough clippings to make an impressive showing at future job interviews. (Eventually, those clippings landed him a job as an assistant editor at a niche newspaper that actually paid him a living wage.) He also started sending out fiction to small literary magazines, a number of which accepted his work.

Later, Tamim went to work for a textbook publisher and eventually worked on a textbook program that earned tens of millions of dollars for the company. But his name never appeared on a textbook cover and he didn't get anything out of it except his paycheck and the privilege of working at home. He started freelancing with other textbook publishers and continued to make a living as a writer.

Then, one day, Tamim's wife was browsing through a magazine in a dentist's office and happened to see that a publisher was looking for people with inside knowledge of various countries to write children's books. Tamim got a contract for a book about Afghanistan, his native land. He had no agent, but he got a book with his name on it and eventually even made a little money from it.

writer and I'm thinking about becoming a cardiac surgeon. What advice do you have for me?"

While writing may not seem like heart surgery, imagine for a moment that it's as hard to become a successfully published writer as it is to become a cardiac surgeon. Imagine all the 90-hour weeks young doctors have to put in before they're allowed to practice on their own. You wouldn't let an aspiring surgeon cut into your heart after a week on the job, would you? As ridiculous as it sounds, many writers expect this kind of immediate success. They think that because they can put pen to paper (or finger to keyboard) and make words come out, these words will be compelling, valuable, page-turning.

So what is the key to a long and successful publishing career? We've asked dozens and dozens of writers and the overwhelming answer is: *Keep writing.*

You never know which piece of writing is going to be the one that makes the world stand up and take notice or sit down and shut up. You never know how long it will take to become a great writer or to write a great book. Even if you plan to work with a coauthor, you still need to continually get your ideas down on paper. You fail and you learn. But you can't learn anything unless you're actually, you know . . . writing.

Some years later, Tamim completed a novel that an agent liked well enough to represent. And then 9/11 happened. On that horrible day, Tamim sent an email about Afghanistan to a dozen friends, who sent it to a dozen friends, who sent it to a dozen friends, until it landed in the inboxes of millions around the world. Suddenly Bill Moyers, NPR, Oprah and a host of others were asking him for interviews. His agent said, "Give me a proposal to sell, anything, just put something on a piece of paper!" It so happened that Tamim had a thousand raw pages of a memoir he'd been working on for years. He thought about how he could carve a book relevant to the times out of that mass of material and he wrote a one-page description of his book. Titled *West of Kabul, East of New York*, it was snapped up by one of the world's most distinguished publishers. Since publication, the book has enjoyed a wonderful life of its own. It has been selected for One Book One City everywhere from Waco to San Francisco. And has been adopted by numerous freshman reading classes in universities around the country. These are the kinds of honors that turn a book into a backlist bestseller and allow authors to enjoy the glorious and rare birds of publishing: royalty checks! Tamim says, "Getting my book published wouldn't have happened without the email. But it also wouldn't have happened without the raw memoir out of which it was carved, already written and waiting to be used. The moral: Always write."

The Power of Perseverance

Acclaimed novelist Charles Baxter got a Ph.D. in English and then wrote fiction and poetry while teaching. He sent off his first completed novel to a few editors. As Charlie says, "I was exhilarated by almost every one of my sentences. I suspected I was a genius but was careful to keep this stupendous secret to myself." Sadly, this was not the conclusion of the editors who received the book. Charlie got the ubiquitous "not for us" response. Two years later, he finished another novel and sent it off to an agent who had agreed to take him on. He called to find out her reaction.

"Charlie," she said, "don't you want to know what I think of your new novel?"

"Yes, Julia, of course I do."

"I hate it," she said.

After an intense recovery period, Charlie hooked up with another agent. With a renewed sense of hope and enthusiasm, he sent off yet another newly completed novel. The new agent, while kinder than the last, told him it just wasn't marketable. "I felt as if my nerves had moved out to the surface of my skin," Charlie says. "I felt humiliated and exposed."

So Charlie resigned himself to the hallowed halls of academia. But just before hanging up his literary hat for good, he wrote one more short story, "Harmony of the World," based on the feelings of brutal rejection and soul-sucking failure these years had inflicted upon him. He sent it out to a local literary journal, expecting to receive one last stinging rejection. But much to his amazement "Harmony of the World" was accepted. And then . . . drum roll . . . it won a Pushcart Prize, one of the highest honors awarded to a short story! It was included in the 1982 edition of *Best American Short Stories.* And it led to a string of book contracts, hefty sales, movie options and that unquantifiable satisfaction of knowing that maybe, in fact, you were right after all—you are a genius!

As you can imagine, Charlie is a major proponent of perseverance. "Part of being a writer is going through dark nights of the soul. In these nights you confront your own doubts, lack of self-confidence, the futility of what you are doing and the various ways in which you fail to measure up. But a lack of self-confidence can be turned to your own purposes if it helps you to take pains, to take care, to avoid glibness."

He also makes the important point that the more you write (and read), the better your writing will become. Which means you need to persevere through the periods when your writing isn't quite good enough. Until eventually it is.

The moral of this story? As Charlie says, "Don't quit. Don't quit. Don't quit. Don't quit."

4. Persevere

You will want to quit. You will question your ability to succeed. You will want to throw your hands up in despair and curse the author gods. And to overcome, you will need perseverance. The vast majority of the world's finest and most successful authors have all had to persevere against oftentimes staggering evidence that they were complete losers who were bound to fail. Now perseverance doesn't mean mindlessly sending out the same stuff over and over and over again. The best kind of perseverance involves continuously evolving and reinventing yourself and your material. Perseverance is the fertilizer that turns a tiny acorn into a mighty oak.

Perseverance is so important because you never know when it's going to be your time. Which agent is going to go gaga over your material? It may be the second person you send it to. But more likely it will be the 42nd or even the 92nd. You never know which publisher is going to scoop you up. Maybe it'll be Penguin Random House or maybe it'll be the house you build because no publisher will bite. And your house may be able to deliver your book into the heads, hearts and hands of readers better than Penguin Random House ever could. You never know what piece of publicity is going to launch your career. It may be the *Today* show (very unlikely), or it may be a blogger who is the go-to gal for everyone interested in books like yours (much more likely). You never know which book is going to connect with the audience you're sure is out there. It may be your first, it may be your seventh. So, please, don't quit five minutes before the miracle.

Setting Up Shop

Writing the Right Idea

"To produce a mighty book, you must choose a mighty theme."

—Herman Melville

PICKING THE RIGHT IDEA—which is different from picking a good idea—is one of the most essential pieces of the book-writing puzzle. The right idea is one that is so exciting, you'll be willing to hack away at it for years and years. The right idea is one you are particularly well suited to write. The right idea will make a real contribution—which can include a good laugh or a good cry or a good cheesecake recipe—to the world. The right idea will get agents, editors and publishers excited. It'll get readers to buy and read your book and will inspire all sorts of media to cover it.

Settle on the right idea before you start writing. But the very first thing you need to ask yourself, before you even choose an idea, is:

Do I *really* want to write a book?

Before you scream YES! let us first run you through the economics and the daily realities of writing a book. Because as Michael Powell, founder of the famed Powell's Books in Portland, Oregon, says, "I don't think authors ask themselves the hard questions. You can't just hand over the pages of your manuscript and then go to the beach. Writing is the beginning point. Then you have to decide how much energy, money and time you can put into your book."

The Economics of Publishing

Even the least labor-intensive book will take hundreds and hundreds of hours of your time; and there's no guarantee you'll ever make a penny, let alone get rich. In fact, your odds of becoming rich in the book world boil down to 1) slim, and 2) none. For every Stephen King (and there is, after all, only one of him), there are hundreds of thousands of people who write books and make NO money. Either they're unable to sell their projects, or they sell them to publishers who pay no up-front money, or they self-publish and have to dig into their own pockets just to get their books into print, and on and on. Marketing maven and *New York Times* bestselling author Seth Godin puts it this way: "Please understand that book publishing is an organized hobby, not a business. The return on equity and return on time for authors and for publishers is horrendous. If you're doing it for the money, you're going to be disappointed." That's why, before you decide to write the book you wish to publish, we ask you to consider the following equation:

$$\frac{X\ (\$)}{Y\ (time)} = Z\ (\$\ an\ hour)$$

Let's say you spend 700 hours on your book. And you make 0 dollars. Now let's do the math:

$$\frac{\$0}{700\ hours} = \$0\ an\ hour$$

Before you start, know that you may make a grand total of nothing. It may actually cost you money to write a book, even if it's simply a matter of new cartridges for your printer, but there may also be travel, books for research, phone calls, postage and so on. Now let's suppose you get an advance of $5,000, which can be, depending on the kind of book you're writing, a nice advance:

$$\frac{\$5,000}{700\ hours} = \$7.14\ an\ hour$$

That's well below minimum wage. But here's the thing: What you receive initially for writing your book doesn't necessarily correlate to the amount of money your book could eventually bring you. As Seth Godin points out, "A book gives you leverage to spread an idea far and wide. There's a quite common worldview that says that people who write books know what they are talking about, that a book confers some sort of authority." In other words, it may be possible for you to use your newfound author status to become an authority and make some dough.

Let's say you've decided to write the complete guide to raising bunny rabbits. You find a small publisher who specializes in pet care, and they agree to publish your book. You're paid a $1,500 advance. That's not big money, but consider this: After your book comes out, you'll be in a position to start the National Bunny Rabbit Social Club—because people now see you as *the* expert on bunny rabbits. You charge bunny fiends $10 a month to be part of the club. If 100 people join, that's $12,000 a year. Build up your membership to 1,000, and that's $120,000! Now we're talking real money, in your bank account.

> "The profession of book-writing makes horse racing seem like a solid, stable business."
>
> —*John Steinbeck*

What this basically means is that you're going to need another source of income while you write your book or proposal, unless a) you're a person with a massive trust fund, or b) you work short hours and make large coin. (If you're in either of these categories, please contact the authors; we have some wonderful opportunities to discuss with you.)

Do You Stay or Do You Go?

You've run the numbers and you've figured out a way to write a book without selling your house. But do you have the time and personality to make a book happen? Answer these questions to find out:

- Do you want to spend many, many hours working on something that may never see the light of day?

- Are kids, partners, job and recreation going to be obstacles that you can get around?

- Do you have the discipline, focus and attention span it takes to make a book and get it published?

- Are you self-motivated enough to grind it out month after month?

- Can you stand being alone in a room, staring at a blank computer screen or an empty piece of paper?

- Can you put aside regular chunks of time to work on your book?

- Do you have the desire to shape your life to make the time you need?

- Besides the hundreds of hours you spend writing your book, will you also be able and willing to set aside chunks of your day in the great time suck known as social networking (which we will be getting to in the following chapter), and then to continue to nurture those networks for an indefinite period of time?

Persistence Pays Off

Susan Wooldridge, author of *poemcrazy: freeing your life with words*, needed seven years to free up enough time to write her book. Between her workshops, her newsletter, her kids, her husband and her generally overextended life, she often had only minutes a day to devote to writing. But Susan embraced an ancient Chinese adage: It doesn't matter how slow you go as long as you do not stop. One day, she would just write chapter headings or cross out one line. Another, she'd add page numbers—anything to move forward, to keep her book alive. After seven years, she had more than enough material for a great proposal. Which landed her an agent. Who got her a book contract. *Poemcrazy*, she's happy to report, is now in its 21st printing.

Christopher Paul Curtis took a totally different approach, but also wound up happily published. After high school, Christopher took a job at a factory in Flint, Michigan. It was miserable work. He would write in his journal during his breaks to keep from going insane. Still, he didn't consider a career as a writer until his wife encouraged him to take a year off and give it a shot (illustrating the importance of marrying a really nice person). To live on one salary for a whole year was not fun. Having a book after a year of writing was. Christopher submitted that book to a contest, whose first prize was publication by a major publisher. Like Rocky, he didn't win but still ended up a winner. The publisher decided to publish his book anyway, and *The Watsons Go to Birmingham—1963* was named a Newbery Honor Book. And his next book, *Bud, Not Buddy*, won a Newbery Medal, the top prize in children's publishing.

Answering these questions with brutal honesty is a smart thing to do before deciding to write a book. Bottom line: Do you have the skill, audacity, brains, drive, the vavavoom and the zazazoo to write a book, find someone to publish it and then convince people to buy it?

You do? Then it's time to choose an idea. Or rather, The Right Idea.

Judging Your Idea

Make a list of the strengths and weaknesses of your idea according to the following categories and questions, which we'll explain throughout the rest of this chapter and, indeed, the rest of the book:

- *Audience.* Who will be interested in reading your book? Is there a big enough audience?

■ *Competition.* What other books like yours are already out there? Is the competition overwhelming?

■ *Marketability.* Do you have a way to reach your audience? Why will your book attract attention from the media and the public? What skills and contacts do you possess that would help get the word out?

■ *Potential costs.* How much will you have to pay for necessary photographs and/or writing by other authors? Will you need to travel?

■ *The "Why me?" factor.* Why are you the person to write this book? What do you have to say that's new and different?

■ *Salability.* Why would a publisher, a bookstore and eventually a reader plunk down money to buy your book?

Who's Your Audience?

This should be the *very first* question you ask yourself when you come up with an idea for a book. Assuming, of course, you want someone to actually read your book. If you don't, by all means proceed without giving your audience another thought. But what is the point of a book without an audience? If you don't have one, you might as well save yourself the grief and keep a journal instead.

We are always shocked by how many people begin to write without giving a thought to their audience. The success of any book—whether it be critical success, financial success, or the kind of success that comes in the shape of a letter saying "Your book changed my life"—is dependent on its readers. Every part of the publishing process is designed to get your book into readers' hot little hands. That's why you must get a handle on who your audience is and why they would want to read your book. Step back from the trees and take a look at the forest where your potential readers live, work and play.

The more specific you can be when imagining your readers, the easier it will be to reach them. As you consider your ideas, picture the people who might buy your book. Go where they go. Live where they live. Make them come to life in your mind.

Assuming that your idea is based on a subject of great interest to you, it's probably fair to say that you're aware of which magazines, TV and radio

▶ In researching competitive titles, be sure to write down the title, subtitle, author(s), publisher and year of publication for each and every book on your list. This will save you time down the line.

shows, newspapers, websites, blogs and the like provide coverage of the subject. Make a list of the relevant media outlets you know of, being as specific as you possibly can. You'll keep updating this list throughout the process.

Think of the world as your personal market research lab. Try to find out if the audience you're imagining really does exist. This process will help you not only in writing your book, but also in marketing, publicizing and selling it. And if you try and try but still can't find the audience you thought was out there, perhaps you should consider another idea.

Discuss, disseminate and get feedback on your ideas from members of your potential audience to see if they spark enthusiasm. You can do this via Twitter, Facebook, online forums, conventions, conferences or your local book club. If it seems too early to be reaching out to your audience (a.k.a., publicizing and marketing your book-to-be), you're in for a shock. These days, depending on the kind of book you're writing, you might want to think not just about reaching but also about actively *building* that audience— drum roll—*before you even have a book*. As publishers devote fewer and fewer resources to publicizing and marketing books, a carefully cultivated and captive audience is becoming an ever more valuable commodity, sometimes even a necessity. Many of the tools you'll need to build this audience exist in a magical hinterland where a keystroke can instantly connect you to a web of readers. Yes, we're talking about the power of the Internet, and you're coming

Overcoming the Competition

I n May of 1763, James Boswell ran into Samuel Johnson in the back room of a bookstore. At the time, Johnson, a prickly, difficult man, was one of the best-known literary figures in England. But Boswell, basically a nobody at that point, was not intimidated. And Johnson took a shine to him and let him hang around.

So Boswell asked questions. And Boswell listened. While Johnson waxed on about, well, everything.

Boswell became passionate about writing a biography of the great man. But he had so much material, and he really wanted to do it right—which meant taking his time. Other biographies popped up. Boswell despaired that no one would care about his—that his moment had passed. Still, his passion burned on. It took him almost 30 years, but he did finally finish his biography. And the book became a huge success. It is still in print more than 300 years later, unlike nearly every other Johnson biography out there. Indeed, Boswell's *Life of Samuel Johnson* (1791) is considered by many to be the greatest biography ever written.

up on a chapter that explains all about how to use it to sow the seeds of literary greatness.

Did the Competition Get There First?

You may have a blockbuster idea with a rabid audience. But if that book has already been done, what's the point? Look around to make sure it hasn't. That said, some degree of competition may demonstrate a public desire for books on your topic; so if there isn't a book out there with your particular, original spin, yours could still have a fighting chance. In fact, publishers look to the sales of similar books as proof that lots of readers are interested in your subject.

Start making lists of books that are similar to yours. Study these books. Get a feel for your competition. Literally. How are they designed? What do their covers look like? How much do they cost? Are they hardcover or paperback? How are they marketed?

Internet bookstores are great for tracking down the competition. Go to Amazon, for example, and do a search on your subject. Once you find a competitive book, click on it and go to the icon that identifies similar books. Boom, you've got five similar books. And five more. And five more. Asking around helps, too—especially at bookstores and libraries.

> "The unread story is not a story; it is little black marks on wood pulp. The reader, reading it, makes it live: a live thing, a story."
>
> —*Ursula K. Le Guin*

Is your book different enough from the competition that a bookseller and a reader will identify its uniqueness just by picking it up, reading the description on its flaps or back and leafing through its pages?

If not, you'll have a hard time convincing any publisher that your book should be published.

Is Your Idea Publicity-Friendly?

As you consider which idea basket to put your eggs in, be sure to contemplate how and where you might be able to publicize it when the time comes. If you can't get people to write and talk about your book, it's going to be difficult to get it bought and read. Here are some things to think about:

- Is there anything unique about your book that the media might pick up on?

- What publications/websites might you write an article for as a means of getting your "byline" out in the world (hence establishing your expertise and heightening your author cred)?

■ What publications/websites would be interested in featuring you and your work? What bloggers could you approach? Which online communities could you reach out to?

■ Which publications/websites might run an excerpt from your book or do an interview with you? (Think broadly but realistically here. Everyone wants *New York Times* coverage; however, it's better to show a publisher what you have a really good shot at rather than clogging the works with what you wish for in your wildest dreams.)

■ What kinds of organizations, groups or clubs might be interested in your book? Do they have websites or publications that might review your book or interview you?

■ Are there universities or charities that will cotton to you and your book, potentially helping to boost promotional efforts or sales?

■ What kinds of events can you see yourself putting on for your book? Is there anything about these events that could be considered newsworthy?

■ Are there any trends you observe in mainstream media or the blogosphere that you can publicly comment on, to bring attention to your book?

Once you've corralled your existing knowledge, it's back to our very first directive: Research. If you're writing about interior decorating, start reading interior decorating magazines, watching all the interior decorating shows on TV, checking out all the websites, forums and blogs on the subject. Pay attention to the differences among them and think about how your book might be featured on each. Go after the obvious targets, but be on the lookout for new or potentially overlooked ways of penetrating the book-buying landscape. And activate your imagination. When your interior decorating tome comes out, maybe you could offer your services to a charity that helps low-income families build homes. Would local and national media do a story on that? Maybe you could do an event at a home improvement store, showing shoppers how to use your techniques while selling a few copies of your book. Maybe you could hold a contest for booksellers—the winner receives a free home makeover. Maybe you could do a series of short videos to post on your website or on a video sharing site, each discussing a particular interior design topic, like color, fabric, bathrooms and basements. Write a series of Top 10 lists that you post all over the web. (Everybody loves a Top 10 list.)

Permissions and Other Expenses

Will your book require photographs, illustrations, song lyrics or excerpts from other books or other people's poems? If so, in all likelihood you'll need permission to use them. Permissions usually require money. Your money. Not your publisher's.

That's why it's necessary to deal with the money/permission issue up front, before you get too far down the line. This way, you can figure out if your idea is one you can actually afford to write.

For archival photographs, you may want to start by calling or going to the website of Getty (the largest photo stock house in the world) to find out the going rate for photographs you might use in your book. This will give you a high-end starting point from which to figure out your costs. If you're going to need original photographs or illustrations, start poking around the web to see if you can find photographers or artists who are young and hungry (i.e., willing to work dirt cheap). Some publishers will want to handle picking, hiring and maybe even paying photographers, but it's best to do your research early so that you're fully prepared no matter what the scenario.

The reason for doing this early research is that sometimes permissions can actually cost more than what you will be paid to write your book. And if you get no advance payment, the costs will all be out of pocket.

Also, obtaining permissions is a huge pain in the keister. If playing detective, administrator and accountant is not your strong suit (or if you can't enlist some unsuspecting underling or family member!), you might consider taking on an idea that does not involve permissions.

As if that's not enough, you'll also need to consider other potential expenses. Will you have to travel for your book? Will you have to hire outside help for research? Will you have to buy supplies for your book (e.g., food for recipe testing, yarn for knitting, lumber and tools for a do-it-yourself book)? How much will it cost to set up and maintain a website? And we're not even taking into account publicity and marketing costs.

Who Are *You* to Write Your Book?

Now it's time for some honest self-assessment. Do you really have something new to say? Something only you can put into words? Neal Sofman, owner of San Francisco's BookShop West Portal, says, "The thing I notice with successful authors is that they have a unique voice that communicates to their audience. They touch you in some way. You know immediately who's speaking because

What *Should* You Write?

People often set out to write the book they think they *should* write. A chef *should* write a cookbook. A manager *should* write a book on getting the most out of employees. A golf pro *should* write about the perfect swing. If you love what you do and want to share your enthusiasm and expertise, fantastic. But you may have a driving passion outside your day job, a driving passion that makes YOU the perfect person to write your book.

This was just the case for psychologist Bob Klein. Bob went out to lunch with literary agent James Levine to discuss writing a book based on his years of clinical practice—what he thought he should write about. As they were looking at the menu, Bob pulled out a long list from his pocket and scrutinized it.

"What's that?" Jim asked.

"Oh, that's my beer list," Bob said. "Wherever I go, I always try a new beer, and I rate it according to color, taste and what food it goes well with."

Jim, a fellow beer lover, asked to see the list. Being the wise agent that he is, the moment he laid eyes on it he said: "There's your book!"

Months later, *The Beer Lover's Rating Guide* was born. It has 220,000 copies in print in two editions and spawned an annual Page-A-Day® calendar. And Bob, well, Bob is now the envy of men everywhere as he travels the world over, reveling in, analyzing the particulars of and drinking . . . BEER!

Which brings us to our deep, philosophical thought on "should": Should shmould. Write about what you love. Chances are, a lot of other people love the same thing. And if you can communicate your passion, people will be drawn to you and what you write.

they're so distinct." Many, many people spend years and years writing and trying to market books that end up as recycled paper precisely because they've failed to capture their uniqueness on the page. And those who fail often become bitter and frustrated, sliding sadly into desperate lives of drugs, booze and literary criticism.

Which gets us back to your idea. "Is it so compelling that a person will plop down his hard-earned money for a copy of your book?" asks Jim Levine, founder of the Levine Greenberg Rostan Literary Agency and author of seven books. "Your friends and colleagues will say, 'That's a great idea,' which is different from saying, 'That's such a good idea, I'd pay $25 if you write it.' Most authors don't realize the difference here." How can *you* tell the difference? Now is the time to put to good use whatever bits of self-knowledge you possess. Consult your therapist, your inner children, your guru, your webmaster, your e-friends on Facebook and as many other people as possible. And not just your mother and BFFs who believe that nothing but sunshine pours out of you.

The more you know in your heart that you are the perfect author for your book and that your book is salable and/or necessary, the better your chances of convincing someone else. Remember: Every day, another writer nobody ever heard of gets a deal to publish a book.

Why Would Anyone Buy Your Book?

If you feel reasonably satisfied that you've got no major competition, a sizable audience, a good shot at garnering publicity, a whole lotta love for your subject and a good argument for why you're the one to write your book, then you need to ask yourself: How many copies will this book sell? To whom? And in what form?

If you're not sure how to answer these questions, you're not alone. Problem is, no one can really answer the question "Will this book sell?" Anyone who could would be swimming in money and the envy of all publishing. But because no one does, people in publishing houses are trained to pick ideas apart—to excavate the reasons an idea *won't* work. Whether you want to self-publish or convince a publisher that your book will buck the odds and rake it in, you need to familiarize yourself with what's selling right now, what's sold in the past, and how your idea can be compared and contrasted

> "Write something to suit yourself and many people will like it; write something to suit everybody and scarcely anyone will care for it."
>
> —*Jesse Stuart*

with successful books in the marketplace. Bestseller lists in *The New York Times*, *USA Today* and *Publishers Weekly* and on Amazon should become part of your regular reading. Check in frequently with general news outlets, both cyber and traditional, as well as websites, online communities and bloggers who write about and discuss the subject around which your book revolves. This way you can anticipate any stumbling blocks that might impede the sale of your book and be prepared to counter them. Tit for tat. Lynn Goldberg, CEO of Goldberg McDuffie Communications, one of the leading public relations agencies in publishing, puts it this way: "From the beginning, you must consider yourself an author and think like a publisher. You can't come into the world of publishing a total virgin. The good thing is that with this attitude you're neither helpless nor hopeless."

IS YOUR BOOK NICHE?

If you're contemplating a small niche subject, think twice before proceeding unless you plan to publish and sell the book yourself, you're okay with your book

The Art of Becoming a Literary Lion

If you're writing literary fiction, you're probably wondering how in the world you might convince a publisher, a bookseller or a reader to buy your book. Sure, there are trends in the world of literary fiction. But let's face it, a literary oeuvre is a lot harder to pitch than the newest fad diet.

Contemporary literary fiction is, sadly, read by few and doesn't attract the media attention that so many other categories of books profit from. And with the death of so many newspapers and magazines and/or the book review sections they contain, it gets even less media coverage than ever. Because it's difficult to get recognition for literary fiction, agents, publishers and booksellers tend to look for literary journals you've already been published in to determine if you're worthy of representation, publication or room on their bookshelves.

Most people have never heard of this plethora of literary journals (online and in print), even the very best of them; their circulation numbers are usually minuscule. But the top journals (and many smaller journals) are publishing our future literary stars. And people in literary circles look to these journals for a stamp of approval. That's why it behooves all literary fiction authors to submit writing to respected journals prior to embarking on a book project. This is just what Caroline Leavitt, the author of eight novels including *Girls in Trouble,* decided to do. "I had been sending out dozens and dozens of short stories to little literary magazines and getting nothing but rejections," Caroline says. "As soon as I got a story back, I redid it and sent it out again. After a while, the rejections started getting a little nicer. Instead of form letters, it would be 'Hmmm, interesting. Try us again.' Finally, I got a story published in the *Michigan Quarterly Review.* Two weeks after it was published, I got a letter from an agent in New York City, asking if I had an agent and did I have a novel. I was flabbergasted and signed on immediately."

You can see from Caroline's experience just how much weight the best of these journals pull! And luckily, there are now plenty of places in cyberspace where literary fiction writers can be happily published. To find out more about which journals to submit your work to, get yourself a copy of Writer's Digest Books' indispensable annual guide, *Novel & Short Story Writer's Market* or research online.

being sold to a small publisher and distributed in limited outlets or you have reason to believe it can transcend its genre. If no books even remotely related to yours have made good money—or exist, for that matter—it's going to be difficult to convince a publisher that yours is about to start a trend. That said, one of the handy things about the Internet is that it can help make the argument for books that appear to have tiny audiences by demonstrating a large and hungry interest in particular topics. Let's say you've put together a book on how to make your own cheese. Prior to the Internet's glory days, the small group of editors who acquire books at publishing houses might have scoffed at such a book, thinking, *How many people want to make cheese at home? I don't know anyone who does. What a silly idea!* That's the way things work with editors. But where audiences were hidden before, they now become obvious with the click of a few buttons. For example, a search for home cheese making turns up over 19 million results! In fact, the book on home cheese making—called, surprise surprise, *Home Cheese Making*—is now a classic.

Unlike niche subjects such as home cheese making, you'll notice that certain kinds of books seem to prove their salability over and over again. There's a famous story about British humorist Alan Coren, who claimed that the most successful, perennial themes in publishing were cats, golf and Nazis. To put his claim to the test, he wrote a collection of essays entitled *Golfing for Cats*. When it was published, Coren made sure that its cover pictured a cat putting on a green—with a Nazi flag flying above the hole!

What's hot (and what's niche) is always changing, so know which way the wind blows—studying the business you want to be part of will help you enter and succeed there. And, most importantly, it will help you make an informed decision of how, exactly, *you* want to publish. With so many options available now, many routes are open. Maybe an ebook sold directly to your audience through your website and other e-outlets is your publishing road of choice. Maybe a niche publisher who knows your audience through and through is going to sell the most books. Maybe the imprimatur of a big publisher is necessary to your vision of success. Pay attention to how the books *you* consider a success were published.

▶ Is your book controversial? Certain stores will not sell a book if it contains particular words or situations that they believe will offend their customers. But everything from *Uncle Tom's Cabin* to the Harry Potter books has been banned and burned. Though you might have more difficulty selling a controversial book to a publisher, such a book may also attract a certain kind of audience.

WHAT'S YOUR CATEGORY?

If you don't know what category of the bookstore your book belongs in, stop everything you're doing and figure this out *now*. Can't find a category that your book fits into? Then you've got trouble, my friend. We've seen far too many writers waltz into agents' and editors' offices and boldly proclaim, "My book is like no book ever written!" Please don't say this publicly. It's going to do nothing but harm your chances of getting published. Booksellers, particularly the larger ones, don't know what to do with category-free books, and they simply don't order many of them. Hence very few publishers will publish a book they see as category-free.

Both brick-and-mortar and online bookstores organize their offerings via a fairly common set of categories and subcategories—gardening, mysteries, history, romance, self-help and so on. "Get to know your category," says James Wehrle, director of sales for national accounts at Workman Publishing. "And get to know the strength of that category." Go to the largest brick-and-mortar bookstore in your area and take a look at how much space your particular category takes up. Familiarize yourself with what has been successful and what has stayed successful over the years. Read a minimum of 25 books on that shelf (though we hope you read many more). Check out copyright dates (usually listed within a book's first three pages). Talk to booksellers and librarians. Poke around the web. Find out what books the bloggers and tweeters are blogging and tweeting about. Check in with online magazines like Salon and The Huffington Post. If you see novels about Alaska popping up on bestseller lists and filling your local bookstore and you've got a mystery centered on the last frontier, then chances are you've got a salable idea.

To be clear, not fitting into any category is different from straddling two categories and residing comfortably in each. A biography of Rosa Parks could fit easily into a bookstore's Biography section as well as the African American, Women's Studies and American History sections. And plenty of books start within an overall category and end up establishing new subcategories in bookstores. Books on feng shui, which were first published under the general umbrella of home decorating, are a good example of this phenomenon; they got so popular that they now have their own subcategory. But if your book doesn't fit squarely into at least one category, you're probably going to find yourself slamming into brick walls.

WHY YOU NEED TO GET THEE TO THE BOOKSTORE AND THE LIBRARY

As you've probably guessed by now, three of a writer's best friends should be: 1) your local bookstore, 2) your local library and 3) your Internet bookstore. Unless you live in the hinterest of hinterlands, you probably have at least one bookstore and one library somewhere in your neck of the woods. Chances are, you've got a couple. Start spending time in them. And read lots of books—especially books that relate to your subject.

Many experienced writers underestimate the importance of reading. We meet memoirists who have never read a memoir, fantasy writers who read only realistic fiction, and picture book authors who haven't read a picture book since they were small children. As Stephen King writes in his inspiring memoir/writing guide, *On Writing*, "If you want to be a writer, you must do two things above all others: read a lot and write a lot. There's no way around these two things that I'm aware of, no shortcut."

Without getting into the merits of reading for inspiration, allow us to remind you that reading helps you understand what other readers are buying, shows you how other authors have presented work on similar subjects and lets you discover who publishes books like yours. Immerse yourself in the business and culture of books, both online and in the flesh. In doing so, you'll start to see if your idea is viable—whether it fits into or expands upon what's already out there. Reading publishing trade publications like *Shelf Awareness* (a daily free online newsletter), Publisher's Lunch (another online publication, which has both a free and a paid version), and *Publishers Weekly* (which has both a weekly print magazine and an online daily newsletter) will turn you on to stories about the book business. Reading online reviews and blogs will give you an up-to-the-second understanding of the zeitgeist and how to capture it. And while you're doing all this reading, you can start accumulating lists of people who might write about your book when it comes out.

> "Read, read, read. Read everything—trash, classics, good and bad, and see how they do it. Just like a carpenter who works as an apprentice and studies the master. Read!"
>
> —*William Faulkner*

While continuing to read, get to know your local bookstore and library. When you visit, take a moment to notice just how many books you see. Several hundred thousand books are published every year in the United States alone—not including print-on-demand titles, which are experiencing exponential growth. To put this into perspective: The film industry releases approximately 400 movies a year. The good news is that you have a much greater chance of getting a book published than getting a movie made. The bad news? The competition is so vast and so fierce that getting your published book noticed will require massive amounts of hard work and a dollop of good luck.

The visual manifestation of the level of your challenge will strike you as you walk into any big bookstore. Look at how few books are displayed with their covers facing out, and how many have only their thin little spines showing. This means that even if your book is lucky enough to land on the shelves of bookstores, it will have to rely on its spine to communicate your very excellent idea.

▶ If you use your bookstore like your own private library, researching and reading there but never actually buying a book, don't expect to get advice from anyone. Quid pro quo. Buy books, get advice. Being nice also helps—a lot.

Now think about logging onto your favorite Internet bookstore. You won't see *anything* except the few titles chosen for the opening screen. How many clicks will it take to get to your book? And will a small image of your cover lure people into wanting to learn more?

One of the great things about bookstores and libraries is that they're often staffed by industry professionals who live and love books. If you're respectful of their time and steer clear when they're busy, you can learn a tremendous amount from them. Take it from Margot Sage-El, owner of our very own local bookstore, Watchung Booksellers, in Montclair, New Jersey, "We love talking books. We love recommending books. And we love authors. Particularly authors who are customers! If a writer approaches us, we're happy to answer questions and pass on the insider knowledge that we have."

Down the line, many booksellers and librarians will be deciding whether or not your idea is compelling enough for them to order your book and have it take up some of their precious shelf space. And unlike agents, editors and other publishing industry professionals, these people are easily accessible. You can talk to them on a daily basis. In the flesh, no less. And for free. So when you go to the bookstore or library, take time to get to know the people who work there. Many bookstores and libraries have a shelf devoted to staff recommendations. Talk to staff about their selections. See who has interests similar to your own. Not everyone is as generous as Margot Sage-El, but when the time is right, ask your librarian and local bookseller what they think about your book idea. Remember, this is not the time to try and convince them that your book would do well. This is just a time to listen.

Writers in Search of Ideas

Are you determined to write a book but have come to the end of this chapter and found that despite your mad skills and creativity you've got no salable idea? Don't despair. You could look for people to write a book with. A famous local figure who's still unknown to the rest of the world. An expert in a field you have a particular interest in. Someone you know who has a great idea but no writing skills. Jessica Hurley has written numerous books, including *One Makes the Difference* (with famed activist Julia Butterfly Hill). She got her start by sending her résumé to an author, care of the publisher's address. "I had seen the author's gift book series," she says, "and I thought the concept was right up my alley. The author liked the fact that I took the initiative and called me for an informational interview. We hit it off right away, and I started out by making lists of ideas for each of the titles and then began writing for the series. Eventually, I ended up managing them."

Another way to build up name recognition in the industry without having an idea of your own is to contact packagers. Packagers produce books, taking projects from idea to ready-to-print files. Since they invent ideas in-house, they often use writers-for-hire to complete their projects. They don't pay well (you typically get a flat fee with no royalties), but you'll get great experience and some excellent résumé fodder. And the packager will be the one to worry about the competition, audience, marketing and publicity, so you can just concentrate on writing. Oftentimes, packagers will put your name on the book (though the copyright will probably be in their name), which is a nice added bonus. It's a great way to get your metaphoric foot in the very real publishing door.

What's Next?

You have found the right idea(s), so naturally you should write your book and start your search for an agent and/or publisher, right? Not! In the Electronic Information Age, it behooves you to first start combing the World Wide Web to find, connect with and become actively involved in the community that's relevant to your idea. Richard Eoin Nash, former publisher of Soft Skull Press, says, "A publisher shouldn't be the first step. It should be the last step. The real work is in the day-to-day writing—and connecting. While you're continuously putting out the poem, the short story, you're doing a reading as part of a series, you're going to your writing group, you're showing up at a writers conference, studying with someone you admire. You're blogging, you're critiquing, you're putting your ideas out there—that's the true work of writing. The writer in the garret cliché created an absolutely alienated producer. Engage with others who are doing similar things. Do it for your own sake—it will make you a happier and more fulfilled writer. And, in fact, agents and publishers are more likely to find you if you are actively participating in your culture." Richard's excellent advice is what the following chapter is all about.

CHAPTER 2

A World Wide Wonderland

"We are advertis'd by our loving friends."

—*William Shakespeare*

TEN YEARS AGO, WHEN WE wrote the first edition of this book, this chapter didn't exist. But in just a decade, the world has fallen down a rabbit hole. Mad Hatters are going viral on YouTube, and Tweedledum and Tweedledee are tweeting away.

What does that mean for you? As we've said, these days it's imperative to start assembling an audience long before you've even written a word. And there's simply no better way to do that than by using social media to connect with like-minded fellow citizens. If your inner voice is screaming, "I just want to write my book!" let us give you 10 persuasive reasons why social media is important for any writer. It can:

1. Expose you to an infinite world of ideas and stories.
2. Instantly connect you to sources of information and knowledgeable experts.
3. Plug you into trends so you know what's hot and what's not.
4. Give you the means to test-drive your material.
5. Help you find your community and future audience.
6. Allow you to become an active citizen in your community.
7. Develop and/or expand your platform and/or brand.
8. Demonstrate to a publisher that lots of people will buy your book.
9. Raise the profile of your name and your work.
10. Help you sell lots and lots of books!

In this chapter, we're going to concentrate on everything you need to be doing at least one year *before* you reach a magical milestone: the publication of your

▶ In world wide wonderland, websites can pop up, flower brightly, then decay, burn out or fade away. So by the time this book is printed and in your hands, it's possible that some of the sites referenced by yours truly may no longer exist. Fear not! Our website, thebookdoctors.com, will keep you totally clicked in and up to date.

book. Everything you need to do *after* publication will be elaborated upon in Chapters 12 and beyond.

We can imagine prospective authors holding their ready-to-launch manuscripts or books in their hands, aghast at the potential implications. Are we telling those of you who have finished writing your books or proposals that you're actually behind the electronic eight ball? Well, in a sense, we are. But all the more reason to get on it, and get on it quick. That's why we've put this chapter so close to the beginning of the book—and why you're reading this right now, before it's too late.

What of the author for whom the very idea of websites, blogs and tweets brings on nausea and lightheadedness? We ask you to at least read this chapter, dip your toe into the pool and test the water. You can always rush back to dry land—but at least you'll know what you're contending with.

The funny thing is, the more you trek around online, the less murky or foreign the terrain becomes. The human nature of the web quickly emerges because, of course, the web is nothing without the people who create and inhabit it. For this reason, the world of the web is, at root, no different from the world outside it. And the four principles overarching this book—networking, researching, writing and persistence—still apply, just with an e-twist. So if you have any fears, put them aside for the moment, boot up, log on and dive in.

A note for hardcore technophobes: While this chapter will teach you the basics of building an audience via the tools of the web, it will *not* tell you the minutiae of how to, for example, set up a Facebook or Twitter account. For that, you must avail yourself of the services of a trained professional or child mentor (see page 23).

The New Platform

Y̲ou send out an e-blast to your one million devoted followers. They imme-diately spring into action and not only purchase your book, but tell all their friends, who tell all their friends, who tell all their friends, creating a viral storm that sweeps from shore to shore. Your book rockets to the top of the Amazon rankings and *The New York Times* bestseller list and lands you a movie

Your Child Mentor

If you're any kind of novice navigating cyberspace, find yourself a Child Mentor. Our two-and-a-half-year-old daughter knows how to use an iPhone better than her 60-something grandmother. No lie. Their brains are just wired differently.

Your child mentor should ideally be between 14 and 21 years old. A mentor in this age range will be able to show you the basics, like how to open an account on a social networking site, how to post on a blog and, for the true Luddites, how to tame your mouse. Bestselling author Pamela Redmond Satran, whose 20 books include *How to Not Act Old,* which grew out of her blog, says, "When I first started blogging, my 17-year-old son would come home and I'd pump him for information. How do I put pictures up? How do I embed something? How do I put up a link?"

Child mentors are not hard to find. You might even have one living in your house. And honestly, a 14-year-old will work for a video game or a month's supply of pizza. Heed well the famous adage, "And the children shall lead them."

---

deal. What a rosy future you have. Only you actually have to connect to those one million followers to begin with.

Marketing guru Seth Godin puts it this way: "If you don't have a better strategy for your book promotion than 'Let's get on *Oprah,*' you should stop now. If you don't have an asset already—a 'permission base' of thousands or tens of thousands of people, a popular blog, thousands of employees, a personal relationship with Willard Scott—then it's too late to start building that asset once you start working on a book. My best advice? Build an asset. Large numbers of influential people who read your blog or read your emails or watch your TV show or love your restaurant."

By *permission base,* Seth is referring to those people whose ears and eyes you've already captured and who welcome correspondence from you—who've given you tacit permission to send communications their way. A permission base is similar to what publishers call a *platform,* which can mean different things depending on the author and the book. A speaking career, a track record as a talking head in the media, demonstrable expertise or recognition within a particular field, a Twitter following of tens or hundreds of thousands, a major YouTube audience—all of these are examples of platforms.

An author with a platform is a real turn-on to a publisher, as a platform is considered a reflection of an author's potential bookselling power. It used to be that authors built platforms via the media or speaking engagements, but lately, platforming has taken an e-turn. VP and executive editor at Crown Archetype Dominick Anfuso puts it this way: "It is certainly a plus to have a website, a blog, a Twitter and Facebook following. All of those things matter—and they grow in importance every day. With fewer review sections and fewer outlets in mainstream media, these resources are becoming more valuable. The ability of a writer to reach out directly to 'fans' is an amazing asset. The size of the following certainly matters—we have had authors with hundreds of followers and authors with over a million. Guess who sold more?"

Of course, the 64-gigabyte question is: How does one go about developing a large following? There are as many ways to amass one as there are human beings with imaginations. Daniel Handler created a fictitious character named Lemony Snicket and then, under that name, wrote *The Bad Beginning,* the first of his young adult novels collectively called "A Series of Unfortunate Events." He devised shows in which he plays the accordion, manipulates nutty props and generally puts on a wild and crazy act. And these events draw hundreds of kids and parents.

Some authors enjoy speaking in front of a crowd and spend days on the road lecturing to whomever will hear them. Others write columns for magazines and newspapers. Still others make their name doing radio commentaries. That certainly suited David Sedaris; his hysterical National Public Radio story of being hired as a Christmas elf launched him into the pantheon of American humorists.

The problem is, all of these non-web routes are tough nuts to crack. But setting up a blog isn't. Tweeting isn't. Creating a weekly podcast isn't. Setting up a video camera, talking into it and posting clips on your website isn't. The web has given those without a platform the hammer, nails and four-by-fours to construct their own. The trick, of course, is to build something that'll actually support you.

Some of you will be coming to this chapter with no platform whatsoever, while others will already have a well-developed stump from which to shout. No matter. If you choose to stump it old school, in the flesh, you'll know what works the moment you look out into your audience—or lack thereof. If you choose to stump it new school, it's easy to track the response you're getting on the information superhighway, with data so hard it sometimes hurts. Then it's a matter of the perpetual tweak to get the formula just right. Editor in chief of *Wired* magazine and bestselling author of *The Long Tail* Chris Anderson observed, "To actually have a presence, to build a following, doesn't happen overnight. Building a community is very hard, but once you build your community, they become evangelists and customers very easily."

Calling All Experts

If you can realistically frame yourself as the leading person on anything from alien abduction to the history of the dachshund, you have a good chance of creating a solid platform and getting some attention. The media—on and off the web—are always looking for experts to consult. And the first place the media goes to find anyone these days is the web. So when that big story hits on the dachshund who won the Westminster dog show and then got abducted by aliens, and you've got the world's top alien abduction dachshund blog, guess who they'll be calling? You, that's who!

Social Networking for Luddites

Social networking. These two words get bandied about so much these days, but for many people—even those who engage in the practice regularly—the term's meaning remains slightly murky. A *social network* is a structure made of citizens, groups, companies and/or organizations connected by shared interests, including but not limited to: friendship, leading an alternative cyberlife, celebrity worship, celebrity trashing, good jobs, bad cats, exchange of goods and services of every kind imaginable, and yes, books. And these connections take place online.

Social media is the umbrella term for social networking and for sites that allow for user participation. This includes major social networking sites like Facebook, Twitter, YouTube, Tumblr and Flickr. But it also encompasses individual websites, blogs and microblogs that serve specific audiences. Take Harlequin's website, one of the cornerstones of the community of romance writers and readers. Says CEO Donna Hayes, "For many years we had Reader Parties. We would go to various cities, and 200 to 300 readers would come to meet each other, have lunch and talk to our authors. It was really a celebration of Romance. That translated very well into a virtual meeting place. Now our website is the center of an online community, where readers and writers and fans can talk to each other. Readers can review books, tell us what they like and don't like, and they can actually talk to our authors. Lots of our authors schedule talks where readers can ask them questions directly. And some of our authors have virtual parties, sometimes in conjunction with organizations like Romance Writers of America."

When we wrote the first edition of this book, we ourselves were pretty socially awkward in these brave new hinterlands. Now we're officially social networking veterans. As the founder and driving force behind a start-up that became a multimillion-dollar company, Arielle has experience interacting with niche groups like mommy bloggers, inspiring a rabid core of followers in the shape of tween girls, and embracing these groups and watching as they spread the word, literally, all over the world. David has been putting up short movies on YouTube, blogging, tweeting, writing for The Huffington Post and developing communities on places like Facebook for years. For those of you with little to no experience with social networking, let us explain what is valuable about this new form of communication. There's a three-minute video that demonstrates social networking at its best. Maybe you've seen this YouTube phenomenon about a guy dancing his brains out at the Sasquatch Music Festival. If not, here's a recap: A shaky camera captures a wacky-looking shirtless guy dancing wildly on a hill at some kind of concert. He is surrounded by people sitting on the hill, watching the concert. It appears to be a lovely day. The dancing guy looks like he's having a really great time. He also looks a little ridiculous—like he might provoke some mocking and whispers. ("Look at the freaky guy dancing!") But he clearly doesn't care. After a decent amount of time passes, one solitary goofball gets up and starts shaking it with Dancing Guy. The cool thing about Dancing Guy is that he welcomes his new friend with passionate abandon. They have a grand time dancing together—and continue to do so for quite a while.

At the point where you may be ready to turn the video off, a second follower comes bolting in. He too is welcomed with open arms and enthusiastic flailing about of body parts. And he too appears to be having as good a time as the first two guys.

Follower Number 2 validates the first dancer and his Tonto, making them into a teeny tiny community. Very quickly after he joins the fray, three new followers leap into the dance party, getting their giddy groove on. Within a few seconds there's a formidable little nation gyrating wildly, whirling like dervishes, alive and inspired. The group then seems to have a gravitational force, pulling everyone toward it like moths to a beautiful flame. Says CD Baby's CEO, Derek Sivers, who wrote a brilliant speech about this video, "This is the tipping point! Now we've got a movement. As more people jump in, it's no longer risky. If they were on the fence before, there's no reason not to join now. They won't be ridiculed, they won't stand out, and they will be part of the 'in' crowd, if they hurry. Over the next minute you'll see the rest, who prefer to be part of the crowd, because eventually they'd be ridiculed for not joining."

Why does this video demonstrate the essence of social networking? A citizen has the courage to publicly do something he loves, something simple and easy to participate in that adds value, whether that be useful information, excellent entertainment or just plain fun. And yes, this person runs the risk of looking like an idiot, opening himself up to snark and player hatred. But don't worry. We don't want you to stand up and dance like an idiot . . . not yet, anyway. For now, we just want you to follow along. And enjoy the ride.

Is Social Networking 4 U?

For many authors, the idea of social networking sends bile hurling up the digestive tract, leaving a very nasty taste in the mouth. This is a perfectly understandable reaction. But before you have a knee-jerk reaction and rule out the possibility of using new technology to help your book career, at least read the next few paragraphs.

What if we told you that the one thing you needed most to be successful in the world of social networking has nothing whatsoever to do with technological savvy? Do you feel a little better? What if we told you that the one thing you need more than anything else is totally doable? Would you perk up a bit? What if we told you that the one thing that could make the difference in the success of your book takes less time than listening to "Stairway to Heaven"? This one thing is . . . seven minutes a day. That's right. If you can spend seven minutes connecting with your tribe every day, you will slowly but surely build yourself a nice e-platform. It's like brushing your teeth. You must make it part of your daily routine. Make it a habit. Habits are incredibly powerful. If you need to, set the timer on your smart phone for seven minutes. It's not much out of your day. Out of your life. But the trick is, you have to do it *every day*. Yes, there are some authors who spend hours and hours social networking. Some people love tweeting it up, commenting on Facebook, blogging up a storm. If that's you, fantastic. But for the rest of you who find social networking a chore, we know you can take seven minutes out of your day for the health of your baby book.

Will a preestablished community significantly increase your book's chance of success? If you're

▶ Are you a visual person who loves to take pictures with your iPhone or troll the web for beautiful images? Then you might be more inclined to spend your time on Pinterest or Instagram. Or are you a video buff who enjoys filming the moment or creating short videos? Then Vine or YouTube might be your medium.

Margaret Atwood on Twitter Fairies

D avid noticed mega-award-winning bestselling author Margaret Atwood was on Twitter. He couldn't resist tweeting her to find out how she felt about being instantly connected to her audience. Whether she felt social media was now an expectation of authors. And whether she believed it benefited a new author to embrace technology and social networking. For those of you who don't know, Twitter only allows for posts consisting of 140 characters. So in order to get a more fleshed-out answer, David asked if she would reply via email—and boy are we glad she did.

"I started Tweeting because the builders of the website for my book *The Year of the Flood* (yearoftheflood.com) told me I should do this 'tweeting' thing. I knew nothing about it, but I did know McLean Greaves, who helped me 'launch' with the aid of several of his Twitter friends," says Margaret, illustrating the importance of a helping hand. "I now have a lot of Twitter pals, not all of whom are from the writing world. Many are readers, it's true, but there are also many from the ecology world and the science/tech/geek area. Many authors tweet; many don't. I think that if you're doing it just because you think you have to in order to sell books, it won't be fun and it will exhaust you. For me, it's a mini-world in which self-invention is ongoing. It's a little like having fairies at the bottom of your garden. Ask them a question, they help you out. Start a game with them, they play inventively. They like jokes and are often mischievous. Sometimes they tease. They have faces that are beautiful or weird, or the faces of cats, birds, masks, plants . . . elementals. Once in a while you get a goblin, but what else can you expect?"

writing a birding book, and you're connected with all the birding bloggers and tweeters, you're going to have an easier time selling your book. If you're writing a vampire romance and you've befriended the rabid online community of vampire-philes and romance devotees, you're going to have an easier time selling your book. If you've written a Civil War history and you've befriended thousands of people on Facebook who list the Civil War as an interest, again, obviously you'll have an easier time selling your book.

Let's say your book falls into a category for which a community is imminently reachable, hence greatly increasing your chances for success. The next question is: What does success mean for you? Is it simply getting a book in print? If so, and all this new media holds no interest, you probably don't want to spend any time or effort social networking. Is all you want the imprimatur of a distinguished publisher on your spine? Then maybe your time is best spent writing a brilliant or brilliantly commercial book, and you can worry later about how you're going to get readers. (Though, again, depending on the type of book you're hawking, your virtual connections may be seen by a publisher as a bankable asset.) But here's the bottom line: If your top priority is to sell lots of copies of your book, whether you self-publish or go with a major publisher, then it certainly behooves you to hop on the cyber wagon. Because while no one has figured out the formula for directly turning e-friends into buyers, we know that the future of bookselling is in the hands of these communities. Are you still hesitant? Kemble Scott, author of the novel *SoMa* and an early adopter of new media and social networking, has this to say: "Don't be afraid of technology. Embrace it. Find someone to help you. So many writers seem mentally blocked when it comes to technology. I get these midnight phone calls from frantic writers who are having nervous breakdowns because they can't change the font size on a Word document. Don't take it personally, and keep your sense of humor." Malle Vallik, director of digital content and social media for Harlequin, adds: "Social media is your friend. It can be the *single best* use of your time because it's from your home and it's all about writing on a regular basis, which is a writer's natural forte."

As Kemble points out, many writers have a knee-jerk fear of computers and new technology. Bestselling author Susan Orlean confessed to her own resistance: "Do I enjoy social media? Yes, much more than I expected I would. I was a naysayer for a long time and was dragged kicking and quietly screaming into it." Often our worst fears lie in anticipation. Understand that it will take you some time to get up and running. But once you do, you'll find that most of the stuff is so basic a 10-year-old can do it. If you don't believe us, go ask a 10-year-old.

The Special Case of Literary Fiction

While literary fiction comprises a tiny percentage of overall book sales, it has an elite and special place in the heart of publishing. The world of literary fiction has its own community, or rather its own club. In this club, commercialism is often disdained, and the old-fashioned image of the writer in a cabin is still celebrated and canonized. So it stands to reason that social networking doesn't carry the same weight for a literary fiction author—at least for the moment. National Book Award nominee Amy Bloom sums up the social networking/writerly balance as she sees it: "I'm not morally opposed to Facebook and Twitter. It's a great way to see videos of my granddaughter. If someone told me I had to, I suppose I would. But for me it's got to come back to the writing. I believe, in the end, if every sentence and paragraph is important, the work will speak for itself. My mother used to say, 'If you don't treat yourself with respect,

A Gift to the Shy

Congratulations, shy people of the world! It's your lucky century. Finally, you can connect with people across the globe without leaving your living room or ever actually engaging anyone in the flesh. Thanks to social networking, you can use your natural skills as a writer to befriend, bedazzle and/or be connected to like-minded citizens who will love your book. Caroline Leavitt, *New York Times* bestselling author of 10 novels, is just the sort of person who's benefited greatly from the Internet. "People told me to network with other writers, and I never did," she says. "I'm very shy. Now that we have the Internet, it's a lot easier. And I've made valuable contacts. Publicity, promotion, blurbs and friendship, the most important of all. Who but another writer understands what you're going through?"

So get your party pajamas on, don't comb your hair and start connecting . . .

no one else will.' It's the same with your writing. If you care more about platform than about the work, then the work will suffer."

It goes back to priorities. As Amy says, with literary fiction, the writing has to be the priority. And because the influential literary journals still hold sway, any time spent away from your writing should first be spent attempting to get your work published in these outlets.

This is not to say that literary fiction authors need pretend the web doesn't exist. If you enjoy, for example, the haiku-like nature of Twitter, please tweet tweet tweet! Or if you enjoy the company of like-minded wordsmiths on Facebook, the more friends you can make the better. These early efforts will pay off, because once your book is completed, you *will* be expected to participate in the online world like everyone else—and you'll certainly need someone to come to your readings! As Pamela Dorman, publisher of Pamela Dorman Books/ Viking and a woman with an uncanny eye for discovering debut fiction, says, "In the case of a literary novelist, I don't think she has to have an online presence to begin with, but she needs to step into it quickly once her book is handed off to her publisher."

Yes, literary fiction is its own beast. And while social networking is not absolutely necessary for writers of literary fiction, if you've written a great book and you want people to read it, and you'd like to actually make a living as a writer, you'll find tons of enthusiastic readers and writers out there waiting for your beautifully wrought, exquisitely written literary masterpiece—if you just connect with them. So why not?

The Four-Step e-Program

Now that we've laid down the state of the nation, let's move on to the basic principles of creating an online community. We've been lucky enough to talk to some remarkable e-genius types, and one thing we've heard over and over is that there are four main steps to getting traction electronically:

1. Finding your online community

2. Connecting with and becoming an active citizen in this community

3. Buying land and building a house in your community

4. Asking your fellow citizens for support

In addition to these principles, this chapter will also explicate some of the ideas, language, etiquette and theories that will guide your efforts in World-Wide-Webification. What you will quickly see is that participating in social media will be an ongoing task. And you will get out of it as much as you put in.

Step 1: Finding Your Online Community

Back in the Paper and Pencil Age, it was very difficult to locate all of the humans in the world who were interested in, say, an ordinary citizen cooking her way through a Julia Child cookbook. But now, in this beautiful new speed-of-light cyberworld, it's possible to locate your audience with the precision of a laser surgeon—and to put your finger right on its pulse.

If you care enough about something to write a book about it, there will surely be others who share your enthusiasm. Roxanne Lott, managing director of the online marketing agency Imerex, says, "There is a circle of influential individuals related to whatever you're writing about. There is a lot going on online that your core group has interest in. Use the power of the Internet to find those people and to interact with them online." Whether your book is a scientific tract on tree frogs, a history of po'boys or a Gothic romance starring Little Red Riding Hood and The Three Little Vampire Pigs, there will be websites, bloggers, tweeters, chatters and potential e-friends for you to connect with.

Track your people down. See what neighborhoods they hang out in. Learn the languages they speak, if they're not already your own. Watch them work and play. Finding your fellow citizens is part art, part science, requiring a combination of experimentation, determination and cyber excavation. Sometimes it's sheer simplicity. A single search may lead you to dozens or even millions of people fascinated by the same things you are. Sometimes it takes a little more doing.

In sussing through your search results, be discriminating. Whether you use Google, Facebook, Twitter or another favorite Internet hideout, start locating the movers and shakers for your subject. "Find the most interesting people, the people you trust, and see who they are listening to, see who they are following," says Sree Sreenivasan, social media expert and professor of digital media at Columbia University.

As you'll see, e-connections tend to be self-perpetuating. Identify a few people in your bailiwick and you'll soon find out who they're connected to. Then who those people are connected to, and who those people are connected to. Ripples in a pond . . .

As you accumulate friends and followers in your online community, it will behoove you to keep them well organized. Categorize your network using very specific lists. You might have a list organized by geographic area, a list of experts, a list of influencers (i.e., big mouths), a list of media contacts and even a list of relatives. Every time you add a new person, either via email or on a social networking site, immediately put him or her on the proper list(s). This early categorization will eliminate lots of annoying busywork down the line.

THE VALUE OF NICHES

Whether you're writing a novel about Albuquerque, a gluten-free cookbook or a manual on robots, there are good reasons to locate the people who populate the nichiest corner of your online niche—that is, the members of the Albuquerque historical society, the fans of the gluten-free cupcake page, the obsessive robot makers. These people will be your first and most precious readers. They will also be the ones who will spread the word about you and your book like honeybees fertilizing flowers with pollen.

As we've mentioned, the value of niche audiences is on the rise. Many forward thinkers believe that, soon, books directed at small niche audiences will command more dollars than books geared toward the general public. It has to do with the gold rush boom of online stores, where shelf space is infinite. What's the connection? Chris Anderson of *Wired* breaks it down: "When consumers are offered infinite choice, the true shape of demand is revealed. And it turns out to be less hit-centric and mainstream than we thought. People gravitate toward niches because they satisfy narrow interests better, and in one aspect of our life or another we all have some narrow interest (whether we think of it that way or not)."

e-Look, e-Read, e-Listen

Before you go barging into a cyber china shop like a virtual bull, take a moment to do these three simple things: 1) Look. 2) Read. 3) Listen.

Now that you've got a list of who's who, the leading lights in your area of interest, start looking for these people's various outposts. Do they have websites/blogs, Facebook pages, Twitter accounts? Do they post movies? Podcasts? What books have they published, if any? Can you see who their influences are? Look at what books and writers they're reading and talking about. Poke around in the corners and closets to find your allies. Read everything you can about them. And listen very carefully to the e-chatter. You'll be amazed how much you can hear. Pay particular attention to what kind of posts get the most attention. Where is the buzz now? Where is it heading?

For example, if you really want to find a book on the mating habits of tree frogs in Yosemite and you try your local chain bookstore, there's very little chance that you will find the book you're looking for. A clerk may offer to order it for you, but who wants to wait? Now you go to your local independent bookstore. Again, very little chance that such a book will be there, even if the store is close to Yosemite. Tree frogs + mating + Yosemite = too niche to take up valuable shelf space. But online, you can find that tiny amphibian-specialized site with the very tree frog tome you're looking for. If it's been made available electronically, you might be able to get it for $0.99 in less than a minute. Bam! The web has made it possible for the tree frog author to thrive.

The theory behind all this niche marketing business has been explained rather brilliantly in Chris Anderson's *The Long Tail*. Chris explains: "The theory of the Long Tail is that our culture and economy is increasingly shifting away from a focus on a relatively small number of 'hits' (mainstream products and markets) at the head of the demand curve and toward a huge number of niches in the tail."

And what good news this is for authors everywhere! Books that populate the long tail don't need to appear on bestseller lists or major media outlets. They just need to be easily locatable by readers through an Internet search. Tap deep into the well of your niche audience—your future readers—and you will set yourself up to reap the rewards of the Long Tail, bypassing lots of stumbling blocks that stop authors from enjoying success and making money. Distribution difficulties, problems with publicity and marketing, inability to get face time with a buyer at a major chain . . . all these obstacles become obsolete if you go direct to your customer, e-door to e-door, riding the Long Tail. Cultivate and grow your niche, and you, like Jack, will come back down the beanstalk with a goose that lays golden eggs.

Step 2: Becoming an Active Citizen in Your Community

In Step 1, you found the places where your fellow citizens live. You learned about the leaders. And you got a feel for the community's language and customs. In Step 2 it's time to start making some connections. This part of community building doesn't involve creating a website or blog, or for that matter any sort of substantial content—by which we mean original writing, be it posts, essays, short stories or chunks of your book. Right now it's just about establishing your citizenship by becoming a fan and a follower, signing up for newsletters and blog feeds, writing reviews and comments, and creating profiles on social networking sites and sites that serve your particular community. Making friends. Harlequin's Malle Vallik says, "When you enter the social media space, you can't expect to be an immediate star. You have to go to the party, check out the other stars, study them, introduce yourself and slowly make your way up to star status."

Get a lay of the cyberland social scene in order to find out how you fit in. Think not only about where your audience might be—also use this time to put out tentacles in the bookish community. Remember Richard Eoin Nash, former publisher of Soft Skull Press, founder of Cursor and independent publishing entrepreneur? He puts it this way: "How do you conceive of yourself as a writer in terms of the cultural mishmash that we find ourselves in? What is your community of books, journals, scenes, zines, bloggers, websites? You need to be creating a cultural context for yourself by engaging with your peers and finding mentors."

▶ Make sure the e-venue you choose matches your style, your substance and your audience. Not all networks are created equal. Each has its own unique audience, focus, pros, cons and user engagement. Obviously your passion for Lawrence Welk will not be well served on a social network that draws mostly Ozzy Osbourne fans. Some networks attract readers, some music fans. Be sure to tool around and research the mediums that interest you before spending the time making them your own.

Before you commit yourself to diving down any particular rabbit hole, really poke your nose around. "Research the mission statement of the website/

community you're interested in," recommends Columbia's Sree Sreenivasan. "It will help you figure out which of the social media outlets best serves your purpose."

DEFINING YOUR IDENTITY

Filling out a profile on a social networking site is one of the best and easiest ways to get started—social networking sites are generally user-friendly enough to suit even the phobiest of technophobes. A profile will allow you access to others people's profiles, and to whatever means of interaction are available on that particular site. Facebook and Twitter are, at the moment, the obvious places to start. But there are many online communities dedicated to books, writers and readers, like Goodreads and Google Plus (see page 346 on the importance of a Google Plus profile once you have a book out). And, of course, all of your e-research will have given you your own ideas of where your community hangs out.

Since you will be known by the information you provide, be meticulous in filling out your profiles. Since no one knows you yet, you get to invent who you want to be. The words you use will define you, so choose them carefully. A good social media profile should also include terms that help your niche market find you.

Study profiles of people you admire. How do they present themselves? You'll quickly see that profiles run the gamut from brief and unsatisfying to total information overload. A good profile captures who you are, gives fellow citizens a taste of your tastes, makes readers laugh if you're funny and be impressed if you're impressive and leaves them wanting to know more so they'll check back often. And on Twitter, in the "bio" field, you have to do all this in 160 characters or less!

Fun or interesting details can make big impressions on profiles. Bestselling author Susan Orlean lists the following under "activities" on her

▶ Be sure to upload a profile photo. Nothing screams "My heart isn't in this" like a profile without a photo. Of course—and this should go without saying—make sure your profile photo captures you on a good day. And we need to see your face—not a speck of you off in the distance. Faces are important. It's human nature to want to put a face to a name.

Your profile photo is often the only visual any web surfer will have of you. Make it memorable, professional, personable and brimming with whatever image you wish to put out into the world. (For photo tips, go to page 353.)

Security and Insecurity, Web-Style

M any people who are unfamiliar with the lay of the cyberland are reluctant to socially network because they're afraid their identity will be stolen, their bank accounts hacked into and their most embarrassing and private pictures and documents displayed for all the world to see. While caution is certainly advised, there are countless ways to protect and preserve privacy. You can put filters on almost every online community or website you care to join, so that your 411 is viewable by only those you deem worthy. That said, on sites like Facebook, the privacy policies change almost daily, so you have to be vigilant about making sure your settings are up to date. See Appendix II for sites that will help you keep on top of the ever-changing privacy game.

Facebook profile: "Procrastination, Dilly Dallying, Fussing, Fuming, Puttering, Chicken Tending"—making us fall in love with her immediately. Author Tamim Ansary sometimes posts favorite quotes, like this one by A.J. Liebling: "I can write better than anybody who can write faster, and I can write faster than anybody who can write better."

Many sites also offer opportunities to craft well-written answers to questions like: What are your influences? Favorite books, movies, music? Religion? College, high school, fan clubs? Have fun with these questions, but make sure your answers are information-filled and truly reflect who you are; in a social networking context, cultural or geographic or institutional references become searchable clues, keywords that can help like-minded people find you.

Think of your profile as a tiny piece of you—possibly the only piece an e-citizen will ever get to see—and you'll understand how important it is to craft your profile with love and care.

FRIENDING AND FOLLOWING

Once you've set up a profile, the next step in social networking is (surprise) getting social. How? The age-old, tried-and-true, playground-tested and caveman-approved way of accumulating friends and followers: befriending and following others. With your profile in place, you can begin cultivating relationships by becoming a virtual "friend," "follower" and/or "fan." Word to the wise: "Friend" is often used as a verb in social networking circles; to "friend" someone means you've just accepted or requested their friendship. You and your new friends will now be able to view one another's profiles to the degree dictated by your privacy settings—and, perhaps best of all, you'll have access to one another's friends.

Sign up for the RSS feeds of bloggers you've taken a hankering to. (Such a feed allows a new post to land in the lap of your inbox, meaning you won't have to take the active step of checking that blog every day.) Start following the interesting people on your list who tweet. Befriend not just individuals but also bookstores, festivals, and reading and writing groups on Facebook and other social networking sites. How do you find these organizations? All you have to do is type in your interests, whether they be the Civil War, humidors or Labradors, hit return and watch groups who adore the same stuff magically appear.

Then what happens? A constant flow of 411. Friending and following will give you daily—sometimes hourly or up-to-the-minute—updates on the movers and shakers of your particular e-world. Many people feel instantaneously overwhelmed by what comes back at them when they take the social networking plunge. Remember, there's no pressure to respond to or even read everything that comes your way. There may be days where you don't read a thing and others where you're on a minute-by-minute watch.

▶ Just because someone befriends or follows you doesn't mean you have to reciprocate. You don't have to go out with the creepy guy because he asks you! You're social networking with a purpose, to find truly like-minded people. Anyway, fewer, more engaged friends and followers is always better than lots of friends and followers with no real attachment. Quality not quantity. (Best-case scenario: You combine high quality with vast quantity.)

REVIEWS, COMMENTS AND LINKAGE

An excellent way to improve your writing chops, establish an online presence, give e-love and generally make yourself useful is to post reviews and make comments in other people's spaces—walls, websites and blogs. Spread around interesting links from people you admire and/or emulate.

With the drying up of traditional book review venues, the phenomenon of what we like to call the Citizen Reviewer has become increasingly important in Book Nation. Becoming a citizen reviewer is one great way to spread the virtual love while simultaneously bolstering your street cred. Authors are always grateful for positive, thoughtful reviews.

Clean Data

From the very millisecond you decide to enter the e-world, make sure your data is squeaky clean. Huh? "Clean data" just means consistent information. For example, David published his first book under the name David Sterry. That was in 2001, when Facebook was just a glimmer in a 13-year-old's eyes and David didn't have a website. Then he discovered there was an Australian pop star named David Sterry. So when his next book came out in 2002, as the World Wide Web was becoming even more prominent, he very consciously changed his professional name to David Henry Sterry, which he's meticulously stuck to ever since. Not David Sterry, not David H. Sterry, not Dave Sterry or any other variation. Same should hold true for any other information that you want to follow you around.

The cleanliness of your data is so important because search engines do not have brains. They simply crawl through the gazillions of characters on the web, and when they see a bunch of characters show up together in one place and then in another, they lump them together. If you give mixed information, entering David Henry Sterry in one place and David H. Sterry in another, you're not search-friendly. And you want to be best friends with all the search engines. So that all the friends you make are able to find and buy your book.

You can post reviews on big sites like Amazon or Goodreads (for more on the value of Goodreads reviews, see page 384), or you can leave comments (complimentary, naturally) on individual author sites. Once you've written a review, cross-pollinate. Write a review of your favorite author's book on Amazon, then post the link on your Facebook page.

Don't stop at reviews. In social networking land, comments are where it's at. When people put posts up on their websites, blogs, Twitter accounts, or places like The Huffington Post, Salon or The Daily Beast, comments are not only allowed but welcomed. Sometimes a particularly provocative post will generate hundreds of comments. Discussions and cross-discussions. You can actually find yourself in the middle of a rabid and/or riveting conversation. Just remember to think carefully. And walk softly. It's not like talk, which evaporates into the ether. Once you make a comment, it can just hang out there forever like a big electronic lox.

To sum up: Be a promoter of others. There's great value in passing along other people's projects and posts, and it's a way to engender goodwill without having to create something brilliant or shattering. You can leave that to the originator. All you have to do is pass it forward—whether by email, status update, tweet or blog post.

Step 3: Buying Land and Building a House in Your Community

We're not ones to mince words. The only reasons not to have a website/blog are if 1) you are ridiculously famous, 2) you don't care if anyone knows about you or your work, or 3) you are a rank amateur and want to stay that way. Fact is, anyone can put up a website or blog, so there's really no excuse not to. But we want to help you make one that actually works for you and your book. Your site is your business card, your calling card, your shrine, your museum, your store, your mirror to the world. "A good website can help you develop a following. It's a way of staying in touch with people and letting them know what you're doing." That's the opinion of Likoma Island founder Bradley Charbonneau, whose company designs many a writer's website.

Some authors have full-blown interactive multimedia websites with whistles and bells up the wazoo, some have bare-bones blogs and some have blogs on their websites. A blog is basically a simplified, single-page website featuring a collection of "posts," or entries; typically, the most recent entries appear at the top of the page, and viewers scroll down to see older entries. But the cyber lines between websites and blogs blur more every nanosecond. As you consider how you want to present yourself on the World Wide Web, contemplate your content, your audience and your personality.

▶ Have you taken to Twitter or some other social networking form, and don't see the need for a website or blog? Before you decide to forgo a site of your own, think about this: A website or blog is completely under your control. It's your home. You choose the paint color, the curtains, the furniture. No large social networking site has this advantage.

A blog might not be right for you if you're developing a book with awesome visuals, design and/or photos, or you plan to support your book with movies or cartoons; you have a wide variety of content you want to display in an organized fashion; or you don't have the time or inclination for regular blog posts.

Website. Blog. You choose. Just be sure to make it as easy as possible to feed the machine on a regular basis.

AN EFFECTIVE SITE OR BLOG

There are as many sites as there are human beings. Yours can be as simple as a white page with a list of posts. It can have animation and music and interactivity.

It can have an elaborate resource section with links to people, places and stuff all over the world. Or it can be a highly profitable e-commerce site. The cyber sky is the limit. If you're not sure what kind of site you want, or you're looking to get more out of your current site, the number one thing to do is, guess what? Research. Comb and surf examples from Web Giants and Tiny Tims alike. See what you like visually. What sites are easy to navigate. What sites make you want to dig deep and hang around.

You also want to think about your *branding*—another publishing buzzword. What is your brand? What is the promise you're making to a reader? To entertain, inform, present an avenue of escape into another galaxy far, far away? Your brand should be exemplified in your site. Not only in content, but through its aesthetic, tone, style, color and design. Look for sites that express a similar brand. The more precedents you assemble, and the more concrete examples of details you like, the cheaper and easier it will be for you to design a successful site. And the more chance it will have of showing you off in your Sunday best all over the e-universe.

▶ Today, you have to be sure that whatever kind of site you choose looks as good on a laptop as it does on a smart phone. As we move more and more of our activities to the palm of our hands, it will become ever more important that your site must be navigable and attractive on every device.

As you surf around, it's easy to be charmed or even blown away by the bells and whistles you see along the way. But don't be fooled. Sites don't have to be fancy to do their jobs. In fact, very often the fancy ones are confusing and overdone, unless they're constructed by a top-notch designer. Sometimes people let the visuals take over the site architecture, making it hard to navigate and get around. Navigation is key. As Lori Culwell, owner of Get Creative, Inc. and author of *Million Dollar Website*, says, "What makes a good website is the million-dollar question and it has a relatively simple answer. It all boils down to a concept called the 'user experience,' which is basically Internet jargon for 'How easy is the website to use?'"

The good thing about a simple site is you can pay a professional as little as a few hundred dollars for one. Of course, you can spend $1 million on a site as well. But no matter how much you spend or don't spend, heed this advice from Fauzia Burke, president of FSB Associates, a pioneering online marketing firm dedicated to helping authors: "The most important aspect of an author website is the quality of its design and content. Authors need to understand

10 Things You Could and/or Should Have on Your Website

1. **Your writing.** Chapters that you've completed or are workshopping, personal essays, rants, raves, how-to articles, opinions on anything and everything—whatever your audience will be interested in reading.

2. **Your bio.** It's great to put fun and interesting facts about yourself in this section. Nowadays, journalists go directly to personal websites to get their facts straight, and if something catches their fancy, they're more likely to write about it.

3. **Photos, both current and from throughout your life.** Photos are eye candy that draw surfers in, so feel free to go to town.

4. **Reviews and interviews by or about you.** Press begets press—and reader interest.

5. **A resource section** where you post items of interest to you and your readers.

6. **A calendar of events, lectures, workshops or appearances.** These can be physical events or cyber events. Just make sure you keep this section up-to-date.

7. **Videos of yourself.** In the flesh, talking about, reading and/or performing from your book.

8. **An easy way to sign up for your mailing list or newsletter.** Your mailing list is extremely important, even if you're a literary fiction writer, because people who give you their names and email addresses are telling you they want to hear from you.

9. **Contact information.** Definitely list at least one way for people to get in touch with you!

10. **Links to outside sites.** Direct visitors to your Facebook and Twitter accounts, or whatever other social networking sites you happen to be on, and recommended blogs.

that a website is their résumé to their readers. An immature site reflects poorly on the author's style and the quality of his or her work."

These days, all you have to do is shake a cyber-tree, and a dozen freelance or unemployed web designers fall out. Most of these can be found via the Internet, with portfolios posted for you to peruse. You can also contact art schools to find people who've just graduated if you're looking for someone on the real cheap.

We used a crowdsourcing design website called 99Designs.com to find a designer for our website, thebookdoctors.com. We were guaranteed a certain number of designs, of which we had to choose one. We were thrilled with the result. Many people said, "Wow! You got lucky." But luck had nothing to do with it. We put together a memo with extensive art direction based on the research we had done, and we recommend you do the same with whomever you decide to hire.

If you don't have any money to spend, and you're good at putting together Ikea furniture, then you are an excellent candidate for making your own site. That's what Lisa Genova, *New York Times* bestselling author of *Still Alice*, did: "I still manage my own website, and I love the instant flexibility this gives me— to post book events, news, quotes, to add links to reviews and other press. It's not sexy or flashy, but I think the trade-off is worth it." Just be sure to keep things simple and stay away from canned graphics. A nice font and a few

To Blog or Not to Blog

We were at a writer's conference recently and a professional giving a workshop said, "Every writer should have a blog." We looked at each other, mouths agape, wondering what to do, considering that this was some of the worst advice we'd ever heard. The truth is, every day, too many writers start blogs that they will inevitably abandon. Blogs become sad, undernourished gardens full of weeds, with no flowers, herbs or vegetables to nourish their famished readers or attract agents or publishers. If left untended, your blog can do more harm than good because it suggests you're not invested in your work. "It's true that blogging is a very effective marketing tool, when done well," says Jane Friedman, top publishing blogger as well as digital media professor at the University of Virginia and publisher of *Scratch*, a magazine about the business side of the writing life. "Unfortunately, many authors pursue blogging without any understanding of the medium, and also as little more than a means to an end. Meaningful blogging requires patience and persistence, as well as a willingness to learn what comprises good, compelling online-driven or online-only writing. It's not the same as writing for formal publication or in other genres/mediums—or even for websites other than your own."

Fauzia Burke puts it this way: "If you enjoy blogging and want a dialogue with your audience, then a blog is a great idea. But blogging is a demanding effort. If you are inundated with other work or obligations, a regular blog schedule may be challenging. Keeping information updated and fresh is very important."

Please, don't just blog because somebody told you to. Blog because you have things to say on a very regular basis, on topics you're excited and passionate about. And let us say now because we neglected to say it at the conference: NOT EVERY WRITER SHOULD HAVE A BLOG!

well-placed images are all you need. Easier still, go with a blog and choose from a predesigned layout.

Whether you hire someone or go it alone, we recommend one particular platform to build and manage your website. That platform is WordPress. It's free. We use WordPress for our website/blog as do the vast majority of writers we know. Unless you have lots of extra cash on hand, you don't want to get stuck having to pay someone every time you want to make an update to your website. Yes, there are many things we still haven't figured out how to do on WordPress, but for the day-to-day stuff, we've found it easiest to master. There are other content management platforms out there, but there are lots and lots of people trained to work with WordPress for a small fee and it's relatively easy to learn yourself.

Once your site is launched, get feedback from everybody who will give it. A website is a living, breathing organism, so you can keep playing with it until you get it just right.

The Name of Your Website or Blog

One of the first things you need to decide when building a website/blog is what the URL will be. Your URL is simply the address of your website.

Site names break into two categories: those that are simply the author's name, like our perennial favorite, davidhenrysterry.com, or those that are titular, like iwillteachyoutoberich.com. One camp of publishing people believes that your website should always be your name—not the (potential) name of your book. This camp believes that your name, not your book, is your brand. David's aforementioned site makes the argument for author as brand. He has information about all his books, movies from his acting career, a blog on subjects as wide-ranging as politics, memoir, baseball legends, soccer lunatics and Ikea. It's a celebration of David in all his diverse glory.

But we choose to use the website for our business for this book because this site features only information related to getting a book published, as well as the services we offer to authors and authors-to-be. People interested in getting a book published will be much more likely to find this site than they would David's, because websites with clear titles are more search-friendly. Though it's not all about the URL—the more subject-specific your content is, the higher your search ranking will be. Of course, we link our site back to David's, and vice versa.

Search factors aside, there's also the issue of personal choice. Nancy Kay, an award-winning blogger and veterinarian, decided to go for the website name speakingforspot.com. "Hey, I never wanted to be famous," Nancy explains. "I just wanted my book to be famous."

If you're concerned about the title of your book changing during the publishing process (and you should be), here's one more piece of food for thought: Authors who successfully establish an audience for their sites almost always get to keep their titles. Examples include *Hyperbole and a Half. The Pioneer Woman. Stuff White People Like.* Publishers don't want to fool with what already works. And they want to make sure they're able to draw on the established web audiences when it comes to bookselling time. So if you've got a title that you think really speaks to your audience, and you're not as concerned about putting yourself in the spotlight, go for it!

DRIVING TRAFFIC TO YOUR SITE OR BLOG

There are many ways to drive camels to the lush oasis of your site. Making absolutely sure that you're using the right words throughout. Putting up links to other sites in your community. Getting your site listed in articles or interviews. Analyzing your site's data to figure out who is visiting and how they're getting there. But you will also want to use your ever-developing networks to spread the word and get the virtual tourism rolling.

The fact is, experts get paid top dollar to do nothing but figure out how to drive traffic to sites. They'll bandy about phrases such as "search engine marketing," "search engine optimization" and "keyword research." We may not be able to turn you into an expert, but we can offer a plain English translation:

- *Search engine optimization* (a.k.a. SEO) increases the chance of search engines finding your site and listing it high up as a search result. Optimization can be a matter of putting keywords into the metatags (a.k.a. code) of your site as well as tweaking your site's contents.

- *Keyword research* is a subset of SEO. Keywords are the words that people put into search engines to find what they're looking for. Use the correct keywords throughout your site and you'll reap the visitors.

- *Search engine marketing* (a.k.a. SEM) helps drive traffic to websites through pay-per-click ads, banner ads and a host of other kinds of paid placements.

We're going to stick to talking about the first two terms, SEO and keyword research; you don't want to spend money on SEM before you have anything to sell, and maybe even not then.

SEO could take all your time and energy, but if you have an active site about something you love and know a lot about, and you have ample and constantly updated content, its magic will happen naturally. No extra hours spent trying to figure out how to beat the system. If you use it right, the system works just fine.

Keyword research is a helpful tool and an easy concept to get your head around. Take this book, for instance. If you go to Google Adword's Keyword Tool program and put in the search term "get a book published," you'll pull up a list of terms related to your search. Terms are numbered according to their popularity. In our case, we found out that "publish book" was approximately five times more popular a search term than "get a book published." This means we would want to use the latter phrase throughout our website, both in what we write and in its internal code (which we have no idea how to do and so have hired an expert to do for us). The right keywords can send tons of traffic to your site. And the wrong keywords, or lack of keywords, can leave your site the road less traveled.

Like its umbrella, SEO, keyword research is an art and science unto itself. If you really want to make the most of this amazing tool, you can do what we did and hire an expert.

But SEO happens in lots of big and little ways— ways that you can affect without the help of an expert. Keywords are, for example, directly related to the actual content on your site. While we will shortly get into the importance of not just a *plethora* of content but a *constant stream* of content, let us just say this for now: *Content is the number one way to drive traffic to your site.* The more concentration of information, references, words on your particular subject you use, the more likely you are to get web visibility. So if there is one and only one thing you can do for your site, it is to create great content. Period.

▶ If you'd like to go from blog to book, make sure you have a name that's bookstore-friendly. Matthew Gasteier's blog enjoyed so much success that it was snapped up by a division of Random House. But he ended up having to change the title of his book from *Fuck You Penguin* to *FU Penguin* (and *F*** You Penguin* for the British edition) because some bookstores won't carry books with curses on the cover. Bummer.

Of course, nothing can take the place of the old-fashioned way of getting attention: networking with your community. When everything is up and running and ready, you want to send out an email blast, as well as a notice on all your social networking sites, letting people know that your site is up! A cyber neophyte we know recently put up a blog. She took great pains to make sure everything was just right. Finally, she got it all up and running exactly the way she wanted. Then she waited for the cyber masses to flock to it. Sadly, no one showed up. Her awesome blog just sat there like a wallflower at a party, abject and lonely, all dressed up and no one to dance with. When we started making gentle inquiries, she quickly revealed that she hadn't actually sent a link out to anyone. Not even her nearest and dearest friends. Please note: Like Dancing Guy, you have to dance in front of people in order for anyone to join!

We've mentioned Pamela Redmond Satran, who created and launched How Not to Act Old, a funny and fantastically successful blog. We asked her what she did to get an audience. "I sent it to everybody I ever met," she said. "I asked people to send it to their friends. I sent it to my friend Debbie Gallant, a popular local blogger, and she wrote something about it. Then someone else sent it to the *Star Ledger,* a larger local New Jersey newspaper. And they named it a Blog of the Day. I took that story and started poking around, looking for journalists. I found someone at the *L.A. Times.* At that point a lot of people were falling all over new media, so I was putting myself out there, saying, 'You should write about me.' Most of the time I was ignored. But then the *L.A. Times* named it one of *their* Top 10 blogs. Which, of course, I sent around. This is all in a matter of days, not months. Then through a friend of a friend it landed in the hands of Meg Cabot— she of *Princess Diaries* fame—all unbeknownst to me. So Meg Cabot wrote about me in her blog. Now I was looking at the traffic incessantly, and it was very consistent, day after day, 300, 300, 300. But all of a sudden it was at 10,000 for the day. I thought the server was broken. I was blinking to make sure I wasn't seeing things. Then Meg wrote to me. And gave me a wonderful blurb. And wrote about the book again. And this was only a month after I started the thing."

As you can see, it's all about researching, networking, writing and persevering. Both in the cyber and real worlds. Some other ways to make your website a major road on the information superhighway:

- Get your site listed as a link on other people's sites. Link to other people on your site or blogroll. Links not only drive traffic, but also lend a sense of authority by showing the reader that you have access to sources of information they might find useful.

- If anyone interviews you for print, ask to have your site included in the piece somewhere. If you get interviewed on TV or radio, mention your site on air.

- If you get an article placed anywhere on the World Wide Web, make sure a link to your site is included.

- Make your site sticky. Give visitors a reason to come to your site, but also give them a reason to stick around awhile. Keep it up-to-date and fresh so people will come back again.

■ Make sure every email you send contains a hyperlink to your web address—this will give people an easy way to click through to your site so they can take a look around.

■ Learn how people are getting to your site by using statistics-tracking software. Some of this software is both free and good; ask your web designer for a recommendation. "In general, the web is great because data is analyzable and you can see what works and what doesn't," explains Malle Vallik of Harlequin. "On Twitter, for example, you can get a sense of trends (like spikes every time you put the word FREE in all caps)."

■ Put free stuff on your website. Everyone loves FREE stuff. (Read on for more on how this works.)

Free Content

We asked social media czar Gary Vaynerchuk what he thought was the best way to cultivate a following via the web. His answer? "Give away content on your website before you have a book in hand. Eighty-five percent of *Crush It* [Gary's book about turning your passion into a career] was consumable on my website and a variety of other places before my book came out." Why would anyone buy a book that was mostly available for free to begin with? Gary explains: "Time and context are valuable to people, so they are willing to pay for aggregation—for you putting it all together for them in a great package. And because I had tested the content and already knew that people liked it before I even put it out there as a book, I was sure that people would buy it." And they did. *Crush It* became a *New York Times* bestseller.

We now live in a time where the reader/watcher/listener has an expectation that they're going to get stuff for free. This is the whole idea behind the Google business model. You don't get charged anything to search. Google makes money by charging advertisers who desperately want to catch the eye of the hundreds of millions of people who march through its portals every day.

So it is with your content. To generate interest, when you're just starting out or even if you already have a following, giving away your stuff can go a long way toward establishing or continuing to grow your online presence. And of course, again, it's a great way to test whether other people share your passion for whatever idea or story you're putting out into the world. See pages 54 and 58–59 for more info on giving away your words for free.

Expressing Yourself

We find that people often get frustrated or even give up if they don't like the first form of online expression they try. If blogging doesn't suit you, don't do it. Maybe you'd prefer to be a regular commenter on other people's blogs. Maybe you'd be comfier with a shorter form than a blog, like a microblog or a Twitter account. Whatever your likes and dislikes, there's sure to be a format that fits you. Malle Vallik adds: "The deal with social media is that you *have* to experiment. Don't spend a lot of time on any one thing until you fall in love or see results. Choose a couple of mediums that you like best."

Of course, there are some people who simply thrive on social media and like to try it all. Not surprisingly, Chris Anderson is one of these: "I do everything. I tweet, I do interviews, speeches, free audiobooks, excerpts, video trailers. You just have to find what works." If you're like Chris and thrive on new media, be an early adopter. Every day brings new online communities and new methods of communication. Keep your ears open and get in early, and you'll be able to build up your audience quicker than those who take longer to hop on the bandwagon.

To bring it all back to the writerly sphere: Consider that finding the right venue is about personal preference, but also about how your voice blends and shines in a particular medium. "Social media is a strange and interesting writing form, much more like performance than publication since it is so immediate and unedited," says Susan Orlean, whose witty and wonderful tweets and Facebook posts charm her friends and followers. "I think it also helps you appreciate what does create a writer's voice—funny to think you can convey voice in such tiny fragments." Like any writing that you put out into the world, your voice—and the voice you intend to use in your book—needs to stand out in some way amidst the billions of chattering voices in the cacophony of cyberspace. Whether it's humorous, lyrical, authoritative or dramatic, the quality of your voice will help you carve out your position in the e-universe. While you will surely develop and hone your voice as a writer, beware of morphing wildly from one persona to another, even when it comes to something as simple as a one-sentence comment on someone else's blog.

BLOGGING YOUR WAY TO SUCCESS

In 2006, Julie Powell won the Blooker Award (a Booker Award for blogs) for *Julie and Julia,* and this marked a shift in the zeitgeist. The fact that there even *was* a Blooker Award meant the world had changed. But the fact that The Little Blog that Could ended up a bestselling book was what really fueled the blog-to-book craze.

Of course, there are a kajillion blogs out there that have never been turned into books or movies. Nor are they well trafficked, unless you consider a nice comment from your mom a big day. So what separates the successful blog from the masses? First, smart bloggers choose their audience consciously and carefully. You can't be everything to everyone. If you try to, you'll dilute your blog to a watery soup that no search engine or individual will care to sample. "I didn't try to include everyone," Ramit Sethi told us about his blog, I Will Teach You to Be Rich. "I was very crisp about my audience. I attracted some people and repelled others."

Mike Shatzkin, author of The Shatzkin Files blog and CEO of digital publishing consulting firm The Idea Logical, gave us his Top 10 things author bloggers can do to effectively build a following:

▶ **Are you planning to turn your blog into a book? If you post and/or solicit photos on your site, make sure you clear the use of the photos beforehand—or keep very detailed records on where they came from so you can track them down at a later date.**

1. Stick to topics that will resonate with a consistent audience. You can't build a following if you jump around among things that interest different people.

2. Post regularly; no less than weekly.

3. Link to others on the web in your posts, particularly to others who might send traffic back to you.

4. Link back to prior posts of yours when they are relevant to what you're discussing.

5. Respond to comments promptly, politely and concisely. And quickly delete spam and abusive comments.

6. Promote each post through your various social networks by using shortened and trackable links.

7. Use Twitter to promote your posts, even if you do nothing else there. Your number of followers will grow.

8. Install Google Analytics so you can watch your traffic.

9. Write more about the topics that attract the most comments and traffic.

10. Keep your posts short. If you've got a lot to say about any particular subject, break it into multiple posts.

And here are three more tips of our own:

11. Make sure your blog's categories make sense. Categories are the umbrella terms for the general subjects you write about on your blog. You want to keep these to under 10. For example, our categories include: *getting published, book proposals, finding a literary agent, self-publishing, book marketing* and *book publicity.* Proper categories lead to better SEO.

The Blog to Book Dream

Allie Brosh likes to draw. And write. She writes her own crazy, kooky, very personal stories alongside her own crazy, kooky, very personal illustrations. If Allie had shown us her work prior to starting her blog and asked if we thought she could have turned it into a book, we would've screamed, *No!* Traditionally, the publishing business doesn't really know what to do with this kind of material. And unless you're already famous, publishers are very reluctant to take a risk on something that is so offbeat and doesn't fit into a neat little category.

But Allie wasn't thinking about writing a book. When she found herself unemployed and bored, she started a blog called Hyperbole and a Half. Through posting personal stories and idiosyncratic illustrations on her site, and meaningfully engaging with her fans on social media, she slowly developed an audience. She made a point not to feature ads or to post anything overtly self-promotional. Often she would post things that were very funny. But she would also post unflinchingly honest and sometimes dark things about herself. Her audience grew. And grew. And grew. To the point where Allie was getting three to five million unique visitors every month. What would normally be seen as unpublishable suddenly became a book that everyone wanted, and Allie found herself with a book deal.

In 2013, after a long absence from her site, Allie posted a very moving and revealing entry about her struggle with depression. It received 1.5 million hits in one day and 5,000 comments on her blog (the maximum allowed per entry). Though she said nothing about her upcoming book, which was due to be released six months later, her readers started preordering copy after copy on Amazon. Her publisher took notice of just how passionate and dedicated Allie's fans were and their high hopes for her book got even higher. Today, there are over 350,000 copies of *Hyperbole and a Half* in print, and it's become a favorite of independent booksellers nationwide.

Although it's tempting to construct a blog in order to get a book deal, this tactic rarely works. Instead, take Allie's lead. Success didn't happen overnight, and a book wasn't the goal when she started. She did what she loved, shared it with others and developed meaningful relationships with her audience. She was in it for the long haul. She persisted. The book deal was just the cherry on top.

12. Make sure each individual post is tagged accurately. Tags are the clickable terms you use to identify an individual post. So, for example, if we were writing a post on blogging successfully, our tags might be: *blogs, tags, categories, links*. Many people neglect to tag, which is a great way to make your post invisible.

13. Blogging, in general, requires a more intimate relationship with your audience than a website. Treat each and every person who takes the time to read and comment on your material as if they might be the last.

Guest Blogging

Wouldn't it be great if you could write a brilliant blog post, a scathing editorial or an inspiring story and have it read by millions of people without having to do any of the networking, connecting and building of community? You can! It's called *guest blogging.* And you can make it happen anywhere from a fellow citizen's blog to a big site like The Huffington Post, Drudge Report or Salon to the website of your local bookstore.

▶ Apply the same effort toward searchability, via keywords and tags, out in the cyberworld as you do on your own site. For example, if you post a video on YouTube and you don't put in tags, no one—and we mean *no one*—will be able to find your video. As Sree Sreenivasan says, "You must search optimize everything you post across all social platforms."

How to create such an opportunity? It's back to e-researching, e-networking, e-writing and e-perseverance. Lisa Genova, author of *Still Alice,* a novel about a woman living with Alzheimer's disease, recounts her journey to guest blogging: "I went on all the social network sites that have anything to do with writers. I would post a profile and start looking for friends and community who were interested in Alzheimer's and might be interested in my book. Next I sent the book to the National Alzheimer's Association. Luckily, they really liked it. And they asked me to blog on their website. It was such a fantastic platform. From there, I got invitations to give keynote speeches to National Alzheimer's regional groups, and I really connected with my audience. A lot of them were like me—they were looking for something about Alzheimer's that wasn't out there." As you can see from Lisa's story, she did a tremendous amount of reaching out before she struck a vein of gold. And once she struck gold, it led her to more riches.

If such an opportunity strikes, remember that you're speaking to someone else's audience and adjust your writing accordingly, while, of course, retaining your own voice and authenticity. Since this audience may not know who you are, be sure to introduce yourself and make it easy for people to find you, should they want to do so.

Building Content

You've chosen your venues, set up your profiles, figured out who you'd like to follow and befriend. Now you have to start putting out. Content, that is. The

> Pepper posts with popular people and phrases who you want to connect with. According to our man Sree, "Smart people see every single tweet that has their name in it."

more content you produce, the more visible you become. You want to build the biggest house you can with as many roads leading to and from you as possible. But your house has to be pretty enough that it'll make someone actually want to stop and come in. If there is one thing we must emphasize in no uncertain terms, it is that all your content has to be of the highest quality you can possibly make it. Don't just put stuff out to put it out. Better to create one great post than five mediocre ones, no matter what platform you're using—blog, website, Facebook, Twitter or whatever hot new site comes along.

Great can take many forms. For cyber guru Sree Sreenivasan, all posts must be at least one of the following:

- Useful
- Informative
- Relevant
- Practical
- Actionable
- Entertaining

- Fun
- Occasionally funny*

  *Unless you're a humor writer, in which case occasionally should be always!

Here's the first item on the what-NOT-to-do list. Do NOT fill people's inboxes with the stultifying dull details of your life. Unless you're Marcel Proust, no one is interested in what you had for breakfast this morning!

Right up there at the top of the DOs is the following: Unless you're already famous, focusing your content and keeping it on track will make it that much easier for you to find and retain your audience. If your management blog opines more on your cat than on your employees, you're going to lose everyone but that small core of management junkies who happen to be felinophiles.

Think about who you're trying to reach and how best to reach them. Again, this is a question of trial and error as well as data analysis, both of which will help your online entity evolve. Pay very careful attention to who is sniffing around your e-door and who is actually coming in. Find out as much as you can about them. These people are golden. They should be treated with all due respect, reverence and love. Here's Sree Sreenivasan again: "Think and rethink what your posts will be—who you are targeting. Study who follows and reads you and give them what they want. Practice and see what works."

Then there's a matter of craft. Yes, what you write on the Internet is usually more off-the-cuff and more roughly edited, if edited at all, than what you put in print. But that doesn't mean that your work shouldn't be crafted and that your voice shouldn't shine through. Susan Orlean has this to say of her posts on social media platforms: "I do think about what I write. I don't deliberate and edit, but I do consider and craft it, so to speak."

And don't forget to feed your online venues regularly, give them lots of sunshine, regular watering, pruning and, of course, a goodly amount of fertilizer. Otherwise, they will become invisible. The more you cultivate your electronic garden, the more fruit it will bear, the more it will grow, the more people it will draw and delight.

BLOGGING THE BOOK JOURNEY

One topic you can feel free to wax poetic on is the progress of your tome-to-be. Updates and queries on your opus are wonderful ways to keep your beloved audience organically involved in your future authordom. Whether you're putting out a call for information or letting readers know you've reached a milestone or have had creative difficulties or a research breakthrough, getting people to feel connected to your book is a good thing. Queries and updates will also help you gauge public opinion on what aspects of your book

▶ Did you know you can synchronize your content across all media? Make sure you only have to post content once. There are a number of tools, such as Tweetdeck and Hootsuite (check with your cyber guru) that allow you to post content just once, yet have it appear on all the various platforms you use for social media. For example, you can set up your website so that when you post something, it automatically gets posted on Facebook and Twitter simultaneously. But please note that auto-posting and cross-posting can overload your audience. They might not want every tweet going to Facebook and vice versa. Curate carefully!

are most interesting and what needs work. "I kept my followers up-to-date about my progress and kept them involved by asking for feedback," says author and blogger Ramit Sethi. Bestselling author Rebecca Skloot took a similar tack: "I sent out emails asking questions about what I needed help with, like the subtitle of my book." The answers Ramit and Rebecca received were not only beneficial to the writing of their books, but also turned their friends and followers into evangelizers.

USER-GENERATED CONTENT

Citizens who are new to the Internet sometimes feel daunted about the prospect of continuously creating content, not to mention top-notch content. One wonderful solution is to let other people create that content for you. This is one of the genius moves employed by Arianna Huffington, founder of The Huffington Post. She gets all kinds of people, from the rich and famous to the talented and poor, to work for her for free.

Blogger and author Matthew Gasteier told us that one of the biggest mistakes he made in creating his blog was not setting up a place for user-generated content: "If you can get people to do your job, there's nothing better. The hardest part of a blog is having to produce the content for it. But with blogs like Awkward Family Photos, people can send in what will comprise an entire post. This means the person who runs the blog can post 10 to 20 times a day. If you post 20 times a day, you have a lot better chance of success."

Contributors aside, you can also repost or retweet content from other people's sites. This isn't plagiarism, as you'll be attributing these posts— common practice in cyberland. (Ask your child mentor for help if you're confused!) You can send around interesting links. Put up favorite quotes. In general, always keep your eye out for user-generated content that fits your platform and will feed your community's hunger.

TEST CONTENT

One of the most difficult components of any business is picking the right idea before you waste time and resources on one that turns out to be a dud. Wouldn't it be great to know for certain that your idea will draw numerous readers and lots of interest *before* committing to writing it? And wouldn't it be great if you could simultaneously kill another bird with that same stone? (The other bird being that many writers are flummoxed by the prospect of filling up a blog or website with content.) Well *voilà!* Testing your idea = content.

Until recently, testing an idea was a very difficult thing to do. Take this book. We had to go on a 20-city tour, which took a tremendous amount of time to set up and to perform and cost several thousand dollars, before we were convinced we had a winner. Today, the web offers fabulously easy and virtually cost-free methods of testing your idea.

Take your idea for a test drive to see if you want to own it before you make the down payment—the hours and hours of work it will take to make a book come to pass. Blogging is a terrific way to work out your writing muscles while figuring out whether there's a large and/or passionate audience for your book. Try your material out on the people you've e-friended. Ask for comments and/ or help. Are people interested? Are you getting consistent feedback? Use any and all comments to make your idea even better. "I treated my blog as my lab," says Ramit Sethi. "Blogging is like meeting someone in a bar. You don't say to someone you just met, 'Will you marry me?' You get to know the person. You ask questions. And you find out what you're not good at."

Blogging is also a good way to stick it to the man. How? Sometimes you have an idea that you just know is good, but the powers that be, the cultural gatekeepers who supposedly have their fingers on the pulse, have told you to take a hike. Used to be, that was the end of the road. But now you have the power to prove all the experts wrong. That's exactly what Pamela Satran Redmond did. "I wanted to do something fast and fun, and I was at a party with my contemporaries. We were all standing around talking. All anyone could talk about was their kids. And we did seem like old people, in a condo, playing shuffleboard. And I realized that, to kids, we do all look old. So there was this whole generation of people who were kind of mystified that people treat them in this condescending way, like they're irrelevant and kind of stupid. I thought it might be a magazine article. I tried to pitch it to a bunch of magazines. Nobody wanted it. I got frustrated. I had one of those F*** You moments, which are so productive. I thought, *Okay, I'll do this as a blog, see how it goes.* I started with a Top 10 list, and I figured if there was more, I'd continue. If it sucked, it could still be anonymous."

As you know, Pamela's blog was so successful that it became a *New York Times* bestselling book. And it happened in large part because she was able to test her idea and prove to publishers that it had excellent legs upon which it could run fast and far. "My blog gave me a great belief in my ability, in my impulses and my vision," says Pamela. "This was a property no one was interested in. And I did it myself, so I could make it exactly how I wanted. It was even more successful than I ever dreamed it would be. Artistically, technologically, it was one of the best things I ever did in my life."

Test your idea. Fill up your website/blog. In one fell swoop.

Walking the e-Walk

I n order to show and not just tell, we were determined to use social networking in the writing of this book. David likes Twitter. He finds great pleasure in composing 140-character haikus. Well, it turns out mega-bestselling author Neil Gaiman also likes getting his tweet on. So David decided to try to interview Neil over Twitter. The result is social networking magic, a pure example of how like-minded people connect:

Sterryhead @neilhimself finishing new edition on how to get book published 4 workman, want to interview you over twitter, r u game, gaiman?

neilhimself @Sterryhead you can try. My twitter stream is kind of heavy, so it's always luck whether I see anything or not.

mollycrabapple @neilhimself You should totally do it. *@Sterryhead*'s book is life-changingly good. *(Note: For those of you not familiar with Twitter, this is a comment by another follower of Neil Gaiman's—as well as a fan of ours!)*

Sterryhead @neilhimself wot do you think r the best ways for a new author to connect to their audience? best device anyone gave you about writing?

Step 4: Asking Your Fellow Citizens for Support

Poke your head around the World Wide Web and the term *influencer marketing* will pop up, a lot. Essentially, influencer marketers are citizens who have the eyes, ears, nose and/or throat of a community. As we've said, with traditional media outlets shrinking and the world growing more focused on specific and niche interests, individual citizens have become more and more important in spreading the word. As Sree Sreenivasan declares, "The scarcest resource of the 21st century will be human attention. The people who can get a slice of human attention will succeed." This means the right mention from the right influencer marketer can send your book shooting through cyberspace at the speed of sound. That's a big reason why you're spending all this time in the social media air space. To gain the eyeballs of these influencers. To cultivate their attention and respect far enough in advance of publication for it to matter.

E-ETIQUETTE

When you're trying to become friends with someone—be they an influencer marketer or an Average Joe—you probably don't go marching up to their house *neilhimself* *@Sterryhead* Whatever's handy. I've used Blogger and Twitter and The WELL and CompuServe . . . they all worked.

Sterryhead *@neilhimself* sorry shoulda been "Best advice anyone ever gave u about writing." i use voice recognition software it has mind of its own.

neilhimself *@Sterryhead* Ah, I was a bit puzzled about what kind of device you were after.

neilhimself *@Sterryhead* "Everything in a contract is negotiable, even the date at the top" from an old Writer and Artist's Yearbook.

Sterryhead *@neilhimself* do you think it's important for a writer to read? What are you reading currently?

neilhimself *@Sterryhead* absolutely. Lots of books on Scottish myth and legend by Otta F Swire.

Sterryhead *@neilhimself* what's more important—2 write a great book, or have 250,000 followers on Twitter?

neilhimself *@Sterryhead* to write the best book you can.

uninvited at midnight and ring the doorbell until you wake them out of a deep sleep. You don't invite them to your party two or three times a day, or every day for two weeks in a row. You don't stalk them when they are at work and demand that they give you their attention, join your club or read your brilliant new piece about Genghis Khan and Jane Austen. Or so we hope. The same rules apply in the e-sphere. You don't want to alienate the very people you're trying to attract. Every community has its own etiquette and language. But here are some general dos and don'ts to abide by as you travel far and wide in cyberspace:

- DO have an attitude of gratitude. Thank others profusely and often.

- DO pay it forward. If you're asking for favors or know you will be in the future, do something to help the person you'll be hitting up.

- DO read your emails before you send them out. Make sure there's nothing egregious, sloppy or unclear. Once it's out there, you can't take it back.

- DO be polite. Hellos, salutations, greetings, pleases and thank-yous are just as important on the information superhighway as they are in the flesh.

57

Web as Testing Ground

I f you want to test out your work online but aren't ready to set up a blog, you can try posting (or even selling) shorter pieces of work on sites such as Scribd, Amazon and Smashwords. These are great places on which to figure out if you have an audience. Elaborate tagging systems allow people to easily find your work by looking for the particular subjects they're interested in; and via the commenting system, you can engage in an ongoing dialogue with your readers. Tammy N. Ham, VP of content and marketing for Scribd, adds: "We have a built-in community, where you just start searching for people with similar interests—you start subscribing to other people. People are great about sharing and critiquing."

Many websites now sell short works as well. Kat Lu, a physical therapist by day and novelist by night, wanted to find out what, exactly, her particular audience was after. She decided to test her appeal by writing short stories that she would post, individually, as ebooks (or e-shorts!). But before she wrote a word, Kat did her research: "I went on forums and discussion boards, finding out what people like in my genre, which is fantasy romance." Then Kat got down to business. Once she completed a number of stories she felt good about, she

- ■ DO make absolutely sure you're sending your emails to the right person before you click *send*.

- ■ DO double-check all links to make sure they're valid before you send them out—people won't take the trouble to track down a broken link.

- ■ DO put a subject in the subject line of your emails. This will help you and others store, organize, search for and find information.

- ■ DO confirm if information is or is not confidential if you're part of an online community. David accidentally passed on an email to someone from a list that was, in fact, confidential. No one told him, and he didn't bother to ask. A lot of people yelled at him after that.

- ■ DON'T USE ALL CAPITAL LETTERS UNLESS YOU'RE E-SHOUTING!

- ■ DON'T tell them how great you are, show them. Don't be one of those people who walk around with shirts that say SEXY on them. Let them be the judge of that.

- ■ DON'T send big huge files unannounced. People aren't set up for them and they can slow down recipients' computers, i.e., be totally annoying.

- ■ DON'T send things out with a bunch of stupit speeling errrs.

uploaded them onto Amazon. To make sure people could find her work, she was very careful about her search terms: "*Sexy, women's fiction, paranormal romance,* and several other words that would make your mother blush," Kat says. "I sold 200 stories in three weeks with no advertising. I am a category bestseller." Now Kat is actively working on her novel, using everything she learned from her bestselling short stories to strengthen her work.

Speaking of fantasy romance, some traditional publishers—Harlequin being the most active in this area—have set up electronic imprints to nurture aspiring writers and to encourage established authors to experiment with new kinds of writing. Here's Harlequin's CEO, Donna Hayes, on the romance publisher's electronic division, Carina Press: "Carina is great for new writers, but also for writers who want to write something completely new and different. It's a great place to test your material, to experiment and see how the audience responds. And, if an author becomes really popular, we may decide to publish her in print."

Instead of slaving away for years on a book only to find out you can't write that book well enough, or that there's no audience for it, you can test the waters before you go plunging in.

- ■ DON'T beg people to forward your stuff. If it's good enough, they will.

- ■ DON'T ask someone a question that's already answered on their website. Do your homework. Look around for the Frequently Asked Questions link.

- ■ DON'T hit reply and vent your bile if/when someone gives you some e-hate. In our experience (and sadly David does have quite a bit of experience with this), fighting fire with fire only makes more fire.

A Bit More on Generosity

Just as Blanche DuBois relied on the kindness of strangers, so will you. But first you have to give some kindness of your own. Now is the time to reach out with a generous hand and a warm heart. Understanding you may not get any love back for a long time. Understanding you have to just keep doing it over and over again, evolving and learning, giving lots of gracious generosity as you go.

It seems to be hardwired into us humans that when someone is generous to us, it makes it easier to be generous back—to them specifically and also just in general. As long as it's genuine.

Nakedly self-serving self-promotion, whether it occurs by email, post or tweet, needs to be balanced by genuine, authentic humanoid content (more on that in a bit). Sree Sreenivasan suggests limiting the number of times you talk about or promote yourself to 1 in 5. Malle Vallik of Harlequin ups the number to 1 in 20. Of course, there is no magic number. But you never want people to feel that your communications are always me, me, me.

So, how can you be electronically generous? By making comments, by rating posts and/or books highly, by writing thoughtful (and yes, nice) reviews, by participating in spirited discussions on other people's websites. If it's done correctly, this kind of generosity is often rewarded in spades, just when you need it. Such is the cooperative promise of social networking.

The Importance of Authenticity

One of the most wonderful things about the Internet is that it allows you a peek into the lives of people you never would've had the opportunity to engage with on terra firma. This is why so many authors—particularly fiction authors—have enjoyed success with their blogs or social networks. People want to find out about the living, breathing person behind the characters or stories. Does this mean you need to tell your friends and followers everything about you? John Scalzi, one of the top book bloggers in the country as well as the author of numerous books, thinks not: "Authenticity is important. But we have to be careful about how we define authenticity. It doesn't necessarily mean vomiting out your life onto a blog. It doesn't mean psychodrama. One thing I'm very clear about is that I'm *personable* but I'm not *personal*. I will write up a cute thing that my daughter said (which I clear with her first), but I don't tell people when she's being an 11-year-old butthead. The point is that what you're receiving is an edited version of my life. But in the context of what I'm telling you, you can believe it 100%."

▶ NEVER EVER EVER (yes, we're shouting) include individual email addresses in the "To:" box of a mass email. You don't want to give away access to people's information without their permission. Use the discreet BCC function instead.

Keep it real. Just as a fake smile can be a turnoff in the real world, an artificial, awkward or deceitful post/email/comment in cyberspace can generate much ill will. There is such anonymity on the World Wide Web, it's very tempting to make yourself into something you're not, to be someone you aren't. Whether you're stretching the truth about yourself and who you are, pretending to be friends with someone you aren't, soliciting people while pretending you're really trying to do something nice for them, having friends and/or fans act as shills in a rude, invasive way, creating fake identities to rave about yourself—all these kinds

Email Lists and e-Newsletters

When we wrote the first edition of this book, we made a very big mistake. We never got the email addresses of the people we met, taught, workshopped, schmoozed and consulted with. We meant to. We even printed out sheets with a space to fill in this information. But we never followed through. By now, we would have amassed a list of tens of thousands to whom we could send an announcement about this new edition, about our upcoming tour, about our workshops, and more. So stupid! At least we learned from our mistakes, and after our second edition came out we got serious about our lists. Please don't follow our early lead. Capture emails on your website, at any gigs, at the PTA meeting. Wherever. Keep your lists current. Separate them out into subcategories (by region, interest, group). Then weed out people who don't make sense. Although a big mailing list is great, you want people on your list who want to be there. That's why it doesn't make sense—even though it's tempting—to hijack email addresses off other people's lists. Just like with e-friending and following, a smaller list of the right people is more effective than a larger list that includes the kitchen sink. Even small but potent mailing/social networking lists make it easier to solicit help and spread the word. (P.S. If someone wants off your list, don't argue. Say you're sorry to see them go and take them off your list immediately.)

One of the best ways to use email lists today is through a revolutionary, cheap and relatively easy way of communicating with your audience: the e-newsletter. It's much like a traditional newsletter, except, of course, it's electronic, which means that you can insert pictures, links, even video. And you can track how many people actually read your newsletter, how many click on links, how many never want to hear from you again, and lots of other fun stuff.

When we first started using our now-extensive mailing list to send out our electronic newsletter, we mainly focused on plugging our upcoming events and/or book releases. Surprise, surprise, that didn't attract a huge number of readers. So we started filling our newsletters with things we knew our readers would find valuable: writing tips, links to interviews that would educate and illuminate the publishing process, shout-outs to other authors. Surprise, surprise, when we did this, our numbers jumped. Of course, we also listed upcoming events and stuff about our various books and projects. Turns out that when they were included with lots of info our readers found valuable, they clicked on our promotional stuff as well.

Most e-newsletter services are free unless you have a mailing list in the thousands. The data, however—including what your audience is interested in and what they're not— is priceless.

of inauthentic behavior will almost always come back to bite you in a very unpleasant place. John puts it this way: "The difference between being part of a community because it's organic, or because you've read in a book somewhere that it's important to be part of the community to market yourself is obvious. People will figure out very quickly if you're there to enjoy or exploit."

The Dark Side of Anonymity

Over and over, we've seen people "say" vile, pernicious, hateful ugly stuff on the Internet, stuff that very few humans would ever say in real life. There is a term for this: *flame mail.* So know this and know it well: If you spend any time at all putting yourself out on the Internet, there is a possibility that people are going to say rude, crude and/or violent things to you. (Sree Sreenivasan says comments on social media platforms are 10 times more likely to be negative than positive.)

The strange thing about getting a smackdown online is that, under the right circumstances, it can actually help make you and/or your book successful. Kemble Scott, one of the first writers to use YouTube trailers to promote his book, had just this happen to him. An online journalist said something snarky about one of his videos on Gawker, a heavily trafficked site. This sent lots of people to his videos, which in turn promoted his book.

Good or bad, we've come to embrace the Godfather model of interacting online: It's always business, never personal.

The Apple of Your Eye

In the meantime, it's back to the precious commodity around which this all revolves. Your book. Did you think we had somehow forgotten? We haven't. It's just that we want the apple of your eye to flourish and thrive when it finally does have its coming-out party in the world.

CHAPTER 3

The Perfect Package

"There is one rule for business and this is it:
Make the best quality of goods possible."

—Henry Ford

EVEN IF YOU'RE A PROFESSIONAL builder, you still need help building a house. So it is with building a book, only instead of a painter, a plumber and an electrician, you'll potentially need an agent, an editor and a publisher. But to get to any of these people, you must put together a package so perfect that it will make a jaded publishing professional perk up. For nonfiction writers, this means an airtight proposal consisting of everything from a bang-up bio to an outstanding outline. For fiction writers, it means an entire manuscript, along with a few bells and whistles.

Either way, in order to prepare this package, you'll need a steadfast support team, a top-notch title and maybe even a doctor in case your proposal or manuscript gets sick.

Selecting Your Dream Team

One of the ironies of the book business is that while writing is generally a solitary art, the publishing process is all about assembling a great team. Linda Bubon, co-owner of Women & Children First, an independent bookstore in Chicago, says she's noticed a common thread among successful authors: "They involve others in their work. They send drafts out to friends. They solicit advice from friends. They are part of writing groups. They go to readings and support other writers. They make other people feel that they're part of the process. Writers who never leave their garrets rarely make successful books."

We can't tell you how many times we've heard the sentence, "I never could have finished my book without my writing group." Particularly for those writing fiction, creative nonfiction or poetry, writing groups and writing partners can be a great source of inspiration, constructive criticism and support in that we're-all-in-the-trenches-together kind of way. Many people have a hard time starting a project (especially one as big as a book), and an even harder time maintaining motivation. So if you have that sinking woe-is-me-I-can't-even-get-started-and-when-I-do-what-will-I-do feeling, see if you can find some kindred spirits to march down that long and winding road with you.

▶ Planning on self-publishing? While you will need only a *few* of the elements included in this chapter (like a pitch and a bio), you will benefit by at least thinking about *all* of them. So before you skip ahead, at least take a speed-read.

The fact is, it's nigh impossible to be a brilliant writer, excellent editor, superb proofreader, social media guru, salesperson extraordinaire, graphics genius and perfect publicist all at once. Instead, you need to build a team. Your first draft pick, if at all possible, should be anyone you know who's actually in publishing. Beyond that, look for people who are erudite, enthusiastic, business-savvy, articulate, selfless readers of books like yours; graphically/visually acute; fab proofreaders . . . and nice enough to tell you when you've got a bit of food on your lip without making you feel like a miserable loser. Start assembling your team early. Prepare to barter for services.

If you're despairing because you don't know a single soul to fill any of these roles, have no fear. We'll show you where these people are and how to find and woo them. No garret for you!

Models for Success

Imagine trying to put together a jigsaw puzzle without a picture. Not impossible, but much more difficult. So it is with a book. Before writing your proposal or manuscript, it helps to have a model—a successful book similar to yours in theme, style and/or approach. You're going to use your model to prove that your book-to-be will succeed. And you're going to learn from your model how to make it so.

When locating a model, there are two rules: 1) Your model must be or have been successful in some way, and 2) Your model must be similar to your book in content or form, but not directly competitive. A model is all about success by association. For example, if you want to sell a book about Peruvian mud sharks and heart disease, you wouldn't choose as your model a bestselling book about Peruvian mud sharks and heart disease. You might, however, choose a bestseller on Peruvian mud sharks and liver maladies. Or a bestselling

"Keep away from people who try to belittle your ambitions. Small people always do that, but the really great make you feel that you, too, can become great."

—*Mark Twain*

Supermodels Are Not Beautiful Airheads

For years, Arielle and her mom, Joann, wanted to write a book about the science, history and culture of color. First, they thought they'd write the book for 8- to 12-year-olds. They developed a proposal. The publisher they sent it to said, "This doesn't feel like a kid's book." Back to the drawing board. Arielle and Joann discovered a book that did everything they wanted to do, but was on a totally different subject. It was called *The Elements: A Visual Exploration of Every Known Atom in the Universe.* This funny, smart, beautiful book was the perfect model for Arielle and Joann. It also happened to have sold about 250,000 copies up to that point (and tens of thousands more since). They studied it to figure out what "elements" made *The Elements* so great. They developed a second proposal, hiring a graphic designer who used the same square format as their model. The publisher of *The Elements*, Black Dog & Leventhal, has since published two more books with the same trim size and the same popular science audience. Arielle and Joann wondered if Black Dog & Leventhal might be interested in publishing one more. They submitted their book exclusively to this inventive publisher. Lo and behold, the publisher was looking for the next book in this unofficial series. Any other publisher would've had a hard time categorizing Arielle and Joann's book. Was it science? Art? History? Nature? It was also very expensive to produce. But Black Dog & Leventhal had been so successful with *The Elements* that they had buyers waiting with bated breath—both in the United States and worldwide—for whatever came next. What would've been a very hard book to sell—both to a publisher and to the public—became very easy due to the great model they chose. Their book, *The Secret Language of Color: Science, Nature, History, Culture, Beauty of Red, Orange, Yellow, Green, Blue & Violet,* has already sold tens of thousands of copies and has been translated into five languages.

book on heart disease and hammerheads. Look, if you're proposing a book that's already out there, editors and agents will naturally question the need for your book. Whereas, if you're proposing a book that's like your model but reinvents the mouse trap in some key way, it will make them excited to sell your book to those same readers. And once your book has found a home, your model will also help you and your publisher figure out how to get you media attention, and how to get your book onto the shelves of major retailers and ultimately into the hands of readers who will give you all the love you so richly deserve.

Comp Romp: The Power of Comparable Titles

Within the publishing business is an insider name for models: "comp titles"— short for "comparable titles." Once a book is bought, comp titles are used by the sales force and the publicity and marketing departments to help the media and booksellers understand exactly what your book is, why it will sell and where it fits on the shelf. Comp titles tell us who your audience is. They tell us how commercial or literary a thriller is. Whether a mystery is cozy or suspenseful. If a dystopian novel is for adults or middle graders.

Many authors are confused when trying to come up with comparable titles for their book. When you're looking for comparable titles, think in big, broad strokes. Which books are like your book in general terms of character, plot, tone, language and category? A great way to find comparable titles is to go to your local library or your local independent bookstore. Find a person who is the expert in your category. Tell her about your book and ask her if there are any similar books that you should know about. (Note: If you're doing this in an independent bookstore, you must pay for this service in a very important way. You must buy a book.)

Although you should be thinking in big, broad strokes, don't go too big. Using comps that are mega-bestsellers makes agents and publishers roll their eyes. It displays how little you know about your category. Good comp titles, on the other hand, demonstrate just how well you know your shelf by trotting out writers/books that people within publishing love and know to be great but that the average reader may not be aware of. You get instant insider status.

If you must compare yourself to the great or famous, be specific or inventive (more to come on this in a few pages when we discuss the elevator pitch). But, please, whatever you do, don't say you're the next *Hunger Games, Harry Potter,* or *Eat, Pray, Love*!

Getting Titular: Titles and Subtitles

America's most famous B-movie meister, Roger Corman, often used to come up with the title and the poster for a movie before the story. And his movies always made money. Corman understood the value of a great title, and you should, too. Believe it or not, in some cases, a great title and/or subtitle alone can result in a book sale.

Titles can be metaphoric, like *What Color Is Your Parachute?* Or practical, like *101 Ways to Cook Chicken.* They can be clever like *Lies, and the Lying Liars Who Tell Them,* poetic like *I Know Why the Caged Bird Sings* or silly like *Captain Underpants.* It doesn't really matter how, but your title must make readers want to pick up your book, buy it and read it. And for nonfiction it must express clearly what's inside your book. *Men Are from Mars, Women Are from Venus* is a terrific title because it's clever and intriguing, and it states a point of view that many humans intuitively relate to. It lets readers know what they'll find between the covers. And it does so in a jiffy.

> "A good title should be like a good metaphor: It should intrigue without being too baffling or too obvious."
>
> —*Walker Percy*

Here's one of our all-time favorite titles, which you're going to hear a lot more about shortly: *No Plot? No Problem!: A Low-Stress, High-Velocity Approach to Writing a Novel in 30 Days.* We love this title because it strikes just the right note of freewheeling whimsy and rock-solid information. The subtitle lets people know exactly what the book is, while the main title communicates both the gist and the hilarious tone of the book.

Speaking of subtitles: For nonfiction, they can be just as important as titles, especially if a title is poetic or metaphoric. A subtitle will clue your potential readers into what your book is about, without requiring them to open the book. And if they can catch on to what your book is about with just a glance, there's a much greater chance that they'll pick it up and buy it. Most people don't take the time to open books in bookstores. Most often, it's that first glance that hooks them—or not.

A common mistake authors make is choosing a title that has a particular meaning to them but that no one else understands. Choosing a title that sounds good but doesn't clue readers in to what's great about the book also smacks of self-sabotage.

A good technique for finding a title and/or subtitle is to create a title pool. Write down all the forms of speech of chief words relating to your book.

Title Torture

Rick Beyer had an idea for a popular history book made up of clever, fascinating and little-known stories. Unfortunately, he didn't have a clever, fascinating title to match. He went through approximately, oh, 50 million different ideas, but nothing fit. Just at the point of giving up, Rick said to one of his team members, "Well, there's one I thought about a long time ago, but I don't think it's any good." Hoping for some sort of seed to brainstorm with, she encouraged Rick to say it anyway. *"The Greatest Stories Never Told,"* he said. Not only did she flip her wig over the title, but every publisher his proposal was sent to loved it as well.

The title, a fabulous twist on a common phrase, perfectly captured the idea behind the book. Interestingly, even though Rick came up with this title himself and had always had it in the back of his mind, he didn't have confidence that it was a winner. This is why it's important to share your title ideas. Yes, you'll get a million opinions. But if you've got a great title, its greatness will be confirmed by others over and over again.

Indeed, *The Greatest Stories Never Told* sold in a heartbeat and has spawned three sequels. The rest, as they say, is history. . . .

For example, if you want to use the word "receive" in your title, also write down "receiving," "reception" and "receiver." Then put all the words into columns based on their part of speech—noun, verb, adjective, adverb. Play mix-and-match.

As we revealed in our introduction, words and terms that are search-friendly have become such important selling tools that we had to scrap a book title we loved. It was search-unfriendly. How can you tell what's search-friendly and what's not? Thanks to Google, you can now get up-to-the-moment information on the most commonly used "keywords" (the professional term for search words) within your subject area of choice. Go to Google Adwords, select the Keyword Tool and start trying out different words and phrases related to your title. You'll get to see which keywords are most commonly used by Googlers. Add these to your pool. For example, if you're writing a tomato cookbook, you might want to consider using the word "sauce" in your subtitle; "sauce" is one of the search terms most commonly combined with tomatoes.

When you're looking for a title, get lots and lots of opinions. Write your options on a piece of paper so your bias is not revealed by the tone of your voice. Go to your support team or writing group and show these around. Ask people you think would be likely to buy your book—this includes booksellers and librarians. Have brainstorming sessions. Sometimes the title is lying right there; you just can't see it. But be forewarned: Other people's opinions can confuse matters. Arielle frequently has clients who've settled on a title only to call in a panic and say, "Tom and Dick didn't like it! But Harry loved it! What should I do?" Take the ideas of people you trust, and then go with your gut.

Perfecting Your Pitch

One of the most egregious and common mistakes that both amateur and seasoned writers make is underestimating the power of the pitch. Your pitch will be both the backbone and lifeblood of your book, from idea through (and past) publication.

The first time you announce to anyone that you're going to write a book, there's an excellent chance their response will be "What's your book about?" Your answer to this question is your pitch. When you approach an agent, you will have to pitch your book. When your agent approaches an editor at a publishing house, she will have to pitch your book. When the editor presents your book at his editorial meeting, he will have to pitch your book to his editorial colleagues as well as his colleagues in publicity, marketing and sales. And they will all be evaluating his pitch to determine whether or not to buy your book. If you're lucky enough to sell your book, the sales force will go out to large retailers and small booksellers alike to pitch your book. And the publicity and marketing staff will be pitching your book to the media. If you get on the *Today* show and Matt Lauer asks what your book is about, you better have a very good answer. And a hundred years from now, when a reader in New York is reading your book on the screen implanted in her wrist while waiting for her molecular transporter to take her to New Shanghai, and the person next to her says, "What's that book about?" . . . you better hope that reader can give one hell of a pitch!

▶ Don't make your pitch a book report. Your pitch is your audition to show us what a brilliant or funny or romantic or authoritative or fill-in-the-blank writer you are. That's why your pitch has to demonstrate the very best of your writing. We like to think of it this way: A pitch is like a poem. *Every word counts.*

Every book makes a promise to its readers: to educate, to challenge, to amuse, to romance, to inspire, to entertain. What does your book promise? A pitch must take your promise and deliver it lickety-split. The beauty of a major league pitch is that it contains the juicy essence of your book, it's over in no time at all and it leaves the crowd oohing and aahing in awe. Your pitch should entertain and delight, pique interest or give pause, depending on what kind of promise you need to deliver. At the end of your pitch, you want the person you're pitching to say, "Wow, I can't wait to read that book!" or "I can't believe I never thought of that before!" or "I know someone who would really love that book!" A beautifully crafted pitch is a skeleton key that will open many doors.

There are two kinds of pitches: 1) the elevator pitch, which is over by the time the elevator gets to the next floor, and 2) your long-form pitch. But when we say long-form, we're talking *under a minute*. Never, ever, let your pitch go longer than a minute. In fact, most long-form pitches can be done in under 30 seconds. Whenever pitches go longer than a minute, eyes start to glaze and boredom sets in. Hey, most people are willing to give you a minute, but often not a second longer.

Elevator to the Penthouse

Elevator pitches usually draw from those comp titles you've unearthed and are often framed in Hollywoodesque combos like the following:

- *The Catcher in the Rye* with Asperger's (*The Curious Incident of the Dog in the Night-Time*)
- *Pride and Prejudice* in modern London (*Bridget Jones's Diary*)
- *Winnie-the-Pooh* meets the *Tao Te Ching* (*The Tao of Pooh*)

There are variations on this theme as well:

"The _____ with/without _____,"
"The _____ for _____," or
"The _____ of _____."

For example, Mark Bittman's *How to Cook Everything* is the "*Joy of Cooking* for the 21st century"; Jon Krakauer's *Into Thin Air* is "*Alive* without the cannibalism." Or one of our all-time favorites that we heard at an early Pitchapalooza: "*The Elements of Style* for Fruit Trees," which became *Grow a Little Fruit Tree: Simple Pruning Techniques for Small-Space, Easy-Harvest Fruit Trees*. If you borrow from a familiar title, you don't have to explain your promise because people already know what the "it" is. Take this book. We pitched it as "the *What to Expect*® *When You're Expecting* of publishing." People think of *What to Expect*® as the leading reference book for women who are looking for friendly, in-depth advice on the entire pregnancy process, written by people who have been through it—who know what you'll be feeling because they've felt it. By associating our book with *What to Expect®,* we were promising the same sort of in-depth, in-the-know, full-spectrum advice. The only adjustment our editor had to make was to replace "pregnancy" with "publishing."

> "I have made this longer than usual because I have not had time to make it shorter."
>
> —*Blaise Pascal*

But as we mentioned in our discussion of comp titles, beware of comparing yourself to the biggest and best authors out there because you're sure to disappoint. "Early Philip Roth with a dash of Jane Austen" can't stand alone as an elevator pitch. You're asking an agent to make a comparison that more than likely isn't going to come out in your favor. Instead, if you must use literary giants because they really do help describe your book, construct a pitch that specifies how your book will speak to the audience of those über-authors: "What happens when the repressed male sexuality of Alexander Portnoy meets the strong-minded, spunky joie de vivre of Elizabeth Bennet? Watch the sparks fly in *The Shiksa of Herefordshire,* a new twist on the old battle of the sexes."

For nonfiction books, your subtitle often makes for a great elevator pitch. Chris Baty's book is a fabulous example of how your subtitle can work double duty. Here's how you'd put this into pitch form: "My book, *No Plot? No Problem!* takes a low-stress, high-velocity approach to writing a novel in 30 days."

Check out the subtitles for these books, which we think also make for standout succinct elevator pitches:

- *The South Beach Diet:* The delicious, doctor-designed, foolproof plan for fast and healthy weight loss

- *The Quants:* How a new breed of math whizzes conquered Wall Street and nearly destroyed it

- *The Happiness Project:* Or, why I spent a year trying to sing in the morning, clean my closets, fight right, read Aristotle and generally have more fun

- *Trattoria:* Healthy, simple robust fare inspired by the small family restaurants of Italy

- *Same Kind of Different as Me:* A modern-day slave, an international art dealer and the unlikely woman who bound them together

- *The Happiest Baby on the Block:* The new way to calm crying and help your newborn baby sleep longer

- *The Backyard Homestead:* Produce all the food you need on just a quarter-acre!

If your elevator pitch doesn't fit into a formula or use its subtitle, that's fine, too. One of our favorite against-the-grain pitches was for *Why God Won't Go Away: Brain Science and the Biology of Belief* by Andrew Newberg, Eugene D'Acquili and Vince Rause. Here it is: "Did God create the brain? Or did the brain create God? The answer to both these questions is a resounding 'Yes!'" This pitch is quick as silver. It uses intriguing questions and an unexpected zinger of an answer to reel readers in. It makes people want more.

Because your elavator pitch is a few sentences long, it has to be jam-packed and drum-tight. A pitch is all about economy.

Magic in Under a Minute

Your long-form pitch is typically more like a paragraph or two. Your elevator pitch often makes a great first or last line(s) to your long-form pitch. But where to go from there? Read lots and lots of flap copy and, particularly, the backs of paperbacks, where the whole kit and caboodle is limited to a paragraph or two, tops. You'll see how concise those copywriters had to be, and how they managed to describe a book—and sell it—in only a few sentences. Online bookstores are great resources as well, and they have an added benefit: Because nearly every book is accompanied by flap or back cover copy, you can cut-and-paste phrases you like into a document and then use these phrases to craft your own pitch. Just be sure that your copy represents the writing style of your book. (And don't copy copy. There's a word for that: plagiarism!)

Make the pitch for your hardcore, authoritative business book hardcore and authoritative. Make your tear jerker jerk some tears. Make the pot boil on your potboiler. Here are a few examples of pitches we think are pitch-perfect, along with why we love them:

- *One Plus One* (Pamela Dorman Books). *Notice the deft and detailed introduction of numerous characters.* Suppose your life sucks. A lot. Your husband has done a vanishing act, your teenage stepson is being bullied, and your math whiz daughter has a once-in-a-lifetime opportunity that you can't afford to pay for. That's Jess's life in a nutshell—until an unexpected knight in shining armor offers to rescue them. Only Jess's knight turns out to be Geeky Ed, the obnoxious tech millionaire whose vacation home she happens to clean. But Ed has big problems of his own, and driving the dysfunctional family to the Math Olympiad feels like his first unselfish act in ages . . . maybe ever.

- *A Series of Unfortunate Events: The Bad Beginning by Lemony Snicket. Observe the brilliant use of voice:* Dear Reader, I'm sorry to say that the book you are holding in your hands is extremely unpleasant. It tells an unhappy tale about three very unlucky children. Even though they are charming and clever, the Baudelaire siblings lead lives filled with misery and woe. From the very first page of this book, when the children are at the beach and receive terrible news, continuing on through the entire story, disaster lurks at their heels. One might say they are magnets for misfortune. In this short book alone, the three youngsters encounter a greedy and repulsive villain, itchy clothing, a disastrous fire, a plot to steal their fortune, and cold porridge for breakfast. It is my sad duty to write down these unpleasant tales, but there is nothing stopping you from putting this book down at once and reading something happy, if you prefer that sort of thing. With all due respect, Lemony Snicket.

- *Trattoria: Simple and Robust Fare Inspired by the Small Family Restaurants of Italy. Check out how this copy actually makes your mouth water:* Whether it's a bustling eatery in the heart of Florence or a tiny alcove tucked away on a side street in Venice, the trattoria is where Italians go for big flavors, great friendship and good times. Patricia Wells now fuels America's undying passion for Italian food with more than 150 trattoria recipes—recipes for honest food, bursting with flavor and prepared with a

Beware of the Plot-Heavy Pitch

Time and again, we see amateur authors pitch by trying to tell the plot of their entire novel or memoir in excruciating detail. Here's the kind of thing we've heard about a squazillion times: "My main character, Frodo Potter, gets up one morning and decides to have breakfast. So he invites his pet rat Bobo to eat an egg with him. But the egg is slightly runny, so they decide to cook it a little bit more. . . ." This pitch, which we heard a few months ago, might still be going on if we hadn't emphatically put an end to it. Broad strokes combined with specific imagery should display how exciting your characters and story are. Universal appeal should be implied via the mention of themes rather than an endless recitation of events. And, again, the pitch should be an amuse bouche that gives your audience a tiny, delightful taste of the delicacy that is your writing.

minimum of fuss. Savor the succulent taste of lamb braised in white wine, garlic and hot peppers, the hearty pleasure of authentic lasagna with basil, garlic and tomato sauce, or the delight of a luscious fragrant orange and lemon cake created by a chef in a tiny hamlet in Tuscany. Patricia Wells' *Trattoria* presents a full range of healthy, homemade recipes for soups, antipasti, dried and fresh pastas, rice and polenta, fish, poultry and meats, with special chapters on breads and pizzas, spreads, broths and condiments, and an irresistible selection of desserts.

■ *Predictably Irrational: The Hidden Forces That Shape Our Decisions. Marvel at the way this makes you go "Really? Wow! I want to know more!":* Why do our headaches persist after taking a 1¢ aspirin but disappear when we take a 50¢ aspirin? Why do we splurge on a lavish meal but cut coupons to save 25¢ on a can of soup? Why do we go back for second helpings at the unlimited buffet, even when our stomachs are already full? When it comes to making decisions in our lives, we think we're in control. We think we're making smart, rational choices. But are we? In a series of illuminating, often surprising experiments, MIT behavioral economist Dan Ariely refutes the common assumption that we behave in fundamentally rational ways. Blending everyday experience with groundbreaking research, Ariely explains how expectations, emotions, social norms and other invisible, seemingly illogical forces skew our reasoning abilities. We consistently overpay, underestimate and procrastinate. We fail to understand the profound effects of our emotions on what we want, and we overvalue what we already own. Yet these misguided behaviors are neither random nor senseless. They're systematic and predictable—making us predictably irrational. From drinking coffee to losing weight, from buying a car to choosing a romantic partner, Ariely explains how to break through these systematic patterns of thought to make better decisions. *Predictably Irrational* will change the way we interact with the world—one small decision at a time.

Once you've figured out the words, then you've got to practice your delivery. Rehearse on your own, then start pitching everybody, everywhere. The more often you pitch, the sooner you'll know what works and what doesn't. If during a certain part of your pitch, people look confused, bored or nonplussed, cut or change those parts. Sometimes it's as simple as reordering your words or trimming some fat. Get feedback. Keep refining your pitch until it rolls trippingly off your tongue. Until people who hear or read it want to be in business with you and your idea. As Valerie Lewis, co-owner of Hicklebee's in San Jose, California, says, "You have to pitch in a way that eliminates the possibility of getting back the word 'No.'"

The Facts About the Fiction Proposal

When it comes to selling fiction, unless you've recently turned up in the pages of *People* magazine or have already sold a treatment of your unwritten novel to a Big Hollywood Film Studio, chances are you'll need to write the whole enchilada before you start marketing it. This doesn't mean you can't show it to readers a chapter at a time for comments. Just don't start marketing it until you're sure it's the best you can possibly make it.

Once you've polished off your fiction manuscript, all you'll need to complete your package is a bio (see pages 80–82), blurbs (pages 98–99) if you can get them and possibly a cover (pages 96–98). If you have a brilliant and/ or unusual idea for marketing or publicizing your novel, or you have a large following on Twitter or some other social media platform, you'd be crazy not to include these as well.

Lastly, we'd like to address the issue of plot synopses. Some agents and editors will never look at such things because they know how difficult it is to boil your book down to a page or two. Others like to scan these first to see if they're even interested in looking at what you've written. Our advice is to work up a synopsis if you feel you can capture the narrative drive of your book and manage to make it seem exciting. If you're unable to do this (and it's particularly difficult with literary fiction), don't submit a synopsis with your manuscript. Just wait and see if anyone asks. To master the art of synopsis writing, start reading flap and back cover copy of novels similar to yours. This can be done without leaving home, since most online bookstores repurpose the publisher's flap copy as the book description.

In the meantime, keep reading, because the rest of this chapter touches on all the oh-so-relevant issues that will pop up down the road.

The Nonfiction Proposal

Think of writing a nonfiction book proposal as an art form like competitive figure skating. First you must perform the compulsory moves, then you have to dazzle the judges with your original material if you want to bring home the gold. And a really snazzy outfit doesn't hurt! Go back to your notes, where you identified your audience, your competition, your marketing and publicity opportunities and the reasons why you're the one to write your book. Now you're going to pull these pieces together with succinct, deep and specific information and wrap them up into a nice package with a shiny bow.

Should You Finish Your Manuscript Instead of Writing Your Proposal?

No. That's the short answer if you're writing nonfiction. As we said, for fiction, you need a complete manuscript. And if you already know you want to self-publish, there's obviously no need for a proposal either.

There's an old show business adage: Leave 'em wanting more. Publishing is no different. The less information you can give and still make an airtight case, the better. Why? Because publishers live off HOPE. Hope that your book will be reviewed in top-tier newspapers and magazines. Hope that your book will speak to Terry Gross and, for that matter, that she'll speak for it. Hope that it will quicken the pulses of buyers at bookstores. Hope that it will spread on the World Wide Web like a virus. Hope that it will beat the odds and become a big fat juicy bestseller. Publishers throw a lot of spaghetti at the wall and hope that something sticks. Because when they score a big fat juicy bestseller, they make lots and lots of money.

▶ As we mentioned in Chapter 2, your chances of landing a publisher will almost certainly increase if you pre-test your material online and make it as great as you can with the help of your audience. Bonus: You can use the material that was best received as your sample to a publisher.

The chilly reality is that few books get reviewed in top-tier publications, wind up on the homepage of the wildly hot website du jour, land on national TV or become bestsellers. But you want to keep potential agents and publishers in fantasy mode for as long as possible. Most often this means shorter is better and less is more. If your idea is particularly hot and timely, this may mean going so far as to exclude actual sample chapters from your proposal. However, 95% of the time, publishers are more likely to shell out good money if they read a dazzling sample chapter or two to get the voice and point of view. More than that is rarely necessary. Indeed, doing too much writing can both harm your chances (if it strays from the agent's or publisher's idea of what the book should be) and waste your time (because the publisher or agent who takes on your project may want you to change large parts of it).

Exceptions to the don't-write-the-whole-nonfiction-book rule: Say you're an English teacher who's writing a popular book about sociobiology. If you have no science background, why would a publisher believe you're qualified to write this book? A proposal alone might not be enough. But maybe you really *do* have something earth-altering to say. If so, you have a much better chance of convincing people when they can see the finished product. Memoirs can be another exception. Because memoirs read like novels, some editors want to see how you handle the plot and writing from beginning to end before making an offer.

The other reason to finish a book is simply because, well, you have to. Some people can't complete a part without completing the whole. If you know this about yourself, do what you gotta do. But this doesn't mean you should submit a finished book. Instead, employ the guidelines below, picking the best chapters as samples.

Braving the Elements: The Nuts and Bolts of Your Proposal

Good proposals have one thing in common. They convince agents and editors beyond a shadow of a doubt that lots of people will want to not just read your book, but pay money to buy it. The particular book proposal form we use (our proposal for this book is reproduced in Appendix V) has been honed over the years by James Levine of the Levine Greenberg Rostan Literary Agency, where Arielle is an agent-at-large. The elements include:

- Table of contents
- Overview
- Bio
- Audience
- Competition

- Special marketing and promotional opportunities
- Manuscript specifications
- Outline
- Sample chapters

Each section should stand on its own, with its own heading at the top of its opening page. You don't want to begin a new section in the middle of a page. And no section—with the exception of marketing and promotion, the outline and the sample chapters—should be longer than a few pages, double-spaced. It's best if you can keep the other sections under two. Sometimes a section may be only a paragraph. In other words, keep it short. Keep it tight. Keep it moving.

▶ With nothing more than a standard word processing program, you can make your proposal look better than most just by keeping it clean. Choose an inviting and readable typestyle (Garamond and Times New Roman are always good stand-bys). Make sure your margins are 1¼" on either side and that your text is unjustified.

We're including an actual nonfiction proposal in this chapter, so you can see what one looks, feels and smells like. We will refer to and analyze it throughout in order to illustrate how to turn your idea into a proposal that will compel people to give you money and publish your book. This proposal was written by Chris Baty for his aforementioned book *No Plot? No Problem!: A Low-Stress, High-Velocity Approach to Writing a Novel in 30 Days,* which can be found at a bookstore near you and has just entered its sixth printing with over 60,000 copies in print!

TABLE OF CONTENTS

Start your proposal with the same kind of table of contents that you'd find at the front of any book, including page numbers. This will give an agent or editor a snapshot of your proposal's organization.

Here's what a table of contents looks like:

TITLE OF BOOK

THE OVERVIEW

If it's comprehensive enough, sometimes your pitch is your overview. Sometimes your overview is an extended version of your pitch. It's like what you read on the inside flaps of a hardcover. (Great flap copy is worth its weight in gold. To master the art, read lots of it.) The overview needs to entice and invite while illuminating how your book is unique yet universal, timely yet timeless. It should touch on nearly every part of your proposal, including your audience and why your book will garner the nation's ovations.

Here's the overview from the *No Plot? No Problem!* proposal:

When I was 26 years old, I accidentally founded an institution that now produces more fiction than all of America's MFA programs combined.

I blame it all on coffee. National Novel Writing Month (NaNoWriMo) began in a moment of overcaffeinated ambition when I sent out an email to friends, challenging each of them to write a 50,000-word novel in July. Since then, the escapade—chronicled on the CBS Evening News *and* NPR's All Things Considered *and in dozens of newspaper and magazine articles around the world—has grown to include a high-tech website, hundreds of spin-off fan sites and discussion groups, and thousands of enthusiastic participants every year.*

Part literary marathon and part rock-and-roll block party, NaNoWriMo is based on the idea that anyone who loves fiction should be writing his own. Not for fame and fortune (though those may come in time). But because novel writing is ridiculously fun once you throw away the rulebook. My rallying cry as NaNoWriMo cruise director (and fellow participant) is simple: No plot? No problem! That low-stress, high-velocity approach has helped tens of thousands of writers set aside their fears and dive headlong into the joys of homemade literature.

Based on four years of experience as the director of NaNoWriMo, No Plot? No Problem! *will be a thoughtful, encouraging and fun guide to blasting out a 50,000-word novel in a month.*

A resource for those taking part in the official NaNoWriMo event, as well as a stand-alone handbook for year-round noveling, the book will break the spree down into five unforgettable weeks, taking writers from the preparation phäse ("If you have children, say good-bye to them now") to the intoxicating highs of Week One, crushing self-doubts of Week Two, critical "plot flashes" of Week Three, and Week Four's victory laps and reluctant reentry into normal life.

Along with the week-specific overviews, pep talks and essential survival strategies, the book will feature checklists, boxed text and anecdotes from myself and other repeat NaNoWriMo winners, i.e., those who completed 50,000 words.

Bursting with can-do literary mayhem, No Plot? No Problem! *will be the kick in the pants first-time novelists need to jump into the fiction fray, an empowering, creative push from the heart of a wildly successful writing revolution.*

Why is this such a good overview? It tells you about the audience, the competition, the market, publicity hooks, even the manuscript specs. But above and beyond all that, Chris makes a profoundly compelling case for why this book will sell. And he makes it sound fun while doing it. Let's break it down:

1. *Chris begins with a Big Bang,* i.e., NaNoWriMo produces more fiction than all MFA programs combined.

2. *Chris uses the same playful voice that he plans to use in his book.* People often write dull, dry overviews, falsely believing that this is like a college assignment where their only job is to get the facts right. Your overview has to be entertaining and informative. Even if you're writing about a very serious subject, you must engage readers.

3. *You see what an interesting, funny and unusual person Chris is.* You can tell right away that he'll be terrific in front of a microphone or camera.

4. *Chris identifies both a rabid fan base and a wide audience.* Rabid fan bases often drive a book's success even if their numbers are relatively small. If you have such a base (a blog with a good number of readers is one example), advertise it right up front in your overview, even though you'll repeat it later.

5. *Chris demonstrates marketing and publicity potential* by pointing out previous coverage. Even if you've never had any media coverage, be sure to artfully point out how your book is both newsworthy and publicity-ripe.

6. *It's clear that Chris has thought out every aspect of his book,* right down to the inclusion of checklists and boxes. This reassures publishers that he will be able to pull off what he proposes.

7. *Chris lets the reader know there's no other book like his out there,* even though he doesn't say it directly. His voice, and the organization from which the idea sprang, is particular, energetic and hard not to like.

YOUR BIO

Just like your overview, your bio should not be a dry, dusty affair. Even more important, it must make the case for why you are the ideal person to write this book and to sell it to the reading public. Whether it's your insider's expertise on a subject, your shockingly compelling life story or your boundless passion for your material, it's up to you to demonstrate why you and you alone are the perfect author for your book. In a page or two. If you've been published, won any awards, been showcased in the media . . . whip all that stuff out. Include any and all information that shows you've got the savvy necessary to publicize and market your book. If you have a Big Time CV, put it in the back of your proposal and pull out the appropriate highlights for your bio. The bottom line is, if you don't toot your own horn (albeit in a way that drips of humble sincerity), who will?

In one of our seminars, a successful businessman mentioned that he'd been homeless for several years. We told him to put this in his bio because it would show what an unusual and resilient person he is. Can't you just see this story on an afternoon talk show? Clearly, this is the kind of information you wouldn't bring up in a job interview. But again, it'll set you apart from the hordes of others trying to storm the gates of publishing.

You also want to try and anticipate any problems that publishers may find with your bio. Bill Parker, a gynecologist, had a stellar résumé—great credentials, media experience, the works. He also wrote a proposal that a number of editors said was the best they'd ever seen. But every one of those editors turned the book down. Why? Because Bill was a male doctor writing about women's health. Bill was well aware of this issue in his practice, but he never thought it would be an issue in a situation where he wouldn't be examining anyone. After a second round of submissions, two thoughtful editors (one of whom was the daughter of a male gynecologist) saw beyond this stumbling block and bid on the book. Before publication, Bill opted against a sex change and instead decided to involve his two female partners in the project. As preventive medicine, he mentioned their contributions on the cover. In hindsight, this might have been the thing to do in his proposal from the get-go.

Once again, in *his* bio Chris Baty knew just what to say about himself:

*Founder and four-time National Novel Writing Month winner, Chris Baty is the Web's most sought-after writing coach. The 29-year-old Oakland, California, freelance writer has been called "an indie David Foster Wallace with compassion" (*Fabula *Magazine) and has been profiled in newspapers ranging from the* L.A. Times *to the* Chicago Tribune *to the* Melbourne Age, *as well as being featured on NPR's* All Things Considered *and a host of BBC radio programs. When not heading up NaNoWriMo, Baty is usually on the road, covering Louisiana juke joints and Parisian thrift stores for such publications as the* Washington Post, *the* SF Weekly, *the* Dallas Observer *and Lonely*

▶ If you're writing a children's book and are inclined to make a big deal in your bio of how you're a mom or a dad, think twice! Editors get this from every freshman children's book writer, and there's nothing persuasive about it. Just because you have kids doesn't mean you can write for them.

Planet guidebooks. His funny, freewheeling style landed him an Association of Alternative Newsweeklies award for Best Music Writing in 2002. Before becoming a full-time writer in 1999, Baty spent several years behind the editing desk, first for Fodor's publications and later as the New York, London and Chicago City Editor for the travel Web site ontheroad.com. Baty holds degrees in cultural anthropology and psychology from the University of California, Berkeley, and the University of Chicago. His quest for the perfect cup of coffee is never-ending and will likely kill him someday.

Why is this an excellent bio? It's got awards, it's got Big Names, it's full of writing cred, and again it displays in its style a rigor, a vigor, a self-deprecating wit and a sense of rollicking good fun. Let's break it down:

1. *Chris shows that he's got a wide reach*—he's the most sought-after writing coach on the World Wide Web. He also tells us that he's the founder of National Novel Writing Month, which makes him sound important.

2. *Information is doled out fast and furious.* In the very first paragraph, we find out how old Chris is, what he does for a living, that he's been compared to a famous guy and that he's connected to media outlets like the *Los Angeles Times,* the BBC and NPR.

3. *Chris has other people saying nice things about him.* Better others than yourself—more believable.

4. *Chris associates himself with top publications,* suggesting that his book has a good chance of ending up reviewed and/or covered there.

5. *Chris identifies his own style: funny and freewheeling.* Yes, he does this by actually telling us, but he also shows us by writing his bio in a comparable tone (as illustrated by the inclusion of juke joints and Parisian thrift stores in the copy).

6. *Chris establishes his writing and academic credibility.*

7. *Chris's bio ends with a joke,* illustrating why it's always good to leave 'em laughing, if you can pull it off.

If, after reading Chris's bio, you feel yours doesn't stack up, do not despair. You, too, can spin a web of magic around your life to make it come up smelling like roses. At first, many people doubt they have anything significant to say in their bio. But if you sit down and make a list of your accomplishments, hobbies and quirks, you'll see an interesting portrait emerge. Have you raised nine kids? Did you ever get a hole-in-one? Do you keep chickens in the middle of Manhattan? All these things count as long as you can spin them so that they help make the case for your book.

YOUR AUDIENCE

Who's going to read your book? Even more important, who's going to buy your book? Describe your audience—and their motivation to buy—as specifically as possible. Prove to an agent or an editor that people are hungering for your book and that you've been actively connecting with your audience and listening to what they say through your company, your workshops, your blog, your social networks or whatever other means you have.

In addition to a display of your knowledge of your audience, bottom-line proof of your audience through numbers is always a major plus. When Jun Chul Whang, Sun Chul Whang and Brandon Saltz put together a proposal for a book on taekwondo, they included the fortuitous fact that there are seven million worldwide practitioners of this particular martial art. Publishers couldn't believe that, given the size of the audience, no major house had ever done a book on the subject. The authors landed a six-figure advance from Broadway Books for *Taekwondo: State of the Art,* in no small part because they drew attention to the staggering number of practitioners.

Reference librarians are fabulous resources for number-related research. And with the power of the Internet, numbers are getting easier and easier to quantify on your own. For example, if you put "taekwondo" into the search field of Facebook, you'll find groups with hundreds of thousands of followers. You'll also find dozens of taekwondo blogs. Use the web to make a compelling case for how big your audience is, and be very specific about who they are, where they hang out and what they buy.

If you're unable to track down statistics proving your audience, or if statistics don't apply, get as specific as possible about your future readers and why they will buy your book. If you say women will be interested in your book, you're not saying much. The question is, which women? If you say women who suffer from depression, then you're getting somewhere. But take it even further. Do they watch QVC or *Sesame Street* on demand? *Masterpiece* or reruns of *Friends*? Do they listen to NPR or Howard Stern? Beethoven or Busta Rhymes? Do they read *Good Housekeeping* or *Wired*? The latest Harry Potter or Charles Dickens? Do they drive Range Rovers or hybrids? Do they buy K-Mart or Prada? Are they downhearted baby boomers or despondent

Gen Xers? Do they read on their iPads or stick with the printed word? Are they active on Facebook or do they prefer to tweet? And lastly, a very important question: Do you have direct access to these women? If you can successfully define your audience and show that you know how to reach it, you've done a large part of your job.

Let's check in with Chris to see how it's done:

The numbers tell the story

NaNoWriMo grew from 21 participants in 1999 to 14,000 in 2002. With a minimum of 25,000 participants expected in November 2003, the built-in market for No Plot? No Problem! *is sizable, international and annually recurring. NaNoWriMo participants are, by and large, an inexperienced group, excited by the prospect of writing a novel in a month but daunted by the creative and time-management challenges of the endeavor. Participants have already committed a large chunk of their lives to the event; many would be happy to spend a little money on a handbook that would increase the likelihood of a higher return (read: completed novel) on their investment.*

The silver bullet: artistic fulfillment made easier

Readers buy how-to books expecting a silver bullet—a magical formula that makes a daunting activity understandable and achievable. This is exactly what No Plot? No Problem! *delivers: a results-oriented plan for people who want to nurture their inner artists without getting tangled in time-consuming classes or ongoing writing groups. After one week of the* No Plot? No Problem! *regime, participants will have already written 46 pages of their novel. By delivering huge results in a short time, the book will have instant appeal for busy people who want to experience the creative joys of writing, but who have limited free time to devote to the project before the demands of real life intervene.*

Also, by framing novel-writing as a short-term, highly accessible activity for everyone, No Plot? No Problem! *casts its line out beyond the confines of "serious writers," tapping into the vast demographic of people who have no fiction-writing experience but who feel they have a story worth telling. The structured creativity of* No Plot? No Problem! *will reassure first-time writers that they already possess all the skills necessary to write a rough draft, and that the only thing standing between them and their manuscript is a month's labor.*

The book will also appeal to those who may not intend to write a novel, but who simply enjoy the thrill of contemplating the project. Studies have shown that 20% of travel guidebooks are purchased by armchair travelers, those who have no intention of buying a ticket to the destination but who appreciate the thrill of a vicarious visit. I anticipate a similar percentage will pick up No Plot? No Problem! *for its gonzo tone and uproarious depictions of the psychological states writers pass through on their month-long journey to literary fulfillment.*

Success stories will reassure hard-nosed, results-oriented book buyers

Though the focus of No Plot? No Problem! *is on personal achievement rather than fame and fortune, there is no question the low-stress, high-velocity technique laid out in the book has led to some surprising success stories in the world of publishing, allowing several would-be writers to transition into new lives as successful, full-time novelists. These stories, detailed in the book's final chapter, will increase the allure of the book for results-oriented writers looking for a creative on-ramp into the world of publishing.*

Why does the audience section of this proposal work? Because it clearly identifies a die-hard, hard-core audience and then branches out to describe several other large yet specific groups of readers and buyers. Let's break it down so you can get to work:

1. *Chris starts this section off with numbers.* Publishers love numbers. Right away, an agent and/or publisher will see how many people are ready to buy this book, and why.

2. *He makes the argument for perennial readers and a long shelf life.* Chris explains that how-to book buyers need a silver bullet. *No Plot, No Problem!* delivers such a bullet in no time at all, hence appealing to the evergreen I'm-too-busy-to-accomplish-any-artistic-goals crowd. This indicates a continuous need for his book, because there will always be those seeking silver bullets for problems they have no time to solve.

3. *He differentiates his book from the competition* (books that apply almost exclusively to the "serious" writer) and so opens up a new audience for himself: people with absolutely no novel-writing experience but the inclination to give it a try. It's a huge leap in numbers when you go from people who

desperately want to write a book to people who have thought at some point in their lives that they might want to write a book.

4. *He closes strong* by explaining why a person who is faced with a shelf chock-full of writing books would choose his over another.

If Chris were to have written this proposal today, he would also have added a very compelling bullet demonstrating how easy it is for him to reach his followers, friends and fans via NaNoWriMo's extensive and highly successful social media platform.

THE COMPETITION

Identifying your competition has two primary purposes: 1) to prove that no one has published the same book as yours, and 2) to associate your book with books that have been successful. In the first case, you need to state quickly and clearly why your book is different. In the second case, you'll want to state quickly and clearly how your book is similar.

Return to your preliminary search of the competition and fill in any gaps. Go to your favorite online bookseller and plug in your keywords (like "taekwondo" and "martial arts" if you're doing a book on taekwondo). Once you've found a book that's a good match, be sure to go to the screen that gives you all the publishing info, reviews and so on. Scroll down until you get to a feature that says, "People who bought this book also bought . . ." Following this lead will take you to many other appropriate titles. Aim for at least 5 books and stop at around 15. Even if your search leads you to dozens of books, you're not likely to come up with more than 15 that fit squarely into our definition of competition.

After you've made your final list, go back once again and ask around at your local bookstore or library. Sometimes librarians and booksellers may be able to point you to obvious titles you've missed. In all cases, you must identify the publisher and author of each book and the date it was published. In a short paragraph, describe the book(s) at hand. Say why your book will succeed where the competition has failed. Speak to an aspect of your subject that the competition has not addressed. Appeal to the same core audience.

Don't trash the competition. You may want to send your proposal to the publisher of one of your competitive books, and if you slag their book, they may not want to play with you.

Call us old-fashioned, but we think it's a very good idea to actually read the competition. That way, you'll really know what you're talking about when you write this important piece of your proposal.

Separating the Bigs from the Littles

I f you're submitting to a major publisher, it's only necessary to track down titles published by major or midsize companies. Sometimes this can be difficult to suss out, because almost every major publisher has numerous imprints that may look like small presses. Check out books' copyright pages. If a book was published by an imprint of a larger house, it will identify the larger house. For example, on the copyright page of a book published by Riverhead, you'll see that Riverhead is a division of Penguin. To help sort out big from little, see the list of major and midsize publishers and their divisions and imprints in Appendix III.

Let's check out Chris's competition section:

Writing vs. writing well

Bookstore shelves are overflowing with tomes from well-known authors quibbling over the tenets of good writing. No Plot? No Problem! does not teach good writing. From my work as a writer and editor, I have come to believe that the most valuable writing lessons are self-taught, and that the most beautiful pieces of literature begin as mediocre pieces of crap. No Plot? No Problem! is essentially a personal trainer in book form, a wisecracking coach who sits down with would-be writers each night for 30 days and gives them the permission they need to make messes and the encouragement they need to keep going.

A pan-genre approach to taskmastering

Unlike craft-based books, where the author's opinions on timing, semantics and plot development may miss the mark for certain genres, the tactics and strategies of No Plot? No Problem! work regardless of novel niche. And unlike the overly broad books for novice writers that cover everything from brainstorming protagonists to handling royalty checks, No Plot? No Problem! brings all of its taskmastering to bear on the first and highest hurdle: surviving the first draft.

The miraculous power of a deadline

Finally, where several of the books below give writers assignments on getting started (3 pages a night, 15 minutes a day, etc.), none of them offers a clear-cut stopping point. The value of a deadline—and a contained writing period—cannot be overstated in helping novice writers pull off the mammoth (and at times painful) task of extracting a novel from themselves.

87

The looming 30-day cut-off in No Plot? No Problem! *helps keep writers motivated, focused and on track.*

*Along with the range of books that have used the time-tested motivational strategy of a month-long exercise (*30 Days to a More Powerful Vocabulary, The 30-Day Low-Carb Diet Solution, Successful Business Planning in 30 Days, *etc.), complementary titles on writing include:*

Immediate Fiction: A Complete Writing Course *by Jerry Cleaver (St. Martin's Press, 2002, $24.95). Simple, straightforward advice on everything from plot strategies to book marketing, written in a reassuring tone from the founder of The Writers' Loft in Chicago. Expounds on the joys of messy first drafts and offers the timeless insight "the less you care, the better you write."*

Bird by Bird: Some Instructions on Writing and Life *by Anne Lamott (Anchor, 1995, $12.95). Inspiring book avoids the quagmire of revision advice and offers humorous insight about the realities of the writing life (including several sections on the utter necessity of not taking first drafts so seriously).*

The Marshall Plan for Novel Writing: A 16-Step Program Guaranteed to Take You from Idea to Completed Manuscript *by Evan Marshall (Writer's Digest Books, 2001, $16.99). Breaks memorable plots down into a series of formulas and concrete charts, and includes information on how to set up a writing area and manage your time while writing.*

How to Write a Damn Good Novel *by James Frey (St. Martin's Press, 1987, $19.95). A colorfully written, character-centric guide to the novel-writing process. Heavily reliant, however, on prewriting.*

How to Write & Sell Your First Novel *by Oscar Collier with Frances Spatz Leighton (Writer's Digest Books, 1997, $16.99). A somewhat celebrity-focused book takes novice writers on the inspirational path from selecting a genre to finding an agent.*

Why does this audience section work so well? Because it clearly illustrates how Chris's book is different from everything else out there. And again, it does so in a gonzo style. Note that Chris decided to put his "why my book is different" info all up front. This is a great thing to do when none of the books on your list is directly competitive. But if you're writing what you claim will be the definitive book on taekwondo and there's already a book out there that purports to do the same, you'll have to get very specific about your competition (for an example, see our proposal for this book in Appendix V). Let's break it down:

1. *Chris faces his competition head on* by telling the reader that he's well aware of the vast number of writing books available. Sometimes writers shy away from the truth because they think the competition will hurt their chances of selling their book. Better to speak the truth and show how your book reinvents the mousetrap for the huge pool of mousetrap buyers always looking for the new best thing.

2. *He's very clear about what differentiates his book* from the competition. For example, when he talks about the power of the deadline, he's making a specific case for what his book will offer that no other book does.

3. *He identifies himself with a well-published category,* yet explains why his book is unique within the category. His enumerating of all those 30-days books makes publishers feel warm and fuzzy because they've sold lots of copies of those same books.

4. *He inspires confidence* by laying out the list of books thoughtfully and carefully. Looking like you know what you're talking about is often more important than really knowing what you're talking about. (We advocate a cozy combination of the two.)

5. *He maintains a consistent tone.* Throughout, he continues to illustrate the zany style of his personality even as he presents information: "most beautiful pieces of literature begin as mediocre pieces of crap." He makes us laugh with his matter-of-fact demystification of art. We can see even here that he'll be a fun interview and put on a good show at events. Which leads directly into . . .

SPECIAL MARKETING AND PROMOTIONAL OPPORTUNITIES

As publishing tightens its belt to the point that its belly is aching, publishers are demanding more and more of their authors. In addition, with the shrinking of space in newspapers and magazines where books traditionally got attention, it has become increasingly difficult for publishers and authors to get the love they need. Luckily, it is now possible for individuals to connect with huge networks, communities and tribes of other citizens interested in their book. That's why we spent so much time in the last chapter talking about how to develop your platform *prior to* developing your book.

Whether you have a big platform, a small one or none at all, you need to convince an agent or editor that you'll make it your top priority to let the public know about your book. Publishers want to know what public venues, both traditional and electronic, you can use to make a speech, post an opinion or grab the ear of the public. The more creative yet concrete your plan, and the more you can show what *you* will do to spread the good word (as opposed to what the *publisher* can do), the better.

Speaking of spreading the word: The only thing publishers like better than a platform is a rapidly expanding platform, something the Internet is particularly well-suited to delivering. So if you skipped Chapter 2, please go back and read it now!

Can you get yourself on radio and television, into magazines and newspapers? Can you get bloggers to write about you? Can you write about other experts on your blog and get lots of people to pay attention? Can you get your material into the hands of people who review books online? Do you write a column for your local paper? Do you have regular speaking engagements? Do you ever appear in the media? Are you affiliated with any large groups? Any specific groups your book will speak to? Do you belong to any trade organizations? Do you have a website with noteworthy traffic? Does your high school, college or graduate school have an active alumni association with a newsletter or magazine? Can you write an editorial, rant or personal essay that you can place prominently on the leading website where your readers regularly hang out? Can you make a short movie that taps into a wave of interest as it streaks down the Information Superhighway?

This is one place where it pays to let the muse flow through you, without resorting to the obvious or the overly pie-in-the-sky. Everyone knows you fully expect that your book will be reviewed in *The New York Times* and that you're a natural for national TV. But unless you have a concrete plan for making that happen, you run the risk of coming off as a rube.

Are you wondering about Chris's marketing strategy? Here it is:

Evangelical participants as advertisers

The NaNoWriMo participants themselves are evangelical advertisers. The growth of the event—which has never sent out a press release or advertised anywhere—has been due primarily to hyperlinked endorsements from a vast network of participants' Web sites and Web logs. These sites would happily promote a book they felt reflected the zany and unique experience that NaNoWriMo provides every year. The incentive of proselytizing for a good cause is further enhanced by the ubiquitous "Amazon.com Rewards" program, which gives Web logs a kickback on any copies of books sold via click-through recommendations.

The primary sales vehicle, though, would be the NaNoWriMo.org Web site. No Plot? No Problem! *could be sold on the site or offered to participants as part of a "donation package," where a donation to National Novel Writing Month would net the donor a free copy of the book. Each year, around 15% of participants donate to the (otherwise free) event. With 30,000 participants expected in November 2004 (the approximate period of the book's release), NaNoWriMo.org–facilitated book sales could range anywhere from one to four thousand units, repeatable annually.*

NaNoWriMo groups around the world

There are about 50 NaNoWriMo chapters in the U.S., and 15 groups overseas. These groups meet informally throughout the year to swap manuscripts and support each other's writing projects. No Plot? No Problem! *would serve as a bible for these groups, and, in the case of a promotional tour, they could be counted on to come out and support the founder of the escapade (and hopefully buy a book or three while they're at it).*

The joys of annual coverage

Because it makes for a fun human-interest story, NaNoWriMo is widely covered by TV, radio and print media every year. Most of the pieces on the event feature interviews with local participants coupled with quotes from me on the history and current status of the event. This recurrent media attention will be a boon to No Plot? No Problem! *creating an annual opportunity to promote the book long after the first publicity push subsides.*

Why does this publicity and marketing section rule? Because it shows concretely that there's a terrific grassroots marketing campaign behind this book as well as real opportunities for local and national publicity. It also indicates that new publicity and marketing opportunities will arise year after year because of the annual nature of NaNoWriMo. Let's take a closer look:

1. *Publishers love authors with direct access to a core audience.* Chris leads with this aspect of his marketing juggernaut, which is just the sort of thing that makes publishers drool.

2. *Chris ties this grassroots appeal to e-marketing.* By placing the website and the Amazon tie-in so centrally, he lets publishers know that he will be exploiting the awesome power of the Internet, and that makes them happy, too.

3. *Chris keeps throwing numbers at them.* He makes a great case for 1,000–4,000 guaranteed sales a year before the publisher has to lift a finger. Granted, this isn't a huge number in publishers' minds, but it's a nice security blanket. The more you can convince publishers that they will sell books without having to do anything, the better your chances.

4. *Chris shows that his audience is worldwide.* An expanding number of groups that meet regularly in America and internationally will buy his book. By bringing in the international angle, he lets publishers know that foreign sales are likely.

5. *Chris makes a compelling case for his ability to get both big- and small-time media.* Pieces that appear in little papers and on tiny radio stations, as well as on national morning television and NPR shows, are the fuel that keeps the media engine purring. And Chris makes it clear he can get behind the wheel and drive that baby off into the sunset.

Best Foot Forward

Most agents and editors have thousands of pages stacked on their desks and tens of thousands sitting in their inboxes, which means they probably won't read your proposal or manuscript in its entirety unless they're so taken in by the first sentence, first paragraph or first page that they're spurred on to read more. So make sure each of these firsts is spectacular. Don't count on anyone getting to the "heart" of your proposal or manuscript somewhere deep on page 10. Count instead on having about one minute to capture someone's attention.

Spend as much time as necessary to get your first words right. Study the first sentences of great books for inspiration. Arielle's predictable favorite is the classic opening line of Jane Austen's *Pride and Prejudice*: "It is a truth universally acknowledged that a single man in possession of a good fortune must be in want of a wife." And one of our more recent nonfiction favorite first paragraphs is from Jonathan Kozol's *Amazing Grace: The Lives of Children and the Conscience of a Nation*: "The Number 6 train from Manhattan to the South Bronx makes nine stops in the 18-minute ride between East 59th Street and Brook Avenue. When you enter the train, you are in the seventh richest congressional district in the nation. When you leave, you are in the poorest."

YOUR MANUSCRIPT SPECIFICATIONS

What is the approximate word count of your book? Are there any special design features? Will there be illustrations? Recipes? How many? How long will it take you to complete the writing of the book?

It's no surprise that Chris had a fun way to deal with even the nuts and bolts.

The book's format—part travel guide and part survival kit—will echo the fun, adventuresome feel of the novel-writing process. The book will be 45,000 words long and will contain 36 illustrations.

The completed manuscript can be delivered in PC Microsoft Word format within six months of signing of the contract.

Even in this little section, Chris displays the joie de vivre that dances through his proposal.

While you may view the manuscript specifications section of your proposal as a throwaway, it has some essential information. By carefully preparing and evaluating your outline, you can reasonably calculate what your word count and delivery timetable will be. Yes, this information is hard to predict. But the more precise you can be, the better the chances that you and your future publisher will be on the same page from day one.

YOUR OUTLINE

First off, your outline is not a final commitment. At this stage, it's enough to show that you've got a solid working plan for moving ahead. The outline should contain section and/or chapter headings; beneath each heading, you'll need to write up to a few paragraphs explaining what the chapter contains and how it moves the book forward.

Again, your outline should maintain the style of your book. Every part of your proposal must be a great read. Here's a piece of Chris's outline to give you a sense of how it's done:

Introduction

The author offers a personal history of National Novel Writing Month, explaining both the absurd origins of the event and the surprising, life-changing effects it had on the first group of 21 participants.

Chapter 1

Enlightenment is overrated: Why you should write a novel now—16 pages. For most people, novel-writing is a "one day" event, as in "one day, I'd like to write a novel." This chapter explores why that day never comes for most would-be writers and offers five reasons why the biggest tasks are best accomplished in a minuscule amount of time.

The chapter opens with a list of common reasons people offer for postponing the writing of their first novel. These include:

"I'm waiting until I'm older and wiser."

"I'm waiting until I get fired from my job, so I'll have more time to dedicate to the book."

"I don't have a quiet place to write."

"My plot ideas are all clichés."

"I'm afraid my novel will suck in unpredictably monstrous ways, and I'll be forced to admit that I'm a total failure as a creative individual."

The author dispels each of these worries, building a reassuring case for the fact that novel-writing is best undertaken as a month-long, anything-goes adventure, where the stakes are low and the rewards are high for writers of all ages and skill levels.

The second part of the chapter delves into those rewards, including the tremendous boost in creative confidence and a deepened understanding of the hell professional writers endure in creating the books we love.

The final part of the chapter explores the supernatural way a deadline enables achievements far beyond our normal powers, and offers a guarantee for would-be writers: Write for two hours a night, five nights a week, and, over the course of a month, aliens will beam a 50,000-word novel onto your hard drive.

Two supplemental boxed texts for Chapter 1 will provide 1) a gauge of how long 50,000 words really is, including a short list of famous 50K novels, and 2) an overview of the magic number 1,666 (the average daily word quota) and about how long it typically takes writers to reach that goal.

Why is this outline so effective? Chris combines his playfulness with a sure-handed description of exactly what the chapters will cover. Appearing to know indicates to publishers that you may, in fact, actually know what you're doing. Here we go again:

1. *Chris explains how he will handle every aspect of the book.* By addressing the components of each chapter (including supplemental boxed texts), he leaves no one guessing.

2. *Chris's chapter descriptions are only as long as they need to be.* The introduction necessitated one sentence; Chapter 1 required several paragraphs. Unnecessarily long outlines are not just boring, they're dangerous. And if

they feel too much like the real book, without communicating the level of information or interest that the real chapter will hold, the publisher may come away thinking your book itself will be thin. On the other hand, if your ideas are highly complex, take the space you need.

3. *The outline is fun to read.* We can't overemphasize the importance of this. Not that "fun" has to be the universal descriptor—heartwarming, authoritative, edgy are all legitimate descriptors for a proposal. But you want your proposal to pop.

Chris does do something out of character that we would like to point out. His impersonal references to "the author" lack the intimacy of the rest of the proposal. Not a big deal, but not in keeping with his voice. As a general rule, don't refer to yourself as "the author" anywhere in your proposal. Either keep it in the first person or call yourself by your given name.

SAMPLE CHAPTERS

You'll need one to three professional-caliber sample chapters, for a total of approximately 20 to 50 pages. Most writers start with the first chapter—it's harder to get a feel for a book when you jump in midstream. But both chapter choice and page count are ultimately dependent on what you think will make the best case for your book.

While the business end of your proposal is the skin and bones, the sample chapters are the heart and soul. They're what agents and editors will look at to see if you have the goods to produce what you say you can. So while a bad overview can hurt your chances of getting published, bad sample chapters will probably kill them dead.

After you've written and rewritten and rewritten, show the sample chapters

First-Person Proposal: Yea or Nay?

If your book will be written in the first person (as in a memoir, for example), it makes sense to write the proposal in the same first-person voice. This will familiarize publishers with the "sound" of your writing. Problem is, not everyone can write an effective bio in the first person. If you can't blow your own horn, use the third person (it will sound as if someone else is saying how great and qualified you are). If you feel that your proposal will benefit from a first-person voice but you're not comfortable with a first-person bio, change the voice for your bio only. That's okay. The same holds true for your overview and special marketing/promotional opportunities sections.

to your team. Take heed of all their advice and criticism. Listen with open ears and ask smart questions. But ultimately, trust that little person in your head who's always right. (We won't include Chris's sample chapters here, simply to save some space. But you can go check out his book if you're curious about how it turned out.)

Looks Are Everything

If it looks like a book, if it smells like a book, chances are it will become a book. Again, agents and publishers are inundated by books and book ideas. At parties. At dinners. From family, friends, friends of friends, friends of family, and family of friends. So the more your document can look like a book, the easier it will be for them to see that it should be a book.

ILLUSTRATIONS

If yours is an illustrated book, it can be beneficial to hire a graphic designer to do between two and five sample spreads, i.e., side-by-side book pages. This typically costs anywhere from $500 to $5,000, depending on the number of spreads and the designer's level of experience. A major investment. However, an illustrated book is all about how it looks. And an agent or editor who has a hard time envisioning the look of your illustrated book is likely to pass on it.

If you go the sample-spread route, the trick is to make sure your spreads have the finished look of a published book. To achieve a professional look, go to a professional. Not just a graphic designer, but a book designer, preferably one who designs for major publishers. Thankfully, these people can be found. Their names are often listed on the back flaps of books or on the copyright page, and many freelancers have websites. Once you've found a designer, let her know if you don't have a deal yet, and she may give you a better price.

COVER DESIGN

Study book design. Find covers that attract the eye. Go to AIGA's website (AIGA is the leading organization for graphic designers) and look up the 50 Books/50 Covers Award for the year. Check out the blog The Book Cover Archive, which displays awesome covers, will lead you to top book designers' websites and discusses all things related to book design. If you can design a great cover or know someone who can, go for it. If you don't know anyone with these skills (and most people don't), you can contact schools that have graduate design programs. For one of his own books, David found a student who created a great cover for $250.

Are You Writing a Children's Book?

One of the biggest mistakes authors of children's books make is to submit illustrations with their text. Even if you think your friend or colleague is a master illustrator, hold off making any sort of recommendation about art until after your book is sold. David Allender, the editorial director of Scholastic Book Clubs, says, "Including illustrations doubles your chances of rejection. If it's essential, include directional sketches." If you're wondering why submitting art could possibly hurt your chances, here's David's explanation: "Children's book editors are a bit like musicians. We can read the score and hear the music in our head, and that's what's exciting. Typically, pictures drain the life out of the text. Of course, the exception is when there are illustrations that are wonderful. But you have a better chance of getting struck by lightning than submitting this kind of quality illustration."

Another question children's book authors face is how educational to make their books. Steven Malk, an agent at Writers House who has represented many of today's top children's authors, says, "The children's book industry is anchored by schools and libraries, so ideally a book will have a strong life in the retail market while also having the support of teachers and librarians. However, your book can't be purely educational." In other words, don't forget the entertainment factor!

Speaking of entertainment, Steven adds a piece of good news for the world of children's publishing: "A lot more attention is now given to children's books because so many have recently been turned into movies." And when Hollywood calls, the publishing industry jumps to attention. . . .

If you decide to include a cover, here's the catch: MAKE IT GREAT OR NOT AT ALL. If it's not a Grade A cover, it will call you out as a rank amateur. The following books have beautiful, elegant, fun and/or vibrant covers that you might want to check out.

A Natural History of the Senses

The Zuni Café Cookbook

Divine Secrets of the Ya-Ya Sisterhood

The Worst-Case Scenario Survival Handbook

I Married a Communist (hardcover edition)

Everything Is Illuminated (hardcover edition)

Gone Girl (original, not movie, cover)

Drive: The Surprising Truth About What Motivates Us

Dry: A Memoir

The Mind's Eye

These range from covers that use only color and type (the graphically intense *I Married a Communist* and *The Worst-Case Scenario Survival Handbook*), to those that elegantly incorporate photography (*A Natural History of the Senses* and *The Zuni Café Cookbook*), to those that evoke a mood (*Gone Girl*). Yet they all scream: Read me!

The Cherry on Top: Blurbs, Press Kits, Photos and Other Enticing Extras

It's easy to get so caught up in your proposal or manuscript that you forget about the additional materials that can be exceedingly helpful in selling your book. Typically, these include blurbs, DVDs or links to video, press kits, speaking schedules and/or a great photo. But don't stop there. Include any others that you think would get an agent or publisher racing to the phone.

BLURBAGE

A blurb is an endorsement from another author or well-known person. An advance blurb can also be used to help sell your proposal. It's slightly shocking how much stock people put in blurbs, but the fact is that a great quote from the right person can push agents and publishers from on-the-fence to in-your-corner. And while it's not essential to have blurbs at this stage of the game, it helps. Just one great blurb can do the trick. If you have a connection to an

Are You Writing a Cookbook?

Let's start with your title. Unless you own an established restaurant or catering business, or you have a title that conjures up images that make people's mouths water, your title must announce the focus of your cookbook. Some classic examples are: *The Cake Bible*, *How to Cook Everything* and *Bistro Cooking*. And unlike other nonfiction proposals, here your table of contents is key. It serves as an outline, rather than just a page locator, so it has to be thoroughly thought out. Instead of just listing soups, salads, vegetables or whatever, you need to be explicit about recipes in the book—not necessarily every single one, but enough to get an agent or editor hungry and interested. An introduction to the book as well as the introduction to an individual chapter should be included in your proposal. If there are sidebars or other bits that will give your book literary flavor, provide samples of these as well. And you'll need at least 10 to 15 recipes with headnotes (the little introductory thoughts found at the beginning of a recipe). Keep in mind that the purpose of a headnote is to let your reader know both what makes this recipe different from others and what makes it something you want to try.

influential person in your field, or if a well-known writer was your professor in your MFA program, or if you can track down the perfect candidate and help him see why it's incumbent upon him to endorse your work, start making your requests now. Many times you'll get no response, but you'd be amazed what people will do for you if you're respectful of their time and ask nicely.

TRAILERS AND VIDEO LINKS

When we wrote the last edition of this book, book trailers were all the rage because they were new and novel. But publishers quickly learned that the vast majority of trailers did not go viral. Instead, they were time and money vacuums that sat unwatched on YouTube and author websites.

If you are an excellent presenter, and the camera loves you; or if you are a filmmaker or know someone who is (and who is willing to help you for free); or if you do have a unique and fabulous idea that just might go viral, it's still worth considering making a trailer. Although the risk/reward ratio is not in your favor, an easily clickable link that shows what makes you or your book special might be just the thing that separates you from the pack.

There are as many kinds of trailers as there are books. Dramatic live readings, how-to demonstrations, highly artistic creations that have very little to do with your actual book and so much more. A trailer doesn't have to be fancy, but it does have to hook its audience. Author Kelly Corrigan became a star when

---

Suzanne Rafer, the editor of such all-star cookbooks as *The Cake Mix Doctor, How to Grill* and the Silver Palate series, says, "I like it when someone can title a recipe well and can give information in the headnote that draws me in. Grilled steak I've seen a million times, but tell me something *new* about grilled steak."

As for photos of recipes, 99% of the time they are not necessary and may scare off a publisher who prefers line drawings or no illustrations at all. The exception is when your photos are so exquisite, so professional, that they'd leave Jacques Pepin drooling.

Suzanne adds one last piece of advice: "Even if you're the best chef in the world, you have to realize that it takes a lot of writerly invention and imagination to translate what you do in the kitchen to the page. A lot of people are good chefs but not good writers. If you're having trouble getting what you want to say down on paper, be sure to partner up with someone who can reflect your talent and passion." This advice applies to anyone who has a great idea and/or brand but lacks the necessary writing chops.

▶ If you happen to have appeared in a TV segment with a long introduction that doesn't include you, cut the introduction out of the recording. People want to see YOU, not an anchorperson. But be sure to keep enough of the intro to identify the show if it's reputable in any way, shape or form.

a simple video of her reading an essay she wrote on women's friendships was viewed by more than four million people. It helped propel her book *The Middle Place* into bestsellerdom.

But trailers aren't the only kind of video that can showcase your voice and talents. Have you been on TV, and do you have a professional-quality video of yourself? If you've been on the tube a number of times, cut together a sampling of your best appearances. Same goes for professional-quality video of lectures you've given or workshops you've hosted. All you need is a couple of minutes—this is just a tease to show how good you'll be at marketing your book.

If you do decide to create a trailer or highlight reel of media appearances or lectures, upload it onto your favorite video-sharing site (like YouTube or Vimeo) and include it as a hyperlink in your proposal. (Agents and publishers are now used to reading proposals on their computers and clicking directly wherever an author sends them.)

But before you put any time, and certainly any money, into making a video featuring yourself or your book, read the advice of the experts we consulted (see pages 355–359).

SPEAKING SCHEDULE

If you speak or hold workshops regularly, include a list of select speaking engagements for previous and upcoming years. Leave out very small venues, unless you're making the point that you will speak anywhere and everywhere, big and small. If, on the other hand, you speak in front of particularly large audiences (500 or more), be sure to include those numbers.

PRESS KIT

Gather together any press coverage that you've received over the years. Your press kit is living proof that you and/or your work have already been recognized. It makes publishers think that someone will want to write about you again. If you can't get copies of the original articles, try to track them down online.

AUTHOR PHOTO

If you've been told you take a great photo, then take one now. What does a great photo have to do with a great book? Nada. What does it have to do with a great marketing campaign? A lot. If you remember Sebastian Junger's book *The Perfect Storm,* you might also remember the author photo on the back. The guy looks like a supermodel! The joke in the publishing industry was that his photo launched his book. Okay, he wrote a great book. But the photo didn't hurt.

The Value of Good Readers

It is an immutable law of the universe that humans simply cannot, under any circumstance, no matter how hard they try, be completely objective about what they've written. That's why, once you finish a draft of your proposal or manuscript, it's important to let it sit and ferment, marinate and settle. Move away from your work for a bit. This will help with your objectivity. In fact, there's a direct correlation between the amount of objectivity you can achieve and the time you spend away from your material. You can test this by going back and reading things you've written over the years—things you thought were deep and witty and spectacular. Yes, there may be lots of great writing there, but there's also a very good chance you'll be shocked by how not deep and witty and spectacular some of it is.

So, during this marinating/objectivity–enhancing time, get other people to evaluate your writing—to tell you what's wrong with it, what's right with it and how to fix it. The more input you have, the more you'll know about how to make your book better. One of the biggest mistakes amateur writers make is sending out their material before it's ready. It's like feeding someone a half-baked cake.

If you subscribe to the theory that Writing Is Rewriting (and if you don't already have a subscription to this theory, buy one now!), you must locate smart, literate, articulate people and then convince them to read your writing after you've finished a draft. Believe us, this is just as hard as it sounds. First of all, where do you find smart, literate, articulate people these days? If you're lucky enough to know any people like this, you know that they mostly have lives that keep them busy. And it takes a lot of time to read a proposal, let alone a fiction manuscript, and make thoughtful, useful comments that will help move your book forward, strengthen plot and characters, and cut away fat.

Friends and colleagues notwithstanding, where can you find people who will have the time and expertise to help you? Who are they? Where are they? And how can you bend them to your will? The first and most obvious group to penetrate in your search for quality readers is, of course, other writers. Because if they're smart (and that's one of our prerequisites for a quality reader), they will one day need readers, too. So you'll have an I'll-scratch-your-back-you-scratch-mine situation on your hands. But where can you find and connect with other writers? At literary events listed in the Events section of your local newspaper or online hot spot. At cool websites and blogs where writers and people who love them hang out. At readings in bookstores. Writing groups. Creative writing classes at colleges, universities and community centers. Writers' forums on the Internet. Poetry readings and coffee shops. Khaled Hosseini, author of the #1 *New York Times* bestseller *The Kite Runner,* read parts of his novel to his writing group and received some excellent advice: "Several members of the group suggested that the beginning of my novel could be better served if I kept the first chapter short (it was initially around 25 pages long)." Heeding their advice, he cut it to one page. "Obviously, not all the suggestions were helpful, but several were. There are always people in a writers' group who are natural-born editors."

> ▶ Stay away from obsequious sycophants! The last thing you want is people telling you your proposal/manuscript is good when it's not. Be sure to let people know you want the you've-got-a-wart truth.

It's particularly helpful if your potential reader is someone who fits into the profile of your audience. The more specific your audience, the more knowledgeable your reader should be. So instead of a general writers' chat room, you might want to find a mystery writers' chat room if you're writing a mystery. But if you're writing a book about knitting, you'll want to track down your local knitting group or the owner of your local knitting shop. You'll want to find and follow the hottest and hardest-hitting knitting bloggers. You'll want to become a member of online communities, both large and small, which cater to knitting in general and to your particular knitting niche.

If you feel like you want to hire a professional reader, read on.

Picking Partners: "Help, I Need Somebody!"

If you've tried to sit down and write your proposal and are questioning your ability to pull it off at the level you would like, you may need to ask yourself a harsh but necessary question: Are you, when it comes down to it, a professional-caliber writer? If you don't think you have the answer, you may want to ask it of a close friend or colleague—or anyone else you can trust to be honest with you.

Unfortunately, neither you nor anyone else in your immediate circle may have the expertise to know whether you've got what it takes. If you're feeling unsure or you're having trouble getting started, staying the course or being a finisher, you might want to bring in a hired gun in the form of a coauthor, cowriter, ghostwriter, writing coach, outside editor or professional reader. These people can help you at every turn, from picking the right idea to starting it up, from finishing your proposal to writing the best book possible.

If you've got the money, hiring a professional could be dollars well spent. Someone who really knows his stuff—and the industry—can give you a major edge over your competitors. This is especially true if you're a beginner at writing genre fiction such as mystery, romance or true crime. Genre fiction has hard-and-fast rules that you may be completely unaware of but that a professional writer or editor will know inside out. With a little help, your novel could go from one of promise to one that contains the ingredients of bestsellerdom. All work can benefit from a professional eye, but not to worry if you can't afford one. You'll just have to outsmart (and outresearch) your wealthier counterparts.

What distinguishes a coauthor from a cowriter? A writing coach from an outside editor? Here's a cheat sheet to help you get a handle on the nomenclature:

- A *coauthor* brings equal and/or complementary knowledge and expertise to the table. Coauthors may be professional writers, may or may not already have a book or two under their belts and are schooled in the subject at hand. Coauthors generally get equal credit on a book cover—same-size lettering, same line. They typically split all money 50-50, although every deal is different.

- A *cowriter* is usually a previously published writer who's in the mix primarily to write—not to provide information. Cowriters usually get their names on the cover, but often in smaller type and underneath the primary author's name. They generally split all advance dinero up to a percentage of 50-50, but may get a lesser percentage of royalties paid from books sold. Sometimes cowriters get paid a flat fee broken down into two parts: a fee to write a proposal and then a fee for the book itself if it sells to a publisher.

Sometimes cowriters are given a guarantee for a certain amount. And, hold on to your hat, sometimes this guaranteed amount can actually turn out to be more than 50%—even up to 100%—of an advance.

■ *Ghostwriters* are typically, but not exclusively, hired for celebrity autobiographies or other works "penned" by famous folk. Ghostwriters are brought in to make readers believe that the person whose name appears on the cover has written what's inside the book. Great ghostwriters are able to capture other people's voices with uncanny perfection. Even some mega-bestselling commercial fiction authors use ghostwriters to churn out book after book, without actually having to write them. Nice work if you can get it, being a well-paid author and not having to actually write anything! Naturally, ghostwriters, being ghosts, don't get their names on the cover, but often you can find them in the acknowledgments. Ghostwriters are typically paid up front to write a proposal and are often guaranteed a certain amount of money to write the book. Sometimes they get a percentage of an author's royalties. Often not. Sometimes they're brought in if a deadline is looming huge and the author won't be able to get the book done on time. Or maybe an author is just stuck. Or maybe an author or publisher wants someone to add some panache, punch and pop to a manuscript. If this is the case, hiring a ghostwriter may be just the ticket.

■ A *writing coach* works with a writer over a period of time, often until the book is sold—or until the money runs out. A good coach will know when to give you a pat on the back and when to give you a swift kick in the behind. She'll hold your hand and midwife your book into the world. She'll help set up a schedule and make sure you stick to it. She'll help you with everything from large structural issues to delicate turns of phrase. She'll help you define and refine what you're trying to say and make sure you're saying what you really mean. A good coach will be a combination cheerleader, taskmaster, master editor, plot guru, devil's advocate, guardian angel and powerhouse motivator. Most writing coaches are paid by the hour, anywhere between $25 and $150 an hour, depending on their level of experience and expertise.

■ *Outside editors,* a.k.a. *book doctors,* diagnose, treat and help you fix your book. Many outside editors have worked in publishing and know the ins and outs of proposals and manuscripts. For a fee, they will identify the strengths and weaknesses of a manuscript and suggest ways to correct its flaws and enhance its best qualities. Their fee depends on their degree of expertise, how fast they're expected to get the work done and whether it's a cosmetic nip and tuck or radical open-heart surgery. Hourly rates typically range between $50 and $250. There are two kinds of edits that book doctors and outside editors offer: developmental edits and line edits. A developmental edit usually includes a thorough read of your manuscript and a detailed editorial letter that outlines overarching conceptual or structural changes, but no markup of the actual manuscript. A line edit includes all of the above plus a line-by-line markup. Depending on the kind of edit you're interested in, as well as the length and state of your manuscript, the cost could range from $250 to $25,000. Again, all fees depend on the editor's level of experience as well as the amount of work involved.

■ *Professional readers* write evaluations that assess the commercial potential of a manuscript or proposal. They can give you an objective opinion of how your writing will fare in the marketplace—for a one-shot price of between $75 and $1,000. The high end is reserved for professional editors who are hired solely for this kind of evaluation.

Where to Find Your Perfect Partner

If you know you want professional help and you've got money to throw around, you can hire someone who's not only great but has publishing connections. While this won't guarantee you an agent or a publisher, it certainly can't hurt. But whether you have a little or a lot to spend, you can find the help you need by returning to our favorite principle: Research, Research, Research.

If you're in the market for a writing coach or outside editor, the first place to look is in the acknowledgment sections of published books. What we like about this method is that the published book is proof of the person's expertise. If you venture onto the web, switch your shyster detector on and check to make sure the person really has done what he says. Check references and, again, check the acknowledgments in any book an editor claims to have worked on.

Writers' conferences, book festivals and fairs are also great places to look for writing coaches or outside editors. So are the continuing education departments of the best universities in your neck of the woods. Many professional writers teach classes in these departments, and many of them work as writing coaches or outside editors on the side.

If you're in the market for a professional reader who won't break the bank, we think your local bookstore or library is a lovely place to look for one. Is there someone who's been there a long time? Someone you rely on for recommendations? Who thoroughly knows the category your book falls into? If so, this person will more than likely make an excellent reader.

If you're looking for a coauthor, cowriter or ghostwriter, start reading magazines and newspaper articles, websites, literary journals and books with coauthors or cowriters. Check out organizations like the American Society of Journalists and Authors that will help you find a writer for whatever subject you're writing about. Many writers have websites. The more you know about them, the better it will go when you make your approach. Use your bio, audience, competition and marketing info to woo said writer by letter, email or phone call. Even with shallow pockets, if you have a great idea and you describe it well, you'll have a good shot at hooking a professional writer. Why? Because many writers spend their days 1) looking for work, and 2) trying to dream up great projects. Some will forgo up-front money for a bigger share of the overall cabbage if they think something has a good shot at selling to a publisher. And if you team up with an experienced writer, you automatically catapult yourself into the ring of serious publishing contenders.

If you're considering seeking an agent before you hire a cowriter, the advantage will be that the agent will likely be able to introduce you to a writer. But be forewarned, you better have a big profile, a substantial press kit and a perfect pitch if you expect a callback from an agent without a fleshed-out proposal.

Hiring Excellent Writers and Editors

You have got to hire top-notch professionals to get top-notch assistance. So, how do you know if you're getting high-end help or low-down bottom-feeders? Naturally, you'll want to ask the typical informational questions: May I have a list of references? How much do you charge? How do you work? Also ascertain the person's previous publishing experience: Have you worked with a major publisher? If so, which one(s)? Doing what, and for how long? Do you have an agent? Do you know any agents, or anybody who knows any agents? What books and/or articles have you written? Have you written and/or sold a book proposal? Do you have publishing contacts to share?

Ask for samples of the person's work. Only a true schmo would hire a writer whose writing he has not read.

After you've asked questions, let the writer/editor/writing coach prove to you that he or she is the right person for the job. The best of these people know what sells. They know the language of books. They should be able to give you a sense of why they can or can't help you. And if they can help you, they should be able to tell you exactly how this will happen and for how much. If you're going after a coauthor/writer and you don't have money to pay someone up front, let the person know from the get-go that you're willing to go 50-50 on everything in exchange for no up-front fees.

Prepare Your Package for Liftoff

Now that your proposal or novel is as close to perfect as it's going to get, it's time to send it out into the world. If your book has a shot at a mid- to large-size publisher of trade books (books for a popular audience), you'll be sending it to literary agents. If it's more than likely to end up at a small, regional or university press, then you'll be sending it directly to editors. If you decide you and your publisher are going to be one and the same, you'll need to investigate which kind of self-publishing best suits you and your book.

CHAPTER 4

Locating, Luring and Landing the Right Agent

"Finding a literary agent is like moving to a new town and having to find a contractor to remodel your house and a mechanic to fix your car all at once. It has a strong element of Russian roulette."

—*National Writers Union*

YOU'VE GOT YOUR TITLE, LOCATED your model, perfected your pitch and completed your proposal. And you've come to the outlandish conclusion that you actually want to get P-A-I-D, up front, for your work. Now you need an agent.

But what exactly *is* an agent? People say to Arielle all the time, "So you're an agent? Can you publish my book?" Agents do not publish books. They do not work for publishers. They work for themselves or for agencies that house more than one agent. *Good* agents have their fingers on the pulse of the publishing world and are skilled in the art of the deal. Notice the emphasis on *good*. Unfortunately, the thing about agents is that they don't need a degree; they don't have to pass a test or get certified. So practically anyone can be an agent. But there aren't that many *good* agents.

Good agents eat lunches with editors from major publishing houses to find out who's buying what and to discover the passions and pet peeves of individual editors. They know how to find the best publisher for you. They'll help with everything from your title to your bio, to the development of your novel's characters, to basic editing and proofreading, to knowing the competition—even brainstorming with you to come up with the best idea for you to write. Good agents will serve as buffers between you and your editor or publisher. They'll come up with publicity and marketing ideas for your book and strategize about getting blurbs for your cover. Good agents will hook you up with good website designers and search engine experts. Good agents will make sure you get every thin dime that's owed to you. And they'll tell you when you should take less money and go with a better publisher. Good agents don't just sell books; they build careers.

Great agents combine all these traits and are part wizard, midwife and guide dog. They'll show you the tricks of the trade, manage your career, introduce you to all the right people, and guide you and your manuscript through the messy maze of the modern book world.

Bad agents, on the other hand, do only some or none of these things, won't return your phone calls, may never send your book out and sometimes will even steal your money. Like bad travel agents, they can send you on some really bad trips, or worse, not even get you off the ground. Naturally, there are many more bad agents than good agents. Sadly, when you meet them, it's often hard to tell the difference. But once you've experienced their incompetence, sloth and/or idiocy firsthand, the distinction becomes painfully obvious.

Do You Really Have to Have an Agent?

If you're looking to get an advance for your book, you almost certainly will need an agent. And even without the hope of an advance there are many reasons to be agented. However, there are a few exceptions to the agent-rule:

■ *Are you writing for a very limited audience?* Most agents will not want to take on a book about the history of Lithuanian movie stars or an experimental novel about the life of a brick in Brooklyn or a how-to on breeding and grooming shitzapoos. Let's say there are 2,000 shitzapoos in North America. Even if every single solitary shitzapoo owner and his mother buy your book, you'll still be selling only a fraction of the number of books that a major publisher looks to sell. In this situation, you'll want to go the small-press or self-publishing route. No agent necessary.

The Slush Pile/e-Trash

f you're an unknown nobody, your stuff will probably end up in a sad, sorry stack of unsolicited letters and manuscripts—the horribly named "slush pile." Or its electronic equivalent, the bloated inbox. Even if it does get read, it will almost certainly be by assistants or junior agents who then pass on any interesting prospects to the appropriate agent(s). Slush has been the primordial ooze from which a teeny tiny trickle of bestsellers have crawled—a great story come press time! That's the good news. The bad news is that agents get thousands of pounds and billions of gigabytes of slush a year. And 98.9% of the time it ends up in the recycle bin. Or gets flushed into the great black cyberhole of nothingness.

Are you starting to understand the importance of researching, networking and making your proposal or manuscript all that it can be?

- *Are you a poet?* Unless you're a Pulitzer Prize winner or a pop icon like Jewel, you stand basically no chance of making any money off your gem of a poetry book. The majority of poets send their manuscripts directly to small poetry and university presses. These publishers rarely offer an advance for poetry manuscripts. The non-Pulitzer, noncelebrity exception to this rule is poetry with a hook or gimmick that allows it to live outside the Poetry section of the bookstore. For example, Hal Sirowitz's *Mother Said* (poems about the truly remarkable rantings of Sirowitz's mother) and David M. Bader's *Haikus for Jews* were both published by divisions of Random House and distributed widely in bookstores because they could be shelved in the Humor section. If you've written poetry that can be shelved someplace other than poetry, look for an agent.

- *Are you writing a book whose subject is of regional interest only?* Say you're crafting a guide to the wildflowers of Oregon, a book that would probably be published by a university press within that state or by a local publisher who specializes in books of local interest. In this case, you don't need an agent.

- *Are you writing a book that needs to be packaged?* Packaged books tend to involve an added product (a DVD, a pen, a bracelet) or lots of illustrations or photographs—anything that may call for multiple contributors or has added sourcing/production complexities. Some agents have the expertise to help you put such books together, but many projects of this type are produced by packagers. Packagers will develop the book and sell it to a mainstream publisher much the way an agent would. Finding a packager involves the same process as finding an agent. If this is your sort of project, read on! Just substitute the word "packager" for "agent" as you read.

- *Are you writing an academic book?* A treatise on polynomial refractors and their impact on mutating quarks could only be published by an academic press. If you ask an agent to sell this kind of book for you, it's extremely likely that you'll get this response: "Huh?"

- *Are you an entrepreneur who wants to bring home a bigger piece of the pie?* With the proliferation of ebooks and print-on-demand technologies, many entrepreneurial folks are bypassing agents and publishers completely and self-publishing instead. Especially if they already have a built-in audience. Yes, this often requires a significant up-front investment. But it also means you have full control of your product and that you get to keep a much larger share of the profits. If you think you fit into this category, check out Chapter 11 for a better idea of the pluses and minuses of self-publishing.

▶ Don't have time for a trip to the bookstore? Many books have been scanned and are available to "leaf" through via GoogleBooks. You can't view an entire book, but if you type a title plus the word "acknowledgments" in the search field, you'll be led right to the page where you want to go.

A Note on Children's Book Agents

Before the advent of publishing conglomerates and the Harry Potter explosion, lots of children's book authors didn't use agents. Not that it would have hurt to have an agent back in the day, but it wasn't a necessity. Oh, how times have changed. Most major publishers of children's books simply do not look at unsolicited manuscripts. This is also true for young adult novels.

Lawyer or Agent?

A few lawyers sell books to publishers on a regular basis, charging clients an hourly fee instead of a percentage of the book's proceeds. This works only if the lawyer has good connections and if you truly don't want or need the myriad services often offered by agents—editorial development, foreign subagents, hand-holding and more.

Note: A lawyer who doesn't have a thorough knowledge of the business can end up costing you more money than an agent costs, with very little or no return.

▶ Sign up for Publishers Marketplace, an e-source that reports deals daily, identifying the agent who sold a book and the editor/publisher who bought it. Then buy a subscription to *Publishers Weekly* (online so you can sign up for the free daily e-newsletter), and scan for agents and editors who are representing/ buying material similar to yours. It's a bit pricey, but this kind of insider info is invaluable. If you don't have the money, read *Publishers Weekly* in magazine form at your local library and sign up online for Publishers Lunch, which offers less information than Publishers Marketplace but will begin to educate you on all things publishing. (See Appendix II for more information.)

Locating an Agent

People ask in wide-eyed terror how they can possibly find a great agent when agents are as rare as unicorns and there are approximately 17 kazillion aspiring authors. We tell them two things: 1) Without authors, there would be no agents. Let's put that another way: Without authors, agents make no money. 2) Every single agent in history has passed on a project by an unknown author that went on to live in the land of bestsellerdom. This is why nearly every agency—whether they admit it or not—looks at query letters. No agent wants to be remembered as that guy who passed on *The Da Vinci Code* or *The Catcher in the Rye*. So, in your quest for an agent, let this be your mantra: THEY NEED ME!

Proceed now with confidence in your search for a top-drawer agent. For those with no personal referral, which is the case for most aspiring authors, fear not! Our system is nearly foolproof. Of course, it all revolves around that old Principle #1: Research, Research, Research. You don't want to send your sci-fi epic to someone who thinks *The Lord of the Rings* is a jeweler, your illustrated history of tea to a coffee junkie, or your Christian self-help book to a die-hard reincarnated Buddhist.

Acknowledging the Acknowledgments

Not every book contains an acknowledgment section, but such a section often holds clues about a book's road to publication, including the names of the author's agent and editor. We're going to show you how to mine these acknowledgments for help in navigating your own road to publication.

First, go back to your extended list of competitive titles. Save it as a new document, then add any books that draw a similar audience as yours, as well as those you have strong feelings for or that inspired you. Eliminate books that are in direct competition with yours. For example, if you're writing a cookbook on vegetarian Thai cuisine, you do not want to go after an agent who has represented a book on that exact subject. You'd be wiser to choose your favorite vegetarian cookbooks and your favorite nonvegetarian Thai cookbooks as models.

Once you've exhausted your library and your memory, recruise the Internet and revisit your local bookstore and library to complete your list. These visits are especially important for ferreting out those books that didn't make it onto your competition list, but have a style and vision similar to yours.

Once you've located at least 5 to 25 books, it's time to check out their acknowledgment sections. See if the author has thanked her agent and/or editor and/or publisher. Make three lists: 1) agents, 2) editors, and 3) publishers. This way, you can call the editor's office to get the name of the agent if none is listed. And these editors and publishers will come in handy later as well. Fishing acknowledgment sections is a common publishing industry trick, but one that few newbies know.

Congratulations! You are now in possession of a list of agents and editors whom you admire or who have demonstrated a proven interest in your subject of choice.

Agents on the Web (and in the Bookstore)

Supplement your acknowledgments research with some targeted snooping. Most agencies have websites, so troll away. What kinds of writers do the agents whose names you've culled represent? Read the agencies' mission statements. Check out the agents' personal bios. Take notes. You'll eventually use this information in writing your query letter. You might even borrow language from a particular agency's mission statement in order to show that you know what they're about and that you've chosen them for a reason.

▶ One of the newest vermin to worm their way into the publishing business is a group of people who are taking fees from writers to submit their work to agents. Arielle has been on the receiving end of these kinds of queries. She—as well as any other agent worth her salt—could pick these queries out in a nanosecond. If someone asks you for money to submit your work to an agent, be sure you very carefully research her services. Chances are, she is an old-school shyster trying to rip you off in a new-school way.

Meeting Your Match

R oxanna Elden spent hours and hours researching the right agents for her book. "My proposal was finished," Roxanna recalls, "and I had queried quite a few agents. Okay . . . about 60. I had gotten some interest from five or six, but had run into resistance because I didn't have enough of a platform and my book was aimed at somewhat of a niche market, namely teachers." Roxanna was frustrated but undeterred. She continually used the information gleaned from her rejections to strengthen her pitch, query and proposal, until she felt that she had an airtight package.

Roxanna then signed up for a local writers' conference where an agent named Rita Rosenkranz was appearing. During her presentation, Rita mentioned the value of niche market books. Roxanna felt she had met her perfect match.

At the end of the presentation, Roxana approached Rita with the 30-second pitch she'd been honing for two years. "I was able to tie my pitch to a point she made in her presentation. I was much better prepared than the other people in line, who were asking her basic questions, complaining about the publishing industry or trying to sell her their work on the spot. I gave the pitch, handed her a card and asked for her contact information." Rita chimes in: "Roxanna was serious about her project, was well positioned to write her book and had done her homework. She was clearly a reliable, dedicated author."

Roxanna followed up by emailing her proposal, and Rita gave a few suggestions that she thought would make the book more marketable. After Roxanna made the changes, Rita took her on as a client. And within a month, she had sold Roxanna's book to a major publisher who focused on education-related subjects.

"In retrospect," Roxanna says, "I feel lucky for the two years of experience I had before meeting Rita. They gave me a level of preparation and professionalism that I would not have had otherwise." That's not hazard—it's hard work.

Check out Jeff Herman's *Guide to Book Editors, Publishers and Literary Agents,* which lists personal and professional information about individual agents. Where did they go to college or high, middle and grade school? You never know, you might have attended the same grade school. Wouldn't that make a great opening line? Tool around. Can you be their friend on Facebook? Can you follow them on Twitter? Do they have a pug, love the Cowboys or adore opera? Are they a nature lover, fashion maven, steak freak? Keep in mind that lots of agents have written books. Read and study these as well.

You will use all this information to personalize your query. A car nut who sells thrillers might be just the right agent for your novel about a vintage Chevy that murders people. Again, an agent who has represented a book directly competitive with yours is not the right agent for you. She will consider this a conflict of interest. And if she doesn't, do yourself a favor and walk away. (However, if she tells you that the directly competitive book is now out of print, she might be perfect.)

Are there other agents that your acknowledgment search might not have turned up but who seem like a good fit? When researching a larger agency, look for the newcomers who are just making their bones. They will be much easier to reach and much more likely to take on a newbie.

Going Face-to-Face

Networking is a great way to meet an agent. The very thought may activate your wallflower instinct, but avoid networking altogether and you'll make your job so much harder. Fortunately, there are lots of ways to network: writers' conferences, seminars, readings, MFA programs and more.

> ▶ If you're not in the right neck of the woods and don't want to travel, you can take online writing classes/webinars for e-face time with industry professionals. There has been a mass proliferation of such classes; do your research and it's likely you'll be able to turn up an e-teacher with a great résumé. Check out Appendix II and our website, thebookdoctors.com, for more information.

WRITERS' CONFERENCES, SEMINARS AND WORKSHOPS

Get thee to the hot spots where agents and published writers lurk and linger. Workshops, seminars and conferences are often free when they're presented at bookstores or libraries, or if an agent is promoting a book she herself has written. The most famous writers' conferences, like Squaw Valley and Bread Loaf, cost a pretty penny—but the quality of instruction is high and food and lodging are included. You also have to factor in your transportation costs, lost work time, maybe extra baby-sitting fees, and so on. These conferences also happen to be very competitive. At their best, however, they will allow you not only to improve your writing skills, but also to meet an agent, live and in the flesh, and even to take a class from an agent. One on one, up close and personal.

As always, inspect and research any and all organizations before giving them your money. Look for conferences featuring agents from reputable agencies. Or, if you hunt down a particularly affordable conference where you don't know the instructors, check out their websites and look them up in agent guides (see Appendix II). Go in armed with as much information as possible. If an agent/presenter is a nut about nuts and you're writing a history of the peanut, you're in luck.

Local writers' conferences, often lasting only a day or two, are usually open to anyone who pays. You may or may not get a lot less personal attention, but you'll usually have at least a shot at a short, private meeting with an agent. The third option is your Learning Annex or Mediabistro–type deal—you get a couple hours of a presentation, some Q&A and a card. Face time is possible but not guaranteed. Of course, many of these workshops are held in New York, L.A. or San Francisco. But if you live in the right neck of the woods or are willing to locomote yourself, we recommend looking into the possibility. Even if you don't actually acquire an agent, you'll probably ingest some juicy morsels about publishing.

▶ Although New York is the throbbing heart of publishing, it's sometimes better to have an agent who lives in your neck of the woods but visits the city regularly or worked there previously. An agent who is out of the New York scene may have a better feel for what's going on in the hinterlands than New York agents would have. She may see success written all over your book when someone in the publishing mecca looks down his snobby nose at it.

READINGS AND OTHER PLACES TO MEET AND GREET

If you're having a tough time meeting an agent in the flesh, try meeting some published writers. Not only is this a great way to become part of the publishing community; it's also a great way to get to agents.

Where does one find published authors? Though they're often somewhat reclusive, many of them give readings. So get on local bookstore and library mailing lists. Locate lecture series that regularly feature authors. Check out your Independent Booksellers Association's regional conferences (they typically occur once a year). Attend any and all readings and lectures, particularly those by an author working in your field. Stay after the reading. And buy the author's book. (More on this later, but understand this: Authors do readings to sell books. They're not supposed to be free workshops or pro bono entertainment. An author whose book you buy will be much more inclined to talk to you.) Try to be last in line at a book signing so no one is breathing down your neck. Ask the author about her publishing experience. See what you can learn. If it feels right, tell the author about your own book. If she's receptive, ask her for advice about finding an agent. Some authors will volunteer their agent's name. If they do, you can use this information in your query letter: "I am writing at the suggestion of AUTHOR X." Including this information lands you in the "referral category"—an elite position that will exponentially up your chances of landing an agent.

Many booksellers have connections with agents, either because they bring agents into their bookstores to do workshops or because their bookstores are so known in the industry that agents go out of their way to promote books there. Many agents have written books themselves and done events in bookstores. The point is, by getting close to your local bookstores, you may even wangle an introduction to an agent.

MFA Programs: Should You Become a Master?

Are you a fiction or creative nonfiction writer? If so, perhaps one of the MFA (Master of Fine Arts) programs is for you. While they can be debt-inducing, they can also be career-launching. The reasons are threefold:

- Well-known writers populate the staffs of these programs. And if one of them cottons to your work, he can introduce you to agents and publishers galore. He can also help you get your writing into important literary journals that will make your résumé thrilling to publishers. Even just a blurb saying how much he likes your work can open some pretty heavy doors.

- A prestigious program at the start of your query letter can light up an agent's eyes. A mention of the Iowa Writers' Workshop (considered by many the most prestigious writing program around) would certainly make a query jump to the top of most agents' enormous piles—it's essentially a *Good Housekeeping* stamp of approval that means your work will probably be worth reading.

- You're immersed in a community of writers with whom you can network, network, network. So if you make nice with your classmates and one of them lands an agent and a book deal, that's one human you know who now can connect you to an agent and publisher—and maybe even give you a blurb someday.

Because many fiction and creative nonfiction writers don't have the days or the dough to go to school year round, lots of schools have "nonresidency" programs. Bennington, Warren Wilson College, Goddard and Antioch are four of the most respected. (For further information, see Appendix II.) These programs require only a few fortnightly visits a year to campus. The rest of the time, you're on your own.

Grande Agents, Little Bitty Agents and All Who Fall Between

Querying agents is a little like applying to college. It's great to have Ivy League schools on your list, but you should also include a few solid midsize colleges and a safety school or two. There's no harm in writing to some Big Shot Agents, but you want to make sure you have your bases covered.

How do you know how big a Big Shot is? Look at the books an agent represents. If he counts Toni Morrison, Danielle Steel, Stephen Hawking and a galaxy of other bestselling and/or prizewinning authors among his clients, you're in Harvard/Yale country. If he's got smatterings of bestsellers and clients with impressive/interesting backgrounds, you're talking competitive midsize liberal arts college. And if you haven't heard of anyone on the agent's list, or if he has a post office where an address should be, that's your safety school.

Of course, you can get a crummy education at Harvard and a mind-altering education at a safety school. At the same time, a Harvard degree can help you throughout the rest of your life. So it is with publishing. Working with a new or smaller agency can be a dream-come-true situation. You may get an agent hungry to make her bones with your book. You may get tons of personal attention and fantastic editorial input. Or your work can get sucked into that ugly publishing black hole. If you're with a Big Shot, there's no doubt your proposal or manuscript will make editors jump to attention. But there's also the very real possibility that you will be low man on the pole—that you will never be able to get the agent on the phone and your work will be sucked into that ugly publishing black hole. Or that the Big Shot Agent will abandon you at sea without a sail if she doesn't make a quick deal.

Luring the Agent

Research in tow, it's time to cast your line. Think of your perfectly polished query letter as the bait, your proposal/manuscript as an irresistible lure and your follow-up letter as the hook.

Now we'll show you how to catch the big fish!

The Killer Query Letter

No doubt about it: A smart, savvy, scintillating, personal query letter can get you an agent. Your query letter should be information-packed yet concise, complimentary without being obsequious, powerful without being overpowering. Be professional, but make sure the letter reflects the best of your personality and style. Show the agent you'll be great to do business with.

A query letter to an agent has three components: 1) the connection, 2) the pitch, and 3) the bio. Make each one approximately a paragraph long, and try to keep the whole letter to a page. As you'll shortly see, we've created three different fictional authors with three different styles of queries. Read them carefully to learn how to craft a query of your own.

THE CONNECTION

Why is this agent the right one for you? Use the info you gathered with your sleuthing to make the connection. If the agent is also an author, say nice yet honest things about the book(s) she's written. When someone starts a query to Arielle with "I bought your book, *The Essential Guide to Getting Your Book Published,* and it has been my go-to resource for the entire publishing process," her ability to focus is immediately enhanced.

Refer specifically to successful books the agent has represented. Tell her what you dig about those books and why yours is similar yet different.

Why so much buttering up? What most writers don't realize is that, generally speaking, agents are anonymous pieces of the pie who get no respect outside the industry. How many bestselling authors can you name? Now, how many of their agents can you come up with? Exactly. So anything you can do to make an agent feel acknowledged, appreciated, acclaimed, affirmed and special will go a long way.

It's now time to find out how our fictional authors approached the connection paragraph of the query:

▶ Every once in a while, Arielle gets a query letter claiming a referral that is pure B.S. Most of the time, the claimed referent is not even anyone Arielle knows. Sometimes the referent is an "editor" at a publishing house of note, but one Arielle has never heard of. When Arielle looks up the person in her database or online, no such editor exists. Need we even say that it's a really stupid idea to lie about a referral?

①

In researching literary agents, I saw that you represented two of my favorite books, poemcrazy *and* Fruitflesh. *I have used these books personally and professionally in my psychotherapy practice. What particularly impressed*

The Magic of the Referral

A re you one of the precious few writers armed with an agent referral? Display the name of the referring person in the first sentence of your letter or the header of your email and there's a grand chance your query will end up in the hot hands of the agent. If you don't, there's an excellent chance it will end up slushed.

Briefly explain your connection to legitimize it—"my good friend/colleague/professor"—if, and only if, the connection is more meaningful than your second cousin thrice removed or someone you met for five seconds at a party. Agents often call the referring person to see what your deal is. If there's any way to get your connection to call the agent before you send your query, much the better. This is a great buzz-builder.

me about them is the incredible amount of heart they display. What brave women Susan Wooldridge and Gayle Brandeis are to reveal their lives in such intimate detail! I can't tell you what an inspiration they have been to my patients and to me. I believe that my book, Writing for Your Life, *shares some of the essential qualities of* Poemcrazy *and* Fruitflesh, *but its roots in my experience as a clinical psychologist make it unique. Because both Susan and Gayle acknowledged you so effusively, and because my book shares many of the same fundamental beliefs as theirs, I hope you'll be interested in reviewing my proposal.*

②

After seeing you acknowledged in Hooligan Killers, *I logged onto your website to check out what other books you represent. I was happy to see so many books that I have on my shelves and that I admire. I am a particular fan of* Goalie on a Rampage *and* Midfielders Gone Mad. *But what impressed me the most was your love of* Manchester United, *as I myself am a Red Devil fan from the days of Bobby Charlton and Georgie Best. At 20, I moved to England and played for Newcastle United's Under 21 Club. I've written a novel about my time as an American soccer player in England called* The Referee Assassin.

③

I recently bought a copy of your book Monkeys in the Bible, *and I read it cover to cover in one night. I loved the chapter in which you had the orangutan come down from the Mount with Moses and the Ten Commandments.*

I see that you've agented a number of popular science books, including Bees Bees Bees *and* Men Are Dogs, Women Are Cats. *I have written a proposal for a book about monkeys called* My Monkey, My Self, *based on the award-winning research I conducted in Kenya.*

REPERFECTING YOUR PITCH

Take the pitch you meticulously crafted (see page 69) and give it a fresh look. Do you need to tailor it to fit the agent you're querying? Do you have to pare it down a bit?

Picking up where we left off with our three made-up author queries, we'll now show you a great pitch for each:

❶

Scientific studies have shown that writing down traumatic experiences immediately boosts your immune system. In fact, your heart rate, brain waves and nervous system are all positively affected by this simple act. Writing for Your Life *follows 12 women as they write about the seemingly insurmountable challenges they've faced and continue to face in their lives. And it dramatically shows how these women are profoundly changed as a result of daily writing. Each chapter is accompanied by writing practices that any reader can do on her own in order to elicit the same kind of results as the women portrayed in the book. Inspired and inspiring,* Writing for Your Life *will speak eloquently to anyone who's had to fight through adversity and struggle for her dreams.*

▶ Do NOT overpromise. Have you called your opus the next *Eat, Pray, Love?* An even better version of Harry Potter? If so, you've got trouble. Better to underpromise and overdeliver. As Daniel Greenberg of the Levine Greenberg Rostan Literary Agency says, "Anytime anyone compares himself to a big bestseller, it's a big turnoff. While it's not impossible that there's a real comparison to be made, it raises my suspicion that the person is overhyping himself."

❷

A supermodel-handsome international soccer star and his pop star girlfriend. A tyrannical, egomaniacal, homicidal national-hero coach. A young stud with a dark, dark secret. A gambloholic sex-starved referee in deep, deep debt. And a lonely psychopath with an uncontrollable urge to kill—who just happens to be the biggest soccer nut in the world. The Referee Assassin *is an international soccer thriller that takes ripped-from-headlines events and weaves them into a white-knuckle thriller, culminating in a wild ride of a World Cup that will leave readers screaming, "Gooooooooooal!" The* Referee Assassin *shoots. And it scores.*

❸

When I left to study the candyass baboons of western Africa's Burrunguguanaptchinwazazie Plains, I was an uptight, unmarried professor with a secret drinking problem and a stack of unfinished academic articles on my shelf. When I returned, I was a hang-loose, loving husband with a profound zest for life, a successful career and an amazing story to tell. And I owe it all to the candyass baboons. While in the wilds of the jungle, I met Zeus, the brooding king of the baboons, struggling to stay the alpha; Madonna, the diva who drove everyone crazy but always came through when the chips were down; and little Tiny Tim, who was born lame in one leg and forced to fight the ultimate Darwinian struggle of life and death. I came away with My Monkey, My Self, *a book that reveals the deep connection we share with our primate friends as well as the many things the animal kingdom has to teach us.*

A BOOMING BIO

Time to let the agent know why you're great. Take your hot bio from your proposal and pare it down to a paragraph. This is not a job résumé—it's an enthusiastic review of your accomplishments. If you've been published, trot out your personal bibliography. If you've won awards, by all means include them. Elucidate on how you've got the savvy and the sass to publicize and market your book. Include interesting tidbits about yourself (you were on Canada's Olympic track team in 1990; in addition to being a lawyer, you are also an ornithologist; you were Marilyn on *The Munsters*).

Let's turn to the bios of three fictional authors who'll be sure to get their targeted agents on the horn pronto.

❶

I am a practicing clinical psychologist as well as the founder of the Writing for Your Life workshop, which now has over 15 active satellite groups in the United States. Since its inception eight years ago, more than 5,500 people have taken the workshop. I have been profiled in the Dallas Morning News *and on my local CBS morning show, and have done at least two dozen radio interviews, a number of which were for NPR affiliates. I believe that my experience leading workshops and with the media, along with my willingness to pound the pavement upon publication, will make* Writing for Your Life *a front-list success and a backlist favorite.*

❷

When not on the soccer field, I spend my days as a real-life referee, a substitute teacher and a writing instructor at San Quentin. When I was 20, I was a merchant mariner; at 30, I was an emergency room technician; at 40, I was a dot-com multimillionaire in the process of losing almost all of that money; and at 45, I'm the oldest player by 10 years in a Division One intramural league in the Bay Area. I'm tied for the most goals with the youngest player on my team; he just turned 22. I think this says all you need to know about my character. I'm tenacious as hell, and I'm a true team player.

❸

I'm a professor of primatology at Rice University, where I hold the Chippendale Chair in biology. I've included my CV so that you can see the myriad of papers I've had published over the years, most in leading academic journals. I've included photographs of myself with Zeus, Madonna and wee Tiny Tim, as well as clippings from a number of national and local papers in the United States and Canada that featured our story and that served as the seed for this book. I am caretaker of several baboons, one of whom, Zippy, has already made several media appearances and is raring to go again. I also have a blog and website you might enjoy, apeman.com, where all this information is assembled (including several YouTube videos, one of which has been seen over 250,000 times).

▶ Sometimes agents get queries with no contact information. Can you imagine? If you are snail-mailing your query, include a self-addressed stamped envelope (SASE). If you leave off the stamp part, you probably won't hear back unless the agent is interested. Include your email and snail-mail addresses, as well as your phone number in case the agent wants to get hold of you ASAP or has lost your SASE (which, sadly, often happens).

Multiple Submissions

You've got your agent list. You've got your killer query. Now it's time to launch yourself out into the world. Unless you have a personal referral to an agent or there's one agent who you feel is a perfect fit, you should definitely send query letters to all the agents on your list at the same time. Many how-to-get-published books tell you not to do multiple submissions to agents. Ignore this feeble advice. Agents can take up to a year to respond. A year! If you wait for each of them, you could easily be dead before you get representation. However, do NOT send your query letter to multiple agents within the same agency. "There's nothing more annoying and frustrating than to find out everyone in the office has received the same query all at once," says Larry Kirshbaum, former chairman and CEO of the Time Warner Book Group and current literary agent. Annoying because: 1) It makes you look like you're just throwing spaghetti at the wall and haven't done your research as to why a *particular* agent is right for you, and 2) If more than one agent is interested, it creates in-house conflict.

The great thing about legitimate multiple submissions is that, if you get interest from one agent, you can use this interest to prod all the other agents to read your material. If someone wants you, it's easier to get other people to want you. Anyone who's been to high school knows that. It's not necessary to write in your query that you're submitting to multiple publishers. But if you're asked, be sure to tell the truth—don't act like you're in a committed relationship if you're still playing the field.

> ▶ If you're sending your query to just one agent because you're sure she's the one for you, be sure to tell her so in your letter. But put a time limit on her exclusive look. Two weeks should be enough time, unless she asks for more.

Should You Send the Whole Enchilada?

Do not, under any circumstances, bombard the agent with written material unless you want to get it shredded and e-trashed. Include a description of what material is available in your query, and then let her tell you what she wants. Some agents want proposals by email so they don't have to handle any paper; some hate e-proposals. You must send your material exactly as the agent wants to receive it, and the only way you'll know that is by asking or looking up submission requirements on her website.

When David first met Arielle, as a writer he was shocked by how many envelopes and packages floated across her desk every single day. Thousands and thousands of authors' dream ships sailing by. So if you're sending your query via snail mail, make yours look classy. Use high-quality stationery. The more elegant, simple and professional the presentation, the less chance you have of bumping up against someone else's taste. Arielle gets lots of query letters on rainbow stationery. She hates rainbow stationery! So she has an instant prejudice against these authors even if they've written excellent proposals.

With both paper and electronic submissions, use a legible, professional-looking font. And if you're a professional graphic designer (or you know someone who is), strut your stuff. Top-notch visuals can turn someone on just as much as rainbows turn Arielle off.

The Underestimated Importance of the Follow-Up

As important as the query letter is, its follow-up may be just as crucial. You have no idea how many letters get lost. In the mail. Under a desk. In bloated inboxes. In the spam blockers that now guard e-gates everywhere. In the slush pile. And once you've made sure your letter has been received, you've got to make sure it gets read. Just because an agent hasn't responded doesn't mean she's not interested. Sometimes she needs a few gentle reminders.

E-reminders are the least invasive and most effective way to grab an agent's attention. If you don't have an agent's email address, to make contact you must negotiate your way through the first layer of defense: the receptionist, and/or assistant.

► For goodness sake, spell the agent's name right! Arielle Eckstut has gotten letters addressed to Arel Ekctuts, Areel Esckstup and Mr. Arilee Etschuck. And while we're on the subject, please make sure the letter you send is to the person named on the front of your envelope. We know it sounds elementary, but make the act of checking the letter against the envelope part of your checklist.

SCHMOOZING THE GATEKEEPER

Almost certainly, the first person you'll speak to at an agent's office is a receptionist or secretary or intern. These are the people who do the grunt work, get none of the credit and yet are responsible for whether your message finds a place on top of the agent's call list or gets eighty-sixed into the wastebasket.

Be extra nice to the receptionist. Call in the late afternoon, when things are less hectic. Be hyper-aware of the mood in the office. If you hear yelling and phones ringing off hooks, suggest that you'll call back another time. But when the time is right, see if you can strike up a conversation with this individual. See what you can find out about him. There's a good chance he'll be the first one to read your material—and an equally good chance that in a year or two he'll be an agent.

You should keep notes on every agent you're contacting. When you call, note the day and time along with any information that could be valuable down the line. When David was in Hollywood, he was courting a prominent agent. He called and got the receptionist, who sounded miserable. David asked her if she was okay. She confessed that her cat had a tumor. It just so happens that David is a cat lover, so they exchanged cat stories for a few moments. David wrote the name of the assistant's cat in his notebook, and the next time he called, the first thing he asked was "How's Max doing?" The assistant couldn't believe that David had remembered her cat's name. More chatting ensued. Three months and 12 phone calls later, David had a meeting with the agent.

If you can develop a relationship with the gatekeeper and the moment feels right, don't hesitate to ask, "If you were me, how would you get my stuff on the agent's desk?" All of a sudden, the person who's been an office underling all day is being treated as an authority. Asked for advice. Humans like to think they're authorities. Humans like to give advice. Use this to your advantage.

THE DID-YOU-GET-MY-LETTER/EMAIL CALL

One week after you send your query letter, contact the agent's assistant to make sure it's actually been received. Again, she might be the first person who reads your letter. BEWARE: She might say, "Oh, what's your book about?" So you

Sounding Out Solo Agents

M any agencies are one-person operations. This can be great—you're more likely to get personal attention—but it also means you need to know exactly what you're getting yourself into. Barbara Moulton, who opened her own one-person agency after years as an editor at HarperCollins, says, "You want to know what qualifies the person to be an agent. Is she a publishing defector? That's usually a good sign. But always check the agent's background."

Here are other essential questions to ask a solo practitioner:

- Do you sell book rights around the world? If so, what is your commission?

- Will you be able to sell serial rights to my book?

- Do you have the ability to sell film and TV rights? If so, what is your commission? Do you work with a TV/movie-selling co-agent? If so, who?

- When you're on vacation, are you available to take my calls if an emergency comes up? If not, do you have an assistant who's capable of taking care of business?

The answers to these questions are very important, because as you'll discover throughout the rest of this book, the agent's role is not necessarily limited to the selling phase.

better be ready to pitch, baby, pitch (have your query letter handy to help). And you *must* be done in less than a minute! So, practice before you get on the phone. Then practice some more. When you're sure you've got it down pat, take a few moments and do some more practicing.

If you're using email to send a query, get an automatic "confirmed receipt" if your Internet provider has this function. You won't have to call the agent, yet you'll know when he's opened his email. If you don't know how to do this, find a tech-friend who can help.

▶ Some agencies don't keep a log of query letters. If you think yours has been lost, email the receptionist and ask if you should send another. Double-check that you're sending it in exactly the way they want it; often agencies will junk queries that aren't written to spec.

THE DID-YOU-*READ*-MY-LETTER/EMAIL CALL

This one calls for delicacy. David, an avid agent hunter for over 20 years, thinks it's best to call the agent or assistant once every couple of weeks to follow up. Arielle, on the other hand, being an agent for over a decade, hates people calling her to find out about query letters. She believes the one did-you-get-my-letter call to the assistant is enough. Or that an email to the agent is okay. But she also believes that persistent calling should be reserved for the months after the agent has received the material he requested. What we both agree on is that you never, under any circumstances, want to be a pest. Pushy is bad. Tenacious, friendly, charming, sweet, thoughtful, kind and professional are good.

Landing the Big Kahuna

Now that you've located and lured some agents, it's time to reel one in. Some writers may have a number of nibbles to work with. Some one. Some none. However, your chances of landing the right agent go up if you systematically apply the guidelines that follow.

Eureka: When an Agent Calls

You wait and you wait, and you wait and you wait. Maybe a week, maybe a year. Then, all of a sudden, you get a call from an agent. Someone's interested! If you've got the money, send the requested material via overnight delivery.

(Remember: Have your materials ready and waiting before your query goes out.) Or, if appropriate, ask if you can email your proposal. Whatever you do, get something off immediately so you're still on the agent's mind when she gets your package. Iron. Hot. Strike.

Next, call every other agent you queried and let them know that you have interest elsewhere. No need to specify that only one person called. However, if more than one person has called, trot this information out. This should vault your query to the top of their lists. With any luck at all, these calls will produce more requests for your material.

Once you've sent out your proposal or manuscript, it's follow-up time again. This time, David and Arielle agree: You're going to have to be persistent—and nice and funny and patient—for the long haul.

Grilling an Agent

As Smokey Robinson's mother so wisely advised, "You better shop around." Or, put another way, you want to find out who you're hopping into bed with before you do the hopping. Even if an agent says she's ready to sign you up as her client, stop doing your happy dance long enough to figure out exactly who you'll be seeing in the morning.

Some agents will never talk to you after they sign you. They will not return your calls. They just want to sell your material. This may not be the kind of agent you had in mind. Or maybe you don't care as long as they sell your book. But most of us would prefer an agent who communicates well and who is great at nurturing and building successful writing careers. Some agents are also talented editors, meaning that part of the joy of their job is shaping material. This can be enormously helpful in selling your book. You want this to be the start of a long, fruitful relationship, not a dark, harrowing nightmare. The point is, you have to find the right person for you.

Here are some key questions you should ask an interested agent:

- What other books like mine have you sold?
- Do you help authors develop their material?
- Will contact be primarily with you or your assistant?
- Will you help me promote my book when it comes out?
- Are you a member of the Association of Authors' Representatives?
- Do you have client and editor references I can call?
- What publishing houses do you work with on a regular basis?
- How many books have you sold in the last year?

- Are you known for selling a particular kind of book (business, science, African American, romance, literary fiction)?
- Have you negotiated terms with all the major publishing houses?
- Do you have co-agents who help to sell your books overseas?
- Do you have a co-agent in Hollywood?

It's perfectly legitimate, logical and human to ask: "How much can you sell my book for?" But be forewarned that the answer, e.g., "big bucks," might be the opposite of what you want. In fact, if an agent gives you the "big bucks" answer, don't take it with a grain of salt; take it with several shakerfuls. No agent can possibly give you the real answer to this question. Books that look like bestsellers often sell for pocket change. Esoteric, quirky tomes sometimes sell for six figures. You just never know. When authors ask Arielle this question, her stock answer is: "Somewhere between $5,000 and $500,000."

An Embarrassment of Riches: When More than One Agent Is Interested in Your Book

Suddenly you're in the enviable position of choosing among several agents. Maybe one agent is young, hungry, attentive and inexperienced, and another is super-high-powered but impossible to get on the phone. Whom to choose?

Eenie, Meenie, Minie, Moe . . .

A first-time writer who wishes to remain nameless found herself on the horns of a choosing-between-two-agents dilemma. Both seemed great, though for very different reasons. The less experienced agent completely understood her book and was delightful to talk to and not in the least intimidating. He flew out to meet with the writer and was accessible to her at all times. He made editorial suggestions that made perfect sense to her. However, he didn't have a client list packed with Pulitzer Prize winners and bestsellers, like the super-high-powered agent. But the super-high-powered agent asked the writer to change her book from nonfiction to fiction. Asked her to change it from a dark, literary story to a light, fluffy one. As flattered as the writer was by the super-high-powered agent's interest, and as awed as she was by this agent's client list (which included two of her all-time favorite authors), she simply couldn't live with those kinds of changes to her book.

In the end, the writer went with her gut and signed with the younger, hungrier agent. Turns out her gut was right. Her agent got her a two-book, six-figure deal. And she was never scared to pick up the phone and call him.

Again, what do you need? A hand-holder? Then young-and-hungry is the one for you. Are you more of a "show me the money" type? Then high-powered might be the solution, especially if you've written a book with big potential.

Make a pluses-and-minuses list based on your interview questions. Are the pluses things you care about? Are the minuses less important? If so, that's the agent for you.

If you want to write for a niche audience, it really helps to have an agent who knows that particular world and the players in it. If she specializes in your category and wants your project, odds are she'll sell your book.

If, in fact, you want to build your career as a writer, the macrocosmic question is less about whether the agent will help you with your current book than whether she'll be able to help you build that career. If you envision a next book that is not in the agent's area of specialty, then you've got a tough decision. It's hard work finding another agent, and most agents want to represent all your work. If you do plan on writing a different kind of second book, this is something you should discuss with the agent from the get-go. Point being, while you're looking at the trees, don't lose sight of the forest.

> If you're a published writer who's not happy with your representation, don't drop your agent until you know someone else wants to represent you. Already having an agent is a position of strength you'll want to take advantage of. And be sure not to bad-mouth your current agent . . . it may come back to haunt you. Who knows, the new agent may be best friends with the old one. Or maybe the new agent will think you'll diss her in the future.

The Lone Suitor Scenario: When Only One Agent Is Interested in Your Book

Getting love from an agent is cause for celebration. But it can be tough if you're not entirely sold on the sole agent who wants to work with you. On the one hand, if the agent can sell your book, at least you'll get your work published. And if you then go on to write a second, it'll be easier to find another agent with a published book topping your résumé. On the other hand, an ineffective or nasty agent can spoil your chances of getting published. Your book may never make it out of the agent's office, or it may go to all the wrong editors, or you and your work may become associated with an agent who sends out bad material. Or she may be a hellion to deal with. But on the whole, it's almost always better to have an agent than to have none at all.

Back to the Drawing Board

We don't know any writer who hasn't been slapped by the cold hard palm of rejection. Often repeatedly. If you have a hard time dealing with rejection (and who doesn't?), you may want to go directly to Chapter 6 to help shore yourself up against the inevitable. Once you've soothed the savage beast, evaluate the feedback you've received. If several agents tell you the same thing, address their concerns. However, you may get rejections that include no feedback at all. In that case, you'll have to reassess the commercial viability of your project and/or the writing while keeping your sense of humor as activated as possible.

If you still feel that your project is salable and your writing professional-caliber, go back and repeat the steps you've already taken. Do more research. Come up with more agents and submit to them. If you do this several times and still get nary a nibble, it's probably time to think about 1) going with a smaller publisher, in which case you won't need an agent, 2) self-publishing, or 3) hiring a trained professional to help make your work more polished and/or marketable.

John Hancocking: Signing an Agency Contract

Almost all agents, whether they're working solo or as part of a larger agency, will have you sign an agency agreement. Specifics may vary, but a standard agreement includes:

- The agency's commission (on advances, royalties and sub-rights sales)
- A description of how the agency charges for out-of-pocket expenses (if it does)
- The agency's obligations to you, and vice versa
- Conditions for termination

Most agencies charge a 15% commission on advances, royalties and most subsidiary sales, except for foreign rights. For these, 20% is standard, because the agent works with co-agents who split the commission. (So in actuality, while you're paying more, your agent is getting less.) The smallest agencies can charge up to a 30% commission on certain sales (such as foreign rights), because they use a middleman to connect them to a subagent and each party gets 10%.

Some agencies charge for out-of-pocket expenses like postage, overnight delivery and messengers. It's perfectly fine to ask for a cap on expenses or to request to be notified if expenses go beyond a certain point.

The Hollywood Agent

U nless your agent works at a large agency with its own film/TV department, he will, more than likely, work with a separate film and television agent to sell these rights to your book (if, indeed, your book screams "movie!"). Many agents have existing relationships with Hollywood agents, known in the book biz as co-agents. Some literary agents have exclusive relationships with co-agents, and some work with a variety of them.

If you think you've got a hot film or TV property on your hands, you'll want your agent to hook you up with a co-agent as soon as your proposal or manuscript is ready to be sent out to publishers. That way, as soon as your book sells, the co-agent can shop it to Hollywood. Why wait until your book sells? Sylvie Rabineau, cofounder of the elite Rabineau, Wachter and Sanford Literary Agency, which specializes in selling books that will be adapted into movies, has this to say on the subject: "In my experience, it's very difficult to get attention for a manuscript without a publishing deal." She adds, "It's unlikely that a manuscript or proposal would even get read."

If your agent doesn't have a connection to a Hollywood agent and you think your idea has silver-screen potential, you need to find your own representation. Be forewarned that the gates to Tinseltown are even more heavily guarded than those to publishing. Head back to the land of research and amass a list of appropriate Hollywood agents. Then ask your book agent

It's important to remember that in life just about everything is negotiable. If any part of an agreement is confusing or simply feels wrong, be sure to ask if it can be eliminated or changed. If this is not possible, make sure you're satisfied with the agent's explanation of why it's in the contract.

If the agent doesn't make you sign a contract and you're comfortable working this way, that's fine. It's much easier to walk away from this type of deal. But protect yourself by getting a signed letter stating how much commission the agency will take on your advance, royalties and sub rights so that there are no surprises down the road.

Contract Red Flags

Most agency contracts are straightforward and harmless. A few are not. Here are the main red flags to look out for:

1. An agent who charges a fee for his services. Most agents charge for their out-of-pocket expenses, but no one should charge "development" or "reading" fees. If someone proposes this to you, don't walk away. Run.

to contact these agents directly. Your book agent is much more likely than you are to get a response from these muckety-mucks.

If you don't have an agent but you're sure you've got a mega-movie on your hands, you can try to query Hollywood agents directly. But don't waste your time approaching studios and production companies unless you have a referral. Legally, the studios and most production companies can't even look at unsolicited manuscripts. What you can do is track down independent filmmakers who are just starting out and see if you can collaborate on a short film or a trailer. You can enter your short film in film festivals and market it on the web. Submit it for a short movie Oscar. It's a crazy long shot and takes two tons of work. But then again, so does the rest of this stuff, and it's so easy to find filmmakers these days. Shake a tree on YouTube and a million videographers fall out.

Yet another way to reach Hollywood is through scouts. These middlemen do just what their name suggests: scout out material for studios and production companies, or, in the case of international scouts, for foreign book publishers. Scouts are listed in *Literary Market Place* (LMP), a great resource guide for all things publishing. (Find a copy at your local library.) If you can convince a scout that you've got a hot Hollywood property, you're in luck—she'll be able to get it into the hands of people who, in all likelihood, you could never get on the phone.

2. A contract that locks you in for a set amount of time and doesn't allow you to leave. Either party should be able to walk away with 30 days' notice.

3. A contract that locks your next book up with that agent (also known as an "option book"). You should be free to work with any agent you choose on your next book without having to pay a commission to the first agent.

Knowing that some agents try to take advantage in their contracts, many writers wonder whether they need a lawyer to look everything over. If you happen to have access to an affordable and competent lawyer who specializes in publishing law, it certainly can't hurt. But if hiring a lawyer means spending money you don't have or don't want to part with, then we don't recommend it. There are two reasons: 1) Most lawyers don't have publishing experience, so they end up asking for pie-in-the-sky clauses, and 2) No reputable agent will put pie-in-the-sky clauses into their contracts. So you may end up spending an arm, a leg and half a lung for nothing.

What's Next?

If, by the end of this chapter, you've found your agent match, please proceed to the next chapter to learn all about how to work with your agent and navigate the shark-infested waters of submission.

If you've decided to pursue a small or university press, walk straight ahead to page 151. If you've decided to take the self-publishing route, skip to Chapter 11, but please go back and read Chapter 9. Much of the information covered there will apply to you as well.

CHAPTER 5

Demystifying Submission

"If you have built castles in the air,
your work need not be lost, that is where
they should be. Now put foundations
under them."

—*Henry David Thoreau*

MICHAEL POWELL, FOUNDER OF the legendary Powell's Books in Portland, Oregon, says, "I believe nearly every book that deserves to be published gets published." We believe him. Now more than ever.

If you've signed with an agent, the submission period will involve working with her to hone your proposal or manuscript; if you have a proposal that's all set to go, you'll be setting up a strategy for the submission and sale of your work. In short, it's go time. Which also means this is the period when the honeymoon with your agent sometimes ends. Gird yourself. There are sure to be rocky roads ahead.

Agent Relations: Snarling Snafus and Scary Silences

Now that you and your agent have moved from courtship into a meaningful relationship, you need to get your proposal or manuscript submission-ready. Whether the agent is an attentive, caring hand-holder or an unavailable, self-centered knuckle-rapper, there are four major areas that can make or break your relationship.

Sweet Appreciation

We've talked about how agents get so little professional love from anyone outside publishing (or in it, for that matter). Consequently, those precious few drops of appreciation from you can go a long way. Most of us don't do nearly enough appreciating in our lives, but here's a circumstance where there's a direct correlation between sincere appreciation shown and benefits reaped. A lot of writers don't even quite know what their agents do, so naturally they don't know what to thank them for. Here's a list of potential thank-yous:

- *"I know how busy you are. Thanks for getting back to me."* Many writers labor under the mistaken impression that they're the only clients in their agent's stable. Clients who act annoyed if their agent doesn't get back to them immediately make the agent never *want* to get back to them. Appreciation beats annoyance in any agent's eyes.

- *"I know how busy you are. Thanks for reading my material."* What you may not realize is that reading material carefully takes a long time and requires much concentration. Just one novel can take hours and hours to read. Even just skimming a proposal or manuscript takes time. Agents are on the phone all day, which means they have to read at night and on the weekends, when they'd rather be having a life.

- *"I know how busy you are. Thanks for your thoughtful comments."* Ditto above. Thoughtful comments are not dropped off by the Thoughtful Comment Fairy. They take a long time to develop and don't take kindly to the phone ringing off the hook.

- *"Thanks for taking the time to explain the process."* Assume that most agents have at least 25 clients (and many have 50 or more). Assume that at least half these clients are first-time authors. That's a lot of time spent explaining the ins and outs of the business and answering questions. If you and every other first-time author the agent represents ask half an hour's worth of questions a week, that's at least six hours total—almost a whole day per week.

Great Expectations

Unless you're not quite human, you have expectations about what will happen to your proposal or manuscript. Your agent will drop everything as soon as your proposal or manuscript comes in, give you brilliant notes immediately, sell your book to a great editor at a great publishing house, then sell the film rights, the foreign rights, the audio rights and on and on.

Go ahead and dream. Part of the fun of this whole process is imagining best-seller lists, a translation into Croatian and a Pulitzer Prize. However, it is your duty to manage your great expectations and not dump them all over your agent. Making your agent into a beast of burden is one of the quickest and easiest ways to alienate her.

Expectations often do not reflect reality, which is why, at the beginning of your relationship, it's a good thing to ask your agent which of your particular expectations are legitimate and which are poppycock. For instance, are you expecting daily, weekly, monthly check-in calls from your agent? Are you expecting a return call within the hour, the week, the decade? Are you expecting the agent to read and respond to your 500-page manuscript within 24, 48, 100,000 hours?

As these numbers illustrate, some people's expectations are simply unmeetable. If you find out at the beginning of the submission process exactly what your agent can and cannot do for you, then you can adjust your expectations accordingly. Ultimately, this is all about . . .

Maximizing Communication

Over and over, we hear writers say: "I'm so scared of my agent, I avoid calling whenever possible." They haven't learned that lack of communication equals bad news for their book. Good agent-client relationships are made up of honest, thoughtful, reasonable, respectful communication, with a dash of humor thrown in to lighten the load. But, again, try to keep it short. The more you respect the agent's time, expertise and effort, and the better you articulate what you want and need, the more you increase your book's chances of getting out into the world successfully. An agent who genuinely enjoys working with you is sure to be a better salesperson for your book.

Many writers and authors feel so lucky to have found an agent that they're afraid to stand up in the boat, let alone rock it. As a result, when they do have a legitimate problem or just a series of reasonable questions, they tend to err on the side of mum. Regardless, here's an important rule of communication: *Ask.* Compile your list of questions carefully and make sure you catch your agent at a moment when she's not crazy with the heat. How do you know? Same rule: *Ask.*

On the other end of the bell curve are complainers who are never pleased, no matter what their agents do. They demand constant attention with useless, irrelevant, I'm-talking-just-to-hear-myself-speak questions and comments. Agent-wise, we strongly advise against nagging . . . unless you want to see your book buried under a massive stack of manuscripts in your agent's office.

▶ Especially when you're starting out in publishing, it's often better to admit you know nothing, even if you know something, than to pretend you know everything when you don't know anything at all. Temper your cluelessness with a dose of humility. Preface a question with "Excuse my ignorance, but" and you'll most likely get a thorough, plain-English explanation.

Many people assume all sorts of outlandish scenarios about why their agent hasn't called them. They get sucked into the ass/u/me vortex, wherein assuming makes Asses out of U and Me. If you're sensing a problem or you're simply in the dark on an issue, what do you do? *Ask.*

DO: "Is this is a good time to talk?"
DON'T: "I need to talk to you right now."

DO: "Am I calling too much?"
DON'T: "Why haven't you returned any of my calls?"

DO: "Have I overwhelmed you with material?"
DON'T: "It's been three weeks since I gave you my material, and I haven't heard a thing."

DO: "Have you lost interest in this project?"
DON'T: "I'm taking your malicious indifference to mean you hate me."

Bottom line: It's much better to know where you stand (and to move on, if necessary) than to stew in your own juices, or worry yourself sick, or any scenario that makes you feel like the loser of the universe.

If you've done all the asking you can do and you're still confused, unsure or disheartened, it might be time to tell your agent how you feel—if you can do it without attacking.

DO: "I know you're busy, so please let me know the best way for us to communicate."

DO: "I feel that I haven't edited my material enough, but I'm unsure what to do. Please let me know if I'm asking for too much help."

DO: "I feel that you've lost interest in this project. I'd rather know now if that's the case, so please be up front with me."

Yes, of course, problems will come up and things will not go as planned. No matter how much you prepare for every contingency, you will be unprepared. But at least, if you've asked all you can ask and you've said how you feel, you'll know you've given 110%. Which is, in the end, all a person can do.

The Saddest Scenario: When Your Material Never Gets Sent Out

A n alarming number of authors sign with agents who never send their work out. Or never say they've sent their work out. This maddening situation is often revealed when you call your agent several times over the course of, say, a month and you get no return phone call, no email, no timeline and no editorial feedback. But this can also take place even when an agent has exhibited all the telltale signs of enthusiasm: warm handshakes; nice words about your work; kind, quickly returned emails.

What gives? For one thing, in almost all such situations, the author, out of fear, ignorance or a combination thereof, has never called the agent to follow up. Big mistake. Imagine entrusting a baby-sitter with your newborn only to find out she sat in front of the TV all day and left the baby wet and crying in the crib. Wouldn't you say something? Of course you would! Well, you put a ton of time and love into creating your baby of a book, so don't let it languish in dirty diapers! Speak up. The book you save may be your own.

The Dangers of Being an Affirmation Junkie

If you're a self-assured, well-balanced, healthy-egoed person, you can skip this section altogether. If you're like the rest of us, you'll want to read this advice more than once. (And perhaps consider needlepointing it for posterity's sake.)

It's natural to want your agent to affirm the value of your project, your talent . . . you. And a lot of agents are very good at supporting their clients and providing positive, encouraging feedback. But a lot simply don't have these skills or are utterly uninterested in anything that smacks of cheerleaderism. Either way, you'll be better served by looking for your affirmation elsewhere.

An agent doesn't have to be warm and cuddly to sell a book. In some cases, a cold and prickly agent can get more money and make better deals. Don't let your emotional needs overcome your business savvy. If you have an agent who's stand-offish but does a great job selling your book to a reputable publisher, count your lucky stars!

"I WANNA HOLD YOUR HAND"

Defined by the OED as "giving close guidance or moral support," hand-holding is only one step beyond standard affirmation—but above and beyond the agent's call of duty. Many agents will do some hand-holding, but frankly it's an unreasonable expectation. You should expect expert advice on all things related

139

to the publishing of your book. You should hope to receive positive feedback on good work well done. But a desire for more than that is a symptom of neediness—a dangerous country to be from. If you inhabit it for too long, your agent may break off all diplomatic relations with you and sometimes even declare war.

Same-Paging

Your agent may let you know at the outset that your project needs minor or major fixes. But sometimes an agent will tell you nothing but how great your work is until after she's signed you. Then she'll tell you everything that's wrong with your manuscript. Don't be surprised if you start to feel that what was once Enthusiasm Central has become Reservation City. This change in attitude might get your antennae twitching, but don't assume the worst. Your agent might have signed you up without carefully reading your proposal (this happens). So, when she told you that you needed to do very little work, she may not have been dishonest, just not fully informed.

Whether or not your agent was up front about the amount of work you needed to do, you'll now want to be sure that you're both on the same page editorially. This means getting the clearest set of directions possible. Start with a conversation. Take notes. Ask questions—even the ones that seem utterly obvious:

- What specifically did you like about my material?
- What specifically stood out in it? What did you find particularly strong?
- What did you feel were the problems?
- Are there specific sections that you feel need strengthening?
- Is there anything that you feel should be added?
- Is there anything else I need to do to make my material ready to sell?
- Do you have the time to mark up my material so I can see exactly what you're talking about?

If you're preparing to submit an illustrated book, ask your agent a few additional questions:

- Do I need sample spreads?
- If so, what quality and format should they be?
- Do I need to make changes on my existing spreads?
- How many copies should I print?

Alan Burns, co-creator of *The Mary Tyler Moore Show*, was once told by an executive that his script needed to be "40% funnier." This kind of generic criticism is useless. Find out specifically what you need to do to make your manuscript as great as it can be. If you've written a humor book and your agent tells you that the story on page 7 isn't funny, find out what in particular isn't funny about it. A sense of humor is, of course, incredibly subjective, but a trained professional can often dissect and deconstruct a piece of humor so that it's clear that the punch line is in the wrong place or the butt of the joke is actually the tail wagging the dog. And even if you don't agree with a piece of criticism, it can sometimes clarify in your own mind exactly what you wanted to say.

If your agent can email or send you an edited, marked-up copy of your proposal or manuscript, all the better. But we still encourage a conversation, because a marked-up submission won't necessarily reveal more general concerns. And the agent may not have taken the time to tell you what she liked best about your work, which is just as important as what she didn't like.

Lastly, you may want to ask your agent if she thinks you can get the job done in one more draft or if it's going to take a number of passes. Some agents will go back and forth on a proposal numerous times. Liz Perle, author of *When Work Doesn't Work Anymore* and a former editor and publisher herself, says, "My agent was really tough on my proposal. I think I redid it 20 times. Sometimes I didn't agree with him, though, and I had to balance what he thought would sell with what I wanted to write." Those 20 drafts resulted in a terrific sale. So if you do end up having to do a lot more work, consider yourself lucky to have a professional paying such close attention to your writing.

Having a sense of how far you are from a finished proposal or manuscript will keep your expectations in check and your frustrations at bay. If you know early on that it's going to go back and forth between the two of you for a few drafts, it's a lot easier to bear. And, as Liz Perle made clear, you have to maintain your own core convictions about your work and communicate any discomfort you may have with your agent regarding dubious changes.

▶ If you know you need a minimum dollar amount in order to write your book, figure out what that is BEFORE you or your agent goes out to sell it. Calculate costs for your time, permissions and illustrations, travel and research. What you want is the bare-bones-honest-to-goodness-bottom-line-minimum amount, not what you fantasize about in your dreams or what you think your agent should ask for. Then communicate this number to your agent. Daniel Greenberg of the Levine Greenberg Rostan Literary Agency says, "Trust me, agents eat off their 15%. They have every incentive in the world to get as much money as possible. You don't need to re-incentivize them."

141

Sending Your Brave Little Book Out into the World

The actual submission process produces excitement and anxiety in equal measure. Will my book sell? To whom? How fast? For how much? Or . . . will it never sell at all? All these questions are on every author's mind. Unfortunately, no one can tell you if your book will sell. But perhaps we can help you get enough clarity to quell some of your agita.

Who Will See Your Book?

Agents submit proposals or manuscripts to editors within a publishing house, or to the publisher himself. Submitting your book to the right editor is key to selling a book, just as submitting your query to the right agent is crucial to landing representation. There is an art to putting together a most excellent submission list—often comprising editors who either specialize in or have a deep personal interest in your subject—and it certainly helps if your agent knows the editors personally. Good agents spend countless hours having lunches and sipping drinks with editors, getting to know their likes, dislikes and personal passions, so that when it comes time to submit your proposal they know just who to send it to.

Within each publishing fiefdom, most editors stake out territories. So while there may be numerous nonfiction editors within a house, there will probably be only a couple who patrol the science provinces, another couple who rule the roost of health, and one or two who command the kingdom of cookbooks. But knowing what these editors specialize in is not enough. If you've written a medical book about breast cancer, say, you want your agent to send it not only to one of the health editors, but also to the one whose mother is a breast cancer survivor.

The More the Merrier?

Sometimes an agent will get a project that is simply perfect for one particular editor, who just happens to work at the perfect publishing house for your book. Sometimes an agent will be unsure about a project. In either situation, the agent may send the proposal or manuscript on an exclusive to one person. In the first case, she believes she has a good shot at a fast and/or high-priced sale. In the second, she's testing the waters, seeing if she needs you to continue working on your proposal or manuscript—seeing if she has the right bait and she's casting in the right river.

An agent may also submit on a not-quite-exclusive basis to a few editors. Maybe she thinks three people feel like particularly good fits. Or maybe she wants a few professional opinions on the commercial value of your work.

At the other end of the spectrum, your agent may go hog-wild and do a large multiple submission, which can mean sending your book to anywhere between 15 and 30 editors. This allows a much wider range of opinions on how big a market there is for your book and can possibly create more competition for it. More Peters, more Pauls, maybe even a few Marys.

Big and small submissions have their pluses and minuses. Small allows you to learn from editors who reject your proposal (in the event that they offer comments). You won't have burned every bridge, so you'll have the leeway to make changes to your proposal and resubmit to a new pool of editors. And since exclusives are given for anywhere from a day to a couple of weeks, they can also make an editor act fast. On the minus side, submitting to one editor at a time can take *forever*. The waiting can get painful. But probably the chief disadvantage is that you can't create a competitive environment. If you accept an offer from an exclusive, you never know how much money you may have left on the table. (Then again, you might get someone to put all his chips on the table in order to take your book off it.) Large submissions allow for maximum competition and

A Cornucopia of Conglomerates

Your agent may be sending your book out to 30 editors but only 5 publishers. How, you may ask, can this be? These days, every big publishing house is owned by a larger company whose holdings go beyond books. Many of these companies have bought up numerous other publishing houses and umbrella'd them under one huge roof. Penguin and Random House merged in 2013 creating the largest publisher in the business. Owned by multinationals Pearson and Bertelsmann, Penguin Random House contains, among others, Crown, Knopf, Doubleday, Putnam and Dutton. These are now called imprints, even though they all started out as individual publishers.

Your book can be simultaneously submitted to several different divisions and imprints within the same company. In fact, the practice can be key to getting a bidding war going. Exciting stuff, but also really tricky. Some publishing houses let their different divisions/imprints bid against each other; others do not. For example, if your agent holds an auction, Random House allows for competing bids within its walls as long as one outside house is part of the auction as well; Penguin does not allow for competing bids. But don't worry your pretty little head about such things. That's what your agent is for!

can drive up the price of a book; but if it turns out your proposal/manuscript has problems that you and your agent did not see, you may come up with a fix only to find that you have no place left to go.

Your Agent Pitches and Fires

Your agent has your completed proposal or manuscript. She's made a submission list of editors who she thinks will be hungry for your book. She then writes a cover letter with her version of your trusty old pitch. She might also call and pitch editors over the phone. Or some combination of the two.

Your agent will then send or email out your proposal or manuscript. Overnight delivery or messengering can be cost-heavy, and typically you'll have to reimburse your agent for the expense. We think it's worth every penny since it makes your work feel urgent and important. Ask your agent how she's sending out your book; if you can afford it, see if she will same-day or overnight it.

The Agony and Ecstasy of "Interest"

Y ou open your inbox. There's a message from your agent. A publisher is interested in your book.

Take a minute to rejoice. But don't start spending your future advance. An excruciating amount of time may go by before an offer is made. The interested publisher may want to meet with you. Then you may receive so much inconsistent feedback that your head will spin. And, sadly, sometimes interest does not

How to Help Your Agent During Submission

In Chapter 4, we had you look at *Publishers Weekly* and publishersmarketplace.com, as well as the acknowledgments of books similar to (but not directly competitive with) yours, for the names of editors and agents who might be interested in what you're writing. We asked you to put the editor names aside for later. That later is now. While agents should have their fingers on the publishing pulse, they can't know what absolutely everyone is up to. Revisit your editor list and gently pass on the names to your agent. You might have a few suggestions that your agent hasn't thought of; besides, it's good for your agent to know which editors' books you admire. Just as you used information about books your agent represented to gain her interest, so your agent can do the same with editors, who will love to hear that you're a fan of a book they've sweated over.

result in a sale. But steel your resolve and gird your loins, because this is where the real fun begins. . . .

Face Time with Your Potential Publisher

Once there's interest in your project, meeting with publishing teams—from potential editor to publicity people, marketing and sales, sometimes all the way up to the publisher—may serve you well. Indeed, some agents, eager to have you meet with editors, may ask you to arrange a trip in conjunction with the submission of your proposal. If you can afford the travel, it's probably worth your while: Face time can make a sale.

It's not just about you convincing a potential editor and publisher of the value of your book, though. It's equally important that you check out a potential editor and publisher to see if you think they're the right match. The editor is like a parent to your project. Imagine that you got the chance to pick your own mom and dad. Would you really choose not to meet them before you made a decision? Madness! So we suggest trying to look your future editor and publishing team square in the eyes, shake their hands and get a good measure of them. Even if you don't get to choose your editor in the end, take notes on everyone. The information you gather in these meetings can help you later on. You can often pick up on what kinds of hesitations a publisher has about your book or you. Address these early and you'll be better off.

If you have a good rapport with your agent, it's great if she can come with you. She can be just the social lubricant needed to ease you into an informative and lucrative meeting.

. . . OR EAR TO EAR WITH YOUR POTENTIAL PUBLISHER

If, after careful consideration, you feel you may not be physically, financially, emotionally, verbally, mentally and/or sartorially equipped to sell yourself and your book to a roomful of hardened publishing pundits, don't ignore your instincts. As Kathy Pories, an editor at Algonquin, puts it, "When we're trying to decide whether to publish a book, the personality of the author is a factor. How will he present himself to the world?" Discuss any doubts about your performance potential with your agent before she starts contacting editors about a meeting. If you're not a presentation-friendly author, you can actually cause more damage than good. But even if, for whatever reason, a face-to-face meeting is a no-go, there's no reason to rule out a phone call—or better yet, a conference call with your agent on the line as well. This way, if you're presentation-phobic, you don't have to worry about pitching to a room full of people, but you still get to check out your potential editor, get a sense of her take on the project and ask any questions you may have.

Same goes if you can't afford to take the trip or the publisher isn't offering up any meeting times. Truth is, these days most books are sold without the author meeting the publisher. P.S. If a publisher buys your book, you'll have plenty of time to improve your presentation skills—if necessary—before you're called upon to help promote it.

"WHAT SHOULD I WEAR?"

Before you meet with a prospective publisher or editor, it's prudent to properly prepare. On the fashion front, follow this easy rule of thumb: Wear what you would wear if you were going on your favorite TV talk show. And if you even suspect that you're fashion-challenged, do yourself a favor and get some help. Unless your book is some glam-fest, always go for elegant over flashy. And be sure to wear an outfit that makes you feel comfortable. You don't want to be fidgeting with a too-short skirt or fussing with an uncomfortable necktie. If you have any doubts, ask your agent for advice.

WORKING THE ROOM

Successfully working a room is an art. You want to be energized but relaxed, a good talker *and* a good listener, confident but not cocky, intuitive and well prepared, eager but not pushy, funny but not shticky. And whatever you do, no matter what you say, display your passion. Remember, passion is contagious. Agents often see on-the-fence publishers get won over by the strength of an author's passion.

▶ Get a card from every single person you meet at the publisher's—not just the editor, but the publicity, marketing and sales people. Immediately after you do your rounds, send thank-you notes. Then squirrel these cards away in a safe place so you can take them out and nibble on them later.

Have your pitch down stone-cold. This way, you'll be able to deliver it with an energetic yet conversational ease. You want an editor to be able to hum your pitch as he leaves the office. Make sure it's a catchy tune—easy to recall, and totally you.

Remember, though, that you also need to make an informed decision about who is the best publisher for you—this isn't just a dog-and-pony show. Take the opportunity to gather as much information as possible. Have good questions prepared in advance. The editor/publisher will likely run the meeting, but it may benefit you to take the driver's

Performers One and All

Nowadays, authors are expected to be able to present themselves and their ideas publicly. At live events, at bookstores, in libraries. And, if they're lucky, on radio and television. Agents and publishers are looking for authors who know how to sparkle. Problem is, many authors prefer the solitude of their writing room and long to remain out of the glare of the bright white spotlight.

Whether you're a shooting star or shrinking wallflower, it behooves you to work on your performance skills. In fact, being able to present in front of people can mean the difference between rejection and a six-figure deal.

Cathy Rose Salit, the CEO of Performance of a Lifetime, helps bring transformational change via performance skills to everyone from Fortune 500 executives to inner-city teenagers to New York City cops. She is also the author of a forthcoming book called *Doing Things When You Don't Know How: The Breakthrough Approach to Enhancing Your Performance at Work and in Life.*

When Cathy's agent got her meetings at several big New York publishers, all she had to do was close the deal. No pressure! Cathy and her agent worked hard to come up with a performance plan. She had never pitched a book before and felt nervous about the prospect. That's why she rehearsed, tweaked and polished until she felt that her presentation shined. Then she put on her best author-going-to-a-publishing-meeting "costume" and performed like a relaxed, confident first-time author with a valuable book proposal. The performance was a convincing one. She got not one, but three six-figure offers.

"We are all performers," Cathy says. "But we often get stuck in performances we've been doing our whole lives. If you're not a comfortable presenter, it's helpful to try new and different performances than the ones you've done in the past. These can be done with your writing group, colleagues, agent or even just by looking in a mirror."

seat, at least part of the time. Julia Fox Garrison, bestselling author of *Don't Leave Me This Way,* says of her meetings with publishers, "I was very clear: I was interviewing them, not the other way around."

Below is a starter list of questions to ask an editor, but, of course, it's imperative that you come up with queries that are appropriate to your particular project.

▶ Will you be speaking to your editor over the phone instead of in person? All the information in this section still holds!

■ What other books have you published that are similar to mine? Have these been successful? Why or why not?

■ What changes do you foresee in the content or direction of my book?

■ What are the weak points in my proposal/manuscript, and how would you fix them?

■ What are the strong points in my proposal/manuscript, and how can I improve on them?

■ What kind of publicity/marketing plan do you envision for my book?

■ What kind of publicity/marketing have you done for similar books?

■ How do you like to work? Do you prefer to receive a complete manuscript or to get several chapters at a time?

■ When do you see my book coming out, and why?

Listen. Aggressively focus in on what the editor has to say. Take notes.

How Long Must You Wait?

Of all the excruciating waiting you'll endure in the publishing business, the period between submission and offer (or rejection) is most likely to make you feel like a pregnant woman who's three weeks overdue. Prepare yourself, because this so-close-yet-so-far waiting can be brutal. Sure, your book could sell super quick. Within a week or two, you could have a publisher and—take a breath—a delivery date! But even if you find yourself a month or even six months into a submission, it doesn't mean that your book won't sell.

▶ Can't get a clear answer from your agent about when she sent your proposal out? Ask for copies of her cover letters for your files. This way, you can track how long your work has been out in the world.

So what should you do to quell the waiting willies? Many authors believe their best course of action is to call their agent every hour on the hour to get a progress report. We advise that you NEVER do this. One of the greatest calls an agent ever gets to make is the one that starts: "Hello, I got an offer on your book." Trust us, as soon as your agent has good news, you'll be the first to know. If, after a few weeks, you haven't heard anything, it's okay to send an email saying, "Any news?" Then, please, do yourself a favor and leave it at that. You can do this every few weeks. If any rejection letters have crawled like sniveling pigdogs into your agent's office, ask for copies. They may prove helpful later. If, after a few months, there's not a bite, it's time to have a conversation with your agent. Ask her what she thinks isn't working. Is there any consistent feedback? Should you start reworking your proposal or manuscript? Also ask if she's gotten any positive feedback and what exactly it is. You want to be sure not to eliminate anything that editors actually liked.

I LOVE IT! I HATE IT!

It couldn't be more common: two smart, successful editors with opposite opinions of your work. At Arielle's agency, there's a story that's become a favorite office joke. James Levine sent out a proposal that he was tremendously excited about. The first call came in, and the editor said, "Jim, the writing here is marvelous, but I just don't think there's an audience for this idea." Then the second call came in, and the editor said, "Jim, the idea here is terrific, and there's clearly a huge audience, but the writing isn't strong enough." Crazy-making? Absolutely. Unique? Absolutely not. The only thing you can do is learn what you can and move on. Incidentally, Jim ultimately sold the book for three-quarters of a million dollars and then promptly sold the film rights for half a million more.

FIRING BLANKS

If your agent doesn't get a bite on the first round, it's important to re-express your appreciation of all he's put into the project thus far. Remember, your agent has been working for free up to this point. He doesn't make a cent until you do.

If you sense that your agent is rapidly losing interest in you and your project, it's important to ask up front if he plans to cut bait or try to do some more fishing. If he says he's willing to continue but you hear some serious waffle in his voice, you have several options: 1) You can approach smaller publishers on your own. 2) You can try to find another agent (recommended only if you've had a nightmare experience thus far with your own). 3) You can, in addition to expressing your sincere appreciation, ask your agent what you can do to improve your proposal/manuscript to make it salable. Do not count on much agent participation at this particular point in the process. Once an agent has received a lot of rejections on a project, its luster can fade. Unless he has an undying passion for you or your work, it will be difficult for him to call up the same enthusiasm he brought to begin with (assuming he ever brought any!). But lack of agent participation doesn't mean all hope is lost. A little of the right advice can sometimes fix your ship. Maybe your agent can suggest a book doctor or editor if the rejections you've received have to do with editorial problems. (You might also want to jump ahead and read our next chapter about making the most of rejection.)

If your agent agrees to cast out his line again, find out his submission strategy. Are there divisions of the bigger houses that haven't seen your work yet? Independent publishers who pay less money but are very good at what they do?

If, on the other hand, your agent tells you he's not sending your work elsewhere, reassess. Once your book has been submitted by an agent and remains unsold, it can be very difficult to find another agent unless your first agent did a very small submission or has a reputation as a loose cannon or an idiot. If you do decide to change seahorses midstream, be sure you know exactly who your book was submitted to (get copies of all letters, both submission and rejection) and ask your agent for suggestions about who you should submit to on your own. Maybe he can give you a list of small publishers who would be appropriate for your book. Ask if he knows any editors at these houses. And ask if he'd be willing to negotiate the deal with a smaller publisher if you get an offer from one. If you decide to fish in a smaller pond, see the directions that follow for submitting your book on your own.

Sweet Victory

We first met Ayesha Mattu and Nura Maznavi at our Pitchapalooza during San Francisco's legendary literary festival, Litquake. Lots of great writers pitched lots of great books that night. But when Nura pitched their anthology about the love lives of Muslim American women, we were blown away. Here's a taste of that awesome pitch: "Everyone seems to have an opinion about Muslim women, even (especially!) those who have never met one. We thought it was about time you heard directly from Muslim women themselves." The book was so timely, so valuable, so necessary. Nura was so full of life, so passionate, so funny, so smart.

It turned out Nura and Ayesha had been working on the book for a long time. They'd even had an agent at one point. But when their agent sent the book out, all they heard back was no. They received lots of nice accolades but also lots of comments that essentially said there was no audience for a book like theirs. Big publishing is, unfortunately, a very white, very Manhattan-centric business. If you're out of the orbit, the assumption is, your book won't sell.

With all the rejections, their agent lost interest. But Nura and Ayesha weren't ready to give up. They were on the lookout for opportunities to make their book a reality when they saw that Pitchapalooza was coming to town.

Nura and Ayesha went on to win Pitchapalooza, but they still had a lot of work to do. We review every winner's proposal so we can introduce him or her to an agent or editor. After taking

Sending Your Book Directly to Publishers

If you've decided to submit directly to publishers, you're going to have your best shot at smaller, independent houses. Some independent presses are mom-and-pop operations and have published only a few books. Some are presses that specialize in niche subjects and tend to be small like their mom-and-pop brothers and sisters. In the publishing industry, a "small press" is defined as one that publishes fewer than 12 titles per year.

Not all independent publishers are small. The category includes university presses, midsize presses and a number of stars in the industry, including Chronicle Books, the top gift book publisher in the industry; W.W. Norton, known far and wide for its anthologies; and Workman, the publisher of this very book. As Richard Eoin Nash, former publisher of Soft Skull Press (a hip, edgy independent with a great reputation) and founder of the independent publishing

a look, we realized another reason why they were getting so many nos. The proposal was stiff and formal, almost academic. It had none of the life and sass we saw in Nura when she was up onstage. We helped them capture this energy on the page and beef up their publicity and marketing section, which was weak.

Once they made these changes, we sent their proposal off to Laura Mazer of Soft Skull Press, a fantastic publisher whose mission is to take readers into worlds that they know little about. As we suspected, Laura fell in love with the proposal, and a week later Nura and Ayesha had a book contract. Lo and behold, their pitch became a book. *Love, InshAllah: The Secret Love Lives of American Muslim Women* was featured in *The New York Times,* and they sold out of the first printing before the book was even released. Nura and Ayesha went on a multicity tour, and *every* venue was packed to the gills (no audience, eh?!). In fact, the book was so successful that they published a sequel, *Salaam, Love: American Muslim Men on Love, Sex, and Intimacy.*

Heed the advice of Ayesha: "Look for any and all opportunities. If you have something important to say, you can't give up. The road to publication can be a very long and arduous process, but the reward of connecting to your audience makes the Herculean effort worthwhile."

platform Cursor, says, "To simplify, at the moment there are two types of independent publishers: One is still looking to make direct contact with writers and readers, through word of mouth and online, of course. The second has already established a reputation to such an extent that now the better agents send them potential projects as well."

Stacks of bestsellers and tons of bestselling authors have been published by independents. Tom Clancy's *The Hunt for Red October* was first published by the Naval Institute Press. *Chicken Soup for the Soul* and its dozens and dozens of offshoots are ladled into the world by Health Communications, an independent press operating out of Deerfield Beach, Florida. And it's not a fluke that these books became bestsellers. Independent publishers may be small, but they're not necessarily run like small businesses. In fact, independent publishing is a multibillion-dollar industry.

Why to Consider Working with an Independent Publisher

These days, many writers prefer independent publishers to the big guys. Here are some of the best reasons you should seriously consider working with an independent:

- *Special love, tender care.* Independent presses are likely to give you more personal attention than a publishing behemoth and to view you as a valued player during each step of the publishing process. Many independent publishers are looking for long-term relationships that help to build writers' careers.

- *Big-time front-list attention.* Let's say your book is published by a division of Random House. The chances of its being one of the few new books that are given the most attention are slim, even if the publisher paid a nice chunk of change for it. So when it's time to publicize and market your book, you may be sadly disappointed over the amount of attention it receives. Because independent publishers are dealing with smaller lists of books, your book has a chance to get some front-list enthusiasm and attention, which can go a long way even if resources may be limited.

- *Long shelf life.* Because they usually publish far fewer books than the big boys, independent publishers do their darndest to keep each book alive for the long haul even if it hasn't had killer sales right out of the gate. You can't underestimate the importance of continued attention. There's nothing more frustrating, heartbreaking and revenue-reducing than putting your passion into print, only to have it languish sadly on remainder tables a year later. Also, you never know when your book will suddenly become relevant. A major worldwide event or your relentless promoting could bring your book into the spotlight and turn it into an "instant" bestseller. But if the book is out of print, you'll be out of luck.

- *Specialization.* Most independent publishers specialize in a particular area. Guess what Motor Books publishes? What about Travelers' Tales? Or Collector Books? Specialized publishers know how to get your book into the hands of your audience. They're chummy with the media people who cover your subject, and they sell into non-bookstore venues that specialize in your area. They know how to get sports books into stadiums, cookbooks into kitchen stores and dog books into pet stores. And many know or are learning how to use social media to go directly to their audiences. Less than a third of books published by independent presses end up in bookstores, precisely because they bypass the general market and sell directly to their sweet niche audiences.

▶ Scared an independent press won't lend your book the credibility it deserves? Think bookstores and reviewers may pooh-pooh your book? Our research indicates that when a title is being considered, the size of the press doesn't matter as much as its reputation. So, if prestige is a concern, look out for the publisher's name in the chains and in your local independent bookstore. Track down reviews and news stories on the publisher's books to ensure that major media outlets pay attention to its offerings.

Why Not to Consider Working with an Independent Publisher

As compelling as the reasons might be for going with an independent publisher, here are the major downsides:

- *Smaller advances.* Independent publishers generally pay less money than the big conglomerates for advances (in the $1,000–$3,000 range), if indeed they pay any at all. While some occasionally pay five- or even six-figures up-front, you are more than likely going to make your money on royalties, which will only accrue once your book is out in the marketplace.

- *Lower royalties.* Standard royalty rates for independent presses run about 10% of net (this is approximately 5% of the cover price). Most major publishers start their royalties at 7.5% of the cover price for paperbacks and 10% for hardcovers. This lower royalty is due not to greed on the part of independent publishers, but rather to the reality that most don't have in-house sales representatives and/or the ability to fulfill orders (many small presses don't have warehouses to stock and ship their books). This means they have to pay extra fees to get their books distributed to bookstores and other retail venues.

- *Small to nonexistent marketing budgets.* A big publisher who gets behind your book might sink thousands of dollars into marketing and publicizing it. That kind of spending power isn't even a remote fantasy with the majority of independent publishers.

- *Potential sales and distribution problems.* Most smaller publishers contract with larger publishers or specialized distribution companies to handle

Going with an Independent Publisher: The Good and the Bad

S hawna Kenney is the author of *I Was a Teenage Dominatrix*, about her very interesting after-school job. If you're conjuring up an image of a mean lady who inspires terror in everyone she meets, you'd be describing Shawna's exact opposite. Shawna is a sweet, warm, inviting person who promotes relentlessly and loves working with a team. That's why going with a respected, midsize independent publisher made sense for her. According to Shawna: "My publisher allowed me complete artistic freedom in choosing a cover. . . . I know their sales people and can call or stop by whenever I like." She also liked their extremely equitable contract and how they continued to feature her book in their catalog well after publication.

Not to say that her experience was flaw-free. Shawna says, "Due to their small size and a more laissez-faire attitude than the majors, I learned that sometimes things run well behind schedule. For example, my book was reprinted almost six months later than the date stipulated in the contract, due to the owner's illness." She also was left to handle most publicity and marketing on her own. Fortunately for Shawna, she's a PR whiz, so the lack of backup was something she learned to live with. And her experience overall was exceedingly pleasing. The book was very well received critically and has been optioned for a Hollywood movie, and well-attended events all over the country attest to her growing fan base.

selling and fulfillment, i.e., order processing and shipping. A distributor normally handles all sales to all trade accounts, including national chains such as Barnes & Noble, Target and Walmart as well as independent bookstores and Internet retailers. But some very small publishers don't have the resources or a strong enough list to be represented by an outside sales and/or distribution company. Instead, they have to rely on local sales, web sales and/or word of mouth only.

While independent presses tend to focus more on nonfiction than on fiction, a number specialize in genre fiction, ranging from sci-fi, mystery and romance to literary fiction and poetry. (Unfortunately, whether the house is big or small, fiction is particularly challenging to sell.) If you're having a difficult time finding a home at a major publisher for your novel, it's worth pursuing independents and university presses or self-publishing.

Not Your Father's University Press

Traditionally, the mission of most university presses has been to publish important books with little or no concern for marketplace demands. That's still true, but over the past 20 years, as more and more individual publishers have been bought by conglomerates, things have changed. The quality of general-interest submissions at university presses has gone up. Opportunistic agents and authors realized that as major publishers were becoming more conservative, university presses were launching books in categories they traditionally left unexplored. It turns out that top-notch books without blockbuster potential or top-notch authors whose books never broke into bestsellerdom were being frozen out of large publishing houses. University presses grabbed the opportunity and began publishing these excellent books and authors, many of whom have dedicated audiences. True, these books don't bring in megaprofits, but they're doing well enough to take care of the bottom line of a university press. And that can mean great things for your writing career.

Nowadays, over 50% of university presses' lists are made up of trade books. You'll see university press books covered everywhere from *The New York Times Book Review* to *USA Today*. University presses are no longer publishing stiff, stuffy tomes on the Fluctuation of Market Trends in Postindustrialized Patagonia. Instead, their lists include memorable memoirs, titillating histories, even fabulous fiction.

Many university presses also have specialty areas into which your book may fit perfectly. And unlike many of the independent presses, university presses often handle literary fiction. The University of Wisconsin Press, for example, has one of the best gay and lesbian lists in the country. It also publishes highbrow mysteries, travel, popular history, even cookbooks. Editor Raphael Kadushin says, "We've probably had better luck with smaller literary books than the big New York houses. We regularly get reviews in *The New York Times* and other national exposure." So, if you can live with a smaller advance and you find a university press that knows just how to publish your book, it might be a better choice than a large house.

Another good time to go with a university press is if you're an academic who's written a popular book but would like the prestige of a university press behind you for career purposes. This is especially true if your book has the possibility of being adopted for classroom use. University presses, as you can imagine, are far better at getting their books into classrooms than a lot of the major trade houses.

▶ If a publisher asks you to send your proposal/manuscript, we recommend overnighting, messengering or emailing your material if appropriate. You'll get the top-priority factor, thus lessening your chances of getting lost in that vast morass of paper. Plus, these methods give you a record of receipt.

Unfortunately, university presses are relying more and more on agents for material (unheard-of 20 years ago), which means it's less and less likely that your book will be able to climb out of the slush pile. That said, most university presses have regional publishing programs (in fact, some university presses are devoted primarily to regional publishing), hence they will be more likely to read direct queries that skew local. One more caveat: university presses also take foreeeeeeeever to respond. So sit tight.

Approaching the Independents

If you read the chapter on finding an agent, some of the following information will ring a bell; you'll be using the same techniques to find the right publisher.

Again, it all begins with research. Which independent publishers do books like yours? Revisit your local bookstore and library and log on to an Internet bookstore. Take time to chat with your local independent booksellers. They often know who's who in the galaxy of indies. Margot Sage-El, the owner of Watchung Booksellers in Montclair, New Jersey, says, "I have worked with writers to identify publishers that have a particular focus that fits their books. Sometimes the sales reps that work for these publishers also like to troll for new, undiscovered writers. So I am able to pass on an author's information."

Track down appropriate publishers. Study them. Find their books and read them. Check the acknowledgments to see who's thanked. Does it look like there was a good relationship between author and publisher? If so, write down names. Repeat as needed.

There may be one independent publisher that seems exactly right for you, but a number of other houses that look good, too. Let's say you're writing about teen pregnancy. You learn that Morning Glory Press of Buena Park, California, publishes books solely on the subject of teen pregnancy. An obvious place to start. But your research should uncover a number of other independent publishers who handle parenting and teen titles. Add these to your list. And if you're writing about the history of race car drivers from Oxford, you'd probably start by looking at Motorbooks, which has an office in Oxford, England.

Within the appropriate houses, it's best to tailor your query letter to a particular editor. Once you've tracked individual editors down, here are the three essential elements to include in your query: 1) *Why your book is right for the publisher's list.* This is where you display the fruits of your research. Talk about the books the editor herself has worked on. This will lower the letter's chances of getting flushed. 2) *Your book pitch.* In order to write the best possible pitch for a particular publisher, you want to study the copy on the back and jacket flaps of their books and write your pitch in their style. 3) *Your "me" pitch.* Let them know why you're the perfect person to write this book—and why you'd be a smashing addition to their list.

If you can find the email address for a particular editor, all the better. Email your query and attach your proposal or, if you're writing fiction, a piece of your manuscript.

It's now time to put a two-week tickler on your calendar. When that tickler tickles, follow up. Do this every two weeks or so. For more information on the art of the follow-up as well as more query letter information, flip back to Chapter 4.

If you'd like to submit your proposal/manuscript to more than one publisher, send queries simultaneously. It's okay to send out multiple submissions even if a publisher wants exclusivity. Publishers can have exclusivity when they give you a contract. But, again, if they ask, be honest. Then, the second you get a nibble, contact all queried publishers and let them know another someone is panting after your book. Since you don't have an agent to represent you, you'll have to leverage interest. So let everyone know someone else wants to take you to the prom.

Again, if your personality is suited to the task, try to meet any and all interested publishers, as well as their staffs. Scope out their organizations. Are they so small that you'd be better off self-publishing? Or have they been doing this for years and know just how to do what they do?

Micropublishers

Sometimes the line between being published and self-publishing can be quite blurry. For example, if you took a poll of people who purport to know the story behind *Fifty Shades of Grey,* most of them would probably tell you it was self-published. But it wasn't. It was published by what we like to call a micropublisher. A micropublisher is a little like a microbrewery. Both almost always specialize in a certain kind of brew or book. They're also usually run by a couple of extreme enthusiasts with small staffs. And they often have a lot more

Beware the Shyster

With the rise of micropublishing, print-on-demand and other nontraditional routes to selling books, it's becoming increasingly difficult for writers to differentiate among publishers who are genuinely interested in their work, and vanity presses (see page 302), who are genuinely interested in their money. These predatory businesses have been around for some time, but this new breed of vanity presses is sneakier and all too happy to capitalize on writers' confusion. They'll call themselves "publishers," but are they really? No! Like good con men, they promise their victims the very things they most desire, offering to turn unpublished writers with stars in their eyes and money in their pockets into international bestsellers.

So how do you know when you're dealing with a shyster? With their "offer" to publish your book will also come a request for money. Money for their expert editing, cover designers and publicity and marketing teams. Or money for a certain number of books you have to guarantee to buy.

To be clear, there are lots of legitimate "author services" companies that help you self-publish for a fee. We'll be getting into what makes for a good author services company in the chapter on self-publishing. But beware when what sounds like an author services company claims to be something it's not: a publisher. These false "publishers" do not actually care about the content of your book. They are not approaching you to build their "list." They are not a curated enterprise. They are there to TAKE YOUR MONEY. Period. We beg you, when someone asks *you* for money to publish your book, *run.*

enthusiasm than resources or money. Micropublishers won't pay an advance, they may not edit your book, and they will produce only an ebook or a print-on-demand book with little to no distribution (i.e., they won't get your book into bookstores). They don't have publicity and marketing departments and may consist of just one person and a website. But they are capable of being a wonderful partner for you and your book. Or at least for some, a better option than going it alone and self-publishing.

Fifty Shades of Grey was originally published by The Writer's Coffee Shop, an Australian micropublisher specializing in fan fiction. E.L. James was already a star in the *Twilight* fan fiction community, so this micropublisher was the perfect match. They knew how to reach her audience and helped get the book off the ground and into the hands of thousands of readers. Thanks to that first boost from the micropublisher, buzz about *Fifty Shades* spread across the globe. E.L. James eventually sold the rights to Random House, and *Fifty Shades* became the fastest-selling book in history with more than 100 million copies of the series in print.

The key to choosing a micropublisher (or any publisher, for that matter) is making sure they do exactly the kind of book you're writing. As always, before you enter into partnership with anyone, make sure you research, research, research.

Going Direct to Your Readers

It's an all-too-familiar story: the writer who, after being rejected by everyone and his uncle, goes on to great self-publishing success and is later wooed by the same publishers and agents who initially turned him down. It's the story of Lisa Genova, the *New York Times* bestselling author of *Still Alice*. After querying dozens and dozens of agents to no avail, Lisa had had enough. She decided to use a print-on-demand publisher and to find her readers herself. Which she did. In spades. With a readership in tow, she quickly found an agent and a publisher. A publisher who offered her half a million dollars. Lisa reflects on her experience: "It's like that scene in *Pretty Woman,* when Julia Roberts goes back into the Beverly Hills boutique where the woman was so rude to her. Only now she comes back with Richard Gere and his credit card and the woman is, well, in awe."

Are you like Lisa—feverishly frustrated and peevishly pissed off at how your work has been received by the world of traditional publishing? Maybe you just want to do an end run and get your work directly to readers so you can see firsthand what works and what doesn't. With the advent of ebooks and print-on-demand technologies, self-publishing is now a more viable option than ever.

One of the advantages of self-publishing in this day and age is that you can test the market. Have you been told that people don't want to read about your subject? That your novel's plot doesn't hold up? That your audience is too niche? Try putting your book up, for a limited time, on any number of websites and sending it out to your mailing list, your Facebook friends or whatever other means you have of reaching as many people as possible. See what happens (you can always take your work down). If you're getting results, you can go back to agents and editors with hard-nosed evidence. Or, if you like the feeling of total control, you can contemplate adding a print edition via print-on-demand or an offset printer.

If you're excited by the idea of going directly to your readers, skip ahead to Chapter 11 to see if self-publishing is right for you.

And in Conclusion . . .

If you've generated a lot of interest in your project, it's time to celebrate. With gusto. If your first round didn't go well, despair not. Many books remain unsold on their first, second or even third submission, then go on to lead long and happy lives. It ain't over till you say it's over. Channel angst and anger into action. This action may be figuring out how to mend your proposal/manuscript. Or it may mean coming up with an alternate publishing plan—developing a platform *before* you sell your book, for instance. Or, as we said, it could mean self-publishing.

New bait, new rod, new pond . . . you never know. If you're finding rejection hard to bear (and who doesn't?), move on to the next chapter. It's important to keep a sense of humor and remember that, time and again, it's the patient fisherman who catches the real whopper.

CHAPTER 6

Rejection Section

"Can't act, can't sing, can dance a little."

—*Hollywood studio hack, rejecting Fred Astaire*

THERE'S NO MORE HEARTRENDING STORY of rejection than that of John Kennedy Toole, author of *A Confederacy of Dunces*. In 1969, three years after the novel was rejected by Simon & Schuster, Toole had become so despondent that he committed suicide. Toole's grief-stricken yet incredibly determined mother asked everyone she could think of to read the book.

Seven years of rejection later, she got it into the hands of novelist and professor Walker Percy. How could he say no to this poor woman with her deceased son's unpublished manuscript? With great dread, he opened the thick tome, hoping it would be horrible so that he wouldn't have to read the whole thing. At the end of the first page, he sighed in dismay. The book was too good to quit reading. As he read on, he groaned. It was so good, he was going to have to read the whole thing. Halfway through the book, he realized he was holding a novel of immense value. In fact, he was. *A Confederacy of Dunces* went on to win a Pulitzer Prize.

If only Mr. Toole had maintained his mother's faith and resolve. Imagine the career he might have enjoyed, the books he might have written.

If you write something that you want someone else to publish, YOU WILL ALMOST CERTAINLY BE REJECTED. It's not a question of *if*. It's a question of *when*. Virtually every great author has been rejected. In fact, as far as we're concerned, you can't be a great writer *until* you've been rejected. James Joyce's *Ulysses*, voted the best novel of the 20th century by The Modern Library, was rejected over and over again, deemed by many "learned experts" to be unpublishable. Jane Austen, J.D. Salinger, Vladimir Nabokov. Name your favorite authors and you'll find a trail of rejections scattered behind them.

So if the greatest writers have been bashed, pilloried, dismissed, railed upon and savaged, what makes you think it should be any different for you?

Unfortunately, we humans hear the roar of rejection hundreds of times louder than we hear the whisper of praise. Lance Armstrong, the great cycling champion, described riding down a mountain during the Tour de France. Even though there were thousands of people cheering loudly, he found that all he could hear was that one booing, jeering jerk screaming, "YOU STINK!" Obviously, no matter how many great things people say about you, it's hard not to focus on that one voice saying you're no damn good. And it's even harder, of course, when no one at all is saying anything nice about you. This is the time to keep the cheerleader on your team close at hand. It's also a good time to devise a means of dealing with rejection. That's what this chapter is all about.

Rejection Rules

Humans can get used to anything. Muhammad Ali once devised a strategy called the rope-a-dope, in which he leaned against the ropes, tucked his head behind his gloves and let his opponent pummel him until the sap wore himself out. Ali would then pounce back and win the bout. Lesson? Rejection can make you feel like a human punching bag. But hang in there long enough and you just might triumph in the end. Below are some coping strategies to help you bear up:

- *It's only one person's opinion.* All agents and all editors have stories about bestselling books they've turned down. Books they thought were downright terrible, books they thought had no market. Or simply books they didn't feel strongly about one way or another. The problem is that agents and editors have only their own experience on which to draw. Maybe they've always been carb fans and thought the Atkins diet was not only distasteful but ridiculous. Think of all the bestselling books that don't appeal to you—that you just don't get and that you can't understand why others are reading. Or, conversely, the books you love that never made it big. The point is, there is simply no accounting for taste.

- *No one wants to give you your first job.* Everyone wants to give you a job after you're already successful. A couple of nutty brothers wrote a script that was made into a movie, and suddenly they had the ear of some Hollywood muckety-mucks, all of whom wanted to know: "Where's your next script?" The brothers had been working on a big, crazy science-fiction idea that they wanted to direct themselves, but the idea was so huge and unusual that no one would give them the money for it. No one would risk giving them their first directing job on a film so large and strange. So they wrote a smaller, easier-to-make movie, much of which takes place in one apartment. Because the budget was so small, and the movie was so good, it made money. So now those Hollywood muckety-mucks, who wouldn't give them money to make their crazy science-fiction movie before their success, were more than happy to give them $70 million. The nutty sci-fi film? A little movie called *The Matrix*.

■ *No one knows what's going to sell.* In a study done at the Wharton School of Business about predictors of success in trade publishing, it was shown overwhelmingly that no amount of number crunching or objective quantifying analysis can predict what will be successful. The best predictor of a book's future success is an agent's or editor's or publisher's gut instinct. Unfortunately, it appears that the guts of those in publishing are particularly unprescient. So, no matter how many people tell you that your manuscript has no value, understand that a large percentage of those people have no idea what they're talking about. (You don't have to tell them that to their faces, of course.)

■ *Let no nabob shake your faith in your writing ability.* Yes, listen intently. Yes, be open to making the changes necessary to mold your manuscript into a lean, mean fighting machine. But don't let the "nattering nabobs of negativity" shake your belief in your own ability to succeed. As Saul Bellow put it, "I've discovered that rejections are not altogether a bad thing. They teach a writer to rely on his own judgment and to say in his heart of hearts, 'To hell with you.'"

■ *It takes only one.* Your book can be rejected by hundreds of publishers and/or agents. But what you've got to remember is that all it takes is one publisher or one agent to make your dream come true. Joe Quirk wrote five novels and collected 375 rejection letters before he got published. Upon finishing his fifth novel, he sent the first chapter to *Harper's* magazine. He got back a form rejection letter. Scribbled across the bottom were the words "Give it a rest, pal." You'd think at this point he would have done just that. Instead, he soldiered on and a month later found an interested agent. Shortly thereafter, his book was sold. We're happy to report that *The Ultimate Rush* went on to become a national bestseller.

■ *Rejection can help you become a better writer.* As Charles Baxter, acclaimed novelist and professor of creative writing, says, "A lack of self-confidence can be turned to your own purposes if it helps you to take pains, to take care, to avoid glibness."

To Learn or Not to Learn

C an you learn from your foul and brutal rejections? Are there consistencies from letter to letter? Is it obvious from these rejections that you haven't made particular points clearly enough? Does your ending fall apart? Or is there a weakness in your writing (stiff, purple, meandering) that is directly addressed or indirectly alluded to?

Most people get so caught up in the rejection that they don't see the gift the rejecter is giving them—free advice! Imagine what you would have had to pay this fancy agent or editor if you hired her for an evaluation. Granted, often you just get a form letter, but sometimes you don't. And the letters that contain advice can help you transform your work from a pile of dusty paper into a book. Rainelle Burton, author of *The Root Worker,* says, "Many writers either become devastated when they get a rejection letter or don't submit their work out of fear of being rejected again—often because they take it as a personal rejection. Some of the best advice on how to shape and rewrite my book—and one of the book's strongest characters—came from agents' rejection letters. I paid attention to what they said the book needed, took their advice and sent it back. I ended up with a stronger, better novel."

Here are three real rejection letters from editors to an agent, all regarding the same novel. Taken together, they illustrate what you can and can't learn from a rejection letter.

❶

Thanks for sending me _____. Although I can certainly see why you are so taken with this, I'm sorry to say that I didn't share quite the same level of enthusiasm.

❷

Thanks for giving me a look at _____. The world portrayed is fascinating, and one senses that the portrayal is authentic. I found the development of the story a little too bare, though, and I longed for more texture and complexity. For this reason, I'm going to pass.

3

Thanks so much for showing me _____. This novel was a really tough call for me. I was very drawn to its sensitivity, its depth and the elegant and sparse language that captured the lives of such interesting people. I was completely transported into a world so very different from mine, and yet so complex and poignant. Overall, I found the story itself to be engaging, deft and extremely touching. However, my main problem with this novel was the fact that I did not feel acquainted with the main characters until halfway into the story. I just didn't know them well enough to care as much as I felt I should until I was well into the book. For this reason, I'm passing on _____.

Letter #1 is a great illustration of what you can't learn from a rejection letter. Even though the editor says, "I can see why you're so taken with _____," she gives no information to back this up. She then goes on to say she doesn't share "the same level of enthusiasm." Why? We have no idea. From this letter, we can't even tell if the person actually read the novel. This is an utterly worthless rejection and should be used as lining for the birdcage.

Letter #2 is also quite "bare"—the word used by the editor to criticize the book. But at least she gives a little bit of detail about why she's passing. As she says, she longed for "more texture and complexity." By itself, it's a little hard to know exactly what this means. What kind of texture and complexity is missing? Is there not a strong enough sense of place? Is the plot thin? Are the characters cardboard? But, when coupled with Letter #3, you can start to put the pieces of the puzzle together to reveal what exactly this novel may be missing.

Letter #3 shows that the editor also has a problem with the story being bare, though she doesn't put it in the same words as the writer of Letter #2. Instead, she says it took too long to get to know the main characters. Okay, now we've got something. There is a lack of character development up until the midpoint of the novel. Might a dose of texture and complexity help? Once you've gleaned this kind of information, you can go back into your work and see 1) if you think the criticism is on target, and 2) how you can fix your book.

While it can be difficult to hear criticism, it can be equally difficult to hear praise. As we said, we humans tend to hear rejection roar and praise whisper. But the kind words contained in a rejection can help clarify what works, which is important if you don't want to make unnecessary changes to your proposal or manuscript. Even in the worst-case scenario—that you don't sell the work in question—these kind words can guide you to your next project by pinpointing your strong suits as a writer or your affinity for a particular subject. For example, a single chapter or character may grab the attention of agents and editors. Maybe this chapter or character can be expanded into a book of its own.

Praise is also a balm for pain. It's proof that you're not busting your buns in vain. And if you don't let yourself hear this praise, it's going to be very difficult to plod on.

If you reread the second two letters, you'll see a solid helping of praise. Letter #2 says the world portrayed in the novel is "fascinating" and "authentic." Two major successes for any fiction writer. And Letter #3 is the kind of rejection letter you long for (an oxymoron, we know). It's filled with praise and adjectives you'd want to pull out and use as blurbs on the back of the book: "engaging," "deft," "extremely touching." And it should definitely make the author hopeful—the editor lets him see how close she came to making an offer on the book. So close that the author could resubmit the manuscript if he goes back in and addresses the editor's concerns. All in all, this letter is cause for celebration. If you get one like it, don't mope around the house thinking how close you got. Go out with friends and toast the great writer that you are!

Of course, some rejection letters are just plain ridiculous. One of Arielle's all-time favorite rejection letters included the line "a novel should not be written in the first person." Go quick! Rip *The Catcher in the Rye* from your shelf and fling it in the garbage! Or there are David's favorite kinds of rejections, the ones that dismiss an entire category of books: "Football books don't sell!" "Cancer memoirs don't sell!" Or, as a famous rejection of George Orwell's *Animal Farm* stated, "It is impossible to sell animal stories in the USA." Statements like these are continually disproven, and when they are, publishers rush to do dozens of books in whatever category they've just lambasted (most of which fail because they aren't nearly as good as the book they're copying). These kinds of rejection letters are for prominent display on your wall of fame or for placing in a favorite scrapbook. As for the educational value of such letters, they teach you only one thing—that publishing, like so many businesses, is absurd, ridiculous and inhabited by fallible individuals who often can't tell a future runaway success from a pointed stick poked sharply into the eye.

Bottom line: Do not ignore your rejection letters and/or choose to simply let them get you down. Please, play through the pain. You can't hit the game-winning home run unless you're up at bat.

The Art of Taking Criticism: "Thank You, Sir, May I Have Another?"

The art of taking criticism can be as difficult to learn as not falling off a rolling log. Our instinct is to become despondent and defensive when we hear negative things hurled at us . . . even when they're being said politely. This is why it's often better to keep ears open and mouth shut when people are telling you what's wrong with your work. No one wants to hear that his child is ugly. But, unfortunately, it may be true. The great thing is, you can actually make yours more beautiful.

If you're lucky enough to have the opportunity to talk to your rejecter in person, on the phone or via letter or email, Do Not Be Defensive. Instead, ask your rejecter what you might do to improve your work, as well as what he liked about the work. If, for example, someone happens to email you to reject a proposal he requested, don't just delete the email and eat a pint of Häagen-Dazs. Take the time to compose a thoughtful reply so that you can get as much information as possible about why the rejecter rejected your work. Here's the kind of exchange that you'll want to shoot for, in this case with an agent:

Rejecter email #1: Thanks very much for submitting your work, but this project just isn't right for me. I wish you the best of luck with it.
Author email #1: Thank you very much for taking the time to read my material. I really appreciate it. I'm wondering if you could give me some specific feedback so I know what I need to work on. Can you tell me what did and didn't work for you? And what you think I need to do to improve the proposal?

Rejecter email #2: The writing isn't strong enough. It's too stiff and academic. I think it would be a good idea to work with an editor or to bring on a writer.
Author email #2: Do you have any suggestions for someone I might work with? If I go ahead and hire either an editor or a writer and rework my proposal, would you be interested in taking another look?

Rejecter email #3: Yes. But I'd like to see an introductory chapter if you resubmit. And Bud Krupke, a freelance editor, might be a good fit for you.
Author email #3: Thanks so much for your helpful advice. I will pursue either an editor or a writer and get back to you with a revised proposal and new introductory chapter once I feel that I've addressed your concerns fully.

As you can see, this rejection went from a shutout to an open door. And even if the rejecter had said "no thanks" to the last request, this writer would still have learned that her writing was stiff and that her submission package was missing a piece: the introductory chapter. And the writer got a great referral for someone to work with. This exchange also gave the writer a chance to make it clear that she would be great to work with. She listens well and is willing to put in the necessary work to polish the proposal so it's publisher-ready. Agents and editors hate it when they have to read a second draft of a proposal or manuscript that's essentially the same as the draft they've already read. By clearly stating that she won't get back to the agent until she's fully addressed the agent's concerns, she lets the agent know that this will not be the case with her book.

▶ If you happen to get a rejection over the phone, be sure to have a pen and paper handy before you ask a single question. Then write everything down. Memory can be a harsh and faulty companion.

So the next time your work is criticized, try the open-minded question approach. Yes, there's a chance you'll receive no reply. But there's also a chance that you will. Anyway, it's preferable to the slinking into silent self-loathing approach.

Many times it will not be possible to face your rejecters. Many times you will hear nothing at all from them, as if a giant black hole has sucked up your manuscript and swallowed it. Sometimes you will get a form letter. If this is the case, we have a suggestion. Turn these wicked pieces of paper into art—a collage or a poem. Or, if it's cold and damp, build a roaring fire and watch it burn, baby, burn.

How to Deal: Developing Thick Skin

David was a professional actor for 20 years before he became an author. So naturally he was rejected tens of thousands of times, by everyone from titans in the industry to the lowliest bottom-feeders. Thus he became the Raja of Rebuff. The Sovereign of the Snub. Master of the Cold Shoulder. To David, a rejection proves only one thing: that the rejecter is the biggest moron in the world for not understanding what a brilliant, astonishing, amazing specimen of humanity he is. He looks at each rejection as a badge of honor. And he's got his own little conspiracy theory going about rejection. Only after he's accumulated a sufficient number of rejections will he be rewarded with an offer.

Hallie Ephron, coauthor of the Peter Zaks mystery series, agrees that a stubborn streak is crucial: "The difference between unpublished and published writers, talent aside, is sticking with it. Don't give up after you get rejected by four agents—a good friend of mine was rejected by 48 before she found one who then promptly sold her book within two weeks."

Unfortunately, a large percentage of us feel as if the word "loser" has been permanently branded on our foreheads when confronted with rejection. Unlike David, we stew in the juices of our limitations rather than taking the "no limits" point of view. So, if you're one of the majority, it's a good time to reread the rejection tenets and then come up with a mantra that comforts you. Bestselling author Barbara Kingsolver says, "This manuscript of yours that has just come back from another editor is a precious package. Don't consider it rejected. Consider that you've addressed it 'to the editor who can appreciate my work' and it has simply come back stamped 'Not at this address.' Just keep looking for the right address."

We know a writer who imagines himself commiserating with James Joyce and Herman Melville about what it feels like to be rudely rejected. Similarly, many writers find it helpful to get together with others to swap war stories. Sometimes the stinging nettle of rejection is soothed by voicing it to others who've been similarly stung. And the great thing is, the worse your rejection, the more entertaining, funny and interesting your stories will be.

These methods may sound hokey, but it's amazing how helpful hoke can sometimes be. So before you throw this book at the wall (another helpful venting technique), at least try commiserating, or ranting, or making badges of honor out of your rejections, and see if it makes you feel better. If it doesn't, we have a surefire technique for one and all. Type up a number of rejections of famous books and pin them up in your work space. These are great spirit buoyers. Here's a good starter list taken from the wonderful book *Rotten Rejections,* edited by André Bernard:

The Deer Park, by Norman Mailer:
"This will set publishing back 25 years."

The Diary of Anne Frank:
"The girl doesn't, it seems to me, have a special perception or feeling which would lift that book above the 'curiosity' level."

Barchester Towers, by Anthony Trollope:
"The grand defect of the work, I think, as a work of art is the low-mindedness and vulgarity of the chief actors. There is hardly a 'lady' or 'gentleman' amongst them."

Carrie, by Stephen King:
"We are not interested in science fiction which deals with negative utopias. They do not sell."

Catch-22, by Joseph Heller:
"I haven't really the foggiest idea about what the man is trying to say. . . . Apparently the author intends it to be funny—possibly even satire—but it is really not funny on any intellectual level."

The Spy Who Came in from the Cold, by John le Carré:
"You're welcome to le Carré—he hasn't got any future."

Lady Windermere's Fan, by Oscar Wilde:
"My dear sir, I have read your manuscript. Oh, my dear sir."

Lolita, by Vladimir Nabokov:
". . . overwhelmingly nauseating, even to an enlightened Freudian . . . the whole thing is an unsure cross between hideous reality and improbable fantasy. It often becomes a wild neurotic daydream . . . I recommend that it be buried under a stone for a thousand years."

Taking Action

If you've ever had someone close to you die, you know too well the frenzy of activity that follows the death of a loved one. Calls need to be made, the funeral planned, the flowers ordered. And in this flurry of to-dos lies a certain kind of relief. Well, rejection is like a very, very small death. And here, too, the pain can be lessened by action. Fortunately, there's a lot you can do—rethinking, revising, resending.

James Bradley, author of the #1 *New York Times* bestseller *Flags of Our Fathers,* which was rejected 27 times before it was bought by a publisher, said this in an interview: "When someone says 'no,' the most important thing you can say to yourself is . . . 'Next'!"

PART II

Taking Care
of Business

CHAPTER 7

Let's Make a Deal!

"The best way to make a good deal is to have the ability to walk away from it."

—Brian Koslow

YOUR AGENT CALLS. A PUBLISHER with great taste has made an offer for your book. If you're lucky, several publishers with equally great taste have made offers. Maybe your agent has just held an auction, and she's calling to tell you which fortunate publisher is the highest bidder. Maybe you've submitted your proposal or manuscript directly to a publisher, and they've just called to say they want to publish your book.

Excitement reigns! You rule! Savor this moment. Then take a step back. You may be inclined to jump at the first offer. Don't. Keep a calm head and cool nerves. This is the time for strategic evaluation of your options so you can make the best possible deal with the best possible publisher.

The Selling of Your Book

Some deals move at the speed of a glacier. Some deals happen lickety-split quick. Some initially sizzle, then fizzle fast. Some crescendo only after fits and hiccups. And there's no way of knowing in advance.

No matter the timeline, almost all offers come in one of three ways: 1) preemptive offers, 2) auctions (either round-robin or best-bid), or 3) individual offers. Preempts and auctions occur only if there's competition. If you've submitted your book directly to publishers, you'll more than likely be dealing with individual offers. Each scenario is complicated in its own special way.

The Preempt

Preemptive offers are made in the hope of eliminating the competition. That's why most publishers will let a preempt sit on the table for only about 24 hours. They don't want the author shopping their offer around.

▶ If you get interest from multiple publishers and are torn, it's tempting to want your agent to make the hard decisions for you. But ultimately you're driving the train. Your agent is there to present you with options and to get you the best possible deal. Get clarity on what you want, and you'll go a long way toward a happy and healthy publishing experience.

Like everything else in life, preempts have pluses and minuses. Here are the pluses:

- A publisher who preempts is a publisher who is really passionate about your book.
- A preempt may be the best offer you get.
- No matter how many birds are in how many bushes, this is a bird in hand.

And now the minuses:

- If you accept the offer, then you can't use it to breed other interest.
- Another publisher might have given you more money, so you could end up leaving money on the table. Bad place to leave money.
- Another publisher might have been a better match for you and your book.

If you're lucky enough to be on the receiving end of a preempt, try to at least talk with the editor who's making the offer. If you're in the same city or you're willing to travel, go meet the editor. Methodically compile an organized list of questions (see pages 147–148).

Auction Action

There are two kinds of auctions in the book world: *round-robin auctions* and *best-bid auctions*. Both occur by phone or email at a preordained time and date. In a round-robin auction, people often start low and end high, whereas in a best-bid auction each editor has to do just that: pony up his one best bid. Only if two publishers make the same highest bid will they be given a chance to give another best bid.

In round-robin auctions, all editors make first-round bids (with the exception of "floor-holders"—see box, opposite). Whoever has the lowest bid in the first round makes the first bid in the second round, and on and on. Each offer has to top the previous bid by a minimum percentage, typically 10%. So, if someone makes an initial offer of $10,000, the next bidder has to come in at $11,000, the

One Man's Ceiling Is Another Man's Floor

Sometimes an editor will make a preemptive offer that isn't as sumptuous as you or your agent would like. Your agent may then ask this editor to "take a floor" in an auction. If you've ever been to a live auction, you may have noticed that someone had submitted a first offer prior to the start of the auction, below which no bids can go. This is a floor. However, in publishing, it has an additional significance. When a floor is accepted, the editor who holds it sits out of the auction. Once all bids have been made, the floor-holder gets an opportunity to make one final, topping bid, typically 10% higher than the last bid.

Floors are great because they guarantee the sale of your book for a predetermined sum of money. But floors can discourage other publishers from participating in an auction; no matter how much they bid, they don't have the option of making a last offer.

next at \$12,100, and so on. However, someone may choose to make a bid that exceeds 10% above the current offer. This is a strategic move that editors make in order to try and knock out the competition.

This bidding goes on until only one editor is left standing. If the auction has a floor-holder, he is now allowed to come back and top the final offer. Whoever makes the highest bid wins and gets the honor and privilege of publishing your book. Or, at least, this is an auction at its simplest. In reality, money is just the largest of many points considered in an auction. Other points that are considered include format (hardcover vs. paperback), rights (worldwide vs. North American), royalties, publicity and marketing commitments, and more—we'll get to these matters shortly.

To give you a sense of how an auction actually works, let's imagine that Crown (a division of Penguin Random House), Putnam (another division of Penguin Random House) and HarperCollins are bidding on your book. Their initial bids for round one are as follows:

Crown: \$25K
Putnam: \$40K
HarperCollins: \$40K

Crown, the low bidder in the first round, then makes the first bid in the second round, which must be 10% higher than the last round's highest bid. Since HarperCollins and Putnam placed the same bid, the agent typically contacts the person who called first and let him know where the action stands. So our second round goes as follows:

Crown: $44K (the minimum bid)

HarperCollins: $49K (they round up from the minimum bid)

Putnam drops out

Third round:

Crown: $54K

HarperCollins: $61K

Fourth round:

Crown: $75K

HarperCollins drops out

You can see that Crown made a risky move in the fourth round, offering more than was required in order to try and knock out the competition. The strategy worked.

Note that if there had been a floor in this auction, the editor who held the floor could have topped the $75K bid by 10% and bought the book for $82,500.

One of the beauties of a round-robin auction is that in a short time you can watch your money grow by leaps and bounds. Another is that the initial lowest bidder can come out on top. One of the downsides of a round-robin auction is that money is the controlling factor. Sometimes the underbidder may be your first choice, and this can lead to unpleasant feelings. Another downside is that one house may be willing to pay a lot more than the others. Let's say one house was willing to pay as much as $100K whereas everyone else will not go above $50K. This means that if everyone's initial offers are low, your book could end up selling for $55K when it could have sold for double.

Sifting Wheat from Chaff: The Right Publisher for You

If a publisher is excited about you and gets behind your book, your chances of getting reviewed in the right places and generating that elusive, all-important buzz rise exponentially. In 2002, for example, Little, Brown was publishing a novel about a dark and brutal subject. But everyone in the house was passionate about this book, so they sent promotional copies everywhere and talked about it to everyone. The sheer force of their efforts, combined with the quality of the book, created a blizzard of big-time buzz. That book hit the ground sprinting, and in almost no time it hit the million-copy mark. The book was *The Lovely Bones* by Alice Sebold, and it became the bestselling novel of 2002. Yes, it's an excellent book, but it's about a very difficult subject, and if it hadn't been handled with such relentless passion by Sebold's publisher, it could have died on the vine. So, if you have a choice of publisher, you want to choose carefully.

> Remember to send classy, funny and/or sweet thank-you notes to any editor you meet or speak with. Not only because it's the polite thing to do, but also because it may result in an editor remembering you and looking out for your next book.

If you're lucky enough to have more than one publishing suitor, you're in a position to be able to actually choose the one who's best for your book.

If you haven't already met with interested editors and you don't live in the same city as the publisher(s) who made the offer(s), ask to speak to all editors by phone (see pages 147–148 for pertinent questions to ask). You can learn volumes by speaking to an editor.

Once you've met with or talked to editors, go over your notes to ascertain their enthusiasm levels. Sometimes the publisher you thought would be least likely to make an offer shows up with the bucks and a passionate letter of intent. Maybe a publisher you love makes an offer, but it's half what another publisher offered or not close to what you'd like the book to sell for.

What about the different styles of editors? Is one quiet and demure? You're in the honeymoon phase now. Imagine this person when the bloom is off the rose. When she's displeased. Or even when she's pleased but doesn't show it. Again, know thyself. Do you need a lot of sweetness and light? Do you think this editor will be able to provide that? Quiet and Demure isn't bad as long as you can live with it and the publisher does a great job with your book. But if you need someone who will be demonstrative and supportive, you're going to have a hard time with quiet demurishness.

Maybe there's an editor who can't stop telling you how fantastic your book is. Maybe you feel a deep personal connection with this editor. You both have cockatoos and spend your spare time creating rubber-band balls. Maybe this editor's ideas aren't as strong as Quiet and Demure's, but you just know that this person is going to be your friend for life and a dream to work with.

It's important to keep in mind that personality does not necessarily reflect talent. You may find yourself with an unexpressive editor who will edit your book to perfection and champion it relentlessly. Let your gut instinct and your listening skills, coupled with each editor's track record, be your guide. Also, consult with your agent, whose experience should help guide you.

Beware of the editor who comes on gangbusters, only to disappear when push comes to shove. You don't want to get swept away by someone who promises the moon and stars and then doesn't have the wherewithal, desire or resources to deliver. Separate the rush of enthusiasm from the actual facts of what he's really putting on the table. You may also want to ask for a list of books he's edited so that you can quietly check out and assess the acknowledgments he's received.

What about the publishing company as a whole? Are they, as a group, excited about your book? Have you heard anything from the marketing, publicity and sales departments? If you met with the publishing company, did anyone from marketing, publicity or sales show up? Do they have someone who understands what keywords are and how to spread the word in cyberspace? If you make a cool promotional video, will they know how to help it get seeded all over the World Wide Web? Keep in mind that at some point your book will be handed off to the publicity and marketing departments. Then to the sales force—the people who are actually going to sell your book. It's crucial to have the whole house behind you.

Another reason to evaluate the whole house and not just the editor is that editors in publishing change jobs as frequently as teenage girls change boyfriends. The editor you fall in love with may be there for only a part of your book's journey through publication. You want to be sure that the enthusiasm for your book doesn't leave with her.

LESS MONEY, BETTER PUBLISHER?

If you have a family to feed, or rent to pay, or a body to clothe, you'll be tempted to take your highest offer. But don't make the mistake of confusing more money with more love. It might seem slightly insane, but publishers often give huge advances for books that they pay little or no attention to when it comes time to publish. This can be due to a regime change, a lackluster finished manuscript or a slow sales start. So you could pay off your mortgage but end up with a book that doesn't do as well as it should have, and your book may be viewed by publishers as a disappointment because of lack of sales. If you want a long career as a writer and/or you'd like to see your book on the shelves in 2, 4 or 24 years, a smaller advance with a publisher more committed to your book and better suited to selling it may be the way to go. A great specialty publisher will know exactly where your audience likes to buy books, and how to get their attention.

Sharing a Vision

Remember Tamim Ansary? The guy who wrote the email about Afghanistan that was heard around the world? He was in the fortunate position of getting to choose among a number of first-rate publishers. He had fruitful, in-depth conversations with each. One of the conversations was with a publisher who has a list of hits as long as your arm. This publisher immediately offered up a pretty pile of money. But Tamim had a sense that as savvy as this publisher was, she ultimately envisioned a different book from the one he wanted to write. He turned down the offer and accepted a lower one from a publisher who shared his vision. His book, *West of Kabul, East of New York*, published by Farrar, Straus & Giroux, became a bestseller, earned out its advance and is now assigned at colleges and universities around the country.

But what exactly makes a publisher "more committed" and "better suited"? Our definition includes:

- A track record in publishing your kind of book.
- Enthusiasm from top to bottom, side to side, stem to stern, foot to mouth.
- An editor who loves your book.
- An established edge in prestige, attention, design or anything else that's important to you and the health and wealth of your book.
- A desire and ability to go the extra mile to get your book into readers' hands.

If you accept a smaller advance from a better publisher who pushes your book the right way, to the right people, it could end up selling a lot more copies. Selling a lot more copies would 1) ultimately put more money in your pocket, 2) make you a hotter commodity, and 3) help you sell your next book. *New York Times* bestselling author Seth Godin adds, "The only people who should write books for money are people who made money on their last book." The upshot being: If your book is brought out by a great publisher and makes a big splash in the world, your stock will soar, making everything you produce worth a little bit more.

What if you're leaning toward one editor in particular and/or don't like a particular editor? In that case, let your agent know right away. She'll probably want to hold a best-bid auction, not a round-robin.

Sometimes an auction will reveal that an editor or publisher who makes the highest bid is not right for you. Another editor may write a passionate letter about why he's the right match for you. Another may make a marketing commitment in her contract. Another may give you a large first payment. Whatever the reason, if you feel that your book will fare better with an under-bidder, it is your prerogative to choose that house instead. For understandable reasons, this will most likely anger the highest bidder. But if you're worried about a grudge against your future work, know that people tend to forget old slights if your next book has the sweet smell of money wafting over it.

ONE LONELY OFFER

Often only one brave publishing house will be willing to take a chance on you and your book. Sometimes this one offer is made by the publisher you like the best and for the money you want. But sometimes the publisher isn't your first choice or doesn't deliver top dollar. At this point, some authors choose to self-publish. If you don't have the energy to be your own publisher, you need to ask yourself: Would you rather have a xeroxed proposal/manuscript in your filing cabinet or a book in your local bookstore? Yes, you want a great publisher with a great track record and a great editor. But, when it comes down to it, you also want a book.

A Lose-Win Situation

In 2007, David put together an anthology with his partner in crime, RJ Martin Jr. He shopped it everywhere: to top agents, junior agents, assistants to junior agents, to big publishers, university presses and small presses. Everybody turned David and RJ's anthology down. And each time they got shot down, rejection-experts David and RJ listened, tightened the pitch and improved the proposal.

Finally, networking led them to Soft Skull Press, a prestigious small press that made a name for itself with hip, cutting-edge books that the big publishers were scared to touch. It was a match. Soft Skull offered David and RJ a small sum—so small that after they paid all the contributors, they actually lost money on the anthology. But that book was beautifully designed. And their publisher understood the anthology's audience. The book and the partnership jived.

Shortly after publication, something impossible happened—something that even some of the world's most famous authors can't claim. Are you ready? David and RJ's labor of love ended up on the front page of the *New York Times Book Review*. That's right: the front page. And, yes, it was a rave. The result? The book went through four printings in six weeks. And David and RJ had earned out their advance before they were able to clink glasses at their celebration dinner.

One Sad Offer, One Bestselling Book

When Geoffrey Moore's book *Crossing the Chasm* was sent out to publishers, it received only one offer, and for an underwhelming sum. At the time, Geoff was a consultant at a prestigious high-tech consulting firm. But he wanted to set up his own consulting practice and thought a book would help to establish his credibility, as he wasn't well known in his industry. His hunch was right. He took the offer, and *Crossing the Chasm* went on to become not just a bestseller, but a business classic—required reading in business schools and corporations worldwide. Since then, Geoff has written four more bestsellers. He's known all over the planet as a guru of high-tech marketing. And all it took was one wee offer.

"IS THAT ALL THERE IS?"

Jerry Stahl, author of the bestselling memoir *Permanent Midnight* and the best-selling novel *I, Fatty,* says it best: "My daughter's 13, and I need to find a better place to live and pay for her college down the road—neither of which I could do by devoting myself to what amounted to the rather expensive hobby of writing books." Because advances rarely translate into minimum wage and considering how much time you'll most likely spend on a book, you often have to make the difficult choice to take an offer that will not support you in the style to which you are accustomed. The sad fact is, your advance may not support you in any style at all.

If the final offer you get doesn't meet your minimum, you or your agent can go back to the publisher and explain your situation. Sometimes seeing an actual budget will make publishers come up with a little more cabbage. Or you can apply for a grant or look for corporate sponsorship. This will almost certainly take lots of work and tons of time. But it can also pay off.

In the end, of course, it comes down to how badly you want to do your book, and what you and the market will bear. Maybe you decide you can't write the book for the money offered. Maybe you can then use the experience you gained to develop your next project, which will get you a larger advance. If you can sell a different project first and it does well, your original proposal will become more valuable. But if your goal is to get a book actually published by a publisher, as bank-breaking as it may seem, this might be your chance. We know a number of people who turned down the only offer they received, and every single one of them has regretted it. If you can find a way, suck it up and get your book out into the world; you never know what it will lead to.

Je Regrette Tout

K aty Butler, a well-known journalist who has written for *The New York Times*, the *San Francisco Chronicle, The New Yorker* and numerous other publications, put together a terrific proposal for a book about the politics of sexual violence. Fellow writers, experts in the field and her agent all said the proposal had "big book" written all over it. Indeed, Katy received offers from editors at two major houses: one a veteran editor, the other a big shot with her own imprint. Both offers were healthy, but they weren't the kind of "big" money she was expecting for her "big book." Nor did she feel they would adequately cover her expenses for the two years it would take to write the book. So Katy turned both down. "I really wish I had taken one of those offers," she says now. "In retrospect, I could have easily rearranged my life to live more cheaply."

Katy continued to successfully publish in many top newspapers and magazines. And we're happy to report that since the last edition of this book, one of these articles—for *The New York Times Magazine* no less—touched a nerve so deep that agents and editors came calling. The result? A mega-book deal and a *New York Times* bestseller in the form of *Knocking on Heaven's Door: The Path to a Better Way of Death*.

Finding a Cowriter or Dumping the One You Have

A n editor or publisher may want to buy your book but insist that you get help from a writer. What to do? Every situation is different, but they all come down to what you're willing to give up and what you must hang on to. The studio that bought Sylvester Stallone's script for *Rocky* insisted that someone else play the lead. But he had written the script for himself, so he refused. In the face of much browbeating and angry posturing, Sly would not relent. The studio did. And the rest is history. He got to be a movie star.

But not all publishers will relent. Sometimes they'll tell you and your proposal/manuscript to go away if you don't do exactly what they want. How much does it mean to you to write the book? Are you sure you're capable of writing the book? Soul-searching and a lot of consultation with your agent, friends and colleagues are required here.

In other cases, an editor or publisher may want to replace the writer you're already working with. This is potentially a *Sophie's Choice* moment. Only you can assess your level of commitment to your writer. Perhaps you want to buy him out and cut him loose. Perhaps he's your best friend and you'd never toss him aside. Either way, find out: What's the problem with the writer? Do they have suggestions for a replacement? Talk to potential writers with an open mind. Sometimes an experienced writer with an established track record is just the person to turn your book into a wild success. Sometimes loyalty to your writer, or your own writing talent, must be honored. Your call.

Negotiating Nuggets for Agentless Authors

Many people feel daunted when they have to negotiate for themselves. Especially when they're in a new business and don't know the lay of the land. How do you put a value on your work? Or accept someone else's value if it seems paltry or downright insulting? How do you know if a contract is fair when your contract looks like a bunch of gibberish? Every deal is different, but here are some guidelines to raise your comfort level and to help you avoid getting saddled with a nasty contract:

- **RESEARCH!** Know the terrain. Have you been reading the deal sections of *PW* and Publishers Lunch? Have you Googled your prospective publisher's backlist to see if you can get some dirt on their deals? Do you have a sense of what books like yours are selling for? Amass as much info as you can, so you don't act like the neophyte that you may be.

- *Let the publisher make an offer first.* Don't fall into the trap of naming your dollar before they do—most authors either greatly under- or over-value their work. That said, a publisher may try to lowball you or give you a crappy contract. And if you've ever been lowballed, you know how painful that can be. So don't just accept a first offer.

- *Use your agentless-ness to your advantage.* Agents are so used to operating within the industry standards that they know not to ask for the unaskable. Thing is, sometimes the unaskable can get you the ungettable. So ask lots of questions: "What are the highest royalties that you've given in a contract?" "What's the range in advances that you give?" "Will you have an advertising or publicity budget?" "Will you build a website for my book?" You may discover answers that an agent never would have.

- *Prepare a book-writing budget.* Demonstrate your costs so your requests don't seem like they're coming out of thin air, left field, the blue. Do you have research, permissions or travel costs? Do you need to take time off from work or hire a baby-sitter? Be specific.

■ *If you can, hire a lawyer with publishing expertise.* They'll know what's kosher. Also, they can act as your negotiator, creating that cushy business buffer that allows you to ask for what you really want. David agented one of his own books, didn't hire a lawyer and ended up deeply regretting it.

■ *Can't afford to hire a lawyer?* Join The Authors Guild. The Guild distributes official contract guidelines and offers a written contract review that provides specific suggestions and comments; the review is not exhaustive, nor will the Guild speak on your behalf to a publisher. As their website explains, "While the Guild does not negotiate individual member agreements, we are willing to answer members' specific inquiries to aid them in securing the best deal possible." Lastly, the Guild has contract seminars around the country. Sign up for one now! (See Appendix II.)

As difficult as it may be, if you don't ask, you most certainly will not receive. Stand tall, be firm, keep your sense of humor. In the end, you may not get what you want, but hopefully you'll at least get what you need.

Million-Dollar Baby

We know three enterprising fellows who came up with an idea they thought was worth some money. They made a prototype, and lo and behold, one of the behemoths of their industry beckoned. They were pleased as punch and happy as clams. They were sure they could get enough money to put down payments on country homes. They convened to come up with the dollar amount. They made a pact. They were dreaming big, and they decided they'd ask for the whopping sum of $30K, or $10K each. (Keep in mind this was 30 years ago.) They wouldn't take a penny less. Furthermore, they were determined not to let the big boys push them around. They were going to go in, control the meeting, name their price and walk out triumphant.

The day of their meeting arrived, and they walked into the conference room in their Sunday best, cocksure and ready to rumble. Before they had a chance to name their deal-breaking, drop-dead number, the Head Honcho talked about how much he loved their prototype and went on to say that his company wanted to make an offer. "We're prepared to offer you one million dollars," he said. "But we can't go a penny more."

Dumbfounded, the three industrious fellows had no idea what to say next. Their plan hadn't anticipated this turn of events. So they just sat there in slack-jawed astonishment until someone mumbled a faint "Uh . . . yeah . . . cool."

The moral of this story? He who offers first often comes in last.

Get It in Writing: The Deal Memo

After much brouhaha and folderol, you've finally decided who's the right publisher. Or the decision has been made for you. You've accepted an offer. But it's always a good idea to get it in writing that you have a deal in place before the contract gets executed and signed, which can take months. The best way to do this is with a *deal memo,* confirming the basic points of the offer you've accepted. This memo should include the advance, royalties, territory, payout, rights, delivery date, bonuses (if any), option information and every other pertinent part of your contract. (In order to understand exactly what you're agreeing to or asking for, read to the end of the next chapter.)

Some agents do deal memos. Some don't. Some do them some of the time. Some do them all of the time. If your agent isn't the type to do deal memos, it's not necessary to insist. Just make sure you understand the basic points of the deal so that you can check that your contract jibes with the original offer. If you're negotiating a deal on your own, you can ask the publisher directly for a deal memo or you can draw one up yourself and send it in. (Email is fine.) Here's a sample of a deal memo to give you an idea of what you'll want to include:

Territory: North America.

Advance: $75,000.

Payout: $37,500 on signing, $18,750 on delivery and acceptance, $18,750 on publication.

Royalties: Hardcover: 10% for the first 5,000 copies, 12.5% for the next 5,000 copies, 15% thereafter. Paperback: 7.5% flat. Ebooks: 25% of net.

Sub rights: Publisher retains audio and first serial. 80/20 split on British rights, 75/25 on translation. (Note: The first number in those ratios represents the author's take.)

Bonus: $10,000 earn-out bonus. Must earn out within one year of publication. Bonus applied to advance.

Option: 30-day option on next proposal, to begin after delivery and acceptance. No matching clause.

Title: Mutual agreement on title.

Cover and jacket: Consultation on cover and jacket copy.

Now put on your eyeshade, roll up your sleeves and channel your inner CPA. It's time to dissect your contract.

Submitting to Hollywood

I f you have a movie-friendly book, you need to determine the best time to go out with your material. Some books will benefit immensely by being seen first in completed manuscript or finished book form, as opposed to just a proposal, so people can grasp the whole breadth of your story. On the other hand, some high-concept ideas scream MOVIE from the moment they're put down on a page; just the promise of what you'll deliver will make some movie mogul plop down a huge chunk of change. A well-known film agent once told Arielle, "There are good reasons to sell your book fast. And there are good reasons to sell your book cheap. But there are no good reasons to sell your book fast and cheap." Unless, of course, you're dying for cash or think the chances of your book being made into a movie by anyone else are super thin.

No matter whether you choose to send your book as a proposal, a manuscript or a finished book, you've got to pick your moment to infiltrate Hollywood. Should you send it when there's still a halo of hope hovering over your unpublished book? Or should you wait until you have something concrete and exciting to dangle in front of Tinseltown? This is a tough call and one that only you, your agent and your sixth sense can make. But be sure to follow trends and developments in the film world. Is the highest-grossing movie of the moment in the style of film noir? Is your book also written in a noir style? Seize the day. Have there been a string of sci-fi flops? Is your novel science fiction? Then hold off.

Remember the scouts we talked about in Chapter 4? If your book has movie potential, it's very likely to land in a scout's hands, whether you put it there or not. It's the scout's job to discover what's new and exciting before anyone else. Scouts create relationships with a whole host of editors who tip them off when something promising comes in. This can be good news if they get their hands on your work and pass it to the right people at the right time. But it can be bad news if they pass it on to the right people at the wrong time, or worse, the wrong people at the wrong time. If a studio or producer rejects your book before it has a chance to blossom, it will be hard to get them to revisit it later, when it's in full bloom. If you have an agent with good relationships with the scouts, she can help manage the timing so that you're protected against premature exposure.

As much as we wouldn't advise anyone putting too much energy into a Hollywood fantasy, you also shouldn't automatically assume that your book isn't right for Hollywood. Rosalind Wiseman's *New York Times* bestseller *Queen Bees & Wannabes*, a sociological exploration of the hierarchy of adolescent girls, has no plot and no heroes. Not a likely candidate for a blockbuster Hollywood movie? Guess again. *Queen Bees & Wannabes* was turned into the #1 box-office hit *Mean Girls*. FYI: Rosalind's next book, *Queen Bee Moms and Kingpin Dads: Coping with the Parents, Teachers, Coaches, and Counselors Who Can Make—or Break—Your Child's Future* (written with Elizabeth Rapoport), was sold just as the movie was hitting screens all over America. We're sure you won't be surprised to hear that it went for a very pretty penny.

CHAPTER 8

Contract Facts

"A verbal contract isn't worth the paper it's written on."

—Samuel Goldwyn

PEOPLE SPEND YEARS AND YEARS and hundreds of thousands of dollars learning how to read contracts. If you're interested in understanding the full nitty and complete gritty of contracts, go to law school. Here, we're not going to teach you about force majeure (not to be confused with horse manure). But we will give you basic guidelines and red flags to look for in dealing with a book contract. The essential purpose of a contract between you and a publisher is the granting of rights regarding your work. Usually a publisher wants to claim as many rights as possible while paying as little as possible, so part of your agent's 15% is earned by making sure you get a fair shake. If you don't have an agent, read this chapter carefully.

An Askance Glance at Your Advance

An advance is exactly that. Cash advanced to you before your book starts making money. The point of an advance, theoretically, is to allow you to write your book unencumbered by the need to make money elsewhere. In reality, advances are typically based on the publisher's projections for the first year of revenues, so they vary wildly in size (the publisher's ideal is that the book earns out its advance within that first year—but more on that in a bit). Whatever its size, however, these days payment structures are such that your advance will probably not cover your expenses, unless you live in the woods and enjoy a diet of nuts and berries or have kind and wealthy relations.

An advance is formally referred to as an *advance against royalties*. To explain how this works, we'll need to take a quick trip through the economics of a book. Say you receive a $20,000 advance. Say that your hardcover book sells for a retail price of $20. Say 10% of the cover price of your book goes to you, which means you earn $2 for every book sold through regular retail channels. This 10% is called a royalty. However, you won't get a check in the mail after your first copy is sold, since you first have to earn out your advance. This means that you must apply your share of the earnings to the amount that was "advanced" to you. In this case, 10,000 copies of your book will have to be sold at retail in order for you to earn out. Then and only then will you start receiving one of the loveliest things an author can get: a royalty check.

The equation below illustrates how the sale of one book impacts your royalties in the preceding example:

$$\$20K \text{ (advance)} - \$2 \text{ (sale of one book)} = \$19{,}998 \text{ (left to earn out)}$$

One of the most frequent questions we hear from first-time authors (often with voices aquiver and terror in their eyes) is this: "If I don't earn out my advance, do I have to pay it back?" Imagine their relief when we say: NO! All advance money is yours to keep even if you end up selling just three books. Only 10% of all books earn out their advances. That being said, if you don't finish your book, or if it's not accepted by your publisher, you *will* be responsible for paying the money back.

► If you're writing an illustrated book or a cookbook with photos, try to get a separate art budget that is NOT part of your advance (typically, you are expected to pay for photographs or illustrations). This way, you'll have a lower advance to earn out.

Payout: "When, Oh When, Do I Get My Money?"

We wish we had a dollar for every time an author has asked us this question. So here's the skinny. Almost all advances are paid out in chunks. Typically, you get one chunk when you sign your contract, another chunk when your manuscript is accepted and the last one when your book is published. However, sometimes there are more payment dates in the schedule, and sometimes there are fewer. For example, a percentage of the money may be released on delivery of only half the manuscript or on publication of the paperback version of a book where the first release is in hardcover.

In general, publishers are set up to spread out their payments over as long a period as possible. Here are a few typical ways advances are made:

⅓ on signing of contract
⅓ on delivery and acceptance of manuscript
⅓ on publication date of book

¼ on signing of contract
¼ on delivery and acceptance of manuscript
¼ on publication of hardcover
¼ on publication of paperback

½ on signing of contract
½ on delivery and acceptance of manuscript

> If you're being paid upon paperback publication, make sure it's spelled out in your contract that you receive the paperback portion of the advance either at that time OR within 12 months of hardcover publication, whichever is earlier. This way, if your book never makes it to paperback, you ensure that you will be paid your full advance.

Two payments are the least common these days. Four payments are most common for hardcovers and six-figure advances. Once you get into these numbers, a publisher is sure to break up the money as much as possible in order to hold on to it longer. The trouble with this is that even a major advance of $200,000 might not provide enough money to live off of, once it's broken up. Let's say you get $50,000 on signing, but it takes you one and a half years to write your book and another six months before it's accepted. That's only $25,000 a year for the most time-consuming part of the process. This is why it's important to get as much money up front as possible—unless there are major tax implications. Let's say, for example, that your publisher wants to pay you in thirds. See if you can get them to change the payout to ½, ¼, ¼. With this arrangement, if your book gets canceled or your pub date keeps getting delayed, you've got more of their money in your pocket. And generally speaking, it's always better to have money in your own pocket than in theirs.

"When Do I *Really* Get My Money?"

Pay attention now. After you make your deal, it may be months and months before you actually have cold hard cash in your hot little hand. Between agent-editor haggling, corporate lethargy and the check clearing through the agent's bookkeeping system, it's not unusual to wait three to six months to get paid. Sometimes more.

Similar snafus can affect the timing of your other payments. Say a publisher makes an offer of $10,000 on January 1, 2015. In your contract, it says you will be paid in thirds. Taking the six-months rule, you'll get your first $3,333.33 check on July 1, 2015. Now let's say you have a delivery date of May 1, 2016. You hand in the manuscript on time and your editor takes two months to read it and get back to you. You then take another month to get changes back to your editor. She takes another month to read the revision and asks you for a few more minor changes. So it's October 1, 2016, before you get your delivery and acceptance check of $3,333.33. Your book is not coming out until October 1, 2017.

Here's how your contract and payment calendar would look:

January 1, 2015: offer made

July 1, 2015: payment due on signing of contract

October 1, 2016: delivery and acceptance payment made

October 1, 2017: publication payment made

▶ With some small publishers who have cash-flow troubles, you may wait much longer for a check than your contract stipulates. If you're signing with a smaller publisher, ask to have it written into your contract that you must be paid within 30 days of each payment date. This way, if they don't pay you for months, they're in breach of contract and, worst-case scenario, you can cancel your deal and take your book on to greener pastures.

So your final check of $3,333.34 will not be in your hands until almost three years after the offer was made. Sad but true.

Bonus Bounty

If you're dissatisfied with your advance or you simply want to see additional royalty dollars, it's a good idea to ask for a bonus. Bonuses typically come in two forms: bestseller bonuses and earn-out bonuses.

To clarify: A bonus in the book world is not like the bonus an employee gets at the end of the year for work well done. It's just more money added to the pool of money you already have to earn out—the equivalent of an added advance check.

Bestseller bonuses usually revolve around hitting the *New York Times* bestseller list—the holy grail of publishing. A typical *New York Times* bonus is based on where a book appears on the list. For example, if your book hits the #1 spot, you get more money than if it hits the #10 spot. Sometimes you get a one-time bonus for hitting the list. But more than likely you'll get a certain amount for each spot and for each

Your Publicity Nest Egg

I f you were lucky enough to get an advance for your book, we recommend that you set aside money RIGHT NOW toward marketing and publicizing your book. Every penny helps. If you can put aside $25,000, fantastic. If you can put aside $2,500, that's good, too. Start small; think big. (As we'll explain in Chapter 12, the work of publicizing and marketing your book will be primarily on you.)

week, up to a specified cap. And, typically, your book must find its niche on the bestseller list within a year of its publication (this usually limits the bonus to the hardcover edition only).

Here are some standard *New York Times* bonus numbers:

(i) $2,500 per week for each week the Work occupies any of the #6–#10 positions,

(ii) $5,000 per week for each week the Work occupies any of the #2–#5 positions, and

(iii) $10,000 per week for each week the Work occupies the #1 position.

The aptly named *earn-out bonus* is given if your book earns out its advance or sells a certain amount of copies within a certain amount of time, typically a year. For example, if you earn out your $25K advance in the first year, you could be given an additional $10K advance. The beauty of this bonus is that it puts more cash in your hands but doesn't require the publisher to take huge risks. In other words: a win-win situation.

The Reality of the Royalty

A royalty, despite its rather kingly connotation, is simply your percentage of the sale for each copy sold. This royalty varies greatly, depending on three major factors.

■ The format of the book, e.g., hardcover, paperback, ebook, illustrated, four-color.

■ The buyers of the book, e.g., independent bookstores, mass merchandisers, or special sales outlets like QVC.

■ The terms on which the book was bought.

Anything special the publisher adds to your book—colored ink, glossy paper, a page that folds out, stickers—naturally adds to the production costs. To offset those higher production costs, the publisher will want to negotiate a lower royalty. Four-color (industry language for "full-color") books or books with special features can have royalties half the size of their traditional brethren. The good news is, if your book does well, the initial production costs (which are the highest) go down as you sell more copies.

Below you will find standard royalties throughout the publishing industry for a typical printed book. These are NOT for unbelievablycheapbooks.com sales, mail-order sales or other sales that vary from the publisher's standard asking price. The royalties pertain only to one-color, standard-size books. And they apply to the book's cover price.

Hardcover	Trade Paperback	Mass-Market Paperback
10% to 5,000 copies	7.5% for all copies	8% to 150,000 copies
12.5% to 10,000 copies		10% thereafter
15% thereafter		

What's the difference between the two kinds of paperbacks? The ones you see on supermarket racks, with pages made from newsprint paper, are called *mass-market paperbacks*. The pricier, often larger ones, filled with nice paper, are called *trade paperbacks*. Not only do they look different and cost more, but they're sold differently. Mass-market paperbacks are often sold through special distributors, as a magazine would be, and trade paperbacks are generally sold through regular book channels.

Riding the Escalator

Often a publisher will reward you with a higher royalty rate if you sell more than a specified number of books. This is called an *escalator*. For example, if you sell more than 50,000 copies of your book, your publisher might be persuaded to go from a 7.5% trade paperback royalty to an 8% royalty. The sale of large numbers of books means an increase in profit margins and more samolians for your publisher, who can then pass some of them on to you.

If you can, get escalators written into your contract. They can be particularly crucial if your advance is small and you think you're going to sell a lot of books, allowing you to make up for that advance with more money from long-term sales.

Escalators can also go down. It's common practice for publishers to reduce the royalty on reprints of a limited number of copies, giving the author

The Size of Your Royalty

M any authors are aghast when they discover that they receive only between 5% and 15% of the sale price of their book while the publisher keeps between 85% and 95%. However, it might be more shocking to learn that the publisher sometimes earns even less per book than the author does. If your book sells for a retail price of $15 and the average wholesale price is $7.50, then the remaining $7.50 has to cover all the publisher's costs. These costs include your initial advance, your royalty, the production costs (paper and binding, for example), warehousing costs, shipping costs, paying for any outside staff who will work on your book (say, a book designer or copy editor) and a very large overhead.

what's called a *small printings royalty*. The smaller the print run, the higher the printing costs for the publisher, so reducing the royalty is often the only way they can manage to keep physical books in print. A publisher never wants books sitting in the warehouse, unsold, so printing and warehousing extra quantities of books is not a desirable option. If your contract stipulates such a reduction, see if you can make it for the smallest number of books possible (most publishers will agree to 2,500 copies or less for one-color books). Be sure that it can occur only once a year, so that if your publisher ends up doing multiple small printings during the year, you get a reduced royalty for only one of these printings. And lastly, make sure this clause applies no earlier than two years after publication so you can depend on at least two years' worth of your full royalty.

Illustration Escalation

Say your publisher wants to start your trade paperback royalty at a lower-than-average 5% because your book is four-color. (He may also want to figure the royalty on net receipts rather than retail price. Fight that one if you can.) Four-color books are so expensive to produce and print that it takes longer for publishers to earn back their money, hence low beginning royalties. But that doesn't mean you can't ask for an escalator that rewards both parties if the book does well. Here's a suggested escalator:

5% for the first 25K copies
6% for the next 25K copies
7% for the next 25K copies
8% thereafter

Even half a percent can make a big difference if your book sells a lot of copies. Let's suppose your book retails for $20 and you sell 100,000 books. If your royalty is half a percent higher, this will mean 10,000 more dollars in your pocket. If you sell a million copies, that's $100,000. What? It could happen!

Electronic Books

The laws are still in the process of being written and tested in the world of electronic books, but we'll try to explain where we are today. Check our website to see whether there are any pertinent ebook updates you'd need to consider in negotiating your contract.

Here's a short history of how ebook pricing has evolved. We'll start at the dawn of ebook popularity: Amazon's Kindle was beginning to take off, and the Barnes & Noble Nook and the Apple iPad hadn't yet arrived. Everything appeared relatively simple: ebooks were priced identically, or nearly identically, to their hardcover or paperback counterparts (whichever edition was most recently released).

It turned out that techies and math nerds weren't the only ones reading ebooks—lovers of romance, science fiction and your average blockbuster were hopping on the bandwagon.

To get readers to hop even faster, Amazon made the bold move of offering Kindle versions of bestselling books for only $9.99. For about half a second, it seemed like publishers, authors and retailers were all happily in bed together. Here's why: A retailer like Amazon buys a book from a publisher at approximately 50% off the cover price. In the beginning, this was true for ebooks as well. So even if Amazon priced an ebook at $9.99, they still had to pay the publisher 50% of the publisher's cover price, and the author received a royalty based on the cover price. You might have heard this called the "wholesale model." Let's do some quick math here: Publisher prices ebook at $24. Amazon pays publisher $12 for ebook. Amazon sells ebook for $9.99. Amazon loses $2.01. Author still gets royalty based on $24 cover price. No harm to publisher. No harm to author.

Why would Amazon be willing to lose $2 on the sale of $9.99 ebooks? To entice consumers to buy Kindles and establish customer loyalty so they'd go on to buy every other conceivable product from the superstore. But publishers quickly realized that consumers might come to expect all books to be priced at $9.99—even newly released hardcovers. And in effect it would be Amazon, not the publishers, who was in control of pricing. Chaos ensued.

Enter Apple with the iPad—and a different financial model (known as the "agency model") that allowed publishers to set their prices (with certain parameters that we won't bore you with) instead so that retailers could not discount wildly. Eventually, this model was shot down by the U.S. Justice Department because they considered it price-fixing. And with that, the price wars were back on—at least for a few years. The Justice Department also stipulated a certain time frame before price negotiations could start up again between publishers and e-tailers—most importantly, Amazon.

The model that has emerged is a bit of a hybrid. But the upshot for you is that most major publishers have decided to pay authors ebook royalties at 25% of the amount actually received by the publisher from the retailer, usually referred to as "net receipts." Why the switch to net when hardcover and paperback royalties are based on the cover price? Because of the crazy scenarios we just outlined, publishers now have only partial control of pricing and are trying to protect themselves against losses by giving you only a percentage of what will, in reality, end up in their pockets.

Independent publishers, on the other hand, have ebook royalties all over the map. From 20% of net, even lower than the big guys, to 50% of net (twice the big guys, for those of you with a math phobia) to 25% or more of the cover price (which, remember, is usually at least double that of the net). So it's important to do the math when you receive a contract. You'll want to compare your hardcover, paperback and ebook royalties. Typically, your ebook royalty will fall in between, but hopefully closer to that of your hardcover.

Flying Without a Net: Calculating off "Net Price"

Some publishers, especially small ones, work off net price, not cover price. Typically, net is approximately 50% of cover price. So your actual royalty will be twice the standard royalty on cover price. For example, if your book sells for $10 and you're getting a 7.5% royalty on cover price, then you will receive 75¢ for every book you sell. If, on the other hand, your royalty is based on net price, i.e., $5, you should receive a royalty of 15%. That's 75¢ a copy as well. Same money. Different math.

The Ouch! of Deep Discounts

Toward the end of the last century, chains like Walmart and Costco accounted for a small percentage of overall sales; today they can mean big business, depending on the type of book. These chains are offered "deep discounts" or "high discounts" by publishers when they order very large quantities of books (the good news is that most of the time these books are nonreturnable). They then offer the consumer deeply slashed prices on these books.

Most authors overlook the realm of deep discounts because they don't know what these are and find them confusing, but it's worth digging in because there can be lots of money at stake. The problem with deep discounts is that they mean a lower royalty. The upside is that they can represent the sale of many more copies of your book. Most deep-discount royalties are set at around two-thirds of the prevailing royalty rate. Still, the math can be confusing, so make sure you're in this range. Also, some publishers will adopt a sliding scale so your royalty won't drop precipitously. And a scant few will give you author approval on deep discounts. But to receive, one must ask.

Delivery: The First Step Toward Blissful Acceptance

Delivery and acceptance are two interconnected yet very distinct activities. The delivery of your book is self-explanatory—it's the moment you hand over the finished manuscript to your publisher. But the delivery date that you put in your contract should not be arbitrary. There are two major points to consider when deciding on your delivery date.

1. *Realistic time frame.* Give yourself more rather than less time. You simply cannot believe how quickly time flies once you've got your contract. And, as we said, a check may take months and months to land in your hand. If you can't start working on your book until you receive your on-signing check, then add another four to six months to your delivery date.

   If you don't give yourself enough time and you end up being late, you will be in breach of contract and your book deal can get CANCELED. While publishers are used to deadline drama and are often willing to extend delivery dates, you need to realize, going in, that they have the right to cancel if you don't meet your deadline.

2. *Publication date.* Discuss with your publisher and consider carefully when you want your book to come out, and work back from there. For example, if you want your book to come out in time for Mother's Day, ask your publisher to give you the latest date you can hand in your book and still get it into stores in plenty of time. Do not under any circumstances agree to a delivery

date you can't meet. Also understand that while everyone wants to get published as soon as possible, most publishers need at least nine months to do the preparation it takes to launch a book properly.

The Beauty and Power of Acceptance

While delivery is self-explanatory, acceptance is not. "Finished" can mean many things, especially where your manuscript is concerned. Is this a sloppy first draft? Or an incredibly polished ready-to-publish manuscript? Or (more likely) something in between? How close your manuscript is to actually being publishable will determine, in large part, whether or not it's "accepted."

Typically, you and your editor will go through at least one round of revisions before your manuscript is accepted. During this time, you may be required to make minor cosmetic changes, or you may find yourself doing radical surgery on your entire book. But at a certain point, with any luck at all, your editor will tell you that the manuscript is ready for the copy editor. The moment your book is handed off to the copy editor (barring any red flags from

The Early Bird May Not Get the Worm

It's not impossible that you will have to finish your book before your contract is done. Talk about an act of extreme faith! But sometimes this will be in your best interest. Let's say, for example, your book is about Christmas. Chances are, you're going to want it to come out a month or two before that date. If you sell your book in September and want it to come out during the holiday season of the following year, in all likelihood you'll have only a few months to write the book. If you factor in the three to six months before you see your first check (let alone your last), you may have to finish your book before a check is even in the mail, never mind in your hands.

If you find yourself in this situation, 1) be sure you get a deal memo before you start, and 2) do not turn in anything before your contract is signed, the check has cleared and the money is in your pocket. If, for some reason, the publisher doesn't like what you've written, they can just decide to cancel the contract, like it never even existed. And that means all work and no money for you.

Also, don't be shy about asking your publisher or your agent to put a rush on the contract and check due to the time constraints. This is possible no matter what any naysayer tells you. Even the biggest publishers can get you a check in a day if they want to. The trouble is, what often is a huge deal to you is insignificant to them.

your publisher's lawyer) is often the moment your book is considered officially accepted. At this point, your "delivery and acceptance" check (often referred to as your D&A check) is released from its gilded cage so it can fly merrily into your pocket.

The Tragedy of Unacceptability

Unfortunately, some manuscripts are not accepted. Be sure you're protected in this sad event, because you could end up having to pay back the portion of your advance you already received.

AVOIDING A "BAD HAIR" CANCELLATION

Your contract will most likely stipulate the circumstances under which your work can be rejected. You want to be sure that your publisher can only reject your work for editorial or legal reasons. This means the publisher can't cancel your book because of changing market conditions, because they disagree with your politics or because they don't like your new 'do. The only reason they can cancel your book is because the manuscript is editorially unacceptable or you're guilty of something heinous like plagiarism. Rejection for editorial reasons is vague enough to cover a wide range of issues: the writing isn't up to professional standards, for example, or the structure is a mess, or they simply don't like the way it's written. But if you have a "for editorial reasons" clause in your contract, and your publisher decides to cancel your book because another book has just been published on the same subject, they have to let you keep your entire advance. Sometimes publishers claim they're rejecting a work for editorial reasons, but in reality they're canceling the book because of changing market conditions, political views or bad hairdos. If this is the case, you have grounds to sue your publisher.

> ▶ If you need to get permissions for your book, you must deliver these with your completed manuscript in order for the work to be accepted. Your publisher may give you a little leeway in terms of the timing, but don't count on it.

Bottom line: If the cancellation clause in your contract isn't specific enough, a publisher can cancel your book on the slightest of whims. In this salt-in-the-wound situation, you will not get the rest of your advance money, you'll have to return the money you've already received and you won't get your book published. Bad bad bad.

FIRST PROCEEDS PROCEDURES

If your book is canceled for contractually legitimate reasons and you've already been paid any money, the *first proceeds clause* stipulates not only *that* you must repay the money, but also *when*. Ideally, your contract should say that you need only repay your publisher out of the proceeds of a sale to another publisher. Many contracts, however, now state that you have to repay all monies within 12 to 18 months regardless of whether you're able to resell your book. This means that 18 months after a publisher rejects your manuscript, you have to pony up the dough. In reality, it's often been the case that many authors couldn't repay this money because, well, because they just didn't have it.

Publishers used to consider these losses part of the cost of doing business, but more and more they're going after authors to get their money back. The bigger the stash of cash involved, the more likely it is that a publisher will try and track you down and get it back. If you're dead-broke and you can prove it, you probably won't be hauled off to debtors' prison. But if you owe money to a publisher because they canceled a book of yours, you probably won't be able to publish a book again until you pay them back. So, if you're unable to secure a first proceeds clause that's only enforceable if your book sells elsewhere, try to make your time span for payback as long as possible.

The Sanity Clause

Ask for your contract to include a clause stating that your editor must respond to your manuscript within 60 days of delivery. He doesn't have to accept the manuscript, but he has to give you feedback. If he doesn't, you and/or your agent can force a response. Your contract will undoubtedly stipulate that you must write a letter to the publisher, demanding a response. You will then inevitably have to wait a while longer, but it's a lot better than having the editor sit on your manuscript indefinitely.

Note that it is often hard to get publishers to agree to this clause because of one of the "unwritten rules" of publishing: Whatever your due date, there's a good chance you will deliver late. Authors or their agents are routinely asking editors to extend the delivery date (and in most cases editors are reasonable about allowing for an extension—sometimes more than one). But if an editor has granted you a three-month extension, and then another two-month extension, he may feel it's not fair when you then try to hold him to the contractual requirement of responding within 60 days of manuscript delivery.

Copyright or Copywrong?

Always retain the copyright to your work. Some publishers write in their contracts that they "may" register an author's book. Some say that *they* own the copyright. Neither situation is acceptable. Under all circumstances, you want it stated in your contract that the publisher *shall* register the copyright in your name.

An exeption: If you're writing a book for a packager, with a corporation or even in certain situations with a coauthor, you may be signing a work-for-hire agreement. In such an agreement, the writer does not retain the copyright. In addition, the writer may receive negligible royalties or none at all.

The Many Faces of Subsidiary Rights

Along with the standard rights to your book, your contract will also contain *subsidiary rights*. These rights (known in the industry as "sub rights") are those that are secondary to the primary rights granted to the publisher. Primary rights include hardcover, paperback or electronic versions of the book sold in North America (or wherever the primary publisher is). Sales of the work in different formats—whether that's an audiobook, a TV show or a large-print edition—are considered subsidiary rights. Sales of the work in a different territory like the United Kingdom, Japan or Brazil are also considered subsidiary rights, typically covered under the "foreign rights" section.

Your contract will stipulate what percentage of each sale of a subsidiary right goes to you and what goes to your publisher. The typical splits between you and your publisher are as follows (the first number represents your share of the pie, the second represents the publisher's):

- First serial (the appearance of an excerpt of your book in a magazine just before or coinciding with its publication): 90/10
- Second serial (the appearance of an excerpt of your book in a magazine after publication): 50/50
- Book club: 50/50
- Permissions (the use of part of your book by another author): 50/50
- Paperback: 50/50
- Special editions: 50/50
- Foreign-language translation: 75/25 (50/50 for four-color illustrated books)

- United Kingdom: 80/20 (50/50 for four-color illustrated books)
- Textbook: 50/50
- Large-type edition: 50/50
- Electronic book: The current rate is generally 25% of net, but since ebook pricing is very much in flux, it's reasonable to try to get it written into your contract that if the publisher's prevailing rate (the rate offered to most authors) changes in your favor, you will automatically be granted the higher rate
- Multimedia adaptation of a book, which may use some of the text and/or illustrations, or additional text or illustrations as well as video or sound added: 100/0
- Audio recording: 50/50
- Commercial and merchandising: 100/0
- Performance (film, TV, stage): 100/0
- Storage and retrieval: 50/50
- Calendar: 50/50

▶ Do you plan to use material—song lyrics, poems, art—that requires permissions? Then ask that your contract include a line to the effect that the publisher will provide you with approved forms for securing any permissions.

We believe you should retain certain subsidiary rights in totality (those marked with a 100/0 split). If you don't keep these rights, they will almost certainly languish and die a sad and lonely death at the hands of your publisher. You and/or your agent have the power to do something with these rights and the chance to make some additional dough. The one exception here is commercial and merchandising rights. If you happen to have a publisher who wants to pursue these rights, give them the option for a limited time period (one to three years).

There are a number of other sub rights you should consider retaining, depending on the circumstances. These include:

- First serial rights
- Foreign rights
- Calendar rights
- Paperback rights

The benefit of retaining all these rights is that if you or your agent can sell them, 100% of the proceeds goes directly into your pocket. But each of these rights has its sticking points.

In order to successfully sell *first serial rights*—less and less likely these days, for a variety of reasons we'll touch on in Chapter 12—it's necessary to have contacts at magazines and newspapers who could publish a section or chapter of your book. If your agent has these contacts, great. If you're a journalist who makes your living selling magazine articles, you may have a shot as well. But even so, remember that the typical split between you and your publisher is 90/10 in your favor (although you won't see that 90% until you earn out your advance). Better to let your publisher keep 10% and take care of all the xeroxing and mailing of your manuscript, because these costs may well exceed the 10% you held on to. And if your or your agent's only contact with the magazine business is a subscription to *People,* you should certainly let your publisher hold on to first serial rights. All large publishers have a department devoted solely to subsidiary rights. Of course, this department may have to deal with literally hundreds of books, so unless yours is one of their leading titles, its chances of getting the level of attention needed to actually make a first serial sale are slim. But slim is better than none. And if you do have magazine connections, you can work in conjunction with your publisher to sell these rights.

Whether or not to retain *foreign rights* can be a particularly difficult decision, because there can be much money involved. Many agents have what are called subagents in countries around the world to help sell these rights. But once again, if neither you nor your agent has the contacts to sell your book abroad, there is little point in holding on to foreign rights.

The Rancor of Returns

It's hard to believe how publishing works when it comes to returns, so listen up. Let's say a bookstore orders 10 copies of your book. Your publisher then sends 10 copies of your book to said bookstore. The bookstore pays for those 10 books. The books then go onto the shelves. Sometimes they're not all sold. The melancholy unsold books can then be returned to the publisher, who has to give the money back or credit the bookseller.

How does all this affect you? It may be written in your contract that the publisher can withhold a portion of your royalty money in anticipation of a "reasonable" number of returns. So, while the bookstore may have sold 10 copies of your book, your publisher can withhold money against future, projected returns—what's called in the business a reserve against returns. Most of the time, this is not more than 25% of your royalties. But it can be more. Try to ensure that the publisher can neither withhold more than 20% of your royalties against returns nor withhold your money for more than two royalty periods (one royalty period equals six months).

Calendar rights are significant only if you're one of the lucky few with a book that can be transformed into a calendar. Does your book have witty aphorisms that are perfect for a boxed calendar? Does it have gorgeous photos that would translate into a knock-your-socks-off wall calendar? If not, pursuing publishers that produce calendars won't be worth the energy.

Paperback rights are relevant only if your book is coming out first in hardcover, and important only if your book is with a midsize/independent publisher. The reason is that, if your book is successful, midsize/independent publishers often sell the paperback rights to large publishers, whereas larger publishers almost always publish both the hardcover and paperback versions themselves.

A large publisher who buys the paperback rights to your book pays your publisher an advance and royalties, half of which gets applied to your own royalties. The problem with allowing your publisher to retain the paperback rights is best displayed in the following numbers: Say your paperback rights sell for a $50,000 advance with 7.5% royalties. Say your book sells 75,000 copies at $15 per copy, or $1.13 per book in royalties. Since you get only 50% of the take, you end up with approximately $42,000 in your pocket. However, if you had held on to the rights, you would have received the full 7.5% royalty, resulting in double the amount: $84K in your piggy bank. But if you don't have an agent, selling paperback rights can be very tricky. Your book has to do well enough for publishers to be coming to you, or for you to interest an agent who can sell the paperback rights.

▶ Whether you or your publisher retains foreign rights, you should know about the power of scouts to help with your foreign sales efforts. These middlemen are employed by publishers around the world to look for titles appropriate for their lists. By getting your proposal/manuscript into the hands of scouts (they're listed in *Literary Market Place*), you may increase your chances of foreign sales.

In the Loop with Out of Print

Because of all the recent technological advances in publishing, most books will no longer really go out of print. Yes, your publisher may decide not to print an entire run of your book once its sales have fallen off, but they're sure to make the book available via print-on-demand or as an ebook. This is why it's so important that you pay special attention to the *out-of-print clause* in your contracts.

Say your publisher is doing nothing to market or sell your book and you want to take the rights back. You will be unable to do so if your book is deemed "in print" by your contract. To avoid this scenario, you'll want to set what's called a performance standard for your book. A performance standard states that if the Work does not sell a determined number of copies (for example, 500) *in any and all formats* within a certain period (say, a year), then either the rights automatically revert to the author or, more typically, the author can request a reversion of rights and the publisher has a certain period to reissue the book—or not. As you can tell by the italics, the crucial piece of this clause is the "any and all formats."

▶ Few authors are sued over their books, but those who are can certainly benefit from insurance. Most big publishers include you in their insurance policies, and some smaller houses will add you to theirs if you ask. But if you're with a house that doesn't have insurance and you don't want to spend the time investigating policies, here's some advice everyone should live by: Don't write anything libelous and don't infringe on anyone else's copyright.

If you're signing with a smaller, more flexible publisher, you will also want to try to set a term for the electronic rights to your book (say, five years). After this period, a new term is subject to a good-faith negotiation with the publisher.

Warranties and Indemnities: Publishers Covering Their Asse(t)s

You wouldn't plagiarize, would you? That's good, because most publishing contracts have a paragraph requiring you to warrant that the writing you say is yours really is. And just in case it's not, you also have to *indemnify* (protect) your publisher from damages in case an aggrieved party sues. This indemnification applies even if you unintentionally err. So, if you're researching a topic and copying down material created by others, be extra sure to keep track of your sources so you can give them proper attribution. And make sure those working with you do the same. If a research assistant forgets to put quotation marks around a passage taken from another source and you accidentally use that passage as your own, you are liable.

While you almost definitely will not be able to change anything in your contract related to warranties and indemnities, it's incumbent upon you to understand what you're getting yourself into. There's a whole world of people with way too much time on their hands and way too much bitterness in their hearts for you to make a mistake in this area.

Author Copies: "You Mean I Have to Buy My Own Books?"

Think you get unlimited free copies of your own book? Wrong! The number of free copies you receive is written into your contract, and there's a good chance you'll get as few as 10. This means, if you want to give copies of your book to friends, relatives and folks you meet along the way, you will have to buy them. That's right, not only will you have to write the thing, but you'll have to pay good cash money for your own book! The good news is, you get what's called an author's discount. This, too, is stipulated in your contract. Most publishers give you a 50% discount, although some won't go below a 40% discount.

Some publishers will also agree to give you many more free copies of your book for promotion and marketing purposes. One of the ways you can get these additional copies written into your contract is to provide a list of great contacts to whom you'll be sending your books. It's not unreasonable for a media maven to ask for as many as 250 copies. If you can't get this stipulation, don't worry. Your publisher will often send books to the media or other important folks—though "important folks" don't include your second cousin.

Covering Your Cover

Do whatever you can to get the *right of consultation* on your book's cover, as well as on your interior design, flap and catalog copy. Not that consultation means all that much. In essence, it means that your publisher can show you your cover design, get your comments, say thank you very much and give you the big kiss-off. But at least, if you get to review these pieces, you have the chance to ask and fight for changes.

▶ If you or your company plans to buy large quantities of your book (say, over 1,000 copies), you might be able to get the publisher to give you a hefty discount (under the category of "special sales"). Similarly, if you expect your own connections to result in direct sales to a company or companies, you might be able to increase your own royalty on these sales. Be sure to negotiate this discount at the time of the initial offer.

Your contract should say that you and your publisher will *mutually agree* on a title or that you get approval on the title. Hopefully you're going to be saying this title for the rest of your life. And you don't want a bitter taste in your mouth every time you do.

Options for Your Option

Most publishers want first dibs on your next proposal or manuscript (especially if your first book does well). This is what's known as an option. Options allow your current publisher to have an exclusive time period to decide whether or not to pursue your next project. So you don't sign over your life, make sure that the language of your option includes some limits:

- Your next book of nonfiction or fiction (whichever your current book is).

- A book written solely by you, if you are the sole author of your current book, OR a book written solely by you AND your coauthor, if you cowrote your current book.

- A detailed proposal only, if you're writing nonfiction.

- An option period that begins as close to delivery and acceptance as possible. If it can begin at delivery and acceptance, that's great. But some publishers will make you wait until your book comes out before you can show them a new proposal or manuscript because they want to see what the response to your first book will be.

- A period of 30 to 45 days for an exclusive look. Once you submit your option book, if no decision is made within this time frame, you should be free to shop it around.

- No matching clause. A matching clause stipulates that you cannot enter into an agreement with another publisher for your option book if your current publisher matches the other offer.

■ If your publisher makes an offer but you cannot agree on terms within a 30-day window, you should be free to move about the cabin at your leisure.

The Rules of Accounting

Your publisher should send you royalty statements at specified intervals (at least twice a year) on specified dates. These statements should be sent whether or not a payment is due to you.

An accountant of your choice should also be allowed to examine the publisher's books at least once a year in case you feel there are errors in your statements. Your contract should stipulate that the publisher will pay for the examination as well as all monies owed within 30 days in the event that the accountant finds errors greater than 5%. This hardly ever happens, but it's very important in this day and age to have proper protection.

It can be a frustrating and difficult thing, but understand that publishers do sometimes "lose" sales of thousands of books. This, of course, can mean thousands and thousands of very real lost dollars. It's certainly not an everyday occurrence, but more than one author has had to sue his publisher over discrepancies in actual sales vs. reported sales. If you're concerned about the accuracy of the numbers on your statement, check with booksellers in your hometown and around the country. Keep an eye on Amazon to see how your book is selling. If you know you've sold books but negligible sales keep coming up on your royalty statements, you may have a problem.

Sign Here, Please . . .

If you're a writer and you don't deal with contracts on a daily, weekly, yearly or even once-in-a-blue-moon basis, you may let your excitement overshadow your obligation to pay close attention to your contract. Do not fall into this trap. Working closely with an agent and/or lawyer, go over your contract with the finest of fine-tooth combs. You don't want to be one of those poor dweebs you read about who signed an odious contract and made a big pile of money for somebody else, only to keep a wee sliver of it for himself.

If you don't have an agent, you should definitely have a lawyer. And even if you do have an agent, depending on your agent's level of expertise, you might want to have your publishing contract looked over by a lawyer who knows the ins and outs of the publishing business. Anyone else will more than likely be a waste of money.

Someone Has to Write the Thing . . .

With the nuts and bolts out of the way, it's time to turn to the dark underbelly of this whole business: the scary netherworld in which you will actually have to WRITE YOUR BOOK!

We truly hope you are in possession of a membership to a nearby warehouse club, because you are going to need a bulk supply of snacks. One note of caution: Do please beware of the potentially deadly combination of beverages and workstations. Amen.

CHAPTER 9

Write Away!

"I think I did pretty well, considering I started out with nothing but a bunch of blank paper."

—*Steve Martin*

SOME WRITERS WRITE ONLY WHEN caffeine-saturated, while others demand distilled water. Some vampirically shut all the shades; others need a room with a view. Edgar Allan Poe is rumored to have written with a head full of opium. Isabel Allende lights candles and begins all her books on January 8. Carolyn See, *Washington Post* book critic and author of numerous books, takes the practical approach. She writes 1,000 words every day.

The important thing is to write whichever way suits you. This may mean following in someone else's footsteps or inventing your own mad ways. While we can't help you put pen to paper or fingers to keyboard, we can help you break down your big scary book into a series of small friendly tasks—from filling in a Master Calendar so you can pace yourself and avoid burning out, to the nourishing and use of your outline, to the creating of your first draft, to the inevitable and seemingly endless revisions and rewritings, to that wonderful moment when you're done.

Getting Your Ducks in a Row So You Can Get Quacking

It may seem slightly ridiculous to methodically organize an artistic activity like writing, but doing so can bring comfort and freedom. You'll know where your milestones are, when you're moving ahead of your deadline and when you're falling behind. Let's break it down. How long is your book? How fast do you write? When is your deadline? When do you want to be finished with your first draft (which is a different question from when you want to hand in your completed manuscript)? Consider that before you deliver a draft to your editor, you should have it read by your team, your agent and/or other assorted readers so you can use their comments to rewrite before you hand in your manuscript. You may want to do this several times; it can take readers weeks or even months to read and intelligently evaluate a manuscript. Factor in your rewrite time. Sometimes a large hairy rewrite. Then consider whether there are photographs or illustrations to find or make, permissions to obtain, research to do or people to interview. When you're estimating, assume you'll have to do more rather than less work.

As the great Yogi Berra said, "It gets late early out there." And you do not want to be scrambling around as your deadline looms, panicked, frantic, sleep-deprived, like an author in the headlights of a runaway train. Generally speaking, people do not do their best work under these conditions.

Making a Place to Write

Before you sit down and make a schedule, create a work-friendly environment. Try to arrange your life so you have several hours every day when you don't answer the phone. This may mean getting up at five in the morning or staying up until five in the morning.

Many years ago, Erma Bombeck was an unknown housewife with less than no time to herself. But she really wanted to write. She wanted to write so much that she made herself a little desk area in the kitchen where she would grab 15 minutes here and 15 minutes there. She turned her desire into a wildly successful publishing career, writing about the everyday trials and tribulations of being a mom and wife in America.

Understand that while writing is certainly time spent at the computer or with pen in hand, it's also time spent thinking about your book between writing sessions. As Agatha Christie said, "The best time for planning a book is while you're doing the dishes." Perhaps you could use the time spent commuting to iron out plot problems. When you're lying in bed at night, figure out what your characters are wearing, what their parents were like, what their hobbies are. Use workout time to smooth out the bumps in your thesis and the chinks in your arguments. While you're making dinner, think about how to present the various elements of your subject in an original, easy-to-understand way.

The Art of the Schedule

Let's suppose you plan on writing a 500-page manuscript. Say you write two pages a day and you have a year to finish your book. This means it will take 250 writing days, or about eight months. And you have to assume you won't be able to write every single day. So you should probably aim to get a first draft done in nine months. That will give you plenty of time to get people to read your draft and give you comments, and for you to do your award-winning rewrites.

Breaking it down further, this schedule means you have to do 55 pages a month. Given the fact that a page equals 250 words, you will have to write 13,750 words a month. That's around 3,437 words a week. If you write 5,000 words a week for two and a half weeks, you'll have almost enough for your whole month. Then you can either forge ahead or go back and rework what you've done. If things are going slowly and in three weeks you've got only 7,500 words, you know you need to put your life on hold a little and churn full steam ahead.

> "When I start a book, I always think it's patently absurd that I can write one. No one, certainly not me, can write a book 500 pages long. But I know I can write 15 pages, and if I write 15 pages every day, eventually I will have 500 of them."
>
> —*John Saul*

To keep on track, it's helpful to construct a motherboard, your Master Calendar, which will lay out all your deadlines from here through launch and beyond. Buy or make yourself a big one-year calendar. You will need to be able to change and modify it. A lot.

You can use your Master Calendar not only in the writing of your book, but in its marketing, publicizing and selling as well. Your Master Calendar won't let you overlook any of the many important details. It's hard to stay on top of everything, but if you're meticulous about updating this calendar and consulting it regularly, you can stay one step ahead of the typhoon that will soon be your book.

By Whatever Means Necessary

Khaled Hosseini had a great excuse not to write a book. He was a full-time doctor. He had no time. Nonetheless he was bound and determined to write a novel. "I would get up at four," he says. "I'd read the paper, have my coffee and then start writing by four forty-five. I'd write until about eight. Then I'd go in and work my shift. Luckily, in residency you learn how to function on very little sleep." Khaled found that there were few distractions at that time of morning, and he was able to finish his novel. His book *The Kite Runner*, set in Afghanistan, became a #1 *New York Times* bestseller, has been translated into 42 languages and continues to sell all over the world. Together, *The Kite Runner* and his second book, *A Thousand Splendid Suns*, have sold over 38 million copies worldwide.

If you're using a calendar on your computer, it's helpful to keep a printout on your wall so that you can see the whole year at a glance. Mark your start date and your deadline. Then determine your various interim deadlines. Where do you need to be by the end of the first month? In six months? Nine months? A year? Lay it all out for yourself very clearly. In number of words, in number of pages. If you're doing interviews or research, jot down when you'd like each completed. If you need to acquire permissions, add these to your schedule. If your book contains original illustrations or photographs, set up deadlines for these as well.

Search and Research

If you're writing a book that requires extensive research, do yourself a couple of favors. First, leave lots of time. Second, document your research meticulously.

Doing research is like mining for gold. It takes time and patience to hack all that rock just to find one gleaming nugget. And you never know if your next hack will be the one that strikes that rich beautiful vein. Which means it's very hard to make a schedule around research. You could take a three-week trip to Bali and come back empty-handed. You could spend an afternoon at your local public library or a weekend on the World Wide Web and find everything you need. That's why it's critical to stuff in sufficient padding when you're making a research schedule. If you haven't done a major research project before, talk to authors who have. And remember, when it comes to research, a great librarian can be worth her weight in the aforementioned gold.

INTERVIEWS AND THE SWEETNESS OF DOCUMENTATION

Keep track of everything. Whether you're gathering information from historical documents, interviewing people, or getting photos and articles from the Internet, magazines and/or books, write down *all* pertinent information: publications, exact dates and times, photographers' names, page numbers. Everything. It's best to keep all this information in one log so you always know where to find it.

This log will hold valuable information for your footnotes or bibliography and for tracking permissions. When we wrote our book about Negro Leagues baseball player Satchel Paige, we did a lot of research in libraries across the country. Much of this involved making xeroxes from microfiche. We naïvely didn't write down the names or dates of the publications, thinking we'd somehow remember them when we got home. Naturally, we couldn't remember a thing. We thought we'd have to spend thousands of dollars making a second trip back to these libraries to get our information straight, but luckily we were able to do heavy detective work from home to figure it all out. Still, we wasted countless hours by not keeping careful records.

If interviews are required for your book, the best way to document them is by recording them. Always test your recording technique before you go to an interview, especially if you're recording for the first time! Also, be sure people know when they're being recorded. And don't deceive anyone by pretending to turn the recorder off when you're leaving it on.

Keith and Kent Zimmerman have spent years and years doing taped interviews, first as journalists and then as coauthors for famous folks. Their advice is as follows:

- End the formal interview before you run out of tape, and keep the mike hot so you can get some great off-the-cuff remarks.

- Try not to interrupt. Silence brings extra insight as your subject attempts to fill up the spaces.

- Transcribe your own tapes. You were there. Nobody you farm it out to can re-create that experience. You can also do double duty by simultaneously doing subtle rewrites—basic cleaning up of grammar and syntax—that don't in any way change the meaning or language of what was said.

- Change rooms every so often when conducting interviews. Familiarity breeds complacency.

THOU SHALT NOT MAKE STUFF UP OR COPY FROM OTHERS

This may seem obvious, but again, say it we must. If you're writing nonfiction, DO NOT claim that something that isn't true is true. And with fiction and nonfiction, DO NOT use other people's words without crediting them properly.

In recent years, a number of memoirists have been accused of making up parts of their books. Some of these memoirists have vociferously defended their truths and others have admitted to writing falsehoods. Some have been sued and destroyed. Others have made millions due to all the attention.

Plagiarism scandals have long plagued authors. Often these cases turn out to be more about sloppiness than bad intentions. But in a court of law, plagiarism is plagiarism. Which brings up another essential point. DO NOT be sloppy. A world of people with way too much time on their hands is just waiting to prove that something in your book is wrong, especially if it becomes successful. And if someone proves one thing in your book is wrong—whether intentional or not—it destroys your credibility. You do not want your credibility destroyed, as this often leads to public disgrace and humiliation, and sometimes to having to pay back all the money you made from your book.

So if you're doing research and copying information directly from a source, put quotes around it so you know which words belong to you and which belong to someone else. Then be sure to get permission for any quotes that exceed "fair use" (see page 218 for details). Better yet, footnote your work. (But if you're working in Microsoft Word, don't use the automatic footnote function or you'll create problems for your typesetter. Instead, label the footnote as such and type it in directly below the referring paragraph.)

The Art of Locating Art

To determine a schedule for your art, first figure out exactly what art you need. If you need an illustrator or photographer to create original art, and your publisher is not helping you locate such a person, head straight for your computer, local library, bookstore and magazine stand.

If you're looking for illustrations, the children's sections of bookstores are great spots to start looking for artists, even if your book is for adults; since nearly every book is illustrated, you can often find someone whose style appeals to you. The next places to look are sites like theispot.com and commarts.com, which advertising agencies, publishers and others use to track down illustrators. These sources are helpful search tools because they include each artist's contact information.

If you're looking for contemporary photographs (or classic photos by famous photographers), there's no easier pit stop than a stock house, which owns thousands of images. Getty and AP are great places to start and are accessible via the web. They do the research for you: Put in a search word and you're likely to find hundreds of potential images. The permission process is simplicity itself. You can pay via credit card. And you get what you pay for—Getty and other high-end stock houses have world-class pics but can be stiff, price-wise. So stiff that you might spend your entire budget for a photo or two. (AP charges somewhat less than Getty but doesn't have nearly as many images.) One thing to be aware of is that many stock houses charge based on the size of your first printing, then recharge for every subsequent printing. So if your publisher is planning a big first printing, as exciting as this may be, if you go with a stock house, you're going to feel some pain in your pocketbook.

Fortunately, with the plethora of user-generated content on the web, there are now lots of other places to go for photos and illustrators. Like Flickr, one of our favorite sites for finding photos. In case you've been hiding under a rock, Flickr allows anyone in the world to post his or her photos and tag them so people like you can find them. While there are numerous professional photographers posting to Flickr, most are amateurs. But many amateur photographers are doing fabulous stuff these days. And if you buy a photo from one of them, you're sure to pay much less, if anything at all. Not to take away from the professionals. A professional is a professional for a reason; even subtle differences like how a pro deals with light, composition and detail can make a huge impact on the page.

Istockphoto is another great user-generated site for both photos and illustration. However, they have a nonnegotiable fee structure in place. The good news is that they don't charge according to the number of books in your first or subsequent printing. It's a one-time charge only.

Art schools are yet another resource for finding very talented people at very low prices. Some students will even hand over their work for nothing in exchange for getting published. But be careful here. While the price may be right, the work might *look* like it was done by a student. Full vetting is advised.

▶ In some cases, a picture may be worth not only a thousand words, but a thousand dollars as well! So never just accept the price a stock house quotes you for art. Haggling, if done with humor and intelligence, can be both fun and profitable. No matter what your source, it will almost always behoove you to consolidate your purchases; you stand a much better chance of getting a lower price per image when buying in bulk. If you ask, that is.

If you plan on hiring a single illustrator or photographer to do original work throughout your book, check out the aforementioned places (even stock houses list the artists' names). Once you have about half a dozen people you're keen on, check to see if they have their own websites; even students have their work up online these days. You want to see as much of each artist's work as possible to make sure his style suits you. You might spot a single illustration or photograph that looks perfect, but upon glancing at the artist's site, realize that piece was the exception to a style, not the rule.

Be forewarned: Original illustrations and photography can cost tens of thousands of dollars. But if an artist is excited about your project and feels it will help his career, you may be able to swing a deal. If the artist has never worked for your publisher (or any publisher, for that matter), you will be opening a valuable door for him. This is particularly important if you have a publisher

215

A Sporting Good Time

D avid loves soccer. So when his friend Alan Black growled in a Scottish brogue about working with him on a guide to World Cup 2010 in South Africa, David jumped at the idea. They wanted to make an edgy, funny homage to the old-fashioned soccer (a.k.a. football) guides they loved in their childhood. These books are heavily illustrated, often with cartoons, little boxes and quizzes. Part of the joy of these books is looking at photographs of players you love and hate. Alan and David sold the book to Dutton, a division of Penguin, for $20,000 with a $5,000 art budget. This $5,000 art budget was supposed to include original art, photos *and* the actual graphic design of the book.

If you were an art director, you'd be rolling around on the floor laughing right now at how stupid David and Alan were to sign such a deal. Any one of these three elements could cost the entire $5K, if not more. A realistic art and design budget for this book would be a minimum of $15,000. Alan and David quickly discovered their stupidity when they went to buy some photographs of hugely famous soccer players. So they each attacked the problem in different ways. David went to Times Square, where some of the best caricaturists in the world ply their trade for next to nothing. He found a remarkable artist named Liu Yuhua, who had displayed at his little spot on the street a hysterical caricature of Michael Ballack, the German soccer star. David

known for illustrated books. Many illustrators and photographers bang their heads on publishers' doors until they're lumpy with knots, so they'll often take a pay cut just to get a toe or two in. But beware: An illustrator or photographer with no book experience might be in for a shock when he discovers what publishing fees look like in comparison to the advertising world. A photographer can make $10,000 in one day when shooting for an ad—as opposed to $10,000 for an entire book's worth of photographs. If the artist won't agree to your offer, consider giving him a small percentage of the royalties.

Your project may also be of personal interest to an artist. Say you're doing a cookbook on pastas from the Ligurian region of Italy. Maybe your top choice for an artist has ancestors from that part of the world and has always wanted to go there. Once again, doing your research, making a personal connection and showing the value of your project are paramount in bringing a top-notch artist on board for a price you can afford.

In terms of setting a price for art, work with your editor and/or agent to determine fair market value and, if you're looking for a bargain, go down from there. In most cases, it's better to negotiate a flat fee for all art than to pay for it piece by piece.

contracted Liu to do a bunch of portraits of World Cup stars. Liu did it for very little money—$100, for everything—because he wanted the opportunity to be in a book. The deft and funny drawings added a unique element, contributing to an overall effect that was both cutting-edge and old-school.

Meanwhile, Alan went out and found the most amazing photographs on Flickr. He narrowed in on a world-class soccer photographer named Ryu Voelkel, who, it turns out, was willing to work within their budget. Alan and David bought 10 exquisite soccer photographs for $100 each. They had now taken care of the lion's share of their art needs and still had 80% of their budget left! They also lucked out with some fantastic photographs by those shockingly talented amateurs who run rampant all over the web. And those photographers agreed to participate in exchange for copies of the book. Cost: $0.00.

With the rest of their art budget, and a little bit of their advance, they hired a graphic artist named Kim Sillen. She also took a reduced fee because she had never designed a book before. One of the things Kim did to keep costs down was to use toys and action figures to create brilliant and funny dioramas of famous scenes from soccer history. They fit in perfectly with the tone and monetary limitations of the book because they're unique, cheeky and cheap. Much like David and Alan.

If original art is not necessary or appropriate for your book, you can look for existing art in any number of places. Do you need historic photos? Period illustrations? Vintage advertisements? Contemporary photos? Japanese anime? Cave drawings?

The Internet has made finding art an art in itself. You can now get all manner of remarkable art from all over the world. If you're looking for anything old, libraries and historical societies are great places to start. The Library of Congress is one of the greatest resources for artwork; its archives are huge and the prices are reasonable.

Permission Slips: Decoding Copyright Laws

If you want to reprint a passage, poem, song or image that was not created for your book, you're likely to need written permission from the person who owns the copyright to the work. Before a major publisher will publish your book, they must have all your permissions in hand. If they don't, they'll ask you to remove the material in question. If you won't, they won't publish your book. They don't want to be sued. And neither do you.

Making a schedule for permissions is tricky because you never actually know what you're going to use in your book until you write and edit it. Books often change significantly from first draft to last. A picture or poem you think is essential early on might prove to be meaningless fluff when the book is laid out. But that's usually quite late in the game.

▶ In Chapter 8, we suggested that your contract include a clause about your publisher providing official permissions forms. Request these forms with your signed contract or very early in your research process; otherwise you may forget about them and end up having to create your own at the last minute. If you're self-publishing, we've included a form in Appendix IV for your convenience.

So don't start getting permissions too soon, because you don't want to waste your time or money. However, since it often takes a while to track down a pesky permission—and all permissions should be handed in with your finished manuscript—we suggest the following process:

1. *Break your permissions into three piles.* Definites, Maybes, Unlikelies. Track down all sourcing and contact information for the Definites as early as possible. Get prices and any necessary forms. This will help you guesstimate total costs and figure out how much you'll have left over for the Maybes and Unlikelies.

2. *Don't pay for a thing until you're sure what's going in your book.* This way, you won't wind up spending money on a Definite that turns out to be an Unlikely.

WHAT DO YOU NEED PERMISSION FOR?

You will almost certainly have to obtain permission to reprint more than two lines of a poem, more than one line of a song or more than a few lines of a book or essay. You will also almost certainly have to obtain permission for a photograph, illustration or painting. One exception to this rule is the use of text in the *public domain*. All works published before 1923 are now in the public domain, but works published after this date can fall into a number of different categories. If you're unsure whether something you want to reprint is in the public domain, we encourage you to go directly to *The Chicago Manual of Style* (which has over 30 pages on the subject) or to the Library of Congress to ask for help.

No permission is necessary if the piece you're reprinting is considered *fair use*. Here's where things get really complicated. There is no easily quantifiable measure of fair use. As the *Chicago Manual* says, "Use of less than the whole [poem, essay, chapter or such] will be judged by whether the second author appears to be taking a free ride on the first author's labor. As a rule of thumb, one should never quote more than a few contiguous paragraphs or stanzas at a time or let the quotations, even if scattered, begin to overshadow the quoter's own material. Quotations or graphic reproductions should not be so long that they substitute for, or diminish the value of, the copyright owner's own publication. Proportion is more important than the absolute length of a quotation: to quote five hundred words from an essay of five thousand is likely to be more serious than quoting five hundred words from a work of fifty thousand." In other words, it's okay for us to quote 122 words from the *Chicago Manual* because that's a tiny percentage of its total word count (the book could double as a doorstop). However, if you took 122 words out of a 200-word poem, you must get permission to reprint it—unless, of course, it's in the public domain. And don't forget, composers' and poets' estates are notorious for going after people who abuse copyright law.

If you've tried without success to track something down, don't despair. The *Chicago Manual* states that as long as the author demonstrates (and documents) a "reasonable effort" to locate the copyright holder, then the piece in question can be printed. Just check with your publisher to make sure they're okay with the associated risk. If, once your book is published, you are contacted by one of the sources, you can negotiate a fee at that time.

The Pangs of Permissions

Acquiring permissions requires the patience of Job and the persistence of a pit bull. When she began writing *A Thousand Years over a Hot Stove,* a book with more than 100 photographs and illustrations, Laura Schenone was ill-prepared for the amount of work permissions required. Not to mention the pounding her pocketbook took in the process. Laura says, "I wish I'd had a better understanding of those permission fees at the outset and how they work with print runs—a huge issue with an illustrated book."

Laura was presented with an unexpected challenge. Many of the people she was dealing with would sell her rights only for the first printing of her book. "My editor told me this would be 7,500 copies," she says. "When I bought the permissions, I wanted to up this number to 10,000 or 15,000 copies to be sure I was covered. But sometimes the fees as much as doubled."

Laura's story illustrates the importance of understanding permission costs before signing a deal or even developing a project. That said, Laura couldn't be happier that she wrote her book, permissions and all. *A Thousand Years over a Hot Stove* went on to win a James Beard Award, the Pulitzer Prize of food writing.

HOW TO GET PERMISSION

To acquire a permission, you'll need to apply by filling in the aforementioned permissions form, preferably provided by your publisher. It should state *what* you're reprinting, in what *form* you're reprinting it, the *territory* you're reprinting it in and in *how many books/editions* the material will be reprinted. This form will constitute a legal agreement between you and the owner of the material you want to reprint.

It's always better for your permission form to cover nonexclusive world rights in all languages and for all editions of your work (including ebooks). Sometimes copyright holders won't want to grant you such rights, or will grant them for a prohibitively expensive fee. If you can afford to acquire only North American rights and you don't predict any foreign sales of your book, then stick with those for the moment. If you're lucky enough to sell foreign rights down the road, you'll have to go back to the source and pay for these additional uses. The same rule applies to different editions, hardcover vs. paperback.

Everyman Power: The Paul Davidson Story

Paul Davidson wrote a book containing dozens of letters he penned to the customer service departments of America's biggest corporations, along with their responses. When he sold his book, the publisher informed him that he would now have to get permission for EVERY SINGLE letter from EVERY SINGLE company that wrote to him. Many of these letters didn't put the companies in the rosiest of lights. And yet, if he wanted his book published, by hook or by crook he had to get these corporations to sign release forms.

What's a guy to do? After tracking down the correct contact people, Paul got on the horn and trotted out his excellent sense of humor. At first, many company representatives didn't believe that it was in their best interest to sign. But Paul made them laugh until they gave in. One time, he had his wife call and leave a message for one of the most stubborn of the bunch, saying that their marriage was taking the brunt of Paul's hunt for permissions and would they please, please, help save a sacred union. In the end, fewer than a half-dozen companies refused to sign permissions. In Paul's words: "It was an arduous process for a non-lawyer, but it turned out to be greatly successful because I was, indeed, not a lawyer. Because I came across as an 'everyman author,' companies seemed more apt to help." At publication, his book, *Consumer Joe: Harassing Corporate America, One Letter at a Time*, found its way into Jamba Juices around the country. Why? Their tongue-in-cheek letters addressing Paul's ideas for a delicious Tuna Melt Smoothie were in his book. In fact, Jamba Juice was one of the first companies to realize that it was good business to have some fun and join Paul's party.

Once you have a form in tow, the next step is identifying the owner of the material you want to use. If you're looking for permission to reprint material from a book, first go to the copyright page to find out who originally published it. For example, if the material is in a paperback edition of a book, you may find that a different publisher did the hardcover; if so, you'll need to go to the publisher of the hardcover to secure permission. Or, let's say you're using an essay from an anthology. It may have first been published elsewhere, perhaps in a magazine. The copyright page will list the source you need to contact.

If you need permission to reprint song lyrics, you can go directly to the website of the American Society of Composers, Authors and Publishers (see Appendix II). Click on the box on the upper right-hand corner that says "ACE/ Repertory." Once there, you can search the database for a title, writer or performer. At the bottom of your search results page, you'll find the information about the publisher/administrator. These are the people you'll need to go through to obtain permission.

Sound like a pain? It is. But there are worse pains in life.

Once you've found your source, it may take you what seems like a billion phone calls to track down a real person. When you do, be sure to get a name and email address as well as phone and fax numbers. Do not count on permission givers getting your permissions back to you in a timely fashion. Repeated follow-up will probably be necessary. You might even have to send another form because the original has been "misplaced" or was "never received."

Don't necessarily assume you will have to pay anything. Some kind souls will give you the piece of material you're seeking free of charge. But even if you get someone's permission for free, you still need his signature on your form.

You may be surprised to learn that your publisher will most likely not lift a finger to help you with permissions. Then again, if you've ever worked with a publisher, you may not be so surprised. However, in some extreme instances, if you've tried and tried without success to secure a permission, your publisher may step in at the end and facilitate. In the big houses, people trained to do such things can assist in a pinch. But DO NOT count on this. Often the publisher just won't let you use the material in your book. Case closed. End of story.

Do not rest until every single permission has been tucked nicely into bed. It's easy to forget about a dangler.

Lastly, make copies of your signed permission forms before you send them to your editor. Put these copies in a safe place. You're going to have to credit all sources at the back (or front) of your book. The more organized you are now, the easier this task will be later.

Getting Started

B efore you write your first word, arrange a meeting or phone conversation with your editor, if you have one, to establish the guidelines of your working relationship as well as the direction of your manuscript. This is where you need to get as much information as possible about the kind of book your editor wants. If, unbeknownst to you, your editor has a different idea than you do of what your book should be, you could be in serious trouble when you hand in your manuscript and she asks you to do massive rewrites or, horror of horrors, rejects your book (for more information on how to work effectively with your editor, see the section beginning on page 235). Once you know the lay of the land it's time to start, you know, writing.

Ernest Hemingway's first rule of writing was "Apply the seat of the pants to the seat of a chair." That's another way of saying something that many people have difficulty grasping: If you want to complete your book, you have to write it. And starting is almost always more difficult than keeping it going. Something about inertia, and bodies in motion remaining in motion.

Resisting the Temptation to Write the Perfect Sentence

M any writers want to write the perfect sentence right out of the chute. And if they don't have the perfect sentence, they feel as if they can't go on. It's extremely difficult to write a great book this way. It's hard to write any kind of book this way.

Try this: Write the best sentence you can at this particular moment.

Then move on.

Never sit with one sentence longer than five minutes. Writing can be like quicksand. If you struggle, you just sink faster. Give in, accept the fact that you're stuck and come back later to fix it. Tonight. Tomorrow. Whenever. You'll be amazed how often the fix seems obvious. Or, more often still, it becomes obvious that you can just throw the sentence away.

We met a man who claimed he wanted to be a writer more than anything. He said he had an idea for a phenomenal book and that he had started writing it. But every time he wrote a sentence that wasn't perfect, he considered it a miserable failure. So, after years and years of writing and rewriting, he has yet to reach page 5 of his manuscript. If you find yourself bedeviled by a piece of your writing, put a moratorium on it. Do not allow yourself to go back and look at anything until you've completed a first draft.

But whatever you do, don't wait for inspiration to write.

Just write.

When you write, it's crucial to turn off the critical part of your brain. The snarky part that snarls, *Who would ever want to read this pitiful drivel? Who do you think you are anyway, trying to write a book and get it published?* When you hear that voice (and you will hear that voice), you have to find a way to push the mute button. Nothing will stop you colder, deader and flatter than the nobody-loves-me-everybody-hates-me-I-think-I'll-go-eat-worms voice. As Samuel Johnson said, "Keep always in your mind that, with due submission to Providence, a man of genius has been seldom ruined but by himself."

> "Every day, every day, I write the book."
>
> —*Elvis Costello*

There are many techniques for dealing with this voice. One effective method is to consciously acknowledge it. Try saying some variation of this:

"I'm afraid nobody will want to read my book."

This alone will keep your brain from doing what it was doing: spreading a virus in your hard drive. Then you can restart your brain, like rebooting a frozen computer, with a new, different, better thought. Perhaps something like:

"I'm so happy my book is getting published. I'm good enough, I'm smart enough, and gosh darn it, people like me."

If this seems hopelessly dorky to you, fine. Make up your own technique. But keep moving forward. Always keep writing your book, even if it seems like the lamest piece of dreck ever. Get that first draft done. Then you can start shaping your book. Making it great. Developing characters, strengthening arguments, jettisoning hackneyed metaphors, sharpening wit.

Nourishing Your Outline

As you move forward, it can be helpful to look back through work you've already done. One of the best places to look is your outline. Some authors like to make elaborate outlines and plot out their books in their entirety before they write word one. Others just start writing, and whatever book comes out is the book that comes out. Many fiction writers make notes on index cards as they do their research, carefully filling in each scene with each character's

▶ Now that you're ready to write in earnest, it's the perfect time to riffle back through any rejection letters you might have filed away. Study them carefully, with a detachment that allows you to take in their truths. And with pen in hand or fingertip to keyboard, take a moment to gloat over how foolish all those rejectors were!

motivation, what the locale looks like in detail, how the scene moves the plot forward. Some writers could care less.

Naturally, most writers are somewhere in between. But we're big proponents of outlining. Here's why:

1. If you're writing nonfiction, you probably included an outline in your proposal. Feeding and watering it as you write will undoubtedly help you organize your book, see where it's going and where it's been.

> "I was working on the proof of one of my poems all the morning, and took out a comma. In the afternoon I put it back again."
>
> —*Oscar Wilde*

2. It's easy to get off track when you're writing. Sometimes going off track can lead you to new and exciting places. But sometimes it can be a huge waste of time. If you have an outline, you can see if your new ideas make sense and, if they do, where exactly they fit. Maybe you're on a tangent that slots perfectly into Chapter 10, not Chapter 2. That's much easier to see with an outline in place.

3. When you get stuck, an outline helps you see the big picture and gives you other avenues to explore. If Chapter 4 isn't flowing, you can move on to another and come back to the bugaboo later.

4. Making an outline is also a good way to break down a book into its smallest components, helping you focus on the individual twigs that you can easily gather in building the nest of your book. The more minutely detailed your outline, the easier it is to visualize and thus write your book. Think of your outline as a living, breathing, evolving thing. Continually revise and update it to reflect changes. Having a good, detailed outline will help you slide right into your first draft.

First Drafting

You have to write a first draft. It doesn't have to be good, but you have to get it done. Anne Lamott, author of the fantabulous writing book *Bird by Bird,* puts "Shitty First Draft" in big letters at the beginning of everything she starts, to remind herself that's exactly what it should be. Once you complete the first draft, you can tell people:

"Yeah, I just finished my first draft."

Nothing quite matches the relief you'll feel when you can say that. Then, once you've finished celebrating the completion of your first draft, you can go back and make it just right.

Writing Is Rewriting Is Rewriting Is Rewriting

As with all clichés, there is utter truth in the statement that writing is rewriting. The way to perfect your writing is not through sitting on a paragraph for an eternity, but by doing multiple drafts of your book.

One of the most important parts of rewriting is cutting away the fat. Go through and fine-tune your manuscript with a fine-tooth comb. Do this many times, always looking for stuff you can lop off. Eliminate redundancy. Streamline every chapter. Every paragraph. Every sentence. Every word.

Occasionally you may have to kill the baby. Sounds gruesome, true, but it's an apt description of what it feels like when you take a piece of your book that displays the full range and depth of your writing brilliance, cut it out and then discard it on the junk heap where old manuscripts go to die. It's important not to fall so in love with a piece of writing that you lose sight of the big picture. As Colette said, "Sit down and put down everything that comes into your head and then you're a writer. But an author is one who can judge his own stuff's worth, without pity, and destroy most of it." The only modification we'd add is: Save the baby you've killed. Store it away in the bowels of your hard drive. Someday you may be able to perform mouth-to-mouth on it and bring it back to life in another book, where it can dazzle the world.

▶ If you're having trouble getting started, try automatic writing. Just write whatever comes into your head, even if it has nothing to do with the subject at hand. No matter how trivial and idiotic it may seem. Laundry lists, grocery lists, childhood rhymes. Whatever. Just the act of writing will often prime your brain's pump.

Do not stop rewriting until you've transformed your manuscript into a thing of beauty. Then read your book from stem to stern, cover to cover. Do you repeat things? How is the pacing? Does it lag at times? Did you rush through information that needs more development? Do you repeat things? Did you cut away from a scene before the drama was fully played out? Are your characters consistent? Is your prose too slick or too flowery? Too choppy or fragmented? Do you repeat things?

Fools Rush In: Turning In a Great Manuscript

Many, many writers do themselves the disservice of presenting material that is just not ready. They assume their editors will wave a magic wand and fix their manuscript. But in this day and age, a lot of editors have neither the time nor the interest

"You know you've achieved perfection in design, not when you have nothing more to add, but when you have nothing more to take away."

—*Antoine de Saint-Exupéry*

required. And, most important, you want your editor to jump for joy upon finishing your manuscript. You don't want him to sit around and stew over how much work he'll have to put into it. Leslie Meredith, a VP and senior editor at Atria Publishing Group, puts it this way: "Why would you hand in something that can be turned down—that isn't your best book? You want your editor to be an advocate of your book, not to be tied down with a laborious revision. And you don't want your book to get a reputation as a problem."

Ironically, one of the best things you can do for your writing is not write for a while. Once you've completed your first draft, give it a rest. Get some distance from all those words your brain coughed up. When you go back to them, many of the problems you struggled with will seem easy to solve. You'll find the perfect words to replace the ones that never sounded right. And you'll discover that distance is a miracle worker when it comes to structure. It's like a Magic Eye poster; where before you saw only dots, now you'll see a fully formed picture.

So, please, don't be the fool who rushes in. We beg you not to turn in your book until you:

- Rewrite until you can rewrite no more.

- Get some distance by stepping away from your book and letting it sit for anywhere from a week to a month.

- Have many readers of all different kinds evaluate your book.

- Rewrite some more.

- Read your manuscript out loud, from beginning to end, to make sure it flows and is free of mistakes.

- Finish off with a couple more rewrites.

- Make sure typographical and grammatical errors have been eradicated.

More Readers

As we said in Chapter 3, good readers don't grow on trees. You have to unearth ones who have the skills, time and desire to read and comment intelligently on your work. Reader candidates include your agent, writing group members or writing partners, coworkers (if your book has to do with your line of work) and the larger network of writers/authors you've cultivated over the book-writing process. You can find all kinds of online writing and reading communities where people exchange critiques. Even friends, family and acquaintances who can read and talk reasonably well are good people to pursue. These people may be more excited to read your work because they've never been asked to do such a thing before.

Asking people to be readers can be awkward for a writer. Look, it takes a lot of time to read a manuscript, and we all know that it's hard enough finding the time to eat, sleep and answer emails these days. But it also means exposing yourself, making yourself vulnerable. Will your readers like it or loathe it? Or, worst of all, will they find it utterly average and ultimately unpublishable? Many writers, when forced to face these fear-based feelings, decide not to pursue readers. This is a mistake. If you're writing a book for the general public, this means OTHER PEOPLE ARE GOING TO READ IT! And it's better to get feedback now than to encounter crippling criticism when you can no longer do anything about it.

> "To write is to write is to write is to write is to write is to write is to write is to write."
>
> —*Gertrude Stein*

The Danger of Turning In a Not-So-Great Manuscript

We know a writer who received a hefty advance for his novel. He was in the very unusual position of having sold a novel on the first 100 pages only, and his editor pushed and pushed to get the finished manuscript, ASAP. He was a fast writer and was proud as punch when he turned in his manuscript ahead of the rushed schedule his editor had him on.

A week later, his agent called and told him the publisher was rejecting his manuscript and not even offering him the chance to rewrite it. The writer was in total shock. He assumed that after he turned in his furiously fast first draft, he'd be working with his editor, getting notes, doing rewrites. But because he gave in to his editor's pressure to turn the manuscript in NOW NOW NOW, because he didn't rewrite until he could rewrite no more, his deal got killed and he got to keep only a pitiful pittance of his advance.

Cue the violins and pass the hankies.

Okay now dry your eyes. This writer has since gone on to write several books, all of which have been published. His secret? Handing in a clean, professional manuscript.

▶ Have you invested a lot of time in developing your relationships with local booksellers? If so, you might want to ask a bookseller or two to read your manuscript. But heed the advice of Linda Bubon, co-owner of Chicago's Women & Children First: "Be humble. Don't make demands. I'm more likely to respond positively to someone who is a regular customer. Who attends programs and book groups. Who has an interest in literature outside their own writing."

Getting the Most Out of Your Readers

When you work with a reader, maximize your time by putting together a list of questions. Some writers prefer to dole out the questions after the read has been completed, because they don't want to color their reader's point of view. A portion of your questions should be extremely general ("Was my story suspenseful to the end?") and a portion should be extremely specific ("Is the dialogue on page 52 between the killer whale and the drowning muskrat really believable?"). And always ask: "What did you like best (or least) about my book?"

Why the questions? Many readers, inexperienced in the art of the critique, will simply say, "I really liked it," and call it a day. This is not helpful. You want as much information as possible about your manuscript. Once you've sussed out its strengths and weaknesses and gathered as much specific info as you can, ask your readers if they have any ideas about how to fix any problems.

After all that writing and rewriting, your perspective will be skewed. If your readers can articulate problems and solutions, they'll have done you the immense favor of letting you see through new eyes. Here's a list of general questions to ask your readers:

- Did the book deliver on its promise?

- Was anything confusing or awkward?

- Was the information easy to understand? Was any information missing?

- Did the arguments make sense?

- Where does it flow? Where is it choppy?

- Was there enough humor? Too much? Did any jokes fall flat?

For fiction writers only:

- Are the characters and the dialogue believable? Do you care about these characters? Are you rooting for them to succeed or fail?

- Did the plot make you want to keep turning the page? Where did the story lag? Are there scenes that should be taken out? Scenes that you think need to be added?

- Was it suspenseful? Predictable?

- Was the ending satisfying?

It's Critical to Take Criticism

Whether you think you're after praise or not, you are. If you're human, that is. And while you may ask for criticism, when you actually hear it you may wish you'd never asked. Learning to take criticism early on is great preparation for rude reviews that may attack or belittle you and your book, often for no good reason at all. Good to toughen the hide before the slings and arrows start flying.

> "It's my experience that very few writers, young or old, are really seeking advice when they give out their work to be read. They want support; they want someone to say, 'Good job.'"
>
> —*John Irving*

The first rule of taking criticism, especially when you've asked people to take their precious time to help you, is to listen instead of defending yourself or your work. If, after serious consideration, you have questions about someone's criticism, that's all well and good. Ask civilly for clarification. But wait until you've had time to calm your emotional beast. Avoid all sentences like "What kind of stupid comment is that?" and "What was the last thing *you* wrote?"

Reading Right Out Loud

After you've sucked all the advice you can out of your readers and made your edits, take the time to read your manuscript to yourself out loud. That's right, your whole manuscript. Out loud. You'll be surprised to discover how you're suddenly able to hear sentences or passages that sound awkward. Reading your book aloud will also give you a sense of scenes or sections going on too long, straying off point, coming across as boring, bad or unclear. Your voice will also naturally find the points of emphasis. And your manuscript will be all the better for reflecting your own personal rhythms.

More on Outside Help

E ven if you're working with an editor at a publishing house, you might need outside help *before* you turn in your manuscript. This depends, of course, on 1) what kind of person your editor is, and 2) what kind of shape your manuscript is in.

If you've received little or no help from your editor and you anticipate he'll only be giving you a light edit, you might want to hire an outside editor/book doctor. Why? We've said it before and we'll say it again: Your book has ONE shot in the world. You want to give it every opportunity to succeed.

But how do you even know what kind of editor you've got? This is where showing your editor a chapter or two (or three) can come in handy. See what kinds of comments you get back. Are they thorough, interesting, thoughtful and reflective of a deep knowledge of what you're trying to do? Even your first conversation with your editor can reveal a lot about her editing skills. Did she give you concrete suggestions, ideas and comments? Did she seem to have a clear vision and real understanding of your book? If your answer is "no" to all of the above, then you can put money on the fact that your editor is probably not going to do the kind of editing you need.

Now, what if you're having a really hard time with your manuscript? You just can't get things to gel. Your readers are reinforcing your fears that your manuscript isn't very, you know, good. Or you've taken the requisite time off, come back and still can't see clearly where to go from here. This may be the time to bring in an outside editor. While readers can help you identify problems, they more than likely won't be able to tell you how to fix them. A good independent editor can. Hiring extra help is shame-free. Many professional writers do it. Your job is to produce a great book. No one cares how you do it. Atria's Leslie Meredith puts a tremendous amount of time into editing her books, but still encourages authors to hire freelance editors because 1) clean manuscripts will excite your editor and make her a full-on advocate for your book, and 2) clean manuscripts allow her to get great sample material around to her colleagues right away so that others can get excited, too.

An outside editor can be an editor who's worked in the publishing business and is now independent, or someone who works for a publisher and is moonlighting. An outside editor may also work as a professional reader or a book doctor. So be specific about what you think you need. (See Chapter 3 for more details.)

Unfortunately, high-caliber, state-of-the-art editors can cost a pretty penny. Well-known editors with great track records can make thousands of dollars per manuscript, depending on how much work they have to do. Some are worth their weight in bestseller lists. But if you don't have the bucks, and you feel you need some truly objective and professional advice, then go with the professional reader option. A smart local bookseller may be just the trick (a nice bonus for paying a local bookseller is that he'll be all the more invested in your book when it comes out).

Don't Let Running Out of Time Drive You Out of Your Mind

After all the writing, rewriting, editing, reading, time off and personality-induced paralysis, is it any wonder that writers have problems hitting their deadlines? Plenty of powerful people in publishing will tell you that deadlines mean nothing in the book business. And while there is a great deal of truth in that statement, it is not entirely accurate.

Most publishers plan their lists 9 to 18 months ahead of time. There's an art to these lists; they want their seasonal catalogs to be well balanced. Naturally, it takes a lot of juggling and planning to pull this off. If you've written a reference book on mental health, your publisher will not want to put out another reference book on mental health in the same season—or maybe even the season after that. And one of the ways they plan their catalogs is by looking at due dates. So, if they think your book will come out in the fall of one year, they'll make sure the other mental health book won't come out until a year later. Trouble may ensue when you hand in your book six months to a year late.

The good news is, unless your book is time-sensitive, your publisher will probably be happy to give you an extension on your deadline with

▶ If you need an extension, don't underestimate the time you require. Publishers lose confidence in authors who repeatedly ask for extensions. And a publisher who isn't happy with what you've been sending in so far can use a request for multiple extensions as a reason to cancel your contract. As one successful author told us, "I was having a terrible time getting my book done. I was new to the book business and slightly clueless. Well, my editor left the company, and all of a sudden I was an orphan. So when I was late with my manuscript, they canceled my contract. Just like that. Believe me, I've been very careful about meeting deadlines ever since."

231

enough advance notice and time to juggle things around. In fact, your editor could be so swamped that she wouldn't mind postponing your manuscript one little bit! But, if you get a substantial extension, be sure to get a written amendment to your contract. That way, if your editor leaves or anything else untoward happens, your publisher will still have to honor a contractual obligation.

Postpartum Depression

We've made the "book as baby" comparison before, and we'll be making it again. But if there is one moment when your book feels especially baby-like, it's when you hand it in. This is when you may feel the pangs of postpartum depression. You've birthed your baby, and now you no longer have control over its fate. You are left to wonder how it will fare in this cruel yet beautiful world.

> "If there is a special Hell for writers, it would be in the forced contemplation of their own works, with all the misconceptions, the omissions, the failures that any finished work of art implies."
>
> —*John Dos Passos*

Or, worse yet, you've birthed a baby that's nothing like the gorgeous one you imagined. That's how it may seem, anyway. We're here to tell you that this, too, shall pass. If one moment you can't imagine a worse book in the history of time, know that this will be matched by a moment when you can't imagine a better one. These mad mood swings are all part of the giddy process of making a book.

Just keep in mind that nobody put a gun to your head and said: Be a writer.

If somebody did, you should contact the authorities immediately and have this person dealt with harshly.

One Last Thing Before You Turn It In

Before you submit your manuscript, give it one more final dress inspection. Make sure that its hair is combed and its shoes are nice and neat. That pages are in the right order, contact numbers are correct, and chapters begin and end correctly.

Writing your book may be the most difficult thing you ever do. But that doesn't mean it can't be fun. If you take an organized, methodical approach, you can minimize the difficulty and maximize the joy.

CHAPTER 10

Working with Your Publisher

"I am a publisher—a hybrid creature: one part stargazer, one part gambler, one part businessman, one part midwife and three parts optimist."

—Cass Canfield, chairman of the board,
Harper & Brothers, 1945–55

IN DAYS OF YORE, PUBLISHING was known as a Gentleman's Business. Run by Gentlemen. Individuals. Families. Yes, they wanted to make money, but they would also produce beautiful books whether they thought they'd make a profit or not. They wined and dined their clients. Threw lavish parties. Made a habit of martini lunches.

You see very little of that these days, although some smaller publishers still hold to the traditions of yesteryear. Maybe not the martini lunches, but the ethos of a family business where long-term relationships are valued alongside the bottom line. If you've signed a contract with a publisher like this, your experience may vary wildly from that of authors who have signed with a larger house. Today, the big publishers are owned by major corporations staffed by thousands of people who have no idea who you are or what your book is about. Welcome to your corporate publishing team—at best, a sleek machine where each department works in tandem to maximize your book's chances for success. At worst? The right hand won't even know what the right hand is doing.

Which brings us to one of the most important things you can do to help your book succeed: Turn your name into a face. When your book goes from

The Sunk Cost Principle

When Dan Ariely, author of the *New York Times* bestseller *Predictably Irrational,* agreed to be interviewed for this book, we couldn't wait to ask him, "So what's predictably irrational about publishing?" Dan, a chaired professor of psychology and behavioral economics at Duke, is one of those rare people who is simultaneously warm, funny and ridiculously smart. Every time you talk to him, you come away with some new fact or story that you tell for the next year or two. No wonder his book is a bestseller!

Dan, of course, had a predictably fascinating answer to our question. "When I first signed a contract with HarperCollins, I met with the big dudes there and they told me that I should be very happy that they gave me a big advance because this meant they would promote the book to a large degree. Which was amusing because this kind of thinking is irrational. And it's what we call the Sunk Cost Fallacy."

"The Sunk Cost what?" we asked, behavioral economics not being our strong suit.

Dan explained. The Sunk Cost Fallacy is all about throwing good money after bad. Imagine that you have a car factory and you're designing a new car. You've allotted $100 million for its design. Everything is going well, and you've just hit the $90 million mark in your spending when all of a sudden you find out that someone is designing something very similar—only better. And the market can only bear one more car of this kind. Do you continue to develop your inferior car? Most people say yes, because you've already invested $90 million. Now let's say you've invested only one million of your dollars when you discover this other car. Would you continue in this case? Most people say no way. The difference here is that the more money we spend on something, the more (in many cases) irrationally committed to it we feel.

So how does the Sunk Cost Fallacy play out in publishing? Imagine a publisher has just bought two books based on proposals. One for a million dollars and another for $10,000. Once the books are delivered, the publisher discovers that the $10,000 book is actually better than the

being a bunch of squiggles and symbols on a piece of paper or computer screen to being the product of a real person with a face, dreams, talent and passion, most people will feel differently about it and you. Many times, this can mean the difference between someone making that follow-up call that gets you an article in a leading magazine, or pitching your book extra hard so it gets reviewed in *The New York Times,* or making sure your book is available in stacks at bookstores around the country or has a cover you'd like to be judged by. Balance advocating for your book with being the best team player you can possibly be. Sometimes that means ruffling a few feathers. Sometimes it means taking one for the team.

million-dollar book. Here's the rub: Almost all publishers will still continue to spend more money on the million-dollar book, even though they recognize that it's inferior to the far less expensive one. Sadly, this is the rule, not the exception, in publishing. It's why so many fabulous books that were bought for very little money never get the attention they deserve. And why a lot of bad books end up getting so much attention. "A lot of ego and pride is involved," explains Dan. "That's why publishers throw good money after bad. It's very hard to give up once your ego is involved."

Because so few authors get large advances, it's easy to get depressed thinking about all those sunk costs that aren't going toward your book. But Dan says his research shows that the Sunk Cost Fallacy can be turned on its head. If investment is directly related to ego and pride, the challenge is to get your publisher personally involved in your book: "You know how people fall in love with what they create, even if it's a crappy piece of Ikea furniture they had to put together? The same thing happens with ideas. Whenever we create something, we think it's more useful, important, etc." If a publisher feels they're invested in the creation of your book, they will be willing to spend more on it.

So how do you go about co-creating your book with your publisher? Let your editor take credit for a seminal idea that came out of a discussion between you. Write a thank-you email to your publicist for the perfect placement she got (even if it was through your connection) and copy everyone else on the publishing team. Be both generally and specifically appreciative and gracious to everyone involved from the top to the bottom of the totem pole. What not to do? "The wrong approach is for the author to take full ownership of their book," says Dan. "If you don't let your publisher take credit, it's a recipe for them not caring."

Turns out that while the ego and the brain may consistently be predictably irrational, the heart may not be. Turns out the more love, respect and credit you give, the more likely you are to get some back. Go figure.

Editor 101

As we mentioned, large and midsize publishing houses have many departments. These include sales, marketing, publicity, art, accounting and so on. The department your editor belongs to is, appropriately enough, called the editorial department. Editorial departments, like other tribal societies, are hierarchical. At the top of the totem pole is the publisher (who also runs marketing, publicity, sales), then comes the editor in chief, then sometimes the editorial director, then

> "Some editors are failed writers, but so are most writers."
>
> —*T.S. Eliot*

executive editors, then senior editors, then editors, then associate editors, then assistant editors, then editorial assistants. The most powerful and successful editors work their way up the totem pole and often become editorial directors, editors in chief, publishers or heads of their own imprints.

Every publisher is different, of course, but nearly all editors, regardless of rank, acquire books and are thus known as acquiring editors. In most cases, they find a manuscript or proposal that they think will sell and that fits their company's list, and then take it up the editorial ladder to what's called an editorial board or acquisitions meeting. There, they try to convince all the other people in editorial (plus, possibly, people from marketing, publicity and sales) that the manuscript or proposal is worth buying. This is undoubtedly how your opus got acquired, unless the publisher or editor in chief acquired it and decided to edit it himself or hand it off to an editor.

▶ Early in your relationship with your editor, ask her to keep you abreast of key dates in the publishing process. Of particular importance are the launch meeting and sales conference, which we'll get to later in this chapter.

Every editor works differently. Some are very hands-on. They go line by line, syllable by syllable. They make sure the voice, rhythm, plot and information are what they should be. From micro to macro, from soup to nuts, they will try to massage your book from zygote to bestseller.

Some editors make only broad changes. Some editors will change barely a word. Most fall somewhere in between.

Your editor is your primary point person, your liaison to every other department. She can be a great cheerleader, shepherd of your complaints, pumper-upper of sales/marketing/publicity. Or she can actually kill your book. Bottom line: You want to do everything you can to make sure your editor never hesitates to go to bat for you.

Walking a Mile in Your Editor's Moccasins

Publishing people are, generally speaking, underworked and overpaid. No, wait, reverse that. Overworked and underpaid. And the epitome of this overworked/underpaid dichotomy is the editorial staff. Editors are often people with multiple degrees from top universities who have forgone higher-paying jobs because of their love of books (or because they have liberal arts degrees and have no idea what to do with them). They stay late and often give up their nights and weekends, hauling home large stacks of manuscripts.

Most editors are also master multitaskers. These days, they're forced to acquire more and more titles every year with the hope that a few will actually make money. And in addition to acquiring and editing numerous books at the same time (yours will certainly NOT be the only book your editor is working on), they are also required to go to numerous meetings, return phone calls and emails and put out the inevitable fires that rage in any modern publishing house. Why are we telling you this? Because we want you to think twice before assuming the worst when a phone call or email isn't returned pronto.

Getting Simpatico with Your Editor

There's something very important about your editor that, in all likelihood, you don't know: Your editor has already done a tremendous amount of work on your behalf. As David Ebershoff, Random House editor-at-large and bestselling author of *The 19th Wife,* says, "The editor who acquires your book has made a big statement in the publishing house about you. Acquiring a book is a very complicated and rigorous process that involves a lot of people, money and time. All these people have to be convinced that you and your book are the ones to bet on. This means that your editor has done something personal by committing to you and your book. And this is why you really have to put a good amount of trust in your editor, because he or she has already put a lot of trust in you."

No matter what your editor's personality is like—even if she appears indifferent or totally unreachable—you should start from the assumption that she believes in you and your book and that she shares a central set of goals with you: those of making you and your book as successful as possible. Which is why you need to preserve and nurture the relationship.

To find everything you need to know about appreciation, expectation, communication and affirmation, which are the backbone of a healthy relationship with your editor, go back and revisit pages 134–138.

▶ Are you an author whose book was bought by a publisher or senior executive and then handed off to a subordinate? Or an author whose book has been orphaned by an editor who has left or been let go? If so, your new editor might be less invested in you than you'd like. Time to panic? Freak out? Fold your hand, cash in your chips and give up on your publisher completely? Quite the opposite. In these cases, appreciation and good communication are even more important.

Same-Paging

Before you start digging into the writing and/or editing of your book, you first want to set up a call with your editor to be sure you are both on the same page. Prepare a solid list of practical, substantive questions. Here are some general queries, but it's important to develop additional questions that reflect you and your project:

■ What would you like me to know about how you and this process work before we begin?

■ Do you want to see chapters as I finish them? Or would you prefer to see a completed manuscript?

■ Do you prefer telephonic or electronic communication?

■ Do you have any general or specific editorial suggestions before I start? Is there anything in my argument/presentation/information/plot/characters and/or tone that needs work? Did you see any stylistic problems in my sample writing/manuscript that you would like me to work on?

■ How closely should I stick to my outline? If there are changes in the outline, would you like me to keep you in the loop about them?

■ What is the ideal pub date? Are there certain key holidays or events you want to plan my book release around that will affect my deadline?

Your editor's responses will give you a lot of information about her. Are her fingers going to be deep in your pie? Or will she simply support you? Or neither? No matter what your editor is like, when she talks, listen aggressively—this is harder than it seems. Write down all suggestions. Thank your editor for taking time out of her busy schedule to formulate her comments. Really think about them. Ask your friends, allies and agent for their opinions. Then formulate a thoughtful, smart, professional response.

Acquiring Editorial Love

While it's crucial to be on the same page with your editor from the get-go, you also want to keep up an ongoing dialogue. When you start working with your editor, it's a bit like going on a blind date that you hope will end up in marriage. It will probably be a bit awkward at first, especially if you don't feel a personal connection. But as you continue dating, you want to establish an increasingly comfortable rapport—a relationship where ideas flow freely and easily. If this doesn't happen, don't panic. Many writers confess in hushed tones that they walk on eggshells around their editors. Your editor doesn't have to be your best friend. She just has to be your professional ally.

Often your relationship with your editor will not heat up until you hand in your manuscript. Then what happens? The whole publishing machine starts gearing up to produce your masterpiece. As word spreads that your long-awaited work has finally arrived, excitement swells through the various departments and *The New York Times* starts calling. Right?

Wrong.

Almost certainly, this next phase of your relationship with your editor involves . . . WAITING. After that, you'll probably have to . . . WAIT. Then, most likely, there'll be more . . . WAITING.

The Waiting Game

The period between handing in your manuscript and hearing back from your editor may make you feel like an old-fashioned father-to-be stuck in the waiting room. However, instead of pacing through a few hours of labor, you will in all likelihood be treading that linoleum for months. Even though most contracts spell out the "waiting" period, many editors far exceed it. This is an utterly brutal time in any writer's life. Your book—indeed, your whole writing career— is hanging in the balance. Will it be the next National Book Award winner? Or shredder fodder? Gwen Macsai, NPR commentator and author of *Lipshtick*, a collection of humorous essays, says this about the waiting period: "I loved my editor, and he was extremely attentive at first. Then he fell off the face of the earth. I sat there thinking: 'He hates me' . . . 'He hates my work' . . . 'If he hates me, he should just tell me he hates me and stop leaving me hanging like this!' It makes you crazy and chips away at any confidence that you have."

To avoid the pain and suffering of the waiting period, we advise making your presence politely felt. Resist the impulse to pop your head into the delivery room every hour, but don't disappear entirely from your editor's life. A friendly postcard or email saying hello and detailing all the great things you're doing for your book is perfectly acceptable. You don't even need to ask, "Have you read my manuscript?" It's implied, and your editor will certainly let you know when she has.

On the other hand, if you haven't heard from your editor in more than two months, you may have a problem on your hands. Be sure to stay in contact with your agent, if you have one, about the state of your manuscript. Your agent can nudge in a way that you can't. And if there's a problem, you want to know about

Two Months and Counting

H as it been over two months, maybe even six, seven or eight months since you turned in your manuscript and you've still heard nothing from your editor? First of all, this situation is not as uncommon as you might think, and it's almost never a good idea to act precipitously, as the timing may have nothing to do with your work. It's possible your editor has gotten in 10 books all at the same time and is simply unable to address yours. Maybe the others are time-sensitive or written by celebrity authors who get star treatment.

Many contracts stipulate that your editor must provide editorial feedback within 60 days. If the editor does no such thing, most contracts require that you send a letter to the publisher asking for a response if you want the lag to become actionable. But this protocol isn't always followed. For example, you may have a very good relationship with your editor and feel uncomfortable being perceived as formal and pushy. If your book is time-sensitive, however, at the very least it's necessary for you or your agent to get your editor to commit to a date by which your work will be edited. Figure out the last possible date when your manuscript can go to the printer and work back from there.

Even if your book isn't time-sensitive, you don't want to give the impression that it can constantly be moved to the back of the bus. By asking an editor to commit to a date, you're forcing her to be accountable. It's important to get this date in writing. This way, if your editor is not able to deliver, you or your agent will have ammunition if you need to go up the publishing ladder.

In these situations, it's always better to have your agent carry the big stick so you can walk softly. Obviously, if you don't have an agent, you have to do both. If after 60 days you continue to hear nothing, send a letter politely requesting editorial feedback.

it as soon as possible. Your agent may be able to pick up trouble on his radar long before you can.

If you're agent-free, stay on top of business in a professional and non-annoying manner.

Hearing from Your Editor: "You Want Me to Change *What*?"

At last, the waiting is over. Your editor has read your manuscript and is ready to roll. Unless your manuscript is completely flawless (not bloody likely!), you will probably receive a letter stipulating the overall changes your editor would like you to make, in addition to line-by-line edits.

Your editor will have an objectivity about your material and an insight into the book business that you almost certainly do not possess. Be thankful for your editor's ability. On the other hand, you have a depth of insight into your material that your editor does not. DO NOT automatically agree or disagree with your editor. Some writers just blindly follow their editor's instructions. Others take the drama queen approach and seem hell-bent on having a series of emotional arguments. We do not advocate either of these approaches. Emily Loose, a former editor for many of the big houses and a current freelance editor, has this advice: "Take a few days to respond to editorial feedback. Then read it over several times so that defensiveness isn't your first reaction."

Author and editor David Ebershoff adds another interesting perspective: "My editor, Kate Medina [a celebrated executive editor at Random House], said something to me that I now tell my authors as well: 'I'm here to represent the reader. I'm here to say a few things to you that a reader might say.' In fact, once when I was in front of my readers after my book came out, I saw directly how they responded positively to Kate's edits. And it was then that I was able to fully appreciate her editorial guidance."

> "No passion in the world is equal to the passion to alter someone else's draft."
>
> —*H.G. Wells*

Sometimes an editor will make a small, one-sentence suggestion that turns out to have a profound effect on your book. Sometimes the suggestion is *not* the right one but will lead to changes you would have never thought of on your own. Sometimes an editor can be flat-out wrong. But even if an editor's comment is off, it can often help you clarify what you want to do. After you've had some time to marinate, calmly and carefully formulate your response to your editor's comments. Where you agree and disagree. And why. Where you have questions about what your editor meant. If you just say "yes" or just say "no," you deprive yourself of going through the process of exchanging ideas. Often a confusing piece of information can be transformed into a brilliant insight by asking a simple question. From this sort of collaboration can come a great book.

Use your agent and allies to clarify and refine your questions before you address your editor. They may see things you don't. A reader or agent may confirm an observation of your editor's and illuminate the point in different words. Carefully lay out your ideas before you have a conversation with your editor. Maximize your editor's time. We're not advocating short, curt conversations. We're suggesting that you go to your editor with a serious, well-informed, intelligent list of questions and comments that can be a springboard for a fruitful dialogue that will make your book good, better, best.

Ideally, this is a time to meet with your editor face to face. If not face to face, then over the phone. Sometimes a five-minute talk can resolve an issue that might take dozens of back and forth emails. Oftentimes you can get information from your editor's demeanor and tone of voice that you never could in a letter. And every scrap of information is valuable.

"WHOSE BOOK IS THIS ANYWAY?"

Sometimes you will come to an impasse with your editor. From plot to argument to character, from the general to the specific nature and tone of your book, there are countless ways you may disagree. When it comes to the details, most editors will bow to the author. But an editor who sees fundamental problems that will impede your book's success is more likely to hold fast. Try to be open to suggestions even as you stick to your guns. It's almost impossible not to react emotionally in these situations and to feel that your editor is a chowderhead who's totally missed the point. Instead of pouting or railing, decide whether to knuckle under or make a case for why the manuscript should stand as is.

If you feel strongly that your editor is mistaken, you need to formulate an argument that convinces her of your position. If this doesn't work, then you have to decide whether to ruffle feathers or roll with the punches. Either decision comes with a price. If you take one for the team and make the necessary changes, hopefully your editor will appreciate the fact that you're playing ball and be more likely to get behind your book with enough enthusiasm to help make it a success. But by taking one for the team, you also run the risk of creating a book that you don't like. Will this still be a book you'll be proud to have your name on? Remember, it will never be your editor's name on the cover.

With that in mind, ruffling feathers may be your best option. But, in general, it's better to be a dove of peace than a bird of prey. A toxic relationship with your editor can spill over past the editing phase and into the publication of your book.

GOOD COP, BAD COP

If you have an agent, let him be your sounding board in terms of figuring out which issues are important and which ones you should let slide. Sometimes what seems like a boulder can be turned into a pebble.

If you both agree that it's time to speak up, let your agent be the bad cop. Judy Clain, editor in chief at Little, Brown, says, "Sometimes it's better for the editor and agent to duke it out and reserve the author/editor relationship for issues that are less contentious." One of the skills a good agent acquires is the ability to get what a client needs without alienating the team. Your agent may already have a relationship with your editor and can speak the language of publishing, articulating what you want better than you can. In addition, most editors don't want to anger agents. They depend on them for the best projects and want to keep them happy.

If you do call in your agent, we suggest following the advice of Mauro DiPreta, publisher of Hachette Books: "What an editor doesn't like is a passive-aggressive author who says yes or gives an implicit yes and then has his agent come in and say, 'What he said isn't what he meant.' Either let your agent handle a situation entirely, which I have no problem with whatsoever, or speak up and say what you really think."

GOING OVER YOUR EDITOR'S HEAD

Few people enjoy the mark of a footprint on their scalp. But there is the chance that if you or your agent can finesse the act of going over your editor's head, you'll be able to get the ear of his boss and convince said boss that you're right—all the while still making your editor look good.

Before you make the decision to stomp on someone's skull, make sure you've exhausted all other avenues. Be extra sure that the thing you're fighting for is crucial. And once you've made the decision to jump rank, tread quietly. Be humble, be charming, lie on your back and show your belly. Do whatever you have to do, but make it as easy as possible for your editor to save face. Jennifer Josephy, a former executive editor at Broadway Books, suggests that you go to your editor before you go above her head, to let her know that you'll be doing so. This allows for one last opportunity for rapprochement and also will not leave you feeling like a snitch. Jennifer suggests this script: "Say to your

Blind Following

One author who wishes to remain nameless sold her proposal to an editor she really liked and who seemed to understand exactly what she was up to. However, when they started working on the first few chapters, her editor steered her in a whole new direction. The author told us, "I followed my editor's advice because I respected her and wanted to please her. But all along I kept thinking that this was not the book I signed on to write, nor was it a book I knew how to write." The author plodded along. When she turned in her final book, her editor was extremely displeased. The author tried to explain that she had only been following orders, but by this time it was too late. "I could see that there was no hope of repairing the relationship or the book," she said. "I knew I'd have to find another publisher. Fortunately, my agent convinced the publisher to let me keep the money already advanced. But I was devastated. And I wish with all my heart that I had just written the book I wanted and knew how to write."

editor, 'I'm feeling frustrated by our communication, so I'm afraid I'm left with no choice but to go to a higher authority unless we can resolve this amicably.'" But she also cautions: "Unless violence is about to ensue, you will have to work with your editor through your publication date. Publishers will only very rarely switch editors on a project, so it's imperative to keep communication open at all times." If possible, try to have a conciliatory meeting with all parties involved and imbue the old all-for-one, one-for-all esprit de corps into the team.

The fact is, there *are* circumstances where you need the aid of a more senior person. You may have an editor who's young and inexperienced. Smart, dedicated and hardworking, yes, but without the experience, time and/or contacts to give you what you need to make your book great and profitable. Or you may get stuck with an editor who's just plain incompetent. If you and your agent, after due consideration, come to the conclusion that you've been shackled with such a dud, remedy the situation by whatever means necessary and as quickly as possible. Build a concrete case with specific examples of how you need help. This way, if you do need to go over someone's head, it'll be clear why you're doing so. It's also important to point out your editor's positive qualities. This will soften the blow and make it clear that you're a reasonable, thoughtful person.

TAKING YOUR BOOK TO ANOTHER PUBLISHER
After receiving Graham Greene's manuscript for *Travels with My Aunt,* his American publisher cabled, "Terrific book, but we'll have to change the title." Greene responded, "No need to change title. Easier to change publishers." If your editorial differences absolutely cannot be resolved, it's time to consider taking your book to a new publisher. That means returning the money to your current publisher. Obviously, this option is fraught with peril. But on the plus side, if you sense things are only going to get worse and that your publisher might be getting ready to reject your manuscript, your preemptive move will make it easier for you to resell your work. The fact is, once a manuscript has been rejected, it's very often perceived as tainted.

Leaving a troubled publishing experience can be like breaking up with someone before he gets the chance to break up with you. Only trouble is, you run the risk of being perceived as "difficult." That's why you need to come up with a good answer to the question: "What happened?" Your answer has to indicate that you are the active party, without calling your ex a bad name. The most popular reasons seem to be "creative differences," "not seeing eye to eye" and "wanting to go in a different direction." Of course, you will want to take one of these phrases and make it your own.

Packing Up and Moving Elsewhere

One well-known writer sold her book at auction for a hefty sum, to a most excellent editor at a top-notch publishing house. The start of their relationship was nothing short of a lovefest. But when she handed in the first half of the book, things changed. To begin with, she had to wait several months to get a lick of feedback. And when the feedback arrived, it made her heart sink. Her editor did not have one single positive thing to say.

The writer had heard only the very best things about this editor, so she figured it must be that her writing simply wasn't very good. She hired an outside editor to help her get the manuscript in tip-top shape. In the meantime, her inside editor never returned her calls, and all the good feelings that had passed between them early on in the process seemed like distant history. Finally, it was time to hand the book in, and all she could do was hope for the best.

Lo and behold, the months ticked by. Not a word. No return phone call. Her agent did a bit of nudging here and there, but still no response. The writer was now not only distraught but furious. She had spent day and night of an entire year getting her book finished and a good deal of money on outside help to make sure it was as good as it could be. She decided that if she didn't get back an edited manuscript at the six-month point, she would move on.

After a call from her editor but still no edited manuscript, she knew that this person was no longer her advocate. When she took a step back, she remembered her book's auction. Many people had wanted this book. After all her work, there was sure to be someone who still would.

Turned out she was right. After canceling her initial contract and returning her advance, her agent resubmitted her book to a half-dozen hungry editors. And within two weeks of pulling her manuscript from this publisher, she got a commensurate offer from a lovely, very enthusiastic editor who edited the manuscript within weeks of a signed contract. Clearly, sometimes yanking a book can be the best thing that ever happened to it.

Before you make any move regarding a change of publisher, have many long, thoughtful conversations with your agent. If you don't have an agent, try to talk to other people in the business or to other writers to help you make the most informed decision. Either way, work out an exit strategy.

Leaving your publisher should be like removing a bandage. You want to do it quick and clean, and you want to spend as little time as possible in publishing limbo. The sooner you can find your book a new home, the better.

CANCELLATION (GOD FORBID)

A tiny percentage of book contracts get canceled. So it's unlikely, but yes, it could happen to you. If you've missed your deadline, or if you handed in a manuscript that's not up to professional standards or doesn't deliver on the promises made in your proposal, your book can be canceled.

On the other hand, if your editor leaves or gets fired, if your publisher decides to go in a new direction or if something unforeseen happens in the world, your book can also be canceled. (This is obviously unfair, having nothing to do with you or your work; turn back to page 198 to make sure it can't happen to you.)

After you (and your agent, if you have one) have exhausted all avenues of discussion and negotiation, you may have to accept the fact that your publisher is cutting you loose. It may be your fault. Or it may have absolutely nothing to do with you.

The first thing an author wants to know is: *Do I have to give the money back?* If your manuscript has been rejected for a contractually legitimate reason (e.g., you missed your deadline), then technically you do have to return your money. If, however, you can show that the cancellation is not contractually kosher, you should be able to keep what you've been given thus far. Even in the first case, your publisher is unlikely to sue you for the money (depending, of course, on the size of the advance and the degree of animosity between the parties). But if you're able to resell your book, then you will almost certainly have to pay back any money you've received.

The good news is that you will once again own all rights to your manuscript. Which means you will have the opportunity to resell your book. The bad news is that your manuscript, as we indicated earlier, may be seen as soiled if it's already been through one company and spit out unpublished. There's not much you can do about that, but you *can* revisit your proposal or manuscript before going out with it. You never know, but if you take into account everything you've learned, you could end up with love money the second time around.

THE MOTHERLESS CHILD

The publishing landscape is dotted with too many books that have lost their parents and been cut adrift in a heartless world with no one to protect them. If the editor who purchased your book leaves your publisher, your book will become what's known as an "orphan." Unfortunately, editors have a glorious tradition of changing jobs more often than a nervous girl changes outfits before her first date. Not to mention the fact that editorial staffs are shrinking faster than a spider on a hot plate. So don't be shocked if this happens to you. As Philip Bashe, author of over a dozen books, says, "It's been 10 years since I started and finished a book with the same editor. Two books ago, the original editor was fired several months into the project; a second editor resigned after a week on the job; and the senior editor who inherited the book was canned just three weeks before publication. It's pretty maddening, especially when you've had a good rapport with editor number one, then have to build a rapport all over again with number two."

Yes, Phil's situation is extreme, but it illustrates the pathos of authoring an orphan. An editor who's asked to take over your project will rarely have the same passion for your book as the editor who acquired it. This means you'll have lost your primary advocate. But resist tossing your manuscript into a Dumpster. Instead, win her over. How? If there's one thing editors love, it's authors who are easy to work with. That's doable. And hopefully by now you have the tools to make an editor see how cool your subject is. In fact, sometimes you can stumble into a better situation with a change of editors. If, however, your new editor turns out to be a wicked stepmother, here are your options: 1) Slog on, cursing your fate, swallowing your rising bile. 2) Have an open, honest conversation about the editor's commitment to your project. Find out where you stand and what can be done to improve your situation. 3) Cut the cord and find a new parent within your publishing house. This is best done with the help of an agent, if you have one. 4) Cut the cord and find a new publisher. Numbers 1 and 4 should be your last options; it's not easy to find a new home, and it's hard to swallow bile.

Reselling Your Rejected Book

I f you're a fan of the online humor site and newspaper *The Onion*, you probably know their #1 *New York Times* bestseller *Our Dumb Century*. And if you've read the book, you'll find it very hard to believe it was canceled by its original publisher.

Our Dumb Century was originally sold to Hyperion, the publishing arm of Disney. The authors received a six-figure advance and wrote a fantastically funny and furiously scathing satire that everyone at Hyperion loved. The higher-ups at Disney, however, thought the book was a bit *too* scathing. And they were particularly upset by a page stating that a Nazi propaganda cartoon was co-created by Hitler and "pal" Walt Disney. Disney demanded that the unsavory bits be eliminated. The Onion refused. And because of the bigwigs at corporate, Hyperion was unable to publish the book.

The Onion went out with their book again. It was resold in a major bidding war for three times the amount Hyperion originally paid. They also had the benefit of the story getting written up everywhere from the *Washington Post* to the *Dallas Morning News*.

Now, that's sweet revenge!

The Hand-Off: What Happens Next?

Ring, ring. It's your editor. Your book has gone into production. What does this mean? Barring a legal review (which some books must go through in addition to copyediting), it means your book has been accepted by your publisher! At this point, you're 99.99% certain that your book is really going to be A BOOK! While it's being groomed, your editor will be discussing it with other members of your publishing team. This is why it's so important for your editor to be a big fan of you and your book. If you've produced a great book and you've been a joy to work with, this information will pass from department to department. So your relationship with your editor affects not just the editing of your book, but how it is received by your publishing house as a whole.

THE ROLE OF YOUR COPY EDITOR

The next stop on your road to the land of finished books is your copy editor. A copy editor nitpicks your spelling, punctuation, grammar and, consistency of language and may check your facts. Depending on the complexity of your manuscript, this work can take from a week to a month or more. You will then receive a copy of your copyedited manuscript, which you will need to go through carefully, approving or disapproving every comment and correction. Typically, you have a week or two to do so—more for a long or complicated book. Don't leave this to the last minute. Reviewing your copyedited manuscript is painstaking work and can take many, many hours. You may disagree with a whole host of changes, which may require some back and forth with your editor (you almost never have direct contact with your copy editor). On the whole, however, most people are delighted when a good copy editor gives their manuscript a thorough cleaning, buffing and polishing.

Can you hear the distant drums? It's now, depending on your particulars, 9 to 18 months until your Pub Date.

CORRECTING YOURSELF

Once you've returned your copyedited manuscript with your comments and revisions, you won't be invited to make any other significant changes. The manuscript will now be sent to a typesetter and turned into page proofs, a set of which will be sent to you for your approval. At this juncture, you just want to be pointing out errors in typesetting and making small, last-minute adjustments.

Making major changes on page proofs is a no-no for two reasons. First, making extensive insertions and deletions opens the possibility of introducing

Correcting the Corrector

I f you're an author who plays with language and sentence structure, or who writes in dialect, you will want to pay very close attention to your copy editor's corrections to be sure they don't diminish the zazazoo of your writing. Raymond Chandler once wrote to his editor: "Will you convey my compliments to the purist who reads your proofs and tell him or her that I write in a sort of broken-down patois which is something like the way a Swiss waiter talks, and when I split an infinitive, god damn it, I split it so it will stay split." On the other hand, James Michener was so pleased by the work his copy editor did on his books that he sent her a round-trip ticket to Paris.

new errors, which may or may not be caught at subsequent stages in the process. Second, your publisher needs to start figuring out the number of pages for the entire book, including acknowledgments, index and so on. This is because most books are manufactured by binding together signatures of 16 or 32 pages. If the total length were to run over from, say, 272 pages to 278 pages, your publisher would have to go up to 288 pages (not likely) or cut 6 pages (not pleasant). So, at this stage, adding and deleting more than a paragraph or two can be highly problematic.

If you know you must make major changes (and we mean *MUST*, as in you're going to be sued, not *must* as in a turn of phrase that's causing you to lose sleep), ask your publisher for a clean copyedited manuscript before your page proofs arrive. This way, you can figure out your changes ahead of time.

If you feel compelled to change large sections of your book after the type has been set, most publishers will charge you if the changes exceed 10% to 15% of the total manuscript (printer's errors aside). This is stipulated in almost every contract and can cost a pretty penny. While the cost is a good enough reason not to make changes after the copyedit stage, another is that those made at a later date just generally annoy everyone at your publishing house. The sections that you change have to be copyedited, and that can affect the entire schedule. All in all, you're making more work for people who already have too much to do.

A GALLEY IS NOT IN THE HULL OF A SHIP

While you're checking your page proofs, the printer may be turning them into *bound galleys* with pages cut to size. If you're the lucky recipient of bound galleys, their arrival is an exciting time because now your book actually looks like a book.

The drums are getting closer. It's now approximately six months until your Pub Date.

To be clear, bound galleys do not include any of the changes you make to your proofs. And these bound galleys will go to a number of book reviewers. However, all bound galleys have a prominent label instructing reviewers not to quote anything from the text without checking it against the finished book, which will contain all revisions. Reviewers are aware that bound galleys are uncorrected proofs and that they should check all quotes and facts in their reviews against the finished book.

THE BLAD

If you've written a book that will be printed in full color, you most definitely won't be seeing bound galleys, which are extremely expensive to produce. You'll review page proofs, maybe more than once (particularly if it's an art book and you're the "expert" who must check for the accuracy of the color). Sometimes the next thing you'll see is a blad (an acronym for "book layout and design"), usually a pamphlet-size sampler of your book. This will be sent to the reviewers and media people who need an early look. (If there's a particular spread you think should be considered for the blad, be sure to let your publisher know as soon as you turn in your manuscript.)

The Mother of All Meetings: The Launching of Your Book

Remember when we said your editor had to convince various departments to buy your book? Well, now these various departments get together to discuss the marketing, publicizing and selling of your book. A plan will start to materialize in these meetings and will be nourished, fed and fussed over until . . . THE LAUNCH MEETING!

The Players

Whether it's in a basement in Biloxi or in a high-rise overlooking the skyline of Manhattan, your launch meeting will in many ways chart the course of your book's introduction to the world. This is where your editor will formally pitch your book to key members of your publishing team. Depending on the size of the house, it can involve anyone from a guy and his cat to a dozen or more key players representing numerous departments. It may surprise you to know, if you've never been published before, that there will be one key person missing from this momentous meeting. The star of your book. You. All the more reason to try to make yourself visible whenever possible with your publisher. If your book is with a larger publisher, this meeting will probably include:

Your publisher

Your editor

Your publicist

The head of publicity

The head of marketing

A representative from online marketing

The head of sales (along with the divisional heads who sell to chains, independents, Amazon, etc.)

A representative from special sales

Sub-rights representatives for first serial and foreign sales (if relevant)

Your editor you know. But if you're like most of the world, the rest of these monikers are nebulous. And yet these are the people who will make the world pay attention to your book. Or not.

The publisher. Your publisher is the big kahuna, le grand fromage, the commander of your publishing ship. Publishers have certain godlike qualities — they're in charge of everything and everyone. If you can get them excited about your project, your chances of succeeding rise meteorically. Your publisher almost certainly has great contacts and knows the right people, or at least some of them. A word of praise about you and your book purred into the right ear can be the tipping point for its success. So if your editor walks into the launch meeting full of enthusiasm, expertise and passion, this can only help your chances of turning your publisher into your cheerleader.

Publicity and marketing. First of all: What the heck is the difference between these two departments? While the line can be blurry, here's a general rule of thumb: Publicity is when you get it for free; marketing is when you have to pay for it. For example, an article in *The New York Times* is publicity and an ad on the *Times'* website is marketing. Being on *Good Morning America* is publicity; sending a life-size cutout of yourself to everyone on *Good Morning America*'s staff is marketing. Having your book end up on a bedside table in the movie *Sex in the City* is publicity; paying for it to be there as product placement is marketing (which is more and more prevalent).

Generally, you'll have much more contact with the publicity department than with the marketing people. In fact, you'll probably be assigned your very own publicist, whereas you may never—or only fleetingly—speak to anyone in marketing. Why? Because publicity is often dependent on you as a speaker or interviewee, or as the subject of an article or TV/radio segment. Marketing, on the other hand, involves disseminating information about you and your book through stuff your publisher pays for. Think ads, postcards and, now, search engine optimization.

Sales. The sales department sells your book. Large publishing houses have their own internal sales force that sells to independent bookstores, chains like Barnes & Noble, online merchants such as Amazon, mass merchandisers and more. Often these houses have a separate department devoted to making what are called "special sales." This department usually makes deals with corporations and other non-bookselling retailers. The sales department can also include regional sales reps. One sales rep may cover the whole of Northern California and another Southern California.

Smaller publishers use distributors or commission groups of reps to sell their books. These are simply hired sales forces.

▶ Both the big guys and independent publishers whose books sell well in gift stores hire repping firms who sell to the gift industry. If yours is a gift book, it can be fun and useful to go to the regional semiannual gift show closest to you. You can meet your publisher's gift reps in person and get an up-close look into how this part of the industry works.

The sales force goes out seasonally to sell the books on the publisher's upcoming list, which means that each book on the list, if it's lucky, will receive approximately a minute of attention. Here comes your pitch again, as your sales person convinces a bookseller to place an order for your book.

Sub rights. The subsidiary rights department sells secondary rights to your book. The two sub rights most likely to be discussed at launch are first serial and foreign rights. If you've retained foreign rights, then only serial rights are relevant. Word to the wise: Serial rights don't have anything to do with Frosted Flakes. They refer to the possibility that a portion of your book will be reprinted in a magazine or newspaper—in days of yore, newspapers published the likes of Charles Dickens in installments. Nowadays, it's very difficult to have your book serialized, because magazines and newspapers are devoting fewer and fewer pages to reprinted material, and there are fewer and fewer magazines afloat. However, a reprint from your book in or on the pages of anything from *Good Housekeeping* to *Rolling Stone* to The Daily Beast can really help your launch.

Foreign rights can also add up to a tidy sum and can make you feel very worldly without your having to leave your living room. In all midsize to major publishing houses, there are people who try to sell your book overseas. In most cases, the person handling foreign rights will be selling your book through subagents rather than directly to foreign publishers. Many small publishers also use subagents.

Preparing for Liftoff: How You Can Affect the Launch Meeting

Most authors are blissfully ignorant of how important their launch meeting is to the emotional, physical and financial future of their book. At launch, your editor has to deliver his version of your road-tested, sweetly honed pitch. If he does a good job, everyone will leave that room understanding beyond a shadow of a doubt why, and to whom, your book is going to sell. Even if it's not "their kind of book."

Understand that this meeting will in large part determine your publicity and marketing budget. Whether you will go on tour. How hard the various players are going to push your book. Luckily, you marked the launch meeting on your Master Calendar and you've prepped your editor with all the information outlined below.

PUBLICITY

Blurbs for your book can go a long way toward inspiring your team members. Especially if they're from well-known, respected people. If your editor can come into the launch meeting with one or more meaningful endorsements, you will go from unknown quantity to bona fide author. In addition, your editor should be armed with a Top 10 list of potential endorsers to see if anyone in the room is connected to any of them.

A great blurb will not only excite your publisher, but may also help them decide to put some muscle behind your book. These days, fewer and fewer publishers are supporting author tours, questioning their cost effectiveness as a publicity and marketing tool. Peter Miller, director of publicity at Bloomsbury USA, recently told the *Los Angeles Times,* "In 99.9% of cases, you can't justify the costs through regular sales." But if you feel that a book tour would be a boon to sales, you need to provide your editor and publisher with compelling reasons as to why such a tour will be successful. Even more importantly, you need to show them through the sheer force of your personality and your expertise that they would be crazy NOT to send you on a book tour. Concretely, you need to let them know what your event/reading/speaking engagement would consist of and your ideas for getting lots and lots of people to show up—one of the most difficult parts of a book tour. If you're already speaking around the country, or you've got good friends all over the blogosphere, this will make their decision that much easier (especially if a university, writers' conference, book fair or business is footing your travel bills!).

And, of course, as publicity dollars shrink, publishers continue to look to authors to connect directly with their audience. The beauty of electronic media is that all it costs is your time. Which is precious, naturally. But if you apply a bunch of cyber elbow grease, you'll actually be able to do your own cost-benefit analysis. Through, for example, your blog, your website and your Twitter and Facebook accounts, you can very specifically track who you're reaching and then use these statistics to possibly pry some money, or least some enthusiasm and expertise, out of your publisher.

MARKETING

Are there essential materials you need in order to help get the word out? Does it make sense to pay for Facebook ads? What about postcards or mailings to specific departments at universities around the country? Do you need a few extra dollars to make an innovative promotional video? Will your publisher help your video go viral by hiring one of the many companies that specialize in seeding short movies on influential websites throughout cyberspace?

Lay out creative marketing techniques that suit you and your book. And try to frame things in terms of a return on investment. Marketing dollars are tighter than tight these days. So, without some numbers to back up your plan, your requests will more than likely go unheard.

SUBSIDIARY RIGHTS

Give your editor a list of book chapters that you think could be serialized, along with publications and websites where it would make sense to place them. This will make the people who handle first serial rights very, very happy. As you can imagine, they don't have time to read each book and then think about which chapters are best to excerpt.

For the foreign rights people in the room, be sure you've supplied your editor with supportable information on why your book might sell to specific countries. Is your blog big in Bulgaria? Do you receive thousands upon thousands of Tweets from Turkey? Do you know that there's a particular market for books on Green Leaf lettuce in France? Do you speak any languages fluently? Do you travel regularly to any particular countries? Have you connected with bloggers and/or online communities in other countries? If so, make sure your editor knows about these selling points and has copies of any articles that have been written about you abroad.

SALES

One of the most important tools you can provide to the sales force is the proper positioning of your book. This means going back to the elevator pitch (see page 70) in which you compared your book to other successful but not directly competitive titles. By describing the bestselling lineage of your book, you'll be identifying your potential audience. It's another way of saying that people who bought these books will also buy your book. Dan Ariely, author of *Predictably Irrational,* put together a PowerPoint presentation that explained his book. "It would be great if all the sales people could read my book," he says, "but I knew they probably wouldn't have the time, considering all the books they had on their list." Dan's presentation included an overview of his topic as well as a two-slide cheat-sheet that gave the sales people everything they needed to know in under two minutes. Dan was lucky enough to be able to do his presentation in person. If you don't have this opportunity, you can drag out your video camera, post your video on YouTube and send the link to your editor. Or create a document that can be emailed around.

SPECIAL SALES

Provide your editor with a list of places or companies apart from bookstores where your book has a reasonable chance of selling. (Take a look back at your proposal, where you may have listed such companies.) If you can come up with contacts at these companies, this will greatly enhance your chances of penetration. For example, if your book mentions Jamba Juice, as Paul Davidson's *Consumer Joe* did, maybe you can convince them to sell it.

Preparing Your Book for Cataloging

Next stop: your publisher's catalog. A book's catalog entry is basically its coming-out party, which is why you want to make sure yours is the belle of the ball. Great catalog copy can mean the difference between minimal orders and big piles of them. Libraries, independent bookstores, gift stores and universities all look at catalogs in making their ordering decisions. There's even a chance that some enterprising Hollywood movie producer or scout may browse your publisher's catalog, looking for their next huge blockbuster, quirky independent film or HBO series.

Generally speaking, your catalog entry will include eight or nine nuggets of information, from publication date and price to cover image and author photo. We'll take you through each of these elements so that you can help your book have a splashy debut.

A Pub Date Is Not a Social Engagement in a Bar

Catalogs are often organized according to season. So what's the best time of year to publish your book? With some books, it's obvious. A Christmas book needs to be out no later than October. A baseball book must be stocked in stores before April. A book about Abe Lincoln should be published on his birthday—and shipped to bookstores at least a month before.

Picking the right date and season can really help you generate publicity and make marketing much easier. If the nature of your book does not suggest an obvious publication date, you and your editor will want to look for a natural tie-in. If your book is about Mae West, maybe you can release it on the anniversary of her birthday. If it's about an African American historical figure, perhaps your release date should be during Black History Month. If it's about supermodels, maybe it should come out during Fashion Week.

If you're still at a loss, study seasonal publishing patterns. Certain books do better in certain seasons (beach reading in summer, diet books at the new year). Study bookstore display tables to see what books are put out when. Booksellers love promotions associated with certain months or holidays: March Madness, Presidents Day, Father's Day. You name it, most bookstores will have books related to the theme of that month or day. See where your book will fit in.

On Lincoln's Birthday, media outlets around the country are looking for new and different ways to talk about Lincoln. They almost certainly won't be so interested in talking about your beach book. The fall is a particularly difficult time to publish a book unless your publisher is putting hefty support behind you. This is because publishers release the bulk of their big, blockbusting books in the fall, all in time for holiday sales. If you've written a health reference book, you'll have a hard time getting any attention in November when the press is concentrating on gift-giving.

Most publishers are juggling so many books that they may want to put yours where they have a slot, as opposed to where it would best be published. Often the open slots fall during publishing downtime, when big books are not released due to awkward timing (the last two weeks of August, when everyone's on vacation) or months with weak consumer spending (like February). In some ways, this can be a good thing: There are fewer books competing for attention and bestseller lists, and the media still needs stories and the bestseller lists still need filling.

Although you might not have much say in the pub date you end up with (especially if you're with a large publisher), let your publisher know your thoughts about the best time for your book's publication. If your book is about guacamole and you heard through the avocado grapevine that June is about to be made National Avocado Month, make sure your publisher knows. With brand-new book in hand, you may be able to land yourself some of those elusive but lucrative National Avocado Month speaking engagements.

▶ The fall season may always be a difficult time to launch a book, but it's nigh unto impossible during an election year (unless your book happens to be about politics). Be sure to keep the presidential election in mind if you're planning a fall publication.

Title and Subtitle

Sometimes the title you used in your proposal will be the one that appears on the cover of your book. Often it won't. You may feel the new title is an improvement—or you may consider it the utter ruination of everything you tried to achieve. To ensure that the latter never happens, every author's contract should include either "approval" or "mutual agreement" when it comes to title. But even with this insurance, sometimes publishers bully authors into titles they absolutely abhor. What to do if this happens to you? While Gallup hasn't done a poll, it seems that about half the time the author is the one with the good instincts and half the time it's the publisher. Are your feelings of loathing toward the new title in the best interest of your book, or did you simply get used to your old title? As you may remember from the case of the very book you're reading, the importance of web searchability means your title and subtitle have to hit the mark.

Below are some common traps that authors fall into:

- *"I've shown it to X number of people, and they all hate it."* Never tell someone your title. Even if you don't start your sentence with "I hate this title, but what do you think?" most people can hear the drip-drip-drip of negativity in your voice. If you're going to ask for people's opinions, then show them the various titles by typing them out on a page. That said, unless you're able to show a very large number of people or a small number of influential people (like booksellers), telling your publisher that your friends hate it means nothing.

- *Fixation on one word or phrase,* especially if it's essentially irrelevant or based on some personal dislike. Just because a word makes your hair stand on end doesn't mean it might not be a great word in your title. Again, think about your readers. You're not going to be the one buying the book.

- *Snippy, combative belligerence.* Enough said.

Publishers have their own share of unhelpful behavior:

- *One muckety-muck doesn't like it.* In which case, it won't fly regardless of what anyone says. It's shocking how much power one higher-up can wield. This is a very frustrating situation because, depending on how big and hot the bigwig hotshot is, there's virtually nothing you can do about it.

- *Groupthink.* Sales, marketing and publicity throw their weight behind what you consider a heinous title. Another tear-your-hair-out situation. While the people in these departments certainly have experience and information that you don't have, they make many of their decisions without actually reading the books under discussion.

- *Snippy, combative belligerence.* Enough said.

Sometimes both author and publisher feel that the title is wrong. Only neither party is able to come up with a title that's right.

Catalog Copy: Making Your Book Sound Exciting

Some people can spin beautiful phrases that make books feel simply irresistible. One of these people may or may not be writing your catalog copy. Since you've been honing your pitch for months and months, you'd be crazy not to work with the person writing your copy to make sure it's enticing. As you may remember from our discussion of contracts in Chapter 8, we recommend that you be ensured consultation on your catalog copy so you're guaranteed at least a look before it goes to press.

Finding a Happy Compromise

Pitchapalooza winner Melissa Cistaro got a call from her editor saying that they wanted to change her memoir's title, which at the time was *The Occasional Mother*. "I wanted to be a team player, so I politely said I would be open to hearing other possible titles." Her editor told her that they had found a title they loved and wanted to move forward with. "When I heard the title, my whole body told me that this was not a title I could live with." Then the president of the publishing company called and told Melissa she was making a big mistake if she didn't take their title. "I was terrified. Somehow, I held my ground and asked if I could come up with more title options." After writing nine pages of titles, she narrowed the list down to 11. Her publisher came up with their own list as well. Guess which title her publisher picked? One of their own. "At first, I was devastated. But at least I'd escaped the title I hated. I could live with this one." *Pieces of My Mother* turned out to be an apt title because Melissa's memoir is about piecing together her mother's past and trying to understand why her mom abandoned her and her brothers when they were all younger than the age of five. And that's how compromising with her publisher made it possible for Melissa's memoir to finally find its true name.

Covering Your Cover

A great cover can make the difference between your book popping off the shelves and languishing on the remainder table. William Shinker, publisher of Gotham Books and an industry veteran, has these words hanging in his office: "The man who said, 'Don't judge a book by its cover,' never sold a book in his life." Take this to heart.

The cover in your publisher's catalog may or may not be the final cover that appears on your book. That said, most of the time it will bear a close resemblance, whether you like it or not.

Be prepared for the fact that your publisher will most likely want to minimize your involvement in the cover design. You won't be included in those art department concept meetings that end up deciding the fate of the look of your book; instead, you'll be expected to react to a finished or near-finished cover that may have been worked on for weeks and may even have already been approved by the publisher. If you have concrete and educated notions about how your book should or shouldn't look, this can be maddening. But play your cards right and you'll find a way to get your voice heard. To begin with, do NOT wait to receive a cover before you state your ideas. Ask your editor from the beginning to let you know ONE MONTH BEFORE work begins on your cover. Make

Living with a Cover You Hate

Before Arielle sold *Pride and Promiscuity,* she had a professional designer create a proposal for her. Since the book is a parody of Jane Austen, she wanted the design to evoke Regency England, and to that end they researched authentic borders and typestyles. The result was a work of art that welcomed the reader into the world of Jane Austen.

When the book was sold, Arielle made it clear to her large corporate publisher that she wanted to be involved with the design. She thought that her own extensive design experience and the fact that she's a literary agent would mean she'd be a welcome participant. The publisher had loved the design of the proposal—so much so that they practically mirrored it in the interior of the book!

Unfortunately, Arielle's designer had not worked up a cover for the proposal. When Arielle asked to meet with the publisher's art director in order to discuss cover direction, she was told it was not possible. When she asked if they could have a phone conversation, she was told of a blanket policy prohibiting authors from talking to or meeting with the art director. Hoping for the best, she let it go. In the meantime, she sent her editor concrete ideas about the design, including the names of typefaces and a recommendation for an illustrator. The publisher did not

it clear to your editor that you would like to communicate with the designer (but that you'll, of course, be sure to loop her in as well).

Early on, start amassing visual examples of what you're looking for. These can include typestyles, other book covers, artwork, photographs and color palettes. Beware: Just because you love a particular image doesn't mean it communicates your book's contents. As Sydne Waller, book buyer for The Hudson Group, says, "The cover should reflect what the book really is. I just read a book that had a cover that looked like it was a Chick Lit book. In fact, it was a murder mystery. A good one, too. But it was off-putting."

When you've been given the heads-up that it's design time, email or color-copy all relevant images and send them to the designer with a detailed note describing the tone and look you're after. You should discuss your thoughts with your editor and agent beforehand to make sure you've success-fully translated your ideas into helpful art direction. If you can't articulate your vision, you'll be wasting the designer's time. But if you can prove your design salt to your editor, she'll be more likely to remove the roadblock between you and the art department. And many designers actually appreciate input. What they don't appreciate are comments like "I hate it." If you get to the designer of your cover before he's spent a lot of time on it, he'll be more like that illustrator but sent Arielle samples from another first-rate illustrator. Arielle liked them and, wanting to seem like a team player (also secretly hoping she could "buy" herself some more involvement), sent a nice note to the art director via her editor, thanking her for bringing on such a talented artist.

Shortly thereafter, Arielle was shown a "preliminary design" for the cover. It had a distinctly Victorian look—a style that was utterly different from the Regency feel she had established in the interior and utterly historically inaccurate. She made sure to be very upbeat in her response to her editor, but was also firm about the changes she wanted.

Turns out "preliminary design" was a euphemism for "totally finished." Barely anything was to be changed. Arielle was beyond frustrated. Still, faced with making a huge stink and alienating her publishing team, she decided to simply live with it.

But wait! There's a happy ending. David happened to mention Arielle's book while at a dinner with his fine, smaller, more collaborative British publisher. The publisher loved the idea and bought the U.K. rights. Arielle got to sit down with the art director, brainstorm, share her thoughts. And, with her help, he created her dream cover.

open to your suggestions (and you won't be forced to think of a euphemism for "yuck").

If you're shown a cover that doesn't reflect your vision, it's time for constructive criticism. *Constructive* being the operative word here. Be specific about what you don't like. The more specific you are, the more likely your request for changes will be met. It's also helpful to show your cover to experts. This could mean graphic designers who can give you feedback in design-speak. Or local booksellers whom you've befriended. John Evans, co-owner of Diesel Bookstore in Oakland, California, says, "Because we see things at the moment of sale, we have a really good idea about what kinds of covers sell. At Diesel, once a season a local publisher brings their design people through our store to look at our displays." Publishers listen to booksellers because they're at the front lines. And a criticism from a bookseller can be just the ticket to getting your cover changed.

Please do realize, though, that unless you're a graphic designer or a bookseller, your expertise on covers is limited or nonexistent. Even David Ebershoff, who has been an editor for years and years, yielded to his editor's advice when it came to the British edition of his book *The 19th Wife*. "I didn't find the photo appealing," he says. "Plus, it had a woman holding a knife. And there's no scene

▶ Michael Powell, founder of Powell's Books in Portland, Oregon, recommends an important blurb be placed on the FRONT of your cover—not just on the back. If you were lucky enough to get a great blurb early, be sure to suggest this to your editor. (For more on blurbs, see pages 98 and 338–339.)

in my book with a woman holding a knife. It just felt off. But my editor reminded me that I didn't know the British audience and asked me to trust her. I'm glad that I did because my book became a #1 best-seller in the U.K."

INTERIOR DESIGN

A catalog will include your book's cover but not the interior design (unless it's an illustrated book, in which case an interior spread might be displayed). If you want a certain look for the interior, this is the time to put forward your ideas. Once again, study the interiors of books you love. Do you want something ornate? Something simple? What type-faces? Icons? A second color? Sepia tone? Artwork denoting each new chapter?

YOUR SPINAL COLUMN

The spine of your book, like its interior design, will probably not appear in the catalog or anywhere online. But it is an integral part of the design process and one you'll want to pay very close attention to. Why? Because when it comes to brick-and-mortar bookselling, much of the time the spine will be the only visible enticement for your book. And yet spines are too often an afterthought. Sometimes they're so visually dull that they disappear into the bookcase as if they're camouflaged. Sometimes they display only a title, when, in fact, the subtitle contains the most important information. And sometimes they feature type so small that anyone over 50 won't be able to read it without a spotlight and a magnifying glass.

The size of your spine will certainly help determine how much information it can contain. But even thin spines can have visual pizzazz, through color and typeface that entice a reader to wonder what's inside.

A number of years ago, a very talented designer had the idea to put a piece of the cover image on the spine. This has spawned a slew of fantastic designs, the best of which practically beg readers to pull the books off the shelves. One of Arielle's all-time favorite spines is by designer John Gall for the book *Che Guevara: A Revolutionary Life* by Jon Lee Anderson. It incorporates vibrant colors, a bold typeface and a piece of the cover imagery in perfect balance. Check it out.

Categorization: Where Will Your Book Live Best?

Imagine your lavishly illustrated soul food cookbook ending up in the African American History section of a bookstore. Or your book about cannibalism coming to live in the Cookbooks section. Sound ridiculous? It happens. You'd be shocked by how many books are categorized incorrectly and, as a result, die sad, lonely deaths in a section where no one would think to come visit them.

Even a subtle mistake can mean a loss of sales. Let's say a customer wants to buy your book about Passover. He goes to the Religion section and finds a subsection on Judaism, where there are many books on Passover. Naturally this is where he looks. But your book has been shelved with the general religion titles. "Oy," he sighs. "I guess they don't have that book on Passover I read about in yesterday's paper." Like so many of us, he doesn't ask for help but picks up some inferior book written by your bitter rival.

Make sure your category is correct right from the get-go. The first time you'll see it will probably be in the catalog. If you're in the wrong category, be sure to tell your editor immediately.

Your category may also be listed on your flaps or back cover. This tiny detail decides how most bookstores end up shelving their books. To prevent your book from being trapped in the wrong neighborhood, check out comparable titles to see what category they're in.

On the copyright page of a book, you'll also notice an additional list of categories filed with the Library of Congress. These categories will determine where libraries across the country shelve your book. They will also give library-goers a cross-referencing system that will help them find your book. According to David Williamson, cataloging automation specialist in the Acquisitions Bibliographic Access Directorate of the Library of Congress, "Unless we [the librarians at the Library of Congress] are totally wrong in our subject analysis, we do not accept requests for subjects. We are cataloging for our needs." That said, "subject analysis" relies on a publisher's submission of

▶ Before your book comes out, your publisher will have it posted on Amazon. As a supplement to a complex search algorithm that combines sales, page views, click-through and subject keywords, Amazon also allows users to tag books. Check out the tags to make sure they reflect the findings of your keyword research. If not, add appropriate tags. If you feel your book has been miscategorized (check the "product details" section), let your editor know.

subject materials for Cataloging-in-Publication data. Every time a publisher fills out the CIP forms prior to a book's publication, the publisher and author are really being given a chance to sway catalogers like David Williamson. The CIP is the cataloger's first look at the upcoming book (it may include a proof or material such as title page, table of contents, preface, samples) and should lead to a perfectly proper categorization. So, if you want your cookbook, *Festive Recipes of the Napoleonic Wars,* categorized under Napoleonic Wars as well as Feasts and Festivals of Europe, you'd better hope your publisher boldfaces and underlines those subjects in your CIP application. (For more information on CIPs, see *The Chicago Manual of Style.*)

▶ Sometimes you carefully pick your category and your book STILL ends up buried in the wrong section of your bookstore. For example, some bookstores do not have a Memoir section. This means that even if your book is categorized as a biography or memoir, it will be shelved according to what that store deems your theme to be. If you write a memoir about depression, it might end up in the Psychology section. Memoir buyers don't usually think to go to this section to buy memoirs. But there's simply nothing you can do. If this happens to you, take a deep breath, go home and scream: "SERENITY NOW!"

Format: Hard, Paper, Trade, Mass or E?

Most of the time, authors and their publishers agree on a format from the get-go. But sometimes publishers will pull the old switcheroo. You might find that your publisher wants to go directly to paperback for your first novel. Used to be that meant you'd miss out on a review in *The New York Times,* which traditionally favored hardcovers. Nowadays, however, publishing what's known as an *original trade paperback* is a common practice and one that may save your book from oblivion—especially if your audience is in their teens and twenties. (Most people in this age group don't have $25 to shell out for a hardcover or just prefer paperbacks or ebooks.)

Different formats hold different associations for people. Hardcovers often spell prestige, while mass-market paperbacks scream supermarket. And the ebook is a beast unto itself.

Ebooks are either sold on their own (as an ebook-only publication) or in addition to a hardcover, trade paperback or mass-market edition. It used to be that publishers would hold back on releasing an ebook until its hardcover

The Power of Paperback

L ots of authors dream of having their book come out in hardcover. It seems more prestigious. Glamorous. Worthy of being taken seriously. On the other end of the food chain from cheap pulp paperbacks. It also used to be much more difficult to get reviews with a paperback. But all this has changed, as Caroline Leavitt learned with her ninth novel, *Pictures of You,* which was originally supposed to come out in hardback. "My fabulous publisher, Algonquin, told me they had big plans for the book and thought it could be a bestseller. So when Algonquin announced they were going to do it in paper, I was panicked and upset—and a little ashamed. I thought it meant that they didn't take the book as seriously as their other literary works, that I wouldn't get any reviews, and that the book would die."

Caroline promptly called her agent, who told Caroline that publishers were putting books out in paperback because people are more likely to take a chance on something that costs half as much. She also talked about how paperbacks, in the age of e-readers, are more portable than hardbacks, which Caroline could see was true. Algonquin also assured Caroline that the reason they wanted to do it was because they wanted to make her big fast, and paperback was the best way to do that. In this format, she could get into places like Target or Costco. And indie bookstores love paperbacks because they can sell so many. Caroline was slowly coming to accept the idea, but she was still worried she wouldn't get reviews.

Six months after publication, the book was in its fourth printing. It became a *New York Times* and *USA Today* bestseller. It was on Best Books of the Year lists from *The San Francisco Chronicle* to *The Providence Journal.* And what about those reviews? Caroline admitted, "I got more and better ones than I ever had, including *Vanity Fair, Elle* magazine, *O* magazine, *Newsweek, The Washington Post, The Boston Globe* and more. I was astonished!"

When they bought Caroline's next book, *Is This Tomorrow?,* Algonquin asked if she wanted paper- or hardback. Her answer? "I begged them to do paperback!"

counterpart had had some time to sell through. But that is no longer the case. Ebooks should be available whenever the first edition comes out so that readers can choose the format they like best.

Keep in mind that though publishers generally know more about the marketplace than their authors do, they're not always right. And a mistake in format can make a significant difference in sales. So, if your publisher changes formats or if you realize that the original format they chose doesn't make sense, don't sit back because you assume the publisher knows best. Just as you search comparable housing sales when assessing the value of your home, the best way to convince a publisher of the value of a particular format is through the success of comparable titles. You don't want to be trying to sell your cute midtown condo at uptown mansion prices.

Cover Price: What Is Your Book Worth?

How much a book should cost has always been and will always be a bone of serious contention. As we discussed in Chapter 8, with the introduction of ebooks and with retailers like Apple and Amazon still feeling their way, prices have been all over the map. But the question remains: How much should your book cost? Usually your publisher won't consult you about cover price, because frankly, what do you know about pricing books? Unless you've spent time working for a bookstore, the answer is probably very little.

Some books merit high prices. For example, Taschen America published *GOAT* (*Greatest of All Time*), a 700-page, 10-inch-thick, 74-pound, lavishly illustrated book on Muhammad Ali that retails for $3,000! But most of the time you won't want to price yourself out of your category or audience.

Publishers sometimes have to opt out of pricing a book competitively in order to cover production costs, especially on illustrated books or books with special add-ons like spiral binding or pocket folders. But if you have the only Chihuahua book that's over $21.95 and your Chihuahua-loving potential buyer has never bought a book on her favorite pet for more than $20, she may decide to let yours go. In addition, if a price is too high, some chains will order fewer books. Or none at all.

Some publishers believe that going slightly under the average cover price is the best route. But if your book is priced as if it were destined for a remainder table, that can be a turnoff to buyers as well. Many people are wary of "bargain books" unless they already know the author's name. The other difficulty with lower-priced books is that if a book is under a certain amount, warehouse clubs like Costco and Target, as well as QVC, won't take it because they need a certain return on their investment.

All in all, the pressures to move the price of a book up or down are complicated, and what might make no sense to you may be very well thought out by your publisher. These complications shouldn't turn you off from doing your own research, though. You have more time than your publisher has to study your particular category or models for your book, and this may lead to great new insights that will help your book scale the heights.

More Publicity and More Marketing

If your book was given a two-page catalog spread, an announced first printing of 50,000 or more and a long list of publicity and marketing commitments, you can be pretty sure your publisher is pulling out all the stops. If it got one page, a 25K first printing and a few other nice publicity and marketing promises, this is quite good, too. But regardless of what your book's catalog copy says, don't count on it being 100% accurate. First printings are almost always exaggerated. Publicity and marketing information is also typically pumped up because publishers want to make booksellers think they're really getting behind a book. In reality, a first printing listed at 25,000 could easily end up at 15,000. A five-city tour can rapidly become a tour of your living room. And the entire publicity and marketing campaign can disappear faster than you can say National Public Radio.

On the other hand, if there's precious little info about publicity and marketing and no initial print run listed, you can be pretty sure your book is at the bottom of your publisher's barrel that season. But don't despair: This is where *most* books find themselves.

No matter which scenario applies to you, your entry in your publisher's

The Power of the Catalog

We asked Mitchell Kaplan, former president of the American Booksellers Association and founder of Miami's Books & Books, about how a publisher's catalog influences his decision to buy a new book or not. Mitchell laid out a number of things he looks out for in a catalog spread.

1. "Whose catalog is it? I use my 30 years of experience to determine the quality of the publisher. And then I consider my track record with that publisher."

2. "Is that publisher likely to give this book attention? What is their promotion plan?"

3. "What is the print run? This shows the publisher's commitment to the book. It won't deter me from buying a book, but it might give me pause."

4. "Is the cover eye-catching? Again, this is not a determining factor, but it does have a lot to do with whether a book will sell or not. So I do definitely consider it."

5. "Do I have other books on this topic and are they selling?"

catalog is important because it introduces your book to the world and signals how your publisher sees it. The good news is, once you know where you stand, you can figure out the best way to hit the ground running.

The Author Photo: Putting Your Best Face Forward

If the publisher wants your photo on the front cover of your book, it's their responsibility to pay for that photo and to set up a photo shoot. Unless you're movie-star pretty or really famous, this probably won't happen. Most of the time, your photo will go in the back of the book or on the back flap, and you'll be required to provide and pay for it yourself. As tempting as it is to ask your loving but amateur husband or your next-door neighbor's well-meaning but untrained cousin to snap a shot, DO NOT take this approach. Your author photo can be a huge sales tool. Get a good one. (See page 353 for more info on achieving the perfect photo.)

The Six-Month Meeting

Remember when we said how important it is to turn your name into a face? Well, now is the time to do just that. Ask for a meeting with the people who will be instrumental in making your book successful. You'll want to pick their brains, to use them as sounding boards for your ideas and to inspire and excite them. Schedule the meeting six months before publication and preferably prior to sales conference. Mauro DiPreta, publisher of Hachette Books, says, "If possible, an author should come in for a meeting with the editor, publisher, publicist and anyone else who can attend. This way, you can come up with a publishing plan together. The result is almost always that the publishing team comes away more focused."

DO NOT expect your publisher to take the initiative to set up this meeting. If you have an agent, let him set it up. If he's willing and able, by all means bring him with you. Your agent knows the right questions to ask and will help maximize your time with your publishing team.

You want to walk into this meeting with your pitch at the tip of your lips and publicity and marketing ideas in hand. If you wrote a proposal, review your competition, publicity and marketing sections. If you didn't, see Chapter 3.

A great way to open your meeting is to pass out goodies from the best bakery in town. This may sound obsequious, but it shows that you want to give as much as you want to receive (and it gets people on a nice sugar high).

Once you sit down, ask everyone for a card so you can refer to people by name throughout and then follow up with them directly if need be. Trot out any new endorsements you've received; as we've said all along, everyone loves endorsements, and this should get things going on a positive note. Calling on all your style and passion, fully communicate your leave-no-stone-unturned attitude. If you're spending time on the marketing and publicity of your book (and you should be), let everyone know what you've accomplished and what you plan to accomplish. Have you set up speaking engagements? Have you made contact with journalists? Written magazine pitches? Gotten your website up and running? Connected with communities of people who love

▶ If it's six months before your pub date and you still feel nervous about meeting your publisher, you should start getting help with your presentation skills. See page 332 for info on media coaches and presentation doctors.

Meeting Absolutely Everyone on Your Team

Sometimes an author has the opportunity to meet far-flung members of his publishing team. Michael Perry, author of the memoir *Population: 485,* about returning to his small Wisconsin hometown as a volunteer EMT, did just that when he toured HarperCollins' distribution center in Scranton, Pennsylvania. It turned out to be a truly moving experience. As he says, "Most people think of books in terms of editors and writers, but all the angst-ridden typing in the world does no good if someone doesn't move the books from point A to point B. During my tour, I met everyone from the folks who handle telesales to customer service to the technicians who put the books in the boxes. For a while, we stood beside a forklift and talked about deer hunting. Perfect. They gave me a cake with the book cover reproduced on the frosting, several neat gifts and, perhaps coolest of all, my own monogrammed safety belt in case I ever need to run up the forklift to fetch a pallet of my books. Man, that made me smile."

While very few authors get (or create) the opportunity to meet all the folks who make publishing happen, it's still important to recognize that your team most likely has individual players you never even knew existed. And all these players are helping (or not helping) your book reach readers. So if you get to meet any of them, spread good cheer. Michael did just that, and it helped generate buzz within his team as well as in the publishing trade journals.

the same thing you do? Amassed a ginormous Twitter following? Take your publishing team through the marketing, publicity and sales opportunities that you've created. Make them see that they have a seriously organized, dedicated, driven, passionate, articulate, good-humored, reasonable author on their hands.

> Can't do an in-person meeting? Then work with your agent to put together a memo that informs your publishing team of all your present and future efforts.

After you've talked about what you've already done, bring up what you'd like to happen. Maybe go through a Top 10 possible blurbers/media coverage/ bookstore or bookselling event/sales opportunity wish list. Again, this is not so different in concept from your where-do-I-want-to-go-to-college list. Every entry on the list should be appealing to you, but you should have a combination of safeties, solid choices, obtainable dreams and maybe one or two "reaches." Most importantly, every entry on your list has to make sense. You have to be able to logically support your inclusion of a promotion on Amazon, a first serial in *More* magazine, a foreign sale to Norway.

The last, yet possibly most important piece of your plan is, as always, your pitch. You want everyone to see what a bang-up job you do with your delivery. And you want to make it extra easy for anyone in that meeting to go out and do a superb, brief yet utterly exciting pitch of your book to anyone anywhere anytime.

If your agent comes with you, try to arrange to have a quick bite or drink together after your meeting. Review what was accomplished and what still needs to be done. Ask your agent for feedback on your performance. What are your strengths? What do you need to work on?

As soon as you get home, send thank-you notes to everyone who sat in on the meeting (good thing you got everyone's card). Personalize your thank-yous as much as possible by using the notes you took during your meeting. Regina Louise, author of *Somebody's Someone,* also happened to be the owner of a hair salon, so during her meeting she observed everyone's hair type and then sent each person a special hair product along with a thank-you note. This practical and thoughtful gift really made an impression on her publishing team.

Also ask your agent to send a follow-up that requests in writing what, exactly, your publisher has committed to doing; you can refer to this later and use it to your advantage if your publisher doesn't come through on some of the beautiful promises they made.

The Sales Conference

Three to six months before your book comes out, your publisher holds a sales conference. Basically everyone who has anything to do with the selling, marketing and promoting of your book will be attending this conference. The ideas from your launch meeting will be solidified here, and a grand plan will have begun to emerge.

During the sales conference, your editor or publisher will pitch your book to the *entire* sales force, usually in under three minutes. Annik LaFarge, former publishing director of Bloomsbury, says, "Our sales force would hear about 600 to 800 books at one meeting. The sales conference is ultimately, in most cases, where the sales force gets swept up by the enthusiasm of its colleagues and becomes passionate about selling certain titles. For every book, they have to think: *How do I sell this? Who is the audience?*" Many of the biggest publishing houses no longer invite editors to these meetings, which means your biggest advocate may not be there when the sales force decides, *Wow! I can't wait to sell that one!* Or not. Hopefully you've spoon-fed your pitch to your publishing team so that it rolls trippingly off even the dullest tongue.

Again, the more ammunition you give your publisher about your audience, comparable books and what makes your book exciting and salable, the easier it will be for the sales force to storm the castle. And this goes back to your pitch, which you've now been working on for months and months and months.

Tipping the Scales

Hopefully, your sales reps will leave the conference stoked about your book and armed with your *tip sheet,* which includes the basic specs of your book (title, subtitle, ISBN, pub date and so on), plus all of the marketing and sales information that is not on the catalog page: comparison titles, audience and what other similar books that audience bought. Please note how much of the meat of the tip sheet comes from information you've been developing from day one. Your tip sheet is the most important tool your sales force will use when going out to sell your book.

Most authors don't get into the book business so they can talk about comp titles, positioning and tip sheets. Yet these are necessary to successfully selling your book. That's why you want to get as involved as you can in the presales process. Otherwise, you'll only find yourself complaining later.

If you have a highly collaborative editor, see if you can get a look at your tip sheet. The better the pitch and the more accurate the comparison titles, the easier it will be for the sales force to sell your book. Elise Cannon, VP and field

▶ Just because you have little contact with your sales reps doesn't mean you can't let them know you're more than a unit number. Time again to pull out your thank-you notes. Ask your editor if you can send notes to the reps, and more than likely she'll cough up the names. But tread very lightly here. Your sales rep does not want to be bombarded by requests for help. And obviously, if you do send a thank-you note, make sure you keep any contact information strictly confidential.

director of sales at Publishers Group West, says, "I think positioning is most important. I need '*The Graduate* meets *The Texas Chain Saw Massacre.*' I spend a really good amount of time prepping my sales call, getting the right comparison book and its sales figures." Getting the *right* comparison book is the key here. Carole Horne, senior buyer of the Harvard Bookstore in Cambridge, Massachusetts, says, "The comp title has to be valid and make sense. Otherwise, you can do more harm than good."

Your Sales Reps Hit the Road

Starting as early as six months before your book is published, your sales reps begin their quest to convince booksellers to order your book. Some of these reps sell to bookstores within a particular region, say, the Pacific Northwest. Others sell to one or more national accounts, like Barnes & Noble or Amazon.

But from the largest chains to the tiniest mom-and-pop bookstores, your sales reps get approximately 30 to 60 seconds to spin their magic for you . . . and for every single other author on their list.

Here's the rub: Your sales reps have to give an honest account of the promise of your book and how it delivers, because at the end of the day all they have is their reputation. Elise Cannon says, "You must establish credibility with an account. You have to tell them what you truly believe. You can't lie. Lying wouldn't serve anything." Linda Bubon, co-owner of Women & Children First in Chicago, adds: "For me, it's all about relationships. Many of the reps I work with have stayed in their jobs for 15 or 20 years. When they say, 'I've read this book and I know you can sell it,' that makes a big difference."

The health and success of your book is shockingly dependent on how well your sales reps pitch and how many books these booksellers buy. In fact, the results of these pitches (especially the early ones to places like Barnes & Noble, Target or Costco) will, in some ways, determine such things as your publicity and marketing budget and the size of your first print run.

Making a Stink:
When to Get Mad and When to Shut Up

Gene Wilder, the brilliant writer/actor, was making a movie with the equally brilliant filmmaker Mel Brooks. Wilder had written a scene that he thought was very funny. Brooks had a very different opinion and wanted to cut the scene out of the script. But Wilder would not let it go. He shot down all of Brooks' objections as he worked himself into a lather over what a hilarious scene he'd written. Brooks was finally worn down by the sheer force of Wilder's passion. He still thought the scene stank, but he agreed to film it just to shut the man up. Guess what? Wilder was right. The movie was *Young Frankenstein.* The scene was a musical soft-shoe shuffle involving Frankenstein's monster doing "Putting on the Ritz." To this day, that moment brings down the house.

You, too, will encounter many situations in which your desires will come in conflict with those of your team members. It's very difficult to know when to make a stink and when to shut up. Sometimes when you put your foot down, it ends up in your mouth. Sometimes the squeaky wheel really does get the grease. Again, weigh all the circumstances carefully before you take any action. "I always believe in what I call 'the plea from the heart.' A real letter to your editor/publisher outlining specifics and asking for help. That's about all you can do. Because being the author from hell doesn't work." Those are the words of industry titan Larry Kirshbaum, former CEO and chairman of Time Warner Book Group.

Have you made your plea from the heart but still see no sign of action? Have you followed up with concerned calls and emails and had your agent step in on your behalf but you're still getting no love? Then it's time to get proactive. If you have the money, spend it on a plane ticket. Go into your publisher's office and convince them with solid evidence to step up to the plate. If you spring into action instead of just being a complaining ninny, you'll undoubtedly receive a much better response.

If they still won't budge, and you've done everything short of the old horsehead in the bed, then you just have to acknowledge that you've either got a sub-par partner or an inflated sense of your book's salability. Still, don't be afraid to ask for what you want. You'll be amazed by how effective asking can be if you do it the right way. And, as always, doing it the right way means less complaining and more solid, research-based requests that your publisher can actually respond to. Bruce Harris, former vice president of Crown and former

Making a Stink Stick

M ichael Moore wrote *Stupid White Men* before the 9/11 attacks. After 9/11, his publisher told him he would have to eliminate what she considered to be unpatriotic pieces of the book. Michael said he stood by every word and would not make changes. There were already many, many copies of the book sitting in a warehouse, but his publisher refused to release them. In fact, she wanted him to buy back the copies of his own book. But he would not bow to her pressure. He thought this might be the death of his book, but he knew he had to take a stand.

It just so happened that Michael had a speaking engagement lined up in New Jersey when all this came down. He told the story of how his publisher refused to release his book. Turns out there was a librarian in the audience, and she was outraged. She started an email campaign to fellow librarians, who then contacted Michael's publisher, demanding that the book be released. The press got wind, and it became a huge story. Due to public pressure, Michael's publisher was forced to release his book. Of course, it went on to be a huge international bestseller.

This story has two morals:

1) Stick up for what you think is right.

2) Always be nice to librarians.

publisher of Workman, put it this way: "What I hate: cursing, whining authors who are unable to be a part of the team. Particularly those who demean the professionalism of our team. What I like: authors who are willing to listen to professionals, who appreciate the work that's being done on their behalf and who are always willing to do more on behalf of their books."

Enjoying the Ride

I f you have a publisher, it's time to make your book fly. Skip to Chapter 12, and buckle your safety belt. Put your seat in the upright and locked position, and enjoy the flight.

If you don't have a publisher, get ready to build your own plane, hire your flight attendants and jump into the cockpit.

CHAPTER 11

Publish Thyself

"My take is this: If a book is solid, it's solid. I don't much care about how it got glued together."

—Mike Cottrill

TRADITIONALLY, SELF-PUBLISHING HAS BEEN SEEN in certain circles as the ugly duckling of the book world. But with the blossoming of print-on-demand and electronic publishing, the ugly ducklings are looking a lot more like beautiful swans. "In the past, if you were lucky enough to find an agent and get a publisher, you were a member of the privileged class," says Mark Coker, cofounder and CEO of ebook publisher and distributor Smashwords. "We're moving from a world where publishers tell readers what they can read to a world where authors have the freedom to publish anything and readers decide what gets read and bought." And this is good news for anyone self-publishing. Between print-on-demand and ebooks, you can have a book in your hands in days or even minutes. All with no agent, no publisher, no rejection. And, sometimes, at little or no cost. Awesome!

Self-publishing is all about making it on your own, doing everything your way, and not caring about whether you're part of the club or not. It's about building your own nation and making it exactly how you want it.

William Blake. James Joyce. Virginia Woolf. Rudyard Kipling. Edgar Allan Poe. Ezra Pound. Mark Twain. Gertrude Stein. Walt Whitman. Carl Sandburg. Beatrix Potter. What do these authors have in common? All self-published. What a cool group to belong to. The fact is, self-publishing can be a ball. It can launch you into superstardom and turn you into a millionaire (okay, rarely, but still). The bottom line? This is not your daddy's self-publishing. The onus of the ugly duckling is gone. Says Arsen Kashkashian, head buyer at Boulder Book Store, "Nowadays, because there is no barrier to publishing, we're seeing people give up faster on the traditional route. These are people who are writing good books and turning to self-publishing. This means the quality of self-published books has gone up."

More people are, indeed, seizing on the new technologies and low costs of publishing on their own because try as they may, they cannot break through the gate of the castle that holds agents, editors and publishers. But more than ever, people are publishing books on their own because they *choose to*. Because they see opportunities in the market and want a bigger share of the pie than publishers offer; because they want full control of their book; because they don't want to have to wait for the sloooooow publishing machine. And, for some, because they just want a polished piece of work to share with a small circle of friends and family.

Why Do You Want to Publish Your Book on Your Own?

These days, there are SO MANY ways to self-publish. That's a good thing and a sign of a healthy marketplace, but it also means that in selecting your method and your means, you need to separate the wheat from the chaff. Choose the wrong course and you could end up with any number of sad scenarios including: 1) $20,000 on a credit card and a basement full of books; 2) an unprofessional-looking book (that you'd planned to use as your business card) filled with spelling errors; 3) an ebook that no one but your parents owns (and which they can't figure out how to download).

Choosing your method of publishing is a Goldilocks situation—you're looking for the one that's going to be *just right* for you. First, let's figure out exactly why you're self-publishing by honing in on your particular situation. Do you want to self-publish because:

1. You have direct access to your audience?

2. You want a bigger chunk of the retail dollar of your book?

3. You have a time-sensitive book and want to publish fast?

4. You want full control of your book inside and out, from your hands to the hands of your readers?

5. No matter how much you rewrite and how hard you market yourself, you can't find anyone to agent or publish your book?

6. You've written a book whose value isn't apparent to a traditional publisher because it caters to a niche audience or particular region, or for any number of reasons?

7. You really want to publish a book, but you just don't have the personality to market it to an agent/publisher?

8. You've written up your family history or the life story of a loved one that will be of great interest to Aunt Coco, Cousin Momo and a handful of other blood relations but no one else?

If you fall into category 1 or 2, congratulations, you are what we like to call an authorpreneur; categories 3 and 4 can also be authorpreneurish. You know your audience and how to reach them, and you may have the ability to make a splash and/or wads of cash from your book or via the ideas you're spreading through your book.

If you're in category 5, and possibly even category 6 or 7, you're a person who firmly believes you've got a valuable book that idiot agents and bone-headed publishers are too thick to appreciate. You want to publish on your own as a springboard for success—or maybe you want to prove to a publisher that you have the audience, the chops, the perseverance to make it in the hopes that self-publishing will be your road to traditional publishing.

If you're in category 8 (and possibly 6 or 7), you're a candidate for a small printing via print-on-demand, or possibly even a small special print run from an old-fashioned printer. If you aren't concerned with selling your book to a wider audience, you'll be focusing on writing and printing the right package for you.

Authorpreneurs to the Moon

Remember Seth Godin? He is the king of authorpreneurs. Seth has been going direct to his audience since he began his book career. Numerous *New York Times* bestsellers later, after being invited into the publishing castle and showered with fine wine and sweetmeats, he still self-publishes in combination with traditional publishing.

One of the ways that Seth was able to self-publish so successfully from the start was that he embraced new technology and was one of the first people to have a breakout ebook—and to give away a third of its "printing" for free.

Show Me the Money

M any people assume that once you've hooked up with a publisher, you're set for life. The truth is, it can be even harder to sell a second book than a first one. In fact, some of the people we've met who are most frustrated with the publishing industry are those who have been successfully published, then gone on to write often better books—only to have rejection thrown like sand by a bully in their faces over and over again. We've been asked by these frustrated folks, as we've asked ourselves: What to do?

JA Konrath, a.k.a. Joe, is the author of numerous thrillers and mysteries including *Whiskey Sour,* the first in his Jacqueline "Jack" Daniels series. Joe is a doer. Among other feats, he's toured 100 blogs in a month, signed at 600 bookstores in one summer and sent 7,000 letters to libraries. He's also a man who doesn't like to take no for an answer. In fact, Joe received more than 500 literary smackdowns before he sold his first book. His particular combination of personality traits led him down the authorpreneur path. He took the books he was unable to sell—even once he had a major publisher on board—and published them himself as ebooks. "I originally made my unpublished books available as free downloads on my website, JAKonrath.com, in order to generate interest for my print titles," explains Joe. "But when the Kindle came along, I was contacted by Kindle owners asking for a way to read my ebooks (the first version of Kindle couldn't read PDF files). So I uploaded these to Amazon, charging a small price—$1.99."

Guess how many people asked for that free sample? A whopping 175,000. And a healthy percentage of those 175,000 went on to buy the print book.

Seth has also used creative packaging to help sell his self-published books. *Purple Cow* was sold in a custom-designed milk carton. Would a traditional publisher ever publish a business book in a milk carton? NO WAY! Which gets back to one of the joys of self-publishing: You can do it your way. No one can tell you why it's stupid or won't work. How it's never been done before, so it can't be done in the future. You get to operate from the standpoint of "yes"—and that's a good thing.

No matter what kind of book Seth publishes, or the form in which he publishes, there's one key ingredient he can always depend on: a built-in audience. Seth has one of the most successful blogs in the world, a top-of-the-heap speaking career and a network of like-minded muckety-mucks. But anyone with a built-in audience, even if it's not worldwide or even nationwide in scale, can enjoy success with self-publishing. In fact, the more niche or localized your audience, the nicer your results may be.

The results? Joe started selling more than 200 units per day, and he earned over $100,000 that year on Kindle sales. His experiment was so successful that he now sees going to a publisher as just one option. "I go where the money is," says Joe. "If a publisher wants to pay me, I'll take it. But they'll have to pay me more than I believe I can earn on my own. That means over 100K per novel."

When we heard these figures, we could only wonder if Joe would prefer to go solo on all his future books. "Self-publishing is two jobs," he told us. "I'd rather just write than have to worry about line editing, proofing, formatting, uploading and cover art. But if I earn more by doing it myself, I'll do it. I'm lucky enough to be able to write for a living. If that means I have to bang my head against the keyboard trying to get Kindle DTP to accept my HTML, so be it."

Yes, self-publishing is a money suck, not a money generator, for most self-published authors. But for those who have enjoyed some authorial success before, or who have established platforms and built-in audiences, self-publishing *can* be a way to pay the bills. True authorpreneur that he is, Joe puts it this way: "I take pride in all of my work, and I'm always thrilled when people enjoy it, but at the end of the day this is a business and the best reward is a full bank account."

Meet Robert St. John. We did, at a book fair in Lexington, Kentucky. We were in the green room of the local NBC affiliate station when we struck up a conversation. Turns out Robert owned three high-end restaurants in southern Mississippi. Arielle, who is always hunting for great restaurant recommendations, was fishing for clues about where to have a delicious dinner that night. But soon she was distracted by Robert's gorgeous illustrated cookbook, *A Southern Palate,* published by him and him alone.

Both Arielle and David's jaws dropped when they learned that this book had already entered the black, to the tune of six figures. Beautifully printed, heavily illustrated books are famous for losing money. Fewer and fewer publishers are producing them. But Robert had figured out a way to not just sell them but make a big ol' chunk of change.

How did Robert do the undoable? First off, he's a known quantity in his neck of the woods, namely, Hattiesburg, Mississippi. Not only does he own successful restaurants there, but he's also a syndicated columnist (his column started off locally and grew to cover a large sector of the South). Robert makes the most of his local presence. As he says, "Big oil companies dig wells where there's lots of oil. But there are pocket wells, too. Pocket wells can be a great source for people who self-publish."

Robert also had the wisdom to choose a perfect partner in his illustrator, Wyatt Waters, a well-known Southern artist whose work is much beloved. "Wyatt was much more well known than I was at the time. So I owe a lot of the success of the book to him." To ensure that his partner's work was shown off at its best, Robert had the book printed on lush, high-quality paper. The book just screams out for a coffee table to sit on.

Lastly, Robert had a staff to deal with the accounting, marketing and shipping of his books. No small thing. Eight books later (three of which were published by a major publisher), he's built a well-oiled machine that knows how to create, market, publicize, sell and distribute books. Robert has certainly made the most of his pocket well!

Of course, your niche doesn't have to be geographic. Roger Gilbertson and a partner started a company related to building robots and developed an expertise with shape-memory alloys, an obscure and unique means of creating motion without motors. One day Roger was on the phone, once again giving out information to a robot enthusiast. When he hung up, his mentor, who'd overheard the conversation, lamented that Roger had answered the same set of questions for the third time that day. The mentor said, "You should write this all down and sell it to people instead of giving it away for free." So Roger wrote up a detailed explanation of a number of his robot-building projects: "It was so esoteric that it didn't even seem worth it to go with a publisher," he says. "I went to Kinko's and made stapled xeroxed copies with card stock covers."

Roger then ran an ad in monthly electronics magazines for what he called *The Muscle Wires Project Book*. For $39.95, buyers would get the book plus a kit of the hard-to-find alloys in wire form, manufactured by a supplier that Roger had known for years. (In the publishing industry, this is known as a "book plus.") There were no other sources for this information, and very few for the materials, so Roger knew he could determine the price—a price that meant he was making $20 per book! "The really cool thing I learned was that not one person (in over 1,000 books sold) complained, because the information was so vital. No one cared that it was xeroxed. They were getting inside info." Roger did eventually print 10,000 copies of his book, using digital printing. To date, he has sold over 40,000 copies of a book whose subject most of us have never even heard of—and couldn't understand if we did.

Then there's Julia Fox Garrison. The second you talk to Julia, you see that she's got authorpreneur writ all over her. "I always beat to my own drum," says Julia. "Everyone said, 'You're crazy, self-publishing will never work.' But that just made me even more determined." Julia is a woman with a singular story, a wonderful voice and the ability to get people to listen to whatever she has to say—which was critical to her success. You see, on July 17, 1997, Julia woke up in the hospital to find herself completely paralyzed on the left side of her body. The story of her paralysis and her life in its wake is the basis for her memoir, originally titled *P.S. Julia: Missing a Piece of Your Mind Can Be Puzzling.*

When Julia decided to publish her book all by herself, she was dead-set on making sure her book did not *look* self-published. "That was very important to me. So I did a very elaborate hardcover. I made my binding sewn and not pasted. I had a linen jacket, with four-process color and parts of the image double-embossed." All costing, you guessed it, lots of money.

Seth, Robert and Roger all had audiences they knew how to reach, making a return on their investment a strong possibility. Julia did not. She had to create her audience from scratch. "One of the first things I did was visit my local bookseller and ask them if they would sell my book. They said, 'We don't do self-published books.' I said, 'I'll take no after you read my book.' Well, they read and loved it. So my first event ever was in that bookstore. Three hundred people came. And one staff member told me they never sold as many books at an event." How did Julia pull this off? She emailed everyone she knew. She made flyers and postcards and bookmarks, and she talked to anyone and everyone. "I took the success of my book on like I took on the recovery of my stroke. I looked at obstacles as learning experiences. I was just relentless. In fact, I was so focused that I was on the *Boston Globe* bestseller list and didn't even know it. My husband came home and showed me the paper. I was number eight. And my reaction was, 'Why am I number eight? I should be number one.' That's just how I am, always striving to raise my bar."

THE AUTHORPRENEUR ROAD MAP
You may have noticed that Seth, Robert, Roger and Julia each used different formats for their books. Seth publishes ebooks or interestingly packaged books. Robert publishes gorgeous, four-color coffee-table books. Roger started his direct publishing career with a Xerox machine and ended with digital printing. Julia went with an old-fashioned printing press for her hardcover memoir. These are classic cases of form following function. Their format of choice reflects their

audience and competition. It also allows them to effectively market, promote and sell their books.

Though we stress the importance of resourcefulness and proper preparation in all authors, these qualities are absolutely vital for the authorpreneur. Imagine if you invented a great product but had no idea what your competition was, no idea how to reach your audience and no way to get your fabulous product into their hands. With authorpreneurs, your book is your product. So you have to know how to do all these things. For each piece that you don't tackle, your chances of success drop exponentially.

What else do successful authorpreneurs need? A lot of times, they need money. Many authorpreneurs sink a decent amount of dough into their books. Sometimes to the tune of tens of thousands of dollars. Printing books ain't cheap—especially if they're four-color or in interesting packages. So if you don't know how you're going to sell your books, you will want to keep costs at a bare minimum, which is doable these days. But, to go back to the product analogy, you wouldn't be surprised to hear that an entrepreneur invested money in a potential product. If you're serious about your book product, you may have to do this, too.

Consider authorpreneurship carefully before mortgaging your house to pay for your book. But do it right and you can have it your way, while still laughing all the way to the bank. As you can imagine, in the wake of Seth, Robert, Roger and Julia's success, major publishers came knocking on their doors. And now three of the four have also worked with major publishers. Roger enjoyed a whole other type of success—his company was bought, book included, by a larger company.

Publishing Yourself to Court Traditional Publishers

Maybe self-publishing wasn't your first choice at all. Maybe you're sick and tired of relentless rejection at the hands of shortsighted, narrow-minded agents and publishing houses. But you know that with an actual book or ebook in hand, you can prove to a publisher that you've got something.

Remember Lisa Genova? She had no interest in self-publishing. In fact, Lisa had no conscious ambition of becoming a novelist. She has a Ph.D. in neuroscience and was doing strategy consulting for a biotech company when the idea for her novel first presented itself: "The seeds came when my grandmother was diagnosed with Alzheimer's. Of course, as a granddaughter, watching her deteriorate was heartbreaking. But as a neuroscientist I was fascinated on a molecular level. I wanted to know, 'What does it feel like?' Sadly, my grandmother couldn't really answer that question."

Lisa decided to write a novel from the perspective of an Alzheimer's sufferer. Seven years later, she finished her novel, *Still Alice,* and immediately sent out queries to agents. "It was very discouraging and lonely. For nine months, I heard nothing but rejection. Finally, I heard from four agents who all wanted to read the first 50 pages. After months and months more, three of them had said no. I'm still waiting to hear from the fourth!" Lisa heard over and over again that there was no audience for *Still Alice.* Agent after agent came back with, "Who wants to read about Alzheimer's? It's too depressing." One agent told Lisa, "You have a Ph.D. from Harvard. You should write some nonfiction. Get back to me when you do." The last agent she talked to actually said, "Whatever you do, DO NOT self-publish. You will kill your writing career."

At the time, Lisa was living with her future husband, an independent documentary filmmaker. He introduced her to a whole world of musicians and indie filmmakers, doing their own thing, making their own art and going right to their audience online, and she saw a new road. "Even after all this rejection, I had a kind of naive confidence. Besides, I had no other options really, except for sticking my manuscript in a drawer. So I decided to go the print-on-demand route with an author services company. I paid $450 and they basically acted as my printer. I edited and copyedited the book and sent in an old head shot, and my husband designed the cover."

Lisa ordered 50 copies of *Still Alice* at a time. She kept them in the trunk of her car. Eventually, through a combination of social networking and PR—she'd hired a firm to get the word out—Lisa's book started to take off. Before she knew it, she had a query from an agent and an offer from Pocket Books, a division of Simon & Schuster, to the tune of . . . drum roll . . . half a million dollars. The Pocket Books edition of *Still Alice* went on to be featured at such retailers as Barnes & Noble and Target—the kinds of stores that are hardest to break into as a self-published author. And . . . hold on to your hat . . . *Still Alice,* the book nobody wanted, became a *New York Times* bestseller, staying on the list for 31 weeks! A dream come true, and yet it's not even the end of the story. After the dust settled, Pocket Books made an offer for her next two books, which Lisa hadn't even written yet, for . . . really long drum roll . . . over a million dollars!

Zetta Elliott also encountered a steady stream of nos from agents and publishers before turning to self-publishing. Zetta wrote a book, *A Wish After Midnight,* about a subject she thought lots of young readers would be interested in: an Afro-Latino teen who travels back in time to Civil War–era Brooklyn. "I chose to self-publish because every door within the traditional publishing industry had been closed in my face. I sent out dozens and dozens of query letters, and initially got a lot of positive interest from editors and agents. But I couldn't find anyone who wanted to represent my work, and all the editors who praised my writing insisted there wasn't a market for the story I was telling."

Zetta had earned her Ph.D. in American studies from NYU. She had several poems published in anthologies. She had won a contest for a children's picture book due to be published that fall. And yet she *still* failed to find an agent or editor who was interested in her work. Zetta couldn't help but wonder why she couldn't get a foot in the door. Then came some help in finding the answer: "Another self-published author introduced me to the statistics kept by the Cooperative Children's Book Center; finally, I had proof to back up my suspicion that racism was at play in the publishing industry. Of the 5,000 books published annually for children, less than 100 are written by black authors." Now it was clear that self-publishing was the way to go. "Three friends suggested I look into print-on-demand. They were scholars and writers. They didn't fit the image I had in my mind of a self-published author—they weren't lacking in talent, desperate for attention and willing to hustle books out the back of their car. So I started to reconsider what self-publishing could mean for a writer who simply wanted her work to live in the world. As an educator, I knew I wanted my writing to be used in the classroom, so I self-published *A Wish After Midnight*, as well as a memoir and two collections of plays."

For Zetta, one of the great benefits of self-publishing was autonomy. "I believe in the idea of organic writing, stories that haven't been tampered with by editors who, for the most part, are completely outside my culture, my community, and have no sense of my people's storytelling traditions. The publishing industry is so homogeneous—the vast majority of editors come from one particular class and one cultural group. They can't always understand nuances or strategies deployed by writers of color. By self-publishing, I got to present work that is truly my own. I am the writer, editor and publisher, and that means I'm responsible for what winds up on the page."

Zetta chose to publish via print-on-demand. Once she had books on hand, she hit the teen blogosphere hard and started racking up kudos all over the web. Her book was also getting picked up by libraries and schools. Then one day she got a call from Amazon. They wanted to publish her book! Her first thought: This must be a hoax. Au contraire, it was part of a new effort by the online behemoth to, in the words of vice president Jeff Belle, "identify great books that we think have been overlooked and bring them to a wider audience." The program is called AmazonEncore. While AmazonEncore does not, at this point, pay its authors advances, they do pay royalties competitive with other publishers.

"What mattered most to me was that my book was simply *available*," says Zetta. "In libraries, especially, since that's where I found most of my books as a child. My ultimate goal, I suppose, is to write stories that are meaningful to me and to others and to open doors not only for myself but for others as well."

Unlike Lisa and Zetta, Andy Kessler had a great start with his book *Wall Street Meat*, about the securities industry. It was the right idea at the right time, and he quickly signed with an agent. But the agent told him a conventional publisher would never buy this idea, because Andy wanted a finished book on shelves within three months and it would be at least nine months to a year before a publisher could get it out. When Andy asked why a publisher couldn't do a rush job, he was told they wouldn't put in the extra dough to rush a book to press unless you're famous or you're writing about something of major national importance.

"The time frame for the launch of books by publishers has gone from silly to unrealistic," says Seth Godin. "When the world moved more slowly, waiting more than a year for a book to come out was not great, but tolerable. Today, even though all other media has accelerated rapidly, books still take a year or more." Instead of throwing up his hands and cursing his bad luck, Andy decided to take charge. He hired an editor for $35 an hour. He found a couple in Florida (Andy lives in California) to design his book cover. He hired a well-known illustrator. He tracked down a printer. He purchased his ISBNs. He set up his page on Amazon.com. And he did all this in a matter of weeks. He shared his rush schedule with us:

End of December: Had idea for book titled *Wall Street Meat*.
January 1: Started writing book.
January 31: Finished book.
March 17: Book for sale on Amazon.com.

Unhappy with his first printing, Andy ordered another from a different printer. In the meantime, he was getting orders. By the end of the first day, he had 50 orders via Amazon. Soon they were coming 100 at a time. Soon a human being from Amazon called Andy and ordered 500 books. And soon he was out of his first printing.

Amidst this flurry of success, Andy was contacted by the editorial director of HarperBusiness, who "dropped some lowball number that I didn't accept." Then Andy got a call from a new agent, who said: "Let's do this right. We'll have an auction." The agent created a feeding frenzy, and HarperBusiness ended up buying the paperback rights to the book—plus a new book—for far more than they originally offered. And Andy even managed to convince Harper to accelerate its typical 12- to 18-month schedule on the new book.

Are You Absolutely, Positively Sure You've Got a Success?

One self-published author we met was convinced he could easily sell thousands of copies of his book. He thought all he had to do was write a good book and get it printed. His reading public—whoever they were—would flock to him. So he went to a traditional printer and had 5,000 copies printed up. After six months had passed and no such flock appeared, his heart sank as he had this sad but sobering thought: He would have to market, publicize and sell his book, too. It sounded like a root canal without novocaine. The result? Three years later, he can't even stand going into his basement because facing those sad and lonely 4,851 copies of his book sends him hurtling down into a shame spiral. The moral? While we encourage you to embrace the authorpreneur spirit, we also encourage a conservative plan—at least to start out with. Don't print more books than you have reason to believe you can sell or want to give away.

Self-publishing has always been an against-all-odds way to launch a book or, for that matter, an entire career. But Lisa, Zetta and Andy's stories illustrate the unprecedented opportunities and options available to authors of every ilk. And how, in this world of quickfire communication, once you have a book in hand (or on your e-reader), the very agents and publishers who gave you the cold shoulder may be fighting to give you a warm embrace.

THE BIG LEAGUES

Sometimes, even if your book is selling at a brisk rate, you won't get that fantasy call from a publisher. But if you've sold (not given away for free—this is a really important distinction) approximately 10,000 books in a year and you're not fond of playing publisher, you may want to consider trying to interest an agent or going directly to a small or midsize publisher. Many major publishers have trouble selling even 5,000 copies of their own books in a year, so it will be impressive to them if you've doubled this all by yourself, especially if your book was not widely distributed. Hopefully, by the time you've sold this number of books, you've become an excellent pitchman, you've received some hot press, you've gotten yourself into some good stores, you've created your own platform and you've got a great web business going. All of these things will entice agents and publishers.

Self-Publishing a Labor of Love

We've talked to many self-published authors who have no dreams of achieving or landing a big publishing deal as a result of their efforts. Nor do they have the time, energy or expertise to take on the tasks of authorpreneurship. They just want a book or two, or 25 or 100. In hand. To give to family, friends or those who share the same passion for whatever their book is about.

Anie Knipping is a visual artist and writer, but she has also worked as a graphic designer and has all the skills necessary to design her own book. Anie wrote and illustrated an 8-by-10-inch four-color book called *Eccentricity* about living with autism. Although publishers and agents were interested in this utterly unique and beautiful tome, it was too financially risky for them to gamble on. The project was technically dead, but *Eccentricity* was her life's work. "I couldn't just let it go," says Anie. "It wasn't possible to self-publish a full-color book of that size at the time, so for nearly a decade I had little choice but to futilely hurl myself against the wall of the publishing industry. I probably still would be, but in 2012 the advance of self-publishing technology finally allowed me to vault over it. I've never looked back."

Bob Viarengo has self-published everything from a memoir to a family photo history to a coffee-table book for first-time visitors to China. "For me, publishing is a hobby. And an expensive one at that," says Bob. Because he's interested in creating beautifully designed books, Bob hires a graphic designer for each of his projects. The designer does everything from choosing the cover images and interior faces and fonts to organizing photos and creating dust jackets to preparing a print-ready file. Bob also hires a proofreader for each book. Bob's printings have run from 25 copies to 150, with individual books costing him up to $60 dollars each. Expensive hobby indeed! But each book is a labor of love that is intended for those closest to him—his friends and family.

Bob is member of a long tradition of bookmaking enthusiasts who produce books not for fame, recognition or profit, but for the satisfaction of creating something beautiful of deep personal value. Though Bob's enthusiasm runs him a pretty penny, in a moment you'll be hearing about wonderful ways to publish on the cheap.

The Costs and Components of Self-Publishing

With the explosion of ebooks, digital printing and print-on-demand, you may assume that you can self-publish on the cheap. And you would be right. But even with an ebook, if you want to do things right, there are a number of costs involved. Expenses to consider include:

- Editor/copy editor
- Proofreader
- Cover designer
- Interior book designer (print books only, except in rare cases)
- Permissions
- Lawyer (to check text so you don't get sued and to set up company for tax purposes)
- Author photo
- Marketing (banner ads, postcards, keyword research)
- Publicity (hiring publicist, paying for book tours or events)
- Website (architecture, design, upkeep)
- Printing (print books only)
- Warehousing (print books only)
- Shipping/handling (print books only)

A good editor can cost thousands of dollars, depending on her expertise and experience. Same goes for a great book designer or publicist, and then there's the cost of printing—if that's how you decide to go. Authorpreneur Julia Fox Garrison sank approximately $50,000 into her book. Lisa Genova invested just $450 to get her book off the ground. But once she got some traction, she hired a publicity firm. Costs can vary widely, but the bottom line is that if you want success, you have to put out a professional product. Arsen Kashkashian, head buyer at Boulder Book Store, puts it this way: "The self-published books that work are the ones that look professional outside and in. These authors are clearly willing to invest in their books and to pay attention to the details."

As in any business, it's best to start out your self-publishing venture with a budget. Decide from there what takes priority. Does your memoir really have to go to a printing press? Of her beautifully printed, embossed hardcover, Julia Fox Garrison says, "If I had to do it again, I definitely would've just printed a paper-back. Aside from the cost factor, paperbacks are more portable, and thus, more salable. And, as I learned later on, book clubs—my target audience—don't tend to select hardcovers."

Yes, you need to spend money to make money. But spend too much on the wrong thing and *make* becomes *lose* so fast your head will spin. Does your website need to be designed from scratch or can you use a WordPress template? Can you start with print-on-demand and then move on to a printer if you see that you have enough of an audience?

Yes, You Need an Editor

If there's only one thing you're able to spend money on, it should be hiring an editor. It's a necessity, especially if you're not a professional writer. Take a moment to consider how much an objective, professional eye can help your book. If you think your manuscript is perfect just the way it is, let us be blunt: It almost certainly isn't. It's the rare book that doesn't benefit from a good stiff edit and/or copy edit. As Lisa Genova says, "I didn't use a copy editor for my book. And I would definitely not recommend going that route under any circumstances. It was a very bad idea. When it's your book, you've been over it so many times you just can't see mistakes anymore."

If you don't have the money to hire a professional editor, your next best bet is to create an editor by committee. Ask friends and colleagues to read and mark up your book. The best readers are those who fit within your audience profile; they are the people who would actually buy your book and have read other books like it. If you don't have any friends who fit the bill, join a writers' group, association or chat room.

After your book has been edited, it will then need to be copyedited and proofread. If you're tempted to skimp on these services, let us just remind you that a book filled with grammatical and spelling errors is one that will not find success in the world.

The Look of Your Book, Inside and Out

Whether your readers are shopping for a book via the web or in a brick-and-mortar store, the first thing they will see is your cover—so don't take it lightly. Mark Coker, CEO of Smashwords, who sees daily the sales effects of good and bad covers on self-published books, says, "A great cover makes an emotional promise to the target reader. It should go without saying (but must be said because not all authors think this way . . .) that the entire cover design process starts with thinking of the target reader, and it should be microtargeted. For example, if the target reader is someone who reads erotic romance, then that cover should look very different from a cover targeting readers of romantic suspense or Christian romance. Some authors make the mistake of trying to make their cover appeal to all readers of a broad genre, though that only sets things up for disappointment."

See if you can hire the cover designer of a book you love in your book's category. Cover designers usually have their names printed on the back of a book, on the back flap or on the copyright page. Many can be tracked down through

A Very Personal Self-Publishing Story

L isa Schenke had a very personal story to tell, and she was passionate about her mission to tell it. She knew she had an audience, and she suspected her story would attract media attention. But she also knew that because her story was a very specific one, it would be difficult to find a publishing partner who understood her audience and would take a risk on an unknown writer with a book on a difficult topic. So she set about determining the best way to reach the audience she knew was out there waiting for her and her book, *Without Tim: A Son's Fall to Suicide, A Mother's Rise from Grief.*

"Before determining whether I was going to self-publish, I began identifying my target audience. My book actually has multiple audiences, primarily those who are grieving, and more specifically those who have lost a child or those who have lost a loved one to suicide. Other important audiences include teens and young adults who are suffering from low self-esteem and *all* parents of teens and young adults."

Lisa set about soliciting supportive blurbs for her book. She contacted numerous celebrities and political figures who had lost someone to suicide or suffered with suicidal tendencies themselves. She reached out to state, local, and national suicide prevention programs, mental health awareness organizations, and hospitals. "Thankfully I did receive a total of five supportive blurbs, a few through random contact, a few through someone I knew who knew someone who knew someone. . . ."

With blurbs in hand, Lisa chose to submit her book to only five publishers. When Lisa didn't get the answers she wanted (or simply no answers at all in a couple of cases), she decided to self-publish. We tell writers over and over again that if they choose to self-publish, and they want to be taken seriously, they have to hire experts to edit, design and promote their books. This is exactly what Lisa did, and it's one of the reasons why her book garnered so much interest from the media, as well as from readers. "After choosing to self-publish, I hired professionals for nearly every step of the process. My goal for writing my book was

an Internet search. (Check out AIGA's 50 Books/50 Covers Award at aiga.org.) We also like design crowdsourcing sites such as 99Designs. Word to the wise: In the case of printed books, don't forget about your spine! Unless your book is displayed face out (an unlikely scenario), this is the only thing potential buyers will see in stores. Make it colorful. Put a picture on it. Make sure your title is legible and stands out. Show your designer covers that are similar in look and feel to what you want (see page 260 for tips on successfully communicating with your designer).

to get my message of hope out to others. I had no plan or desire to learn to become a publisher."

Of course, there were bumps along the road as there are with any endeavor of such complexity and difficulty. "After choosing Amazon CreateSpace as my POD [print-on-demand] alternative, I did not realize that laying out the book would be complicated—even more so because I wanted pictures within the text. At first I panicked. But after some research and asking around, I hired a book formatting company and the cost was reasonable."

Lisa also didn't realize how much it would cost to hire a publicist. After getting a few estimates, she provided publicists with a number she was willing and able to pay and asked what exactly she would receive for that price. This turned out to be a great tactic because she was able to negotiate a deal with the publicist of her choice for far less than the original bid.

Lisa also wanted to make sure her book was for sale at several indies in her area. *Without Tim* is tied to a local series of suicides and she wanted to reach teens and families who might come across the book in one of the downtown stores. "I remember reading that indies are likely to keep 30% to 50% of the price printed on the book. What I did not realize was that I first have to purchase the book from Amazon CreateSpace (at the author discount) before I can even bring it into the local bookstore!" It may have been another bump, but it was a worthwhile one because her book flew off the shelves at her local independent bookseller on the day of her launch party, outselling all other titles. The store immediately became one of her biggest supporters.

Lisa worked extremely hard to write her book, but she worked just as hard to get the word out. So far, she's appeared everywhere from her local television station and newspaper to *The Christian Science Monitor,* National Public Radio and the *Daily Mail* in the United Kingdom. And more important to her, she's touched the hearts of readers all over the world with her story of hope and inspiration.

As for the insides of your book: If the interior design is very simple, it may be possible for you to lay it out on your own, using a simple Word document or filling in the boilerplate forms of an author services company (more on those in a moment). But if you hire a designer, you may want to use the same person for both the cover and interior. Or you can go with a flashy, splashy cover that costs a pretty penny and a more straightforward interior design done by a less expensive designer. This decision comes down to talent, money and the kind of book you want to make.

COVER INFORMATION

In addition to being good-looking, your book cover needs to include some specific information. Figure out exactly what should appear where—on the front and back of your cover (and on the front and back flaps, if you decide to print hardcovers). For print books, your cover should include:

ISBN and bar code. A must for every cover if you want a retailer to stock your book. (See opposite page.)

Category. A crucial detail to include on the corner of your book's back cover. Since the right category allows bookstores and libraries to shelve your book correctly, it's not surprising that the best way to decide on a category is to walk the aisles of bookstores. You'll see where your book fits best. (For more on this subject, see page 263.)

Blurbs. Beautiful blurbs have a way of allaying potential skepticism about a self-published book better than almost anything. They stamp approval on you and your book.

Cover copy. Trot out your A-game pitch to show how wonderful and captivating and profound and useful the contents of your book are. Most people who aren't in the book business don't really care which publisher published a book; they just want something that satisfies their needs, and they look to the jacket copy to see if your book fits the bill. They will most certainly be judging your book not only by its cover, but by the promise on that cover.

▶ Think about searching for a book on your phone. The cover will be smaller than a postage stamp. At such a diminutive size, the image becomes more important than the words. And on a Kindle, it may be seen only in black and white. As you design your cover, make sure to view it with all these caveats in mind.

Bio. A short bio for the back of your book or the back flap: your credentials, any awards and where you live. You can have a more complete bio inside your book if you so desire. Either way, your bio should help answer the "Who are they to write this book?" question.

Author photo. Yes, a good author photo can sell books. So, if you choose to put a photo of yourself somewhere on your cover or flaps, make sure it's flattering, high-quality and nicely reproduced. As opposed to dorky and out-of-focus. (For more info, see page 353.)

The Name Game

Survey bookstore shelves and you'll see that almost every book has a company name and/ or logo on its spine. Your book needs these, too. You and your company should not have the same name, as that screams "self-published"—and not in a good way. Because there still remains a prejudice against self-published books by reviewers, book business professionals and booksellers, it's important to make yourself as bona fide as possible.

Consider adding other information and features particular to your book that you think will draw readers in. When Roger Gilbertson finally decided to print *The Muscle Wires Project Book* professionally, he went to hobby stores and found out what the owners wanted to see on the cover. He learned keywords and phrases that needed to appear on the top half-inch of the cover to help attract readers. He also learned that hobby store owners like "third edition" to be highlighted in the top corner. And he added a gold sticker for the gold medal one of his robots won. These are the kinds of small details that can make the difference between someone pulling your book off a shelf or not.

Permissions

While your book is being edited, take care of any permissions you need to secure. Self-publishing doesn't exempt you from needing to clear permissions for artwork, photographs, song lyrics, poems or other writing that's not your own. The last thing you want is someone coming after you because you used something for which you have no permission. See Chapter 9 for more info.

ISBN and Bar Code

An International Standard Book Number (ISBN) is like your book's dog tag. It allows instant identification, so your book should always be wearing one—even your ebook. If you want to sell your book outside of small mom-and-pop shops, you will need not only an ISBN but also its partner-in-crime, the Bookland EAN bar code that retailers scan when your book is taken to the register. Bowker offers a single ISBN for $125, or they come in groups of 10 and currently cost $295 if you're not ordering a rushed service. But if you do your research on the web and buy ISBNs separately, you can get them for less (if you're publishing an ebook, you can buy them individually through such sites as Smashwords). EAN bar codes can be bought individually. On the ISBN website, they currently cost $25 each. If you do a hardcover, a paperback and

I'm in the Library of Congress!

I f you're self-publishing, you won't be eligible for Cataloging-in-Publication (CIP) data from the Library of Congress, a tool that makes it easier for librarians to shelve books. But you can apply for a Library of Congress Catalog Card Number, also called a Preassigned Control Number (PCN), which enables librarians to actually find and order your book. One catch: The Library of Congress has to believe your book will be of interest to libraries before they assign you a number, so there's no point applying if your book is not appropriate for libraries. But don't be lazy here. Librarians all over the world use the cataloging system, so having a PCN can be beneficial.

PCNs are free (except for the copy of your finished book you're required to send) and assigned before publication so that the actual number can be printed on your copyright page. Be sure to apply three months before your pub date.

an ebook edition of your book, each one will need a separate ISBN; so any extra codes you buy may come in handy.

Copyright

Your book is automatically copyrighted once you write it, but since you're publishing on your own, you may want to go for an additional layer of protection by registering with the U.S. copyright office. Copyright should be in the author's name. A bargain at $35.

Lawyer/Accountant

Larger publishers have lawyers vet books that present the risk of a lawsuit. Memoirs and other works of narrative nonfiction are top candidates for vetting.

Do you need a lawyer? If you've written a memoir that names real people, or attempts to disguise them, you might need a good stiff vetting. If you've written a work of nonfiction where a description of a character could be seen as defamation, the same holds true. Even if you've written a work of fiction that includes a thinly disguised account of something that actually happened, a lawyer might be in your future—and hopefully before, not after, you publish your book.

If hiring a lawyer is in your cards, find one who specializes in intellectual property—even better, a lawyer who specializes in intellectual property as it relates to publishing. We all know how lawyers can be overzealous, and you don't want a shark eating your entire budget.

Post Office Box

Somewhere near the beginning of almost every book, there is a copyright page. On that page is listed the name and address of the publisher. For those of you printing books, do not put your home address on your book. Not only will it make you look both rinky and dinky, but it could also be dangerous. You can get a P.O. box at your local post office. Fees vary by location and start as low as $24 for a six-month period.

A Wicked Website

Unless you are publishing without a sales goal, you'll need a site or blog.

Making It Your Business

With all those costs, it might make sense to officially establish a business so that your expenses count for something on your tax return. For most self-published authors, this would be a sole proprietorship. In a sole proprietorship, you are the business. What the business makes, you make. What the business owes, you owe. It wouldn't hurt to get some expert advice from a lawyer or an accountant, though, as you begin building your publishing empire.

▶ Need help funding your project? Consider crowd-funding (we'll cover this in a minute) and be sure to check out the grant info in Appendix II and/or subscribe to *Poets & Writers Magazine,* which lists all kinds of grants and awards for writers.

Crowd-Funding

We were teaching at a writer's conference last year that featured a workshop on how to successfully pull off a crowd-funded campaign on sites like Kickstarter. We checked our schedules, crossing our fingers that our workshop wasn't at the same time. Fortunately, we got to attend Safwat Saleem's absolutely fabulous class on the subject. An artist and designer who has been using crowd-funding sites for the past several years to fund his projects, Safwat is not just a master fundraiser, but a master entertainer as well. So when we decided to write this new edition, he was on the top of our list to call.

As we've established, self-publishing done right can cost a big chunk of change. Add any bells and whistles—illustrations, color, cool packaging—and most people are priced out of the game. Enter crowd-funding. A good

Kickstart Your Kickstarter Campaign

1. **Use a presale rather than donation strategy.** Use crowd-funding platforms in order to sell products at market value. Doing otherwise amounts to asking for a donation. And it's very difficult to have a successful crowd-funded project with a donation strategy. For example, let's say that you'd like to give backers T-shirts with some clever illustration on them. You buy high-quality tri-blend shirts wholesale and research how much these types of shirts sell for in online shops. You find that they typically sell for $25 each. A presale strategy would mean that you would also sell your shirts for somewhere near $25 each, not $50.

2. **Use simple reward levels.** Don't overcomplicate your reward levels. Complex options will make production and distribution very difficult. Let's say you have men's and women's fitted T-shirts, and each shirt comes in sizes XS through XXL. That's already 12 different items you'd need to produce, assuming that every shirt size is ordered at least once. Toss in five or six different T-shirt designs, and then complicate things further by having reward levels where your backer gets more than one T-shirt, and you've got a mess on your hands if you are a small operation. So stick with the number of T-shirt designs that is practical for you.

3. **Keep your campaign around 30 days.** On most crowd-funding platforms, you get to select the number of days that you want your campaign to last. Crowd-funding much shorter than 30 days is typically not long enough to build sufficient buzz to reach goals, but go beyond 30 days and it will be difficult to maintain momentum. If your campaign is too long, people will forget about your project.

4. **Have a marketing plan in place before you start.** You can't just post a project and expect people to back it. There is a tremendous amount of work required in order to spread the word about your project—think through everything from your current networks to the networks of people within them. Consider who you will reach out to and how you will get them to pay attention. Make a list of relevant blogs and other social media outlets and write individual emails to every single one (mass emails are the worst).

5. **Tell stories.** Tell stories that make your audience want to share your project with their friends, family, coworkers and so forth. If your project has a video, photos and copy that tells a compelling story, your contacts will be more likely to share it with their networks. Using humor can be a very powerful tool as well.

6. Steal ideas. If you want to see what works (and what fails), steal ideas from other successful crowd-funding campaigns. Take note of how others leverage storytelling and the creative approaches they take to their videos and reward levels.

7. Maintain momentum. Your work doesn't stop when your campaign finally (after weeks of planning!) goes live. In fact, that's where some of the heaviest lifting begins. You should have a week-by-week strategy to market your idea that will maintain energy for your project. Think about how you can use the crowd-funding platform's "update" feature for backers, as well as what you can add to your campaign page each week to keep people coming back and wanting to see more.

8. Have a plan for production and distribution before you start. Make sure you have a plan for how you will produce all of the products you are promising in your reward levels—as well as for how you will capture shipping addresses and how you'll store, package and mail products.

9. Make sure the numbers add up before you start. Carefully think through all of your costs—taxes, crowd-funding platform fees, production, shipping (including international) and so on. (And, yes, you do have to pay taxes on your crowd-funded revenue.) Consider what you think will be the most popular reward level and how many backers you'll need in order to be successful. Generally speaking, the $20 to $29 reward level is the most popular. Given that fact, this is also the reward level where you should try to have the largest profit margin.

10. Be flexible with your plan. The best plans go awry when it comes to crowd-funding. Be prepared to problem-solve creatively if you are going to launch a campaign. You might run into a situation where it's one week from the deadline and you've reached only your halfway mark. Be prepared to pull together the time and energy needed to reassess your plans and seek creative solutions.

Wanna get some inspiration for your crowd-funding campaign? Check out Safwat's Kickstarter projects and videos at safwatsaleem.com.

crowd-funded campaign can help an author produce a professional-quality book he doesn't have the resources for on his own, as well as launch a book (and particularly a self-published book) into success before it's even published. What a wonderful time to be a writer, right?!

But who makes a good candidate for a successful crowd-funded campaign? We learned three important prerequisites from Safwat:

1. You have to have a network you're willing to market your project through. This doesn't have to be your own personal network, but you have to at least know what networks you're going to reach out to.
2. You have to be able to tell a really good story. (Good thing you're a writer!)
3. Most importantly, you must be willing and able to put yourself in the shoes of the audience and ask, Would I back this project? Having the ability to empathize with your audience and respond to their feedback cannot be emphasized enough.

If you meet the prerequisites and want to go for it, here are Safwat's top 10 tips for a successful crowd-funded campaign on pages 296–297.

Self-Publishing Roulette

With so many options available, what's the right publishing formula for you? You can don the hats of publisher and printer, production manager, cover designer, marketer, distributor, shipper and doer-of-everything. You can hand all those hats to a print-on-demand author services company. You can be super green and publish an ebook. Or some combination thereof.

Your format is determined by your type of book, your pocketbook, your audience and your desires. See which formats appeal, both aesthetically and functionally. Do you want a spectacularly elaborate photo-filled opus printed on the finest paper money can buy? Or are you simply looking for a way to make your book look like the average trade paperback from Random House? Go to a bookstore and look at books. Open them up. Feel the paper. Get your hands on a print-on-demand book; you might be able to find some in bookstores, or you can buy one through whatever company you're considering using as a printer. If you're thinking ebook but have never actually read one, borrow an e-reader and make sure the user experience is right for your book.

You need to fully understand the costs associated with your wishes. Analyze these costs from beginning to end—and not just the per-book cost. It might appear that an author services company is going to supply you with books for next to nothing. But add in the cost of a copy edit, the cover design, shipping and the charge for each copy sold and then see where you stand.

Making an ebook

"There is a collision of publishing and technology today," declares Mark Coker, founder and CEO of Smashwords. Bookselling is shifting more and more to the web, and although the growth of ebooks has slowed, they are still a major force in today's and certainly tomorrow's marketplace. One of the truly liberating things about ebooks is that their avenues of distribution are open to all—in direct opposition to printed books, where having a publisher makes it much, much easier to get distributed into chains, nationwide independent bookstores, mass retailers and so on. Ebooks are so easy and cheap to distribute that, if your book is straight text, there's almost no reason *not* to e-publish it, even if you offer a print book as well.

So, what does it mean, exactly, to publish and distribute an ebook? And how can you make sure it is available on all e-readers? Our favorite answer (at the moment) is Smashwords. Smashwords is simply the most advanced ebook publishing and distribution platform there is. And it's by far the easiest. "We're a one-stop shop for authors," says Mark Coker. "Smashwords is for those who want to focus on writing and not on starting a publishing business. You don't need to be a computer programmer to get your work published and distributed with Smashwords. All you need is a Word document. We've also turned the compensation model upside down to the author's advantage by returning 85% of the net to the author." This means authors earn 60% of the cover price for sales originated by retailers, 70.5% for affiliate marketers.

Smashwords also has two helpful merchandising tools. The first is a preorder tool where all accumulated preorders credit toward the first day's sales rank at iBooks, Barnes & Noble and Kobo, which causes the book to spike on those retailers' bestseller lists and typically leads to more sales. The second tool is enhanced metadata management

▶ If your format of choice is an ebook with hyperlinks, make sure the hyperlinks are valid, i.e., lead to the intended web page, not to one that reads "URL NOT FOUND"— so annoying! Another bit of housekeeping: tags will play a colossal role in your readers' ability to find and devour your ebook—so don't slack on your tagging.

for series authors. Series authors are the highest-earning self-published authors. And this tool can help make series books more discoverable to readers.

Even with good discoverability and cool tools, are we at a point where an ebook can stand alone? The answer depends on your audience. If you're giving away your ebook for free in order to spread your ideas, then you'll surely want to stick with an ebook exclusive. As Seth Godin says, "If you give away your book and your idea catches on, you can sell the souvenir edition. The printed book. The thing people keep on their shelf or lend out or get from the library. Books are wonderful (I own too many!), but just remember they're not necessarily the best vessel for spreading your idea."

If you're not planning on giving away your book for free or courting romance lovers, sci-fi fanatics or übertechies, make a print-on-demand version of your book available. (See page 303 for the pluses and minuses of this newish technology.)

Old-School Printing

If you're looking for high quality at a good price, *offset printing* is the name of the game. Offset printing looks beautiful and is what most trade publishers use to print their books. It will help make your book look truly professional and up to industry standards. The main problem for self-publishers? While for large print runs of over 500 or 1,000 books, it's less expensive per copy than print-on-demand, it's much more expensive for small print runs. If you don't have a slew of baited-breathed buyers waiting at your doorstep, 500-plus books is a

Getting Help

Whatever the form, and whatever the distribution medium, once you've made the decision to self-publish, you should join the Publishers Marketing Association, the Small Publishers Association of North America and/or a local self-publishing association. These organizations offer all manner of help and guidance. And because they have hundreds of members, they're able to provide discounts on things like shipping, much as AARP provides discounts to seniors. They'll set you up so you can take credit cards, and they'll give you the latest skinny on wholesalers and distributors.

We also suggest you take a look at two important resource guides: 1) *Literary Market Place,* which in the publisher's own words is "the worldwide resource to the book publishing industry" and lists all kinds of crucial industry services that you'll need to know about along the way, and 2) self-publishing guru Dan Poynter's *The Self-Publishing Manual,* which will supply you with all the nitty and gritty you'll ever need.

pretty big risk. But if you're after quality and quantity, offset printing may be for you.

Should you decide to offset print, you have much to learn. There are many people to track down. Bargains to hunt. A mammoth amount of research ahead. But there will also be a lot of rewards to offset (heehee) the printing risks. You'll learn every aspect of publishing, which will be great training for selling future books, either on your own or to an established publisher.

So, of course, the burning question remains: How much will it cost to print your books? According to self-publishing guru Dan Poynter, that's like asking how much a car costs. The format of your book, the kind of paper, the number of colors and the number of copies—all these factors will determine price. And the more copies you print, the cheaper each book will be.

Many offset printers specialize: big or small print runs, one-, two- or four-color printing. Make a list of printers who do the kind of book you want. Ask for page proofs so you can make sure all mistakes are eliminated before your book is printed. Get price quotes that itemize the cost of each element (e.g., paper, binding, cover, illustrations). That way, you and your printer are sure to end up on the same page.

FORMAT AND SIZE

When it comes to format, if you're approaching an offset printer on your own, you're going to have to do the grunt work in educating yourself on the available options. But here's the simple answer: Unless you're aiming to get your book into supermarket racks (an unlikely option, as this distribution channel is generally only open to the big guns), you'll probably want to go with a "perfect-bound trade paperback," a standard-quality paperback book. A "notch-bound" paperback is a step up. Hardcovers may feel more substantial, but we're going to assume you want to get more bang for your buck—as does your audience. If your book is lavishly illustrated and made for coffee-table viewing, or if your audience habitually buys hardcovers, then . . . okay.

Want to keep even more money in your pocket? Go with a standard-size book, the most common being 5.5" by 8.5" for a trade paperback and 6" by 9" for a hardcover.

THE RIGHT PAPER

There are so many paper types out in the world, a person could spend weeks going through the options. Luckily, most printers offer only a few choices. Typically, uncoated book stock is your best choice for a standard, nonillustrated book. It's decent quality for a good price. But if you're doing an illustrated book—especially a four-color one—you'll want to bump up your paper quality. Ask to see heavier papers as well as coated papers.

The color of your paper is also important. Arsen Kashkashian of Boulder Book Store told us, "You used to be able to tell if a book was self-published by its stark-white paper. If you look in any Random House book, you'll never see that. The paper is always off-white." Off-white is easier on the eyes. Arsen said he's now seeing self-published books that look up to industry standards. So make sure your book is up to snuff, paper-wise.

FIRST PRINT RUN

How many books should you print? The industry standard is to print as many as you reasonably think you can sell in the first year. A thousand copies may sound like very little—until you actually try to sell them. Even though the unit cost is cheaper when you print more, again, you do not want to be stuck with boxes and boxes of unsold books. On the other hand, you need to account for books you're going to give away. Family, friends, booksellers, bloggers, reviewers and media will all want—even expect—a free book. Designate around 10% of your print run to giveaways.

Vanity Publishing

In days of yore, vanity publishing and self-publishing were virtually synonymous. Not anymore. In fact, you want to stay as far away from the first kind of "publishing" as humanly possible.

But what exactly is it? Here's our definition: a company that publishes your book (which includes the cost of designing, laying out and printing) but—and here's the major catch—gives you NO royalties on books sold and keeps ALL the rights to your work. In other words, you not only give up the rights to your own work, but you actually pay someone to take them from you. This payment could be in the tens of thousands of dollars. And if you thought that, at the very least, these "publishers" would work hard to sell lots of copies of your book, you'd be sorely mistaken. These "publishers" make the bulk of their money by overcharging you for production costs (and then by overcharging you for publicity and marketing materials). There is no incentive for a vanity publisher to sell your book. And bookstores will most certainly be leery of these sharks in sheep's clothing.

Please understand that just because you pay a company to help you publish your book doesn't mean you're dealing with a vanity publisher. If you pay a company to publish your book, take all rights to your work and give you no royalty, *then* you're dealing with a vanity publisher.

REPRINTING YOUR BOOK

With offset printing, it takes four to eight weeks from the point when the manuscript arrives at the printer for the book to land in your hands. From there,
keep an eye on stock and always know how long it will take to reprint your book.
Then do your best balancing act to figure out when to reprint. This is part art,
part science. Big publishing houses have employees devoted solely to this task.
But if you keep meticulous records of how many books are going out the door
(and how many are bouncing back in from returns), you should develop a sense
of when to place orders for more. The game of guessing supply and demand is
another reason to consider POD or digital printing, where you never have to
worry about having too many and can always get more, lickety-split.

THE SHIPPING NEWS: COSTS AND SUPPLIES

If you're going to sell your book yourself, you have to be ready to ship books all
over the world or hire someone to do your "fulfillment" for you—stamps, envelopes, labels, space, all that mess. It takes time, organizational skills and lots
of heavy lifting. Another reason to join the Publishers Marketing Association
and/or the Small Publishers Association of North America is that you can get
your shipping costs reduced—though you certainly won't get them eliminated.
So it's back to research on the web, in bookstores and libraries, and with other
self-published authors. Your goal is to have your books arrive at their destination right on time, all the time.

If you're doing your own shipping to customers, you can add a shipping
and handling charge to all orders. But we recommend keeping this to your true
costs, as no one likes to pay hefty shipping charges and you don't want to piss
off your customers.

New-School Printing

What's print-on-demand, or POD, and why do many people in the know see it
as the future of the printed book? POD is a form of digital printing that allows
you to print books *one at a time,* fast, for a nonprohibitive cost. Sounds perfect,
right? But it has its limitations. POD doesn't do well by color, embossing, books
in unusual shapes or sizes, or hardcovers, at least at the moment.

To clarify: Though POD is considered a form of digital printing, "digital
printing" is technically a category unto itself. Digital printing gives you more
options than POD and still allows for very small print runs—as in 25 copies—
for cheap. "Now we simply order the number of books we need at a time," says
authorpreneur Roger Gilbertson of going from an "offset" (traditional) printer

to digital printing. "We still have a professionally bound, full-color cover, and the interior is a crisp laser-printed original. Plus we can update the contents quickly so we can keep the book up to date."

If you plan on publishing a small number of books (say, 1,000 copies or less) or need to limit up-front costs, or have nowhere to put boxes and boxes of books, you'll most definitely want to explore POD and/or digital printing. And you'll have many providers to choose from. There are companies that simply print, companies that offer printing plus distribution and companies that offer "author services."

POD/DIGITAL PRINTERS

Want the least expensive route? Go straight to a POD/digital printer and hand them a print-ready file. (That includes a smashing cover.) If you're a do-it-yourselfer who wants to be in charge of your own publishing process, this is a wonderful option, but it will require the potentially tech-heavy step of preparing the book file—a task you may want to outsource.

Digital printing is very different from offset printing, and you have to design around its limitations. Each printing company has its strengths and weaknesses. If possible, send your file to a prospective printer and get a sample copy made ahead of time. If you don't like what you see, find out if your disappointment is due to a limitation of the printing technology, a poor job on the printer's part, a problem with the file or flaws in your design. Ask if your particular issue can, in fact, be worked around. If not, decide: Can you grin and bear it? If the printer will not agree to produce a sample, ask them to send you something similar to what you're after so you can see the quality for yourself, up close and personal.

A common bugaboo is that authors send files that aren't to the printer's specifications. Discuss your particular printer's specs before you send anything. Once they have received the file, be sure that you have done what is expected.

▶ Going with an author services company? Remove their branding from your finished book if you can. In its stead, create your own name for your new publishing company. (See page 293 for more on naming your company.)

"AUTHOR SERVICES" COMPANIES

The easiest way to get a printed book in hand is through an author services company. Author services companies are popping up like mushrooms in a damp forest. These companies will edit and copyedit your manuscript; they'll design your cover and interior; they'll assign your book an ISBN and bar code; they'll help you with marketing and publicity; and they'll distribute your books to places such as Amazon, Barnes & Noble, Kobo and iBooks. (You keep all rights to your work.)

Such a company can greatly simplify the self-publishing process—but at a premium. "You need to determine to what degree you want to be a publisher. Do you need the support of an author services company? If you don't think you need these services, be clear about what you do need and expect out of the company you choose to print your books," says Ashley Gordon, publisher of Mockingbird Publishing and a POD/digital printing expert.

These days the simplest of Internet searches (i.e., Googling the word *publishing*) will harvest a plethora of options. Companies we like include CreateSpace (owned by Amazon), BookBaby and Blurb. Each company offers different packages, but for between $500 and $1,000 you can have many of the basic self-publishing needs covered. For a few hundred dollars more, you can get editorial services and help with marketing. And for anywhere from $2,000 to $15,000 you can get help with every aspect of the publishing puzzle.

The base prices sound good, but some author services companies have downsides that can offset some of the advantages of self-publishing. A lack of options may mean you don't wind up with full control over the look of your book. The company may also keep a chunk of your profits. As a rule (and there are exceptions), author services companies:

1. Provide templates for you to choose from when it comes to your cover and interior. This will significantly limit your chances of having an original- and professional-looking book.

2. Determine the price of your book. They determine what they charge based on page count, not on the value of your information or what your audience might be willing to pay.

3. Determine the discount to retailers.

4. Determine the discount at which you buy books. Typically, you're given anywhere from 0 to 10 books for free but will need to purchase anything above and beyond. And discounts can be low or nonexistent. Some companies give you no discount but offer an 80% flat royalty across all copies sold. Some offer discounts that can start as low as 20% for less than 10 copies and escalate to 80% for more than a thousand copies. Some companies increase their discounts for larger orders, and some don't. Like Mama said, you better shop around.

White-Glove Author Services

I f you're looking for the finest in author services companies and you're willing to pay, there are some excellent options to choose from. The problem is, they also have to choose you. Companies like Wheatmark, Inc., and Greenleaf Book Group are different from the majority of publishing services providers, which will publish anything (for a price) without regard to its editorial content and quality or an understanding of its intended audience. Grael Norton, director of marketing at Wheatmark, says, "We're selective in who we work with and what projects we take on. An ideal Wheatmark client is someone who has serious commercial ambitions for their project, whether it be through book sales alone or the marketing of an existing business via a book."

These companies don't offer publishing packages. They work by custom proposal only, meaning they tailor their services to each individual author and book. And you can quickly lay down beaucoup bucks, as in north of $20,000. These fees sometimes include a first print run, if you choose not to use print-on-demand. These print runs typically fall between 1,000 and 2,000 copies (but they can go higher as well). But you're not just paying for books. You're paying for everything that goes into producing the book as well. If you don't have the time or energy to track down professional editors, copy editors, cover designers and so on, and you do have the budget, these white-glove author services companies can be just the way to go.

5. Provide subpar editorial help. We're not fans of using the editorial services of these companies because you don't know who is editing your book. There are so many top-drawer, seasoned professionals out there for the same price. It's worth the extra time and research to get the right editor for your book.

6. Provide subpar marketing and publicity help. Ditto #5. Look elsewhere for this piece of the puzzle. Each author services company does things a little— or a lot—differently from the rest. For example, maybe you really want a square, gifty format for your book. If so, you'll have to pick one of the few companies, like Blurb, that offers such a format. Make a list of the features and business practices that are most important to you, and then make your choice accordingly. (For a list of the largest and most reliable author services companies, see Appendix II.)

PRINTERS PLUS

Looking to handle the printing of your book yourself but don't want to have to deal with distribution? There are a number of printing and distribution companies for you to choose from, BookMasters Group and Lightning Source among them.

BookMasters Group started as a printer, adding services as clients requested them. They are almost identical to an author services company but won't force you into a cookie-cutter mold. "We give authors the flexibility of deciding what they want," says Bob Kasher, business development manager for integrated solutions at the BookMasters Group. "We offer different packages or just one or two services." The BookMasters Group also has a sales and distribution arm, which authors can take advantage of, along with customer service reps available to talk you through any problems that arise. But their fees can add up quickly, so do your math.

Lightning Source, one of the largest POD printers in the United States, has established a division for self-published authors called Ingram Spark. It allows more flexibility on the printing end and has distribution programs with Barnes & Noble, Amazon, Ingram and Baker & Taylor. But they do not offer editorial, marketing or design services. The standout feature of Ingram Spark is that they allow you to choose whether your books can be returned by retailers. If you want to see your book in brick-and-mortar bookstores, returnability is a *must*. More on this on page 437.

> If you're looking at a company that falls somewhere in between an author services company and a printer, be sure to ask if they handle distribution—that's a major bonus. But remember, just because your book is being made available to outlets doesn't mean it's being actively sold. That's still up to you.

Publicity and Marketing

We wrote the publicity and marketing sections of this book with the assumption that you probably wouldn't get enough help from your publisher even if you had one, so in general those sections still hold true for self-publishers. There will be parts that don't apply, but not many. That said, there are a few things that are particularly relevant to self-publishers.

If you self-publish, and you want to sell more than a handful of copies, then you MUST MUST MUST develop your audience. It all goes back to what we discussed in Chapter 2: researching your community, participating in your community, developing a presence in your community and then asking your community to support you. With very few exceptions, every successful self-published author we

Finding the Voice of Your Media Representative

A ward-winning radio show host Leonard Lopate, when asked about the best way to approach him and his staff, offered this advice: "Writers shouldn't make the call themselves. They should have an intermediary do it." In many instances, like this one, it may be to your advantage to create the illusion that you're not self-published. That's why it's a good idea to find someone who will act as your media representative or screener. Set up a voice mail with an outgoing message that says the name of your company, in the voice of your media representative. This way, when Leonard Lopate's people call "your people," they won't get your two-year-old's super cute message.

have come across has taken these steps. Some, years before their books came out, some once they published. Obviously, the sooner, the better.

Bookselling has always been a word-of-mouth business: You and your friends tell one another about what you're each reading. But it has also always heavily relied on reviews and bestseller lists from major newspapers and magazines—the Achilles' heel of self-publishing. These days, though, as more and more major media outlets fold, word of mouth (or tap of keyboard) is becoming all-powerful. With this democratization, suddenly it's the wisdom of crowds, not a single powerful reviewer, that catches readers' attention.

In light of this, Zetta Elliot, author of *A Wish After Midnight,* forced herself to develop stronger networking skills online and off: "I met some incredible women bloggers online, and they embraced my young adult novel and reviewed it for free. I met literacy coaches and educators here in New York and they welcomed me into their classrooms. Word of mouth is pretty powerful these days, especially with all the advances in social networking." Zetta's visibility online helped her to get discovered by AmazonEncore, and she sold her young adult novel to them exactly one year after she self-published it.

Lisa Genova tried to sell her book, *Still Alice,* to bookstores but didn't have much success. So she focused on online sales. She designed her own website. She went on all the social networking sites that had anything to do with writers, posted profiles and started looking for other people who were interested in Alzheimer's. Lisa also sent *Still Alice* to the National Alzheimer's Association. They really liked it and asked Lisa to blog on their website. Suddenly she started to get invitations to give keynote speeches to regional

National Alzheimer's groups. To supplement her national outreach, Lisa started looking around for local authors who had originally self-published novels, then sold them to big publishers. She found Brunonia Barry, who self-published *The Lace Reader,* which went on to become a *New York Times* bestseller. Brunonia had used a PR firm in Lisa's backyard. Lisa hired the same firm for three months, which resulted in a stellar review in the *Boston Globe.* You know the rest of the story.

Speaking of reviews, don't forget about those Amazon and Goodreads reviews (see pages 384–385 for details). As important as they are for authors with publishers, they're even more important for self-published authors because your chances of getting any traditional reviews are almost nil.

As we've said, the good news is that there now exists a way to reach your audience directly. The bad news is that there's a lot of noise out there and you've got to scream loud enough so someone will hear. If you want to successfully self-publish, and to you that means selling lots of books, be prepared to shoulder the full load of letting the world know—in the flesh, electronically, globally and locally.

▶ A number of newspapers, including *The New York Times,* have a policy of not reviewing self-published books. They will, however, mention self-published books in the body of an article. So don't waste time and money sending books to the book review sections at major papers, but do try to spin a news angle or hook through which your book can be cited or about which a feature article can be written.

Selling Your Book

You've written, edited, designed and produced your book. Now it's time to sell it—the single most difficult part of this whole endeavor. Heavy sigh.

We'll cover this process in detail in Chapter 14, but here we'll focus on what's unique to selling a self-published book. If you're selling an ebook, it will be relatively simple to hit the key bookselling spots. But just because your book's up on a website doesn't mean anyone will actually buy it. If you've got a printed book, you're going to run up against the issue of distribution over and over again—in addition to the problem of getting books to sell once they're sitting on shelves. The bottom line is, as an individual you can reach out to only so many places.

Which is why it's so important to have already staked out an audience that's just waiting for your book to go on sale. If you've done that, stop reading now and start selling! If you haven't, all is not lost. With the right stuff and attitude, you can still climb the sales mountain. By properly capturing your audience's attention via social networking, publicity and marketing, and by identifying where your audience lives and where and how they like to shop, you can gain sales traction. Now let's stroll down the different sales avenues open to you.

Your Pub Date

When you're preparing a writing schedule for yourself, the best deadline may be a date of publication for your book. Don't be arbitrary. The season, the simultaneous release of competitive titles and any pertinent anniversaries or historical dates should all be considered when setting your pub date.

Because you're publisher-less, you don't have to worry about competing with bigger titles on a publisher's list. But you still have to compete with all the other books coming out all over the country. Troll the web to see what books are due out. And this is where your subscription to Publishers Lunch and *Publishers Weekly* will be extremely helpful. *PW* not only reviews a wide range of books one to three months before they come out, but also previews many publishers' upcoming releases by season. Try to position your pub date so that your book won't compete with other, bigger books similar to yours.

If you have it in your budget, attend the Book Expo of America, a.k.a. BEA. This yearly event is the trade show for the publishing industry. There you can collect catalogs from many, many publishers to ascertain what books will be released in the upcoming season/year. Plus it's a huge schmooze fest, and you can bring home a ton of free books.

Pricing Your Book

How much to charge? What the market will bear. Study prices of similar books. Nobody's going to buy an overpriced book. Certain kinds of books can bear high prices, however, like Robert St. John's lushly illustrated, $34.95 four-color cookbook.

If there's demand for your book and little or no supply, readers may be willing to pay more, just like they did with Roger Gilbertson's robot book, which at the beginning was really just a bunch of xeroxed pages bound together.

Comparison titles and competition aside, it's standard for both large and small publishers to charge 8 to 10 times what it costs to produce a book. But

Selling for Free to Build Your Business

One of the reasons marketing guru Seth Godin is a fan of self-publishing is that he gets to set the price. At zero. Seth's book *Permission Marketing* posited the idea that if you want to grab someone's attention, you first need to get permission with some kind of bait. Free bait. On publication, he gave away a third of *Permission Marketing* for nothing and the sales went through the roof.

With *Unleashing the Ideavirus,* Seth took his idea one step beyond. He decided this one would cost $0.00. That's right, he gave the whole thing away over the Internet. The book has been downloaded over two million times.

Yes, it's hard to make money selling books for free. But Seth has this wisdom to share about why you should at least consider the possibility of dangling free bait no matter what your book: "If you're writing a book to make money, you're doing the wrong thing. Every once in a while, someone wins. But every once in a while someone wins the lottery, and that's not a reason to buy a ticket."

With the advent of the ebook, the idea of giving away your book is no longer a nutty proposition. For Seth, the payoff was seeing his speaking career skyrocket because he was successfully getting his ideas out to lots and lots of people. "If your book costs money, it introduces friction to your idea. It makes your idea spread much more slowly than an online meme because someone has to buy it in order for it to spread."

If you're like Seth and your ideas are valuable, you may want to give them away and harvest the fruits of your labor through consulting, speaking, starting a club with a monthly fee or creating something that your audience needs.

this formula applies only if you're using offset printing for a large number of books.

If you plan to sell your books to independent booksellers or other brick-and-mortar retailers, you're going to have to sell them at 40% to 50% off your cover price, plus pay for the shipping. Make sure you include these discounts in your calculations. A very common mistake is to estimate earnings based on cover price, but these calculations only work if you're offering your book directly to customers.

What about your ebook? Frankly, ebook pricing is all over the map, especially when it comes to the self-published market. J.A. Kornrath, author of numerous thrillers and mysteries including the Jacqueline "Jack" Daniels series, felt that $2.00 seemed like a fair price for a download: "After all, an ebook is intangible and can be duplicated and delivered for free, so it isn't worth the same as a print book." Joe did some experimentation (always a good thing) and played around with \$0.99 and \$2.99. He saw no discernible difference in sales, so now all of his ebooks are \$2.99. This means he earns \$2.04 per download—almost as much as he gets on the sale of a \$24 hardcover through his publisher!

Making Amazon Work for You

E va Lesko Natiello and Cari Noga self-published two very different novels. But Eva's domestic thriller, *The Memory Box,* and Cari's literary novel, *Sparrow Migrations,* have something in common: They were both published by professionals with capital "P"s. They also both used the Amazon's Kindle Direct Publishing (KDP) program to help draw attention to their books.

Eva and Cari did their homework. They're both publicity and marketing experts, and they put their experience to work. How could they make the most of this platform? How could they show the agents and publishers who had been so close to taking them on that these books did indeed have large audiences? They quickly learned that free giveaways and playing with pricing were key ingredients to KDP success.

By coordinating all your efforts around a KDP giveaway, it is possible to create a perfect storm of attention. But they also learned that the work doesn't start when the giveaway begins. Follow these steps and you'll make the most of KDP giveaways:

1. Before you can sign up for the KDP Select free ebook promotion, you need to amass at least 25 reviews with a four-star or higher rating on Amazon.

2. Once you've got your reviews in place, you'll want to contact sites that will help you promote your ebook giveaway. Some to consider: Digital Book Today, Books on the Knob, Free Ebooks Daily and Pixel of Ink. Email these sites two weeks in advance.

3. Research book bloggers and reviewers in your genre and request an author interview or review. Pitch these people way in advance so that you may be able to have the review posted during your free promotion. Send them a solid pitch with a book description, your Amazon star rating and number of reviews, and a link to the Amazon page. If you already have a Q&A in your media kit, send it! Book bloggers love it when you make their job easy. Do the work for them and you increase your chances of getting an interview.

4. Try to have the interview coincide with the promotion. "I used my promotion as leverage to get the interview," says Eva. "I wrote, 'I'd love for your readers to benefit from my free Kindle

Distributors and Wholesalers

If you don't want to sell and ship books on your own, there are *distributors* who will do this for you for a fee. The equivalent of a publisher's sales force, these companies will go out and try to sell your book to stores and specialty markets.

download promotion, so perhaps you'd consider publishing an author interview during my Amazon promotion?' And it worked!"

5. Coordinate your giveaway with a free promotion on Goodreads (see pages 384–385), and, if you also have a print version of your title, maybe an autographed book giveaway.

6. On the first day of your promotion, email Addicted to Ebooks, which is great at getting the word out. They'll only post books that are currently free, so don't email them before your promotion begins.

7. The day your KDP promotion begins, also be sure to announce it on social media with a link to the page. Remove any additional steps people have to take and increase your chances of success. Eva adds, "I believe I received a ton of readers through Twitter. There are hashtags that you can use throughout the day, every day, that will attract people looking for free Kindle books. Some of them are: #freeKindlebooks, #freeKindle, #freebook, #KindlePromo. Don't forget to hashtag your genre so you attract your truest readers."

In addition to free promotions, you may also want to try what's called a Kindle Countdown Deal. This is where you lower the Kindle edition price incrementally for a limited time. Cari did this and watched her numbers spike. "I dropped my price to 99 cents for two days and advertised it on BookBub. Then I raised it to $1.99 for two days, then $2.99 for a day, then back to my regular $3.99. I sold about 1,400 over the period, most on the BookBub day. The really nice thing is Amazon lets you keep your normal royalty rate during the countdown period."

Using these techniques, both Eva and Cari sold tens of thousands of copies of their ebooks (although KDP is an ebook-only program, both Eva and Cari had print-on-demand books available as well, which also sold, but at a much slower clip). Due to their stellar sales, both received offers from agents and publishers. Touché! As of the writing of this edition, they are deciding whether to continue to go it alone and reap the majority of the profits or to sign on with an agent/publisher to relieve them of the production work. We'll update you in the next edition!

They buy your book at between 60% and 65% of the cover price, then resell it to booksellers for around 50% off.

Andy Kessler was shipping books out of his garage. The more success he had, the more tiresome the shipping became. So he found a distributor in Maryland who would give him 40% of the cover price on all books sold (he was currently getting 45% with Amazon) and get his books to Amazon, Ingram and Baker & Taylor. They said they would be his sales force, but in reality they didn't do anything to help sell his book; they just handled the shipping and payments. But Andy says, "I would do it all again with them because beyond Amazon no one was going to deal with me directly."

▶ Distributors, wholesalers and most bookstores work on a commission basis, i.e., they can return your books anytime they want. So be sure to remember that a sale isn't really a sale until a reader buys it and doesn't return it! Another hitch: you may wait up to four months to get paid by a wholesaler. Do not count on immediate cash in pocket!

Wholesalers are similar creatures, only they won't actively try to sell your book. They simply stock it so that booksellers around the country have easy access. (Many booksellers and libraries don't want to have to place individual orders to different publishers; it's much easier for them to do one-stop shopping.) Zetta Elliot was also not up for dealing with fulfillment, so she signed on with Baker & Taylor, the leading wholesaler to libraries. "I had to pay quite a large sum to establish a relationship with Baker & Taylor so that public libraries could order my book. But I did this because packing and shipping books just isn't my cup of tea."

Ingram, the largest wholesaler, is now accepting books from self-published authors, which makes life much easier if you want to get your book into independent bookstores.

Distributors are understandably harder to land than wholesalers since they put more effort into selling. As always, you need to have the proper materials and pitch to make these companies believe they will make some money and are not just acting as a large storage unit.

For a comprehensive list of book distributors and wholesalers, check out *Literary Market Place* at the library or online.

Your e-Commerce Site

Some self-published authors have created such a strong Internet presence that they don't need to sell in stores or other online outlets—their websites are their sales hubs. Cutting out the middlemen means more money pours into their pockets, and they save an enormous amount of time trying to get people to sell their books for them. Of course, they also spend a moderate to enormous amount of time packing and shipping their books and running their self-publishing enterprises.

If you do sell your book directly off your website, you need to make sure people can click to buy with ease. As you've probably experienced yourself, if you go to a site, try to buy something and come up against any sort of complication or barrier, you will in all likelihood "abandon your cart"—the most feared phrase in the land of e-commerce. It means that someone actually wanted to buy something, took the effort to put an item in their cart and started to go through the process of buying, only to leave your store without going to the cash register. This is why you want to do EVERYTHING you can to make sure the process of buying your book is hassle-free. Here are the three things that can cause the most sales friction:

- *Navigation.* Is it easy to find where to go on your site to buy your book? No one wants to go on a treasure hunt. Make buying your book an option that's visible no matter what part of your site a customer is on—preferably via a tab on the top or on the left side of the screen. If customers can't find where to buy, they'll ABANDON THEIR CARTS!!!

- *The sales path.* Once you click on "buy," do you have to fill in lots of information that doesn't seem necessary? Like your age? Your phone number? Who you went out with in high school? Lots of people use this process to find out more information about their customers, which is a good idea in theory. But if filling in this information isn't optional, people will ABANDON THEIR CARTS!!!

- *Payment.* Make sure you take credit cards. Better yet, whatever credit card someone may want to use. Set yourself up, through your bank of choice, with a "merchant services" account (see your bank's website for more information)

▶ Like any craftsman, you have to have proper tools. In the book biz, one of the essential sales pieces is the tip sheet, which lets potential sales outlets know why your book is worth selling. A typical tip sheet includes your book's title, a short pitch, any relevant models or comparison titles, blurbs/press, price and format. Make your own tip sheet and keep it with you always. You never know when a good sales opportunity will rear its beautiful head. (See our website for a template.)

or use PayPal. Pay attention to little details here, like having a box users can click if their shipping address is the same as their billing. This way, your customers don't have to enter their information twice—another reason to ABANDON CART!!!

Once your site is set to sell, get some friends to go through the process. Have them note anything that was annoying, difficult or even just mildly confusing. Eliminate these hurdles before your site goes live.

Internet Booksellers

One of the easiest and fastest ways to get your book up and running is to get accepted into Amazon and Barnes & Noble's Internet sales programs, both of which have straightforward application processes. Amazon's Advantage program is slightly buried in the "Make Money with Amazon" section of their website. B&N's can be found under "Publisher and Author Guidelines" in the Services section of their site.

Amazon's program requires a $29.95 annual fee. They buy your book at 55% off the cover price (which they have the final say on). Typically, they will order two to five books at first. B&N's program has no annual fee and lets you determine the discount and the cover price (which has to be over $1). But the better the deal you give, the better your chances of having your book carried. B&N will typically order one to two books as a first order; they also warn that it could take two to four months to find out if you're accepted. There's no guarantee that you'll be accepted into either program. But if your book isn't pornographic or blatantly offensive and has the requisite requirements (ISBN, EAN bar code, etc.), then you should be able to get it onto at least one of these sites. And if you can get both, all the better.

If you do set up an account with Amazon and you're not selling books off your own website, be sure to become an Amazon Associate. You'll be given a link for your website leading directly to your book's page on Amazon. Every time someone clicks through from your site and buys a book, you get a small percentage of the sale.

Bookstores

As strange as it may seem, you'll probably have the most difficult time selling your book into bookstores. Independents are problematic because they're, well, independent, which means you have to go after them one at a time. Chain stores are problematic because they've got one buyer per subject for all the books out there in the universe. It's harder to get in front of this buyer than it is getting an audience with the president, and you certainly won't be the only one trying. However, there are ways to sell to both kinds of bookstores.

Because of the traditional prejudice against self-published books, the importance of finding a model that generates genuine excitement is accentuated. Demonstrating how your book will attract the audience of a book that's already been successful (but is not directly competitive to yours) will help you convince stores to carry your book.

INDEPENDENTS

Independent bookstores are much easier to approach than chains, and they're more likely to stock your book while typically asking for a lower discount—more like 40% than 50%. The problem is, as we said, unless you have a distributor, you'll have to call each and every bookstore individually. This could take over a thousand calls, since there are over 2,000 members of the American Booksellers Association alone.

The best tactic is to first approach all your local independent booksellers. Most independents want to help local authors and are willing to take at least one copy of your book if it fits in with what they sell. Arsen Kashkashian, head buyer at Boulder Book Store, explains why self-published authors are an asset to independent bookstores: "Selling local authors' self-published books is great PR for us because they bring in so many people from the community. These writers feel that they have part ownership of the bookstore, which is good for us as well." In fact, Boulder Book Store has a special marketing program for self-published authors that other independent bookstores around the country are now adopting as well. Even bookstores that are not inclined to take self-published books can be persuaded if you simultaneously play your local card and your why-my-book-is-unique-and-salable card. "We had some success with a self-published cookbook about gluten-free baking called *Cookies for Breakfast,* written by a teenager," says Mark LaFramboise, a buyer at Politics and Prose, D.C.'s famous independent bookstore. "We took it because a) the author is local, and b) it's an interesting and useful subject."

Know your independent stores before you approach them. Since independents are not beholden to a corporate office, they each have their own individual flavor and color. You'll want to show them why your book fits their shelves. Arielle Gronner, formerly of Powell's Books in Portland, Oregon, suggests having the answers to the following questions ready before approaching a bookstore:

"How will people know about the book?" "Who will be looking for it?" "Is there a marketing plan?" "Are you working with a distributor or wholesaler?"

To learn more about independent booksellers, go to the website of the American Booksellers Association (ABA), which lists its members by state. Also check out the list of participating members on the website for Indiebound, a marketing organization created by the ABA to help independents.

Barnes & Noble

The great thing about B & N is that if they order your book, it'll have national distribution or, at minimum, distribution throughout an entire region. This means orders in the three and four figures—a bonanza when you're used to dealing in ones and twos. The bad news is that it's very, very difficult to get a self-published book into B & N stores. In most cases, booksellers in individual stores cannot make the decision to take your book, no matter how much they would like to. All they can do is recommend it to the head buyer.

That said, Barnes & Noble is not completely impenetrable. You will have to go through corporate headquarters, where you can contact the person in charge of:

- Small press relations, or
- Your specific category, or
- Your region

Marcella Smith, former director of small-press and vendor relations at Barnes & Noble, had this to say: "Yes, B&N orders self-published books. The author usually calls and then sends materials—the finished book and the marketing plan for review by the buyer. B & N orders self-published books under the same conditions as they order all books. Does the title have sales potential in a general trade bookstore? Is it competitive in the marketplace? Is there a marketing plan? If it's a nonfiction book, does the author have credentials in the subject? If it's fiction, has the author been published in magazines or journals?"

Libraries

If libraries are interested in your book, congratulations, you've got a great opportunity to sell a mess o' books. There are just over 120,000 libraries in the United States. Find out which ones your book belongs in. Check out the distributor Baker & Taylor, which makes the bulk of their sales to libraries. Also, go to the "Facts About Libraries" section of the American Library Association's website to find out how to locate libraries around the country.

One of the many nice things about libraries is that they generally expect lower discounts than bookstores do. These discounts typically range from 10% to 45%.

Other Sales Channels

Don't limit yourself to bookstores and libraries. You can sell thousands of copies of your book without it ever seeing the inside of a bookstore. The fact is, there are as many places to sell a book as there are books.

If you can line up a bulk sale to one specialty retailer or organization, you have a best-case self-publishing scenario. Your profits will be much bigger than what you'd receive with a publishing house. And the typical work associated with self-publishing is minimized. You ship books to far fewer locations. You don't spend your life going store to store. You can use this sale to open many doors that would typically be hard to access. These kinds of special sales are typically nonreturnable. The only downside is that the discount demanded is usually higher than at your average store. Even so, if you line up a big special sale and get a purchase order before you print your books, you're in a great position to make some serious coin. One key sale to the right place can mean a sold-out printing.

To nail a sale of this kind, you have to approach the right person at the right place at the right time. For a mass retailer, start with corporate headquarters. If, however, you hit brick wall after brick wall, develop a relationship with regional or individual managers and see if you can get any love out of them.

Inventiveness pays off. Remember Seth Godin's milk carton book? It bypassed bookstores altogether. Instead, Seth hooked up with the hip business magazine *Fast Company* and sold the books directly through them as a special one-time promotion. In five days, they sold 5,000 copies. This got the buzz jumping, and buyers flocked to Seth's website, where he offered an unusual deal: 12 copies for 60 bucks. You had to buy a dozen or none at all. This multicopy deal encouraged buyers to circulate copies to colleagues and friends. Which, of course, spread buzz like butter. Within 14 days, Seth had sold his entire 10K first printing.

Robert St. John printed 24,000 copies of his second book, *Southern Seasons,* and had 10,000 sold before the books touched ground. Four thousand of these were special editions that Robert presold to three universities and to the Mississippi chamber of commerce. "The deal I made was that these organizations each had to commit to buying 1,000 books at the full cover price of $34.95

each, and they had to pay up front," Robert explains. "But on the back cover, in place of the author photo, we placed an iconic photograph of the particular university campus. We also included a special signed print inside." These extras cost Robert a lot, but the effort gave him $140,000 up front and paid for the printing of the book. The organizations were able to give these special books to their donors. And while they paid the full price of $34.95, the signed prints upped the value of the package to over $90. Clearly a win-win situation.

Live, Learn and Prosper

When it comes to self-publishing, no one gets everything right. But hey, Random House doesn't get everything right, so why should you? As Robert St. John says, "There are so many unknowns the first time you self-publish. It gets infinitely easier with each new book." While your learning curve will certainly be steep, the process of self-publishing is one that will forever inform your life as an author—whether you choose to publish on your own again, move on to a publisher or agent, or simply continue to sell the book you originally self-published.

We have truly entered the golden age of self-publishing. With the seemingly limitless ways to connect with your audience, the explosion of POD printers and ebooks, and the resulting destigmatization, it behooves all self-published authors to look long and hard at taking the bull by the horns and publishing the one writer who most deserves success: YOU!

PART III

Getting the Word Out

CHAPTER 12

Prepub Publicity and Marketing

"To be prepared is half the victory."

—Miguel de Cervantes

LISTEN CLOSELY AND YOU'LL HEAR a faint ticking. That's the sound of time marching toward destiny, toward the point where your manuscript is finally (cue drum roll) . . . a book. Time for you to morph from author into publicity and marketing machine. Who, me? you ask. Won't my publisher handle all that stuff? Or, won't everyone just go out and buy my book because it's so great? If we haven't made our point yet: Dream on.

Most authors feel it's much more difficult to sell a book than it is to write one. But unless you're very lucky, it will be on you to deliver your book into the heads, hearts and hands of readers all over the world. We want to make the process of getting your book out there as stress-free as possible. That's why, if you're working with a publisher, we're offering this piece of advice: When it comes to publicizing and marketing your book, pretend your publisher is your printer—and that's all. This way, you won't be disappointed in the event that your publisher disappoints you. (If you're self-publishing, publicity and marketing will be all on you anyway.)

It's not your publisher's fault, per se. This is just the nature of the beast. The fact is, in today's world, a traditional approach to getting the word out— book reviews, bookstore events, a publisher-sponsored tour—just doesn't cut it. Publishers know this, but they don't necessarily have the money or manpower or time to fly your book's banner into outer space.

Luckily, all the work you did in figuring out your audience, crafting your pitch, becoming part of a larger community and building up your social networks is going to serve you over and over as you publicize and market your book. If you've been lax networking-wise, don't despair. You can pick up the ball right now and get in the game. Just as you made writing a part of your daily life, you must now make the promoting and marketing of your book an ongoing activity.

Putting Yourself in Expert Hands

If you're working with a traditional publisher and you're lucky, you'll have a publicist. If you're really lucky, you'll have a great publicist. Your publicist will be assigned by your publisher. Sometimes the person is a good fit and sometimes not. While you don't have to be her BFF, you will want to do everything you can to get and stay on her A-list. To achieve this platinum status, you'll want to make her job simple by being easy to locate, easy to work with and quick to come up with anything she needs on an ASAP basis.

Your publicist is there to start, stoke and keep the media fire going. Hopefully, this will apply to print, TV, radio and online media. But she'll also be handling other activities, like speaking to booksellers to set up store events. Elaine Petrocelli, owner of Book Passage in Corte Madera, California, says, "There are certain publicists we trust implicitly." If your publicist communicates enthusiasm about what you've written, this enthusiasm can ripple out into the universe. Roberta Rubin, owner of The Bookstall in Winnetka, Illinois, adds: "One of the best ways to get me excited about your book is to have a publicist be excited about it."

A publicist's reputation is dependent upon whether what she promises in an author is what the media and bookstores actually get. So if your publicist tells the *Today* show that you're a smart, attractive, articulate, responsible person and you turn out to be a curmudgeonly, slovenly, inarticulate bum who arrives an hour late, the *Today* show won't return her calls the next time she has a "great" author she wants to book. That's why you and your publicist should get together, or at least have an in-depth phone conversation, as soon as possible. "It's much easier," says Pru Rowlandson, publicity director of Granta and Portobello Books, "to 'sell' someone once you've met them and you can confidently say that they're great personalities and good talkers. If they aren't, that's useful, too, because there's no point setting someone up for something that they are completely unsuited for." In your meeting, be clear about what you're comfortable with and what you're not. Are you afraid to fly? Are you nervous about doing "shock jock" radio? Shows whose political agenda you don't agree with? "I never mind authors who have preferences and dislikes," Pru continues. "It's easy to work with people if they tell you in advance what they will do and what they won't."

Sadly, publicists are almost always saddled with many books to promote simultaneously. And while you don't want to be a thorn in your publicist's side, you do want to maintain a steady happy presence in her mind. One excellent way to do this is to give regular status updates. This can be done primarily via email and the occasional phone call if something particularly great or particularly horrible occurs.

What if you do all these things but your publicist hasn't gotten that *New York Times* book review? Or, for that matter, the *Tinytown Tinkerbell* review? First of all, no publicist can control whether or not you get reviews. Secondly, your book may not be served through the traditional routes of reviews, a book tour or getting on *Good Morning America*. No matter how great your book on incontinence is, it probably won't get reviewed in *People*. But if it gets a simple mention in AARP's online bulletin, you may have struck gold. The point is: You want your book to be featured in the outlets that reach your readers, no matter where that may be. You need to be sure that your expectations make sense—no publicist can fit a square peg in a round hole.

If you find that your publicist is pitching to media outlets that don't address your audience (or address only one small part of your audience) or is setting up events at places where your audience doesn't go, speak up gently and make a compelling case for who and where your audience actually is. Rainelle Burton, author of *The Root Worker,* a coming-of-age novel about an African American girl, had this experience: "On my book tour, my publisher targeted only an African American audience. I thought the book had more mainstream appeal, as it does not fit the popular notion of an 'African American book.' With the exception of one book club that showed up at a bookstore, only four or five African Americans showed up in five cities despite publicity in black community newspapers." Beth Lisick, author of *Everybody into the Pool,* had a similar experience. Beth had booked her own tours in the past and was relieved to finally have a big publisher do this job. The problem was, Beth's publisher didn't know her audience as well as she did. "At one stop on my tour, two people showed up," Beth says. "I knew this would happen the moment I heard where I was booked: in the suburbs, rather than in the heart of downtown Seattle, where my audience congregated and lived. But I didn't want to be a pest, so I didn't say anything."

If your publicist is not making anything happen, period, then it's time to review the situation. You may find yourself with a wet-behind-the-ears publicist who doesn't yet have the roster of connections that make senior publicists so effective. This is not to say young equals bad. A young publicist can be a highly motivated go-getter who wants to prove herself. But lack of action, from a novice or seasoned veteran, is a red flag. Discuss your thoughts with your editor and agent to see what must be done.

After that, if you still feel that you're not getting the love you deserve, it might be time to hire an outside publicist.

Hiring an Outside Publicist

Even if your assigned publicist is as good as can be, she might have many, many books to promote and not enough hours in the day to do justice to them. Sometimes the right independent publicist is the midwife you need to give your book a proper birthing.

When our book *Satchel Sez* came out, it became clear that our in-house publicist had neither the time nor the sports contacts to handle our promotion. So we went out and found Duffy Jennings, a former publicist for the San Francisco Giants. This guy knew everyone who was anyone when it came to baseball. He turned out to be worth every penny we paid. He got us everything from an appearance on Armed Forces Radio (which goes out to millions of people in dozens of countries) to a boxed mention in *Sports Illustrated,* the holy grail of sports publications. We ended up getting over $100,000 worth of publicity (it costs this for an ad in *Sports Illustrated* alone) for $2,500. Interestingly, this also freed up our in-house publicist to concentrate on the areas he knew best, such as pitching us to local radio shows all over the country.

It's very hard to be a good publicist. A good publicist has extraordinary media contacts, the smarts to know the perfect show, magazine or newspaper in which to place a piece about you and your book, the timing to know when to make the move and the ability to spin your story differently for each target. So good publicists almost always charge a lot of money, anywhere from $1,000 to $25,000 (or more if they stay on past your initial launch), depending on the scope of the job and their level of experience.

Every publicist works differently. Some get paid by the hour, some by the job, some by the market. Get a lot of quotes, do some haggling (if you're haggle-friendly) and strike the best deal you can.

A lot of authors look to hire publicists who specialize in books. But book publicists aren't always the best choice for nonfiction titles. Publicists who specialize in particular areas may better understand your book, your audience and the right people to slip it to. Book publicists know the media people who write about books. But they don't necessarily know the people who write about fashion or cars or food, or whatever your book might be about.

Publicists who specialize in a local territory have a similar edge. If you're going with a home-grown strategy, consider hiring a well-respected local publicity firm that will concentrate on your hometown.

Keri Levitt of Keri Levitt Communications, a top fashion publicity firm in New York City, has this advice for those hiring a publicist:

- Make sure the person has a background and expertise in your subject. This way, you know she has the necessary connections to publicize your book. Another benefit of hiring someone who works specifically within your field is that her connections may prove helpful even beyond publicity by contributing to building your business or creating marketing or special sales opportunities for your book.

- Check out the potential publicist's website and online presence. Verify that her work is in line with what you have in mind. And be sure to check clippings; if they're all from a year ago or more, look elsewhere. A publicist's press kit should be as up-to-the-minute as her contact list.

- Before you make the decision to work with a publicist, ask for names of media contacts that are appropriate for your book. Be wary if these aren't quickly forthcoming.

- Ask for a proposal outlining your publicist's objectives so that you can be sure you're on the same page. This should include a detailed list of initiatives spanning three to six months.

- Be sure to get an activity report at the end of each month, detailing all communications up to that time. Even if you part ways after a couple of months, you'll know when and to whom your book was pitched.

We also recommend asking for referrals. And whatever you do, don't pay the entire fee up front. Break up the payments so you can be sure the person you hired does the job she said she would do.

Lastly, publicists' jobs are very different today from what they were when we wrote the first edition of this book. These days, the lion's share of your publicity may very well be online. That's why you want to be sure the publicist you hire isn't stuck in the mud of print, TV and radio only. As Sarah Burningham, CEO

Inside and Outside Publicists Playing Nicely

If you have an in-house publicist, you'll need to be somewhat political about hiring an outside publicist. Ask your in-house publicist if she can recommend someone she has worked with and likes. These two people need to get along; if they don't, you could end up spending more time putting out fires than getting the PR you desire.

Once you've hired an outside publicist, make sure everyone is clear about who's doing what. You want to make sure the communication channels are open. Again, you can ask your agent to help you with this bit of intricate diplomacy. In the best of all possible worlds, the publicist you hire and your in-house publicist will have complementary contacts and skills so that your work is landing in the hands of twice as many of the right people. While most publicists are sweet, lovely humans, some of them are prickly and sensitive about guarding their territory and their contacts. Make sure everyone feels open and generous. If you can, take both publicists out to lunch and discuss how you can all best work together. At the very least, arrange a get-acquainted conference call.

of Little Bird Publicity and former publicist at some of the biggest and best publishers, says, "My job has changed pretty drastically over the past ten years. I used to focus on tours and local media. But now I spend so much time online. I'm able to do a lot more without me or my authors having to travel. I can also make a budget stretch much farther."

Consulting an Online Marketing Expert

The advent of online marketing has spawned a whole new area of outside help: search engine marketers and optimizers, keyword experts, and all manner of online marketing experts. Should you hire one to consult on the publication of your book? Maybe, maybe not. Search engine marketing is a shadowy underworld full of nefarious and unscrupulous operators who are looking for suckers to skin. And it's packed with incompetents who promise the moon and deliver a turd. Roxanne Lott, managing director of the online marketing firm Imerex, feels that most people end up spending money on Google ad words and search engine optimization, or lots of time trying to figure out how to do these things themselves, but don't wind up getting it right. "Don't waste your time or money trying to learn the ever-changing worlds of SEM and SEO," Roxanne advises. "It's creating and managing your online reputation that's critical and time well spent." While you can certainly get help with this, unless you're made of money, you're simply not going to be able to outsource all of your online efforts.

We'll assume that you're not drowning in Benjamins. So here's a mini-lesson in online marketing to get you started on your merry way. As we learned in Chapter 2, *search engine optimization* (SEO) is the science of increasing your visibility on search engines. Optimization can be accomplished in various ways; one is through inserting keywords into the metatags (a.k.a. code) of your site or blog posts, as well as through tweaking the content of your site or blog. The question is, what keywords? *Keyword research,* a subset of SEO, should provide the answer. The right keywords can send tons of traffic to your site. And the wrong keywords, or lack of keywords, can leave your site the road less traveled.

Search engine marketing (SEM) helps drive traffic to websites through paid online ads. It includes pay-per-click ads, banner ads and a host of other kinds of paid placements. With *search engine/pay-per-click ads,* you only pay each time someone actually clicks on your ad. If no one clicks, you don't have to pay. (You may know these as the small ads on the right-hand side of search engines or sites like Facebook.) If someone takes the time to click on your ad, it means you successfully grabbed her attention and that she's interested. (As opposed to being forced to watch an ad because it's interrupting her TV program.) Bonus: These ads come with statistics, so you'll be able to test different ads or different audiences, and then adjust accordingly.

Okay, now that that's out of the way, here's the lowdown: You don't need to be a computer technician (or a search engine optimizer) to develop and maintain an online presence. Again, keeping up an active blog or website and involving yourself in online communities whose passions mirror yours will go a long way to establishing a strong online presence.

The truth is, if you follow the advice we laid out in Chapter 2, you will organically optimize your site. You will organically employ keywords that will drive traffic. And, rather than paying for banner ads, you will end up having a good shot at getting others to write about you—which is great news, as the most effective kind of advertising is often the free kind.

If you have not gotten around to or succeeded in establishing an online presence and your book is coming out within the year, a specialist in the field of SEM/SEO may be helpful. The best in the field can drive significant traffic to your website/blog or beef up your online presence much more quickly than you can do it alone. And you don't have to spend thousands on their services (though you certainly can). A well-researched list of keywords can be had for a few hundred dollars—from there you can start the work of building your online empire or have someone do it for you. "Good keywords combined with strong

▶ If you decide to get help with SEM and/or SEO, please be sure to hire a firm that uses ethical search engine practices. The whole reason search engines rank search results is so that the most relevant information comes up first—this is Google's whole reason to exist. They want users to say, "Yes, that's exactly what I was looking for!" But beware of those who use dirty tricks to get highly ranked. Google always catches on to these tricks and then punishes these sites. So while you might come up as #1 within a specific search for a short amount of time, instead of dropping back to where you were, once the search engines figure out your trickery they'll drop you to 400 (or ban you altogether).

writing and social media can make the difference between a well-known web presence that catches on (and sells books) and a complete nonperformer," says Get Creative, Inc. owner and SEO expert Lori Culwell.

SEM/SEO experts can also help sort out your online marketing priorities. Let's say yours is a gardening book. Someone who performs a search using the word "gardening" is very unlikely to find your book—there are so many existing sites on the subject, sites that are most certainly more heavily trafficked than yours. But let's say your book is about rooftop gardens, or even just includes a chapter on rooftop gardens, and you know that there are lots of people searching for this subtopic. Employ good SEO practices and you just might end up in the top 20 results of searches for rooftop gardens. "Using the right keywords in your site will put you right in the middle of the conversation about your topic," says Lori. "You need to know how people are talking about your subject so that you can respond accordingly."

If you've hired SEM help and the person you've hired advocates paying for search engine ads (also called pay-per-click ads), or you're doing your own SEM and are sure such an ad is your silver bullet, read this before you leap: Let's say you're writing a book on a new, effective way to manage employees. You decide to buy pay-per-click ads on Google. Problem number one: People generally don't search Google for books to buy to help them with a business issue. They search for free information on that issue. Then, if they decide they need more, they go to Amazon or the Barnes & Noble site and search for business books. Only a small percentage of people look for books on search engines. Problem number two? These ads are very expensive. (The more common the search, the more expensive the ad.) You could be shelling out up to $5 a click. At that rate, even if 50% of the

When Hiring e-Marketing Help Makes Sense

SEO and SEM business aside, managing your online presence and reputation is simply time-consuming. We asked Fauzia Burke of FSB Associates, a pioneering online marketing firm dedicated to helping authors, why hiring someone to help in this area could be dollars well spent. Here are the top five reasons she came back with:

1. **Access and attention.** Although gaining access to online journalists and bloggers is easier than hounding the gatekeepers of traditional media, getting their attention has never been more difficult. Online trendsetters are inundated with information and rely more than ever on their relationships with good publicists.

2. **A sustained effort.** The timing for a marketing campaign is very different now. It's not about shock and awe blitz; it's a sustained effort to continue the dialogue and build communities.

3. **Connections.** Reaching niche markets through web and blog outreach is something anyone can do—but it takes a lot of time. We have an extensive database of contacts that we've built over many years.

4. **Amplified noise.** Social media has made it possible for authors to engage with their readers directly, which is great and highly encouraged. However, a good publicist can elevate the noise about your book through their social media campaigns and encourage reviews and content to go viral.

5. **Your rep.** Reputation monitoring has never been more important. A publicist can monitor the client's online reputation and jump on any hot-button issues.

---

people who click through buy your book, you still won't be making any money. And that's a highly unlikely prediction. In reality, it would be more like 1%. Do the math. It just doesn't work.

There are a few types of books that are searched for directly online—diet books, for example. But again, the competition is so stiff in this category it would be almost impossible to see any return on your investment.

Search engine ads are certainly not the only kinds of online advertisements, though. As you surf the web, you've surely noticed ads on your favorite blogs or websites. Display or banner ads on targeted websites where your audience congregates are a much better way to reach your target audience and generate awareness about your book, and they tend to be less cost-prohibitive. Even so, Roxanne Lott warns, "I wouldn't expect to see direct conversions from such an effort, but I would expect to see a lift in search volume for the subject and hopefully traffic to the site (and/or to the book's page on Amazon)." It's not all going to result in immediate sales. Part of this is building an awareness of you and your book, establishing a presence, becoming a known quantity electronically.

By now, you should know which websites your audience visits on a regular basis. And for this reason, if you decide to test out an ad or two, you wouldn't need to hire someone to figure this out for you. Facebook and Goodreads are just some of the general sites you can advertise on. And then, of course, there are sites that specifically deal with your subject matter, whatever that may be.

Working with a Presentation Doctor/Media Coach

Is public-speaking anxiety impinging on your excitement about your book's release? Tamim Ansary, author of *West of Kabul, East of New York,* has these heartening words for introverts: "One consequence of publishing *West of Kabul* was that it revealed something I never knew about myself: that I can really do this get-up-on-stage-and-talk thing. I was, for most of my life, so painfully shy I couldn't even speak at funerals or in front of a few friends, so this was a life-changing experience for me."

If you're not convinced that this kind of major change in personality is going to happen to you, a good presentation doctor or media coach can help you feel comfortable with yourself and your message in front of an audience, a TV camera, a radio mike or a web cam. Presentation doctors and media coaches may come from the world of publishing, from the world of public relations or from the world of acting/directing. A good one will evaluate your presentation skills, determine your strengths and weaknesses and help you with everything from your appearance to eliminating unconscious nervous tics, to relaxation techniques, to making eye contact; from something as simple as what to do with your hands to something as complex as comic spin. A good coach will also help you find your message, hone your pitch and learn to deliver it in graceful, potent 15-second sound bites.

David has been a media coach for years. One of his most effective techniques is to have you videotape yourself making a presentation or doing a mock interview, then have you play the tape back for yourself. You will see all of your Achilles' heels, step-by-step, frame by excruciating frame. It will not be pleasant. But then, you will be able to work on eliminating those detractions and accentuating your strengths (yes, you've got to look for your strengths, too). It's shocking how often authors unconsciously tap their fingers, twiddle their thumbs, fiddle with their collars and say "uh" every seventh word. And they don't even know they're doing it!

If exposing yourself to a professional is so scary that you never, ever want to hire a media coach, consider this: A little humiliation in front of a nonjudgmental professional is much easier to take than watching yourself stutter, phumph and fidget in front of millions of Americans. Also, if you do it a few months prior to publication, you'll have the time to practice.

Selling Yourself: An Overview

In this new democratized e-universe, the big advertising and PR firms that dominated the world of marketing and publicity are becoming less and less powerful by the day. Average citizens are the new marketers and publicizers, spreading the word on products they like with frightening speed and power. In the first edition of this book, we still placed a major emphasis on old-school marketing and PR. We asked people to think about how to get their books into the hands of the *Today* show, *The New York Times* and the other major hitters, and then to work their way down the food chain (or to start at the other end and work their way up). But so many books, especially niche books like this one, are never going to find their way into the big media. And, as it turns out, that's no biggie. Because the web is all about finding community, about locating people just like you, no matter how esoteric you and your subject may be. So suddenly all the little fish who used to despair when it came to publicity and marketing can celebrate. Yes, getting a great review in *The New York Times* can make your book, but so can the right blog post by the right cyber celebrity. And the fact is, the plates are shifting beneath us, and no one quite knows what works and what doesn't anymore. Pamela Dorman, publisher of Pamela Dorman Books/Viking, puts it this way: "There is so much more outreach to the blogging community. Not long ago, we thought of this community as ancillary. Not anymore. Still, at this point, it's very hard to quantify what online reviews do. On the flip side, even the most sought-after reviews, like those in *The New York Times,* are not always doing what they used to do in terms of moving books."

In the olden times (a.k.a. ten years ago), there was a certain rigidity or predictability to PR and marketing campaigns. Publishers would make their standard lists of who to pitch, and they might or might not send you on tour.

▶ As soon as you hand in your manuscript (or six months to a year before publication, whichever is sooner), devote 15 minutes per day to promoting your book. Then at six months before your pub date, try to up the ante to a half-hour. Then go up to an hour (or as many hours as you can handle). Sound like a lot of work? It is. But it's the kind of work that nearly every successful author needs to do.

Now the only limit to your marketing and PR plans is your imagination. Well, some smarts don't hurt, either. That's why it's important to study successful publicity and marketing strategies for other books—as well as for movies and any other products whose sales are dependent on word of mouth. Dig into the business section of your local paper. Read *The Wall Street Journal*. Listen to NPR. Sign up for the RSS feeds of marketing and publicity blogs. Follow marketing and publicity leaders on Twitter. Surf the web for trends and information that will help you generate interest in your book. Go to events. Study how authors present themselves. What works and what doesn't? What do successful authors have in common? What mistakes do you see authors make? Which of your ideas will make people passionate about your book? All of this information will spark ideas that will help you develop a full-fledged publicity and marketing strategy. Most of all, be proactive. As Kathy Pories, an editor at Algonquin Books, put it: "A lot of successful authors seem to be good problem-solvers. They don't view their publisher as a maternal entity. They're always thinking about who their book will appeal to. They're engaged. They don't wait around for someone else to do something."

Your Author Questionnaire

Your publisher probably gave you an author questionnaire soon after you completed your deal or when your book went off to the copy editor. Filling it out may seem like a trivial afterthought amid the wild excitement of landing a book contract or finishing your book. But the author questionnaire is, in many ways, the backbone of your publicity plan. It will help you to start organizing the publicity and marketing side of your brain. And, out of it, you'll want to develop a comprehensive publicity and marketing strategy that you can hand off to your editor (and publicist, if you're assigned one) shortly after your book goes to copy edit. A strong idea for a plan will rev up the publicity, marketing and sales departments and help to register you and your book in their over-crowded brains.

Here are some of the questions you will probably be asked, with a brief explanation of why your publisher is asking them:

1. *What is the summary of your book?* Here comes your old friend: The Pitch. Trot her out in her Sunday best. Your pitch will be used by publicity and marketing in all contact with the media, including your press release. And it will give the sales department the handle it needs for its various and sundry accounts.

2. *Who are you?* At this stage of the game, your publisher needs a concise bio that they can use in your press release and other publicity, marketing and sales materials. We're talking a paragraph here. Make it too long and your publisher will end up shortening it for you. You can also provide a one-paragraph bio *and* one-page bio. This way, if there's extra stuff that you believe your publisher might want to use, they have the option.

3. *What current books directly compete with yours?* Your publisher needs to know about any and all directly competitive books. Don't try to pull the wool over anyone's eyes here. If you don't provide this information, you're doing yourself and your publisher a huge disservice, because booksellers are sure to ask, "How is this different than such-and-such?" Supply these titles and explain how your book is both different and better.

4. *What well-known people might provide blurbs?* Make your list an exhaustive one. On top of those people you'll be trying to track down yourself, add a wish list of people your editor, publisher and/or someone in publicity or marketing just might be connected to. If you have a Top 5 list, mark those names with asterisks so your publisher will pay special attention to them. And make it clear with whom you rub elbows.

5. *Who is the audience for your book?* Again, go back to your notes or your proposal to see if you've got solid, up-to-date info on your audience. If you've been building up your platform via your blog, website or social networking, do you have new information about your audience that you'd like to add as well?

6. *What is your presence on the World Wide Web?* Your publisher needs to know if you have a website, a blog, a Twitter/Facebook or other social network following and/or a large email list. The more you give the marketing, publicity and sales staff to talk about, the more chance you have of 1) getting them excited, and 2) getting them to get others excited. Because web

presence is so much in the zeitgeist, it's one of the first things these departments will look at. It will also let them know that you are going to be a useful partner in helping them with the incredibly difficult job of publicizing and marketing your book. If you already have the tools in place to get the word out in a meaningful way all over the information superhighway, it will help them be more confident about putting their resources behind you. And, of course, if you're already a known quantity in cyberspace, that just makes it easier to get traditional mainstream media outlets interested.

7. *Where have you appeared in the media?* If you've done a lot of media, don't just mention a few of your biggest hits. Cast a wide net here. Write down every appearance/mention, regardless of whether or not it relates to your book. This isn't about bragging, it's about networking. It's much easier for your publicist to approach someone who already knows and loves you. And you never know what tiny mention in the *Podunk Gazette* could lead to a big ticket segment on the *Today* show.

8. *Are there publicity angles for your book that we might not know about?* What was the inspiration for your book? What interesting things happened during the writing of your book? You might not realize it, but the genesis of your book could serve as a great hook for media. Any curious tidbits the media can sink their teeth into, or any connections to current events, will help get coverage for your book. Think widely and weirdly here. You never know what's going to grab someone's attention.

9. *What publications and bloggers should receive a free copy of your book?* If you've established an e-community, make a list of all the bloggers, tweeters and other new media voices who might review or talk about your book. Make a list of newspapers and magazines. And then move on to associations and organizations whose newsletters or other publications might help get the word out. Also point out any outlets where you yourself have been published and/or featured. In all cases, include any contact information you have.

10. *Where have you lived?* The more places you've lived, the more places you can "go local." Local connections are a great way to generate marketing, publicity and sales. It's much easier to get a story in the local media than in the national media. And local attention can help build your press kit and eventually make you more credible to those large national media outlets.

11. *Do you have lecture or seminar experience?* If you already give lectures on the subject of your book, supply a list of the places where you've spoken. It's also helpful to create short synopses of these lectures, along with ideas for lecture outlets to pinpoint once your book comes out. If you have glowing testimonials from people who've hired you to speak or who've seen you speak, attach a best-of document. If you have a link to one of your best lectures, be sure to include that as well.

12. *Are there any special sales opportunities?* Oddly enough, many books sell better outside bookstores than in them. Are there stores or organizations that might want to buy your book? Might your book about decorating in the bedroom sell best in Bed Bath & Beyond? Or your book about how to find your way in and around Medicare to AARP? Publishers love these kinds of sales, in part because the books are rarely returnable. Don't just give this a second of thought. Dig deep. P.S. We'll discuss special sales in depth in Chapter 14.

13. *Do you have any other comments or suggestions?* Here's the place to show your publisher how motivated you are—how much you want to help, and what you've done that didn't make it into the rest of your questionnaire—as well as your game plan. Susan Edsall, author of *Into the Blue,* ended her questionnaire this way: "I've already contacted 500 organizations by email and letter and gotten significant positive response. I recognize that your publicity people are champions at garnering major media. I hereby volunteer to bird-dog the smaller but highly motivated audiences that you realistically don't have the time to chase down. I see it as my job and responsibility to support your publicity department in continuing to generate and follow through on this interest."

Like your book proposal, your answers to the author questionnaire should sound as much like your speaking voice as possible. The more engaging the answers, the more engaging the author—or so the publisher will assume.

▶ Are you in the unfortunate position of having your book enter the marketplace at the same time as or on the heels of another book on a similar topic? If so, you'll need to get your defensive strategy in order. Part of your pitch will have to explain how your book is different, how it's better or how it adds to the story that's already out there.

Reassessing Your Pitch

You may remember us saying that your pitch will constantly evolve. You may also remember us saying that there will be key points along your book's journey where your pitch will, again, become paramount. Now is one of those times. The sales force is beginning to pitch your book to retailers, the publicity staff is about to pitch your book to media and to bookstores for events, and you are about to pitch your book to everyone from your next-door neighbor to the lead blogger on your subject to the NPR producer you're sitting next to on the plane.

As you can see, your pitch will be at the center of your publicity and marketing efforts. This is why you must now ask yourself: Is the pitch you began your journey with the pitch for the book that just went into copy edit? Or do you have the same book, but you've figured out a stronger pitch from having done it so many times? Here's where things get a bit complicated. Not only are you going to need an up-to-date pitch, but you'll also have to customize your pitch according to whom you're pitching. Obviously you're going to pitch your book differently to Martha Stewart than you would to *Sports Illustrated*. Your local paper is going to want the angle that suits your hood. Whereas a national news outlet will want to know how your book fits into worldwide trends. And your pitch to a niche publication or blog will need to display your insider take. Wherever you're pitching, make sure you're as up-to-date as possible. You want to appear to be part of the current conversation.

Blurb Wrangling

One of the best ways to show that you're part of the current conversation is to have people with active and big names touting your work. Not only is it a relief to have someone else saying nice things about you for a change, it's also a major selling tool. Blurbs (also called endorsements) can act as great additions to or even replacements for your pitch. Over and over again, we've seen blurbers write better promotional copy than the author or publisher does!

A great blurb from the right person wrangled early on can garner you instant respect. That's why tracking down blurbs, or adding to the ones you've already got, should be a high publicity and marketing priority. These blurbs will be used to entice members of the media, in-house sales reps, book buyers, you name it. As Jonathon Keats, author, freelance journalist and member of the National Book Critics Circle awards committee, says, "For a critic, blurbs are hugely important. If I get galleys of a book by someone I've never heard of, a good blurb is pretty much the only thing that makes me pay attention. (Acknowledgments next.) Blurbing is also really important from the standpoint of readers who haven't heard of you but have heard of the person giving you the blurb."

Hopefully your editor will help you to get blurbs. Editors, at their best, mine their own and their colleagues' lists for appropriate people to approach, and write killer letters introducing you as the next big thing. Editors, at their worst, depend solely on you to find endorsers. (Remember how we said to consider your publisher your printer?) Since you've already made blurb lists, you have a leg up. Go over that original list with your editor and agent. Also ask your agent if there's anyone you're missing that she may be able to reach out to.

Many people feel shy and uncomfortable approaching well-known writers and authority figures. That's normal. But if you approach a well-known person in a way that makes it easy for them to say yes, you'll be amazed by how often you'll get results. When we were putting together *Satchel Sez,* we had a tough time getting blurbs. We'd made a great list of potential blurbers, and we were going after them hard. Phone calls, emails, faxes. But we couldn't get even a whiff of a blurb. Finally, through an editor who had shown interest in our original proposal, we made contact with TV sportscaster Bob Costas. We sent him our stuff with a very nice letter. And guess what? He not only blurbed but wrote a beautiful foreword to our book.

> ▶ Reaching out to a potential blurber? Unless you have a connection, there's a good chance that your 300 uninvited manuscript pages will end up in the recycling bin. Rather than waiting for a finished book, ask your publisher for an electronic copy (or a link to a file that can be downloaded onto an e-reader) or ask them to send you bound manuscripts. If they won't, go to a copy shop and have your manuscript bound yourself. Flipping through a neatly bound set of pages feels much more manageable to blurbers.

As soon as a blurb comes in, write a personal thank-you note. When you get finished copies of your book, send a personalized, signed copy to each blurber.

Audience Angling

Just as we've asked you to reexamine your pitch, we also would like you to get a fresh read on your audience. Where does your audience go to find out what books to buy? Do you know their likes, dislikes, ticks and what makes them tick? Have you made your core audience aware of the fact that you have a fabulous book that's about to emerge? If the answer to these questions is yes, then clearly you have participated in the community in which your readers live, work or play. And you've also clearly begun to develop—or have already made great strides in developing—your platform.

If you don't know the answers to these questions, developing this knowledge base as you work to build your platform should be your number one priority.

SOCIAL NETWORKING REDUX

We've discussed, at length, the importance of building networks, becoming part of an e-community early on in your book's life and developing an online reputation. We asked you first to research these communities, then to participate in them and then to set up your own tent in the vast e-jungle. We've also emphasized the importance of being a selfless member of your community.

If you've been active in your e-community, hopefully you have proven that you're one of the gang and not just a momentary intruder looking for your 15 minutes. Now it's time to get strategic. In the year before your book comes out, check out what other members of your community have books coming out. Start actively reviewing these books. A rave review is always great, but only if you believe it. If not, think of other complimentary ways to feature the author. Maybe an interview with him/her. Maybe pull some nice quotes from the book and feature a quote a day for a particular week. Maybe spread the word about the author's tour. The idea here is quid pro quo. I do this for you now, you do the same for me when my book comes out.

> ▶ If done with style, wit and intelligence, a chronicle of your book's journey to publication can delight your existing audience. Getting a book published is, as you know, no small feat. Why not create a weekly post about your bookish trials, tribulations and successes? Create a buildup to your book release so that when the big day arrives, your following will joyously click their way through to purchase.

Apply the same principles to influential bloggers, regardless of whether they have books. Conduct interviews. Talk up their sites. Share or retweet a particular posting. Send some general goodwill their way.

Once you've given everything you've got, you can call on these e-friends to help you start to spread the word. This help can be in the form of reviews, links to your site, tweets, mentions and more. If you've become friends with bloggers with large followings, ask if you can do a guest post or two, or if they would interview you for their site. Bloggers with big audiences tend to be generous, because they can be. People already like them and

The Facebook Debate: Personal or Authorial

We've talked to lots and lots of writers who are confused about how to use Facebook. Most of them have personal accounts on which they post pictures of their kids, trips to the Grand Canyon or giving a haircut to their dog. Now that they have a book, they want to let people know about their work and their lives as authors, but they're hesitant to muddy their personal waters.

Just to be clear, there are two types of Facebook accounts: the personal *profile,* where you can "friend" others, and the public *page,* which is typically used for professional personas, businesses or topics. Unless you're famous, it's difficult to get a lot of people to follow a public author page. It's much easier to friend people and have them friend you back via a personal profile. In addition, because Facebook wants people with public pages to pay to get their posts seen, they tend to bury posts that aren't what they call "boosted" with bucks. This is not the case with personal posts in people's news feeds. Personal pages, as a result, get more visibility.

Antonella Iannarino, literary agent, brand manager/digital consultant and Facebook aficionado, says, "Originally, having a public page versus a personal profile allowed you to keep your personal and professional life separate. Now that audiences can follow a personal profile and the author can decide who sees what content, you can maintain both personas on your personal profile."

But there are also many reasons for an author to maintain a public Facebook page in addition to a personal profile, whether you're just starting out or have a loyal following. For example, instead of a standard "author" page, you could focus on your subject. Maybe you want one of the characters from your novel to have her own Facebook page in her own voice. Or if you're writing nonfiction, the page could be devoted to your research or to a particular time in history. Ellen Meister, bestselling author of the novels *Farewell, Dorothy Parker* and *Dorothy Parker Drank Here,* maintains the public Dorothy Parker Facebook page. She posts quotes and trivia about the great authoress. These quotes get bounced around like a pinball, creating interest in both the inspiration for her novel and the novel itself.

Ellen also uses her personal profile to connect with her audience, but she uses it differently: "My personal profile is where I let my hair down, and I think readers appreciate that. People want to feel a personal connection with the authors they enjoy. As for my nonpersonal page, maintaining it can be a lot of work, especially if you're eager to build a big following. You have to keep the content engaging and update it constantly. So it really helps if it's a labor of love and you truly enjoy your subject matter. For me, it's a win-win because I'm a big Dorothy Parker fan and I love sharing her quotes and poems with the Facebook world. The fact that I now have an excellent platform for two of my books almost feels like a bonus. But it really does help, because as of this writing I'm connected to over 140,000 Dorothy Parker fans, and that's a huge audience."

like to see them supporting smaller players. Blogger and author John Scalzi says, "One of the things I do on my site is give space for other writers, to help them get publicity themselves." This kind of support is imperative. No matter how strong your own site is, readers look to the recommendations of others, first and foremost. Roxanne Lott, managing director of the online marketing firm Imerex, explains it this way: "Let's say I'm really interested in Civil War weapons. If Jim Smith wrote a book titled *Civil War Weapons,* which is exactly what I'm interested in, I wouldn't simply go to his site, read an excerpt and then buy it. I would expect that Jim Smith would have an online reputation. That there would be places where people spoke of his expertise, search results that showed lectures he may have given on the subject or sites that had reviewed his book."

UP CLOSE AND PERSONAL

Now that you've been inculcated in the realm of e-connections, stop hiding behind that screen and start pressing the flesh. It's time to give your devices a break and come outside for some fresh air. As Truman Capote counseled young writers: "Socialize. Don't just go up to a pine cabin all alone and brood. You will reach that stage soon enough anyway."

Get the first bits of buzz going in your own backyard. Let your local booksellers know that publication is near. Same goes for local authors you've befriended. But don't stop with book people—tell your letter carrier, tell your hairdresser. Tell people who know lots of other people. And definitely tell anyone who's connected to the media. Maybe the local anchorperson's kid goes to your kid's school. Ask other parents if anyone knows this person.

If your book has to do with your job, try to go to as many conferences and trade association gatherings as you possibly can in the months leading up to and through publication. Ask colleagues to help talk up your book. Trade-specific newsletters are also a terrific way to get the word out to a very targeted audience. Can you get one to do a Q&A?

If you're writing a literary work that relies on poetic language rather than plot or is more experimental and does not fall into a traditional genre like romance, chick lit or thriller, network with as many authors as you can. Readings and other promotional book events, writers' conferences, book fairs, festivals and expos are all wonderful ways to meet other authors.

You also can't underestimate the influence of friends and family. Due to the power of citizens in today's electronic world, your very chatty aunt might very well be the key to your book's success. Her monthly ladies' luncheon might be filled with other Chatty Cathys who would love nothing more than to claim responsibility for making you a bestselling author.

HANDY HANDOUTS

When you do meet a potential reader or buzz-builder in person, it's great to have a physical nugget ready to pass on. Prior to publication, this can be a postcard, a bookmark or an eye-catching or funny tidbit that'll help people remember you and your book. Master marketer Nancy Levine, coauthor (with her philosopher dog Wilson) of *The Tao of Pug*, had some fun with the fact that her book was published during an election year. She had "Wilson for President" buttons made. Bob Klein's publisher made bottle cap openers for his *Beer Lover's Rating Guide*. If you go with a doodad, just make sure it's something that's easy for people to carry. And don't spend your entire marketing budget on some overly clever object. A novelty item is a nice added touch, but it's not worth breaking the bank on.

▶ If it translates, create an electronic version of your novelty item so you can email it to cyber friends and colleagues.

If you're sticking with the tried-and-true postcard or bookmark, here are the basics of what you should include: your book's cover, title and subtitle; the name of your publisher; your website address and your contact information; a blurb if you have one; your ISBN. Better not to add your pub date, as you want to be able to use your handout after your book is published. If you're printing a postcard, simply put the book cover on the front and the rest of the info on the back.

Ask your publisher to pay for postcards (this is relatively standard in the business). But if they refuse, don't put up a fuss. You can now get postcards made for very little money via the web. And you can then use the fact that you paid for postcards later on: "Since I paid for those postcards six months ago, could you please pay for . . ."

Your Web Presence

Tech grinches, if we haven't already driven our point home, please heed the words of Lori Culwell, novelist, SEO (search engine optimization) guru and author of *Million Dollar Website*: "It is no longer acceptable for you to be out there promoting your book without some kind of web presence. Websites/blogs help you organize your thoughts and target your demographic. They can attract traffic and earn you extra money (through Amazon affiliate programs and the like). They are a great place for reporters or book reviewers to go when they are considering covering your book. They are a place where you can post reviews, tour dates and anything else anyone says about your book. Your website is the nexus point of your PR campaign."

Even if you are very active on other social media, having a website is more important than you might think. A recent study showed one of the key ways people find out about books is through author websites. Annik LaFarge, former publishing director of Bloomsbury Books and author of *The Author Online: A Short Guide to Building Your Website, Whether You Do It Yourself (and you can!) or You Work With Pros,* told us this:

"Surprisingly, in terms of new book discovery, Facebook and Twitter are much less influential than author websites. Some of the reasons for this have to do with SEO (search engine optimization) and keywords. When you type in an author's name, his/her website is the first thing that comes up. To be the first result that pops up in a Google search is reason enough to have a website. This visibility gives you the opportunity to control your message and to craft the experience that you want that person who is interested in your work—that person who has taken the time to Google you—to see."

If you have yet to set up a website or blog, please return to Chapter 2 before proceeding because it is now time to tailor your site for your book's launch. Here are the basics:

1. *Homepage.* Your cover image and the text of your elevator pitch.

2. *Book(s) tab.* Your book's jacket copy.

3. *Bio tab.* Trot out the fun and interesting history of you.

4. *Excerpt tab.* This can be up to 5,000 words or whatever your publisher will allow. (Check your contract, under Licensing, for the exact word count.) Choose the intro, first chapter or whatever passage will lead people to exclaim, "I have to buy this book!"

5. *Press tab.* As soon as any blurbs or reviews come in, get them up, either through a link or via PDF.

6. *Contact tab.* Your email address, or a virtual form that enables you to receive messages without providing your address. We recommend the former. You can set up a book-related email address that you use only for business.

7. *A link to buy.* This link should appear on your homepage and can be available on every page as well. You don't have to wait until your book has hit the shelves. Your book will be available for preorder as soon as it's in your publisher's catalog. It's important to spread the love around here. Try to make your book available for sale electronically not just at the largest sites like Amazon and Barnes & Noble, but also at Powell's and Indiebound, which will connect buyers to their favorite independent bookstores.

8. *Newsletter signup form.* You want to capture as many names as you possibly can. These are the people who are asking to hear from you, and you want to make sure you keep them up to date.

Once you take care of the basics, you can get creative. Are you photogenic? Then a photo gallery might be right for you. Put up pictures of people or places from your books, photos from events, even photos from your childhood, high school or college—anything that might help make your site more sticky.

Have you made any promotional videos for your book or videotaped any of your readings? Then a video tab would be great.

Do you offer workshops? Then you'll need a workshop tab.

If you're writing fiction or narrative nonfiction, you might want to create a reading guide for book groups. (If your publisher is including one in your book, see if you can get a digital copy to upload.) Readers' guides ask 10 to 15 questions to spur discussion. Questions like: "Why is the protagonist so protective of her red shoes—what does this reveal about her character?" "There is a change in narrator mid-book; how does this new voice lead to a different understanding of the crime that took place in Chapter 2?" "We are never told the name of the protagonist's brother, even though he appears throughout the book. Why?" If you're having trouble coming up with these sorts of discussion questions, check out some examples on a major publisher's website. Many books have attained bestseller status due to book group support, so the more group friendly your site can be, the better.

Do you have a list of upcoming events? Then you'll need a calendar tab. One word of warning, calendar-wise: If someone comes to your site and sees only three dates from six months to a year ago, it's going to seem like not much is happening with your book. So, don't include a calendar unless you can really keep it filled. Which leads us to . . .

THE TOP MISTAKE AUTHORS MAKE WHEN DESIGNING THEIR WEBSITES

We see it every day: Great intentions + time = very sad website. "You need to have a plan for your website—a monthly and yearly plan," says Annik LaFarge. "What sort of content will you launch with? What will you add as time goes by? How frequently will you post new material? Enough to blog? If so, what will the voice of your blog be? What will be the first 10 things you write about?" And, of course, once you come up with a plan, you have to stick to it. Better to start small and follow through than have tab after tab that is either empty or three years old.

Make sure that your website address is listed on your publisher's site. Your publisher's site most likely gets more traffic than your own, whether from readers or from story-happy media people.

YOUR ONLINE PROFILES

In addition to ensuring that your site is up or up-to-date, make sure your author profiles on other book-related sites are current. "You only get so many owned or controlled presences online," says Peter McCarthy, of the Logical Marketing Agency, a digital marketing company for the publishing industry. That's why you want to make sure to have in-depth and well-thought-out profiles on Amazon, Google Plus, Goodreads, LinkedIn and other social media sites. Not only do *you* get to decide what to put in these profiles, but you also get to take advantage of the fact that Google ranks these sites highly for searches. So let's say someone is looking for a book on how to get published. If we have profiles on all these sites with well-chosen keywords and phrases on this very subject, *The Essential Guide to Getting Your Book Published* is likely to come up higher in this person's search than someone else's book on the same subject. And the higher up you can get on Google searches relating to your book, the more books you're likely to sell.

But don't put up the exact same profile on all four sites. Differentiate slightly among them so that you can broaden the number of searches that might find you. Within Amazon, for example: Because people visit Amazon to buy stuff, your profile should facilitate those transactions. You want to be much more specific in describing the types of books you write. On LinkedIn, which is mostly for professional networking, you want to be more focused on credentials: Why should a reader trust you on your area of expertise? On Goodreads, which is more social in nature, you can be more informal and talk about your kids, your dog and the books (preferably within your subject area/genre) you love and admire. On Google Plus, where biographical data help Google identify you in searches (we'll explain in a minute), it's just the facts ma'am.

Although all of these platforms provide lots of opportunities, we're going to concentrate on Google and Amazon because they are the leviathans at the moment. First, a quick primer on how Google works. The search engine tries to identify people, places and things and to understand who and what they are in a particular context. It wants to know, for instance, that we are authors who specialize in helping people get their books published. But identifying people is one of the greatest challenges for Google. It understands our behaviors, but not so much *who* we are. If you do a search for a famous author, for example, you'll notice her photo, birth date and books will likely show up on the right-hand side of your screen. Google often pulls these from Wikipedia, one of its primary sources for identifying people. Because not everyone has a Wikipedia page, a social-networking tool like Google Plus is Google's way of enhancing its ability to identify people. It is not, as many people mistakenly think, Google's attempt to create a social network in the image of Facebook.

Google's ultimate goal is to answer questions. Your Google Plus profile can help by equating your name with the profession of author, the titles of the books you've written, the publishers you've worked with and your biography (which includes what kind of author you are and who you are in addition to being an author), and then linking to your other various presences online (articles, interviews, blog posts, social media profiles, Amazon pages, etc.). Google will follow those links in order to verify them—in other words to make sure that you're really the author you claim to be. Here are Peter McCarthy's tips for making your Google Plus profile as strong as it can be:

- Say you're an author! You want to be linked with this word wherever possible.

- Connect to people via "circles," Google's equivalent of Facebook's friending. Circles add greater authority, credibility and relevance to whatever you post.

- Connect to people who are more popular than you in your particular community (science fiction, romance, self-help, etc.). These connections make *you* more credible and relevant.

- You don't need to do regular status updates, but you do need to keep whatever you post relevant to your subject matter or genre.

- "Plus one" (Google's equivalent to liking something on Facebook) things that are in your sphere of interest.

■ Write for the general population, not just for insiders. So, if you're writing for young adults, don't use the term *YA,* which is an industry term, use *young adult.* Remember, you're hoping to show up in the searches of as many people as possible.

■ Relevant links are a must. The more the merrier.

Because Google considers Amazon a highly credible source of information on books and authors, your Amazon profile is your second-most important tool when it comes to Google searches. Your Amazon profile is yet another way to strongly reinforce your presence as an author, to stake your claim in the publishing jungle. When someone does a search for your name, if you have a robust Amazon profile, Google is going to understand that you (not someone else with your same name) are a good result to give that person.

A good Amazon profile is also of primary importance within searches on Amazon itself because it helps the site understand more fully what you write and how to display your book(s) in searches. Ultimately, your profile gives both Google and Amazon more words to search with than your book description alone. Here's what Peter McCarthy suggests you do to help Amazon check as many boxes as possible to get you higher up in searches:

■ The more info Amazon gives people about the product, the more likely the person is to purchase it. If Amazon sees more stuff on your profile than on that of an author with a similar book and sales pace, Amazon will rank you higher and you will outperform the other author. So, the more you fill out in the author profile, the better.

■ Add your blog posts and Twitter feeds.

■ Include a (good!) photo.

■ Post upcoming events.

■ Upload videos.

■ Keep abreast of updates as Amazon rolls them out—stay informed of your options!

Don't underestimate how many Amazon sales come through Google searches and how much Amazon information helps you get ranked higher on Google. One cyber-hand washes the other.

Your Publicity and Marketing Plan

With your author questionnaire done and dusted off and your basic publicity and marketing tools in place, it's time to create a detailed publicity and marketing plan cementing all the good things you set up at your six-month meeting (page 268). If you're working with a traditional publisher, you'll hand this document off to your editor and publicist. It will keep you and your publisher on your toes and help provide accountability. "No matter how enthusiastic or capable the publicity and marketing team assigned to your book, they are generalists, not specialists," says Jim Levine of the Levine Greenberg Rostan Literary Agency. "When it comes to nonfiction, in particular, they rarely know the audience or how to reach them as well as you do. So having your preliminary launch plan will be a terrific help to them, as long as you present it in a cooperative spirit."

Your publicity and marketing plan covers the months leading up to and immediately following publication. Your plan should:

■ *Start with your pitch.*

■ *Summarize your overall strategy and goal(s) for publication.* Not: "I want to sell millions of books and get on national TV!" More: "Connect with a variety of large and small, but specific players in the blogosphere (include names and URLs); do in-person appearances at X bookstores, Y universities and Z organizations; execute virtual presentations consisting of podcasts, videos or webinars (these should each have their own mini pitches); target appropriate mainstream media outlets."

■ *Summarize your efforts to date.* This summary should include what kind of web presence you've built; the community (or communities) you've become a part of; any early media coverage; links to workshops, presentations, readings or other video that can be used to promote your book. Include numbers (site visitors, mentions, etc.) wherever possible.

■ *Identify opportunities in print/TV/radio.* Make a local and national media wish list. Make sure the list has a nice balance of long shots, realistic choices and safeties. Especially helpful here are specialized media outlets that your publicist might not be aware of. If it isn't obvious, you will want to supply the appropriate pitch or angle for a given media outlet. Note any contacts you have.

- *Carve out your niche in online media.* Tell your team about the websites, online communities and bloggers they wouldn't know about. Supply information about how these online communities tend to handle book launches. For example, some places like to serialize a piece of the book; some like to bundle several similarly themed books together; some prefer interviews, some editorials, some just straight-up reviews.

- *Display your platform.* Make a list of all seminars/workshops/events you've booked yourself leading up to and past publication. Then make a list of places you'd like to be booked. Indicate which of these places you can approach on your own and which you'd like your publisher's help with.

- *Highlight any cross-promotional opportunities.* What other authors on your publisher's list speak to the same audience as you? Suggest events and panels with like-minded authors, or guest posting on their website. Ask your team to use the resources they have to bring you and your book more visibility.

Your Press Release

If your publicist wrote your press release, we think there's no reason you shouldn't put your two and a half cents in—you've been pitching your book longer than anyone else. By this time, you should know what grabs people's attention and what turns them off. Do keep in mind that your publicist is a trained professional who knows what the media respond to. Hopefully, working together, you can create a press release that educates, excites and entices.

Consider that journalists, reviewers, bloggers and other media people get hundreds of press releases in the course of a week. That's why your press release should be short and attention-grabbing. On paper, it should be no more than a page long (approximately 250 words), and should include the following elements:

1. The name and address (and perhaps the logo) of your publisher at the top of the page.

2. The contact name, phone number and email address of your publicist.

3. The title of your book, and your name. Your website address, prominently displayed.

4. Your pitch, in a paragraph or two, rewritten in a journalistic voice. Essentially, you want a pitch that can be pulled and used by the media as is. The easier you make their job, the more likely you are to hit pay dirt. A

note: It's really important to avoid absurd, over-the-top descriptions and superlatives. Seasoned media people will see through these!

5. Edited-down versions of blurbs. Always better to have someone else say great things about you than to say them about yourself. If you've managed to get a great blurb from a well-known person who can really speak to your subject, feature that one up top. Journalists who don't know you may know the blurber.

6. Edited-down versions of any great reviews. Ditto above.

7. A small, self-contained chunk from your book, particularly if it's a novel or a work of creative nonfiction. Or, for a how-to book, a list of hot topics covered. Something that illustrates the points in your pitch. Something that shows you off to your best advantage and makes the reader excited about your book.

8. Your bio, reduced to one paragraph, with any pertinent information that makes you seem like an interesting interview. If you've got big credentials, trot them out. If you don't have a particularly impressive bio, blurbs become all the more important.

9. Any relevant information about events, speaking engagements, teaching gigs or seminars.

10. Your ISBN (the number assigned to your book for retail purposes).

While publishers will create only one press release, you might be called upon to write many in the course of publicizing your book. Be sure to update yours, including any glowing reviews and mentions of media appearances. You can also easily customize your release for particular publications or events.

If a media person requested material directly from you, always follow up to make sure they got the material from your publicist. If you simply gave your publicist a list of people you don't know and who don't know you, add the name of a good friend to your list and see how long it takes for him to receive something. If he doesn't get it, ask your editor and agent for advice on how to rectify the situation.

Your Press Kit

You already have a number of the elements you need for your press kit. Now it's all about assembling them into one professional, visually smart package that makes you look good. Larry Mantle, host of public radio's *AirTalk with Larry Mantle* on the NPR affiliate KPCC-FM in Los Angeles, says, "Having a nice package really helps. Something that's professionally presented, that doesn't

Pearls from a Publicity Pro

L ynn Goldberg, CEO of Goldberg McDuffie Communications, one of the leading PR agencies in publishing, shares some thoughts on capturing the media's attention:

- "Press releases are generally viewed as formulaic. That's why customized letters, emails and handwritten notes are so important."

- "Press kits are essential for broadcast media, as producers need a package with topics for discussions and show ideas. The Q&A can be very important—it's a terrific place to pull out an author's ideas and show the consequences of these ideas."

- "For fiction, the voice is key. I often have authors do anecdotal bios that run a page. These don't begin 'I was born . . .' Instead, they feature what is unique or surprising about the authors and how their background has informed their work."

- "For nonfiction, you need a good journalistic lead. It could be about current events or a recent survey. But don't overreach or make extraneous connections. Instead, distill the information in a thoughtful way so reviewers will pick your book out of the pack."

- "If you have a how-to book, provide user-friendly nuggets like lists and tips."

- "The media are not anxious to hear from authors directly. If you're handling your own publicity, follow up on your press kit with prudence. You want to be a helpful resource, not a pest."

- "The good news? The media like ideas. They are thirsty for them."

look homemade. How it looks really does make a difference. I get 50 to 70 books a week. So I often have only 20 seconds to spend looking at a press kit."

Nowadays, electronic press kits are just as useful as the pulpy stuff. But if you need a physical package to send out with your book pages or manuscript, it should look great. For paper press kits, use an attractive folder. For electronic kits, make sure you use a format that won't go wonky over email—PDFs are one way of maintaining your document's visual integrity. Regardless of form, here are the essentials of any press kit:

1. Your press release
2. A full bio (like the one you included in your submission to publishers)
3. Author photo
4. Reviews/blurbs

5. Articles about you

6. Topics for discussion, article and show ideas, plus Q&A

7. CD, DVD

8. A one-paragraph description of what kind of talks/content you can offer as a speaker or workshop leader

About Number 4: Since you're still in the prepublication stage, any reviews will be from trade publications such as *Publishers Weekly, Booklist, Kirkus* and *Library Journal,* or from bloggers, as opposed to general-interest publications. That's fine. If you're worried that your press kit looks a bit skimpy to begin with, aspire to have it keep growing as your book garners more acclaim!

All articles and reviews should be cleanly reproduced, with the name of the publication and the date it appeared clearly displayed. Your Q&A should include the questions you'd like to be asked by the media along with your very pithy one-paragraph answers. This can be a critical element. Award-winning WNYC radio host Leonard Lopate explains why: "I'm always looking for beautiful writing or for someone who's saying something important or someone who I feel is really going to make an impact. But, for example, not everyone who writes beautifully has interesting things to say, or has had an interesting life. So it's a combination of a great book, and someone who I think I could have a great conversation with." The Q&A is the teaser for that great conversation.

A major publisher may send out your book with a press release, as opposed to a full press kit. So the latter may fall to you to create. But run your finished kit by your publicist to make sure that what you're sending out yourself is up to snuff.

A GOOD AUTHOR PHOTO IS NOT AN OXYMORON

It's so important to include an attractive, professional photo in your press kit—an enticing author photograph can really help your book. This doesn't mean you have to look like a model; it just means you have to look your best. Book critic Jonathon Keats says, "Author photos are an often overlooked opportunity. As much as nobody wants to say it, a good photo really matters in terms of getting a feature. Reviewers actually ask about this on the sly."

▶ Make sure you and/or your publicist obtain digital copies of your photos, so they can be emailed along with your press release. Load your favorites onto your website; make sure you're using high-res files, and mark them as such. That way journalists or fans can pull them off your site and use them—to help promote you and your book.

A Pretty Picture's Worth an In-Store Event

Author photos can make booksellers take notice. Barbara Morrow, co-owner of Northshire Books in Manchester Center, Vermont, told us this story: "An unknown author named Prill Boyle wrote a book called *Defying Gravity: A Celebration of Late-Blooming Women.* She sent us a copy of the book along with a press packet that included a great author photo. She is an attractive woman, and she looked like she would present herself and her subject well. We didn't know who she was (she had no track record), but I decided to bring her in to do an event. She was so appealing, and she presented herself and her material so well. Fifteen people showed up, but the amazing thing was that everyone bought books. That hardly ever happens."

This story shows just how powerful a good author photo can be. On the flip side, though, Barbara adds: "Authors who send pictures that look deadly dull do themselves a disservice by including them in their press packet."

Don't be cheap. A six-year-old, semi-cute pic taken by your cousin will not do. Whether you're going for a head shot, a full-body shot or something in between, it's usually worth the money to go to a professional photographer with a studio and lights. Your agent or publisher may know a good one. If not, ask around or look online. Peruse photographers' portfolios. Most of all, find a photographer you're comfortable with. This will make for more natural shots.

Make the most of your photo shoot. Do a whole series of poses: serious to goofy, sexy to thoughtful. This way, you have a number of choices for the media. Interesting, beautiful or unusual photographs have a way of ending up in "pick of the week" sections of newspapers, on the homepages of websites, or in the posts of bloggers, because arresting visuals arrest readers. Sometimes a small, appropriate prop can be fun, as long as it doesn't dominate the picture. When award-winning monologuist Mike Daisey was photographed for the show that became his book, *21 Dog Years,* a friend brought in a toy dog bone. Mike put it in his mouth and made a crazy, wide-eyed dog face. It became the poster for the show. Then the cover for his book. Then a much-published photo in newspapers and magazines around the country. Simple prop. Used beautifully.

If you don't feel comfortable in front of a camera, bring a friend to loosen you up or have a

▶ If you're super photogenic, don't be shy about sending your picture out with ALL promotional materials. And if you have several different and fun shots, go ahead and include more than one!

glass of wine to relax. Try engaging in a conversation as you're being photo-graphed. But if you absolutely cannot tolerate the idea of a photograph, you can forgo it. Remember, a bad picture is worse than none at all.

MEDIA FRIENDLY, WITH CLIPS TO PROVE IT!

If you've appeared on TV or radio and you were able to be your brilliant, charming, lovely self, you'd be crazy not to put together an excerpt of one or more of your appearances via a link on your website or a video sharing site like YouTube. This video will make a fantastic addition to your press kit. It can also serve as your publicist's calling card for more TV and radio spots, speaking engagements and any number of other events.

Just make sure you have a top-quality copy of your appearance(s). Do not include out-of-focus, grainy tape or third-generation cable access footage. You want crisp, sharp footage that makes you look scintillating, deep, funny and/or brilliant.

Running time should be under five minutes, total. Begin the presentation with you, not a long lead-in from whatever program you happened to be on. No one has time for the boring parts. However, if you were on a national show, it's good to start with its logo or a few seconds of the host saying, "In the next half-hour, we'll be talking to (insert your name here) about his fabulous new book."

At the end of the clip, make sure you include a still shot of your book cover accompanied by your website's URL.

The Rise of the Book Trailer

Ever since it became easy enough for anyone to make a movie on their telephone and get it seen by millions of people, authors and publishers have been trying to figure out how to use this remarkable medium to sell books. Some writers spend mucho dinero making elaborate promotional videos for their books and see no bump in sales. Others have made very simple videos for nada and launched their books onto bestseller lists.

Just as you did for your website, poke around and see what's out there before you spend a penny. See what works and what doesn't. Look for some-thing that suits you and your style.

You'll see many different approaches. Bestselling author Kelly Corrigan's video is as straightforward as it gets: she is reading an excerpt from what would become her memoir, *The Middle Place,* in front of a group of women. There are a few snap-shots cut in and some simple guitar music playing in the background. The video is clearly made with your average home video camera. No fancy outtakes. No bells.

Film School for Authors

K emble Scott, author of *SoMa*, and a knight of networking, was one of the first authors to make and post promotional book videos on YouTube. Here's his wisdom on making great videos:

- **Keep it short—2 to 3 minutes only.**

- **Don't spend a lot of money.** "I've noticed lots of authors do these very slick looking trailers, with tremendous production value. But there's absolutely no correlation between slick and success. You will never make back the money you spend. It's just not necessary. My videos cost nothing—zero!"

- **Make sure your video reflects your book.** "When my novel *SoMa* came out, I asked a friend with a fantastic broadcast quality camera to shoot my movie. It looked beautiful, but it was completely wrong for my book, which is a gritty urban story. It needed to look like the real world, not like *Lawrence of Arabia*. So I went back and shot it again. With a $200 camera and a cameraman who had never shot anything in his life. It was like shaky cam by accident. But it was absolutely perfect."

- **Rate your movies PG.** "My books have some fairly graphic things in them, but the movies were all very carefully constructed so that they would be PG-rated. There's lots that's inferred, but there's nothing graphic. That way they can be played on any website anywhere."

- **Get the word out.** "I sent my videos to everyone I know and to lots of people I didn't. This was before Facebook and Twitter, which now make it so much easier to get the word out."

No whistles. But the content is so good, smart, powerful and funny that her video got over four million viewings on YouTube and launched her book career into the stratosphere. All from a very simple five-minute trailer that cost nothing to make.

On the other hand, Melissa Cistaro's video for her memoir, *Pieces of My Mother,* feels like a trailer for a professional documentary. It's beautifully shot, and it looks like it benefited from a tremendous amount of time and thought. The visuals are part of the narrative and enhance Melissa's story. This short movie was also made for next to nothing, by Melissa's husband, who is a professional filmmaker. Remember to use the resources you have!

No matter what your category or genre, you just want to be sure your video showcases your voice and style. Have you written a business book? Then maybe a lecture is the way to go. Have you written a craft book? Then maybe a demo of a how-to project is right for you. Have you written a potboiler? Maybe you can pull a series of images along with some heart-stopping music to create an at-the-movies experience. Most of all, you want to be sure your video entices readers.

Getting Your Hooks and Angles Ready

The perfect publicity materials will only go so far if you don't have a wide array of hooks in your vest. A hook, simply put, is the nugget on which an article, an interview or an appearance can hang. Hooks should be custom-built for the media you're courting. Oddly, sometimes your hook will be about some interesting facet of your personality, your hobbies, your vocation, your background or your heritage and not about your book.

Sometimes you can slant a story about a time of the year (Mother's Day, Christmas, the World Series), a news event, your relationship with your wife. "You gotta have a gimmick," says Debbie Galant, cofounder of Baristanet, a highly trafficked local news website dedicated to Montclair, New Jersey. "Any local angle that ties into your book is great." For example, before Christina Baker Kline became a *New York Times* bestselling novelist, she had to figure out how to promote her book, *Bird in Hand.* She approached Debbie with a great hook: "Her novel revolves around a car accident at an intersection. So she connected her book to the fact that the town had just put up a bunch of four-way stop signs. It was a weirdly great fit."

> The first places you want to hook into are long-lead magazines, i.e., ones that are published monthly or less frequently. These magazines plan their issues six months ahead of their publication dates. So if you want to get an article in such a magazine near your pub date, you need to pitch early and often. Cast your net wider as you get closer to publication date—weeklies, dailies and websites.

The media business is like a two-headed snake that feeds on itself. A hook that grabs the interest of a popular local blogger may then beget a feature on the local news, which may then beget a feature on a national TV show. That's why you should always be looking for trends, both macro and micro, that relate to your book. Scour the news sources: *The New York Times,* NPR, The Huffington Post, *The Wall Street Journal,* all the way down to your neighborhood newsletter, and so on. Keep track of what's being said and written about your subject so you have specific ammunition for your pitch. Then pull out your running list of journalists and bloggers who are reporting

How the Making of a Cover Made a Movie

When Phyllis Theroux finished her memoir, *The Journal Keeper,* she turned her search for the perfect cover into an opportunity: She would make a video book trailer and a book cover simultaneously.

Her initial concept was an organic outgrowth of her writing experience. "I thought about the wingback chair I wrote the book in," says Phyllis. There was her cover image, Phyllis thought—but where should it be shot? In search of the perfect setting, she decided to load the chair onto the back of a truck and go for a ride.

"I called my videographer/website person, Kathy Abbott, who has big ideas—she was a documentary maker for NBC." Kathy told Phyllis that the epic cover quest could be a story in and of itself. "She said this had YouTube written all over it," explains Phyllis. "I was aware from the beginning that the whole publishing scene has changed, that you have to work like a dog to help your publisher—and I want to try as best I can to keep up with the groovy dazzlers—so I said I was game."

Phyllis first took the chair to a nearby farm, then to the railroad tracks in the middle of town and finally to the front lawn of a friend's yard, which became the scene of her cover. In the video you follow Phyllis from spot to spot as she talks about the chair's journey. Since Phyllis's book is a memoir in the form of a journal, it connects the viewer to the book by engaging us in the simple yet deep, funny, powerful, down-to-earth style she uses in the book. We come away feeling like we got to go along for a ride with this very wise, lovely person.

Kathy and Phyllis's collaboration is a great example of how the writing and/or publishing process can provide a wealth of audience-enlarging material.

on subjects similar to yours. Spin your story in such a way that it's an inspired editorial fit for the publication you're pitching. For example, if your book is about Mae West, you might spin an article to the politically minded site Daily Beast about West and censorship, since it would relate to current attempts to censor Internet content. For fashion-centric *Vogue* magazine, you might pitch Mae West as a fashion trendsetter whose effect is felt to this day. For advice-obsessed *Cosmo,* you might talk about how Mae West can spice up your sex life.

If you're pitching journalists and producers directly because you read or saw something that they wrote or produced, let them know what you liked about it, then show them how your book is appropriate for them as well.

You never know when your idea will fit in with someone's upcoming issue. Just be sure to let your publicist and/or publisher know what you're up to. They may want to use these hooks themselves! (Also, they won't be happy if you and/

or your outside publicist are simultaneously pitching the same places they are, so keep those lines of communication open.)

Galley Action

You won't have copies of your book in hand until just before publication. If you're very lucky, you will receive copies of your finished (but uncorrected) book, known as galleys, shortly after you receive your page proofs. These are what your publicist sends out. Galleys look like a book and are, as a result, much easier for people to read than a series of unbound pages or thousands of words on a computer screen. If your publisher isn't printing galleys, your publicist will likely be using bound copies of the page proofs.

Nowadays, your galleys are more likely to be electronic than paper. But if your publisher does print bound galleys or page proofs, get as many as you can! Often, in the case of galleys, your publisher will give you as few as five—they're very expensive to produce, even more expensive than your book itself. But if you ask early enough, you can probably get more.

Look at your media wish list and the hooks you've just developed. Who are the people and places you most want to have an early look at your book? Think bloggers or long-lead journalists (those who work at monthly magazines). You'll

Movie Deal as Mega-Hook

My book is being made into a movie. In our experience, few things make people's eyes light up faster than hearing these words. Even the rumor of a Hollywood deal can create enormous buzz. And the boost in sales if your book actually ends up on the screen can be life-altering. As Pulitzer Prize winner Jeffrey Eugenides said (with his tongue firmly planted in his cheek), "For me, the key to getting on the bestseller list was first to have my book turned into a movie by a member of the Coppola family, then to get a bunch of pretty good reviews. That's it."

Should you be lucky enough to have your book optioned and then made into a movie or TV series, use each step of the often very long process to spin stories and pitches, to get some public love for your book. Cinematic flirtation and rumor, the contract terms being agreed upon, the script being written, the director and actors being hired, the cameras rolling, the grand opening, the release of the DVD—every one of these events is a potential buzz-builder. And since the chance of an optioned book becoming a TV show ranks right up there with getting into Harvard, there's all the more reason to capitalize on any Tinseltown action you do get.

also want to use these for all endorsers you haven't yet approached. If there are booksellers or prominent loudmouths you know well, you will want to get an early copy of your book into their hands, too, since these people are great at creating buzz.

If your book has movie/TV potential, galleys or bound pages can be a terrific way to court Hollywood before your book has actually come out. You will also need them if you've retained the foreign rights to your book. This way, you can get them to foreign publishers for an early look.

▶ Are you one of the lucky few who actually sold the first serial rights to your book? First serial deals are almost always exclusive, meaning they preclude other publications or websites from featuring excerpts from your book up to (and possibly through the first month of) publication. Make sure you're not allowing anyone to excerpt your book until after this period of exclusivity is over.

Be sure to include a personalized letter with each galley (electronic or paper), along with a press kit. If you were referred by someone, put that person's name in the first line. If you're sending a galley to a journalist who wrote an article on a subject that relates to your book, get this info right up front. Again, the more you know about the people you're approaching, and the more *they* know about why they're being approached, the better. And, it bears repeating, be sure that you coordinate with your publicist so that you're not muddying the waters by duplicating work.

Free Content as Buzz-Builder

You might be aware that Charles Dickens's novels started out as serialized newspaper pieces. Serialization or excerpting has been a common practice throughout modern publishing. And it has been a wonderful way for people to get a taste of a new book. As author Kevin Smokler says, "To let a book, an author, into your life, is very intimate. The book has a very high barrier of entry. A movie you can watch in 90 minutes, an album you can listen to in half an hour, a painting you can look at for five minutes. A book is asking someone to invest a big chunk of his life. Particularly in this day and age, when time is so scarce, I believe it's important to tread carefully when asking for people's time. If you offer me a small piece of great content, like the free cube of cheese at the supermarket, you have a much better chance of getting me to nibble. And if I like it, I may even buy it."

With the death of so many magazines and newspapers, the number of print publications who could possibly excerpt your book have plummeted. But bloggers and websites are hungry for content that's appropriate for their readers. As a result, the excerpting of books has had a new and powerful e-resurgence. "Almost any book and author can be syndicated online," says web marketing expert Fauzia Burke. "We have found that nonfiction titles offer a stronger response for content syndication than fiction. If an author has a strong presence in a particular community, then any good content will work well. Editors want content that is self-contained, can stand alone and is not a flat-out promotion of the book. Many editors will not run articles that promote a book too heavily; the book will be mentioned alongside the article in most cases."

Contests, Giveaways and Preorders

Contests and giveaways are great ways to generate excitement. Are you a nutritionist who's written a book on the importance of dark chocolate? Hold a contest for people's best chocolate stories. The winner receives $100 worth of the healthiest dark stuff on the market. Are you a musicologist who has written a novel about the world of Beethoven? Post a quiz on the most interesting Beethoven facts. Everyone who gets all answers right will be entered into a pool from which you'll pick one random winner. That person will receive a Nano filled with your favorite Beethoven recordings. Are you writing a book about how to get published? Ask your followers to send in pitches of 100 words or less. The best pitch will receive a half-hour consultation from you.

Ramit Sethi, master blogger and author of *I Will Teach You to Be Rich,* came up with yet another way of enticing his audience to buy his book. First, he told his followers as soon as he got a book deal. "I kept them up-to-date about my progress and kept them involved by asking for feedback," explains Ramit. Then he rounded up 300-plus members of his community to receive an exclusive six-week personal finance program (including a weekly podcast)—all in exchange for preordering the book on Amazon. These preorders helped launch the book to the #1 spot on Amazon on its publication date, which in turn helped *I Will Teach You to Be Rich* become a *New York Times* bestseller!

Preorders are becoming more and more important. They can help a book get noticed by its publisher, who may see a fat preorder and change their mind about a book's salability— and about the paltry first printing they had planned. Same principle applies to the publisher's publicity and marketing budgets. If you're planning on using sophisticated marketing techniques to drive presales, concentrate your efforts. One day a month, starting three months before publication, see if you can get 50 to 100 people to preorder from a single online retailer. These numbers are enough to grab a publisher's attention, and the concentrated bumps will be more impressive than an overall trickle.

Unlike days of yore, when a publication would pay you for the right to reprint an excerpt of your work, now you usually have to give it away for free. But that's okay. Online content can reach more people (or more people closely tied to your exact demographic) more quickly and for a lot longer (because information online is usually archived, not chucked in the trash when the next issue comes out). Which means that excerpting your book online can quickly build buzz and, if done correctly, keep the buzz buzzing.

Go back to your media wish list and your online community to decide who to approach about excerpts. The key here is to offer ready-to-use excerpts that can be plopped right onto a site on or after publication. Pay close attention to what kind of content each site features and tailor your excerpt (and your pitch for this excerpt) precisely. Most sites prefer excerpts of 700 to 1,000 words in length, unless you're offering up, say, an entire chapter from your novel. Just be careful, as you slice and dice up your book, that you're not offering overlapping pieces to competing sites. Each excerpt should be unique and suit a site that represents a different chunk of your audience. For example, if you're a 60-year-old female author of a memoir about being raised in an Indian American community, you'll want to offer one excerpt of your book to the leading site for Indian American issues. Another excerpt to a leading women's site. Another to a site for baby boomers. And on and on.

You can also offer excerpts or "Look Inside" privileges to heavily trafficked sites like Scribd, Google Books, Amazon and Barnes & Noble. "Just be sure to have a holistic plan," counsels Andrea Fleck-Nisbet, director of digital sales and marketing at Workman Publishing. "Post a free, specially selected chapter to a targeted group. Send out an email blast to the group you've targeted to let them know when you're posting and when your free offer is ending. If you're offering your book for free in a vacuum without letting anyone know, no one will find it."

Getting Bloggers to Review Your Book

"Getting a printed review for a book is like trying to catch a falling knife—one in a million," says Debbie Stier, author of *The Perfect Score Project* and former director of digital marketing for HarperCollins. For decades, reviews were viewed by writers and publishers as the best way to spread the word about a book without spending a dime. However, magazines and newspapers keep shrinking and shriveling. Fortunately, readers are now turning to their favorite bloggers, websites and online communities to find new and interesting books and authors. Or they're getting virtual recommendations from their friends and colleagues. And, again, this kind of buzz is targeted and it lives forever. Bestselling author Seth Godin went so far as to exclude pitches to traditional media for his last book, *Linchpin*. Instead, he went straight to bloggers and other online denizens—the population whom he calls "the short head of the new long tail: the group of professional and semipro writers and journalists who are increasing in influence daily."

From four months out to a day before pub date, call on all those bloggers you've befriended or admire for review attention. Sarah Burningham of Little Bird Publicity shared with us her step-by-step guide to getting bloggers to review your book. Here goes:

- Only approach blogs that you know inside and out. Be sure that the blog is a good fit for your book. You may love and subscribe to a baking blog, but that doesn't mean it's going to review your memoir of horse racing.

- Email the blogger, address him/her by name and say, in one paragraph or less, why your book is a fit for the blog. Short and sweet! Include a link to your site and more info on your book.

- No matter what, do not send a form letter. And don't mass email or bcc. Would you want to be blind-copied as part of a mass email? Neither does a blogger.

- Be nice. This goes a long way with anyone, including bloggers. Treat them the way you would any journalist or reporter who is considering your book.

- Ask for the blogger's feedback. Then listen to that feedback. Even if you think you're the next James Joyce, not everyone will feel the same way, and that's okay. You have to have thick skin to be an author.

- If a blogger doesn't respond, wait a week to 10 days before emailing again. Don't just resend the same pitch. Write a new email and mention that you sent something back on whatever date.

- But . . . waiting and sending a follow-up email does not open the door for going back again and again. NO STALKING! In the same way that form letters are annoying, stalking is another hint that you can't be taken seriously. If a blogger is interested, he or she will get back to you after you've made two thoughtful attempts at contact. If you haven't heard back, the blogger is probably just not that into you.

- When a blogger does get back to you, get a review copy of your book in the mail, stat. Ask if he or she would prefer a hard copy or an electronic file.

Don't make anyone wait. Send it off or hit the post office that day and let the blogger know the book is on its way.

■ When the review goes up, thank the blogger. Send the link out to your readers by posting it on your website, on Twitter, on Facebook. Share the love and get that blog some traffic!

■ And finally, now that you have a good relationship with the blogger, keep it that way. NEVER add a blogger (or anyone else, frankly) to your mailing list without their permission—not even your mother.

One last thing: Give all the folks with a cyber voice the chance to speak about your book in any way they like—even negatively. As Oscar Wilde said, "The only thing worse than being talked about is not being talked about." If someone does dole out some snark in your direction, don't get snarky back. Either let it go or use it as an opportunity to show your humor and good will. "One of our authors received a bad review from a blogger," says Harlequin's Malle Vallik. "After stiffening her upper lip, the author wrote a very funny Top 10 list of what it was like to read the review and posted it to the blogger's site. This won her a lot of brownie points!" And possibly some readers.

▶ In setting up your tour, don't forget about libraries, which often host wonderful author events and series. Sally Reed, director of Friends of Libraries, USA, says, "Try to set up events with libraries in whatever city you go to. Call up each library's program office. If they don't have one, ask for the local Friends of Libraries group." Then, try to get a local bookseller to sell your books at these events.

To Tour or Not to Tour

If you're not shy, and you're excited about getting out on the road to promote your book, great. But unless you are a former president of the United States, it's in your best interest to assume that your publisher will not give you one dollar, euro or peso to help. They may have initially told you that they were going to send you out on a tour, but the next time you brought it up, had no memory whatsoever of their sweet-breathed promises. The question you must now face is: Does it make sense, as well as cents, for you to front the cost (and time) to take your book on tour? A tour requires hard work and expertise. Money and time, energy and effort, and almost certainly frustration. At its best, a book tour will give local media an angle to spin a story around. But will you be able to get local media to pay attention to your event? Will you really sell books by doing events? How will you get people to show up? What if no one does?

Before you make a decision, consider this: You may get a real sense of completion when you stand up in front of an audience and read your work aloud. When you go on a bookstore tour, you also get a great education about yourself, your audience, your book and the entire process of writing and publishing. It's a fantastic feeling to see your book on display. To be introduced to people who are actually interested in your book. To read your words out loud, to sign your books and to engage with those who are actually selling your book.

But if you're going to take the plunge and do it, do it right. You don't want to show up for your big event only to find an empty house and a bookseller who has no idea that there's an event on the schedule. Trust us, we've been there!

> Are big things happening with your book? When lightning strikes, take advantage of the excitement to ask for monetary help. When one of David's books appeared on the cover of the *New York Times Book Review,* he asked his publisher to help defray the costs of the tour he had set up and that he'd planned to pay for on his own. They didn't cover the entire budget, but they did offer a nice chunk of change.

Setting Up Your Own Events

If you choose to organize your own tour, it's best to start in a place where you have a built-in audience, like your hometown, or where you have connections to the media. For the most part, if you select random places where you have no support or no chance of getting media attention *before* your event, very few people will show up. And a couple of sparsely attended events can deflate even the healthiest ego, not to mention take a chunk out of your wallet.

Once you decide on your cities and towns, it's time to pick your venues. If you plan on doing events in bookstores (and we highly recommend that you do, if bookstores are where your audience hangs out), try to get a feel for the different stores before you call. Look them up on the web. Check out their event calendars. Do they host authors who've written books that are similar or complementary to yours? Are they known for hosting successful events? Get suggestions for stores from your publisher, your agent and, most importantly, your audience.

The Book Tour of a Lifetime

I t took Rebecca Skloot 10 years to complete *The Immortal Life of Henrietta Lacks*. After all that hard work, Rebecca fantasized about driving across the country in a hand-painted bus. Her publisher, though very supportive of her book, thought that a tour wouldn't be dollars well spent. They were more interested in building up Rebecca's already strong social networks. Rebecca's agent agreed, so Rebecca was left with only one option: to create a tour on her own. And she did—with the help of her brain-damaged father. Sound crazy impossible? No! Rebecca's tour was a bona fide success. "I don't believe *all* tours are dead," says Rebecca. "Just the old-fashioned kind, where publishers organize events and writers simply show up hoping for a room full of people. I agree that social networking and online campaigns are the most important tools in book publicity. But I don't see book tours and the online world as separate entities. Rather than replacing tours, I believe the new virtual world of book publicity can help keep them alive."

To set up bookstore events, contact event coordinators three to six months in advance (the more popular the store, the longer the lead time). This will give you and the stores plenty of time to promote the event. Be sure to have your pitch down cold so that you can tell the person on the phone in under a minute who you are, what your book is and why she should have you in her store. If you can put together a mailing list of friends, family and colleagues in the area, let her know. Tom Campbell, co-owner of Regulator Books in Durham, North Carolina, says, "If you have a mailing list with 50 names on it, and you tell us lots of them will come to an event, that's great. It's hard to just blindly put out publicity about an unknown book and expect people to show up. If we know an author will bring in people, there's a very good chance we'll book them."

Create a variation of your press release that is specific to your book events. Have it ready to email as a follow-up or as an introduction if you aren't able to get through on the phone. Be sure to include any information about why your event will sell books. Will a local book group be attending? Are you bringing in a musical act with a following? Do you have connections to the local media? All these efforts will make your case much stronger. Jennifer Ramos, director of promotions at Vroman's in Pasadena, California, puts it this way: "If the author can convince me he's going to be very active in promoting, getting press, getting people to come to the event, that really helps." Putting on events actually costs bookstores money. So if they don't sell a requisite number of copies (anywhere

Rebecca set about using her social networks to promote her book events, events that took place not just in bookstores, but also at universities that would pay for her expenses. In no time, she had a 14-city, all-expenses-paid tour set up through first-, second-, and third-hand social networking. And before she knew it, The Immortal Life of Henrietta Lacks jumped onto the New York Times bestseller list.

It should come as no surprise that a tremendous amount of work was involved: "I didn't have a sense of how big it would become," says Rebecca. "I'm not a professional event organizer. And neither were most of the people who helped me organize my talks in each location, because my tour was so grassroots. So we didn't think of some really basic things. For example, when I arrived at a university, I would realize I had no idea where to park. But overall, these problems were really minor." No, Rebecca didn't get to drive her Partridge family bus—but her dream of traveling America certainly came true!

between 15 and 40, depending on the size of the store and how much promoting/ marketing they do), it's not worth it for them.

Be sure to check with your publisher before you set up any events. They'll need time to get your books to the location—at least a couple of weeks and often more. Plus, there are very strict but unwritten rules about how many venues you can do in one city, as well as how to set up events with the chains. Trust us, if you do two identical events for the same book within the same month in the same city, there's a very, very good chance that you'll wind up with two very unhappy bookstores. Once you've got your ducks in a row, ask your publisher if they can help out with media or chip in a night at a hotel.

YOUR BOOK'S LIKE MY BOOK: THE MULTI-AUTHOR EVENT

Through your research and networking, you've probably already amassed a list of authors who have written books complementary to yours. And hopefully you have read these books, are signed up for these author's blogs and are e-friends with some of them. If you approach an author as a fan and now colleague about teaming up for an event, you could end up with not only an advocate but a real friend as well.

"We don't allow author readings because so many times they are dull. Instead we do panels," says Clay Smith, program director of the San Antonio Book Festival, one of the biggest and best book festivals in the United States. It's not only that panels and other multi-author events tend to be more exciting than readings (and kinder to those who aren't natural performers). They also:

- Allow you to rub elbows with more well-known authors and raise your own profile as a result.

- Mean bigger crowds, because each author brings her own peeps.

- Attract more media love, especially when the panel is dealing with newsworthy or current issues.

- Endear booksellers, because panels tend to sell more books overall.

So start reaching out, brainstorming panel themes and making your multi-author event an Event.

Writers' Conferences, Book Festivals and Fairs

As part of your tour or your ongoing event schedule, contact the organizers of any and all appropriate public events—conferences, festivals and fairs—where writers and readers gather. If you can get yourself on a good panel and things go reasonably well, you will certainly sell some books. And you don't have to generate the crowd yourself. All you have to do is show up, do your job, be your fabulous self and sell tons of books.

If you're writing about a particular religion, ethnicity or sexual orientation, there will be seminars, art festivals and book fairs where you'll find your exact readers discussing, mingling and/or partying. For example, if your book is of Jewish interest, there are well-regarded Jewish book festivals that run between the High Holidays and Hanukkah. They draw large crowds of avid booksellers and buyers, and they're a great place to get some face time with your audience.

Conferences, festivals and fairs are wonderful opportunities to meet writers from all over the country. And again, it's important to meet other writers, famous, infamous or unknown, so you can add them to your bookish community and watch them closely, observing what they do well and what they don't. As the San Antonio Book Festival's Clay Smith says, "At a good book festival, new writers can see how it should be done. A lot of writers are so isolated, and I think it's very important for unpublished authors especially to see how readers interact with writers around their books. And you just never know who you're going to meet."

Most book festivals group authors together for events under a particular topic. So don't be insulted—or complain—if you don't get a solo event. In fact, you're far more likely to draw a crowd if you're alongside other, hopefully more famous authors.

Workshops, Seminars and Keynotes

Whether you have been doing workshops, seminars and keynote addresses for years or are hoping to use your book as an entrée into the world of speaking and teaching, you want to try to schedule a flurry of events during the first three months following the launch of your book. You can start up to a year beforehand. Many venues book a minimum of six months ahead, so figure out ahead of time where you can speak and when.

As a general rule, try not to schedule events that fall before your book is for sale. Most people have short attention spans—they want to buy on the spot, and if your book's not there, it's out of sight, out of mind. If, however, you're offered a fabulous opportunity that'll only come once and can't be booked after your publication, go for it. Just be sure to hand out postcards and gather addresses so you can let the attendees know when your book drops. (Or better yet, try to get people to preorder on the spot.)

Again, be sure to coordinate with your publisher. As you accumulate new events, send an updated list. And ask your publicist/publisher to tap their media contacts and to pitch stories and interviews surrounding your speaking schedule. For these precious first few months, it is perfectly reasonable to ask— and to push, if necessary—for this kind of help.

> ▶ Wanna be the best panelist you can be? Heed this advice: *Listen* to the other panelists and the moderator. There's nothing worse than an author who's clearly sitting there like a spider, waiting for a chance to read from his new novel or tell some long, prepackaged story. Panels are only interesting when they're spontaneous. The best panelists come with an open mind.

Doing Events in Small Towns and Cities

If there's one place your publisher is sure NOT to book an event, it's in Smallsville, USA. In fact, publisher tours are defined by how many "cities" they include, and these cities tend to be both large and geographically consistent. For example, you'll rarely find yourself in the Deep South. And large swaths of the Midwest are nonexistent to most publishers as well. But Smallsville may be home to your target audience. As Britton Trice, of Garden District Bookshop in New Orleans says of nontraditional tour spots: "If there is *any* connection to a place—whether it's in the context of the book, personal connections in a city or a contact with someone in the local media, then these should be used to generate interest in an author's book or an event."

David and the Y

W hen David's second memoir came out, he decided to put on an event called The Art of the Memoir, consisting of a panel of two to four memoirists. He spent the months prior to his publication finding appropriate panelists and setting up events around the country. The first one, at a bookstore in our neighborhood, was packed, and David knew he was onto something. Out on the road, he perfected the event with numerous and varied authors. And all this time, David had his sights on one of the meccas of book events in New York City: the 92nd Street Y, whose event catalog is a veritable *Who's Who* of publishing.

Everyone said it couldn't be done, but David wasn't deterred. He decided to contact Phillip Lopate, a friend of a friend, and an extraordinary memoirist/professor of writing at Columbia University. Phillip agreed to be on the panel. Next David contacted Kathryn Harrison, a bestselling memoirist and fiction writer. She, too, fit the Y's elite writer profile. David found Kathryn's website and simply sent her an email asking if she'd be interested in appearing on such a panel. He told her that Phillip was already signed on. She agreed.

Next, David went to the event coordinator at the Y. He told her about his very successful previous events and how he already had both Phillip Lopate and Kathryn Harrison signed on. The event coordinator was intrigued. She said she'd get back to David, and she did. Not only did they want to do the event, but they had asked David Carr, whose memoir had just hit the *New York Times* bestseller list, to join *and* invited Leonard Lopate (Phillip's brother and a celebrated radio host for New York City's NPR affiliate) to moderate.

The event sold out. And David has 92nd Street Y bragging rights in perpetuity!

The thing is, Smallsville often knows how to pack 'em in. In big cities, you're competing against multiplex movie theaters, five-star restaurants, pyrotechnic musical acts, the symphony, poetry slams, nightclubs and the opera. It's hard to get noticed if you're not a famous person. It's difficult just to get word out that you're having an event. But in small towns there's a chance that you're IT. Better to get 50 people in Smallsville than a drunken yahoo and some lunatic with too much time on his hands in Big City, America. The drunken yahoo and the lunatic probably won't even buy books. "Most of the publicity and marketing people in publishing look at a potential spot on an author's tour only from the perspective of the media there. But you've got to have more than a talking head to get people to a bookstore, and more importantly to buy and read the book," says John Evans, owner of Jackson, Mississippi's Lemuria Books, a beloved hotspot for that community and for many authors nationwide. "By working with a store on an individual level, you develop a relationship with them. And a book comes to life because people talk about it and care about it. Not because someone is hustling it."

Events in Crazy Places

Please, we beg you, don't limit your events to bookstores. Keith and Kent Zimmerman, coauthors with Ralph "Sonny" Barger of *Ridin' High, Livin' Free: Hell-Raising Motorcycle Stories,* know just what we're talking about. "Signings need to be directed toward your audience, and that might not be via a conventional bookstore. For us, it's a Harley-Davidson dealership, a giant motorcycle rally, a cross-country road trip/signing campaign."

If you have a cookbook, consider having an event at a bakery or a restaurant where your book could sell long after you're gone. If your book is about birds, maybe you could do a bird walk benefit for your local Audubon Society in some gorgeous spot. If your book is about childbirth, you might do an event at a local Lamaze clinic. If you have a book about dogs, host a doggy beauty show at a local park.

Martha Manning, author of *Undercurrents,* a memoir about clinical depression, spoke at numerous gatherings of local mental health associations. Larry Dossey, author of *Healing Words,* a book about the healing power of prayer, speaks both in churches and at medical schools. Kirk Read, author of *How I Learned to Snap,* a memoir about growing up gay in the South, did a monthly reading series at a gay men's health clinic. Jamie Byng, publisher of Canongate in the U.K., was bringing out *Loaded* by Robert Sabbag, a book about drug smugglers. Jamie thought it would be wild to bring several notorious ex-smugglers together and tour them in nightclubs and cool, happening venues. Thus was born the Smugglers' Tour. Their talk of high times and fast living was mediated by the author. Needless to say, the tour was a huge success and made *Loaded* a bestseller in the U.K.

If you have a book that's hard to make an event out of, you can do what we did. Look for a hole in the market—something people want and/or need—and make up an event around it that's tangentially connected to your book. Then do it wherever anyone will have you. Who knows where it may lead you. For us, it led straight to writing this book!

Living Room and Virtual Tours

Are you reluctant to appear in public, or convinced your book wouldn't draw big enough audiences? Strapped for travel dollars? Then consider a living room or virtual tour.

The Power of the Small Town

Paulina Springs Book Company in Sisters, Oregon (population 911 at the time), was the only store of the dozens we contacted that had any interest in doing an event on our book *Satchel Sez*. We'd been told that books about baseball don't draw crowds, so we just assumed that Paulina Springs didn't know any better. We got to Sisters at 4:40 on a Saturday for our 5:00 event, and apart from Kate Cerino, the owner of the bookstore, none of the Sisterites were there. Our expectations, already low, plummeted as we spied the 30-some empty seats sadly facing the lonely microphone. We walked out to find a place to get a cup of tea, and as we strolled around Sisters, we noticed that no one was around—anywhere. It was like a *Twilight Zone* episode. We began to wonder if we were about to be abducted by author-starved aliens.

Well, imagine our surprise when we returned at 5:00 to find Paulina Springs Book Company packed with 50 of the town's 911 occupants. Our jaws hit the floor. Those melancholy chairs were now brimming with Sisters' readers, all waiting for us to say something insightful and witty. We scanned the crowd, and it suddenly hit us that there were only two people under the age of 60. Exactly our target audience—old enough to remember Satch. Afterwards, the crowd asked great questions, and many of them shared their own stories. It was America at its best, oral history flying all around us. Near the end, the oldest man in the room, who looked 90 going on 120, raised his hand. In a voice weathered with age but still going gangbusters, he told us that he had been a batboy for Satchel Paige when he was 15 years old. He stole the whole show in about 20 seconds.

We signed book after book, with some people buying two or three. It was our most successful event on that tour, monetarily and emotionally. Obviously, Kate Cerino knew exactly what she was doing. Later on, we asked her for her thoughts on why the event worked so well:

A living room tour means taking the backyard model on the road. You call on friends and family around the country to host events to which they invite other friends and family. You're guaranteed a captive audience. You almost always get a free place to stay. And you're surrounded by people who want to see you succeed. What could be better?

Stephen Elliott, author of the literary memoir *The Adderall Diaries,* had ruled out a tour for his book: "The thought of going to all those bookstores and doing events where hardly anybody shows up, then staying in some sterile hotel, just sounded depressing." But when the idea of a living room tour surfaced, Stephen got excited. As he strategized about how to make it work, he came up with two stipulations: 1) Whoever was hosting the event had to guarantee that

US: Why did you buck conventional wisdom and bring in an event revolving around a deceased, fairly obscure historical figure?

KC: Someone in the store heard David being interviewed by Scott Simon on National Public Radio and thought it would make a good event.

US: The subject of the book was an African American. How many African Americans live in Sisters?

KC: Probably under five. But I don't really think about it like that. We try to do great events; the people who come know it's going to be interesting. Like all independent bookstores that have managed to survive, we have loyal customers and they support us.

US: Your event was the most successful on our tour. And there are only 911 people in the whole town! How is that possible?

KC: Well, that's a little deceiving. There are about 10,000 people who live in and around Sisters. But I think Paulina Springs Book Company is in many ways an intellectual center. Besides, Sisters is a very special town with a lot of smart, interesting people.

US: Do you think publishers sometimes underestimate small-town bookstores' ability to sell books and stage successful events?

KC: Most definitely! We have a very hard time getting publishers to send their authors here. We just hope they realize that independent bookstores in smaller towns can put on great events and sell lots of books. We really make sure to get the word out so people know who's coming.

20 people would show up. The people didn't have to buy books, they just had to show up. 2) The hosts had to agree to let him sleep on their couches. Stephen emailed 400 people from his in-person and virtual community. "It could never have happened if I didn't have those people," Stephen says. "That community made it possible. These people had all become friends. Each event was a party and so much more intimate than a bookstore reading because it was in someone's living room, with all their friends." There were two other great advantages to Stephen's living room tour: "The problem with doing events in bookstores is that a lot of times people don't buy books. I sold lots more books in people's living rooms that I ever did in bookstores. And I unearthed an untapped audience—hardly any of these people have ever been to an event at a bookstore."

Speaking Agents

O ne of the fastest ways to build a platform is to speak in front of large groups. (It's also a way to make some money.) But tracking down the contacts you need to get yourself speaking gigs is a grueling grind that takes particular expertise. The expertise of a speaking agent. The bad news is, many speaking agents want you to be *already* speaking to large groups of people, with a published book in hand, before they'll take you on. With the right package, however, including a top-quality press kit, photos and videos, and a list of past and future speaking events you've set up on your own, you can at the very least whet a speaking agent's appetite, if not get one to bite. And once you've interested someone, you can keep following up as your profile grows.

Virtual tours are cost-free, have the potential to attract people from all over the world, and, of course, don't require you to leave your house.

Putting the Fannies in the Seats

Many authors who haven't read our book assume that just because they have an event in a bookstore, flocks of wild readers will show up. This is not true. Even at the biggest and best bookstores, with newsletters that go out to thousands, you can wind up with an empty house. Sharon Kelly Roth of Books & Company in Dayton, Ohio, says, "I don't think authors understand how much work goes on in putting together an event. With the high price of books these days and the enormous effort it takes to put on events, it's even more crucial for writers to make sure lots of readers attend their events." Guess who's ultimately responsible for putting the fannies in the seats? You, the poor slob who wrote the book! Even if you're on a publisher-sponsored book tour. Think you can just lie back and watch your readers stroll on in? Wrong again!

The first thing to do in your epic struggle to get people to show up is to pick the brain of the bookseller or event coordinator where you're presenting. (Provided there is one, and that he'll let you.) Work with him to come up with a list of concrete things you can do. Let him know you'll do whatever it takes to get people there the day of your event.

Among the things to ask are:

- What successful events have other authors done?
- What media should I contact?
- Will you be sending information to calendar listings? If not, can you suggest some for me to approach?

- Will you write and send out a press release or flyer?
- Do you know any organizations I should include in my mailing?

To attract media attention, pull out those old hooks and start fishing. Make an event press release or flyer, and use it to saturate the local media. Websites and online communities locally and nationally. Journalists and bloggers. TV and radio producers and hosts. Calendar listings online and in daily and weekly papers. Everything. Everybody. Everywhere. Start about a month before your event to let them know you're coming. Send out another press release 10 days to a couple of weeks later. Then a final notice three days before your event. Present your information in the form each media outlet requests. It's very difficult, but if you can, and it's appropriate, get them on the phone and pitch your little heart out.

"It's My Party!"

Many authors count their book parties among their all-time favorite events. A book party can be a great way to begin your tour. This is where you announce your book to the world, celebrate yourself as a writer and thank all those who've helped. It can cost a lot and have little value in terms of book sales, but the right party at the right time can raise your profile (and be a blast).

For the most part, publishers no longer pay for book parties. Not even the invitations. Certainly, let your publisher know about your party and ask if they'll contribute, but don't count on it. So throw your own book party only if:

- You're independently wealthy.
- There's a chance of luring the press with a newsworthy cause.
- You have a fun theme around which you can construct a party on the cheap.
- You can get a company or organization to sponsor the party.
- You can tie it into a charity event.
- You can turn your party into a "must" event.
- You can get a local or national celebrity to be the host.
- You just want to celebrate.

Jack Boulware, author of *San Francisco Bizarro,* co-creator of the San Francisco literary festival Litquake and veteran book-party thrower, says, "If you make your book party more of an event, it stands a better chance of getting press attention. Get a press release out with plenty of advance time. And an image that can be printed in papers and magazines." We also recommend inviting a local bookseller to sell books. And if you can, get a band, a musician or a DJ.

375

A Rogues' Gallery

R emember those wacky, interesting, fun, sexy or unusual pics we encouraged you to take along with your regular author photos? Well, use them when you send your event info to the calendar sections of local newspapers and weeklies. An outstanding, compelling, jump-off-the-page picture can make all the difference between a prominent feature and a visit to the slag heap of wasted opportunity.

Regina Louise, author of the memoir *Somebody's Someone* about growing up in the foster care system, timed the opening of her nonprofit organization to coincide with the release of her book and hosted a gala event for 400 people. Local dignitaries, clients of the salon she runs, friends, admirers and social butterflies were invited. So were a dozen young women who were currently in the foster care system. During the event, Regina asked these young women to come up on the stage. One by one, they talked about their dreams in life. There wasn't a dry eye in the house.

Regina then read from her book and showed her documentary. She raised a bunch of money for her charity while everyone had a ton of fun and ate great food (much of which was donated). She also sold all 250 of the books her local bookseller brought to the event. You can be sure that bookseller became an instant fan and mouthpiece for Regina and her book.

Preparing for Your First Interview

Y ou've got your first interview. Your book hasn't even come out yet, and you're nervous because this is the FIRST ONE. How do you tackle your jumpy stomach? What do you do if your brain freezes? What if someone attacks you? How do you get your agenda across while appearing to answer the questions you're being asked? What if your fear of being exposed as an inarticulate buffoon leads to you acting like an inarticulate buffoon?

First and foremost, there are three things you can do immediately to make sure you're at your best:

1. Rehearse,
2. Rehearse, and
3. Rehearse.

Almost everyone is going to ask you: "So what is your book about?" You must have a pithy, fascinating answer that lasts under a minute. Sound familiar? If it doesn't, start popping the ginkgo biloba. This is, of course, YOUR PITCH! It will be the backbone of your media presentation.

So take your pitch, then write and rewrite and practice and repractice. Don't just do it by yourself into the mirror. Do it for friends. Do it for relatives. No matter how comfortable you are in private, the natural instinct when you're on the spot is to freeze up and squirm. And the first step toward overcoming that instinct is to have the pitch for your book down so cold you can do it in your sleep. Which will help when you have to do a radio interview at 4:15 in the morning.

Reread your book. Funny how, after all that time away from it, you can forget a lot of what you wrote. Once you've refreshed your memory, come up with several additional stories from your book. Add interesting anecdotes about the writing process. These are all weapons in your entertainment arsenal, and you will need them. Again, rehearse until it's all second nature.

Have a clear agenda. Focus on what's funny, interesting, unique and special about your book. Entice without giving away the whole story. Slip in your title, but do NOT force it; you don't want to come across as tacky and self-serving. If you have any events lined up, try to slip them in casually as well.

Study the interviewer beforehand if you can. If your publicist has lined up the event, find out what the show or journalist is like. Do your research. If you can, read or watch their work, find out what kind of stuff they like or dislike.

Wade in the Shallow Water
Before You Dive into the Deep End

When you're first starting out, it's a great idea to appear on or in smaller shows, publications or websites. It gives you a chance to practice. Watch or listen to yourself afterwards, preferably with a friend/colleague. Critique where you could've been better, and where you knocked one out of the park.

When we first started touring, we'd never been interviewed together. Fortunately, our first live television appearance was on a morning show in the small city of Bend, Oregon. It was a tiny operation. The cameraman/soundman/production assistant was a high school student. It was in the wee small hours of the morning, and we got the feeling that very few people in the greater Bend area were actually watching. Which made it much less stressful. And easy for us to be ourselves. We had a grand time, and it was fantastic practice for when we did bigger markets later on. Plus it gave us a nice piece of footage we could use to generate more appearances.

10 Essential Rules
for Being a Good Interviewee

1. Maintain good posture.

2. Don't play with/pick at your sleeve, hair, face, fingers.

3. Make eye contact.

4. Breathe deeply.

5. Have lots of energy without being manic.

6. Don't force a smile.

7. Don't panic if something goes wrong. Try to play with it.

8. Keep your sense of humor.

9. Listen carefully.

10. Have fun.

Then, on the day of, be sure to listen to the segments that precede yours. A great way to get an easy laugh, through what professionals refer to as a "callback," is to make a comic reference to something that has already transpired. Portland radio journalist Daria O'Neill says, "If it's a TV or radio show and you've seen or heard some of it prior to your appearance, absolutely bring up the content of an earlier moment if it can be tied in at all. This will a) endear you instantly to the hosts/listeners/most avid viewers, and b) make you seem like a necessary segment of a greater whole."

Start getting in the zone well before your interview is scheduled to start. Stretch your body out. If you know any yoga, do some; if you don't, learn some. Do some deep breathing. Go over your pitch and your stories once again. Picture yourself having a great time. Being funny, relaxed, totally in control.

If you're doing a live interview, bring a glass of water with you. For dry mouth, of course. But also to give you a moment to compose yourself if you need it.

Most people think being interviewed is all about talking. They're wrong. Being a good listener is as important as being a good talker. Be present. The best interviews almost always have some wonderful improvisation in them. Being in the moment makes it possible to react spontaneously to anything that comes your way. And it's so much easier to be relaxed and spontaneous if you're well prepared with material you know like the back of your hand.

No matter how much you've prepared for being interviewed, you cannot possibly be completely prepared. Yes, of course, control what you can control, look good, be well-spoken, have a pitch you love, some stories you're confident in and an agenda that makes sense. But once it starts, be open to the fun that presents itself. Don't freak out if something goes wrong or you make a mistake. Sometimes the most human, endearing moments come from snafus, dropped balls and brutal mistakes. Laugh at yourself and show you don't take the whole thing too seriously. A little good-natured self-deprecation goes a long way.

One more word: *passion*. Whether it's new-media fueled or old-school driven, we keep hearing that word over and over and over again. *Passion*. Hopefully that's what has been fueling your book the whole time, and that's what will make you a good interview. Your passion, in the end, is what will sell your book and make you an interesting, captivating speaker.

Diana Jordan, whose show *Between the Lines* airs on the AP Radio Network, puts it this way: "Of course you have to be able to say what your book is about. You have to nail it. But I want to have an animated dialogue with someone who's relaxed and confident, who knows his topic inside and out. People like that don't just know the basics; they know the nuances, and they have a great breadth and depth of knowledge. But, most of all, I'm looking for passion. I want them to communicate their passion. The driest of subjects can come to life that way." Leonard Lopate adds, "Great guests tell great stories. They engage in lively, fun conversation. They don't give 'yes' and 'no' answers, or answers that lead to a dead end. They don't go off on five-minute rants. They give you answers that lead to other questions."

> ▶ When you're rehearsing for your interviews, have a friend or colleague do things to trip you up. Ask you the questions you fear most. Misquote facts. Throw Styrofoam balls at you. If you can survive that, you're ready.

An interview is quite a juggling act. You want to make sure your message is delivered, while simultaneously leaving your hosts satisfied by fulfilling the obligation of the show/magazine/website. And as in every discipline, you want to make it look easy. The more you practice, and the more you do it, the better you'll be.

Building Buzz

In a sense, everything you've been doing from the time your book was accepted has been to generate and maintain buzz. But what is buzz? Where is it? And how do you get some of it?

Buzz is ethereal. It flits about, coming and going with seemingly random whimsy. If you could bottle it, you'd be a kazillionaire. Some people can create it. Sometimes it appears to have a mind of its own.

Just one word at the right time from the right person at the right place can create huge buzz. Buzz can be sparked by a celebrity, a member of the literati or the aristocracy, the right reviewer or blogger, or that big-mouthed friend from nursery school you just found online. We all know that an appearance on *Fresh Air* or the *Today* show can make a whole career. But most of us don't hit these jackpots. And so we have to keep putting ourselves out there.

> "The difference is slight, to the influence of an author, whether he is read by five hundred readers or by five hundred thousand; if he can select the five hundred, he reaches the five hundred thousand."
>
> —*Henry Adams*

Because buzz is so much like the wind, there is no one way to create it. And you never know which of the things you're doing will be the tipping point that launches your book. Maybe it's the book fair you attended, maybe it's friending an old college roommate who happens to work for *USA Today* or reaching out to your favorite blogger at the hot new website.

But one common denominator we've noticed is that buzz seems to follow people who are willing and able to stand out from the crowd, think outside the book box, take a few calculated risks.

Since you never quite know whence the buzz will come, cultivate it constantly. Those who wait for buzz to find them often wait forever. Every once in a while, you get lucky with some free buzz, but most of the time you have to earn it.

Often we humans wait until a bandwagon is already moving before we jump on board. If you do get buzz from a raving review, an enthusiastic endorsement, a boffo blurb or really any interest WHATSOEVER in your book, jump on it and run with it until the cows come home and you've milked them for all they're worth.

CHAPTER 13

Launching Your Book and Keeping It Alive

"No one interested in being published in our time can afford to be so naïve as to believe a book will make it merely because it's good."

—*Richard Curtis*

YOUR BOOK HAS COME KICKING and screaming into the world, and it's time to enjoy the kudos and, more importantly, the envy of your peers. All your inspiration, perspiration and determination have finally paid off. Time to kick back and party. Right? WRONG! Now you have to get people to actually BUY your book.

In an ideal world, you want the perfect buzz storm you've been generating to peak on your pub date. Remember Rebecca Skloot? That's just what happened to her. All her incredibly hard work paid off and she landed on a *Publishers Weekly* cover, on *Fresh Air* with Terry Gross, on *The Colbert Report* and CBS *Sunday Morning,* among others, just before, on and just after publication. The result? A *New York Times* bestseller. Yes, Rebecca's one in a million. But everyone can and should work to get buzz on and just after publication.

The sad fact is, your book is considered new for just the first three months of its life. After that, it's old. In a year or two, unless you do something to prevent it, your book can die an early death. At least the paper version, anyway. So you have to pack everything you can into those first three months. And we mean EVERYTHING. If you STILL haven't gotten on the cyber bandwagon, here's the last thing we're going to say to you: Hello? Anybody home???

▶ Many publishers are now selling books directly to customers. If this is the case with your book, you may be able to work out a promotion strategy. Readers get, say, 20% off any orders placed on the publisher's site during the first day or week of publication. Discounts are great incentives to get people to buy a book pronto.

Creating the buzz necessary to successfully bring your book into the limelight is a bit like juggling 14 balls of various weights. Some balls might not come down for a very long time, some you'll be catching and tossing every day. So you'll need to be pretty organized and aware of what you need to focus on and when—which balls need immediate attention and which can float around for a while.

Seem overwhelming? Of course it is. But like every part of the process, buzz juggling can be broken down into a series of small, daily, doable tasks. And it's amazing what a cocktail of caffeine, adrenaline and desire can do!

Throughout this book, we've endeavored to lay things out chronologically. In this chapter, that's impossible. Many of these tasks come at you too fast; often they arrive all at once. But we've got to start somewhere: the day your book goes on sale.

Your Pub Date

The intelligent use of social media can make it possible for authors to accumulate massive preorders and have them all tabulated as part of the first week of sales—regardless of when, prior to publication, they were placed. As we mentioned in the last chapter, preorders can get your publisher and major booksellers excited about your book. But when these preorders kick in all at once—on that first day your book goes on sale—they can mean the difference between success and oblivion. Because bestseller lists are based on weekly sales, as opposed to cumulative sales, some authors have been able to use prepublication sales to launch themselves onto bestseller lists. And when you land on bestseller lists or in Amazon's Top 100, bookstores start ordering more books. And most importantly, readers become interested as well. Reader interest leads to actual sales, which is what you're after.

Pub Date Mania

R emember Ramit Sethi, author of *I Will Teach You to Be Rich*? This master of marketing had it all going on the day his book hit the shelves. His pub date marketing efforts included:

■ An extensive email campaign to his blog readers

■ A special blog post that he'd been building up to for some time

■ Several detailed guest posts on other sites

■ Twitter exposure

And the pièce de résistance:

■ A live eight-hour webcast during which he answered questions ALL DAY. "I forgot to order lunch," Ramit recalls, "but luckily somebody sent me a pizza! And my publisher sent me champagne when they saw how we sold out at Amazon in just a few hours."

Preorders or no preorders, you'll certainly want to take action on your pub date. Send a blast out to your mailing list directing people to your website, asking them to tell everyone they know about the publication of your book, encouraging them to write reviews on Amazon, the Barnes & Noble website, Facebook, Twitter or wherever their fellow readers may congregate. This is not a time to be selective. Lori Culwell, novelist and social media expert, says, "Every once in a while, it's okay to send an email to your entire list of friends, family and everyone you have ever known. The day your book is published is that time."

Coordinate with your publisher to see if your book can be featured on their site on its birthday. Can you guest-blog on their site? Also contact bookstores' and fellow bloggers' sites. Interviews on pub date are great, as is anything that will help drive traffic to your site and to online and brick-and-mortar bookstores.

Reviewing Reviews

A s newspaper and magazine space has shrunk so precipitously, and as fewer and fewer book

▶ If you, your friends and/or fans post a bunch of ridiculously stupendous reviews of your book, and they're all posted in the same kind of language, possibly around the same time, it will be painfully obvious to anyone with any online experience that the reviews are not authentic. Not only can these kinds of hijinks get you in trouble with the sites on which you're posting, they also make your cred plummet rather than making you and your book or posts shine.

The Goods on Goodreads

G oodreads has become a major player in launching books into the world. The website is a place where you can set up a profile page that features you and your book(s). It also allows you to friend other writers, readers and reviewers; list, review and recommend your favorite books; and enter into discussions about everything from dystopian political satire to euphemisms that do and don't work for romance writers. Goodreads also allows you to give away copies of your book to get people reading and talking about it—a tool that has gotten the buzz ball rolling for many writers.

How can you best utilize the site to make your book a success? We turned to two Goodreads aficionados to break down this behemoth. One of our favorite publishing gurus, Jane Friedman, cofounder of *Scratch* magazine and professor of digital publishing and media at the University of Virginia, has two primary pieces of advice when it comes to Goodreads:

1. *Reviews are essential.* No surprise there, right? Reviews help readers discover your book. The more people who review your book, the more visible it will be. Goodreads reviews also appear on sites like Powell's and Google Books. They help readers take a chance on an unknown book. Books with just five written reviews are added almost six times more, on average, to a user's "to read" shelf than those with no reviews.

2. *Giveaways are a powerful promotional tool.* Give away as many copies as possible. This goes straight back to the first point. The more books you give away, the greater your chances of getting reviews because more than half of giveaway winners review the books they win.

Eva Lesko Natiello is a professional publicist and the author of *The Memory Box*, a suspense novel that she self-published to great success due, in part, to how she utilized Goodreads. Here's her top 10 list of her Goodreads Must-Dos.

1. Set up an author profile page and make it robust: photo, bio, favorite books, videos and so on.

reviews are appearing in these outlets, you just can't count on traditional reviews in this day and age. What you can count on, and to some extent have some control over, are reviews by readers on sites such as Goodreads, Indie Reader and Amazon. Reviews on these sites can help not just launch your book, but also keep it chugging along months after publication.

On your book's pub date, ask friends and family to post reviews to help you build the buzz about your book. Just make sure every single review isn't five stars or people will start to get suspicious. The more reviews, the more

2. Link your blog/website to your author profile page so that every new post you write also appears there.

3. List upcoming events so readers can find you: readings, book signings, presentations and so on.

4. In the Settings tab, turn on "Ask the Author." This feature allows readers to ask you questions about your book(s) or the writing process.

5. *Answer* those questions! This is a perfect opportunity to engage with your readers.

6. List a Goodreads book giveaway. Read other giveaway book descriptions to get a sense of how to write yours. Autographed books get more entries. Start your description with a great review or award your book has won. Goodreads allows you to use many tags for your giveaway. Browse the tags (there are 1,000!) and use all the ones that apply to your book.

7. Make your giveaway approximately two weeks long. This way, your book is featured on the "recently listed" and "ending soon" lists, which means lots of visibility in a crowded field. Every reader who enters the giveaway automatically adds your book to their "to read" shelf! Do this several times a year.

8. Write a personal note to the winner when you ship the book, thanking her for her interest and asking for a review.

9. Join a book group or two to talk about books other than your own.

10. Create a short quiz (Goodreads has its own quiz section) about your book and link it to your book and author profile page. Readers love quizzes! This is another great way to create some buzz and engagement.

likely your book is to get attention by people who aren't your friends and family. Obviously, you want strangers—lots and lots of strangers—posting reviews as well. Once they do, thank your readers for taking the time to do so. If it is a good review, say what you liked about the review. If it is a bad review, do *not* get defensive. We try to write something like "We're so sorry our book disappointed you. Can you tell us a little more about why the chapter Launching Your Book and Keeping It Alive annoyed you so much? We'd like to improve it in the next edition and any comments would be greatly appreciated." We've had lots of people actually change their negative reviews to positive ones after receiving such a reply. Most importantly, you are engaging directly with your audience. This is not only fun to do, but exciting for your readers who don't expect and aren't used to hearing directly from the authors of books they have read.

Giving Away Books
(Yes, That's Right, *Giving* Them Away)

E veryone loves freebies. That's why giving away your book is an excellent way to get people excited about it.

If you have a publisher, we're assuming your contract finagled you as many free books for publicity and marketing purposes as possible (see page 205). Now's the time to use them. While you want your publisher to send your book and publicity package to many, many people, sometimes it helps if the book comes directly from you. The following people should be the first to get hot-off-the-press copies along with personal notes: bloggers and online columnists; blurbers and tweeters; newspaper, magazine, radio and TV journalists; booksellers and libraries; and favorite loudmouths who have helped get your book ball rolling. But also send copies to the most important people you've already contacted but who have not yet responded.

> ▶ Writing a book, getting it published and then having to buy it back to give it away can cause a slightly woozy feeling. And because most people are unaware that authors have to buy their own books, you can depend on friends, family and strangers asking for a free copy of the printed book. But don't worry, it's okay to say no.

One of the most difficult things for any writer, especially when you're starting out, is simply getting people to read your book. Yes, of course you want all manner of media paying attention to you, but the quest for readers is another good reason to consider giving books away. A printed book has a special power to entice, but an ebook is free to produce and much easier to get into people's hands. Dangle free ebooks like carrots for a limited time and you may entice thousands or even hundreds of thousands to actually buy your printed book. Sites like Scribd, Google Books and Amazon are excellent platforms for free books, but there are many others as well. Do an email blast to accompany all free offers of your book and try to get your e-friends talking up your offer. You want to be sure people know about your generosity so that your free book doesn't end up in an electronic black hole. In addition to creating buzz and helping with word of mouth, free books help to generate reader reviews on all of the aforementioned sites. And reader reviews are absolutely key to drawing in new buyers.

Remember Chris Anderson, editor in chief of *Wired* magazine? Appropriately, he gave away digital copies of his entire book, *Free*, shortly after publication for a limited time all over the world. And he chose to keep his audiobook free forever. Chris says, "*Free* was read more than 500,000 times over the five weeks it was available. The point was to let people sample the book in full; if they liked it, we hoped that some would buy the hardcover to keep or at least spread the word." Of course, this tactic begs the question: Why would anyone buy a book that's available for free? Well, they did. The hardcover edition of *Free* became a *New York Times* bestseller—while it was downloadable for nary a penny. As marketing guru Seth Godin says, "The reason to write a book is to spread ideas. If your ideas spread, you can do so many things. That's why you need to find as many ways to give as many copies of your book away as you can afford."

Connecting with Your Readers

A uthor. That's what you are now. An author with readers. Hooray! But be aware that with this change in status will also come a change in expectation. People will expect you to be friendly, interesting, witty, intelligent, informative or whatever qualities your book promises, and if you can convince them that you are, they will be that much more likely to buy your book. We'll leave the character building to you, but as for the medium, one thing is clear: Social networking is the best one-stop shop for reaching out to your fans, making new ones and proving that you are all these adjectives at once. As Malle Vallik, director of digital content and social media at Harlequin Books, says, "The thing about social marketing—particularly with fiction—is that people fall in love with authors and want to enter their worlds. Blogs and tweets allow readers to feel like they're in their favorite authors' worlds and are actually friends with them."

Social networking is also the best way to keep people informed about your book and your journey as an author, from great reviews (or terrible ones—these can be real sympathy builders!), to where you're appearing and when, to heated conversations on the topic of your book. Rebecca Skloot, author of *The Immortal Life of Henrietta Lacks,* found that despite having garnered megamedia hits like

Fresh Air and *The Colbert Report,* along with an appearance on the *New York Times* bestseller list, most of her events were packed due to word of mouth—passed on via the stroke of a thousand keyboards. Which is wonderful news for any author who won't have the luck of the media draw that Rebecca had.

Crossing Over

Once you've established your social networking platform(s) and start hearing from your readers, you will get a new and more clearly defined sense of your audience. Yes, if you've written a book for toddlers, your core audience will be parents. A book on menopause will be for women primarily in their fifties and sixties. The definitive tome on tree frogs will attract tree frog aficionados. These groups of readers will be the first wave of the storm that you hope to build as your book arrives on shelves. These are the people you'll want to give the most love to. But knowing and loving the tree frog aficionados as you do, wouldn't it be great to find out that your book also appealed to readers beyond your core? If it does, you're experiencing what we call "crossing over." For example, maybe your children's book, *Mr. Poopy Pants* is extremely popular with high school students. Your book on Barbie may sell like hotcakes in Boys Town. Your tree frog book may fascinate fans of Mark Twain's "The Celebrated Jumping Frog of Calaveras County." Tamim Ansary, author of *West of Kabul, East of New York,* discovered that his memoir was being picked as freshman reading by a large number of colleges and universities. "Most of these institutions brought me in as a speaker," says Tamim. "Which gave me, for five or six years anyway, a lecturing career." What a wonderful and wallet-expanding example of finding an audience you didn't expect!

If you refine your knowledge of your audience, refine your publicity and marketing plan. If you pick up on niche audiences, try to access them through the virtual media that speaks to them. Pitch niche publications. You may even discover special sales opportunities.

There's No Place Like Home

In this ever-shrinking world, the word "local" has taken on a whole new meaning. Yes, you can reach anyone, anywhere in the world, but that doesn't mean you should neglect your own backyard. Cuz if you can't find love there, it's going to be hard to find it anywhere. We asked Mitchell Kaplan, past president of the American Booksellers Association and owner of Miami's Books & Books, about the commonalities of successful authors. His response? "They make the book a bestseller in the town they live in first." Making your hometown the epicenter of your efforts and aftershocks will sometimes result in sales at bookstores hither and yon.

Your local bookstore should be the first stop on your list. By now, you should be tight with your neighborhood bookseller. So pick the fruits of your labors. Ask about doing a reading. Make it known that you'd love to speak at local book clubs, conferences or events. Ask about any local critic or reviewer you can send a book to; any journalist who might do a story about your book; a radio show that might have you on; or of other bookstores that might be interested in hosting you.

Many bookstores now have blogs. If your local bookseller does, ask if you can guest-post on a semiregular basis. Pitch the local angle—remember, you're a local author!

Once you've gotten jiggy with it at your local bookstore, take a tour of the neighborhood. Take your book with you to the grocery store, to your favorite restaurant, to baseball games. Show it off. Go back to those mail carriers, barbers and barkeeps. Local authors, social gadflies, event organizers, gossipmongers. These are all great sources of local buzz.

Bookstore Love

Tome in hand, it's time to get booksellers outside your hometown jazzed about your book as well. And don't just talk to the managers. Try to talk to everyone in the store at one time or another, from the events people to the people staffing the cash registers. Show them all in your charming, humble yet persuasive way that you're going to help them sell a lot of copies of your wonderful book.

Anytime you go someplace, whether it's for publicizing your book, attending your Uncle Rodolfo's wedding or beaming in for the annual Star Trek convention, make time to visit local bookstores. As many as you can. Introduce yourself. Sign stock (insider lingo for "copies"). Some writers we know have packed their cars with books and traveled across the country, introducing themselves in person to booksellers from coast to coast. Including us. Of course, it doesn't work every time, but we've actually had many, many booksellers order our books right there on the spot when we went in and presented ourselves and our book politely.

▶ While most booksellers are delighted to meet authors, a few curmudgeonly sorts won't want to give you the time of day. Odd as it seems, they may treat you like a hungry mosquito on a muggy afternoon. Just remember, in the words of Don Corleone: It's always business, never personal.

Grass Roots at Work

After David did his first Art of the Memoir event at our local Watchung Booksellers, the owner, Margot Sage-El, suggested he contact her friend Rob Dougherty, manager of The Clinton Bookshop. The Clinton Bookshop was about 40 minutes away, just far enough to have a completely different demographic. David mentioned Margot's name, and Rob immediately became receptive to David's pitch. Within 30 seconds, an event was set up. Rob helped David put together a fabulous panel and packed the place. The cherry on top: Out of this event, David got a unique paid gig as the featured reader accompanying a prestigious local classical choir—something he'd never done before and will probably never get to do again!

Use bookstores nicely and make it easy for them to use you. Thank everyone. Being a friendly, helpful, sweet professional can mean the difference between one lonely copy of your book and a prominently displayed stack that gets reordered whether you're there or not. From buried in the bowels of the website to a nice juicy spot on the front page.

The Power of Independents

While we absolutely advocate pursuing bookstore chains, it's imperative that you get independent bookstores excited about selling your book. This is something you *can* do on your own, without the help of a publisher. At many independent stores, employees are encouraged to write little reviews of books they're enthusiastic about and make picks of their favorite new releases. Which means that individual opinion (and, by proxy, connections with individual booksellers) can lead to a quantifiable result: prominent placement.

In fact, a number of years ago, independent booksellers got together and created Indiebound, an organization that solicits recommendations from independent booksellers all around the country. Indiebound's "Indie's Next List" picks of the month are front and center in hundreds of participating bookstores. And one of the best ways to get your book on this list is to ask your independent booksellers (or to have your friends and colleagues ask), wherever you travel, to send in a recommendation for your book. The more recommendations you can get, the better your chances of landing on the list.

Stock Tip: Signing Books

When you walk into a bookstore, wait for a lull, then introduce yourself to the staff *as the author of your book* and ask if they have any copies for you to sign.

John Evans, co-owner of Diesel Bookstore in Oakland, California, advises, "Authors will come in and say things like 'Do you have such-and-such book?' But it's *their* book. Better to be straightforward."

It's so gratifying when your name comes up in a computer, your book magically appears in front of you and you get to sign copies of it. We urge you not to deprive yourself of this thrill. It helps to have your book and a postcard in hand when you go around to bookstores. This makes it easy for booksellers to look up your book. If you don't have a handout/postcard, or your handout/postcard doesn't list any blurbs or reviews, print these separately to distribute. If a bookstore doesn't have your book, a card can help you seduce them into buying it.

While you're in a store, make sure that the number of books on the shelves jibes with the number of books in the store's computer. Bookstores will not reorder your book if they think they already have copies on hand. And while you're at the computer, see if there's a way to ask if they'd be willing to order more copies of your book. Here's what Bob Nelson, author of *1501 Ways to Reward Employees*, did: "In three out of four stores of a particular chain, an employee would say, 'Well, the computer says we have four copies. Let's go see if we can find them.' They wouldn't be on the shelf. The clerk would say, 'Let me go check in back.' And after 20 minutes he'd return with two copies. When you've gotten the same thing from 43 outposts of this chain, you know something's wrong. I'd say something like 'If all your books are ordered centrally, and your computer says you have books in stock but they aren't actually on the shelf for someone to purchase, it seems to me you will never reorder this book!'" Because Bob went out and asked, his book went from two or three copies in 60 of these stores to three to five copies in 140 stores—and on automatic reorder when the number of copies dropped below five. Bob would then focus his attention on another bookstore chain or on the independent bookstores.

If the store doesn't have your book and the clerk you're talking to isn't the person who orders books, you may need to take a step up the ladder. (If you do this right, you can turn what seems like a setback into an opportunity.) But sometimes just showing

> When you sign books, you get to meet store employees, your book gets a little sticker that says "autographed copy," and the value of your book rises. That little sticker draws people's attention. There's a good chance the booksellers will display your signed books in some nice spot. And last but not least, booksellers will be less likely to return your books. A win-win-win situation.

up and making polite conversation will result in a book order. We know authors who've walked into independents and chains looking for their book, been told there were no copies in the store and had clerks take it upon themselves to order some on the spot. The authors didn't even have to ask. It's cool walking out of a bookstore knowing that copies of your book are already winging their way toward your readers—for more on selling your book to bookstores, see Chapter 14.

Bookstore Real Estate: Placement in Stores and Online

You know those big display windows that stare at you as you walk into a bookstore? The ones full of blockbuster bestsellers and the bestsellers of tomorrow? Or those books that beckon to you from front display tables? Or by the sides of cash registers? Or on the homepage or category page of your favorite online bookseller? Often they're in these center-stage positions because a publisher paid for them to be there. This is an example of *co-op marketing*, a joint venture by publisher and bookseller to promote your book.

This whole co-op marketing business begins with the bookseller. "Your book has to be wanted by a bookseller before a publisher even has the chance to pay for a promotion," explains James Wehrle, director of sales for national accounts at Workman Publishing. It's a big decision for both parties. Because booksellers make so little on each book, they don't want to give up valuable space to what turns out to be a dud. Michael Powell, founder of Powell's Books in Portland, Oregon, says the average net profit is between 0% and 2% per book. And often there are losses. This is why booksellers have to be sure that the books they accept co-op dollars on are going to fly off the shelves.

A bookstore and publisher might decide to maximize these co-op dollars by keying them to a holiday or other theme (pets, politics, back-to-school) or perhaps to your upcoming event in the store. Your publisher sweetens the bookstore's pot by helping to defray the cost of calendar listings, mailings, press releases or signage.

This special treatment not only improves your location in the bookstore, but also increases the number of copies the store will order. And the more copies the bookstore orders, the harder it tries to sell them.

Let's imagine there are 100,000 books in a bookstore. In all likelihood, 90,000 are single copies displayed with only skinny spines showing. Of the remaining 10,000, 7,000 are written by Dan Brown or James Patterson. Okay, not exactly. Point is, multiple copies of a small number of bestselling titles make up those 10,000 books. Of these, let's say 5,000 are placed face out in the stacks. Of the remaining 5,000, maybe 4,965 are on display tables. Of the remaining 35, let's say 25 are near cash registers and 10 are in the window. That's .0001%. So you can see why competition is so dog-eat-dog for this space. Let's face it, many a book buyer has walked into many a bookstore just to "browse" and walked out with some cool-looking book whose cry of "Buy me!" from the window or a display table couldn't be resisted. You want that book to be yours.

Here's the sad truth. It's unlikely that your book will be getting any of that sweet co-op money. Still, there are a number of ways to get out of the slums and onto the Rodeo Drive of bookstores. First off, don't just assume that your publisher will never give you co-op money if it wasn't forthcoming at the time of publication. Come up with hooks to convince your publisher that these dollars are worth spending. Remember how we talked about bookstores loving tie-ins to holidays, anniversaries of events, special months (Black History Month, National Poetry Month, Children's Awareness Month)? Find out what bookstores are promoting on their windows and tables. Notify your publisher of any possible tie-ins to your book and see if you can go along for the ride.

Secondly, whenever you sign books, ask the bookseller if your book can be placed in a more prominent position. This is obviously more of a grassroots approach, but one that has potential to yield results over time.

You can also call bookstores around the country and dazzle them with your amazing pitch or hook. If you get a nibble with your hook, follow up with an email or fax of a tailored press release. Give them the information they need to determine that your book is display-worthy. While you're at it, suggest an event if it seems at all doable.

> Don't go into a bookstore and move your book to a more prominent location without asking first. No one will be able to find it if it's not on the shelf where it's supposed to be. And if someone asks for it, the bookseller will look it up on the computer, see that it's in stock and fail to reorder it. So, in the end, no one will be able to find or buy your book and the bookstore will never order it again! However, you *can* rearrange copies (or the one copy, as the case may sadly be) of your book so that your cover is facing out.

Making an Eventful Event

You've already put in all the work in setting up your events, getting written up by pertinent and powerful bloggers, scoring prime listings in real and virtual event sections, inviting the media to cover you and contacting friends, relatives and other interested parties. If all goes as planned, you'll show up at your event and the throngs will be waiting with open arms. You'll be witty, smart, articulate and thoughtful, and you'll get a standing ovation and sell boxes of books. You'll get invited to speak at other events all over the country. A movie producer who just happens to be in the audience will option your book and make a boffo film.

Okay, the chances of all this happening aren't huge. However, if you do the necessary work to get the word out, if you prepare an event that perfectly suits you and your book, if you show up on time and smell good, you can make any number of these things happen. *Timoleon Vieta Come Home* author Dan Rhodes, named a Best Young British Novelist in 2003 by Granta, met his wife at one of his readings!

What to Do, What to Read at Your Event

Author escort Crofton Diack of Portland, Oregon, told us, "I get authors who show up at events and ask me, 'What should I read?' And in my head I'm always thinking, 'Are you kidding? Kinda late for that question, isn't it?'" Preparation is key. You should be thinking of your event as a show. As Melissa Mytinger, events coordinator at The Booksmith in San Francisco, says, "In this day and age, people expect authors to be entertainers. That's an unfair expectation. If you don't feel entirely comfortable in front of an audience, forgo bookstore readings and talks. It's okay!" But if you're up for it, embrace your inner entertainer. Even if your presentation is about something as serious as death and taxes, or as dry as the history of the Gobi desert, more people will come (and, more importantly, buy books) if your event is entertaining.

"How many readings can you go to and hear the same lament: 'I am deep and I am in pain. It is raining outside.'"

—*Greg Gatenby*

Your show should be tailored to what you do, who you are, what your book is, where you're performing and what you're comfortable with. Melissa adds, "The best presenters are people who enjoy what they're doing. Lots of authors don't, and it really shows." Melissa also recommends our favorite activity, research: "Talk to other writers or experts who have toured and pick their brains about what to do and what not to do. You should also do a little research about the store you're doing an event at. Just take 10 minutes and look at their website, see what kinds of events they've done in the past, get a feel for the place."

You may not be a professional comedian, a master storyteller or a highly trained entertainer. But if you display your expertise, joie de vivre and passion, people will leave your event feeling excited about you and your book. Remember, passion is contagious. Your goal is to make sure everyone at your events catches yours.

LOOKING, FEELING AND SMELLING GOOD

People are often confused about what to wear to an event. There are no fashion "shoulds" here. It's more important to feel comfortable in your favorite outfit than to go out and buy something that makes you feel as if you're not in your own skin. David often wears one of his vintage sports jerseys, even when he's promoting a book that has nothing to do with sports. Not only does he feel most comfortable in these, but they're great conversation starters as well.

Just as you need to feel comfortable when you walk into the room, so it helps to create a feeling of comfort around you as you do your event. Do you prefer to sit or stand? Do you prefer a cup of green tea to water? Are you more comfortable mingling and talking before the show or going off on your own and gathering your thoughts?

Susan Wooldridge, author of *poemcrazy*, has these words of advice about events and appearances: "Make sure you've got the right shoes. You want to feel spiffy. You also want to get there a bit early and create a little of your own atmosphere. I sometimes bring my own lamp or flowers. Something to create a setting. And I try to sit quietly and ground myself beforehand."

Have your hair nicely coiffed. Don't wear clothes that are so tight they make you feel uncomfortable. Again, avoid nervous fidgets, tugs, picks and pulls. Yes, check your zippers and/or buttons. Give yourself a once-over, twice. Bring a fashion-friendly friend to check you out. Or, if the vibe is right, ask the host to give you a final inspection. If done with charm, this can be very endearing.

KEEP IT SHORT

Unless you're doing a workshop or you're the greatest reader ever, 15 minutes is the perfect amount of reading time. Leave them wanting more. Your whole event, including Q&A (more on that in a moment), should last approximately half an hour—even if it seems like everything is going well and people are loving it. After a certain point, people drift away and then they don't buy books. You can always hang around afterward and chat if you want.

THE IMPORTANCE OF STALLING

Whatever you do, DO NOT start on time. First of all, a certain percentage of people show up late. Second, it gives the audience time to bond in their admiration and respect for you. Third, it's just gauche to start on time. That's why they call it *fashionably* late.

The general rule of thumb is that one should start an event not less than 5 and not more than 10 minutes after the announced starting time. Sometimes a store employee will want to start right on time. Ask nicely, without being a pain, if you can wait a couple of minutes—you're just sure some friends are going to show up.

MANAGE YOUR INTRODUCTION

Have someone introduce you. Make sure she tells the audience that you'll be signing books after the event. Also make sure the same person comes on afterwards and thanks everyone and reminds them that you'll be signing books.

Some people at bookstores go to great lengths to write introductions for writers. Some do not. Here's a generic introduction you can customize and present to your introducer if she is unprepared:

"(Insert your name) has been a (put in relevant work information here) for many years and has written (insert your writing credits if you have any). This is his/her first/second/whatever book. (Title of book) has been called (short, pithy quote from a review or endorsement). She/he has also (insert any additional interesting information here—awards, colorful jobs, etc.). There will be a brief question-and-answer period, and the author will sign books afterward. And now, ladies and gentlemen, please welcome (your name)."

START WITH A STORY

Connect with your audience by beginning your event with a story, an anecdote or a joke. Your story could be about how you came to write your book and get it published. About the subject of your book. Or about something completely different. But it must be entertaining, funny, inspirational, witty, honest, revealing or deep.

You should have a couple of these stories prepared, written and practiced. Write them out longhand on index cards; this will help you remember each word. Also, you can take the index cards with you during your performance. Even if you don't need them, they're a wonderful binky.

In addition to being prepared, be open to the spontaneous anecdote. What happened to you on the way to the event. What you read in the paper that day. Something that's occurring in the moment. Melissa Mytinger says, "Make speaking extemporaneously your goal. Yes, it's a skill, but it's one that can be learned and developed, and it will make your event so much better if you can do it well. This is certainly no substitute for writing a great book, but writers can work hard at and improve their public-speaking skills."

It's important during your event, as indeed it is in life, to be in the moment, aware of your surroundings and in tune with any comedy and/or tragedy that's happening while you're speaking. We once witnessed writer/comic/actor Kevin Meaney ("Uncle Buck") at an event. Observing that a man had fallen asleep in the audience, he quietly placed the microphone under the man's schnoz, and the sounds of the guy sawing logs echoed through the room. The whole place cracked up. No, it had nothing to do with what he was talking about, but Kevin made lots of fans that night.

Have some fun. It will loosen everyone—you, included—right up.

LEAVE 'EM GUESSING

You want to give your audience the real flavor of your book, without giving too much away. Many savvy authors like to read up to a climactic scene and stop just before the climax. If your audience wants to know what happens, they have to buy the book. You should probably read a little from the beginning of your book, unless there's some compelling reason not to. This will give people a context. Then read a couple of self-contained passages that do not need much setting up. Do not tell the whole story of your book. Better to think of it as reading a couple of short stories.

Try to memorize as much of your presentation as you can. Then, when you go up and have the book with you, you'll be able to make periodic eye contact with the audience.

Take your time. Pick out places within your chosen passages where you can pause and look out at the audience. Vary your rhythm and tempo. Find places to go fast and places to go slow. Places to be loud and places to be soft.

Bruce Lane, former director of the South Carolina Book Festival, adds: "This may seem obvious, but more writers than not sound bored and emotionless when they read, as if they've done it a million times or just never got past that singsong 'reading in front of your high school English class' method. So it's exhilarating to hear writers read their own works with a joy and excitement that almost makes you feel they're hearing their own words for the very first time."

Do not ignore the importance of a Big Finish. You want to go out with a bang. Something that's tragic, or hysterical, or lyrical. It should be you at your best.

But again, DO NOT give away the ending of your book.

▶ Always bring a copy of your book with you to any event. We were at the L.A. Book Fair when suddenly a crazed publicist came by, screaming, "Does anyone have a copy of Oliver Sacks's new book? He's reading in five minutes and he lost his copy!" And there was the bestselling author of *Awakenings,* following the bellowing publicist and looking very much like a man who mistook his wife for a hat. They finally found a copy, but they actually had to buy it!

THE QUESTION & ANSWER PERIOD

One of the biggest problems with the Q&A portion of the reading is that it's hard to get started. Often, people feel shy about asking questions. Nobody wants to be first. But usually, once you get the ball rolling, people will ask interesting questions; and if done right, the Q&A can be the highlight of the event. The give-and-take between audience and author can be provocative and exciting.

To avoid an awkward silence after you ask, "Does anyone have any questions?" prepare a couple of options. Now might be a good time to talk about your blogs or online presence. It's also fun to ask questions of yourself. Raise your hand and say something like "I have a question. Is this book based on something from your real life?" "Why, thank you, that's an excellent question." And then whip out your clever, witty, charming answer. Again, adding a laugh will loosen everyone up.

Jen Reynolds, former director of publisher relations and events at Joseph-Beth in Cincinnati and current sales rep for Publishers Group West, has another great suggestion for starting off a Q&A: "Ask the audience what they'd like to hear

Outside-the-Box Eventing

Don't be afraid to step outside the box and do something totally unexpected. But make it reflect the nature of your book. Beth Lisick, author of *Everybody into the Pool,* does many of her readings with a live band behind her—a perfect complement to her hip stories about pop culture. Jamie Oliver, a.k.a. The Naked Chef, cooks fabulous dishes from recipes in his cookbooks at his "readings." Gayle Brandeis, author of *Fruitflesh: Seeds of Inspiration for Women Who Write,* created events that perfectly reflected the content of her guide to writing: "Because *Fruitflesh* is very much about tapping into the body, the senses, as a source of creativity, I offered hands-on experiences, sensory meditations with fruit, at the beginning of my readings. I thought that engaging the audience's senses would help draw them into the heart of the book more quickly. People seemed to appreciate that."

about." If silence reigns after this question, you can again make some suggestions yourself: Would you like to hear about the inspiration for this book? What the research was like? How long it took to write? How my parents feel about the book? Am I available? Sharon Kelly Roth, director of public relations at Books & Company in Dayton, Ohio, adds: "Many people in the audience are aspiring authors looking to get published. It's therefore important to talk about the process or journey of writing. How did you write your book? How did you get published? People are hungry for this knowledge." Peppering your Q&A with these bits of info will keep it spicy.

Whatever you do, don't let the Q&A go on too long. Nothing takes the steam out of an event like a Q&A that drones on and on. And one of the most difficult moments in an author's life is watching potential readers walk out the door before buying a book.

CUTTING OFF THE LONG-WINDED

Some people are so enchanted by the sound of their own voice that they'll use any excuse to harangue the world. And often, once they get started, they just will not stop. One of them may show up at your event and start a filibuster during the Q&A session. Cut him off and shut him down without alienating him or anyone else. This is just as hard as it seems. If a person talks for more than a minute and hasn't come to a question yet, ask him if he can phrase his comment as a question. Or break in as if you're wicked excited about responding to the "question" and segue into your next talking point. If that doesn't work, politely tell him you have to move on but you'll be happy to answer any question he may have after the event.

This may seem harsh, but we've seen sad lonely loudmouths put huge crimps in wonderful events. And your audience will appreciate and respect your ability to set limits.

HAVE A PLAN B

Anything can go wrong at any time. That's why you need to have a Plan B. And probably a Plan C. Let's say your book is about an adult subject and a bunch of kids are in the audience. Or there's a room full of people waiting, but you know more are on the way. Or your books aren't there yet. Or someone else on the bill is late. You may have to stall, or stretch, so you need something you can rely on to help you out in a pinch.

If you have any unusual talents, such as birdcalls or playing spoons, be prepared to dust them off to help you fill time if you have to—or to throw in for fun when nothing else seems to be working. Recite a classic poem. It's so great

▶ When you're finished signing books for attendees, sign as much stock as you can. Again, if you've signed it, they probably won't return it. And returns are the scourge of the writer!

to have something like that to fall back on, and if done properly it will endear you to your audience.

Dan Rhodes, author of the short-story collection *Anthropology,* was faced with just such a conundrum while doing an event in New York. The event had been advertised to start at 7:30 in one place and at 8:00 in another. So at 7:45 there was a big crowd waiting, starting to fidget, getting a little antsy. But he knew there would be people coming at 8:00. What to do? Well, Dan Rhodes was a man with a Plan B. He had brought along a wonderful short story from Jane Austen's *Juvenilia.* Familiar, yet totally unique. So he was able to trot out his party piece and keep everyone beautifully entertained until the 8:00 crowd strolled in.

TAKE TIME TO SIGN BOOKS

When you're signing, it's important to give everyone who buys your book a little piece of you. Look people in the eye and ask them something about themselves. Ask how they found out about your event, about your book. This will give you an idea of what kinds of publicity and marketing techniques are effective. Your readers are precious gems, and you want to find out all you can about them. Be grateful and sweet and humble. These are people who actually took time out of their lives to come out and see you, then stuck around afterwards and paid good money to buy your book and have you sign it for them. If they tell five people, and those people tell five people, and those people tell five people . . . well, you see where we're going with this.

That being said, you want to walk that fine line between keeping the queue moving and giving everyone the individual attention he wants. If there's a small line, this won't be a problem. But if there's a long line (and we should all have this problem), you want to give people their moment in your sun and then gently guide the next person into place.

Make sure you have a sign-up sheet for your mailing list by your side. Ask people if, while you sign their books, they would sign your list. While you're at it, ask how they found out about the event. It's always helpful to know what's working publicity and marketing wise and what's not.

Doing an Event with a Book that Can't Be "Read"

Let's suppose you have a book that doesn't lend itself to a reading. A medical text, or a statistical analysis of postwar swallow migration. You can't very well

What to Write When You Sign

M any first-time authors are confused about what to write when they sign someone's book. First and foremost, find out if your buyer wants you to dedicate your book to him or if he simply wants your signature. People who collect books often want only your signature, because it increases the value of your book. If your buyer does want a dedication, be sure to spell his name right. Some authors have a standard dedication they like to use; others like to make things up spontaneously. Some authors give advice; others write pithy and funny lines. Judy Budnitz, author of the short-story collection *Nice Big American Baby,* draws cartoons. Obviously, do whatever suits you, but know that a lot of buyers want something personal—something that shows you connected with them. Undoubtedly, you will feel on the spot at this moment. So it's good to have a couple of prepared options that you can personalize.

go into a bookstore and read facts and stats. Well, you could, but what would be the point? So what to do? Luckily, you've got a lot of options. Arrange a debate with someone whose views oppose yours. Ask a local luminary or journalist to interview you (another way to get journalists interested in your book). Give a lecture about your topic. But not a dull, drab academic lecture. A fun, charming, well-rehearsed, informative, passionate lecture. A demonstration or workshop might work. Or a slide show (if the images are professional-caliber). If you're addressing a medical issue, a generous Q&A session may be just the ticket.

Joann Eckstut, Arielle's mom and the author of *Room Redux: The Home Decorating Workbook,* gave interior design classes at bookstores. Not only did she draw book buyers, but she attracted new clients as well.

Sharon Kelly Roth of Books & Company says, "We've had authors who write about antiques invite people to bring in an antique for them to appraise. That's a big hit with customers. One customer found out that the lamp she paid $1,500 for was actually worth $25,000. Just remember, make it fun and they will come!"

Bill and Rachel Parker, authors of *A Gynecologist's Second Opinion,* knew it wouldn't be easy to do events in bookstores for their opus. With their usual wit and aplomb, they illuminated their thoughts on books that don't lend themselves to readings:

Bill: "Having events in bookstores for medical books can be deadly—"

Rachel: "No pun intended—"

Bill: "Thank you. Because nobody shows up. The best thing for me is going to medical conventions. Doing medical shows. If you give good advice and plug the book at the end, shows are happy to do it."

This strategy has worked out well for Bill and Rachel's book, which is now in a second edition.

And remember the idea of a virtual book tour? Virtual events are particularly fabulous for niche books that can't be read. Webinars, e-chats, podcasts and the like allow you to do all kinds of stuff you couldn't do in a bookstore.

Selling Books at Non-Bookstore Events

If you decide to do an event somewhere other than a bookstore, you have to figure out how to get and sell books there. It's tempting to buy books from your publisher at your discounted rate (typically 50%) and then resell them at full price. You make a lot more money per book than you would by raking in your standard royalty, and it may seem a lot easier than figuring out the logistics of getting someone else to sell your books for you. For example, if your book retails for $10 and you buy copies for $5 apiece from your publisher, you can make $5 a book. Whereas, if your attendees purchase their books from the bookstore, netting you your standard 7.5% royalty, you'll make 75¢ a copy.

If you're strapped for cash, this may be your best route. Otherwise, you're better off either bringing in a local bookseller or having a sponsoring organization buy books. Why?

■ Most contracts technically bar the resale of books bought at the author discount (though most publishers look the other way at this very common practice as long as the author isn't buying books in very large numbers).

> If you're asked how many books a bookseller or organization should order, always overestimate without being pie-in-the-sky. It's a form of torture to witness people asking to buy a copy of your book and being turned away because there are none left.

■ Making contact with a bookseller can lead to other events and general support of your book.

■ A sponsoring organization that's buying books may decide to put information about your book in its website, newsletter or gift store. And if it buys in large enough quantities, getting a higher special sales discount, the organization will be motivated to get people to the event so that it won't be left with a stack of nonreturnable books.

■ If you're selling through a bookseller, all sales count for bestseller lists—they won't if you buy your own books.

If you're not personally lugging books with you to an outside event, don't just assume your books are going to magically show up. MAKE SURE the books have been sent and will arrive on time. What's worse than not having enough books at an event? Having NO books. It happens. David remembers one event where he contacted the assistant publicist at his publisher to confirm that plenty of his books would be showing up. As a backup, he actually lugged 20 copies of his book with him. When he got there, he contacted the person in charge of books and was horrified to learn that his publisher had not only been a nightmare to deal with, but hadn't sent any of his books. After the event, David quickly sold all his copies, and there were still numerous people waiting in line to buy more. When he called his publisher, they said, "Well, we didn't set up the event in the first place, so . . ." As if he'd done a bad thing by setting up his own event. When he got home, David called the head of publicity and expressed his displeasure. Thankfully, David got an apology and a free box of books.

What If No One Shows Up?

Read this sentence carefully: An event at a bookstore is a good thing, even if nobody comes to it.

If you happen to have an event and no one shows up, and you're standing in front of a table loaded with your books and there's a room full of empty chairs where your readers should be, and your publishing career is flashing before your eyes and you feel like the loser of the universe, it may not seem like a good thing.

And yet it is. Here's why. The booksellers will have a bunch of your books in their store. They may have a sign or poster or flyers up in their store. They may have contacted the local paper, which may have announced the event in its calendar section. They may have put you in their own calendar, which they may have sent out to their mailing list. They may have put the event on their website (hopefully you put the event on yours). And, hold on to your hat, the store may have actually put your book in the most coveted spot in the joint, the Boardwalk of the bookstore kingdom: THE FRONT WINDOW. The place everyone has to walk past to enter the store. So, even if no one comes to your event, your name and your book may be seen by hundreds, maybe even thousands, maybe even tens of thousands.

Plus, they may give you a nice pen or a lovely paper bookmark. You will almost certainly be given a free beverage, hot or cold. Don't count on it, but you may even get a muffin.

Using Everything You've Got: Creating Content from Events

W hen Native Americans were lucky enough to kill a buffalo, they used every single scrap, from horns to hooves. If you're going to be a presence on the web, you have to continuously feed the beast. So you need a steady stream of excellent content. If you're doing events, there's your content. Blog or tweet or whatever about the event as you're setting it up. Then deconstruct what worked and what didn't. Take pictures. Post them on your site and send them to the event's host to post on theirs. Videotape the event. Slice it up into little bits (no more than five minutes long). Put it up on your favorite video-sharing site, embed it on your website, post it on your author profiles at Amazon and on the Barnes & Noble website, forward it to all the other online communities where you've established contacts. Send a link to appropriate friends, colleagues and media contacts. Spread it around to all your e-people and to whatever destinations you've hitched your tent poles.

Use everything you've got. Feed the beast.

Plus, you will probably get to meet the events coordinator and, if you're smart, a bunch of the people who work at the store. The people who, you know, sell your book. If no one shows up, you'll have a lot of time to bond with all of them. If you play your cards right, and keep a good attitude, you can make everyone feel better while simultaneously—believe it or not—sowing the seeds for the hand-selling of your book.

Caroline Leavitt, *New York Times* bestselling author of *Pictures of You,* has this to share: "I went to a bookstore reading and no one showed up. No one! Three people from the bookstore felt sorry for me and sat down in the chairs (they had put out 50 because they expected a crowd) and sat there with their name tags on while I read. Afterwards, Michael Dorris, author of *A Yellow Raft in Blue Water,* soothed me and told me how he read in front of four people once and the cops came in mid-reading and arrested three of them, who happened to be bank robbers on the lam."

Thank You, Thank You, Thank You!

Remember to get business cards from everyone who's working your event! After the dust has settled, make sure you're very generous with your thank-yous. Yes, an email is nice, but people really appreciate a handwritten thank-you in this day and age. This kind of goodwill is priceless. John Evans, owner of Diesel Bookstore in Oakland, California, told us: "The people who really make an impression are those who are respectful. Acclaimed British author and Whitbread prize winner Jeanette Winterson went directly up to each person (including the person at the counter) and said, 'Thank you so much, I really appreciate all the work you've done.' Five years of booksellers' recommendations came out of that."

Jen Reynolds, sales representative at Publishers Group West and former director of publisher relations and events at Joseph-Beth Booksellers, expressed similar sentiments in this story: "Jimmy Carter was the greatest. He was very clear about what he wanted: a chicken salad sandwich. That was it. And afterwards he dropped us a note right away, thanking us, saying he appreciated the event and our efforts. I was blown away. People often come in on edge and complaining, making demands. And then I think of Jimmy Carter, how easy he was, and he was the *president,* for goodness sake!"

A Tour of Your Book Tour

If you're being sent on tour by a publisher, the organizational work will fall to your publicist. She will make sure books arrive at each location. She will provide each bookstore with promotional posters and make sure you end up on its calendar and in its newsletter. She will confirm your listing in the calendar section of local papers and websites. She will send your book and press release to local and national media. She will try her hardest to coordinate a landslide of attention to hit just before and all during your tour. This may include reviews, interviews, puff pieces, you name it. Without your even lifting a promotional finger, you stand the chance of getting an itinerary with a number of juicy interviews and events.

Of course, your publicist isn't a magician. Even with publisher-driven tours, there may be spots where you get little or no media attention. Or maybe the media has to bow out due to late-breaking news. There are all sorts of good reasons why, even though your publisher may be doing all sorts of amazing things for you, you need to supplement these efforts in any and every way you can. Now is absolutely the time to crank up the social networking machine.

▶ If you go on tour, make sure you're in great shape, fully rested, with your battery completely charged, at the very top of your game. Pick out a couple of great outfits that can be easily packed and repacked without having to be ironed and reironed. Travel light. It's a huge pain lugging big bags.

▶ Phone, minibar and room service are often not covered by your publisher, so keep your sticky fingers to yourself. You don't want to end up paying $10 for 12 macadamia nuts, no matter how good they were.

Despite all the wearisome traveling, the grueling grind of being dragged hither and thither signing stock at store after store, all the maddening glad-handing, the utterly draining interviews (sometimes, if you're lucky, five or six in a day where you have to say all the same things but make it seem like it's the very first time you've ever said them), you will still be expected at the end of the day to go to a venue and deliver a slamming show so that a room full of strangers will want to lay down their hard-earned money to buy your bouncing baby book.

Tour Tips from a Master

Escorts have wisdom about the ins and outs of author comportment because they observe it day in and day out. The legendary Kathi Kamen Goldmark, whose untimely death left a gaping hole in the book industry but whose spirit and expertise live on, gave this advice:

ON THE BASICS
- You want to be sure you're presentable, sober, well rested and alert.
- Stay off your phone. Concentrate on where you are in the moment.

ON HOW TO LOOK
- Make sure your clothes are on right. Zipped, buttoned, tucked.
- Bring clothing that doesn't wrinkle.
- You don't have to wear heels!
- If you're not good at putting on makeup, have your escort take you to a department store for a free makeover before a media or bookstore appearance.

ON INTERVIEWING WELL
- Try and make eye contact and a real connection with your interviewer.
- Even if you just have three minutes on air, don't rush. Speak clearly and in a relaxed manner.
- Drop your prepared spiel; allow the interview to be more of a conversation.
- Try not to say, "In my book . . ."

ON GENERAL SELF-CARE
- Every city you go to, no matter how busy you are, do one thing that you can't do anyplace else.
- If you've been on a pretour diet, assume you're going to have to bust loose on tour. You never know what you're going to have to eat, when.

Michael Perry, author of *Population: 485,* has this to say about touring: "It's tough to describe a book tour. It's intense, not in a heavy-lifting sort of way, but in a sort of nonstop way. You're always driving or talking or trying to find a radio station or a television station or a hotel or a departure gate. Your life boils down to showing up and talking. Showing up and talking. Over and over. But at every stop, people listen and smile, and then say gracious things. I've spoken with several other authors during the course of the year, and they all confirmed what I feel: Writing is a mostly solitary existence and we prefer it that way, but when we see someone in a chair at a reading it reminds us that a reader is someone who gives us his time, and this leaves us frightened and deeply grateful. So to everyone in the chairs, thank you so much."

Luckily, provided you're in the best shape of your life, you have the right attitude and you make an extra special point to HAVE FUN, there's a huge upside. Being on a publisher-driven tour bestows upon you a higher status than if you're just Joe or Jane Author walking in off the street. This status should lend you some extra-special face time with employees at bookstores. Cherish these contacts and make the most of them. They could be a lifeline for the rest of your writing career. Ditto when you're interviewed by local and national media. Get cards! From everyone! Make sure you get links to and scans of all media attention and post them to your website.

In the end, you'll improve your event and your presentation skills. You'll accumulate great war stories. You'll come home a more successful, experienced, respected author. You'll get to rub elbows with your public far and wide. Treat them like gold, and they will make you golden.

An Escort Is Not What You Think

If you're lucky, your publisher will hire an escort for you when you go to another city. Hold the off-color comments: An escort is someone who picks you up at the airport and takes you to your hotel; drives you to your event, your interviews, the local bookstores; introduces you to local bookstore owners, managers

▶ After the high of a show, it can be depressing to end up in a lonely hotel room feeling alienated and alone, with nowhere to go and no one you know. Bring a great book or two with you. Write up the day's events while they're fresh in your mind and post them on your site. Tweet to fill empty minutes while simultaneously building your platform one message at a time. Work out. Eat some healthy food. Take care of yourself physically, mentally and emotionally.

and employees; helps you sign books; shows you the local ropes and hips you to the local lingo; and generally makes your life much easier. As is true with every profession, there are outstanding escorts and there are terrible ones. What makes for a great escort? All you need to do is meet Ken Wilson. He's not just good; he's an escort god. Ken works out of Los Angeles. In under four hours, he'll take you to 15 bookstores from Santa Monica to Hollywood to the Valley. He knows everyone's name at every bookstore and how many kids and dogs each bookseller has. He knows how to pitch and position a book in a quick, skillful 30 seconds. With style and wit.

Should you be lucky enough to meet Ken or any of his escort colleagues, be sure to befriend them. Pick their brains, learn from them, observe and absorb. Push them to take you to each and every bookstore in the area. Remember, this could quite possibly be your one shot at this town in your three-month, winner-take-all window. Take advantage of this precious opportunity while it exists and get maximum mileage out of your escort.

Know that escorts tend to be chatty people. Read: It's very likely that you will become drive-time conversation with the next author under your escort's protection. Not to mention telephone and/or email gossip fodder for your publicist (who is your escort's contact at your publisher's). So be generous with your gratitude. And when you're tempted to throw a hissy fit because some producer keeps you waiting or a journalist blows you off for a bigger story, take a deep breath and count to 10.

Satellite Tours

Publishers sometimes pay to send authors on satellite radio or TV tours. These are virtual tours set up and run by companies that specialize in this handy form of publicity. You either sit in a room and get interviewed, via satellite, over and over again by different stations around the country; or you do a taped segment that's sent out to various stations.

▶ Satellite TV interviews can be particularly awkward because you can't see the person who's interviewing you. It's tough to connect with someone when there's no eye contact. All the more reason to listen carefully.

Satellite tours are great when you want to saturate the marketplace in a short period. They can, if done right, get you seen or heard by hundreds of thousands of readers—which is why you might want to consider hiring a company to set one up for you if you can't convince your publisher that it's a good idea. But let us repeat: Satellite tours *do* cost money.

The Medium of Media

Each form of media has its own rules and idiosyncrasies. Sometimes an interview will be a *phoner*. This is an interview on, you guessed it, the phone. Sometimes you'll be asked to go to a radio or TV studio where you'll be interviewed live or on tape. There might be an audience, or you might be alone with the interviewer and the crew. You might be part of a panel of interesting or uninteresting people who have something or nothing in common with you (David was once interviewed on a panel with Yoko Ono!). Sometimes the interviewer will come to your home. Sometimes the interviewer will take you to a location. Sometimes the interview will be conducted via email. And sometimes—the worst—you'll sit in a room with just a camera or a microphone, unable to see the faraway person who's interviewing you. This is when you really need to listen carefully to the questions and keep up your energy while still being intimate with your unseen listener.

Before we give you tips tailored to each scenario, here are some general rules:

- Prior to your interview, try to watch or listen to the show or read the work of the journalist, writer or blogger. This will help eliminate surprises.

- Show up 20 to 30 minutes early.

- Don't eat right before you're interviewed, unless part of your shtick is regurgitation. If you're being interviewed over lunch, eat light and be sure to wipe your mouth regularly.

- Have a beverage close at hand. Again, this is not only for dry mouth, but also for use as a prop if you need to stall.

- Do a physical warm-up beforehand: yoga, stretching, jumping jacks.

- Prep yourself; go over your key points and your pitch before you go live.

- Try to establish a personal connection with your interviewer; asking a few questions of your own can loosen both of you up.

- Gently ask the interviewer beforehand to mention your book, your website and any events you have coming up.

- Before you go on a show, ask if someone can send you a link to your performance after the interview (almost everything is online at this point). If it will not be available online, ask if they can burn you a DVD that you can take home with you. For print, ask the interviewer to have the publication mail you a hard copy of the interview.

On the Air with Larry Mantle

L arry Mantle, host of public radio's *Airtalk* (on NPR's L.A. affiliate KPCC-FM) and one of Southern California's most beloved radio interviewers, shared some of the insights he's gleaned from years of talking to the famous and the infamous:

US: What can a first-time author do to attract your attention?

LM: Demonstrate that you really know the show. If you're a fan and you know who you're pitching to, this can make a huge difference. Make your pitch highly personalized. In addition, relating your book to something that's going on in the world can make a big difference. The more of a hook you have, the better.

US: What makes for a good interview?

LM: You've got to know the style of the host and what the audience is used to hearing. I'm on public radio, so we like depth. Do your research. Past interviews are often available online. Study the list of guests.

US: What makes radio different from other media?

- If you're in the same room as a host, make eye contact. The more you can focus on having a real conversation, no matter how nervous you are, the better the interview will be.

- Be aware of everything that's going on around you. For TV and radio, someone will almost always signal the host 30 seconds before the end of the segment. When you see that signal, know you have to wrap up.

- Don't mention the name of your book over and over again. However, for TV and radio, if your host hasn't mentioned it at all, be sure to say the name at least once.

- Try not to be combative or argumentative. Unless that's your persona and it will help sell your book.

- Don't say, "You'll have to read my book to find out" or "People always ask me that question." It can seriously alienate your interviewer and make you seem self-serving.

- Make sure you have a clear understanding of what kind of language they want you to use if you're going on air. How sophisticated, racy or old is the

LM: Radio is intimate. The best interviews feel like the subject is talking to one person. And, in fact, typically a listener is alone in a car or at home. Never say "you listeners." Always assume you're talking to an individual.

Also, radio is driven by imagination, so you want to provoke a listener's creative imagination. Terry Gross is a great interviewer because she introduces you to a world that may be entirely different from your own. She gives you an insight into what it would be like for you to be doing what her guest is describing. She uses words to open up your mind and make the subject personal. I want the audience to say, "You drew me in." I want the listeners to feel like they're riveted, in the same room, overhearing an intimate conversation.

US: Any general tips for authors going on the air?

LM: I prefer the person I'm interviewing to have high energy without being overwhelming, funny without being shticky, intelligent but accessible. If it's too complex, it's boring. If it's too simple, it's dull. No abstract concepts, just real stories that people can relate to. In the best interviews, it's like the audience is eating greens, but they feel like they're popping Gummy Bears.

audience you're speaking to? Tailor your interview accordingly, especially if it's live.

- Don't give one-word answers unless you're doing it for a specific reason (to create comedy, for example).

- Get contact information from the interviewer, the producer and/or the host before you leave.

ELECTRONIC MEDIA

As journalists have more and more work to do, the popularity of the email interview has grown exponentially. And email interviews can make life easier for you as well. They don't necessitate coordinating schedules. You can do them at your own leisure. You can control what you want to say. You can take your time coming up with your answers. You can never be misquoted—or if you are, you have the proof and the pudding. And, if you're shy and prefer the written word to the spoken one, electronic interviews are a boon.

One of the difficulties of communicating electronically is that all the nuance of voice and face are obviously absent. Something that you may intend as a sarcastic aside may be taken out of context to portray you in a bad light. With so many reviewers relying on snark these days, you don't want to provide fire for someone's fuel. Unless your thing is lighting fires. So measure your words carefully before you send them flying down the information superhighway.

RADIO OR PODCASTS

Are you live or being recorded? ASK! If you're being recorded and you make a mistake or don't like the way you expressed something, you can start over again. If you're live and you make a mistake, do yourself a favor and have fun with it. Live or taped, be sure to develop a nice relationship with the microphone if you are in a studio. Before you go on, find out how far away or how close you should be. Should you have to clear your throat, cough or burp, avert your mouth from the mike.

If you're interviewed over the phone, even if you're in your bathrobe, be sure you're warmed up both physically and vocally. Get the blood moving. Also, make sure that you have privacy, so you can stay focused and relaxed, and that you won't be interrupted by wandering family members. Have notes you can refer to. DO NOT use a phone that has call-waiting (unless you can suspend it). Don't use a cell phone unless you have to. If it's a live radio interview, don't have the show playing on your radio at home—this will create feedback. And don't be surprised if the call doesn't come in on time. Very often, live radio runs late. In fact, there's a good chance you'll be bumped to another day. Also, there's a chance you'll hear a bit of the show, over the phone, just before your segment. Listen closely for anything you can refer to.

Try not to speak in run-on sentences. It's hard for listeners to take in the information when they can't actually see you speaking.

One thing to know is that there's a subspecies of the radio world whose bread and butter is meanness. If you find yourself in an interview with a "shock jock" who attacks you viciously, you have several options: 1) have fun with it, 2) act wounded and hurt, or 3) attack back. If all three make you want to puke, be sure to tell your publicist that you don't want to do this sort of thing.

TELEVISION

If you're appearing on TV, there's a chance that a makeup artist/hairdresser will make you look beautiful. Some men cringe at the idea of makeup. If you fall into this category, it's time to get in touch with your feminine side. You have no idea what those TV lights do to your skin. If you're on a low-budget show that doesn't supply a makeup artist, at the very least apply a thin layer of powder to get rid of the shine. For ladies, a little color in the cheeks and some mascara wouldn't hurt. Those of you who regularly wear makeup should know that the camera and the lights create a different environment than you're used to. Unless you have a good reason not to, let the trained professional do his/her job.

Watch that posture on TV! Yes, appear comfortable and relaxed, but try your best not to slouch into a human question mark. If you can, chat with the host beforehand. Don't assume, however, that just because the host is chummy before the camera's on, he'll be chummy on air, or vice versa.

Sometimes you'll find yourself in front of a live studio audience. Be sure to include your audience from time to time (with eye contact and/or gestures) as you speak. For example, if it's a show that has a Q&A, you can refer back to a previous question an audience member asked. This can go a long way toward gaining their support.

Find out before your interview where the producers would like you to look. Unless you're a seasoned professional, it's almost always better not to look at the camera.

PRINT

Arrange for print interviews to be held someplace where you're comfortable. Have the reporter come to your home or meet you at a favorite coffee shop or at an outdoor spot you enjoy. Just make sure there's not a lot of background noise. Also, journalists need what are called "color" paragraphs, i.e., writing that describes the setting or mood where the interview takes place. So if you pick the right spot,

Who's the Boss?

Develop the art of slipping your critical information into the answer of any question you're asked. It's very difficult to do this and make it seem natural. That's why it helps to practice in front of a video camera. If you can in essence run the interview, you will often be much happier with the results. Of course, it's a fine line between running an interview and running roughshod over the interviewer. Both the interviewer and your audience will want to feel that you're a good listener. So always be sure to respond to questions, even if you end up taking the questions in new directions. It's also important to be open to whatever avenue your interviewer leads you down, because you never know what fun is lurking down there. A question out of left field may result in an animated, engaging conversation that has a greater effect on book sales than your normal shtick.

▶ Get contact information from everyone who interviews you, and stay in touch. If the moment feels right, ask if you may add their name to your email list. You never know when one of them might suddenly need a story on your topic and be reminded to call you when they receive an update. A media contact is always a good thing.

you may be able to get more ink. And even if no one's taking your picture, look as good as you can.

As with TV, don't assume that journalists who get very chummy and intimate with you are doing this to be your friend. Sometimes they're just trying to get you to say something you'll wish you hadn't said. Do not, even off the cuff, say anything to a journalist that you don't want plastered all over creation. Even if you tell a journalist that something is "off the record," you may find that your wishes aren't granted.

Be prepared to be misquoted and know that there's absolutely nothing you can do about it. Don't start sending letters to the editor (unless a journalist has written something that will cause physical harm); you'll most likely come off as a whining boob.

If someone from the media comes to photograph you for a newspaper or magazine, do yourself a favor and employ the techniques described in the last chapter. Bring a friend, engage in conversation, keep physically loose. Be a cooperative subject, but if you're asked to do something you're not comfortable with (like putting on a dumb hat or removing your shirt), JUST SAY NO.

Keeping Track and Keeping It Real

If you're extremely fortunate, you'll be interviewed over and over and over again. Sometimes on the same day. Starting at four in the morning. And guess what? People will ask you the same questions over and over and over again.

Not only do you have to have great answers for all these questions, but you also have to make the answers seem fresh as a daisy every time they pop out. You have to make it seem as if the interviewer is asking you insightful, intelligent, really-makes-you-think questions. Even though you've answered them over and over and over again.

One way to keep it fresh is to consciously reconnect with the origin of your idea. Another is to constantly try to improve your stories. Weed out weakness; add strength. Whether it's changing the words or tweaking the delivery, by attempting to make it better, you will keep a little edge in your stories. Whenever you improvise a great line, be sure to write it down afterward so you can use it again.

If you're being interviewed back-to-back-to-back, it's difficult to keep track of what you've already said and what bon mots you delivered in your last interview. If you end up repeating yourself or doing something stupid, admit you're an idiot. In small, appropriate doses, self-deprecation can actually be sweet. Remember, if you handle it right, a mistake might lead to the best moment in your interview.

Evaluate your presentation after every interview and see what you can do to make it even greater. Keep it real. The late great George Burns put it his own way: "Sincerity is the most important thing in life. Once you can fake that, you've got it made."

Back to Pitching and Hooking

For the 99% of you not being sent on a book tour sponsored by a publisher, it's back to pitching and hooking now that you've got an actual book in hand. You want to keep things moving. Movement can take the form of nice things being said about your book by people you do and do not know on the likes of Amazon and reader sites like Goodreads. It can mean blogosphere chatter. Some nice local press. Debbie Stier, former director of online marketing for HarperCollins, says, "It doesn't happen the way it used to, where media begot media. It doesn't start with the media anymore. Things start to percolate online, and the media picks up on it from there."

If the media hasn't answered any of your past knocks on their door, use any online traction you've accumulated to go back and knock some more. But know that each time you go back to the well, you have to produce new angles and hooks. They need to be tailored to the person you're pitching, and they need to be current.

Rick Beyer, author of *The Greatest Stories Never Told,* is a serious hook-meister who knows how to keep a book in the public eye. He's had particular success with regularly creating new hooks for radio interviews. Whether it's Presidents Day, Memorial Day, Thanksgiving or graduation, Rick writes terrific pitches with great, original hooks that his publicist can simply forward on to her radio contacts. Here's a sample of his Presidents Day pitch:

Did you know that . . .

George Washington was not the nation's first president, but was actually number eight?

While John Wilkes Booth assassinated President Lincoln, his brother saved the life of Lincoln's son?

President James Garfield was shot by a lawyer but killed by the ineptitude of his doctors?

Author Rick Beyer is ready to fill your audience in on these and other fun tidbits of presidential history. He is the author of The Greatest Stories Never Told: 100 Tales from History to Astonish, Bewilder and Stupefy. *Rick has appeared in more than 100 radio and television interviews, entertaining audiences with fascinating little-known stories from history.*

The truth is that the media constantly needs nourishment. You just have to find the right meal to feed the beast. What's happening in the world right now that is different from when your book came out? Has some hot story developed that's related to your book, even tangentially? Can you hook up with a larger story than your own? If so, jump on it, because the news cycle moves very quickly, and an op-ed piece in the right publication can be a major boon for your book. The early—and well-informed—bird gets the worm.

Andrew Exum, author of *This Man's Army: A Soldier's Story from the Front Lines of the War on Terrorism,* noticed a nationwide debate heating up on

Always Say Yes!

When someone extends an invitation related to your book, just do it. Period. Susan Wooldridge, author of *poemcrazy,* was asked to attend an event where, essentially, she'd be sitting listening to others make speeches all day. But the keynote speaker didn't show. So guess who filled in? That's right, Susan became the keynote speaker in front of several thousand people and took them by storm. "It ended up being marvelous and has led to workshop after workshop, even another keynote. Say 'yes'! I regret the things I canceled or that I didn't go to."

Tamim Ansary, master storyteller and author of *Destiny Disrupted,* had this wonderful account about the benefits of saying yes: "The best thing about *Destiny Disrupted* so far is that I accepted an offer by my Kazakhi publisher to bring me to Almaty, all expenses paid, to help him launch the book. I spent a week there."

Tamim continues: "The publisher turned out to be not a company, not a 'house,' but Nurlan Ablyazov, one guy with a laptop and a two-day growth of beard, who didn't even have a home office but worked out of a chair in one corner of a three-room flat he shares with his wife and two children on the campus of Kazakhstan Institute of Management and Economic Prognosis. Nurlan whether or not there would be a new draft. He quickly wrote an op-ed on the subject. Next thing he knew, he was in *The New York Times*. It's easy to find email addresses for editorial sections in newspapers all over the world, either in the paper itself or online.

One author we know is an avid listener of NPR's *Talk of the Nation*. She noticed how, every single day, Neal Conan did a teaser for the show in the form of a few questions followed by a short pitch. So when her book came out, she sent an email to a producer at *Talk of the Nation* in this exact form. Boom! A month later, she was on the show.

For local media, you can ask for references from the owner of the bookstore you're working with, a fellow author, a professor at a respected university in town—a name that the press already knows is a great door-opener. In Kansas City, we asked Geoffrey Jennings of Rainy Day Books whom we should talk to at their NPR affiliate. One phone call later, we were booked for the premier arts show one day before our event. The next day, 300 people showed up for our Pitchapalooza.

Following Up

Do not be put off if you don't hear back from the media outlets you contact. Even if a lot of time goes by. Do not assume your ideas and updates are going

---

used to be a quantum physicist in St. Petersburg, played guitar in a rock-and-roll band in his twenties, played on the European championship volleyball team, later started a newspaper—but took the audacious step of reporting that the president of the country was under investigation for corruption by international agencies. He issued a special edition of his paper to get this news out on the very day that the whole country was celebrating the great man's sixtieth birthday. The result: He had to flee to Chicago and spend a year there with his wife, Julia.

"My book is (at the moment) his only book. This is how publishing works in Kazakhstan. There are no publishing companies, only individuals who get a jones to publish some particular book; and when they do, they gather sponsors to finance the project, put together a network of freelance editors, translators, artists, whatever and get it done. It's kinda the way movies are made here—a publisher is an independent producer. The sponsors for my book included a mysterious former KGB colonel named Igor. But then, apparently, you can't throw a stone in Kazakhstan without hitting a former KGB colonel." Talk about a once-in-a-lifetime experience!!! Why on earth would you possibly want to pass that up?

unnoticed. Do not assume that no one's interested. You never know what's happening on the other end. Use any good news as an excuse to follow up with your media wish list.

Getting Snarked

If you're getting any media attention, you will sooner or later get smacked upside the head with some snark. Snark is ugly, mean nastiness for its own sake. Sadly, in this cynical age, some people mistake snark for journalism. They may use you and/or your book for target practice as they pepper you with potshots.

If you're a member of the human race, it's hard not to take this personally. David was repeatedly snarked when his book *Chicken* came out. Not for the quality of his book or writing, but because his nose was too big and his eyes were too close together. And this was from highbrow papers like the London *Times*. After resisting the urge to book a big block of time with a plastic surgeon, David realized that this was more about the need to sell papers than about him.

Back to author Dan Rhodes (*Timoleon Vieta Come Home*) for a moment. He actually puts his snark to work by using it as fodder for comedy. He keeps a running list of some of the nastiest things ever written about him and his books, and then reads the highlights as entertainment at some of his events.

Heidi Julavits, editor of the San Francisco journal *The Believer,* defined snark in her manifesto on it as "hostility for hostility's sake." She sees snark passing for literary criticism more and more, as book critics become more concerned with being "funny and smart and a little bit bitchy" than saying anything about a book's merits and deficiencies. And the anonymity of e-reviews has spawned a whole new level of ugliness and despicability.

▶ Again with the thank-yous! If anyone interviews you, or writes about you, or helps in any way to get the word out about your book, slap a thank-you note on them. Appreciation goes such a long way.

If you're worried about bad reviews or cyber hate, you're not alone. There are several tried-and-true methods for dealing with reviews. Your first option is not to read them. There's a lot to be said for this approach. After all, they're just some people's opinions. And you don't want their voices in your head the next time you sit down to write something. If you want constructive criticism, you can always find smart, fair people who'll give it to you.

Some writers have a trusted friend or colleague read the reviews first and just pass on the nice and/ or instructive bits. This makes sense, too. You don't get that critic's voice in your head, but you still learn from constructive criticism and register the nice things people are saying, filtered through the lens of a friendly protective voice.

Some writers read their reviews and take them with a very large grain of salt while extracting whatever useful information they can from them. Again, this makes a lot of sense, but it's a tactic fraught with difficulties. For one thing, it's not always easy to find that grain of salt when you need it. As much as you say you won't take it personally, it's almost impossible not to. On the flip side, it's wise to take raves with a small bit of salt as well.

Some writers read their reviews and memorize the worst bits, rage against the cruel world, grow bitter and never produce that masterpiece they were meant to write. We consider this a last-resort option.

But just know this: If you write a book, you will get bad reviews. Just like every writer—great and not so great—before you. So next time you get bashed, pilloried, dismissed, railed upon or savaged, don't despair. Instead, embrace the words of Oscar Wilde: "The only thing worse than being talked about is not being talked about." Be prepared. Always business. Never personal.

Book Club Heaven

As we write, Christina Baker Kline's #1 *New York Times* bestseller, *Orphan Train,* is also the #1 book club pick in the nation. "I know about the power of book clubs!" says Christina. "There's no doubt in my mind that book clubs played (and continue to play) a huge role in the success of *Orphan Train.* They're filled with passionate readers who spread the word among friends and on social media. Once a book is embraced by the book-club community, it's destined for a long and happy life."

From *Good Morning America* to *USA Today* to your Aunt Grizelda's living room, there has been an explosion of book groups in America. Many publishers now put reading guides in the backs of books; they may even directly contact individual book clubs that have an interest in your particular kind of book. There's no reason you shouldn't do the same. Engaging with book groups—in person, over the phone or on the Internet—can be a great way to get your book bought, read and talked about. Most groups are tickled pink to know that an author will speak to them. And remember when we told you to post discussion questions on your website? Well, here's where they can pay off big time. Bestselling author Caroline Leavitt, says, "I did EVERYTHING to get my book out into the world. I offered to talk via speakerphone or email to every book club I could find." It all helped the book get a fantastic write-up in *The New York Times* and a desirable spot in the Amazon rankings.

Track down book groups on the web, in chat rooms, through bookstores and by asking everyone you know. Offer intimate access. You can even use a videochatting program like Skype so people can actually see you. Make it easy for groups to say yes to you. Hop on the bandwagon and enjoy the hayride!

Awards as Buzz

When we see an award next to a person's name, we humans seem to automatically think better of him. Which is why a great way to get buzz is to be nominated for or win an award or to get a fellowship or a grant. Enter your book for as many awards as you can afford (awards typically have "reading fees," or application costs that run from $10 to $50). Better yet, ask your publisher, if you have one, to do it for you. Apply for fellowships and grants.

Lists of awards, grants and fellowships, with specifications and deadlines, can be found on the web and in writers' magazines. *Poets & Writers Magazine* is a particularly great place for prize listings. There are also certain awards that your publisher needs to nominate you for. But don't assume they will automatically do so—make a list of any relevant awards and gently nudge and follow up with your publisher to make sure they're on top of it. Also, for some awards, you can be nominated in more than one category. This may cost your publisher more money, and if you don't push them, they simply won't do it. But if you ask, you're more likely to receive. And this can make the difference between your becoming an award winner and remaining an also-ran.

Keeping Your Book Ball Rolling

Yes, your book is new for only three months. But even if it doesn't jump off the shelves when it's new, don't despair. A book can catch fire six months, a year, even decades after it's published. Virginia Woolf's *Mrs. Dalloway* hit the bestseller lists 80 years after it was written. Why? Because she inspired and was a character in Michael Cunningham's Pulitzer Prize winner *The Hours,* which then became a movie starring Nicole Kidman as Virginia Woolf.

Paperback Publication:
More Beautiful the Second Time Around

Sometimes a publisher will bring a book out in hardcover and then, a year later, bring it out in paperback or sell the paperback rights. One of the great things about having your paperback come out a year after the hardcover is that now you have a second chance to get it right. Even if your hardcover didn't do well and your publisher isn't doing much with the launch of your paperback, in the eyes of the media and the world at large, this is a fresh start. You can learn from your mistakes and capitalize on all the contacts and knowledge you've gained in the year since the hardcover came out. You can set up events at places you couldn't get to the first time around. And it's a particularly good time to book events at colleges, libraries and community centers, because students (and readers who frequent libraries and community centers) are far more likely to pay $15 than $25 for your book.

You'll also want to let those who have already interviewed you know about the release of your paperback. All the bloggers and tweeters who helped you, or didn't. This is a great excuse to go back to the well.

Now is a good time to renew your quest to get more media attention. Reviewers who passed on reviewing your book in hardcover might take a crack at it when the paperback comes out. Make sure you go back to your media wish list and try, try again. Pursue any and every newspaper, magazine, radio and TV show/journalist/blogger/tweeter who might be interested in your book.

New Edition Is Not a Boy Band

Every time David looks at any of his books, he sees things he wants to edit. Editing is but one of the beauties of a new edition.

Perhaps the world has changed in some significant way that makes your book more relevant than ever but necessitates a new chapter or two. Perhaps your book is enjoying particular popularity with book groups, and a reader's guide would make for a great addition. Perhaps a movie is being made of your book, necessitating a new cover featuring movie stars. All of these scenarios give your book fresh legs to walk another mile.

The book in your hands is what's known as a complete revision. Revising and updating this book—now twice—gave us the amazing opportunity to take out everything that, five and then ten years after publication, no longer seemed relevant or up to snuff. It also allowed us to make it the most up-to-date book on the subject, giving us a serious competitive edge in the crowded market for books about getting published. Moreover, the process gave us perspective.

Striking Paperback Gold

M any books have a much richer life in paperback than in hardcover. And there's no better example of this phenomenon than Anita Diamant's novel *The Red Tent*, which takes place in biblical times and is told in the voice of Jacob's daughter Dinah.

When *The Red Tent* came out in hardcover, it sold in the neighborhood of 10,000 copies. For Anita, this was a rather disappointing neighborhood, because she knew there was a big bountiful audience just waiting for her book. So when her publisher told her that the hardcover was going to be remaindered and that what didn't sell would be shredded, she took this shudder-inducing moment and turned it into an opportunity. She convinced them to use those books instead as a promotional tool for the paperback edition, which was coming out shortly. They agreed.

Anita decided that she would begin her efforts with what she identified as her core audience: female Reform Jewish rabbis. Her publisher agreed to send her book to 500 of these women. The response was good. So Anita then cast her net a little wider and sent her book to another 500 rabbis, male and female alike. These mailings became the epicenter of the quake that spread throughout the Jewish community and rumbled into the general population.

Anita followed up with relentless speaking engagements and readings at Jewish book fairs, synagogues and community centers. Her publisher, smelling success, continued to spread the word to religious leaders of many denominations. They also approached book groups, offering discounts to bookstores that ordered in quantity for these book groups.

Because of Anita's constant diligence and relentless effort, *The Red Tent* has to date sold more than 3.3 million paperback copies worldwide. From the slag heap of the remaindered and shredded to the bestseller list. How sweet it is.

Coming back to your book years after writing it is a unique and precious occurrence that should be savored and enjoyed. While these two revisions had their headaches, they are among our favorite publishing experiences. To use the book-as-baby analogy, it was like being able to revisit the birth, first steps, first words, first day at school and ultimately, with your help, graduating from college summa cum laude!

Turn Your Book into Some Other Cool Thing

One-person shows. A line of T-shirts. Making something else out of a book can really help you expand your audience. And it can be profitable and fun.

Let's take the example of turning your book into a one-person show. Even an unknown play by an unknown writer, put on at a small but respected theater, is more likely to get reviewed than an unknown book by an unknown writer from the biggest publisher. It could also help raise your book's profile as a possible movie or TV project.

Nancy Levine is the author of three books of photographs of her pug, Wilson. She contacted a top greeting card company about doing cards of Wilson, and today he has his pug mug on cards across the country. If you like the idea of turning your book into a product, go back to the research drawing board. Just as you looked for agents, editors and publishers, look for licensees, manufacturers or whoever else produces the kind of stuff you'd like to make. You'll use the same techniques to approach these companies as you have all along. And if you succeed, you may be able to develop a whole line of products, each of which will raise your visibility another notch and hopefully put some gold in your pot.

Electronic Availability

Make sure your book is available in electronic form somewhere. Let us say it again. Make sure your book is available in electronic form somewhere. There are many reasons for this. More and more people are reading electronically. If the gods and goddesses of books bestow a smile upon you and your book blows up in some enormous way, without an ebook, you'll very quickly be in the sad position of having an enormous demand for your book and no supply. Bookstores will run out quickly. Online retailers will have to back-order the book. But if it's available electronically, it's ALWAYS FOR SALE.

Similarly, if it's available electronically, your book will NEVER GO OUT OF PRINT. Many forward-thinking publishers have had lots of success putting their out-of-print titles back into print as ebooks.

Caveat: If you have a picture book, or an illustrated book, it's going to be much more difficult and, in some cases, impossible to put your book out electronically—at least for the moment.

The Golden Rules Are . . .

The more we researched, the more we realized that there are definitely three rules to publicity and marketing of all kinds. Unfortunately, no one knows what they are. But we've laid out the basic principles. Given you some simple and some sophisticated tools to use. In the end, you never know which thing will lead to the thing that will lead you to the thing that gets your book the attention it so richly deserves. The one truth we know for certain is that your chances of getting into the spotlight increase exponentially with every intelligent, passionate, properly directed drop of energy you put into the process.

CHAPTER 14

The Fine Art of Selling

"Writing books is a whole lot easier than selling books."

—*John Grisham*

IT IS A TRUTH UNIVERSALLY acknowledged that in order to sell books, someone has to buy them. After all your work—thinking up your book, writing the thing, generating publicity—it's now time to figure out how to get your readers to lay down some cold hard cash.

There are as many ways to sell a book as you and/or your sales reps can invent and pull off. From the utterly obvious: bookstores, both independents and chains. To the slightly less obvious: drugstores, home improvement centers, flower shops, catalogs, mass merchandisers, warehouse clubs. To gigantic cyberspace booksellers and down to your very own website. And to whatever brave new frontiers those World Wide Web wizards may dream up.

You just want to be sure your book is where your readers actually are. And you want to make it easy for them to buy. Here's Harlequin CEO Donna Hayes, on connecting with readers: "We realized years ago that many of our readers lead very busy lives. And if anything, that's even truer today. So we tried to put our books where our readers shop. At the grocery store. At Walmart and Kmart. Places where books weren't traditionally sold. And the web is just a logical extension of this philosophy. We want our readers to be able to buy a book from their bedroom, in their pajamas, at three o'clock in the morning, if that's what they want."

Who are your customers? Where do they shop? And how can you entice rather than annoy your potential readers into buying your book? You know the answers to all these questions because they've come up over and over again in the process of getting your book published. Now you have to put them together in a cohesive sales plan.

"*How* Many Copies Did You Say?"

D oes the size of the first printing of your physical book seem utterly arbitrary? The fact is, no one knows how many of your books are going to sell and at what rate. What your publisher has to rely on are guesses (which are turned into cold hard numbers at sales conference) based on the preorders, early reviews and other early signs of potential success or failure generated by your publisher's sales reps and marketing/publicity team.

For instance, one of the crack members of your sales team is in charge of the Barnes & Noble account. The size of a Barnes & Noble order is, in many cases, more important than any other and thus influences the size of your first printing in no small way. Sadly, even if your sales rep delivers a dazzling pitch, the B&N buyer in charge of your category may still place a low order.

As we've said, nowadays, your first printing may also be determined by the number of preorders you're able to rack up. "As an author, a lot of times you have to make it through layers of sludge to get what you need from your publisher," explains Debbie Stier, former director of digital marketing for HarperCollins. "If you want books on the shelves at Barnes & Noble, first you have to have your editor pitch the Barnes & Noble sales rep, who then has to go to the Barnes & Noble buyer, who then has to go to her boss. Everyone is looking for reasons to say no. But one way to step out of this sludge is to make some early sales action happen on Amazon to get people's attention." Preorders on sites like Amazon and B&N can prompt these booksellers to as much as double their initial orders. Start trying to move the needle a few months out. Again, if once a month, for the three months prior to publication, you can sell 50 to 100 books on a single day, you're not only going to get these booksellers' attention, but you may get your overall print run significantly upped.

If you think you have the stomach for it, find out how many copies of your book your publisher is going to print initially. Keep in mind that a publisher can't print 20,000 copies of your book if they project sales of only 5,000. And since their projections are hardly scientific, they're doing the best they can to estimate demand. But if you feel that your publisher isn't paying enough attention to the demand for your book, speak up, speak loudly and speak often. In publishing as in life, windows of opportunity present themselves rarely and shut with alarming speed. If your window opens, do everything you can to dive through before it closes. Go back to your publishing team with the solid facts you've amassed to back up your claim. For example, if you have a book on medieval animal husbandry and you have good sales figures for a similar book, by all

How the Big Guys Stock

M any people are confused or even mystified by how the largest booksellers like Barnes & Noble decide on the number of copies of a book—if any—they will buy. One of the most common questions agents and editors are asked is "Why is Barnes & Noble only carrying one copy of my book?" or "Why isn't Barnes & Noble carrying my book at all?" "The short answer is because they don't have to," explains James Wehrle, director of sales for national accounts at Workman Publishing. "When a buyer looks at your book, he has to ask himself: How is this going to bring people into our stores? What does this book do so well that I *must* have it in my assortment?" With brick-and-mortar stores, there is only so much shelf space. "Online retailers have no need to get the assortment right—they carry every title," James adds. In other words, online booksellers don't have rent to pay. If a bricks-and-mortar buyer decides to carry your book, he often has to remove another book from his shelves to make room for it. That's why he has to believe that your book is *necessary* to his assortment. Your book has to be a piece of his particular jigsaw puzzle. If the buyer orders too many copies, they'll sit on the shelves and take space away from other necessary titles in the allocated space and budget. James adds this last bit of wisdom: "The challenge of getting the assortment right is much greater in a bricks-and-mortar store. When it's successfully done, though, the reward is a well-curated section. Such a section is pleasing in all the ways that form the basis of a bookstore's traditional appeal—it makes you happy to be there and to browse and discover." And a happy browser often translates to a happy buyer.

means pass these along. Have you convinced the head of the animal husbandry department at Texas A&M to include your book on her syllabus this year? Will this result in 2,500 copies sold in one fell swoop?

Don't despair if your initial print run is smaller than you anticipated. Your publisher can go back and repitch to get more orders if you get good reviews or media coverage, or if your book is selling well in other markets. More good news: If your book flies off the shelves after a small first printing, you may quickly go into a second, third and fourth printing, and multiple successive printings get people very excited. *The Artist's Way* by Julia Cameron started out with an initial printing of under 10,000 copies. It took two years before this book about the daily practice of becoming an artist started to take off. Now, 25 years later, it has more than two million copies in print! Joel Fotinos, publisher of Tarcher (the company responsible for *The Artist's Way*), put things in perspective: "Of course, publishers, like agents and authors, like to start out with a big first printing. But the business being the way it is these days, that doesn't happen very often. I've had some books with first printings of 5,000 to 7,000 copies that went on to sell 15,000, 20,000, 50,000 or more copies. Those books are particularly gratifying, because they're the books that found their audience despite the many roadblocks in their way."

In this competitive market, with the price of printing and paper and the risk of returns being what they are, publishers often under- rather than overestimate the number of copies they'll sell. So you may find yourself in a situation where readers want your book but aren't able to buy it because the publisher didn't print enough copies. This is particularly gnarly when you have a four-color illustrated book that is produced overseas and takes months to reprint.

One author had this tale of woe. His beautifully illustrated history book was published one September with a modest first run. The author worked his tail off to secure reviews, radio interviews and speaking engagements. And lo and behold, his book started selling really well. It was listed in numerous holiday gift roundups in newspapers across the country. Thanksgiving rolled around, the beginning of the holiday shopping rush, and suddenly his book was no longer available. Because it was produced overseas, no more copies could be had until January. So, in what should have been the best season for selling his book, he had to sit and watch as the demand he had created went unfulfilled.

At the height of demand, the author and his agent took a measured but persistent approach, but by that time it was too late. In retrospect, when the book first started getting good reviews, they should have gone to the publisher and rattled whatever cages they needed to in order to get more books printed. All the more reason to make sure an electronic version of your book is available!

Back to the Bookstore

We've talked about chains, independents and discount retailers. Chain bookstores are owned by large corporations. Independent bookstores are more often owned by individuals and/or small companies. A subcategory here is independents that have branched out into several locations. Then there are the discount retailers like Costco, Target and Walmart. And then there's Amazon, the Barnes & Noble site and a million other websites where you can sell your book.

Now it's time for some surprising numbers. It seems almost counter-intuitive, but the fact is, even though discount retailers account for a large percentage of all book sales, they carry only a fraction of the titles stocked by more traditional bookstores. Discount retailers tend to concentrate on best-sellers and reference books; by comparison, only 5% of B&N's total sales are bestsellers. For many independents, this percentage is even smaller. So if you're the next J.K. Rowling, many of your sales will come from Costco. However, you're going to have a very hard time getting your 500-page epic poem about a heroic apricot into these discounters.

Many authors are confused about how to approach and work with the various kinds of bookstores. So we're going to go into the matter in detail to dispel all confusion and quell your anxieties.

Ch-Ch-Chains

When we wrote the last edition of this book, there were two nationwide chains in the United States: Barnes & Noble and Borders. Now we're down to just the former, plus a few regional chains. Barnes & Noble remains a powerful player in the industry. They offer thousands of titles. They hold author events and help to kick-start new writers' careers through programs like B&N's Discover Great New Writers. They've also created reader-friendly, kid-happy environ-ments where you can get a cappuccino, a baked good and read anything you want in peace, browsing to your heart's delight, basking in all those books.

> "Where is human nature so weak as in the bookstore?"
>
> —*Henry Ward Beecher*

Every chain, whether it's Barnes & Noble or a regional chain like Books-a-Million, has a central headquarters and individual stores that each have a similar look and feel. Headquarters does most of the ordering of books and

Where Bookstores Buy Books

Oddly enough, most bookstores order many of their books not from publishers, but from *wholesalers*—companies that stock books for publishers (so that bookstores can order them with ease) but do not necessarily actively go out and sell them.

Ingram is this country's largest wholesaler of books to booksellers. And booksellers like to do business with them because they can do one-stop shopping and receive one bill. In general, bookstores tend to order front-list books directly from the publisher. Then, when a book becomes backlist, they go to Ingram.

There's a whole host of other wholesalers, too. (Baker & Taylor is a major wholesaler that primarily services libraries.) And then there are numerous regional wholesalers.

makes most of the decisions about where they're placed in the stores around the country. Indeed, just about everything that happens in the individual stores is determined by headquarters personnel. Although the stores may have some autonomy, their hands are often tied when it comes down to the act of buying books or scheduling readings.

Some chains, like Barnes & Noble, have buyers who order only for particular regions. Confusingly, sometimes the regional buyer has the power to buy for the entire country. Say, for example, you've written a southwestern cookbook. Chances are, the regional buyer for the Southwest has a much better sense of your book's potential than the head buyer based in New York. So your sales rep may pitch this buyer instead of the national cookbook buyer.

If, however, you have an Italian cookbook, chances are your rep will want to go straight to the main buyer. This one person is responsible for nearly every cookbook buy for the entire chain. If that buyer thinks Italian cooking is on the outs, you're in trouble. Want to convince her otherwise? Making contact with her is extremely difficult because, as you can imagine, every author and every publisher in this category would like to speak with her. As a result, attempts to contact a buyer can actually do more harm than good. What you can do is get to know the sales people who go out and sell your books to the chains, and give them the ammunition they need to convince the buyer that Italian food is where it's at. James Wehrle of Workman Publishing says what a sales rep needs to know is "why your book is needed and why it will stand out within a category—ultimately, what is going to make someone come and seek out your book among all the other titles?" Again we see how placing yourself in a larger context and being able to clearly demonstrate value helps propel books into the hungry hands of your readers.

You can, of course, approach individual stores in a chain and get to know the people there. The manager at your local outpost of a chain can become a big ally. In fact, he can contact headquarters and suggest that they carry your book or tell a regional buyer to take a serious look at it.

And if you're lucky enough to get a VIP on the phone, make sure your perfected pitch is on the tip of your tongue.

> ▶ Worried that your book is selling like gangbusters in far-flung locations, miles and miles away from and unbeknownst to headquarters? Put your mind at ease. Headquarters scours sales reports daily from the biggest to the teeniest outpost. And if they see that your book is moving, they'll beef up orders accordingly.

How to Get Your Book in the Door

To help you understand the world of retail, we interviewed some of America's most beloved independent booksellers about how to get in their stores. You'll start to identify some common themes . . .

- **Elaine Petrocelli,** owner, Book Passage, Corte Madera, California: "The best way to approach a bookseller about carrying your book or holding an event is to shop there and to express your enthusiasm so that they know you're part of their community."

- **Carole Horne,** general manager, Harvard Bookstore, Cambridge, Massachusetts: "Be nice and low-key. Don't insist on talking to a manager or a buyer. The worst thing you can do is be pushy and rude, and yet so many authors do just that. Low-key and nice: good. Pushy and rude: bad."

- **Nancy Peters,** co-owner, City Lights Bookstore, San Francisco, California: "Introduce yourself briefly and leave a catalog or flyer and ordering information. Of course, buying a few books is never going to hurt!"

- **Margaret Maupin,** retired trade buyer, The Tattered Cover, Denver, Colorado: "A great thing to do is come in and say you're going to be on the local news on Saturday at noon and you'll mention that people can buy your book at our bookstore. You should also say you're going to link our bookstore to your website."

- **Linda Bubon,** co-founder, Women & Children First, Chicago, Illinois: "Sometimes having someone else introduce your book for you can be more effective. Ask your friends or another writer who has had some success."

- **Valerie Lewis,** co-owner, Hicklebee's, San Jose, California: "Many authors think they're the first ones to come in here and pitch a book. You've got to understand that I have boxes of books waiting for me to read. The best way to approach us is to come in and say, 'Hi, I'm a local author and I've written a book, and I'd love you to sell it here. What's the best way for me to follow up?' And be sensitive. When someone takes a giant step toward you, you tend to take a giant step back. Approach gently."

- **Tom Campbell,** co-owner, Regulator Books, Durham, North Carolina: "Walk into the store with your book in hand and show us the goods. It's important that your book fit in with our store. We're a general bookstore, but we don't sell romance novels, for example."

■ **Jill Bailey,** former buyer, BookPeople, Austin, Texas: "Do not show up unannounced. Be respectful of people's time. Do your research. Make sure you're talking to the right person. And get to the point. Sometimes people send me 10 pages of quotes without giving me a real sense of what their book is about or letting me know how to get in touch with them. Make it easy to find you."

■ **Ty Wilson,** buyer, Copperfield's Books, Sebastopol, California: "It's better to call first than to just walk in cold. That way, you don't put instant pressure on the buyer. Be upbeat. It's better to soft-sell. Your pitch has to be content-oriented. The more articulate you can be about your book, the better."

■ **Roberta Rubin,** former owner, The Bookstall, Winnetka, Illinois: "Attitude is so important. Authors have to be sensitive to what's going on in the store when they come in. If I'm in a good mood, and it's not crazy, I'm much more likely to be receptive. But please, don't pester me. Don't make me feel like I'm a publisher. I'm a bookseller."

■ **Rick Simonson,** buyer, Elliott Bay Books, Seattle, Washington: "If I were to give a one-word answer, it would be: patience."

■ **Frank Sanchez,** head buyer, Kepler's Books, Palo Alto, California: "The best way to present your book for consideration is to call and set up an appointment. I review most titles coming into the store, and the things I look for, besides content, are physical quality of publication and a willingness to work with us. Many authors I speak with are understandably enthusiastic about their book, but they need to be realistic as well. Getting books into the store is just a first step."

■ **Deb Covey,** buyer, Joseph-Beth Booksellers, Cincinnati, Ohio: "Walk in with your book in hand and a good press release, not just a mock-up. Attitude is also very important. Some authors come in all cocky; they don't understand that we're inundated with books. It really helps to be honest and open and friendly."

■ **Debby Simmons,** inventory and distributed products manager, Deseret Book Company, Salt Lake City, Utah: "We're in a niche market, so it's really important to do your research and make sure your book fits in with what we sell. Then bring or send us your book with a press release, and make sure you follow up."

Declaration of Independents

Independent bookstores tend to be more mom-and-pop (though by no means necessarily small) operations, started by an individual or a family with a great passion for books. Melissa Mytinger, the events coordinator for The Booksmith in San Francisco, says, "Our staff throughout the store are well read, and they're encouraged to express their opinions. We do take chances on smaller books. Small, university and independent publishers are welcome here." This is why it's so important to make connections with people in these bookstores. They can buy and sell your opus one copy at a time.

Since we published the first edition of this book, the world of independent bookselling has gone topsy-turvy. In the old days, general independent bookstores had to carry some of everything. Now they've become more curated. "For people to get in their car and travel to my store, they'd have to have the expectation that they'd find what they want," says Mitchell Kaplan, owner of Miami's Books & Books and past president of the American Booksellers Association. "Now, with the Internet, it's my job to make sure my stores are attractive to my customers through our selection. Differentiation is what customers want now. For example, we opened with a very strong Art, Architecture, Design section. That's something the Internet doesn't do very well because people want to *look* at books like these."

A Man and His Passion

I f you want to experience the height of independence, visit Powell's Books in Portland, Oregon. Starting in the 1970s in an old car dealership, Michael Powell and his father, Walter, a retired painting contractor, created a bookstore with an unorthodox modus operandi. They put used and new books, hardcover and paperback, all on the same shelves. People said they were mad—it would never work. But Michael Powell had a vision. He hired knowledgeable staff to gently guide customers to the books of their desire. He brought in amazing writers to read and talk. And he stayed open 365 days a year.

They were so successful that today Powell's Books is a vast empire, a truly wondrous emporium of all kinds of books under the sun, with book-loving staff to show you where everything is. It is also one of the most successful independent ebookstores, serving customers around the globe. And it is also a store that will carry a great book even if it was published at Kinko's. Because Michael Powell is, as he says, "committed to giving all worthy books, big or small, easy or difficult, a chance to meet their readers and win them over."

Obviously, each store's niche will vary. The neighborhood around a bookstore will tell you a lot about how, exactly, to pitch your book. In fact, the best independent bookstores are the beating hearts of their neighborhoods. Plugged into what's happening all around them, they're centers of learning and knowledge and fun. They know their readers, and their readers trust them to know what books are relevant to them. Gary Frank, who owned and ran San Francisco's Booksmith for many years, describes his relationship with his neighborhood: "We're in the Haight-Ashbury, so we have a lot of quirky stuff here. That's one of the things that makes independent bookstores unique—we cater to our neighborhood. In terms of how I order my books, I look at lots of catalogs, and book companies come and pitch me their lists. And then I use my instinct and my knowledge of the community." The more you can convince an independent bookseller that your book represents an interesting and valuable addition to his niche, the better your chance of getting a hit.

Selling Books in Unexpected Places

S pecial markets are places you wouldn't normally expect to sell a book. Doctors' offices, hair salons, the backs of cereal boxes. But if you do it right, you can sell lots of books in these very special places. Sometimes a book can do very poorly in bookstores yet sell thousands of copies to special markets. *The Recovery Book* by Al J. Mooney, M.D., and Arlene and Howard Eisenberg sold minimally in bookstores but did fabulously with hospitals and treatment programs and nontraditional groups. This book now has more than 324,000 copies in print.

Some special markets make immediate sense, but some require more imagination. For example, maybe your book about humor in the workplace can be sold to Southwest Airlines as an employee giveaway since Southwest considers humor a job prerequisite. Maybe your book about famed flatulence artist Le Petomane would make a great special promotion for Beano.

Here's Jenny Mandel, director of special markets at Workman: "Special market sales are the forgotten stepchild of publishing because people don't understand them. They can be bigger than independents and chains, and these opportunities to sell books are more and more valuable. But they are extremely hard to come by. You face a lot of rejection."

It's hard to sell to special markets with anything but a finished book, because people want to see the final product. But in the meantime there's no reason why you shouldn't ask to meet with a special sales person at your publisher's. Prepare a list of companies you think your book would be appropriate for as a tie-in or as a giveaway. Include mail-order catalogs. Don't forget the obvious. You may also want to prepare pitch letters tailored for each company that you can hand over to the appropriate person. It's back to the old formula: 1) Make a connection. 2) Personalize your pitch. 3) Provide information about you that will entice buyers.

If you're going after a special sale yourself, follow the advice of Frank Fochetta, director of special sales and custom publishing at Simon & Schuster: "Before calling on a potential buyer, learn as much as you can about the company. If the company is nearby, go to its offices to pick up its literature. If you can afford the time and money, go to trade shows and talk with the company's salespeople. Try to make an appointment with your particular prospect, who is likely to be the product manager or, if you're dealing with a consumer products company, the brand manager."

Even if your publisher puts only minimal effort into special sales, there's no reason you can't take the ball and run with it. As Jenny Mandel says, "Nothing about special markets is rocket science. It's all about staying after it. Usually you don't get a callback, or you find out the book's been passed on to someone else. It's a scavenger hunt."

One of the tricks with special sales is locating the right person to target within a company. And then it's all about follow-up. Jenny has this final advice: "This job is really about finding the needle in a haystack. The best thing authors can do is go out and see what kinds of special markets would be interested in their book. There has to be a place for their book. It has to fit."

Sales on the Web

The web, if used correctly, can be a deep sales well for your book. "To optimize sales, make your book as discoverable as you can possibly make it," says Mike Shatzkin, the man behind the Shatzkin Files blog and one of publishing's most relied-upon oracles. Mike adds, "You want to be sure you have as much of your book online and searchable by Google as you can. The more you put up there, the more people can find it and buy it."

Most authors find selling books off their own websites a big hassle due to the space, time and attention it takes to warehouse, ship and process orders, as well as the effort it takes to make their sites e-commerce friendly. If you fit into this category, your best bet is to become both an Amazon and an Indiebound affiliate. Establish accounts, and these affiliate programs will allow you to set up a direct link on your site to your book's page on Amazon and, in Indiebound's case, to local booksellers. For each sale that comes through a link on your site, you make a small percentage. No hassle, plus a little dough in your pocket. And each sale counts on your royalty statement and toward bestseller lists.

> Are you hesitant about the free content available via search engines and through "look inside" programs? Mike Shatzkin says, don't worry! "If you want to read a book, you don't want to read the whole thing on a computer. You'll either buy a hard copy or download the ebook and read it on your reading device."

That said, your own website has the potential to be a powerful sales outlet *if* it's optimized, i.e., if people are able to easily find your site when searching for your book. If people find you before they find your book at a large e-retailer, you'll be in a position to rack up some sales. And if you handle the warehousing, shipping and processing of books yourself, you get to keep a larger piece of the pie. Especially with small presses or self-publishing, your website's sales could represent the bulk of your overall sales, so you'll want to be sure your site is easy to find AND easy to order from. (Return to Chapter 11 for information on how to do this.)

To entice readers to buy directly from you, you may want to offer a special bonus. Dr. Nancy Kay, author of *Speaking for Spot,* offers personalized signed books plus a donation to a charity related to her book. Just remember, since you're not a bookstore, any books you sell will not count toward bestseller lists.

Moving Up the Ranks

Amazon has not only become a great way to sell books electronically, but it's also become every author's favorite way of monitoring sales. Amazon has a feature called the Amazon Sales Rank, which rates your book in comparison to other books they sell. It's hard to know how your book is selling, so it's extremely tempting to check its status on Amazon regularly. Okay, hourly. Okay, every 30 seconds.

Truth be told, Amazon rankings may or may not relate to the overall sales of your book. If you're on the *Today* show, you might see your book fly up through the ranking system—a good indicator that it's selling well around the country at that particular moment, sure, but as many published authors can tell you, moments have a tendency to come and go. On the other hand, your book may sell well on Amazon but not do particularly well elsewhere. Or, conversely, you may have a book that's selling fabulously in hip-hop shops around the country but ain't doing diddly-squat on Amazon. Better to focus on what you *can* control. Send a tweet, post a comment, write a brilliant chapter of your next book. That said, if you were to pop in on us unexpectedly, you'd be sure to find Arielle glued to the screen, checking the ranking of one of her books.

Lovely, Luscious Libraries

There are just over 120,000 libraries in the United States, and you want your book in as many of them as possible. Libraries are also potential event spaces for readings or author panels. And librarians can be a great source of word-of-mouth buzz if they know about your book. You simply cannot underestimate the power of the librarian. Remember Michael Moore's story about how *Stupid White Men* finally got published? His book was saved from the recycling bin by the networking power of librarians.

> "I have always imagined that Paradise will be a kind of library."
>
> —*Jorge Luis Borges*

One of the other great things about libraries is that no matter how offbeat your subject is, there's sure to be a librarian who has a collection it will fit right into. Libraries also tend to be great buyers of regional books. If you have a book that concentrates on a specific area, be sure all your local libraries know about it. Use your local libraries, and befriend your librarians. Show up at events and fund-raisers. When the moment is right, be prepared with your pitch, promotional material and book.

Back to School

Getting your book taught in elementary and high schools or at colleges and universities can result in backlist manna. Some publishing companies have marketing departments and sales reps specifically devoted to targeting schools across the country and around the globe.

If you feel your book is worthy of course adoption, rejigger your pitch accordingly and get it posthaste to the appropriate people at your publisher's (ask your editor who handles this type of sale). Ideally, they will send an email/

flyer to every applicable department in the country (it's expensive to buy these lists, so your publisher may start with one particular group).

If your publisher isn't active in this area (or if you are your own publisher), don't be discouraged—but do anticipate some heavy lifting. Internet searches are your best bet for tracking down colleges and universities, but breaking into curriculum is no snap of the fingers. A track record of lecturing and/or presenting at well-known schools will be a tremendous help. You can use this pedigree to lure prospective academics to buy your book, put it on their reading lists and maybe bring you in to lecture.

Rotten Returns

Remember our warnings about returns? They're about to rear their ugly heads again. In this day and age, when a bookstore's margin of profit per title is tiny, booksellers often exhibit very little patience when it comes to waiting for a book's success. If a title doesn't sell within a few months, it goes back to the publisher with its tail between its legs.

While the percentage of books returned tends to fall somewhere between the 10% and 25% mark, it can run as steep as 75%. If you have returns, know that you're in excellent company. Almost every book suffers from returnitis.

Should you want to know how many of your books are being returned, check your royalty statement, which lists sales, returns and reserves. (For more on reserves, see page 202.)

The War of the Remainder Table

If your book is shortly coming out in paperback or if it's not selling well, your publisher may take the copies they have on hand and remainder them because of the steep cost of warehousing them. Remaindered books are sold at such deep discounts that neither you nor your publisher makes much money from the sale.

If this happens to you, don't freak out. Check the remainder table at your local bookstore. What do you see? Lots of bestselling authors? Books that were on the *New York Times* bestseller list? Yes! Remaindering happens whenever a publisher prints beyond the demand, so you're in very good company. Often, the best of company. Only when you're remaindered can you say, "I saw my book sandwiched between Philip Roth and Toni Morrison!"

The Last Word on Royalties

One of the most common questions we hear from first-time authors is "When do I get my royalties?" If you're among the lucky few who do manage to earn out their advances, there's likely to be a long lag time before you get your cut. Sometimes up to a year, and occasionally, with a smaller or (gasp!) disreputable publisher, never.

If and when you receive statements, you want to know how to decipher the gobbledygook. Some royalty statements seem almost purposely gobbledy-gookish, as if meant to confuse authors about how many copies their book has sold; in fact, their opacity is a reflection of publishing's byzantine accounting process.

Note that your royalty statement will probably reflect sales that occurred a number of months ago. Be sure to check the end date of the royalty statement so you know exactly what period it covers.

A good royalty statement should include:

■ The number of copies sold, returned and held in reserve.

■ The number of copies sold as ebooks, at a high discount, as exports, through mail order and all the other types of sales detailed in your contract.

■ Sub-rights income (for foreign sales, book club, audio, serial rights, etc.).

■ Sales made in the particular period of the statement as well as total sales to date.

If your statement does not include this information, ask your publisher or agent. It's your right to know.

Once you've gathered everything you need, it's time to check the accuracy of your statement. This is a huge pain, and yet it's very important. The royalty statement is put together by someone in the accounting department at your publisher's who undoubtedly works on many royalty statements; therefore, human errors crop up. One decimal point in the wrong place can be the difference between a trip to the Bahamas and an evening at Chuck E. Cheese. Daniel Greenberg, co-owner of the Levine Greenberg Rostan Literary Agency, was nitpicking his way through a client's royalty statement when he discovered an error. He checked it several times, and the math didn't lie—his client was owed just shy of $100K! Imagine the client's delight when he received that phone call.

You may not have as meticulous an agent, if you have one at all, so hone your own nitpicking skills. Here's how:

1. Ask your editor or the appropriate person in your publisher's royalty/accounting department how many books were in print up to the end date of your royalty statement. Then add up the total number of books sold, returned and held in reserve. Is that number close to the in-print number?

2. In all likelihood, your contract stipulated a "reasonable" reserve for returns. Does the reserve for returns on your royalty statement really seem "reasonable"? If your book has been out for more than a couple of years, this number should be small.

One Man, One City, One Book

Remember Tamim Ansary? His memoir, *West of Kabul, East of New York,* was published in 2003. Five years after it came out (the five-year mark being a time when many books go out of print), Tamim's book was selected for the One City One Book program in Waco, Texas. The phenomenal program has participating cities choose a single book for everyone to read at once. The hope is that conversation, intellectual stimulation and friendship will occur when everyone's reading list is the same. It also gives a sensational sales and publicity spike to the chosen book.

They say lightning doesn't strike twice, but it did for Tamim. After Waco came San Francisco—his hometown. Tamim had the pleasure of walking around his very own city and seeing people read his book. It doesn't get much better than that for an author!

How did Tamim get so incredibly lucky? He picked a timely subject. He established himself as an expert. He continually keeps his book in the limelight by writing essays and articles for local and national media outlets. He makes sure that he lectures, speaks and presents locally—which, in combination with the small tour his publisher sent him on when the book came out, has led to speaking engagements across the country. He reaches out to his core audience. He runs a well-known and respected writers' workshop in San Francisco, where you can find him almost every Tuesday night. And for years, he has involved himself in the largest literary festival in the Bay Area: Litquake.

Clearly, Tamim's success isn't really attributable to luck. It's expertise, skill and relentless dogged persistence that led Tamim's book to blossom and bloom, just at the time in its life when so many others are withering and dying. And, of course, it doesn't hurt that it's a most excellent book.

3. Most contracts have escalating royalties. This is one of the biggest trouble spots in royalty statements, especially if your escalators are not typical. Publishers sometimes continue to calculate your royalties at the original rate. So pull out your contract and make sure that if, for example, your royalty rate is supposed to go up after 5,000 copies, this is reflected in your statement.

4. Does your statement account for all sub-rights sales? Does it list exactly who the sales were made to? If your book sold to Italy and you want to know how it's doing there, you can request those royalty statements as well.

It doesn't happen often, but occasionally there will be an irreconcilable discrepancy between the number of copies you think you've sold and the number of copies your publisher claims they've sold. This is usually an accounting/ mathematics problem; however, a few publishers have knowingly underreported sales of books. Should you find yourself in either situation, you have recourse. If your contract includes a stipulation that an accountant of your choice is allowed to examine the publisher's books (see page 207), now is the time to ask for an audit. Be sure to hire an accountant who has experience with publishing audits. Contact The Authors Guild if you have trouble finding the right person.

During this audit, your accountant will actually get to look at how many orders have been placed by bookstores, distributors and other sales channels. By delving deep into the publisher's numbers, he'll be able to determine exactly how many books have sold and exactly how much money you're owed. While this may be a last resort and can possibly result in strained relations, sometimes it's the only way to make sure your publisher SHOWS YOU THE MONEY!

Keep the Sales Train Rolling

Print books can lead long, healthy lives or they can disappear in the blink of an eye. But ebooks and print-on-demand technologies mean books can now live forever. Which means you'll be using the techniques we've described in this chapter as guidelines in the ongoing quest to sell your book. From bookstores, websites, universities and libraries to conventions to pet stores, yoga centers, beauty salons and candy stores, the whole wide world is a fertile breeding ground in which you can plant the seeds from which the sales of your book will grow.

Happy sales to you!

CHAPTER 15

Okay, What's Next?

"Writing is like prostitution. First you do it for the love of it, then you do it for a few friends, and finally you do it for money."

—*Molière*

YOU WROTE A BOOK. YOU GOT IT PUBLISHED, or published it yourself. People bought it—maybe a lot of people, maybe not a lot of people. But no matter what, you put your passion into print. Bravo for you.

So, what now? We recommend conducting a Post-Publishing Experience Exercise. Think about your own book—everything from your first I've-got-an-idea moment to your appearance on the *Today* show or at your mother's reading group. Then make two lists. A FUN list. And an UNFUN list. Put all of your publishing experiences into one of those lists. Relive the fun, then relive the pain. Which list is longer?

The Zimmerman brothers, the Glimmer Twins of publishing and the authors of numerous books, remind us of some of the things we love about being an author: "For example, reading a post on the Internet from a reader who was helped out emotionally or inspired by reading your work. We've had men read our books aloud to their fathers as they lay dying in the hospital. Seeing people buying the book. Getting published in other countries is cool, too!"

Jemiah Jefferson, award-winning author of three books, including the vampire novel *Wounds,* reminds us of some of the things we hate about being an author: "I have had my cover ideas ignored. I've had the titles of my books changed—and then gotten no publicity budget. They ignore my corrections on the proofs, and, of course, I don't get paid very much. Just because you have good intentions and skills and whatnot doesn't mean anything. It's a crapshoot almost as vicious as Hollywood. The only advantage is that you don't have to go to Hollywood."

If, after careful consideration, you decide to write another book, make two more lists. Your RIGHT list. And your WRONG list. Evaluate your choice of agent, publisher, editor and your relationship with each. Review how you handled publicity, marketing, sales. Reread your book and see how it holds up.

You may feel the urge to disappear. Resist! Instead, ponder what you can do next time to enhance and expand upon your successes. How can you eliminate your mistakes and avoid the publishing pitfalls? Can you write a better book? Get more online love? Take advantage of more promotional opportunities? Improve your events? Attend more book festivals and writers' conferences? Kickstart your speaking career? Turn your social networking from a small lunch gathering into a massive rave?

To paraphrase an old Chinese proverb: *Those who do not learn from the past are stupid.*

Don't Make the Same Mistake Twice

Did you enjoy working with your publishing team? Or, if you self-published, was your team of one enough? Did they/you get the job done? Again, if you had a publishing team, you don't have to be in love with them as long as they did right by you. Conversely, you may have the sweetest, nicest agent and/or publisher in the world, but sweet and nice don't feed the baby. We highly recommend having a where-have-we-been, where-are-we-going talk with all of them. Ask which parts of the process went well for them and which didn't. And vice versa. Many people will avoid confrontation at any cost and thus leave an agent or publisher without resolving any differences or voicing their disappointments. We always advocate open discussion before jumping ship. It can lead to a better, more successful relationship if you decide in the end to work together again.

At the same time, keep your eyes, ears, nose and mind open to what and/or who is out there. Meet with everyone you can. You never know when you might need them or they might need you. If you decide it's time for a change, consider this before you do anything rash: It's much easier to find a new agent or publisher when you already have one. Of course, if your old agent or publisher doesn't want to work with you anymore, you won't have this option; you'll have to go out and find a new one.

Have other agents or publishers come up along your publishing journey who seem like a good match? Do you have new author friends who would like to introduce you to their own agents or publishers? If not, return to Chapters 4 and 5 to start the selection process all over again.

Look at the Numbers

B efore you start thinking about your next project, take a serious look at how your book has done in the marketplace. Unless it's sold like hotcakes, this can be a depressing task, which may explain why many authors don't do it. But if writing another book is something you want in your future, then do it you must. Have you earned out your advance? Was your publisher happy with your sales? Has your book gone through multiple printings?

The cold hard truth is this: If your first book didn't sell as many copies as expected, your publisher will be less inclined to do another book with you. And if your sales were disappointing and meager and you go ahead and write a second book, the big accounts like Barnes & Noble will more than likely order no more copies (and maybe fewer) than they sold your first time out. This can be a huge drag, especially if you're convinced that your new book can do much better. When you choose an idea for a second book, be aware of this reality. You have to either fight it or circumvent it. You can fight it with a pitch that has a promise so persuasive that it turns everyone's eyes into slot machines cranked and landing on dollar signs. Or you can circumvent it by writing a book in a totally different category. For example, if your first book was a reference book, your second book could be a novel. When an author's books are in such divergent categories, booksellers don't compare numbers. If neither of these choices makes sense for you, you can always push forward knowing that you will receive a smaller advance (if you got an advance at all) and that you may get the same number of copies out as your first book sold. Maybe shop this new book to a smaller publisher who would be satisfied by those numbers. Consider self-publishing. But no matter what, don't fool yourself into thinking that the numbers will have no effect on your next sale.

Have the Next Idea Ready

Make sure to have a few excellent ideas in your pocket. Just in case the gods shine down upon you, and right out of the gate your book takes off and you're suddenly hot-hot-hot.

But even if your book doesn't fly off the shelves, you never know where or when opportunity may knock. Even if you wrote a book that few people bought, if it got some decent reviews or won an award or if, in fact, it was a really great book, someone somewhere will probably want to publish your next one. Or maybe you'll be at a book conference and you'll meet an editor who casually mentions how much she wants a book just like the one you've been pondering. If you've got a good pitch, or maybe even a proposal that you can send out, you may just have your second book contract. After David's first memoir came out, he was approached by a Young Adult editor. His memoir is decidedly not suitable for YA, but the editor loved the style of his voice and thought it could translate really well to a younger audience. David, who never stops writing, happened to have a YA book he had been developing for years. Six months later, he had a six-figure, two-book deal!

For those of you looking for a career as a professional writer, we turn once

Go, Girl

Although we all have fantasies of how life-changing the publication of that first book will be, it rarely happens that way, and there are very good reasons why. It's incredibly hard work to both write and publish a book at the top of one's game, and it takes time—a lot of time—to do these jobs well. It also usually takes more than one book to improve our craft, learn from our mistakes, build up our networks and so on. This couldn't have been more true for Gillian Flynn, author of the mega-bestseller *Gone Girl.* "If there is a recipe for the success of *Gone Girl,* I think two of the most important ingredients are Gillian's first two books, *Sharp Objects* and *Dark Places,*" says Gillian's literary agent, Stephanie Rostan of the Levine Greenberg Rostan Literary Agency. *Sharp Objects* was written over a seven-year period during which Gillian had a full-time job as a TV critic, which required a very different kind of writing from her. "I think *Sharp Objects* is an outstanding example of a writer working to find her voice, her unique point of view on the story she is telling," adds Stephanie. *Sharp Objects* was published to good reviews and very strong endorsements from fellow writers, sold respectably and received a nomination for the Best First Novel Edgar Award.

After such a successful debut, many writers would be tempted to retread similar ground again to the Zimmermen: "Here's some advice we never got but learned through the process of getting published. When your book is published and turned in, don't just stop there and wait for it to be released. You should be working on your next project. Then, besides that, you should have one or more additional projects in development. As a professional writer, you must always be a book or two ahead of what's in the stores. That keeps you fresh and eliminates being the needy writer in case that book doesn't do as well as you thought it would. You're already on to the next thing. Don't be a one-trick pony. Have various interests so you can come up with new ideas. Challenge yourself by writing about many different worlds. If you just put out one book and it doesn't do well, then your self-esteem suffers. But if you're aggressively chasing new projects all the time, the possibilities are expanded. Don't be overly precious about that one published piece. Move on right away! While it may be your masterpiece, it's still only one book. We see too many writer friends hanging their reputations as writers on one work."

If full-time writing isn't your thing but you know you want to pen another book down the line, it's still important to keep the idea mill churning. Either way, the question will always be:

What to write?

with their second book, but Gillian expanded her horizons with *Dark Places*. Structurally more ambitious, *Dark Places* uses multiple points of view and two different time periods to weave together a story that is part murder mystery and part family drama. It took fewer than seven years—but more than two—to write. While she dove further into the voice she honed in *Sharp Objects,* she also pushed herself to tell a bigger story and to explore what happens when you dig down to the foundation of more than one character. "While *Sharp Objects* is an excellent book, you can see her evolution as a writer in the challenge she takes on in *Dark Places,*" says Stephanie. *Dark Places* also received solid review attention, had respectable sales and really established Gillian as a writer who was not a one-hit wonder, but instead someone who was serious about her craft and intended to experiment and evolve.

With two books under her belt, Gillian had laid the groundwork for her publisher to take a bigger risk on her career. So when she delivered *Gone Girl*—another leap forward in terms of what she was trying to do as a writer—the Random House sales force, the booksellers and the critics already knew this would be the book they had been waiting for her to write. With more than nine million copies sold to date, it was clearly worth waiting for!

Write a Sequel, or Give It a Rest?

Many people want to do sequels to their first book. A good way to gauge the validity of Your Book, Part Two, is to see if anyone wants you to write it. If no one's calling, you better have a convincing argument. Because a sequel is 99% about the numbers.

This is not to say that you should just give up on the idea of a sequel. But make sure it's the project that you MUST do next. Sometimes people do themselves a disservice by writing a sequel without a compelling reason to do so. You don't want to repeat yourself, and you don't want to dilute the continuing sales potential of your first book. On the other hand, if you have a good idea for a sequel and feel passionate about writing it, why not?

Another idea is to wait on your sequel. Write another book first about an entirely different subject and come back to a sequel later, if it's justified. It may be a good thing for you, mentally, emotionally and monetarily, to write about something else.

Becoming a Writer for Hire

If you're looking to make writing a career, you might want to take a break from your own projects and instead hook up with a celebrity, a person with a great story or an expert who wants to write a popular book. Cowriters can earn good money, learn a lot and have fun. Who to cowrite with? Sometimes you'll want to go after a person of particular interest yourself. But sometimes you can get your agent or editor to help you track down someone you can write a book with. Or you can get in touch with agents, packagers (see page 19), and/or publishers who could potentially hire you as a writer or ghostwriter. We've personally ghostwritten books with academics and business leaders, as well as for companies. Ghostwriting can be a great gig. It can also be a gigantic pain in the derrière. So a word of warning: Before you accept a ghostwriting job, be very clear about what you are going to do and what you're not. Look for red flags before you start the project. And be sure to get a contract that spells everything out.

If you decide to become a hired gun, use the research techniques laid out throughout this book to find and woo the people who could hire you.

Corralling Ideas

If you've ruled out a sequel and aren't interested in writing for anyone but yourself, then it's time to draw on your passion, your skills and your new understanding of how this madcap business works. What sections of your book did people most respond to? What did people find most interesting? What part of your pitch attracted the most media attention? What did you have the most fun talking about? Revisit old lists and try to match up your new ideas with your past successes.

Once you've narrowed down your ideas to a few, it's time to . . . start all over again!

Remember that you're an already published author, with a network of readers, media, booksellers, other writers and people who share your interests. So, once you've found your idea, start spreading the word. Blog, tweet, get your Facebook on or whatever floats your boat to start testing your idea. If you didn't do these things the first time around, try one or all of them now. With your past experience, you'll now be able to make the most of these networks and mine them for the information you need—namely, which ideas fly and float or crash and sink.

When to Send

N ow that you have a track record, your timing will influence the sale of your second book—big time.

Let's start on a positive note. If you had success with your first book, it's likely that your publisher will want to sign you on for another sooner rather than later. But don't count on this feeling lasting forever. Strike while the iron is hot. Windows of opportunity take a long time opening but close in a second.

If you didn't have the success you or your publisher dreamed of, buck up. You might have to wait a bit, but your opportunity may be closer than you think. Watch the news, continue to get out into the world, network, research and keep writing. Read the publishing trades. Search for your window—and then open it yourself. As Michael Cader, creator of Publishers Lunch and publishersmarket place.com, so eloquently puts it, "Writing in a way that connects with known and reachable audiences and publishing *well* remain the rare, and valued, skills."

Th-Th-Th-That's All, Folks!

A s we put our baby to bed, we reflected back on how it all started. After we'd both put our passions into print and written our books on our heroes, Satchel Paige and Jane Austen, our publishers told us there was no way to publicize our

"Without passion, man is a mere latent force and possibility, like the flint which awaits the shock of the iron before it can give forth its spark."

—*Henri Frédéric Amiel*

beloved babies. So we dreamed up an event called Putting Your Passion into Print. We got on the phone and cold-called enough bookstores to set up our own tour. *Et voilà!* We were on the road. A funny thing happened. Putting Your Passion into Print became our passion. And then it made it into print.

And now, as we gratefully put our new improved baby to bed, we feel inspired and alive with the possibilities of this amazing new world.

Please let us know your publishing triumphs and setbacks at thebookdoctors.com. Many of our readers, clients and students were featured in this new edition. We'd love to share *your* stories in the next one.

See ya online and at the bookstore!

Appendices

Great Books on Writing

■ *The Artist's Way* by **Julia Cameron**
Though this classic addresses artists and artists-to-be of all stripes, its method is founded on the daily practice of free-writing. Generations of productive creators have used it to incorporate writing into their lives—it's a great tool for becoming unstuck.

■ *Bird by Bird* by **Anne Lamott**
Reading this book is like talking to a great friend you've known forever—a friend who just happens to be the smartest writer you've ever met. Anne Lamott combines a poet's sensibility with a memoirist's self-awareness, and her much-beloved book stands up to countless re-readings.

■ *Eats, Shoots & Leaves* by **Lynne Truss**
We have read thousands of manuscripts by aspiring writers, and one of the things that distinguishes them from professionals is their inability to correctly use the simple but crucial tools of spelling and grammar. This book is not only a funny, dry and tongue-in-cheek read, it also hammers home how tiny things like commas, apostrophes and colons can completely change the meaning of a sentence. Panda eats shoots and leaves. Panda eats, shoots and leaves.

■ *The Elements of Style* by **William Strunk, Jr. and E.B. White**
For half a century, students and writers have turned to this book to figure out which end is up. Although *The Elements of Style* is a detailed manual on language, form and style, it is also a poignant and effective reminder that precision, brevity and clarity are the very heart and soul of great writing.

■ *Forest for the Trees* by **Betsy Lerner**
Betsy Lerner has a lot to say—she has been a writer and a poet, a big-time editor at a major New York publishing house and a very successful book agent. Her enjoyable book is a unique collection of insider publishing information and writers' dos and don'ts.

■ *If You Want to Write* by **Brenda Ueland**
The wise Brenda Ueland convincingly illustrates how a good sense of humor can overcome fear and anxiety. This book has been around for over 25 years, and it continues to speak to writers everywhere. The reason is simple: Show us a writer who doesn't suffer from fear and/or anxiety, and we will show you a leprechaun riding a unicorn holding a goose that lays golden eggs.

■ *Making a Literary Life* by **Carolyn See**
Critic, teacher and novelist Carolyn See is quite simply a class act—riotously funny, unsparingly honest (especially when it comes to writerly activities like snacking and procrastination) and just downright deep. Particularly for fiction

451

writers and memoirists, she offers an irresistible mix of anecdote and advice: "Sneak up on your material. Don't go crashing after it through the forest with a machete."

■ *The Making of a Story:*
A Norton Guide to Creative
Writing by Alice LaPlante
Weighing in at 667 pages, this is the hard-hitting textbook of the bunch, a truly comprehensive, encouraging and practical guide for fiction writers that both edifies and inspires. With tons of examples from master writers.

■ *No Plot? No Problem!*
by Chris Baty
A gonzo form of book writing has taken America by storm. Every year, during National Novel Writing Month, tens of thousands of otherwise apparently sane writers decide to write an entire novel in one month. How? The answer is contained in the title of this book: No plot, no problem. This is your guide to the wildly liberating exercise of churning out 50,000 words in 30 days. Even more intriguing? Many published novels have come out of its madness.

■ *On Writing* by Stephen King
Several people we've recommended this book to seemed surprised by the notion that Stephen King, master of commercial fiction, could write a smart, wise, useful book about writing. Those people need to wise up. Do you have any idea how difficult it is to write a book where the pages actually seem to be turning themselves?

■ *poemcrazy* by Susan Wooldridge
A glorious meditation on finding inspiration everywhere around us. Playful, deep, wise and insightful, this book will help anyone who's interested in conveying information, emotion, thoughts or feelings through words. It reminds us how art and language are all around us. We just have to pay attention.

■ *Writing Down the Bones*
by Natalie Goldberg
This book has been a writer's best friend for over three decades. Beautifully written in an easy-to-read colloquial style, it combines metaphysics, philosophy and practical tips that help unleash creativity.

■ *The Writing Life* by Annie Dillard
A brilliant writer brilliantly writing about how to write brilliantly. At 128 pages, it may be pound for pound the best value on this list. Here's one tiny example: Annie Dillard tells writers to envision an audience of terminal patients, urging them to consider what they could say that "would not enrage by its triviality."

■ *Writing the Memoir*
by Judith Barrington
With examples from great writers like Alice Walker and Frank Conroy, this practical guide shows writers how to navigate the stormy seas of the memoir. Balancing emotional honesty with artistic skill and commercial savvy with the discipline of a craftsman, this book addresses the ins and outs of what has become an extremely popular category.

■ *Zen in the Art of Writing*
by Ray Bradbury
A collection of essays from a great master, *Zen* includes a potpourri of information, inspiration, philosophical musing, poetry and a play adaptation of Bradbury's classic *Fahrenheit 451*. If you're serious about writing, there is much to be learned here.

Resources

Publications

- *2015 Guide to Literary Agents,* edited by Chuck Sambuchino (Writer's Digest Books)

- *2015 Novel & Short Story Writer's Market,* edited by Rachel Randall (Writer's Digest Books)

- *Booklist*
  P.O. Box 607
  Mount Morris, IL 61054-7564
  Tel: 888-350-0949
  booklistonline.com/subscribe

- *The Chicago Manual of Style* (University of Chicago Press) chicagomanualofstyle.org

- *Jeff Herman's Guide to Book Editors, Publishers, and Literary Agents: Who They Are! What They Want! How to Win Them Over!* by Jeff Herman (New World Library)

- *Literary Market Place (LMP): The Directory of the Book Publishing Industry* literarymarketplace.com

- *Poets & Writers Magazine* See Organizations Offering Information on Grants. pw.org

- *Publishers Weekly*
  71 West 23 Street, Suite 1608
  New York, NY 10010
  Tel: 646-746-6758
  Fax: 646-746-6631
  publishersweekly.com
  To subscribe, call 800-278-2991 or 818-487-2069
  Email: pw@pubservice.com

- *The Self-Publishing Manual* by Dan Poynter (Para Publishing) For more information on self-publishing by Dan Poynter, go to parapub.com.

Online

PUBLISHING INFORMATION AND SOCIAL MEDIA INSTRUCTION

- arstechnica.com, search for "Facebook Privacy"
- http://scratchmag.net
- http://shelf-awareness.com
- IMDB Pro: imdb.com
- mediabistro.com
- Publishers Marketplace: publishersmarketplace.com

FIND AN AGENT

- agentquery.com
- agentresearch.com

FIND A COAUTHOR

- Check out the referral service at the American Society of Journalists and Authors: asja.org

ART AND DESIGN RESOURCES AND INSPIRATION

- 99designs.com
- aiga.org, search for "50 books 50 covers"
- apimages.com
- bookcoverarchive.com
- commarts.com
- corbis.com
- flickr.com
- gettyimages.com
- theispot.com

Low-Residency MFA Programs

- Antioch University
  MFA in Creative Writing
  Los Angeles Admissions Office
  400 Corporate Pointe
  Culver City, CA 90230
  Toll-free: 800-726-8462
  Tel: 310-578-1080 x 100
  antiochla.edu

- Bennington College
  MFA in Writing
  One College Drive
  Bennington, VT 05201
  Tel: 802-440-4452
  Fax: 802-440-4453
  Email: writing@bennington.edu
  bennington.edu

- Goddard College
  MFA in Creative Writing
  123 Pitkin Road
  Plainfield, VT 05667
  Tel: 800-906-8312
  goddard.edu

- Lesley University
  MFA in Creative Writing
  29 Everett Street
  Cambridge, MA 02138
  Tel: 888-LESLEY-U or
  617-349-8300
  Email: luadmissions@lesley.edu
  lesley.edu

- Pacific University
  Master of Fine Arts in Writing
  2043 College Way
  Forest Grove, OR 97116
  Toll-free: 800-677-6712
  Tel: 503-352-1533
  Email: gradadmissions@pacificu.edu
  pacificu.edu

- Queens University of Charlotte
  MFA in Creative Writing
  1900 Selwyn Avenue
  Charlotte, NC 28274
  Michael Kobre, On-Campus Director
  Tel: 804-337-2200
  Email: kobrem@queens.edu
  queens.edu

- Spalding University
  MFA in Writing
  851 South Fourth Street
  Louisville, KY 40203
  Toll-free: 800-896-8941 x 4400
  Tel: 502-873-4400
  Email: mfa@spalding.edu
  spalding.edu

University of Southern Maine in Portland
Stonecoast MFA in Creative Writing
98 Bedford Street
Portland, Maine 04104
Tel: 207-780-5262
Fax: 207-780-5795
Email: stonecoastmfa@usm.maine.edu
usm.maine.edu

Vermont College of Fine Arts
MFA in Writing
36 College Street
Montpelier, VT 05602
Jason Lamb, Assistant Director of Admissions
Tel: 802-828-8829 or 866-934-8232 x 8829
Email: jason.lamb@vcfa.edu
MFA in Writing for Children & Young Adults
Ann Cardinal, Director of Student Admissions and Alumni Recruitment
Tel: 802-828-8589 or 866-934-8232 x 8589
Email: ann.cardinal@vcfa.edu
vcfa.edu

Warren Wilson College
MFA Program for Writers
P.O. Box 9000
Asheville, NC 28815-9000
Tel: 828-771-3715
Fax: 828-771-7005
Email: mfa@warren-wilson.edu
warren-wilson.edu

Associations

Academy of American Poets
75 Maiden Lane, Suite 901
New York, NY 10038
Tel: 212-274-0343
Fax: 212-274-9427
Email: academy@poets.org
poets.org

American Library Association (ALA)
50 East Huron Street
Chicago, IL 60611
Toll-free: 800-545-2433
ala.org

American Society of Composers, Authors and Publishers (ASCAP)
ASCAP Building
One Lincoln Plaza
New York, NY 10023
Toll-free: 800-95-ASCAP
Tel: 212-621-6000
ascap.com

American Society of Journalists and Authors
355 Lexington Avenue, 15th Floor
New York, NY 10017-6603
Tel: 212-997-0947
asja.org

Association of Authors' Representatives, Inc. (AAR)
676A Ninth Avenue, Suite 312
New York, NY 10036
aaronline.org

The Authors Guild
31 East 32nd Street, 7th Floor
New York, NY 10016
Tel: 212-563-5904
Fax: 212-564-5363
Email: staff@authorsguild.org
authorsguild.org

■ Communication Arts
110 Constitution Drive
Menlo Park, CA 94025
Tel: 650-326-6040
commarts.com

■ Directors Guild of America (DGA)
dga.org
Go to DGA Members'
Directory to track down who
represents which director.

■ Independent Book Publishers
Association (IBPA)
1020 Manhattan Beach Boulevard,
Suite 204
Manhattan Beach, CA 90266
Tel: 310-546-1818
Fax: 310-546-3939
ibpa-online.org

■ International Thriller Writers
P.O. Box 311
Eureka, CA 95502
thrillerwriters.org

■ Mystery Writers of America
1140 Broadway, Suite 1507
New York, NY 10001
Tel: 212-888-8171
Fax: 212-888-8107
mysterywriters.org

■ Romance Writers of America
14615 Benfer Road
Houston, TX 77069
Tel: 832-717-5200
rwa.org

■ Science Fiction & Fantasy
Writers of America
P.O. Box 3238
Enfield, CT 06083-3238
sfwa.org

■ Screen Actors Guild (SAG)
5757 Wilshire Boulevard
Los Angeles, CA 90036-3600
Toll-free: (855) SAG-AFTRA
sagaftra.org

■ Sisters in Crime
Tel: 785-842-1325
Fax: 785-856-6314
Email: admin@sistersincrime.org
sistersincrime.org

■ Society of Children's Book Writers
and Illustrators
8271 Beverly Boulevard
Los Angeles, CA 90048
Tel: 323-782-1010
Fax: 323-782-1892
scbwi.org

BOOKSELLERS' ASSOCIATIONS

■ American Booksellers Association
(ABA)
333 Westchester Avenue, Suite S202
White Plains, NY 10604
Toll-free: 800-637-0037
Tel: 914-406-7500
Fax: 914-417-4013
bookweb.org

■ The Association for Christian Retail
Formerly known as Christian
Booksellers Association (CBA)
1365 Garden of the Gods Road,
Suite 105
Colorado Springs, CO 80907
Toll-free: 800-252-1950
Tel: 719-265-9895
Fax: 719-272-3508
cbaonline.org

■ Great Lakes Independent Booksellers
Association (GLIBA)
2113 Roosevelt
Ypsilanti, MI 48197
Toll-free: 888-736-3096
Tel: 734-340-6397
Fax: 734-879-1129
gliba.org

■ Independent Mystery Booksellers
Association
123 South Eastbourne
Tucson, AZ 85716
Tel: 520-326-8533
Fax: 520-326-9001
mysterybooksellers.com

■ Indiebound
indiebound.org

■ Midwest Independent Booksellers
Association (MIBA)
2355 Louisiana Avenue North, Suite A
Golden Valley, MN 55427
Tel: 763-544-2993
Fax: 612-354-5728
info@midwestbooksellers.org
midwestbooksellers.org

■ Mountains & Plains Independent
Booksellers Association (MPIBA)
MPIBA Administrative Office
208 East Lincoln Avenue
Fort Collins, CO 80524
Toll-free: 800-752-0249
Tel: 970-484-3939
Fax: 970-484-0037
mountainsplains.org

■ New Atlantic Independent
Booksellers Association (NAIBA)
2667 Hyacinth Street
Westbury, NY 11590
Tel: 516-333-0681
Fax: 516-333-0689
naiba.com

■ New England Independent
Booksellers Association (NEIBA)
1955 Massachusetts Avenue, Suite 2
Cambridge, MA 02140
Tel: 617-547-3642
Fax: 617-547-3759
newenglandbooks.org

■ Northern California Independent
Booksellers Association (NCIBA)
P.O. Box 29169
San Francisco, CA 94129
Tel: 415-561-7686
Fax: 415-561-7685
nciba.com

■ Pacific Northwest Booksellers
Association (PNBA)
338 West 11th Avenue, Suite 108
Eugene, OR 97401
Toll-free: 800-353-6764
Tel: 541-683-4363
Fax: 541-683-3910
pnba.org

■ Southern Independent Booksellers
Alliance (SIBA)
3806 Yale Avenue
Columbia, SC 29205
Tel: 803-994-9530
Fax: 309-410-0211
info@sibaweb.com
sibaweb.com

■ Southern California Independent
Booksellers Association (SCIBA)
3005 Rhodelia Avenue
Claremont, CA 91711
Tel: 909-938-5809
Fax: 619-315-0427
scibabooks.org

ORGANIZATIONS OFFERING INFORMATION ON GRANTS

■ The Authors Guild
31 East 32nd Street, 7th Floor
New York, NY 10016
Tel: (212) 563-5904
Fax: (212) 564-5363
Email: staff@authorsguild.org
authorsguild.org

■ Funds for Writers
fundsforwriters.com

■ National Endowment for the Arts
400 7th Street, Southwest
Washington, DC 20506-0001
Tel: 202-682-5400
arts.gov/grants

■ PEN American Center
588 Broadway, Suite 303
New York, NY 10012
Tel: 212-334-1660
Fax: 212-334-2181
pen.org/awards

■ Poets & Writers, Inc.
90 Broad Street, Suite 2100
New York, NY 10004
Tel: 212-226-3586
Fax: 212-226-3963
pw.org

■ Writer's Digest
writersdigest.com

Self-Publishing

AUTHOR SERVICES COMPANIES

■ Blurb
blurb.com

■ Book Baby
bookbaby.com

■ Createspace
createspace.com

■ Greenleaf Book Group
greenleafbookgroup.com

■ Ingram Spark
ingramspark.com

■ Wheatmark
wheatmark.com

PRINTERS PLUS

■ BookMasters Group
30 Amberwood Parkway
Ashland, OH 44805
Tel: 877-312-3520
Fax: 419-281-0200
bookmasters.com

■ Lightning Source
1246 Heil Quaker Boulevard
La Vergne, TN 37086
Tel: 615-213-5815
lightningsource.com

TO ACQUIRE YOUR PCN

■ loc.gov/publish/pcn

TO ACQUIRE YOUR ISBN

■ isbn.org

FOR INFORMATION ON DISTRIBUTORS, WHOLESALERS, SCOUTS AND MORE

■ literarymarketplace.com

PROGRAMS FOR SELF-PUBLISHED WRITERS

■ Amazon.com Advantage
Email: advantage@amazon.com
amazon.com/exec/obidos/
subst/partners/direct/
direct-application.html

■ Barnes & Noble
barnesandnoble.com/help/
cds2.asp?PID-8153
Search for Author &
Publisher Guidelines.

Selected Publishers

Adult Publishers and Imprints

► Abbeville

► Abrams (LA MARTINIÈRE GROUPE)
- Abrams Books
- Abrams ComicArts
- Abrams Image
- SelfMadeHero
- Stewart, Tabori & Chang
  - Melanie Falick Books

► Amacom

► Amazon
- Amazon Publishing
  - 47North
  - Amazon Crossing
  - Amazon Encore
  - Jet City Comics
  - Lake Union Publishing
  - Little A
  - Montlake Romance
  - StoryFront
  - Thomas & Mercer (incorporating Avalon Books)
  - Waterfall Press
- Audible
- Brilliance Audio
  - Grand Harbor
- Powered by Amazon

- Alloy Entertainment
- The Domino Project

► Andrews McMeel

► Barron's Educational Series

► Beacon Press

► Berrett-Koehler Publishers

► Bloomsbury Publishing
- Bloomsbury USA
  - Bloomsbury
  - Bloomsbury Press
  - Continuum

► Chronicle Books

► Counterpoint, Inc.
- Counterpoint Press
- Shoemaker & Hoard
- Soft Skull Press

► F+W Books (F+W Media)
- Adams Media
  - Polka Dot Press
  - Tyrus Books
- Crimson Romance
- David & Charles
- Impact Books
- Interweave

- Merit Press
- North Light
- Prologue Books
- TOW Books
- Writer's Digest Books

▶ **Grove/Atlantic**
- Atlantic Monthly Press
- Black Cat
- Grove Press
- The Mysterious Press

▶ **Hachette Book Group**
- Center Street
- FaithWords (INCORPORATING WARNER FAITH)
  - Jericho Books
- Grand Central Publishing
  - 5 Spot
  - A Chelsea Handler Book
  - Black Dog & Leventhal
  - Business Plus
  - Forever
  - Forever Yours
  - Grand Central (INCORPORATING BUSINESS PLUS; WARNER; AND WARNER BUSINESS)
  - Grand Central Life & Style (INCORPORATING SPRINGBOARD; WARNER WELLNESS; AND WELLNESS CENTRAL)
  - Twelve (INCORPORATING WARNER TWELVE)
  - Vision
- Hachette Books
- Little, Brown and Company
  - Back Bay Books
  - Bulfinch
  - Little, Brown
  - Mulholland Books
  - Reagan Arthur Books
- Octopus USA
- Orbit
  - Redhook
  - Yen Press

▶ **HarperCollins** (NEWS CORP.)
- Harlequin Books
  - Carina Press
  - Harlequin
  - Harlequin Teen
  - Heartsong Presents
  - HQN
  - Kimani
  - Love Inspired
  - Luna
  - Mira
  - Rogue Angel
  - Spice
  - Worldwide Mystery
- Harper Christian
  - Thomas Nelson (INCORPORATING INTEGRITY HOUSE; INTEGRITY PUBLISHERS; NELSON BUSINESS; NELSON CURRENT; RUTLEDGE HILL PRESS; AND TOMMY NELSON)
  - Zondervan
    - Zondervan Gift Books
- Harper Morrow
  - Amistad
  - Avon
    - Avon A
    - Avon Impulse
    - Avon Red
  - Broadside
  - Dey Street Books (INCORPORATING HARPER ENTERTAINMENT AND IT BOOKS)
  - Ecco
    - Anthony Bourdain Books
  - Harper (INCORPORATING COLLINS)
    - Collins Reference (INCORPORATING HARPER INFORMATION AND HARPER RESOURCE)
    - Harper Business (INCORPORATING COLLINS BUSINESS)

- Harper Design
  (INCORPORATING
  COLLINS DESIGN)
- Harper Paperbacks
  - Bourbon Street Books
  - Harper Paperbacks
- Harper Perennial
- Harper Wave
- Infinitum Nihil
- It Books
  - Newmarket
- Rayo
- Voyager (INCORPORATING EOS)
  - Voyager Impulse
- William Morrow
  (INCORPORATING COLLINS LIVING)
  - Dennis Lehane Books
  - Morrow Cookbooks
  - Witness Impulse

► **Harvard Common Press**

► **Hay House**

► **Henery Press**

► **Houghton Mifflin Harcourt**
- American Heritage Dictionary
- Houghton Mifflin Harcourt
  (INCORPORATING HARCOURT;
  HARVEST; AND HOUGHTON MIFFLIN)
  - Eamon Dolan Books
  - Mariner
  - Otto Penzler Books
  - Rux Martin Books
- Peterson Guides

► **Kaplan**
- Cleveland Clinic Press
- Dearborn

► **Kensington Publishing Corp.**
- Aphrodisia
- Brava
- Citadel

- Kensington
- Lyrical Press (INCORPORATING EKENSINGTON)
- Pinnacle
- Twin Streams
- Urban Soul
- Vibe Street Lit
- Zebra

► **Macmillan** (FORMERLY HOLTZBRINCK)
- Farrar, Straus and Giroux
  - Faber
  - Farrar, Straus
  - Hill & Wang
  - Sarah Crichton Books
  - Scientific American
- Flatiron Books
- Henry Holt
  - Holt
  - John Macrae Books
  - Metropolitan
  - Times Books
- Macmillan Science
- Palgrave
- Picador USA
- St. Martin's Press
  - Griffin
  - Minotaur
  - St. Martin's
  - Thomas Dunne Books
  - Truman Talley
  - Weight Watchers
- Tor/Forge
  - Forge
  - Orb
  - Tor

► **McGraw-Hill**

► **The New Press**

► **New World Library**

► **Nicholas Brealey**

▶ Overlook Press

▶ Oxford University Press

▶ Pearson Higher Education (PEARSON)
  ■ Financial Times/Prentice Hall
  ■ Peachpit Press
  ■ Pearson
  ■ Pearson Education Benelux
  ■ Pearson Education France
  ■ Pearson Education India
  ■ Prentice Hall
  ■ Que
  ■ Sams
  ■ Wharton School Publishing

▶ Penguin Random House
  ■ Penguin Group USA
    ▪ DK
    ▪ Penguin Publishing Group
      ▪ Acento
      ▪ Alpha Books
      ▪ Avery (INCORPORATING CHAMBERLAIN BROS.)
      ▪ Berkley/NAL
        ▪ Berkley
          ▪ Ace
          ▪ Berkley
            ▪ Intermix
          ▪ Berkley Heat
          ▪ Berkley Jam
          ▪ Berkley Prime Crime
          ▪ Berkley Sensation
          ▪ Jove
        ▪ InkLit
        ▪ NAL
          ▪ Caliber
          ▪ NAL
          ▪ Obsidian Mysteries

          ▪ Onyx
          ▪ Roc
          ▪ Signet
      ▪ Blue Rider Press
      ▪ CA Press
      ▪ Celebra
      ▪ Current
      ▪ DAW
      ▪ Dutton (INCORPORATING PI PRESS)
        ▪ Dutton Guilt-Edged Mysteries
        ▪ Redeemer
      ▪ Gotham
      ▪ HP Books
      ▪ Hudson Street Press
      ▪ Penguin eSpecials
      ▪ Penguin Pintail
      ▪ Penguin Press
      ▪ Perigee
      ▪ Plume
      ▪ Portfolio
      ▪ Prentice Hall Press
      ▪ Putnam
        ▪ Amy Einhorn Books
      ▪ Riverhead
      ▪ Sentinel
      ▪ Tarcher
      ▪ Viking Penguin
        ▪ Pamela Dorman Books
        ▪ Penguin
        ▪ Viking Penguin
        ▪ Viking Studio
  ■ Penguin Random House Grupo Editorial
    ▪ Aguilar
    ▪ Alfaguara

- Beascoa
- Debate
- Debolsillo
- Electa
- Grijalbo
- Literatura Random House (INCORPORATING LITERATURA MONDADORI)
- Lumen
- Montena
- Objectiva
- Plaza & Janes
- Punto de Lectura
- Random House Mondadori
- Random House Mondadori Mexico
- Reservoir Books
- Rosa dels Vents
- Santillana
  - Manderley
- Santillana Mexico
- Santillana USA
- Sudamericana
- Suma de Letras
- Taurus
- Random House, Inc.
  - Crown Publishing Group
    - Broadway
    - Clarkson Potter
      - Potter Craft
      - Potter Style
    - Convergent
    - Crown
    - Crown Archetype
    - Crown Business (INCORPORATING DOUBLEDAY BUSINESS)
    - Crown Forum
    - Harmony
      - Deepak Chopra Books
    - Hogarth

- Image Books (INCORPORATING DOUBLEDAY RELIGION)
- Random House Information
- Ten Speed Press
  - Celestial Arts
  - Crossing Press
  - Tricycle Press
  - Watson-Guptill
    - Amphoto Books
    - Back Stage Books
    - Billboard Books
    - Lone Eagle Publishing
- Three Rivers Press
- WaterBrook Multnomah (INCORPORATING MULTNOMAH AND WATERBROOK PRESS)
- Knopf Doubleday Publishing Group
  - Anchor
  - Doubleday (INCORPORATING HARLEM MOON AND MORGAN ROAD BOOKS)
  - Everyman's Library
  - Flying Dolphin
  - Knopf
  - Nan A. Talese
  - Pantheon
  - Schocken Books
  - Vintage
  - Vintage Español
- Random House Publishing Group
  - Alibi
  - Ballantine Bantam Dell

- Ballantine
  - Ballantine Trade Paperbacks
  - Fawcett
  - Ivy
- Bantam Dell
  - Bantam Discovery
  - Bantam Spectra
  - Delacorte Press
- Del Rey
  - Del Rey Manga
- Delta
- ESPN Books
- Loveswept
- One World (INCORPORATING STRIVERS ROW)
- Presidio
- Villard
- Dial Press
- Flirt
- Hydra
- Modern Library
- Random House
- Random House Trade Paperbacks
- Spiegel & Grau

► **Perseus Books Group**
  - Avalon Travel
  - Basic
    - Basic Civitas
  - Da Capo (INCORPORATING MARLOWE & COMPANY AND THUNDER'S MOUTH)
    - Merloyd Lawrence Books
  - Nation Books

- Public Affairs
- Running Press
- Seal Press
- Vanguard Press (INCORPORATING CDS BOOKS)
- Westview

► **Phaidon**

► **The Quarto Group**
  - Aurum Publishing
    - Apple Press
    - Argentum
    - Aurum
    - Frances Lincoln
    - JR Books
    - Union Books
  - Quayside Publishing
    - Creative Publishing International
    - Fair Winds Press
    - MBI Publishing
    - Quarry Books
    - Quiver
    - Rockport
    - Voyageur
    - Walter Foster
    - Zenith

► **Quirk Books**

► **Reader's Digest**

► **Red Wheel/Weiser/Conari**

► **Rizzoli**
  - Rizzoli Ex Libris
  - Rizzoli USA
  - Skira Rizzoli
  - Universe
  - Welcome Books

► **Rodale**

► **Routledge**

▶ **Sellers Publishing**

▶ **Shambhala Publications**
- ■ Shambhala
  - ▪ Roost Books
  - ▪ Snow Lion
  - ▪ Trumpeter Books
  - ▪ Weatherhill

▶ **Simon & Schuster (CBS)**
- ■ Atria Publishing Group
  - ▪ Atria
    - · 37 Ink
  - ▪ Beyond Words
  - ▪ Emily Bestler Books
  - ▪ Howard Books (INCORPORATING HOWARD PUBLISHING)
  - ▪ Keywords Marble Arch Press
  - ▪ Strebor Books
  - ▪ Washington Square Press
- ■ Gallery Publishing Group
  - ▪ Gallery (INCORPORATING SIMON SPOTLIGHT ENTERTAINMENT)
  - ▪ Jeter Publishing
  - ▪ Pocket
    - · Downtown Press
    - · G-Unit Books
    - · Juno
    - · Karen Hunter Publishing
    - · MTV Books
    - · Paraview Pocket
    - · Pocket
    - · Pocket Star
    - · VH1 Books
- ■ Scribner Publishing Group
  - ▪ Scribner
  - ▪ Touchstone (INCORPORATING FIRESIDE AND TOUCHSTONE FIRESIDE)

- ■ Simon & Schuster Publishing Group
  - ▪ Free Press
  - ▪ Simon & Schuster
    - · Simon451
    - · Threshold

▶ **Sourcebooks**
- ■ Cumberland House
- ■ Sourcebooks Casablanca
- ■ Sourcebooks Landmark

▶ **Sterling Publishing** (BARNES & NOBLE, INC.)
- ■ Barnes & Noble
- ■ Hearst Books
- ■ Lark Books
- ■ Puzzlewright Press
- ■ Sterling
  - ▪ Splinter
- ■ Sterling Epicure
- ■ Sterling Ethos
- ■ Sterling Innovation
- ■ Union Square Press

▶ **Unbridled Books**

▶ **Walt Disney Company**
- ■ Disney-ABC Television Group
- ■ Disney Publishing Worldwide
  - ▪ Disney Book Group
    - · Disney
    - · Disney-Hyperion
    - · Kingswell

▶ **Wiley Professional/Trade** (JOHN WILEY & SONS)
- ■ Capstone
- ■ For Dummies
- ■ J.K. Lasser
- ■ Jossey-Bass
- ■ Meredith
  - ▪ Fisher Investments Press

▶ **Workman Publishing**
- Algonquin
- Artisan
- Storey
- Timber Press
- Workman

▶ **W.W. Norton**
- Countryman Press
- Liveright
- Norton

Children's Book Publishers

▶ **Abrams** (LA MARTINIÈRE GROUPE)
- Abrams Appleseed
- Abrams Books for Young Readers
- Amulet Books

▶ **Amazon**
- Amazon Publishing
  - Amazon Children's
    - Marshall Cavendish
    - Skyscape
    - Two Lions

▶ **Bloomsbury Publishing**
- Bloomsbury USA
  - Bloomsbury Children's
  - Bloomsbury Spark
  - Walker Books for Young Readers

▶ **Candlewick**

▶ **Charlesbridge**

▶ **Chronicle Books**
- Chronicle Children's

▶ **Hachette Book Group**
- LB-Kids
- Little, Brown Children's

- Little, Brown Books for Young Readers
  - Poppy

▶ **HarperCollins** (NEWS CORP.)
- Harlequin Books
  - Harlequin Teen
- HarperCollins Children's
  - Balzer + Bray
  - Greenwillow Books
  - HarperCollins Children's Books (INCORPORATING BOWEN PRESS)
  - HarperFestival
  - HarperTeen
  - HarperTeen Impulse
  - Harper Trophy
  - Joanna Cotler Books
  - Julie Andrews Collection
  - Katherine Tegen Books
  - Laura Geringer Books
  - Walden Pond Press
- Harper Christian
  - Zondervan Children's

▶ **Houghton Mifflin Harcourt**
- Clarion
- Graphia
- Harcourt Children's Books
- Houghton Mifflin Harcourt Children (INCORPORATING HARCOURT CHILDREN'S & HOUGHTON MIFFLIN CHILDREN'S)
- Sandpiper

▶ **Kensington Publishing Corp.**
- Dafina
- Kensington Children's
- Kensington Teen

▶ **Macmillan** (FORMALLY HOLTZBRINCK)
- Macmillan Children's
  - Farrar, Straus and Giroux Books for Young Readers
    - Frances Foster Books

- Margaret Ferguson Books
- Feiwel & Friends
  - Swoon Reads
- First Second
- Henry Holt Books for Young Readers
  - Christy Ottaviano Books
- Kingfisher
- Priddy Books
- Roaring Brook Press
  - Neal Porter Books
- Square Fish
- Starscape/Tor Teen

▶ **Penguin Random House**
- Penguin Group USA
  - Penguin Children's
    - Dial
    - Dutton Children's
    - Frederick Warne
    - Grosset & Dunlap
    - Kathy Dawson Books
    - Philomel
    - Price Stern Sloan
    - Puffin
    - Puffin/Speak
    - Putnam Children's
    - Razorbill
    - Viking Children's
      (INCORPORATING FIREBIRD)
- Random House Children's Group
  - Crown Children's
  - Delacorte
  - Disney Books for Young Readers
  - Dragonfly
  - Golden Books
  - Knopf Books for Young Readers

- Random House Books for Young Readers
- Robin Corey Books
- Schwartz & Wade
- Wendy Lamb Books
- Yearling

▶ **Perseus Books Group**
- Running Press Kids

▶ **The Quarto Group**
- Aurum Publishing
  - Frances Lincoln Children's
- Quayside Publishing
  - Walter Foster, Jr.

▶ **Quirk Books**

▶ **Rizzoli**
- Rizzoli Children's

▶ **Scholastic, Inc.**
- Arthur A. Levine Books
- Blue Sky Press
- Cartwheel
- Chicken House
- Graphix
- Little Scholastic
- Little Shepherd Books
- Klutz
- Michael di Capua Books
- Orchard
- Point
- PUSH
- Scholastic Paperbacks
- Scholastic Press
- Scholastic Reference
- Scholastic Nonfiction

▶ **Simon & Schuster** (CBS)
- Simon & Schuster Children's
  - Aladdin
    - Simon MIX
  - Atheneum (INCORPORATING GINEE SEO BOOKS)

- Beach Lane Books
- Jeter Children's
- Little Simon
  - Little Simon Inspirations
- Margaret K. McElderry Books
- Richard Jackson Books
- Saga Press
- Simon & Schuster Books for Young Readers
  - Paula Wiseman Books
- Simon Pulse
- Simon Scribbles
- Simon Spotlight

▶ **Sourcebooks**
- Jabberwocky
- Sourcebooks Fire

▶ **Sterling**
- Flashkids
- Sterling Children's

▶ **Walt Disney Company**
- Disney Publishing Worldwide
  - Disney Book Group
    - Disney-Hyperion Children's
    - Hyperion Children's
    - Jump At The Sun
    - Kingswell

▶ **Workman Publishing**
- Algonquin
  - Algonquin Young Readers
- Workman

Contact Information

Imprints may have their own contact information.

■ Abbeville Press
137 Varick Street
New York, NY 10013
Toll-free: 800-ART-BOOK
Tel: 212-366-5585
Fax: 212-366-6966
Email: Abbeville@abbeville.com
abbeville.com
@AbbevillePress

■ Abrams
115 West 18th Street, 6th Floor
New York, NY 10011
Tel: 212-206-7715
Fax: 212-519-1210
Email: abrams@abramsbooks.com
abramsbooks.com
@abramskids

■ Amacom
1601 Broadway, 9th Floor
New York, NY 10019
Toll-free: 800-250-5308
Fax: 518-891-3653
amacombooks.org

■ Amazon
500 Boren Avenue North
Seattle, WA 98103
apub.com

■ Andrews McMeel
1130 Walnut Street
Kansas City, MO 64106
Toll-free: 800-943-9839
Fax: 800-943-9831
andrewsmcmeel.com

- Barron's Educational Series
  250 Wireless Boulevard
  Hauppauge, NY 11788
  Toll-free: 800-645-3476
  barronseduc.com

- Beacon Press
  25 Beacon Street
  Boston, MA 02108
  Tel: 617-742-2110
  Fax: 617-723-3097
  beacon.org

- Berrett-Koehler
  1333 Broadway, Suite 1000
  Oakland CA 94612
  Tel: 510-817-2277
  Fax: 510-817-2278
  bkconnection.com

- Bloomberg Press
  Tel: 212-617-8585
  bloomberg.com

- Bloomsbury Publishing
  1385 Broadway, 5th Floor
  New York, NY 10018
  Tel: 212-419-5300
  bloomsbury.com
  @BloomsburyPub

- Candlewick Press
  99 Dover Street
  Somerville, MA 02144
  Tel: 617-661-3330
  candlewick.com
  @Candlewick

- Chronicle Books
  680 Second Street
  San Francisco, CA 94107
  Tel: 415-537-4200
  Fax: 415-537-4460
  chroniclebooks.com
  @ChronicleBooks

- Counterpoint/Soft Skull Press
  2560 Ninth Street, Suite 318
  Berkeley, CA 94710
  Tel: 510-704-0230
  Fax: 510-704-0268
  counterpointpress.com
  @CounterpointLLC

- Food & Health Communications
  P.O. Box 271108
  Louisville, CO 80027
  Tel: 800-462-2352
  Fax: 800-433-7435
  foodandhealth.com

- F + W Media
  38 East 29th Street
  New York, NY 10016
  Tel: 212-447-1400
  Email: contact_us@fwmedia.com

- Grove/Atlantic
  154 West 14th Street, 12th Floor
  New York, NY 10011
  Tel: 212-614-7850
  Fax: 212-614-7886
  groveatlantic.com
  @groveatlantic

- Hachette Book Group
  237 Park Avenue
  New York, NY 10017
  hachettebookgroup.com
  @HachetteUS

- HarperCollins
  195 Broadway
  New York, NY 10007
  Tel: 212-207-7000
  harpercollins.com
  @HarperCollins

Harvard Common Press
535 Albany Street
Boston, MA 02118
Tel: 617-423-5803
Fax: 617-695-9794
harvardcommonpress.com

Hay House
250 Park Avenue South, Suite 201
New York, NY 10003
Tel: 646-484-4950
Fax: 646-484-4956
hayhouse.com
@hayhouse

Henery Press
Plano, TX 75024
Tel: 469-298-2100
henerypress.com
@HeneryPress

Houghton Mifflin Harcourt
222 Berkeley Street
Boston, MA 02116
Tel: 617-351-5000
hmhco.com
@HMHCo

Kaplan
30 South Wacker Drive, Suite 2500
Chicago, IL 60606
Toll-free: 800-245-2665
kaptest.com

Kensington Publishing
119 West 40th Street
New York, NY 10018
Toll-free: 800-221-2647
Tel: 212-407-1500
kensingtonbooks.com
@KensingtonBooks

Macmillan
175 Fifth Avenue, Suite 300
New York, NY 10010
Tel: 646-307-5151
us.macmillan.com

McGraw-Hill
1221 Avenue of the Americas
New York, NY 10019
Tel: 877-833-5524
Fax: 614-759-3823
mhcontemporary.com

The New Press
120 Wall Street, 31st Floor
New York, NY 10005
Tel: 212-629-8802
Fax: 212-629-8617
Email: newpress@thenewpress.com
thenewpress.com
@thenewpress

New World Library
14 Pamaron Way
Novato, CA 94949
Toll-free: 800-972-6657
Tel: 415-884-2100
Fax: 415-884-2199
newworldlibrary.com
@NewWorldLibrary

Nicholas Brealey Publishing
20 Park Plaza, Suite 610
Boston, MA 02116
nicholasbrealey.com
@NicholasBrealey

Overlook Press
141 Wooster Street, Suite 4B
New York, NY 10012
Tel: 212-673-2210
overlookpress.com
@overlookpress

Oxford University Press
198 Madison Avenue
New York, NY 10016-4314
Tel: 212-726-6000
oup.com
@OUPAcademic
@OUPMusic
@OWC_Oxford

■ Pearson Higher Education
One Lake Street
Upper Saddle River, NJ 07458
pearsonhighered.com
@PearsonNorthAm

■ Penguin Random House
375 Hudson Street
New York, NY 10014
uspenguingroup.com
@penguinrandom

■ Penguin Random House
1745 Broadway
New York, NY 10019
penguinrandomhouse.com

■ Perseus Book Group
250 West 57th Street, 15th Floor
New York, NY 10107
Tel: 212-340-8100
perseusbooksgroup.com

■ Phaidon
65 Bleecker Street, 8th floor
New York, NY 10012
Tel: 212-652-5400
Fax: 212-652-5410
phaidon.com

■ The Quarto Group
400 First Avenue North, Suite 400
Minneapolis, MN 55401
Toll-free: 800-458-0454
Fax: 612-344-8691
quartous.com
@Qbookshop

■ Quirk Books
215 Church Street
Philadelphia, PA 19106
Tel: 215-627-3581
Fax: 215-627-5220
quirkbooks.com
@QuirkBooks

■ Red Wheel/Weiser/Conari
665 Third Street, Suite 400
San Francisco, CA 94107
Tel: 978-465-0504
redwheelweiser.com

■ Rizzoli
300 Park Avenue South, 4th Floor
New York, NY 10010
Tel: 212-387-3400
Fax: 212-387-3535
rizzoliusa.com
@Rizzoli_Books

■ Rodale
733 Third Avenue
New York, NY 10017
Tel: 212-697-2040
rodalebooks.com
@RodaleBooks

■ Routledge
711 3rd Avenue, 8th Floor
New York, NY 10017, USA
Tel: 212-216-7800
Fax: 212-564-7854
routledge-ny.com
@routledgebooks

■ Scholastic
557 Broadway
New York, NY 10012
Tel: 212-343-6100
scholastic.com
@Scholastic

■ Sellers Publishing
161 John Roberts Road
South Portland, ME 04106
Tel: 207-772-6833
Fax: 207-772-6814
rsvp.com
@SellersMedia

■ Shambhala Publications
300 Massachusetts Avenue
Boston, MA 02115
Tel: 617-424-0030
Fax: 617-236-1563
shambhala.com
@ShambhalaPubs

■ Simon & Schuster
1230 Avenue of the Americas
New York, NY 10020
Tel: 212-698-7000
simonandschuster.com
@simonschuster

■ Sourcebooks
1935 Brookdale Road, Suite 139
Naperville, IL 60563
Toll-free: 800-432-7444
Tel: 630-961-3900
Fax: 630-961-2168
sourcebooks.com
@Sourcebooks

■ Sterling Publishing
1166 Avenue of the Americas
New York, NY 10036
Tel: 212-532-7160
sterlingpub.com
@SterlingBooks

■ Unbridled Books
8201 East Highway WW
Columbia, MO 65201
Tel: 573-256-4106
unbridledbooks.com
@unbridledbooks

■ Walt Disney Company
125 West End Avenue, 3rd Floor
New York, NY 10023
Tel: 212-456-5500
disneybooks.com
@DisneyHyperion

■ Wiley
111 River Street
Hoboken, NJ 07030
Tel: 201-748-6000
wiley.com
@wileytweets

■ Workman Publishing
225 Varick Street
New York, NY 10014
Tel: 212-254-5900
Fax: 212-254-8098
Email: info@workman.com
workman.com
@WorkmanPub

■ W.W. Norton
500 Fifth Avenue
New York, NY 10110
Tel: 212-354-5500
wwnorton.com

Standard Permission Form

[Name of copyright holder] authorizes *[your name]* and his/her publisher, *[name of your publisher]*, and its licensees, to use the following *[photograph, article, poem, recipe, pages, lines, etc.]* from *[title of book, poem, song, article, etc.]* to use in *[title or tentative title of your book]* by *[your name]* in all versions and media and in the advertising and promotion thereof throughout the world. As full consideration for the contribution and all rights therein, *[your name]* shall pay *[name of copyright holder]* a one-time fee of _____ dollars ($_____) due within thirty (30) days of publication of the Work.* *[Name of copyright holder]* waives any claim *[name of copyright holder]* may have against the aforementioned parties, their licensees, and assigns based upon such use, including any claims for copyright infringement or violation of any right.

    [Name of copyright holder] warrants that *[name of copyright holder]* has the right to grant the above rights, that the work does not infringe upon the copyright, or other rights, of anyone. *[Name of copyright holder]* agrees to indemnify the author, *[publisher's name]* and its distributors, customers and licensees against all costs and expenses, including reasonable attorney's fees, that may result from any alleged breach of the aforesaid warranty.

_____

SIGNATURE

_____

TYPED OR PRINTED NAME

_____

DATE

* Delete this sentence if there is no fee involved.

Our Proposal for This Book

Putting Your Passion into Print

BY ARIELLE ECKSTUT & DAVID STERRY

Open This Book and Discover How to:

- Find a Top-of-the-Heap Idea

- Come Up with a Blockbuster Title

- Write a Door-Opening Query Letter

- Create an Airtight Proposal

- Find the Perfect Agent, Editor and Publisher for You

- Get People to Actually Buy Your Book

- And Much, Much More

Summary

A 61-year-old grandmother in Iowa, a 43-year-old academic in Boston, a 21-year-old surfer in Laguna Beach. What do these people have in common? THEY ALL WANT TO WRITE A BOOK! But how to get a book successfully published remains a mystery to most aspiring authors. Literary agent/author Arielle Eckstut and author/pitchman David Sterry demystify the publishing process and reveal the secrets of putting your personal passion into print.

During a recent coast-to-coast tour of their workshop of the same name, people across the spectrum of the publishing process—even published authors with agents— attended Arielle and David's workshop and came out with a whole new arsenal of bookselling weapons. Booksellers and attendees alike had only one complaint: they wished they had a book to take home with them containing all the information they had learned. Indeed, there is a profound need for a soup-to-nuts guide that illuminates each step of the bookselling process, answering every question a writer could ask. A book that addresses the particular concerns of today's authors. A book by those in the publishing trenches who know the tricks of the trade. A book that will speak to the literary fiction writer, the new age guru, the romance novelist and the high-tech businessman alike.

Putting Your Passion into Print will be this definitive tome. Written in a lively, encouraging and humorous tone, it will inspire the millions who want to get a book published.

Audience

In the days when a book cost as much as a farm, only the rich or the religious could even dream of producing a book. Well, things have changed. Now any Tom, Dick or Martha has the chance to get a book published. From those who fantasize about appearing on *Oprah* to Goth Ann Rice wannabes to the heir to the Atkins diet throne, this book will appeal to a wide (and growing) audience. Our audience breaks down into the following categories:

■ **Workshop and Conference Goers:** These are the people who populate writing workshops from Bread Loaf to Squaw Valley to the multitude of local Learning Annexes around the country. These people write predominantly literary fiction, genre fiction, creative nonfiction and children's books. They are avid readers. They often have professional writing experience and some publishing knowledge. Many have finished manuscripts in hand. What they don't have are agents or publishers.

■ **Academics Who Want to Reach a Popular Audience:** There are tens of thousands of academics out there who feel their work merits more than 12 readers. They are looking for a way to bring their work out of the ivory tower and onto the streets. Usually, these folks have little to no knowledge of trade publishing, nor have they developed a voice that will speak to Jane Q. Public. Academics will find this book particularly suited to their needs because we address questions like: Under what circumstances does it make sense to hire a writer or editor to help with style and readability? What are universal tips to "popularizing" academic work? How can you parlay your academic success into a hefty book contract?

■ **Professionals with a Message:** Just like academics, many professionals have a dream of getting their message out to those outside their immediate grasp. They also know that there's no better business card than a book. From management consultants to interior designers to taekwondo instructors, this book will help professionals take their expertise to the page and bring them business in return. We'll also show professionals how to develop a platform based on what is unique about their business and how to use this platform in each stage of the bookselling process.

■ **Hobbyists with a Mission:** Whether their passion is beer, Jane Austen or tracking down their family's genealogy, many hobbyists dream of writing books about their personal obsessions. These obsessions can make for excellent books because usually thousands, if not millions, of others are obsessed with these subjects as well. However, hobbyists often know the least about putting a book together of any of our potential audience. They may not be readers at all, and they may have very little professional or writing experience. These are the people who will want to read this book from cover to cover, so that we can hold their hands through each step of the process.

■ **Mystery Mavens, Romance Lovers, Sci-Fi Freaks and Other General-Genre Junkies:** These folks have usually read hundreds of books within a genre. And now they're at the point where they believe they are ready to write their own. Unlike the workshop junkies, they've never put pen to paper. Like the hobbyists, they need all the help they can get.

■ **Students and Educators:** When we have brought our PYPIP workshop to colleges and universities, the attendance and interest has been overwhelming. So many students want to write books and get them published. But hardly any academic programs provide this kind of information. After attending our workshop, several professors have already told us that as soon as we have a book out there, it will be required reading for all their graduate students.

■ **Published Authors Who Want to Do It Differently with Their Next Book:** Originally, we never would have thought that these people would be our audience. But our workshops proved otherwise. So many authors have had publishing experiences that either did not live up to their expectations or didn't live up to the publisher's expectations. These people want a chance to do things differently the next time around. This book will help them answer the myriad questions they may have, including: Should you have taken a lower offer from a more creative and passionate publisher? Did you start your marketing and publicity efforts as early as you could? Is a sequel your best option, or should you come out with something entirely different?

Our audience also includes people who will come to the book with specific questions: What is the proper format for a proposal? Do you need a subtitle? How do you write a query letter that someone will read? How do you write a bio that blows your own horn without making you sound like a blowhard? When does it make sense to self-publish? How do you get an agent you've queried to return your call? How do you get your editor/publisher to invest in the promotion of your book? What do you do when your agent/editor makes a suggestion that you're uncomfortable with? How do you make sure you don't get stuck with a cover you hate? Should you hire an outside publicist? How do you get on a bestseller list? All this, and so much more, will be at our readers' fingertips in *Putting Your Passion into Print*.

Competition

After doing an extensive search, three things became clear:

■ Almost every competitive book concentrates on only one aspect of getting a book published, whether it's finding an agent, writing a book proposal or publicizing your work. You'd have to buy at least three books to get the amount of information supplied in *Putting Your Passion into Print!* Who would spend $45–$75 when they could spend under $20?!

■ Competitive books also tend to divide between those writing fiction and those writing nonfiction. We believe the essential principles apply across categories (though where there are differences we will have sections or boxes in the book with tips for addressing each), and we've found that many writers want to write both fiction and nonfiction. Again, the issue of buying more than one book vs. one book arises.

■ There is only one nicely packaged book out there, and this one has a Vintage-esque feel that will scare off those with more practical than literary sensibilities. All the other books have the look of a résumé primer published by Adams or McGraw-Hill; in other words, they look like amateur PowerPoint presentations. They're bland, they use only text (with the exceptional stock photo here and there) and they're plain ugly! Maybe you shouldn't judge a book by its cover, but that doesn't mean you won't buy a book because of one. We believe the packaging alone could make our book a category killer.

N ow for the three truly competitive titles. They are:

1 *How to Get Happily Published* by Judith Applebaum (HarperCollins, first published in 1978; latest edition, 1998). The information in this book is very good. Applebaum's voice is clear and authoritative but not intimidating. This book has sold over half a million copies and is now in its fifth edition, proving that there is a huge audience out there for our book. But as good as the information

in this book is, we feel it has a number of significant drawbacks.

■ **Bad packaging:** "Zzzzzzz" is all we can say about this dud of a cover. It has absolutely no presence on the shelf. And if you're just looking at spines and can't see the "fifth edition, half a million copies sold" seal (which is the case 99% of the time), your eye would never seek it out. The size is 5 x 8, which reinforces its lack of presence. The text itself is 242 pages, but 82 of those are on self-publishing. This means Applebaum spends only 160 pages on the entire process of getting a book published from idea through and past publication! As a reader on Amazon wrote, "Great book—if you want to self-publish. Otherwise not so helpful."

■ **Dated material:** It's almost 25 years old. Yes, it was updated in 1998, but the lion's share of the book has not changed since it was first published. The problem is, publishing is not the same as it was 25 years ago. Hence the information has a dated feel about it even though there are a number of current anecdotes sprinkled throughout.

■ **Poor organization:** We had to look in three different places before we found Applebaum's tips on writing a good query letter—one of the most-asked questions by those trying to get a book published. And to go back to the datedness of the material, the author never actually gives tips on writing a query letter to an agent—only on writing them directly to book editors. Since nary a book editor looks at query letters these days, we felt that this was a case of giving not only dated information, but bad information as well.

■ **Slim on e-information:** So much has changed since the proliferation of e-business. From marketing to research, to selling your book, we'll show you how to make your computer your best friend. And while the Applebaum book does have some information about the web world, we will cover it in much greater depth and breadth.

■ **Limited expertise:** While Applebaum is a publishing veteran, she has never developed and sold books on a day-to-day basis nor has she written books on a wide variety of subjects (this is her only book). She's written primarily about the industry or worked as a book publicist. With three books under our belt (and counting), Arielle's experience developing and selling dozens of titles day in and day out and David's experience as a professional pitchman, we have many more publishing bases covered.

All in all, we believe, with up-to-the-moment information, a great package, a larger word count, easier navigation and our upbeat voice to give people encouragement, we've got a book that will be the standard for generations to come.

② *The Shortest Distance Between You and a Published Book* by Susan Page (Broadway, 1997). This is another book with good information and a clear format.

But we think our book has much more to offer than this one.

■ **Limited packaging:** This is the book with the delightfully literary cover. It's nice to look at, but we believe it appeals to the female buyer and to those with New Yorker sensibilities (the font is the giveaway). We want these people, too, but we also want to reach out to a much broader audience.

■ **Limited scope:** While this book covers a wide range of issues, it does not cover them in detail. *Putting Your Passion into Print* will leave no stone unturned, so writers will never have to go out and buy another book on the subject, no matter what genre they write in or what dilemma they face.

■ **Limited experience:** Page has only been on the author side of the publishing equation. She's never tried to sell, edit or publicize any book other than her own. We, on the other hand, are both an agent and a professional pitchman. We know the ins and outs of selling from doing it every day for the past 30 years combined. However, we also have the personal author experience and can empathize with our readers every step of the way.

③ *From Book Idea to Bestseller* by Michael Snell, Kim Baker and Sunny Baker (Prima, 1997). This book is not stocked in any independent bookstore in the Bay Area, nor is it on powells.com. We assume it has been remaindered and is on its way out of print (it is listed on Amazon, but Amazon lists remaindered books as still in print).

Lastly, *Putting Your Passion into Print* will be unique because we are a married couple who continues to capture the media's attention (see next section). The playful banter, which is so much a part of our collective voice and makes our events so much fun, will in turn make *Putting Your Passion into Print* not just the definitive book on the subject, but also the most entertaining.

The Authors

A RIELLE ECKSTUT is a literary agent with James Levine Communications, Inc. She worked in their New York office for seven years before opening up JLC's West Coast office in the Bay Area in 2000. Arielle represents numerous bestselling and award-winning authors and has sold millions of dollars worth of books. She made her first publishing deal at the age of 23 for $300,000. Ever since, she has made it her mission to nurture and develop the talent of those she represents while never losing sight of the art of the deal.

After almost a decade of acting as midwife to other people's creations, Arielle coauthored two of her own books: *Pride and Promiscuity: The Lost Sex Scenes of Jane Austen* (Simon & Schuster, 2001) and *Satchel Sez: The Wit, Wisdom, and World of Leroy "Satchel" Paige* (Crown/Random House, 2001). She was finally able to experience, firsthand, the excitement (and disappointments) involved in making a book. Going through the publishing process strengthened her skills as an agent and gave her a much broader perspective on the world of publishing.

Arielle is a graduate of the University of Chicago, where her major required her to ask a "grand question" and to back up this question with six essential texts. While many doubted the sagacity of such a major (What job will you get? How will you be able to pay for health insurance?), it turned out to be the perfect preparation for a life in publishing. By reading texts so closely and examining every last detail, Arielle was able to understand what makes for a great book. She continues to bring this attention to detail to all her work.

Arielle has also baked pastries for Madonna and the President, cut karyotypes and performed improvisational comedy at the Edinburgh Fringe Festival.

D AVID HENRY STERRY is the author of the *San Francisco Chronicle* bestseller *Chicken: Self-Portrait of a Young Man for Rent* (ReganBooks/HarperCollins, 2002) and coauthor of *Satchel Sez: The Wit, Wisdom, and World of Leroy "Satchel" Paige* (Crown/Random House, 2001). He is also a published poet.

David started his acting career as a stand-up comedian, at the Holy City Zoo, the Punchline and the Comedy Store, performing with everyone from Robin Williams to Milton Berle. As an actor, he has worked everywhere from Lincoln Center to the Magic Theater, with everyone from Will Smith (in *The Fresh Prince of Bel Air*) to Michael Caine to David Letterman (*Cabin Boy*) to Zippy the Chimp. He has been a TV pitchman for companies such as AT&T, Levi's and Isuzu and performed in over 500 commercials, winning 4 Clios.

He starred in Children's Television Workshop/HBO's Emmy-winning *Encyclopedia* and was the emcee at Chippendale's Male Strip Club in New York, winning Cabaret Performer of the Year. His plays have been performed at P.S. 122, the West Bank Café and the Duplex. He has written screenplays for Disney, Fox and Nickelodeon Pictures. He is also a presentation doctor who goes into companies and works with their executives on how to improve their presentation skills.

David has also worked as a soda jerk, a barker, a cherry picker, a chicken fryer, a building inspector, a shoe salesman, a bike messenger and a marriage counselor. He graduated from Reed College and loves his woman, his cat and any sport involving a ball.

Why We're the Best People to Write This Book

To successfully write a book on how to get published, you've got to cover all the bases. While anyone can do the research, it's much better if the authors themselves have an insider's knowledge of a wide range of publishing experiences and access to the top professionals in every area of the world of books.

Arielle is an agent who not only sells books but spends an extraordinary amount of time on editorial development, editing, packaging, publicity and marketing, and many other aspects of the publishing process. Over 75% of her clients are first-time authors (90% of whom go on to be second-,

third- and fourth-time authors) so she knows the trials and tribulations of the novice. She has worked with dozens of people from a wide range of backgrounds, such as doctors, MFA grads, moms, professional writers, academics, amateur scientists, baseball nuts and interior designers. And because she herself is an author, she understands the frustrations, joys and pitfalls a writer goes through each and every step of the way.

David is a bestselling author who knows the nuts and bolts of how to put together a book from soup to nuts, proposal to bestseller list. His years as a professional actor, pitchman and presentation doctor have given him a unique understanding of how people should market and present themselves so they can shine like the stars they are.

Publicity and Marketing

Because of our unique background and training in improvisation, stand-up comedy, emceeing, acting and presenting, along with our years of writing and agenting, our appearances are not just informative, they're also fun. And the fact that we're a married couple, with our own style of playful banter, sets us apart from all the other stars in the literary firmament.

■ **Events**
When we did our *Putting Your Passion into Print:* The Pacific Northwest Tour, we were overwhelmed by the reception. The tour taught us all about the art of the event, from the independents to the chains, from the big city to the small town, from universities to book fairs. It also

taught us how much fun we have together in front of an audience.

Print

There are numerous opportunities for print publicity for *Putting Your Passion into Print* beyond the review attention we hope the book will garner. For one, to coincide with publication, we will pitch original articles to magazines that target their particular audience or subject matter on how to get a book published. Secondly, we recently realized that our personal story seems to be of interest to the general public and could help sell our book. We were featured in *New York* magazine a few weeks ago and then called by *Good Morning America* as a result. This response showed us how remarkably easy it should be to market us as an interesting couple with a unique take on the world. And the fact that our story as a couple begins with putting our own passion into print will be the cherry on top.

TV

Again, our story as a couple combined with our experience as performers (we're both extremely comfortable in front of a camera) and our clear presentation of the information contained in *Putting Your Passion into Print* will help us gain the interest of the *Good Morning America*s, *Oprah*s and local morning and afternoon shows of the world.

Radio

Radio is one of our favorite publicity mediums, and we have a wealth of experience in this area. We have appeared repeatedly on National Public Radio, with Scott Simon, Rene Montagne, Neal Conan and Larry Mantle. We have also done local radio from Hawaii to Portland to New York to Los Angeles, honing our on-air skills to become masters of the sound bite and the extended storytelling information-giving format.

Appearances

Collectively or individually, we have appeared at, on, with or in (among others): *The New York Times, Washington Post, SF Chronicle* bestseller list, *Portland Tribune, Los Angeles Times, New York Daily News, The Oregonian, Baltimore Sun, New Orleans Picayune, St. Louis Post Dispatch, Associated Press, Sacramento Bee, Dallas Morning News, Chicago Tribune;* Reed College, San Francisco State University, Sonoma State; *New York* magazine, *Sports Illustrated, Details* magazine, Cooperstown magazine of the National Baseball Hall of Fame, *Pages* magazine; *Sally Jesse Rafael, The Other Half* (with Dick Clark), *Mornings on 2, Northwest Afternoon at 4, Good Morning Central Oregon;* NPR's *Morning Edition, Weekend Edition, Talk of the Nation, AirTalk with Larry Mantle, The Gil Gross Show,* ESPN Radio, *BookTalk, Between the Lines, Radiozine, Cover to Cover, Mancow & Muller, Lydia & Gunther, The Bob and Tom Show;* Book Passage, Cody's, A Clean Well-Lighted Place for Books, Elliot Bay Books, Eagle Harbor Books, Powell's, Book Soup, Paulina Springs Book Co.; Barnes & Noble in Philadelphia, Berkeley, Vancouver,

Seattle, Colma, Fremont and Bend; San Francisco Public Library (Lila Wallace Reader's Digest Writers on Writing series); the Edinburgh Fringe Festival and Lincoln Center.

■ **The Radio Show**

When we brought *Putting Your Passion into Print* onto National Public Radio's *Talk of the Nation,* the switchboard lit up with calls from one corner of America to the other. In fact, *Talk of the Nation* was so inundated with calls that they brought Arielle back later in the week to answer follow-up questions. We were subsequently approached about the possibility of launching our own *Putting Your Passion into Print* call-in radio show and are now working to have the show up and running in conjunction with the release of the book. We will pitch the show as "*Car Talk* meets Publishing" and will approach Barnes & Noble as a sponsor. We expect the show to start as a segment on an already nationally syndicated NPR show or as a weekly in the San Francisco Bay Area out of KQED or KPFA. Each week will feature a different expert from some segment of the book world: from editors to illustrators, booksellers to agents, book doctors to lawyers, along with a wide range of writers of nonfiction and genre fiction, children's books and cookbooks. We'll have segments like the Pitch of the Week, where an audience member gets to pitch his book on the air in two minutes or less, a Name That First Line contest and a Worst Rejection Letter of the Month. *Putting Your Passion*

into Print: the Radio Show will, of course, give us a regular platform to reach a broad-based demographic.

Manuscript Specifications

We see *Putting Your Passion into Print* in a trim size of at least 6" by 9" and a page count of approximately 500–600, including references and index. Each chapter will include:

■ Boxes (or some kind of call-out visual) with dos and dont's, tips and reminders, FAQs and our personal favorite: the "Think Outside the Box Box."

■ Sample writing from query letters, proposals, pitches, etc.

■ Stories and advice from those within the publishing industry. We plan to interview over 100 people, including authors, agents, editors, media escorts, publishers, publicists, marketing, sub rights and sales directors, booksellers, publishing lawyers, Hollywood book agents and more.

■ Workbook elements for helpful exercises such as our title word chart.

■ Templates for sample letters to agents, editors and booksellers for each stage of the game.

There is also the possibility of adding a software component to this book, as Jeff Herman has done with his *Guide to Book Editors, Publishers, and Literary Agents.*

Endnote

A suburban mom from suburban England, a southern lawyer, a new-age guy who talks to God. What do these people have in common? Their grandchildren's grandchildren's grandchildren will never have to work a day in their lives because they put their passion into print. And this, too, can be true for the millions of authors—aspiring and otherwise—who read this book!

Sample Material

LOCATING AND QUERYING THE RIGHT AGENT FOR YOU

You've found your passion, located your model, perfected your pitch and completed your nonfiction proposal or novel. You've also determined that you want to go for a big-time publisher so you can receive money up front—an advance (see p. XX)—for your book.

Now you need to query an agent.

For those without a personal referral (which will be about 99.9% of you), don't despair! We have a system that is as close to foolproof as you'll get.

[REMINDER: Yes, there are millions of aspiring authors and only a few hundred agents. But while you need an agent, it's fair to say that an agent needs you even more. Without authors, agents wouldn't be in business, and we all know the reverse is not true. It's also important to realize that every single agent has passed up or passed over a project by an unknown author that went on to sell hundreds of thousands of copies. This is precisely why nearly every agency—whether they claim to or not—looks at query letters. Just keep saying to yourself: THEY NEED ME MORE THAN I NEED THEM! Because nobody wants to be remembered as the agent who passed on Harry Potter or *The Catcher in the Rye*.]

PERSONALIZING YOUR LETTER

The key to catching any agent's attention is to personalize your query letter. How do you personalize a letter to someone you don't know? The first thing you'll need to do is make a list of the books you love that have something in common with your book. Do not pick books that are in direct competition with your own, but ones that draw the same audience, that you have read thoroughly and that you have strong feelings for. For example, say you're writing a cookbook on vegetarian Thai cuisine. There may already be a book out there on this exact subject. But rather than choose this book for your list, choose your favorite vegetarian cookbooks and your favorite Thai cookbooks (that are not exclusively vegetarian). We'll explain why shortly.

How do you find books like yours? A few years ago, you would've had to wade through Books in Print. But now, just log onto amazon.com and you'll amass a list in no time. Amazon is extremely helpful even if you think you know what's already out there. In the search field, plug in key words (like "vegetarian" and "Thai") and see what comes up. Or if you already have a book you love and want to use on your list, put that into the search field. Once you've found a book that looks like a good match, scroll down until you get to the feature that says "people who bought this book also bought . . ." This will point you in the direction of potentially dozens of other books on your subject that you can then buy or check out at your local library or bookstore. Once you've located 5 to 20 books of this nature, take your project notebook with you to the bookstore. Then look in the acknowledgment sections to see if the authors have thanked their agent or editor. Make two lists: one of agents, the other of editors. This way you can call the editor's office and ask for the name of the agent if none is listed. The names of these editors will come in handy later as well (see Chapter XX).

[TIP: No agent or editor listed in the acknowledgments? All you need to do is call the main number for the publisher and ask for the sub-rights department. (All major publishers have websites that list their numbers. These numbers are also provided in the publishing guides listed in the Appendix.) Tell them you're interested in acquiring the film or television rights to the book and need to know who the author's agent is. No one will ask who you are or why you need to know. If on the off chance they do, just make up a production company name!]

Once you've culled a list of agents—the more the merrier—find out everything you can about them. Many agencies have websites that list the bios of the individual agents who work there. Another great resource is Jeff Herman's *Guide to Book Editors, Publishers, and Literary Agents,* which lists personal and professional information about individual agents (see Appendix). Find out what other books the agent has represented. Study these books. Figure out how your book relates to the other books and other authors this person represents. Find out if the agent has ever written a book, as many agents have. Read agents' books to find out about their personal likes and dislikes— in other words, their passions. Do they have a dog? Are they a vegetarian? A soccer player? A nature lover? A world traveler? Depending on the subject of your book, you may be able to use this information to personalize your letter. For example, a vegetarian world traveler might be just the right agent for your vegetarian Thai cookbook!

What most authors don't realize is that agents are an essentially anonymous piece of the publishing puzzle. They don't get much credit outside the industry. Guess how many literary agents the average Jane can name? None. So anything you can do to make an agent feel acknowledged, smart, interesting or special will go a long way.

If you don't do your research, chances are, you'll send your sci-fi novel to a sci-fi hater, your illustrated history of tea to a coffee drinker, your Christian self-help book to a die-hard Buddhist. The fact is, most people do NOT do their research.

This means that if you do, you've put yourself leagues ahead of your competition.

Continue your research until you've put together a list of at least 10 agents who appear to be legitimate matches for your book. These are all people who have done similar but not identical books. Do not send your Thai vegetarian cookbook proposal to an agent who has already done a Thai vegetarian cookbook. Most agents will not want this conflict of interest. And any agent who does is not the agent for you.

[BOX: An agenting story from Arielle. One day, I got a query letter with lots of children's stickers and rubber stamps covering the envelope. It was both playful and goofy and caught my attention immediately. Susan Wooldridge, the person who wrote the query, had most certainly done her homework about me. She found out I grew up right by Columbia University in New York City and then went on to the University of Chicago. She also found out I was a poetry lover. It turns out Susan had grown up right by the University of Chicago and went to school at Columbia. And her book was about how writing poetry can help us get to the root of our creative selves. I certainly can't remember the exact words of this letter, but I remember the connection she made with me and how she used our similar histories to pique my interest in her book. Indeed, I sold this book. It's called *poemcrazy* and is now in its 18th printing.

Soon after *poemcrazy* was published, I got another query letter. This one was from someone who had no connection to me—except that she had read and LOVED *poemcrazy*. She wrote a beautifully detailed letter about reading the acknowledgments in Susan's book, telling me what she thought was so special about *poemcrazy* as well as how her book was both similar and different. She made a very convincing case for why the agent for *poemcrazy* should also be the agent for

her book, *Fruitflesh*. And she convinced me. *Fruitflesh* came out last month and became a Book Sense top 10 bestseller (see Publicity), and she just won the Bellweather prize, juried by Barbara Kingsolver, Toni Morrison and Maxine Hong Kingston, for her first novel!

Neither of these women had ever written a book. There was nothing particularly special about their résumés, and their books were not obvious bestsellers. But the work they put into researching agents turned them both into successful published authors. Follow their lead, and you won't be agentless for long.]

WRITING YOUR QUERY LETTER

Now it's time to actually write your query letter. The query letter is one of the most important pieces of the publishing puzzle. A smart, interesting, well-crafted personal query letter can open many doors for you.

A query letter consists of three parts:

Connection with the Agent

Using your research, you need to make your case for why a particular agent is the right person to represent your material. You'll also want to add any possible personal connections you may have discovered (you both graduated from the University of Wisconsin, own three pugs or spent your youth in Florence). Make specific references to books the agent has represented or written. Tell him or her what you liked about the book and why your book is similar to the successful books he or she has represented. Here are three different styles of sample paragraphs:

① In researching literary agents, I saw that you represented two of my favorite books, *poemcrazy* and *Fruitflesh*. I have used these books both personally and professionally in my psychotherapy practice. What particularly impressed me about these books is the incredible amount of heart they display. What brave women Susan and Gayle are to reveal their lives in such intimate detail! I can't tell you what an inspiration both women have been to my patients and me. I believe that my book, *Writing for Your Life*, shares some of the essential qualities of *poemcrazy* and *Fruitflesh*, but is rooted in my experience as a clinical psychologist. Because both Gayle and Susan acknowledged you so effusively, and because my book shares many of the same fundamental beliefs as these, I hope that you'll be interested in reviewing my proposal.

② After seeing you acknowledged in *Hooligan Killers*, I logged onto your website to check out what other books you represent. I was happy to see so many books that I have on my shelves and that I admire thoroughly. I am a particular fan of *Goalie on a Rampage* and *Sweepers Gone Mad*. But what impressed me the most was your love of Manchester United, as I myself am a Red Devil fan from the days of Bobby Charlton and Georgie Best. At 20, I moved to England and played for Newcastle United's Under 21 Club. I've written a novel about my time as an American soccer player in England, so it made my day to find an agent who shares my love for the game. I hope at the very least you'll get a kick out of reading *The Referee Assassin*.

③ I recently bought a copy of your book, *Monkeys in the Bible*, and I read it cover to cover in one night. I loved the chapter where you had the orangutan come down from the mount with Moses and the Ten Commandments. I'm telling all my friends in the scientific community about your book, and some of us quote lines back and forth from it. My favorite is: "When Moses slipped on the banana peel, one of the tablets broke and suddenly, instead of 13 Commandments, we only had 10." I also saw on your website that you have agented many popular science books, including *Bees Bees Bees* and *Men Are Dogs, Women Are Cats*. I myself am a leading primate biologist, and I have written a proposal for a book about monkeys based on my award-winning research in Kenya called *Everything I Need to Know I Learned from My Monkey*. Thanks for your time, and I can't wait to read your next book.

[TIP: Don't be fooled into writing a dull, boring query. Yes, be professional (see p. XX), but make sure the letter reflects your own personality and style. Show the agent you'll be great to do business with.]

The Pitch

Take the flap copy you have meticulously crafted (see p. XX), and condense your pitch to one paragraph.

This means getting your story down to its essential ingredients and making them exciting. Here are two examples of great paragraph-length pitches:

1 My book is called *Why God Won't Go Away?* and it asks the age-old question: Did God create the brain, or did the brain create God? It's based on my long-term study at the University of Pennsylvania in which I used high-tech imaging techniques to examine the brain functions of Buddhists meditating and Franciscan nuns praying. And my answer to both questions, based on my study and research, is a resounding Yes!

This is a pitch for a bestselling book Arielle agented called *Why God Won't Go Away* by Dr. Andrew Newberg, Dr. Eugene D'Aquili and Vince Rause (Ballantine/Random House, 2001).

2 My book is extremely unpleasant, for it tells a terrible tale about three unlucky children. Even though they are charming and clever, the Beaudelaire siblings lead lives filled with misery and woe. In this short book alone, the three youngsters encounter a greedy and repulsive villain, itchy clothing, cold porridge, a disastrous fire and a plot to steal their fortune. My book is best described as "*Home Alone* meets Edgar Allan Poe," and it's called *The Bad Beginning,* the first in a series of unhappy tragedies about the brave, resourceful, talented Beaudelaire children as they suffer one cruel blow after another, surviving by the skin of their teeth and the pluck of their mettle.

This is an example of how we would have pitched the wildly successful young adult book *The Bad Beginning* by Lemony Snicket (HarperCollins, 2001).

Your Bio

In a paragraph, tell the agent what is interesting about you and why you're the person to write this book. This is not about a dry job résumé. This is a wet, fun-filled paragraph that lets the agent know how great and yet modest you are, and why you and you alone are capable of pulling this book off. If you've been published anywhere else, this is a good thing to add. If you've won any awards, include them. It doesn't matter what the award is, as long as you won it. No need to add it's from junior high school—the award alone will do. And feel free to put in any information that shows you've got the savvy to publicize and market your book. In one of our seminars, a successful businessman told us he had been homeless for several years. We told him to put this in his query letter because it helped show what an unusual and resilient person he was—and it was a great story for publicity. Can't you just see him on *Oprah!* Clearly, this is the kind of information that doesn't go on your CV, but again, it would set you apart from the hordes of others trying to get a book published.

[TIP: The more professional your presentation, the better off you are. Use high-quality stationery, folders and visuals. Be sure to have someone else proof your letter. And whatever you do, spell the agent's name right. Remember that God is in the Details!]

FAQS

Q: *Should I send query letters to more than one agent?*

A: Absolutely. The more competition you can generate for your book, the better off you are.

Q: *If I get interest from one agent, should I tell the others?*

A: Oh, yes. If anyone expresses any interest at all, notify the rest of your list. Make them know they're going to miss out on a good thing if they don't jump on board fast. This is a variation on the old Peter-Paul gambit, in which a person plays one potential buyer off the other to jack up the price of whatever is being sold.

Q: *How long should my query letter be?*

A: The whole thing should fit on one page, unless you have a very good reason for it not to.

Q: *Should I send a whole manuscript with my query letter?*

A: Do not bombard the agent with material. That is a good way to get your material shredded and trashed. Just send a query informing them of what material you have available (see p. XX), and let them tell you what they want.

Q: *Should I send a self-addressed stamped envelope?*

A: Yes. And be sure to include a phone number, an email address and a snail mail address. Seems pretty basic, but you'd be shocked how many people leave out this information.

CHAPTER-BY-CHAPTER OUTLINE

1 Writing the Right Idea
- Preparing a Tool Kit
- Finding a Support Team
- Looking at Salability
- Making Friends with Your Local Bookseller

2 Building Your Book
- Locating a Model
- Titles and Subtitles
- Finding Coauthors, Cowriters and Ghostwriters
- Crafting Your Pitch
- The Nuts and Bolts of the Nonfiction Book Proposal
- Your Fiction Manuscript (with a subsection on poetry)

3 Selling Your Book to an Agent
- Finding the Right Agent for YOU
- Writing a Killer Query Letter
- The Art of the Schmooze (with a section on secretaries and assistants)
- Follow-Up
- Picking an Agent (if you have a choice and what to do if you don't)
- Maximizing Your Agent
- How to Be the Dream Client
- Rejection

4 Selling Your Book to a Publisher
- Picking Editors/Publishers
- The Waiting Game
- Choosing the Right Editor/ Publisher for YOU

- The Deal
  (auctions, advances, rights,
  contracts and more)
- Rejection

5 Self-Publishing
- Should You or Shouldn't You?
- With Whom?
- The Look of Your Book
- Distribution
- Pitfalls
- Advantages

6 Writing Your Book
- Making a Schedule
- How to Work with Your
  Editor Effectively
- Differences of Editorial
  Opinions
- Writing Is Rewriting
- Permissions
- Illustrations/Photos
- Title
- Legal Questions

7 Prepublication
- The Look of Your Book
  (the cover and interior)
- Blurbs
- Setting up a Tour
  (with or without your
  publisher)
- Prepublication Print,
  Radio and TV
- To Hire or Not to Hire
  an Outside Publicist
- Getting Media Savvy
  (coaches, rehearsal, etc.)
- Publicity Kits

8 Post-Publication Publicity
- Making the Most of
  Where You Live
  (bookstores, media, etc.)
- Bookstore Placement
- Getting Yourself on TV
  and Radio and in Print
- Buzz
- Getting on a Bestseller List
- E-Marketing
  (a gift to the shy!)

9 Keeping Your Book
Alive for the Long Term
- Movie Deals
- Course Adoptions for
  Colleges and Universities
- Speaking Agents
- Conferences
- Revisions
- Special Marketing
  Opportunities

10 Figuring Out Your Next Project
- Sequels
- Not Making the Same
  Mistakes Twice
- Do You Need a New
  Agent or Publisher?
- Maximizing Your Success

Acknowledgments

WE ARE SO GRATEFUL TO the dozens who have helped us write this book. Numerous authors and publishing people put in their two cents, and we simply could not have done this without the information and advice they ponied up. Unfortunately, our acknowledgments would be as long as this book if we gave props to each and every person. So, instead, we've settled for thanking the "team" behind this book and then listing everyone who graciously agreed to be a part of it—either by telling us their stories or by lending us their words.

First, we'd like to thank the team in order of where they came into the picture. Jessica Gillard, our seriously gifted and talented former Reed intern helped us put together our first tour, which led to this book. Our wonderful colleagues/friends at the Levine Greenberg Rostan Literary Agency—in particular, Jim Levine, who has been the dad our book always had, giving us ideas and fantastic feedback and making sure our book was nurtured, well fed and tucked in nicely. Margaret E. Boyle contributed her big brain, her hard work and her eternal good nature. Danielle Svetcov always came through in a pinch. She is an übermensch, top-drawer researcher, fantabulous writer and generally all-too-talented human being. Jessica Goldstein has been a constant and generous supporter, and this book would never have been born without her. Chris Baty was kind enough to let us make an example out of his exemplary proposal. Bruce Harris spent a good chunk of his time sharing his wisdom. Suzie Bolotin has been the kind of editor you think exists only in your wildest dreams. She asked all the tough questions while making sure all the t's were dotted and i's were crossed. And she's read this thick tome too many times to count. She is also a truly loving, sweet, good-natured, good-humored person. Lynn Strong is a copy editor with a capital "C." She fine-tuned this manuscript in an awe-inspiring manner. Megan Nicolay provided invaluable assistance (and fellow commiseration) at every turn.

On the second edition, we were in the enviable position of getting yet another fabulous editor in the form of Savannah Ashour. Savannah's meticulous edit kept us on our toes and was always true to the spirit of the book. She also helped us work through a terrifically tight deadline with her most excellent sense of humor and just a wee crack of the whip.

First, thanks on our third edition goes to Kristi Tuck Austin. Assistant doesn't even begin to express the breadth and depth of what Kristi does. We like to think of her as the Neil deGrasse Tyson of organization and research. We've also had the good fortune to work with Sam O'Brien as our editor on this new edition. Her attention to detail and her ability to find those sentences that don't quite read right has made all the difference. Other invaluable members of our Workman team include: Andrea Fleck-Nisbet and Justin Nisbet extended their e-kindness and e-genius. Selina Meere put together our tour just moments before her maternity leave—you're a saint, Selina! James Wehrle set us straight with his deep insight on the sales process as well as his sales prowess—which helped make this third edition possible. Steven Pace kept us connected and in tune with all the wonderful independent booksellers we interviewed. Page Edmunds gave us valuable contacts and help on technical publishing jargon. David Schiller wrote our excellent copy and gave advice from the beginning of the project. Walter Weintz was, once again, helpful in a pinch and an all-around supporter.

All in all, the Workman team simply couldn't be more creative, smart, together, fun, talented and lovely. We feel eternally grateful and lucky to be working with what we always heard and now believe is, indeed, "The Workman Magic."

Many thanks as well to:

David Allender	Jack Boulware	Melissa Cistaro
Jonathan Ames	Gayle Brandeis	Judy Clain
Peter Andersen	Deb Brody	Miek Coccia
Chris Anderson	Armin Brott	Doris Cooper
Dominick Anfuso	Linda Bubon	Amanda Cotten
Tamim Ansary	Judy Budnitz	Deb Covey
Dan Ariely	Fauzia Burke	Molly Crabapple
Kristine Asselin	Rainelle Burton	Lori Culwell
Margaret Atwood	Katy Butler	Mike Daisey
Sarah Bagby	Jamie Byng	Dennis Dalrymple
Jill Bailey	Michael Cader	Stacey Dastis
Philip Bashe	Tom Campbell	Michael Datcher
Charles Baxter	Elise Cannon	Karen Davidson
Andy Behrman	Kate Cerino	Paul Davidson
Rick Beyer	Bradley Charbonneau	Barbara DeMarco-Barrett
Amy Bloom	Amy Cherry	Calla Devlin

Crofton Diack

Anita Diamant

Mauro DiPreta

Pamela Dorman

Larry Dossey

Jill Dulber

Jim Eber

David Ebershoff

Susan Edsall

Zetta Elliott

Hallie Ephron

Jeffrey Eugenides

John Evans
  (Diesel Books)

John Evans
  (Lemuria Books)

Andrew Exum

Michael Farello

Frank Fochetta

Joel Fotinos

Gary Frank

Jane Friedman

Neil Gaiman

Paul Gamarello

Julia Fox Garrison

Matthew Gasteier

Lisa Genova

Roger Gilbertson

Mary Gleysteen

Seth Godin

Lynn Goldberg

Jesse Goldstine

Ashley Gordon

David Graham

Daniel Greenberg

Arielle Gronner

Eve Grubin

Tammy Han

Donna Hayes

Carol Hoenig

Carole Horne

Khaled Hosseini

Jessica Hurley

Antonella Iannarino

Sherril Jaffe

Janis Jaquith

Jemiah Jefferson

Duffy Jennings

Jennie Johnson

Diana Jordan

Jennifer Josephy

Raphael Kadushin

Mitchell Kaplan

Caryn Karmatz-Rudy

Bob Kasher

Arsen Kashkashian

Nancy Kay

Jonathon Keats

Shawna Kenney

Andy Kessler

Wayne Kirn

Larry Kirshbaum

Bob Klein

Christina Baker Kline

Anie Knipping

J.A. Konrath

Thea Kotroba

Karen Kozlowski

Annik LaFarge

Mark LaFramboise

Bruce Lane

Alice LaPlante

Caroline Leavitt

Nancy Levine

Keri Levitt

David Levy

Alan Lew

Valerie Lewis

Beth Lisick

Emily Loose

Leonard Lopate

Roxanne Lott

Regina Louise

Kat Lu

Gwen Macsai

Steve Malk

Jenny Mandel

Martha Manning

Wendy Manning

Larry Mantle

Ayesha Mattu

Margaret Maupin

Nura Maznavi

Peter McCarthy

Damian McNicholl

Leslie Meredith

Jackson Michael

Dottie Mitchell

Geoffrey Moore

Barbara Morrow

Barbara Moulton

Maria Muscarella

Melissa Mytinger

Jill Nagle

Richard Eoin Nash

Jan Nathan

Eva Lesko Natiello

Bob Nelson

Jan Nelson

Andrew Newberg

Cari Noga

Grail Norton

Carla Oliver

Daria O'Neill

The Onion
Marilyn Paige
Rachel Parker
William Parker
Karen Perea
Liz Perle
Michael Perry
Nancy Peters
Elaine Petrocelli
Kathy Pories
Michael Powell
Joe Quirk
Suzanne Rafer
Meg Cohen Ragas
Jennifer Ramos
Vince Rause
Kirk Read
Sally Reed
Jen Reynolds
Dan Rhodes
Marion Rosenberg
Andy Ross
Stephanie Kip Rostan
Sharon Kelly Roth

Pru Rowlandson
Roberta Rubin
Bob Sabbag
Margot Sage-El
Cathy Salit
Brandon Saltz
Frank Sanchez
Pamela Redmond Satran
John Scalzi
Lisa Schenke
Laura Schenone
Joan Schwieghardt
Kemble Scott
Mike Shatzkin
Susan Shaw
William Shinker
Debby Simmons
Rick Simonson
Rebecca Skloot
Marcella Smith
Kevin Smokler
Matthew Snyder
Neil Sofman
Jerry Stahl

Debbie Stier
Robert St. John
Valerie Tomaselli
Britton Trice
Malle Vallik
Gary Vaynerchuk
Bob Viarengo
Sydne Waller
Jodi Weiss
Karen West
Jun Chul Whang
Sun Chul Whang
Crystal Wilkinson
Ken Wilson
Ty Wilson
Rosalind Wiseman
Susan Wooldridge
Carolan Workman
Katie Workman
Bria Young
Lisa Zamarin
Keith Zimmerman
Kent Zimmerman

We also thank these people (both alive and long dead), who we've never had the pleasure of speaking with, but whose inspirational stories or words were essential to our book:

James Boswell
Prill Boyle
Alan Burns
Alan Coren
Christopher Paul Curtis
Daniel Handler
Heidi Julavits

Jonathan Kozol
Anne Lamott
J.T. Leroy
Hilary Liftin
Ray Magliozzi
Tom Magliozzi
Kevin Meany

Michael Moore
Heru Ptah
Alice Sebold
Ramit Sethi
Rachel Simon
Gene Wilder
David Williamson

Index

About the Authors

ARIELLE ECKSTUT is the author of nine books including *The Secret Language of Color: The Science, Nature, History, Culture, Beauty of Red, Orange, Yellow, Green, Blue & Violet.* She is also an agent-at-large at the Levine Greenberg Rostan Literary Agency, where for more than 20 years she has been helping hundreds of talented writers become published authors. Lastly, Arielle cofounded the iconic company LittleMissMatched and grew it from a tiny operation into a leading national brand, which now has stores from coast to coast, everywhere from Disneyland to Disney World to Fifth Avenue in New York City.

DAVID HENRY STERRY is the author of 16 books, from memoir to middle grade fiction, sports to reference. His work has been translated into a dozen languages, optioned by Hollywood, and appeared on the cover of the Sunday *New York Times* Book Review. He regularly contributes to the Huffington Post. Before writing professionally, David was a comic and an actor, working with everyone from Will Smith to Michael Caine to Zippy the Chimp. His one-man show, based on his memoir, *Chicken,* debuted internationally at the Edinburgh Fringe Festival and was named the number one show in the United Kingdom by *The Independent.*

Together, David and Arielle have been featured everywhere from *The New York Times* to *The Wall Street Journal,* from NPR's *Morning Edition* to BBC Radio 4, from *Sports Illustrated* to *Nature.* They are married and live in Montclair, New Jersey, with their daughter. They are the founders of The Book Doctors and can be reached at thebookdoctors.com.